OTHERS DURING THE CONSTRUCTION
(about OCT/NOV 1943)

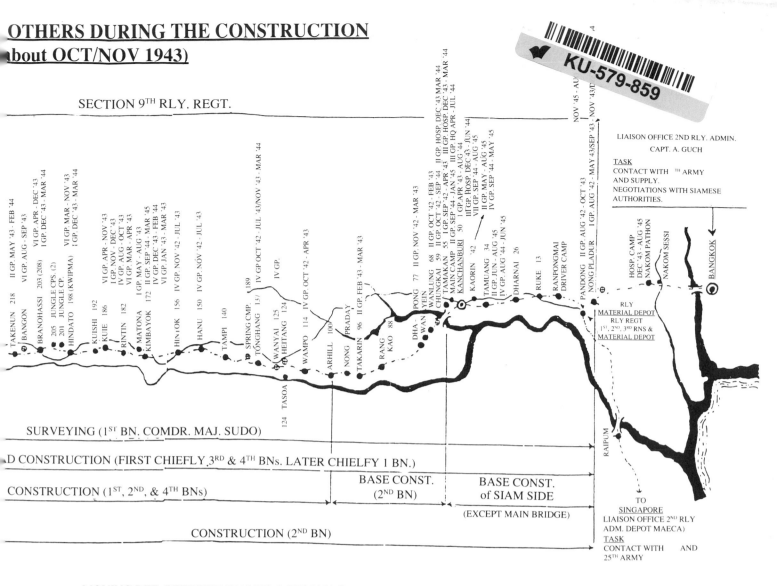

SECTION 9TH RLY. REGT.

LIAISON OFFICE 2ND RLY. ADMIN.
CAPT. A. GUCH

TASK
CONTACT WITH ᵀᴴ ARMY
AND SUPPLY.
NEGOTIATIONS WITH SIAMESE
AUTHORITIES.

SURVEYING (1ˢᵀ BN. COMDR. MAJ. SUDO)

...D CONSTRUCTION (FIRST CHIEFLY 3ᴿᴰ & 4ᵀᴴ BNs. LATER CHIELFY 1 BN.)

CONSTRUCTION (1ˢᵀ, 2ᴺᴰ, & 4ᵀᴴ BNs)

BASE CONST. (2ᴺᴰ BN)

BASE CONST. of SIAM SIDE
(EXCEPT MAIN BRIDGE)

CONSTRUCTION (2ᴺᴰ BN)

RLY MATERIAL DEPOT
RLY REGT
1ˢᵀ, 2ᴺᴰ, 3ᴿᴰ RNS &
MATERIAL DEPOT

TO SINGAPORE
LIAISON OFFICE 2ᴺᴰ RLY
ADM. DEPOT MAECA)
TASK
CONTACT WITH   AND
25ᵀᴴ ARMY

MOVING DET. BETWEEN WAMPO & TAMAJAO
3 DET. I GROUP
APR - SEP 1943

Site of massacre of Japanese troops by Australians, Feb 3/5th 1942, in excess of 1,300 killed.

Changi Beach where more than 2,000 Chinese men, women and children were murdered by the Japanese.

Approximately 1,000 civilians were murdered here by the Japanese, mainly government employees including Chinese, Eurasians and Indians.

Elizabeth Walk, the site of Japanese land reclamation which was used to conceal the remains of many murdered civilians.

Site of the original British POW cemetery.

Site of the original Australian POW cemetery.

Kranji Cemetery, once one of the largest ammunition dumps in the Pacific.

Japanese ceremonial execution site.

Mandai quarry, one time British observation post.

0 The site of Nee Soon warehouse, completely demolished by Japanese bombers.

1 Victory Hill built at the side of the Ford Motor factory and where more than 25,000 Japanese bodies were cremated. The hill was ordered demolished by the British goverment between 1953/60.

2 Tanglin garrison church windows and silver were buried at this spot 9/10th Feb. 1942.

3 Singapore general hospital.

4 Site of Changi POW camp.

5/16 River Valley and Havelock Road camps were built in this area.

WHEN YOU GO HOME

*Tell them of us and say
"For your tomorrow
We gave our today".*

When You Go Home

Arthur Lane

A. Lane Publications

First published in 1993 by A. Lane Publications, 61 Charles Street, Stockport SK1 3JR
© Copyright Arthur Lane 1993.

ISBN 1 897666 00 4

Designed and Typeset by Richard Netherwood Limited, Huddersfield.
Printed in the UK.

Contents

Foreword

by

Sir Peter Herbert

As the words convey to the reader, this book is a dedication to the British men and women of the three services who gave their lives in the battles for Singapore and Malaya and afterwards in the treacherous hands of their Japanese captors. The manuscript describes, in general, a compacted history of the campaign in Malaya from the 8th December 1941, the invasion and following advance of the Japanese, with the Allied soldiers fighting an unequal battle to defend this small portion of the British Empire.

I commend this book written so sensitively by Arthur Lane. He has been back to the sites of battles and engagements, and he has been able to personalise much of the book by calling upon his own experiences in that unhappy campaign.

As a gesture to the memories of the many who will not have come home, Arthur Lane is donating part of the proceeds of his book to The Soldiers' Sailors' and Airmen's Families Association, for which we are extremely grateful.

Sir Peter Herbert KCB, OBE, Chairman SSAFA

(*Author's note:* I am very grateful to Sir Peter Herbert for his generous support of this book, and I must make it clear that the opinions expressed in the following pages are mine and mine alone and Sir Peter's comments should therefore in no way be construed as an endorsement of my very personal views and recollections.)

Acknowledgements

To produce a book of this nature requires the help and assistance of as many friends and helpers as possible. To produce one for a charitable purpose however requires assistance from far more people than I imagined. The idea came to me more than two years ago, when I read in a newspaper that donations to various charities were beginning to diminish. At the same time, in the back of my mind was the thought that by producing a book of this kind, it would as well as providing money for a very worthy cause also ensure that the names of the comrades we left behind will never be forgotten. I have received many letters in the past from relatives and friends of those men who were either killed in battle or later died in the prisoner of war camps, seeking information of the last resting place or a description of the camps where their husband/brother/son or friend had been held captive. So I decided to try to put together a book which would allow all those who were unable for one reason or another to visit those places to be able to at least glimpse something of what the last resting place and the surrounding countryside looked like.

To be able to thank all those people who have given their time, money, ideas or physical assistance, would require several more pages. So I will name a few in the hope that this will suffice and that in my haste to get to the printers, I have not left any major helpers out. My list includes those generous people who donated a total of £1,250 towards our photography and research costs. For which I must thank Joe Green, Henry Beard, Les Paine, B Card, James Wilkinson, R Adam, K Christie, V Finney, J Baynor, E Stockton, E Blackman, Mr. Dear, Julie Birchill, Mrs. H Johnson, Les Picton, Betty Kenny, *Sunday Sport* newspaper, Charles Hall, *The Sun* newspaper, J Fleet ex RN, J & M Onley, E Marriott, Eddie Coan, Joan Brimelow, Mrs. M Midgley, Mrs. Carleston, Maj. Inshaw RN Ass'n, J Baker, Mrs M Bushen, Henry Higgins, J G Smith, Watford Hughes, B/Star Ass'n, Maj. Brett Collier, Joe Bagnaro, Colonel Rex King-Clark, Chuck Stewart, Lord & Lady Boynes of Powys, The Sovereign Rubber Co., Peter Walker and Stockport Council Leisure Committee, Bob Butler Vet Services, W Holloway, Royal Regiment of Fusiliers Ass'n, Mrs Gill and Sigma Graphics. Also Tim Dennis, Carol and the staff at Smith Fort & Symonds for banking the cheques etc., Steve Brindle and Thai Air, for our assisted passage, the Thai Embassy London and the Tourist Authority of Thailand, British Embassy Thailand, Chan and Teing for letting us use their house as our HQ, Mike Mirren at Dean Print for his patience and trust, Joe Metcalf for keeping faith and continually pushing us on each day, Phil Cawley, not just for being our photographer, but also for being our 'gofa', our listener, our confidante and our mate. My family, Glennys & Bill, Julie & Oliver, Philip and last but not least my wife Dot for her continued patience and for encouraging me to carry on when the task seemed impossible.

On the production side the project would not have really taken off without the assistance of The Co-Operative Bank, Stockport, Leeds Cameras, who entrusted us with some very valuable cameras and equipment, Fuji Film Manchester, for the donation of a quantity of film, Colour 061 of Manchester who processed and developed all our film, Philip Lane Photography for the supply of certain special film. The Director and Staff of the Commonwealth War Graves Commission for allowing me to extract information from their records, The Imperial War Museum for the use of several black and white photographs, Squadron Leader Les Evans for his wartime Kwai photographs, Singapore Oral History Museum, Dr. John Miksic of Singapore University, Tan Teng Teng for being able to speak Thai, The Royal Navy records office at Scotland Yard, RAF Brampton for the use of photographs and the British Library for providing maps and finally Richard Netherwood for his patience in designing, typesetting and advertising.

PHIL CAWLEY
PHOTOGRAPHY

IMPERIAL WAR
MUSEUM

CAPE COWLEY
ASSOCIATES

SERVING THE PROFESSIONALS

Leeds Photovisual Ltd

Thai
Thai Airways International Ltd

The CO-OPERATIVE BANK

DISTRIBUTORS OF PROFESSIONAL PHOTOGRAPHIC EQUIPMENT

Colour 061

A member of
the RS Colour Group

This book has been produced in memory of those British and Allied service men and women who trustingly placed their lives in the hands of influential leaders of government and whose sacrifice has never yet been fully recognised.

It is also produced so that in some small way, we, the men who were fortunate in surviving, can carry on the true tradition of the British services by lending a hand to all those servicemens families who are in need.

Opposite page: *Main Picture; The cave at Kinsyok inside which are the remains of at least two British POWs. They were buried after the Japanese engineer Kiyioki Tanaka prematurely detonated an explosive charge in order to teach other prisoners not to rest inside the cave. Inset; The Author.*

PREFACE

In the columns featured in this book are the names of some 22,602 British service men and women who died during the war in Malaya and Singapore and afterwards whilst prisoners of the Japanese, mainly due to starvation and malnutrition: this figure being about 35% of the total number of combined British, Australian, Indian, Chinese and local forces of some 63,000. Included in the total are the names of 21,356 who have no known grave and of this figure 9,295 were British. I have not listed these separately, so that they appear with their respective units where possible.

Added to this, there are 7,015 Allied civilians who also have no known grave and were not afforded a formal burial. Also included in this group are some 130 civilian, military and paramilitary nurses who went missing on the 15/16th February 1942.

During my research for this book I was made aware that most of these nurses were taken by the advancing Japanese army, and that on the 17th February 1942 an order was issued by General Yamashita that all such captured female civilians and nurses should be taken to his headquarters at the Ford motor company. On arrival each was murdered and her body cremated in the large incinerator at the rear of the factory. At this particular time the incinerator was being used by the Japanese to cremate the bodies of their men killed in the fighting, their ashes being transferred to the top of the hill at the side of the Ford plant. Later the hill was topped with a large monument, dedicated to the Japanese fallen and named Victory Hill!

I hope to be able to write a further book, depicting the last days of these brave nurses.

A great deal has been said in the past concerning compensation from the Japanese and when one considers recent trade figures which show Japan with a trade surplus of some eighty billion pounds it makes one wonder just how true was the prediction of Captain Asada in 1945 at Uttaradit. While we were discussing the war he told me, "We will not win this one, not this time. Although our soldiers, sailors and airmen have shown themselves to be far superior fighters to the Allies in all parts of Asia, it has not been enough. We had failed prior to the commencement of hostilities to achieve economic superiority over the West. Although the time was not really of our choosing, it had been assumed that our military power allied to our superior fighting qualities would have ensured a quick and decisive victory, which would have enabled Japan to have taken control of the whole of Asia. We nearly succeeded, but like England, we are only a small nation with few natural resources and we were unable to equal the vast economic superiority of the Americans. There is no doubt in my mind, that if we are to achieve world superiority, we must first acquire world economic domination. To do this, our people must give the same devotion to their country as that which our soldiers, sailors and airmen have given. Once we have acquired economic mastery, it must surely follow that we will be in a position to control the world. Once the Western powers become bankrupt they will in no way be able to offer any threat. Today the Americans are the world dominating power, but in thirty to forty years from now, Japan will be a nation to be reckoned with. Time means little to our great nation and while we wait we learn. The wise sheaf must surely bend before the wind".

At the end of hostilities when asked how many troops were used in the invasion of Singapore, the Japanese reported 30,000. They lied then and have always lied. When asked what had happened to more than sixty thousand missing persons including service men and civilians they claimed ignorance. Again they lied. A little over 1,000,000 persons vanished between the 7th of December 1941 and the 16th August 1945, yet the Japanese claim to know nothing about their disappearance. Today we are asked to accept them as civilised partners?

This book has been published primarily to help raise funds for SSAFA and so that former FEPOW (Far Eastern Prisoners of War) and the families of those who did not come home might glimpse a little of the terrain where the death railway was constructed.

When the Far East prisoners of war returned home, there were insufficient funds to allow for individual counselling or therapy. The funds of most of the charity organisations were exceedingly low and it is with the modern service men and women in mind that this project was undertaken.

The history of those fateful seventy odd days some fifty years ago are etched in the memory of all those who took part. Stories have been written again and again, so I must apologise if the version given herein is found to be somewhat similar to that of other writers, who like myself are dependent on their memory and the memories of others. The reader may well find that he himself took part in the operations mentioned and will therefore see things from his own personal point of view, whereas I can only rely on what I remember and that which I have since discovered.

To provide the list of casualties, I have personally extracted from various registers and from the Ministry of Defence and Commonwealth War Graves Commission the names of all British service men and women only. To have included the names of Australian, Canadian, Dutch, Indian and Chinese forces would have required a further one hundred and fifty pages.

If in the process of compiling this Roll of Honour I have inadvertently missed out any individual, I most sincerely apologise.

The return to Thailand, and our trek along what still remains of the railway, created in my mind absolute admiration for those of my comrades who were involved in its construction. At the same time I felt sorrow for the many relatives and comrades who return to Thailand to pay their respects and are only shown the cemeteries, when just for a few pence they could travel to the various sites where camps existed or where parts of the line still remain intact as a memorial to those who worked there.

In today's modern air conditioned coaches it is only a low - priced one and a half hour drive to Hell Fire Pass. Instead, the tour operators choose to take their patrons to visit the crocodile farms, rose gardens, jewellery stores and similar places, where they are assured of a good commission.

To hire an air conditioned mini bus to hold from four to six persons costs as little as two hundred and fifty pounds for six or seven days, and an air conditioned bus to Hell Fire Pass would cost three pounds fifty at the most and this includes refreshments en-route.

Although our photographer took in excess of 3,500 photographs and I filled three typist's note pads, it would not be possible to print every photograph or transpose every word from the pads. So we have selected the pictures which we feel are most appropriate in the hope that they will be of interest to former Far Eastern POWs and the families of those we left behind.

In closing, may I thank each one of you who purchased a copy of *When You Go Home*, the profits from which will be forwarded to SSAFA in the name of all those listed in the Roll of Honour.

Following page: '*A sleeper for every man who died*'

The Bridges at Tamakan (Kwai Bridge) prior to destruction by Allied bombing 24th June 1945.

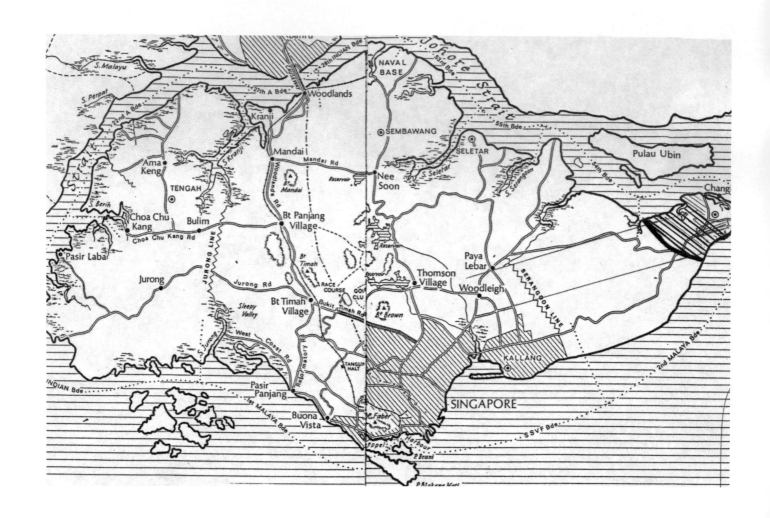

This map shows Changi prisoner of war camp area on the North East coast of Singapore.

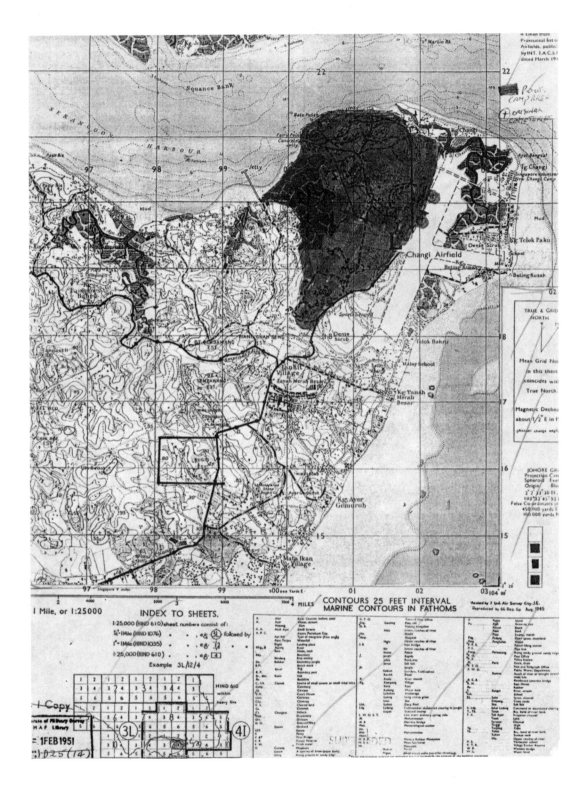

Hundreds of prisoners died within the first few weeks and two cemeteries were created outside the prison camp living areas. After the war, it was found that the cemeteries would be in the way of the new military airfield and the bodies were exhumed and transferred to the former ammunition dump at Kranji on the North West of Singapore, known today as Kranji War Cemetery. The shaded area is where all prisoners taken in Singapore and Malaya lived after capitulation.

The cemetery at Kranji, Singapore. At one time this was the largest ammunition dump in the entire Pacific region.

The Official Version

The Campaign in Malaya

In October 1940, Air Chief Marshal Sir Robert Brooke-Popham was appointed Commander-in-Chief Far East, and G H Q Far East opened at Singapore on the 18th November 1940. The Commander-in-Chief was responsible for the operational control and direction of training of British land and air forces in Malaya, Burma and Hong Kong, and for the co-ordination of plans for the defence of these territories; also for the control and training of British air forces in Ceylon and of reconnaissance squadrons in the Indian Ocean and the Bay of Bengal. His headquarters was an operational one, not administrative, and had no control over any naval forces.

In November 1940, the army strength in the whole of Malaya was 17 battalions, with 1 mountain regiment of artillery. Reliance for the defence of the Far East was to be placed on air power until the fleet was available. The strength of the air forces in Malaya in November 1940 however, was only 88 first-line aircraft, of which only 48 could be counted as modern. The previous month, the Singapore Conference had recommended a strength of 582 aircraft for the Far East; but it was admitted that this was an ideal, and far beyond the bounds of practical possibility. At this time it was the British goverment's policy to avoid war with Japan

When in July 1941, the Japanese spread into Southern Indo-China, the potential danger to Malaya and Burma increased, as the move gave them a naval base within 750 miles of Singapore and airfields only 300 miles from Kota Bharu, the nearest point in Malaya and by the latter part of November 1941, information accumulated which showed that an early Japanese attack was likely, despite the negotiations in progress in Washington. Both land and air reinforcements had been reaching Malaya. By 7th December, the eve of the Japanese attack, there were 158 first-line aircraft available, with 88 in reserve; the land forces counted 31 infantry battalions, plus the equivalent of 10 volunteer battalions with some artillery, engineers, and a small armoured car unit, 5 battalions of Indian States forces, with 7 field regiments, 1 mountain regiment, 2 anti-tank regiments, 4 coast defence regiments and 5 anti-aircraft regiments of artillery and 10 field and 3 fortress companies of engineers … a total strength of close on 87, 000 men. Almost one quarter of them were British, about one-sixth Australians, nearly one-half Indian Army, and the remainder local forces. Even then, the R A F Far East Command was not in a position to fulfil its responsibility of being the primary means of resisting Japanese aggression, while the army strength was far short of what was required to compensate for the deficiency in aircraft. There were only two-thirds the number of infantry required, no tanks and few armoured cars, and the lack of mobile anti-aircraft guns was serious.

In May 1941, Lieutenant-General A. E. Percival had been appointed General Officer Commanding, Malaya Command, and about three weeks earlier Air Vice-Marshal Pulford had assumed command of Far East Air Command.

The Attack

In the afternoon of 6th December word was received of Japanese convoy movements to the South of Indo-China, but reconnaissance conditions were bad, and it was impossible to maintain contact … one flying-boat which attempted to do so was shot down. The first clear evidence of the opening of hostilities was when, in the early morning hours of 8th December, Japanese troops started to land from about ten ships at Kota Bharu, in the extreme North-East of Malaya. Later reports stated that large Japanese forces were also landing at Singora and Patani in Thailand and in the Southern part of the Kra Isthmus. Very soon after these reports reached Singapore, the first Japanese air-raid on the city took place; the results achieved were small, but it was the first indication to most of the citizens that war had begun. At almost the same time the Japanese attacks on Hong Kong, Pearl Harbour and the Philippines had been launched.

At that date, the 3rd Indian Corps were in Northern Malaya, with the 11th Indian Division to the West of the peninsula in Kedah, Perlis and Northern Perak, and the 9th Indian Division to the East with the 8th Indian Brigade Group at Kelantan and Kota Bharu airfields. The weaker 22nd Indian Brigade Group was in the vicinity of Kuantan. The Corps headquarters was at Kuala Lumpur, in the South of the peninsula. The Australian force in Malaya, a part of the 8th Australian Division, were responsible for Johore and Malacca; comprising the 22nd and 27th Australian Imperial Forces (AIF) Brigades with Divisional Artillery and Engineers. Singapore and Penang had their own fortress garrisons which included the heavy artillery defences of Singapore. The 12th Indian Infantry Brigade formed a Command reserve, and there were a number of Command troops, and base and other administrative units. These troops had to defend a country approximately the size of England, their Command headquarters and principal base being on an island roughly comparable in size and position to the Isle of Wight.

On the first day of the campaign all the airfields in Northern Malaya were subjected to Japanese air attacks, and there were losses which could be ill afforded; the airfield at Kota Bharu had to be evacuated in the afternoon. Attacks on the airfields and considerable fresh Japanese landings in Thailand just North of the border were the main events of the next two days. On the Western side of the peninsula reconnaissance forces of the 11th Indian Division had crossed the Thai frontier in the afternoon of 8th December, meeting with some resistance from the Thais, and had made contact with the Japanese. Farther to the South-East a force based on Kroh (hence forth known as Krohcol) also crossed the frontier and met similar opposition from the Thais. They occupied positions a short distance within Thailand, but both forces were compelled to withdraw by 11th December.

Meanwhile, on the 10th disaster had befallen the Royal Navy. On the 8th the new Commander-in-Chief, Eastern Fleet, Admiral Sir Tom Phillips had left Singapore with the battleships Prince of Wales and Repulse and four destroyers. Japanese reconnaissance aircraft spotted this naval force on the evening of the 9th and picked them up again the following morning; Soon after noon on the 10th both capital ships were sunk by Japanese torpedo-bombers. Many were saved, but the Commander-in-Chief and the Captain of the Prince of Wales both went down. This, following the Pearl Harbour attack, gave the Japanese undisputed command of Far Eastern waters.

On the 11th, a heavy Japanese air raid on Georgetown, on the island of Penang, caused many casualties; as a result the greater part of the population left the town.

In the early hours of 12th December the Japanese launched an attack on the Indian troops in Northern Kedah, who, after a delaying action at Jitra, were obliged to withdraw to positions just north of Alor Star. After two more days of heavy fighting, our forces on the left were pushed back twenty miles South of Alor Star. Farther East, Krohcol also had to retreat and then came under the command of the 12th Indian Brigade, which on 12th December was ordered to move up from the South as reinforcements.

The forces in Kelantan, just south of Kota Bharu, were in the unhappy position of having no road communications with Southern Malaya and had to withdraw. Fresh Japanese landings farther South on 10th December, which threatened the British communications and also the two airfields at Gong Kedah and Machang, South of Kota Bharu, forced the decision to abandon these airfields. Once that decision was taken, the principal task of the Kelantan force was gone, and on 12th December orders were issued for the evacuation of Kelantan by the only route, the single-line railway.

The Withdrawal to Southern Malaya

On the West coast, the Japanese attack at Jitra against the 11th Indian defenders had reduced the Division to a state where they would normally have required relief … but there were no reserve troops available. The situation in the West soon began to cause great concern. The 11th Indian Division had withdrawn to a position at Gurun, half-way between Alor Star and Butterworth, but they were allowed little time to settle into this position. Within a matter of hours the Japanese were attacking forward postions. The 6th Indian Brigade, on the left of the front, guarding the vital road and railway, was overwhelmed by a strong Japanese force early on 15th December. A further withdrawal to the river Muda, the Southern boundary of Kedah, was ordered. On the 15th, the final decision to evacuate Penang was taken. The following day, the 11th Indian Division was ordered to withdraw to the Southern boundary of Province Wellesley, to the Krian River line. Very soon, however, a serious threat to this position also developed, as a considerable Japanese force advanced down the main road farther East, which leads South from Patani, and threatened to cut off the 11th Indian Division by reaching Kuala Kangsar.

Although the Northern airfields had all been captured or evacuated, it was still thought essential to keep the front as far forward as possible, in order that the reinforcements now promised might be landed in safety. The Japanese could not be permitted to establish air bases within close striking distance of Singapore. This policy was emphasised at an Allied conference held at Singapore on 18th December. On that day, however, yet another withdrawal, behind the River Perak, was sanctioned, although the enemy were to be held West of that river as long as possible. That day, too, it was decided that the remnants of the 6th and 15th Indian Brigades, both of which had suffered severely, should be amalgamated to form a single Brigade. The 9th Indian Division, now withdrawing from Kelantan, was assigned the duty of protecting Kuantan airfield and of securing the 11th Indian Division and its communications against attacks from the East.

The withdrawal behind the Perak River was soon inevitable, and was ordered to commence on the night 21st/22nd December. In sixteen days the Japanese had taken all of Malaya to the North and West of that river, and also the State of Kelantan; the State of Trengganu, on the East coast, lay undefended. But even so, there is no doubt that they had not progressed as rapidly as they had hoped.

On the night of 27th/28th December the 12th and 28th Brigades began to withdraw to positions some twenty miles South of Ipoh. During the last few days of December and the early part of January there were various changes in command: General Sir Henry Pownall relieved Sir Robert Brooke-Popham as Commander-in-Chief; when the headquarters of the Eastern Fleet moved first to Batavia and then to Colombo, Rear-Admiral Spooner was left as senior naval officer at Singapore; and General Sir Archibald Wavell was appointed Supreme Commander of the new Allied South West Pacific Command, General Pownall becoming his Chief of Staff when on 15th January Command Headquarters was established in Java.

The New Year opened with the hope of early reinforcements. A fresh Indian Infantry Brigade was expected soon, and the whole of the 18th British Division later in the month. Fifty Hurricane fighters with their crews were also in a convoy due to reach Singapore about 13th - 15th January. They, along with other aircraft that were promised, would do something to counter Japanese air superiority. The Japanese also, however, were known to have received reinforcements at the end of December.

On the night 29th/30th December the Japanese commenced what developed into a four-day battle for the positions South of Ipoh held by the 11th Indian Division. That Division had to deal not only with frontal attacks but with a threat to its rear and its communications by landings from the sea and across the River Perak at Telok Anson against the 12th Brigade. This menace to the rear of the main positions forced a withdrawal on 2nd January, after a determined struggle. No respite was granted by the enemy, who continued to press forward and at the same time made a further landing in some strength some thirty-five miles farther South on the West coast.

In the East too, the early days of January saw withdrawal. On 30th December the Japanese began their attack on Kuantan, defended by troops of the 9th Indian Division. There was some fierce fighting around the town and the airfield, and early on the morning of 3rd January orders were issued for a withdrawal towards the West. In the evening of that day the rearguard suffered severe losses when it was attacked by the Japanese. Heavy casualties were inflicted on the Japanese during these few days.

On 7th January came a disaster in Western Malaya. The 12th and 28th Brigade Groups were holding positions astride the road near the Slim River, which forms the boundary between the States of Perak and Selangor. For a few days there had not been much fighting, then in the early morning of the 7th the Japanese launched an attack with tanks. Despite gallant opposition, they broke right through and captured intact the bridge by which the road crosses the river. Both Brigades were thrown into confusion, and, obeying the order that the Division must remain in being as a fighting formation, had no alternative to cutting their losses and withdrawing as best they could. The losses in both men and materials were very heavy.

The Defence of Johore

Plans had been made for a withdrawal to the southernmost State of Malaya, Johore, and for its defence. It had not been expected that this would be necessary before the middle of January, but the Slim River disaster made it essential to establish a front in Johore at once; General Wavell, who visited the front on his way to his new headquarters in Java, issued instructions to this effect. It was decided that the 3rd Indian Corps less the 9th Indian Division should be responsible for operations in Southern Johore, south of a line Endua-Kluang-Batu-Pahat, absorbing the 22nd Australian Brigade Group. Major-General Gordon Bennett with the remainder of the A I F formations, the 9th Indian Division and the 45th Indian Brigade Group (just arrived from India) was responsible for Johore to the North of that line.

This withdrawal into Johore meant the abandonment of the States of Selangor and Negri Sembilan and of the ancient colony of Malacca; also of Kuala Lumpur, the capital of the Federated Malay States. By 14th January all the 3rd Indian Corps troops had passed through Gordon Bennett's force, carrying out demolitions on all roads, and by mid-day the dispositions of the Australian force (known as Westforce) were completed.

The first Japanese attack came in the afternoon of the 14th, when a Japanese column fell into an ambush prepared by the Australians at Gemas and suffered several hundred casualties and the loss of a number of tanks at comparatively small cost to the Australians. Unfortunately this success was soon cancelled by a series of disasters on the Muar River at the Western extremity of the front, where Japanese troops penetrated the area held by the new and untried 45th Indian Infantry Brigade and practically destroyed one battalion. A serious threat to Australian communications resulted, as the Japanese penetration was not far from the main road seventy miles south of the forward troops. At the time it did not seem necessary to withdraw these forward troops, but the strength of the threat from Muar had not been fully appreciated. Despite efforts to reinforce that sector, by the evening of the 18th a withdrawal on the whole front was inevitable. This withdrawal could only be carried out at night because of Japanese air superiority. The force at Muar was in fact cut off on the l9th, and less than 1,000 of the 4,000 or more who were there succeeded in escaping and rejoining the main force. From the 15th to the 22nd, Australian and Indian troops held a Division of the Japanese Imperial Guards at Muar, gaining valuable time for the withdrawal of their comrades farther to the East.

Already the defensive line was that which had been planned as the Northern limit of the Indian Corps' responsibilities. Reinforcements had arrived from India and Australia, but almost all were raw and untrained troops … the only ones available at the time. The main body of the 18th British Division had not yet arrived.

By this time the Japanese had obtained possession of airfields sufficiently close to Singapore to enable them to escort their bombers with fighters, and so Singapore became the target of two or three daylight attacks each day, directed mainly against airfields on the island, but also against the docks and the naval base.

The defence on the mainland was now formed into three separate commands, all of which came under the 3rd Indian Corps. To the East was a group under Brigadier Taylor, commander of the 22nd Australian Brigade, which was already in that area. In the centre, defending the railway and the main trunk road, were the remainder of the A I F and the 9th Indian Division, all under Major-General Gordon Bennett. On the West coast was the 11th Indian Division, under Major-General Key.

Again, as at Muar, the Western sector proved the critical one. Japanese troops landed near Batu Pahat on 16th January, and before long were driving between the Western and central sectors, threatening to cut off the 11th Indian Division. That Division was forced to withdraw its forward brigade during the night 25th/26th January, and on the same night the troops on the central sector also had to withdraw, thereby leaving the Japanese in control of a main road from East to West across the country. These withdrawals, coupled with fresh landings on the East coast and attacks upon the defenders in that sector, made it clear that a retreat to Singapore was inevitable; it was too risky to attempt to hold a line in Southern Johore, with only a single line of retreat across the causeway to the island. It was, therefore, decided that the whole force still on the mainland should be withdrawn across the causeway on the night of 30th/31st January. During the preparations for this retreat the 22nd Indian Brigade of the 9th Indian Division were cut off by the Japanese, and only some 100 officers and men of that brigade were later ferried across the Strait of Johore to safety. The withdrawal of the remainder of the troops across the causeway was carried out successfully with little interference from the Japanese air force. About eight o'clock on the morning of 31st January the last troops crossed the causeway, which was immediately demolished.

The Battle of Singapore

The Battle of Singapore was about to begin, with only a few days in which to make dispositions to counter the assault. Some reinforcements had just arrived: a number of Hurricane fighters flown off an aircraft-carrier, a light tank squadron from India, and the main body of the British 18th Division under Major-General Beckwith-Smith.

The defences were divided into three main areas. The 3rd Indian Corps was responsible for the Northern Area; it now comprised the 11th Indian Division, into which the remaining brigade of the 9th Indian Division had been incorporated, and the 18th British Division, commanded by Lieutenant-General Sir L. M. Heath. The Southern Area, which included the city of Singapore, was defended by what remained of the original Fortress troops manning most of the fixed defences, the 1st and 2nd Malaya Infantry Brigades and the Straits Settlements Volunteer Force. The

Fortress Commander, Major-General F. Keith Simmons, remained in command. In the Western Area, believed to be the danger point, was the Australian Imperial Force, with the 44th Indian Infantry Brigade, under Major-General Gordon Bennett. The Australian troops were the freshest of those that had experience of fighting on the mainland.

The anti-aircraft defences, under Brigadier A.W.G. Wildey, had been re-organised; the Command reserve being constituted by the 12th Indian Infantry Brigade, under Brigadier Paris. In addition, detachments of a force of Chinese irregulars (known as "Dalforce" from their commander, Lt.Col. Dalley) were placed under orders of the Area commanders ... but they were not fully armed or equipped.

During the first week of February there was artillery activity on both sides, and there were Japanese air attacks, mostly on the docks and the civil airfield. Early on the morning of the 8th, Australian patrols returned from the mainland to report that large Japanese contingents were now opposite Singapore Island. Shelling on this front started later that morning and increased in intensity until evening. A little more than an hour before midnight the first Japanese landings took place, and soon the whole of the Australian 22nd Brigade front was engaged. Although there was fierce fighting on the beaches, the Japanese got ashore at many points. They drove a wedge between two of the Australian battalions, and the situation soon became confused. The weight of the attack was not at first realised; two Japanese Divisions were engaged in the assault, 13,000 troops being landed during the night and a further 10, 000 soon after dawn. Later a third Division joined in the attack, the total enemy force now numbered some 70, 000 infantry supported by 150 tanks, 168 guns and more than 500 aircraft.

What British reserves were available were soon thrown in, but by eight o'clock in the morning on the 9th the Japanese were attacking the airfield in the Western sector, and were advancing towards Bukit Timah and Singapore City. In the evening came a further Japanese attack across the Strait of Johore, this time in the North, close to the causeway, and once again the enemy gained a footing. Already it was proving necessary to withdraw units from the Northern sector to reinforce the West. General Wavell visited Singapore on the 10th and before he left issued orders that the island must be held to the last. On the 11th the Japanese continued to advance both from the West and from the North and, despite all efforts to save them, the food and petrol dumps near Bukit Timah were lost. This meant that little petrol and only fourteen days' military food supplies remained to the defenders although the civilian food situation was less critical.

On the 12th, it had to be agreed that there was no point in leaving forces in the North-Eastern part of the island when Singapore City itself was imminently threatened and orders were given to withdraw all forces within a perimeter around the city, which included the water supply reservoirs and civil airfield though the sole remaining fighter squadron had left it two days before. There was heavy fighting along the whole front on the 12th; the Australian 22nd Brigade held an advanced position south of Bukit Timah until evening, when after forty eight hours' stubborn resistance it was withdrawn.

On the 13th the main Japanese attack was made along a ridge to the West of Singapore City. It fell chiefly upon the Malay Regiment, which held its ground that day and the next until forced by heavy losses to yield. In the afternoon at a staff conference all the senior commanders were agreed that, owing to the exhaustion of the troops, a counter-attack would have no chance of succeeding. A start was made that evening with the evacuation of surplus staff officers, nurses, technicians and others whose knowledge would be of value to the Allies for the later prosecution of the war. Among those who left were Rear-Admiral Spooner and Air Vice-Marshal Pulford; the patrol boat on which they travelled, pursued by a Japanese destroyer, ran aground on a deserted island and more than half the party died there, including these two officers. Many of the small ships that took off evacuees on that day met a similar fate, and those on board were either drowned or taken prisoner.

Early on the 14th the water situation became serious; mains broken by bombing and shelling were causing losses which repairs could not keep pace with, and it was estimated that the supply would only last for forty-eight hours ... possibly only for twenty-four.

General Wavell, in reply to a report on the situation, urged that resistance should continue and said, "Your gallant stand is serving a purpose and must be continued to the limit of endurance".

During the night 14th/15th February, Japanese infantry infiltrated in the Western central sector, and there was bitter fighting on the extreme left, where the 2nd Bn. The Loyal Regiment, which bore the brunt of the attack, was reduced to only 130 fighting men. The water situation was reported in the morning to be critical, ammunition reserves were very low, and only a few days' military food stocks remained, although there were large reserves in the area now occupied by the Japanese, and there were civil reserves. There were only two alternatives: a counter-attack to regain control of the reservoirs and the food reserves and to drive Japanese artillery back; or capitulation. A counter-attack was judged by all to be impossible; so at a meeting in the afternoon terms of surrender were agreed with the Japanese commander Lieutenant-General Yamashita, and hostilities ceased at 8. 30 in the evening of 15th February (British time).

This was the end of the fighting in Malaya after seventy days of struggle without respite. In both naval and air strength the Japanese had overwhelming superiority On land, it is estimated that at the time of the surrender they had some 120, 000 troops and 150 tanks on Singapore Island and in Southern Malaya, compared with a total of some 85, 000 troops of the British Commonwealth and Empire in Singapore (among whom were a fairly high proportion of non-combatant units medical, pioneer, etc.).

Operations in Borneo

Borneo came within the Malaya Command, but through lack of resources only token forces could be stationed there. These could be expected to do little more than gain sufficient time for the demolition of the oilfield installations. In December 1941 the garrison of Borneo consisted of the 2/15th Punjab Regiment. They were stationed at Kuching in Sarawak, where there was an airfield, and at Miri, some 400 miles as the crow flies to the North-East. At Miri and at Seria, near by in Brunei, were the oilfields. On 8th December 1941 orders were received by the local garrison for their demolition. This was carried out successfully, the troops, oil company officials, and a detachment of Straits Settlements police being evacuated by sea to Kuching on the 13th. On the 16th, Japanese troops landed at Seria.

On 23rd December, orders were received at Kuching for the demolition of the airfield, which, as well as the town, had suffered several air attacks during the previous days. On 24th December, Japanese landing-craft made their way up the waterways between the sea and Kuching, and by the afternoon of that day the Japanese flag was flying over the residence of the Rajah of Sarawak. The following morning, the British garrison commander, Lt.Col. Lane, decided to withdraw his force Westwards into Dutch West Borneo. On reaching Sanggau on 29th December, the battalion came under the orders of the local Dutch commander. There it fought alongside the Dutch to prevent the Japanese from taking the airfield at Sanggau, the principal Anglo-Dutch air base in West Borneo. Finally, through February and March, after fighting a rearguard action, the Punjabis made their way through wild and difficult country to the South coast of Borneo, which they reached, exhausted, towards the end of March, having covered a total distance of some 800 miles since leaving Kuching. But the Dutch had by then been forced to surrender, and on 3rd April the 2/15th Punjab Regiment became prisoners of war.

Prisoners of War

The end of hostilities was only the beginning of fresh tribulation for many of those who survived the battle, A great many of the men who are commemorated on the Singapore memorial to those who have no known grave, died as prisoners of war. Some perished on the Japanese transports which were sunk while carrying them to permanent prisoner of war camps elsewhere. Many more died of illness, frequently from malnutritional diseases. During the years in captivity many were employed by the Japanese in the construction of the railway from Thailand to Burma, and thousands lie buried in the two cemeteries at Chungkai and Kanchanaburi. The completion of the link between Bangkok and Rangoon was completed by October 1943 after a year of intensive forced labour by many thousands of British, American, Australian and Dutch prisoners of war and local civilians. An example of the death rate is given by the fact that of one party of 7,000 who were sent from Singapore to Thailand in April 1943, 25% were dead by August and 90% of the remainder were ill. The total number of deaths of Allied prisoners was estimated at 24,000.

There are two war cemeteries: at Taiping, which is on the line of the retreat down the east coast of Malaya and at Kranji on the island of Singapore, where the memorial referred to stands. A number of those who died are buried in civil cemeteries in Singapore and Malaya, but the majority lie in the war cemeteries.

The Air War in the East

The Singapore memorial bears the names of men of the Royal Air Force who gave their lives not only in Malaya, but in India and Burma and throughout the Far East.

In 1941 the Far East Air Command included Hong Kong, Borneo, Malaya and Burma and it stretched across the Indian ocean to Ceylon and on to Durban and Mombassa. Air power was to be the basis of the defence in the Far East and in planning it was assumed that the Japanese would not be able to strike simultaneously at several widely separated points, and that therefore the British, Dutch and American air forces would be able to reinforce each other when required. By the time the Japanese attacked however, the necessary air power required to withstand them was not available and they delivered such simultaneous attacks as had previously been thought impossible.

The campaigns of 1941 and 1942 present a story of continual retreat. The airfields in North Malaya were useless almost from the beginning. Thereafter, until the fighting came within range of the airfields of Singapore, the army had to carry on without air support. The Allied air forces strove nobly to carry out their many tasks: they were called upon to bomb airfields held by the Japs, to perform long-range reconnaissance in search of possible enemy reinforcements and landings, to protect incoming British reinforcements, and carry out photographic reconnaissance. And all this with few machines, many of them obsolete. When reinforcements did arrive, in January 1942, some of the machines were not suited to local conditions, and the crews were inexperienced in the tropics. Moreover, the airfields they had to use were already subjected to heavy bombing. In the first ten days of February, the fighters were almost continually airborne, striving to ward off the continual Japanese attacks.

By 16th January, all Allied airforce units in Malaya had been driven back to Singapore island. To lessen the congestion there the bomber squadrons were transferred to Sumatra where there were two airfields near Palembang. Operational and maintenance facilities were primitive and accommodation of personnel presented a problem. From Sumatra, bombers made long flights to attack Japanese-held airfields in Malaya and maintained daily reconnaissances across the South China Sea, while fighters escorted shipping in the waters between Sumatra and Malaya and operated in defence of Sumatra against air-raids. The Japanese soon closed in on Sumatra however. They landed parachute troops near the main airfield on 14th February and on the 15th made an attempt, which was thwarted by British air attacks, to sail a convoy up the Palembang River. A steady stream of British aircraft attacked troop transports, landing craft and barges, and causing very heavy casualties among the Japanese, sinking three transports and several landing craft. There were further landings of parachute troops that day; the Japanese established themselves near Palembang, and it was decided that all Allied airforce units must withdraw to Java. This they did that evening and on the 16th, but were forced to leave much valuable equipment behind.

The End in Java

In Java, organisation was not easy, as on the one hand units from Malaya and Sumatra were arriving partly organised and equipped, while on the other hand the Japanese were expected to land in the island before long (they came twelve days after the evacuation of Sumatra) and a great exodus of civilians had begun. On 22nd February the withdrawal of General Wavell's headquarters was ordered, and it was decided that the British forces that remained should operate under the Dutch naval and army commanders. The change took place on 25th February.

Air reconnaissance was to be maintained over the whole of the Java Sea and as far North as possible on both sides of Borneo, and an invasion was to be opposed as far out to sea as possible by air action. The first invasion convoy was sighted by reconnaissance aircraft on 26th February. By the 28th, other convoys had been located, and it was evident that about midnight there would be simultaneous landings at the Eastern end of Java near Sourabaya and at two points in Western Java near Batavia (now Djakarta). The Eastern convoy was twice attacked by American and British aircraft during the night 28th February/1st March, and considerable damage was done. The same night, British aircraft made several attacks on the Japanese convoy which was approaching the East of Batavia, and on Japanese troops as they landed. The airfield from which these attacks were launched was captured by the Japanese the following morning, and with it several aircraft which could not take off in time, though the majority of the ground staff escaped. Fighter aircraft from another airfield continued to attack enemy columns and to carry out reconnaissances, until on 3rd March they had to withdraw to Andir, near Bandoeng. By 4th March, the Japanese were advancing rapidly in both Eastern and Western Java. Surplus air force personnel, a great many of them without arms, were evacuated as fast as shipping permitted, and from 3rd March till the 7th reconnaissance aircraft were flown to Australia and Ceylon. By 5th March the Japanese were closing in on the final Western stronghold at Bandoeng, and on the 8th the Dutch Commander-in-Chief issued the order to surrender. Altogether, more than 5,000 men of the Allied air forces were involved in this surrender, many of whom had escaped first from Malaya and then from Sumatra.

The Air Forces in Burma

The part played by the Allied air forces in the defeat of the Japanese in Burma cannot be described here in full chronological detail, but tribute must be paid to the immense value of their contribution. The Eastern Air Command which from early in 1944 waged the air war in Burma included Royal Air Force and United States Air Force formations. The Strategic Air Force, under the American Brigadier-General H. C. Davidson, included No. 231 Bomber Group, and in the 3rd Tactical Air Force, commanded by Air Marshal Sir John Baldwin, the R A F elements were Nos. 221 and 224 Tactical Groups. There were also RAF elements in the Photographic Reconnaissance Force and the Combat Cargo Task Force. From the nature of the country and the way in which the campaign for the liberation of Burma was fought, the army was more dependent upon air support than in any other campaign. Units were operating far behind the Japanese lines for prolonged periods; they were taken there by air, were supplied by air, had their wounded and sick removed to base hospitals by air, and could call on the Allied air force for help in battle. All this was a matter of gradual growth. Experiments were made in the ways of carrying and dropping supplies, in the methods of calling up air support and co-ordinating ground movements with fire from the air. It was on the Burma front that large formations were first moved long distances by air and maintained by air supply. In March, 1944, in the second Chindit expedition, thousands of men and animals were landed far behind the enemy's lines and were maintained by air for months. Small wonder that the Fourteenth Army has been described as "the most airminded army that ever existed".

The work of the Strategic Air Force was carried out over a vast area from bases in India. Japanese bases and lines of communication stretched some 900 miles from Bangkok to Myitkyina, and were very vulnerable to air attack; but the raids upon them involved round trips of anything up to 3, 000 miles. A quarter of Strategic Air Force operations were directed against railway communications - in particular the new line between Burma and Thailand. Roads along which Japanese supplies had to be brought, and oil installations in Burma, were also among their targets. Reconnaissance aircraft searching for targets, observing the results of sorties, and surveying Burma and Malaya photographically, also covered amazing distances. More than other branches of the service, they had to combat the weather, and some of the aircraft they used were not suitable for the tropics. Tropical storms took their toll of all branches of the air arm, as did the hazards of flights over jungle country.

When victory was within sight, General Slim in an Order of the Day said: "There could have been no victory without the support of the Allied air forces. They never failed us, and it is their victory as much as ours". There was a peculiar appropriateness in the fact that the first man to enter Rangoon, on 2nd May 1945, was an RAF officer of 221 Group, who landed his machine at Mingaladon airfield, walked into the city, and having assured himself that the Japanese were gone then sailed down the river in a commandeered sampan to meet the troops advancing from the South.

The Burma-Siam Railway

The notorious Burma-Siam Railway, built by British, Australian, Dutch and American prisoners of war, was a project inspired by the need for improved communications to maintain the large Japanese army in Burma. During its construction more than 16, 000 prisoners of war died … mainly of sickness, malnutrition and exhaustion … and were buried along the railway. Impressed Burmese and Malay labourers died in their thousands; exactly how many will never be known. The Japanese kept no records and it was impossible for anyone else to do so, nor were the graves marked, but between 80,000 and 100,000 perished. (After the war the railway was purchased by the Thai government, from its starting point at Bampong to the Burmese border and it is now part of the Royal State Railways. It is open to general traffic from Bampong to Hintock, about 33 miles). Japanese communications depended upon a long and exposed sea route to Rangoon via Singapore and the Strait of Malacca, and a road (quite unfit for prolonged heavy traffic) from Raheng through Kowkareik to Moulmein. The decision to complete the railway connecting Moulmein with Bangkok, which had been commenced before the war but abandoned by the two countries concerned, was taken in June 1942. More than 250 miles of railway, from Thanbyuzayat in Burma to Bampong in Thailand remained to be constructed, much of it through mountainous country and dense jungle, in a region with one of the worst climates in the world. The Japanese aimed at completing the railway in 14 months or at least by the end of 1943. They utilised a labour force composed of prisoners of war taken in the campaigns in South-East Asia and the Pacific, and coolies brought from Malaya and the Dutch East Indies or conscripted in Siam and Burma. From June 1942 onwards large groups of prisoners were transferred periodically to Thailand from Burma, Java, Sumatra and Borneo. Two labour forces, one based in Thailand and one in Burma, worked from opposite ends of the line towards the centre. When the first of the prisoners arrived in June 1942 their initial task was the construction of camps at Kanchanaburi and Bampong in Thailand, and Thanbyuzayat in Burma.

Accommodation for the Japanese guards had to be built first, at all the staging camps along the railway. The cook-house and huts for the working parties came next and accommodation for the sick last of all. Frequently men were sent to work on the line long before their accommodation was completed. Throughout the building of the railway, food supplies were irregular and totally inadequate. Brought up by barge on the Kwai Noi river, or by lorry on a road which was merely a converted jungle track, a consistent food supply could not be maintained by either method, and rations were nearly always below even the Japanese official scales. Vegetables and other perishables long in transit arrived rotten. The rice was of poor quality, frequently maggoty or in other ways contaminated. Fish, meat, oil, salt and sugar were on a minimum scale. Although it was often possible to supplement this diet by purchases from the local civilian population, men sometimes had to live for weeks on little more than a small daily ration of rice flavoured with salt. Red Cross parcels helped, but these were invariably held back by the Japanese. Malaria, dysentery and pellagra (a vitamin deficiency disease) attacked the prisoners, and the number of sick in the camps was always very high.

The Japanese demanded from each camp a certain percentage of its occupants for working parties, irrespective of the number of sick. To make up the required quota, the Japanese camp commandants insisted on men totally unfit for work being driven out and sometimes carried out. Those who stayed behind were accommodated in camp "hospitals" which were simply one or more crude jungle huts. At main camps such as Chungkai, Tamarkan, Non Pladuk and Thanbyuzayat there were "base hospitals" which were also huts constructed from bamboo and thatch, and staffed by such medical officers and orderlies as were allowed by the Japanese to care for the sick prisoners. To these base hospitals desperately sick men … the weak supported by the less weak, since no fit men were allowed to accompany them … were evacuated from the camp hospitals, travelling by the haphazard means of hitch-hiking on a passing lorry or river barge. At both camp and base hospitals, for the greater part of the time, the doctors had only such drugs and equipment as they had been able to carry with them from Singapore. Neither drugs nor surgical instruments were supplied by the Japanese, and although later on certain medical supplies were made available they were always inadequate. A great deal of equipment was improvised by the medical staff with food and medicine being clandestinely obtained. Only the skill, devotion and enterprise of the doctors saved the lives of thousands of prisoners and gradually created an organised system to control certain diseases.

Work on the railway started at Bampong on 1st October 1942 and somewhat later at Thanbyuzayat. The two parties met at Nieke in November 1943, and the 263 mile long line was completed by November 1943. Thereafter work on the railway consisted of maintenance, and repairs to damage caused by Allied bombing. Allied reconnaissance flights over the Burma end of the railway started early in 1944, followed by bombings at intervals. These became more and more frequent when, towards the end of October 1944, trains full of Japanese troops and supplies began to go through from Thailand to Burma. The Japanese would not allow their captives to construct a symbol (a white triangle on a blue base) indicating the presence of a prisoner of war camp, and consequently these air raids contributed their quota to the death toll along the line. Most of the camps were built alongside the railway track, some were near bridges and other vulnerable points. The only cover for prisoners was that afforded by their flimsy bamboo and thatch huts, under which they were made to shelter while the raids were in progress. The inevitable casualties were heavy. In one raid alone on the camp at Non Pladuk situated next to a railway marshalling yard holding petrol, ammunition and protected by an anti-aircraft post in contravention of the Geneva Convention, the prisoners were not allowed to leave their huts and 95 were killed and 300 wounded.

In March 1944, when the bulk of the prisoners were in the main camps at Chungkai, Tamarkan, Kanchanaburi, Tamuan, Non Pladuk and Nakom Paton, conditions temporarily improved. The Japanese had been surprised by the reaction of world opinion against their treatment of prisoners of war, and there is evidence that they began to feel apprehensive about the heavy POW casualties of 1943, and made efforts to counteract their reputation for uncivilised treatment of prisoners. But this phase soon passed, and from May 1944 until the capitulation of Japan in August 1945 parties of prisoners were sent from the various base camps to work on railway maintenance, cut fuel for the locomotives, and handle stores at dumps along the line. Other parties were employed on cutting and building roads, some through virgin jungle, or in building defence positions. As before, their food and accommodation were minor considerations to the Japanese. The railway was overworked carrying troops and military supplies, and local traders seldom visited the camps of the working parties, now small compared with those of 1943 and therefore not so profitable, so that supplementary food supplies were scarce, and again sickness took its toll. The only redeeming feature was the ease with which the sick could be evacuated to base hospitals in trains returning empty from Burma.

The remains of those who died during the construction and maintenance of the Burma/Siam railway (except Americans, who were repatriated) have been transferred from the camp burial grounds and sites along the railway into three war cemeteries. At Chungkai War Cemetery and Kanchanaburi War Cemetery in Thailand rest those recovered from the Southern part of the line, from Bampong to Nieke, about half its length. In the War Cemetery at Thanbyuzayat in Burma lie those from the Northern half of the line.

Those who have no known grave are commemorated by name on either the Rangoon or the Singapore memorial, depending on which theatre they were presumed to have died. The RAF dead are commemorated on the Singapore memorial, and the Royal Navy casualties on memorials at their manning ports.

The Recapture of Borneo

In April 1945 it was decided that the role of the Australian Corps in that year would be to capture bases in Borneo, possibly as a prelude to an advance Westwards into the Netherlands East Indies. It was believed that the Japanese force in Borneo numbered 32,000, of whom 15,000 were combat troops. The 9th Australian Division were given the task of taking Tarakan in Dutch Borneo (now Borneo), the Brunei Bay area and the oilfields in British Borneo (now in Brunei and Sarawak). The 7th Division was to capture Balikpapan in Dutch Borneo.

After prolonged naval and air bombardment the 26th Brigade Group was landed on a beach near Tarakan on 1st May. The Japanese defenders fought with great resolution and it was 5th May before both the town and the airfield had been taken. The task of destroying the Japanese garrison remained.

On the Western flank the infantry advanced fairly swiftly into the centre of the island, but north of the town there was much close fighting. By the last week of May the attackers controlled most of the island, but a strong Japanese force was dug in on high ground near the town. On 14th June after a series of attacks the defenders began to withdraw Northwards. By this time 923 Japanese out of a total force of 1,800 had been killed and 37 taken prisoner. The Japanese force was pressed hard as it withdrew and was dispersed. In the final stage of the operations an additional 600 Japanese were killed and 125 were taken prisoner. The Australians lost 225 killed.

Among the aims of the operations in British Borneo were the establishment of an advanced fleet base at Brunei Bay and the recapture of the oilfields. The task was allotted to the 9th Division (Major-General G. F. Wootten) less the 26th Brigade, but augmented by other units until the strength of the force totalled 29,000, including squadrons of the Royal Australian Air Force. On 10th June the 20th Brigade landed on Muara Island and at Brunei Bluff on the South side of the bay, and the 24th Brigade on Labuan Island off the Northern end of the bay. Both landings were unopposed. The 24th Brigade quickly occupied most of Labuan Island, but a strong pocket of Japanese on hilly ground West of the airstrip held out until 21st June. At this stage 389 Japanese dead had been counted and 11 had been taken prisoner; the Australians had lost 24 killed and 93 wounded. Meanwhile the 2/32nd Battalion had landed at Weston on the North shore of the bay on 17th June and the 2/43rd Battalion and 21/11th Commando Squadron at Mempakul at the Northern headland of the bay on 19th June. These forces advanced Northwards and on 27th and 28th June Beaufort was attacked and captured. Thence the 2/32nd Battalion advanced to Papar and thus completed its task of protecting Brunei Bay against attack from the North.

Meanwhile, advancing against only slight resistance, the 20th Brigade cleared the enemy from the area South of the bay and moved along the coast to Seria (21st June). On the 20th the 21/13th Battalion had been landed farther South at Lutong, from where it advanced to Miri. The Australians lost 114 killed in the operations in North Borneo.

The 7th Division (Major-General E. J. Milford) was given the task of taking Balikpapan in Dutch Borneo and the surrounding area. Including R A A F units and other attached troops the invading force was 33,000 strong. After heavy air and naval bombardments, and after sea lanes had been swept clear of mines and underwater obstacles had been demolished, the leading battalions landed on 1st July. On the left the 18th Brigade captured the high ground crowning the Eastern headland of Balikpapan Bay and, on the 3rd, entered Balikpapan town. The 21st Brigade advanced East along the coast, captured Manggar airfield on 4th July, and advanced to Sambodga. The 25th Brigade landed on 4th July and advanced inland from Balikpapan towards Samarinda. It was strongly opposed but by 22nd July had overcome the enemy force. In the Balikpapan operations the Australians lost 229 killed.

The RAAF joined in the operation against Borneo in mid-April when heavy bombers, based on Morotai Island attacked targets at, or near to, Tarakan. Heavy bombers based on the Australian mainland also undertook strikes over Java, Bali and Celebes in support of the main campaign. Large American forces carried the main burden operating from bases in the Philippines and ranging far afield in the Indies. As the date of landing approached these attacks were intensified, and targets which might impede the ground forces on Tarakan were hit. Although the airfield at Tarakan was soon captured it could only support light aircraft, and this prevented early build-up of the air force there. Instead, the fighter squadrons operated from the nearby Sulu Archipelago, from where targets in Dutch and British Borneo were visited. For the seizure of Labuan and British North Borneo the tasks of Allied heavy bombers were similar to those for Tarakan, while Australian fighters strafed selected targets and after the landings did close-support work for the army. By 17th June Australian fighters were based on Labuan. The landing at Balikpapan called for even greater efforts from the Allied heavy bombers and although, as elsewhere in Borneo, there was little chance of hostile air opposition, the Japanese anti-aircraft defences were strong and during operations before and after the landings exacted a price for the heavy air attacks. Australian fighters were able to use Tarakan in time to undertake operations designed to assist in the Balikpapan operation, and by 13th July were based at Balikpapan and performing a close-support role for the troops.

Hostilities ceased on 16th August. Australian commanders took the surrender of the Japanese commanders in the Netherlands East Indies, in Borneo, and in Australian territories.

The Royal Australian Navy had a major role in the Borneo campaign, in May-July 1945. The landing ships Westralia and Manoora, with Hobart, Warramunga, and frigates, took part in the initial assault on Tarakan in May. On the 9th June Hobart (flagship of Commodore Farncomb), Arunta and frigates formed part of Rear-Admiral Berkey's bombardment and covering force, and the three landing ships Westralia, Manoora and Kanimbla took part in the assault landings. H M A S Shropshire was flagship of the Australian squadron (including Hobart and Arunta) at the landings at Balikpapan on 1st July. The three vessels also took part in these landings, and ships of the R A N Survey Group also did most valuable work in these operations.

The R A N was represented at the Borneo surrender by representatives from Burdekin, Gascoyne, Inverell and ML 1359 at South Borneo on the 8th September, 1945; Bundaberg, Kapunda, Wanganella, and smaller craft at Kuching, Jesselton and Sandakan on the 9th September.

One of the great ships which gave so much confidence during the early days

Motor Launch 311 patrolling the Strait. This launch was later used in an attempt to evacuate approximately 500 civilians to Java. She was attacked and sunk by the Japanese air force.

Top left clockwise:

Men of 18th Division arrive Jan. 29th 1942 only to be taken prisoner four weeks later!

Australian hospital ship Wanganella arrives in Singapore

Too hot to operate indoors, scenes outside Fort Canning

East meets West

This page and opposite: *As well as manning their machine gun posts, the men of the Manchester Regiment were required to erect wooden boat obstacles offshore. These obstacles became submerged at full tide and it was expected that they would rip the bottom from any approaching Japanese boats carrying soldiers.*

The nursing staff showed no discrimination with casualties. The first Japanese and British casualties arrive in Singapore together, 13th December 1941

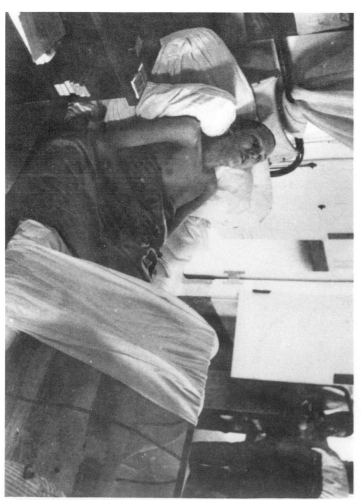

'Manchesters' at 10th Milestone Camp

Bandmaster Grey and the band of the 'Manchesters'
play 11th Division ashore

Colonel Holmes (Manchester Regiment
C.O.) examines a Thompson machine gun

Setting up a road ambush on the mainland

Personnel carriers on manoeuvres

The Singapore Civil Memorial is dedicated to more than 1,000,000 civilians of all nationalities who died between Dec. 6th. 1941 and Aug. 16th. 1945 as a result of Japanese bestiality

The War Cemeteries

Kranji War Cemetery

Kranji, in the North of Singapore Island, lies South of the 1,100 yard causeway across the Straits of Johore which joins the island to the mainland of Malaya. Before 1939 the Kranji area was a military camp, and at the time of the Japanese invasion of Malaya was the site of a large ammunition magazine. On February 8th, 1941, the Japanese crossed the Johore Straits in strength, landing at the mouth of the Kranji River within two miles of the place where the war cemetery now stands. On the evening of February 9th, they launched an attack between the river and the causeway. During the next few days fierce fighting ensued, in many cases hand to hand, until their greatly superior numbers and air strength necessitated a withdrawal. After the fall of the island the Japanese set up a prisoner of war camp at Kranji, and eventually a hospital was organised nearby at Woodlands, staffed by British and Australian personnel, the British predominating. The small cemetery started at Kranji following the re-occupation of Singapore has grown to become what is today the main war cemetery in the Far East.

Kranji War Cemetery is about three miles from the nearest habitation, on a hill overlooking the scene of the Japanese landing in 1941, and commanding good and extensive views across Johore Straits to the North and over the hills and peaks of Singapore Island to the South. It is just off the main Singapore-Johore road. Its development as a permanent war cemetery began when it was found that the large cemetery at Changi, where the main prisoner of war camp in Singapore had been situated, could not remain undisturbed. A large camp hospital had been set up there by the Australian Infantry Force, and the burials at Changi were mostly from this hospital. The site on which the cemetery lay was required for the expansion of Changi Airport. In 1946, therefore, the graves were moved by the Army Graves Service from Changi to Kranji, as were those at the Buona Vista prisoner of war camp. Many graves from other parts of the island were transferred to this cemetery, and also all the 1939 … 1945 war graves from Saigon Military Cemetery in French Indo-China (now Vietnam), another site where permanent maintenance could not be assured. The Commonwealth War Graves Commission later brought in 306 of the 1939 … 1945 War graves and 61 graves of the 1914 … 1918 War from Bidadari Christian Cemetery Singapore, where again permanent maintenance was not possible. There are also three special memorials commemorating three soldiers who died during the years 1914 … 1918 and were buried respectively in Saigon European Cemetery, Singapore (Alexandria Road) Chinese Cemetery and Singapore (Waiyang Satu) Chinese Cemetery but whose graves are now lost.

The central avenue of the cemetery rises gently from the Stone of Remembrance near the entrance, to the Cross of Sacrifice beyond which flights of steps lead to a terrace on top of the hill. On this terrace are four memorials, the largest of which is the Singapore Memorial to 24,346 soldiers and airmen who died during the campaign in Malaya and Indonesia, or in subsequent captivity, and have no known grave. Grouped around it are; to the east a memorial to 107 servicemen buried with some 300 civilians in a mass grave in the grounds of Singapore Civil Hospital; to the west a memorial commemorates 55 casualties of the Malaya campaign whose graves elsewhere cannot be maintained: To the south stands the Cremation Memorial, which honours 789 soldiers, the great majority of whom were Indian, who died during the same campaign and were accorded the last rite required by their religion … committal by fire.

The Chinese Memorial is a collective grave, in which were buried 69 Chinese … all members of the British Commonwealth Forces … who were massacred by the Japanese during the occupation. The inscription on the memorial is in English and Chinese, and reads "The men whose names are recorded on these panels perished in captivity in February, 1942, and lie buried here in one grave with ten comrades whose names are not known".

The cemetery, enclosed by an evergreen hedge within a row of trees, has smooth grass grave plots. Groups of evergreen and flowering trees and shrubs lend colour and beauty; while above all towers the huge central pylon of the Singapore Memorial rising to a height of 80 ft. and surmounted by a star.

The total number of burials in the cemetery is 4,465. It has been necessary to commemorate 730 of these casualties (182 soldiers and 1 airman of the United Kingdom Forces, 497 Australian soldiers, 17 soldiers of the Indian army and 33 Malayan soldiers) by special memorials, inscribed " Buried near this spot". They had been buried from

Singapore Hospital in various cemeteries and during the occupation the identities of the individual graves had been lost. While it is known that they were transferred to Kranji War Cemetery, within a certain groups of graves it is not possible to precisely locate the actual grave in which each has been buried. Four other graves are marked by the special memorials type D, which bear the superscription "Believed to be".

Opposite Page: *Kranji Memorial*

Taiping War Cemetery

Taiping is about 60 miles south-east of Penang in North-Western Malaya, and is a centre for the rubber and tin mining industries. Formerly a permanent British garrison town, it has good road and rail communications with Penang, Kuala Lumpur and Singapore.

At the time of the Japanese invasion of Malaya, Taiping was on the British line of retreat down the West coast. Its normal garrison of one Indian Infantry Battalion had been augmented, a casualty reception station organised and arrangements made with the civilian authorities for provision of 500 beds for military patients, and 20 Combined General Hospital (Indian Army) had been posted there.

During the fighting the Indian 6th and 15th Brigades used Taiping as a rest and re-fitment centre for a few days; and as the withdrawal southwards developed, numerous Indian Army medical units worked there for short periods before each in turn had to move towards Singapore with the fighting forces.

Taiping War Cemetery was created by the army after the defeat of Japan for reception from numerous temporary burial grounds, and from village and other civil cemeteries where permanent maintenance would not be possible. It is one mile west of Taiping, on a level site with forested hills to the South and East. There are separate entrances to the two sections, the plots of Christian graves lying on the South-Eastern side of the road and the Muslim and Gurkha graves on the opposite side. An avenue of peltophorum trees leads between the Christian graves to the Cross of Sacrifice, and in this part of the burial ground there are groups of bauhinia trees. Flowers bloom in the headstone borders. In the Muslim and Gurkha section the Stone of Remembrance stands in front of a high bank which forms the North-Western boundary. This has been planted as a shrubbery, with allamanda, gardenia and scarlet hibiscus, and there are headstone flower borders here too. The two small shelters in the cemetery have been constructed of local stone, and a low stone wall flanks the road on each side.

Chungkai War Cemetery

Chungkai does not appear on any map, but will be well remembered by those who stayed there as prisoners of the Japanese for many long months from the middle of 1942 onwards. It is a hamlet on the river Kwai Noi about 73 miles West of Bangkok, capital of Thailand about 3 miles West of the little town of Kanchanaburi. Visitors go by train from Bangkok to Kanchanaburi and then by river launch to Chungkai.

The war cemetery is in a forest clearing about 200 yards from the river bank, and is approached from the landing stage through an avenue of flowering trees. The entrance pavilion is built of local materials, roofed with coloured Siamese tiles which blend well with the surroundings. A few very large mango trees, which were growing on the site originally, and a number of other specially planted trees give shade. On the opposite side of the river, and clearly visible from the cemetery, are steep tree-covered hills reminiscent in profile of Chinese paintings.

Chungkai, now a peaceful pleasant spot, was one of the base camps on the Burma-Siam railway, and contained a hospital and church built by Allied prisoners of war. The original burial ground was started by the prisoners themselves, for men who died in the hospital. The total number of burials is 1,740.

Previous Page: *Maintenance staff of the Commonwealth War Graves Commission attend Allied graves.*

Thanbyuzayat War Cemetery

Thanbyuzayat is a village in Burma, 40 miles from Moulmein and 15 miles from Amherst, and can be reached from both towns by road. There is an air service between Rangoon and Moulmein and sea communications with Rangoon.

Thanbyuzayat (pronounced Tunboozyat) took its name from the Than Byu Zayat rest house built many years before the war by a devout Buddhist for the accommodation of passing travellers. With a wooden floor and corrugated iron roof, its sides open to the air, the zayat afforded a pleasant place for the tired traveller and gained merit (kuthu) for its builder. It was at this point that work on the railway line finished.

The first group of prisoners of war to work on the railway reached Thanbyuzayat, via Moulmein, at the end of September 1942, and the camp they established became prisoner of war administration headquarters and a base camp. In January 1943 a base hospital was organised for the sick, then numbering 600, but in March the patients were sent to a new hospital base a few miles away at Retpu. However, in May the Retpu hospital was closed and the patients were transferred back to Thanbyuzayat.

Between March and June 1943 the administration headquarters and the hospital, situated close to a railway marshalling yard and workshops, were visited three times by Allied bombers, once in March and twice in June and numerous casualties among the prisoners of war occurred. The camp was then evacuated and the prisoners, including the sick, were marched to camps further along the line where camp hospitals were set up. For some time, however, Thanbyuzayat continued to be used as a reception centre for the groups of prisoners arriving at frequent intervals to reinforce working parties on the line up to the Burma-Thai border.

Thanbyuzayat War Cemetery lies at the foot of the hills which separate Burma from Thailand and is one of the three cemeteries in which are buried men who lost their lives in the building of the Burma-Siam railway. It was created by the Army Graves Service for the assembly of graves found in burial grounds or isolated sites along the railway track between Moulmein and Nieke, which is just over the border in Thailand. The total number of burials is 3,771.

Yokohama War Cemetery

Yokohama, the second largest city in Japan and formerly the most important of the treaty ports, is on the West side of Tokyo Bay in Honshu, the main island of Japan. It lies about 40 kilometres south of Tokyo. Yokohama War Cemetery is about 10 kilometres from the centre of the city.

Attractively situated in Kariba-Cho, Hodogaya Ward, the cemetery was constructed by the Australian War Graves Group. It comprises four main parts; the United Kingdom section, the Australian section, the Canadian and New Zealand section and the Indian Forces 1939-1945 section. A Cross of Sacrifice stands in each of the first three sections. Instead of a cross, a specially designed monument in the form of a pylon with four faces dominates the plots in the fourth section. This is inscribed on two faces ''Indian Forces 1939-1945'', with ''India'' on one face and ''Pakistan'' on the other. In a niche on the north wall of this section are commemorated men who died while serving with the occupation forces in Japan, for whom no burial or cremation information exists.

The total number of graves is 1,518. Special memorials commemorate men known to be buried in the cemetery whose graves could not be precisely located. Each consists of a bronze plaque bearing the name and service particulars of the casualty with the superscription ''Buried near this spot''.

In this cemetery stands the Yokohama Cremation Memorial, a beautifully designed shrine which houses an urn containing the ashes of 335 soldiers, sailors and airmen of the British Commonwealth, the United States of America and the Kingdom of the Netherlands who died as prisoners of war in Japan. Their names (except for 51 who were not identified) are inscribed on the walls of the shrine.

Labuan War Cemetery

Borneo is a large island in the Eastern Archipelago, immensely rich in oil and rubber. The Northern part, comprising Sabah (including the island of Labuan) and Sarawak is in the Federation of Malaysia; while the Southern and larger half was Dutch, but now forms part of Indonesia.

From 1880 until over-run by the Japanese in 1942, the State of North Borneo was governed by the North Borneo Chartered Company, the last chartered company to administer any part of the British Empire. It did not become a British Crown Colony until 26th June, 1946, when the Chartered Company transferred the sovereign rights and assets to the Crown. In July 1946, Sarawak was ceded to Britain, and thus was formed the new Crown Colony of Sarawak, Brunei and Independent Sultanate.

Strategically important after Singapore as the key to the area between Malaya and Australia, and a springboard for any large scale operations on Malaya and Java, Borneo came within the Malaya command, and North Borneo was the first of the British possessions in the Pacific to fall to the Japanese. Through lack of resources only token forces could be stationed there, and they could be expected to do little more than gain sufficient time for the demolition of the oilfield installations. In December 1941 the garrison consisted of the 2/15th Punjab Regiment stationed at Kuching in Sarawak where there was an airfield, and at Miri, some 400 miles as the crow flies to the North-East. At Miri and at Seria, in near by Brunei, were the oilfields; and on December 8th 1941 orders were given for their demolition. This the local garrison carried out successfully, the troops, oil company officials and a detachment of Straits Settlements Police being evacuated by sea on the 13th. On the 16th, Japanese troops landed at Seria.

After the fall of Singapore several thousand British and Australian prisoners of war were sent to camps in Borneo, mainly in the Sandakan area on the Eastern coast of North Borneo, where they were employed on airfield construction. The Australians belonged to the 8th Australian Division ("B" force numbering 1, 494 and "E" force 500). In October 1943 most of the officers were separated from the men and sent to Kuching. Thereafter conditions at Sandakan greatly worsened; the men were starved, beaten and overworked by their captors. In February 1945 the Japanese, anticipating Allied landings in North Borneo, decided to move the prisoners of war Westwards to Ranau, more than 160 miles inland from Sandakan. Although many had already been transferred to other centres, more than 2, 000 British and Australian servicemen remained to take part in the "Death March to Ranau". Those who fell, sick or exhausted, on the journey were killed; the survivors who reached Ranau were made to perform superhuman work on starvation rations. Of the 2, 400 men who left Sandakan only 260 arrived at Ranau, and most of these succumbed later. Only six survived to the end of the war. They had escaped from Ranau and were living with the natives when rescued.

When the Australian Army Graves Service entered Borneo they followed the route from Sandakan to Ranau, and found many unidentifiable victims of this infamous march. They had other casualties from battlefield burial grounds and from scattered graves throughout Borneo were taken in the first instance to Sandakan, where large numbers of prisoners of war were already buried. This flat coastal area, however, was subject to severe flooding and it proved impracticable to construct and maintain a permanent cemetery. The Sandakan graves, numbering 2,700, of which more than half were unnamed, were therefore transferred to Labuan War Cemetery, specially constructed to receive graves from all over Borneo.

Labuan is a small island in Brunei Bay, and became Federal Territory on 16th April, 1984.

Labuan War Cemetery is about 3 kilometres from Victoria, on high ground overlooking the harbour. It is the only war cemetery in North Borneo and contains, as well as the graves from Sandakan, about 500 from Kuching where there was another large prisoner of war camp. The total number of burials is 3,905. The preponderance of unidentified graves is due to the destruction of all records of the camps by Lieutenant Colonel Suga, the Japanese commandant, before the Australians reached Kuching, his headquarters. When apprehended, this man committed suicide rather than face questioning on his conduct of the Borneo camps.

In this cemetery, forming a forecourt immediately inside the main entrance gate, stands the Labuan Memorial commemorating 2,327 officers and men of the Australian Army, the Royal Australian Air Force and the local forces of North Borneo, Sarawak and Brunei who died while prisoners of war in Borneo and the Philippines from 1942 to 1945, and during the operations for the recovery of Borneo, and have no known grave. Beyond this forecourt, in an open grassed space in the centre of the cemetery, stands the Cross of Sacrifice. The graves are in level mown turf, each marked by a bronze plaque on a sloping concrete stool. Throughout the cemetery grow flowering trees and shrubs, adding colour and beauty to the peaceful scene.

To the extreme right of the main entrance, by the Club Road entrance and the rest room, is the Indian Section, in front of which is a memorial to men of the Indian Army, mostly men of the 2/15th Punjab Regiment, who died while prisoners of war and were buried at Sandakan. They have since been accorded the last rites required by their religion … committal to fire.

Kanchanaburi War Cemetery

Kanchanaburi is a little town on the Me Khlong (Kwai) river about 80 miles West-North-West of Bangkok, the capital of Thailand. It is best reached by rail from Bangkok but can also be reached by road (liable to flooding) when it is passable. Shallow-draught boats ply between Bangkok and Kanchanaburi.

Kanchanaburi War Cemetery lies about two hundred yards from the railway station, on the North-Eastern outskirts of the town. The entrance is on the main Kanchanaburi road and the surrounding country is light jungle and hills. The cemetery is only a short distance from the site of the former Kanburi prisoner of war base camp, through which most of the prisoners passed on their way to other camps. It is the largest of the three war cemeteries (two in Thailand and one in Burma) on the notorious Burma-Siam railway and was created by the Army Graves Service who transferred to it all graves (except American graves), from camp burial grounds and solitary sites along the Southern half of the railway from Bangkok to Nieke. Most of the base camps and hospitals were in this area and the total number of burials in the cemetery is 6,982. This figure includes 300 men who died during an epidemic at Nieke Camp and were cremated, whose ashes now rest in two graves in the cemetery. Their names are commemorated on Portland stone panels in the shelter pavilion which stands at the end of the two main avenues, facing the Cross of Sacrifice. Over the two graves are bronze plaques bearing the inscription "Here Are Buried The Ashes Of 300 Soldiers Whose Names Are Inscribed In The Memorial Building In This Cemetery".

In the entrance building is a bronze memorial tablet recording the names of 11 soldiers of the Indian Army buried in Muslim civil cemeteries in Thailand, whose graves are unmaintainable.

IN HONOURED REMEMBRANCE OF THE FORTITUDE AND
SACRIFICE OF THAT VALIANT COMPANY WHO PERISHED
WHILE BUILDING THE RAILWAY FROM THAILAND TO BURMA
DURING THEIR LONG CAPTIVITY
THOSE WHO HAVE NO KNOWN GRAVE ARE COMMEMORATED
BY NAME AT RANGOON SINGAPORE AND HONG KONG AND
THEIR COMRADES REST IN THE THREE WAR CEMETERIES
OF KANCHANABURI CHUNGKAI AND THANBYUZAYAT
*I will make you a name and a praise among all people of the earth
when I turn back your captivity before your eyes, saith the LORD*

*Japanese memorial dedicated to
Allied POWs who gave their lives
in the construction of the railway.*

*Kanchanaburi War
Cemetery.*

A Simple Soldier's Narrative

What became known as the Death Railway was built by British, Australian, Dutch and American prisoners of war. It was a Japanese project inspired by their need for communications and a supply line for their troops fighting in Burma. During its construction more than thirty thousand prisoners died, mainly of sickness, malnutrition and sheer exhaustion.

The Japanese kept no records of fatalities and it was very rarely possible for any of the prisoners to maintain any true record, this being left to individuals recording the deaths of particular friends or comrades in secret. To be found in possession of writing materials … even a pencil … could mean the death penalty for the unfortunate prisoner.

The total number of deaths including British, Australian, American and Dutch servicemen was in excess of 150,000. Of these about 100,000 were forced labourers from Burma, Malaya, India, Thailand, Indonesia, and Chinese living locally, or driven from their homes in Malaya, Singapore, Java, Sumatra and other Asian countries.

The railway, which was purchased by the Thai government immediately after the war, has been depleted and now there remains only a 35 mile stretch of line, running from Bampong/Kanchanaburi to Hintock, of the original 250 miles.

Japanese communications depended upon a long treacherous sea route and it was imperative that the railway be completed as soon as possible. The decision to have it completed by mid 1943 was taken at a meeting of the Japanese general headquarters as early as June 1942.

The railway was to be constructed through the most difficult terrain in Thailand, through dense jungle and the worst climate in South East Asia, if not the world.

The target set by the Japanese for completion was fourteen months, beginning in July 1942. The labour force, it was decided, would be prisoners of war from all theatres, coolies from Malaya and labourers from Java, Sumatra, Borneo and Singapore. Two forces, one based in Thailand and one in Burma, would commence work at the end of July working from opposite ends of the line towards the centre.

The first prisoners to arrive had the job of building camps at Bampong and Kanchanaburi. But before constructing their own living accommodation, they were compelled to build the Japanese living and administration quarters, and had to sleep in the open. This rule applied at all prison camps along the line. The prisoners' living accommodation and cook houses were the last structures to be built. After many 'Heath Robinson' attempts, the Japanese brought in local artisans to teach the prisoners the art of building massive huts to accommodate anything from fifty to one hundred and fifty men.

Throughout the building of the railway, supplies of food were very irregular and in a number of cases non-existent. The basic food was plain boiled rice with the occasional sprinkling of what was commonly known as Chinese lettuce, a vegetable which grows freely alongside stagnant water. Once a month the Japanese issued a very small token portion of fish, Ghee, sugar in the form of Geula mallaca and a very thin cow or water buffalo, to be shared with the Japanese soldiers en route to Burma, with prisoners and labour gangs. This worked out at one 224 lbs beast to be shared between around two thousand men per month. Occasionally the Japanese would send up fresh vegetables from Bangkok, but by the time they arrived at the prison camps they were rotting and stinking.

Red cross parcels started to arrive around the end of 1943, but these were almost all confiscated by the Japanese officers and men, who in turn sold the contents to their comrades en route to the Burma front.

Dysentery, malaria, pellagra, cholera, beri beri, typhus, scurvy, yellow fever and black water fever were the main killers. This caused a large problem for the Japanese who would not believe that so many men could be ill at the same time. It never dawned on them that a body needs sustenance to survive.

The task masters demanded a certain quota of work from each group of prisoners and the fact that any working group had been diminished by men being too ill to work or some having died during the night was of no avail. The quota had to be completed before each group of men were allowed to return to their sleeping quarters. The quota of earth moved per man in the early stages was set at four cubic metres per shift, later increased to six. The movement of railway lines was achieved by dozens of men working like ants, carrying each length. Bridge building was of a primitive nature and every tree used had to be carried by the prisoners without any help, mechanical or otherwise. Trees too heavy for the men to lift were left where they had been felled.

Men who were unable to crawl to the railway site were made to do menial tasks, breaking granite and making dynamite sticks. Others were carried to the quarry sites, where they were made to sit and hold a steel drilling rod while one of the fitter men struck it with a hammer to make holes for the dynamite preparatory to blasting. On some occasions sick men lost their lives through not being agile enough to move away before blasting began.

As work progressed and the number of sick increased, base hospitals were organised with permission from Japanese headquarters, the main ones being at Chungkai, Non Pladuc, Nocompatan in the South and at Retpu and Thanbazayat in Burma. These hospitals, built on the same lines as the working men's huts and usually holding about 200-250 patients, were built away from the main part of the work camps and the stench emanating from the hospital area was enough to deter any potential visitors. Each month parties of sick men were sent down river in search of treatment, accompanied by one or two men who were slightly less sick than the majority. Even by men of their own units, the sick were mostly ignored. For to have offered to assist would have meant a severe beating. Some of the sick were told to make their own way through the jungle on foot. Most of these never arrived and those who did manage to struggle through were generally too far gone for any form of treatment to have helped them.

The doctors in these base hospitals worked night and day to try to keep the slightest flicker of life burning in their patients, but without medication or medical equipment their task was an almost impossible one. Towards the end of the building of the railway, the Japanese did bring some medicines into the camp but the amount was so small and their uses so negative that they did very little to relieve the suffering. A great deal of equipment and medication was improvised by the doctors and the phrase necessity is the mother of invention was never more obvious. Some even tried using native medicine acting purely on the instructions given by the donor. Devotion and skill was never more required and these medical men excelled themselves in every degree.

Work started at the Burma end on the 1st November 1942. The first sod had been turned at Tamarkan the previous month. Both parties met at Neiki on the 23rd November 1943, where a supposed golden nail was struck at the exact centre.

After 23rd November 1943 the main work consisted of repairs and maintenance, plus attending to bomb damage. The Allied bombing accelerated within three days of completion, causing many deaths to the prisoners and forced labourers. These raids increased with the volume of Japanese traffic and because the Japanese would not allow the prisoners to show a symbol indicating their presence, the prisoner of war camps came under some very intensive bombing, resulting in the deaths of hundreds of Allied prisoners of war. At Reptu and Thambazayat more than 200 prisoners were killed and 300 or more injured, while in the Tamarkan/Non Pladuc area more than 260 lost their lives with hundreds more injured, plus hundreds of civilians. Although Thailand was occupied by the Japanese military, no precautions were taken for air raids, consequently hundreds of civilians died along the route of the railway and in the towns and villages at each end.

By 1945 most of the smaller camps along the line had been evacuated, the prisoners being sent down to base camps at Chungkai, Tamuan, Non Pladuc, Kanchanaburi and Nakompaton while the native work force were left to fend for themselves. Many starved to death in the inhospitable jungle.

The Japanese now commenced sending prisoners to various tasks around the Pacific. In Singapore they were required to rebuild the airport, while other parties were employed in land recovery during the day. At night the Japanese engineering units were busy burying evidence of their atrocities beneath what is now known as Princess Elizabeth Walk.

In Kanchanaburi the Kempetai (Japanese military police akin to the Nazi Gestapo), assisted by the engineers, were also disposing of the evidence of their work. What had once been the Kanchanaburi administration building was the main Kempetai headquarters where hundreds of prisoner and native miscreants were tortured and murdered, their bodies being buried in the banana plantation situated at the rear of the building.

In the meantime the railway was being used over and above its capacity and the repair gangs were working at full stretch. Food was still at a premium and it was not only the prisoners who were now suffering.

Occasionally it was revealed that one or two prisoners were selling the rations supplied by the Japanese to local inhabitants at the expense of their comrades. The timely deaths of these so called black marketers dispensed with the necessity of a trial.

It was not until some time after the war that the Commonwealth War Graves Commission really commenced the gigantic task of exhuming bodies from their hastily constructed graves in the jungle. Those nearest to Thambazayat were transferred to that cemetery and all those South of Neiki were sent down the line to Kanchanaburi, while the cemetery at Chungkai remained untouched until about 1957, when it was found that the river was eroding the South Western corner and the entire cemetery was moved some fifty metres to the East and 560 metres North.

Of the fifty odd thousand servicemen and women who lost their lives between December 1941 and August 1945, twenty seven thousand have no known grave. Some walked into the jungle never to be seen again. Others were buried by comrades at the side of the railway without a marker. Others were killed en-mass by their Japanese guards on the completion of their respective tasks. In Labuan a party in excess of 400 men had completed their job of rebuilding a runway for fighter aircraft. The Japanese guards had no further work or instructions, so they forced the prisoners down one of the two large concrete air raid shelters, poured kerosene and petroleum spirit down the steps and set it alight by means of a phosphorous grenade. In 1945 the Japanese in Borneo found the prisoners of war an embarrassment, so more than 2,500 of them, mostly Australian, were force-marched more than 250 miles. Any prisoner dropping out for any reason was immediately shot. Of the 2,500 commencing the march, only 200 finished it. Of these just six remained alive to tell the tale at the end of the war six months later.

There were others who perished at the hands of their sadistic captors, and were thrown into the rivers alongside the railway. Others, similar to those after the air raids on Tamakan, were hastily buried in bomb craters close to the Japanese administration building. Many died during the blasting of cuttings and were in most instances left beneath the rock fall.

Today we are asked to accept the Japanese as full partners in life, we are urged to forget and forgive, while at the same time we are asked to remember the sacrifices our comrades made in Europe and to ignore the fact that had Singapore and the Far East been given the correct defence potential, many surviving ex-prisoners of the Japanese including myself would have no reason to look back in anger.

Had anyone kept a diary from that first day when the Japs dropped their bombs on Singapore, all the controversy innuendo and speculation of today would be totally unnecessary and the families of those men who lost their lives to a vile and despicable enemy would have known the truth immediately the war came to an end.

So many armchair historians, theorists and authors have made a name and not a little financial gain for themselves out of the subject without so much as checking their prose. I recently read an article written by a well known author. In large capital letters the headline claimed that NINE HUNDRED THOUSAND Allied soldiers had been taken prisoner at the fall of Singapore. This is the type of fatuous untruth which perpetrates the fog of misinformation which still surrounds these events. A further well known author claimed that the Allied soldiers had run away from ''a smiling advancing Japanese army''. Such men are supposedly responsible writers and as such the reading public accept what they say as gospel.

The families of those men who died are ordinary people who don't pretend to be able to understand what it was all about. So it was up to these authors who profess to be intelligent, to tell the truth wherever possible and if they should assume that the truth would cause distress, then avoid the matter altogether.

It is now fifty years since that first bomb which was to lead to the destruction of so many lives physically and mentally, was dropped on Singapore, and it is about time that the government released the real truth concerning the Far East and do away with the lies and deceit which created the inescapable situation which led to the fall of Singapore and the loss of so many lives during the battle and afterwards.

Many returned prisoners of war have claimed that they kept a secret diary, but every one I have read so far fails to mention what would have been the consequences if the writer had been found with a pencil and paper, let alone a diary.

I never claimed to have a diary, just a few pieces of army issue buff toilet paper, possibly worth in those days, and those circumstances, about five shillings a sheet. Every one who owned a note book, reading book or even a copy of the bible, would most certainly have sold most of it at some time, in order to purchase food or cigarettes. Paper was extremely valuable, especially after 1943 when one page of the bible sold for the equivalent of around five shillings in Chungkai.

The Begining Of The End

On the 7th December 1941 the defence of Singapore consisted of just four British battalions, two battalions of Australians and three battalions of Indian and Gurka soldiers, plus ancillary service units and three coastal batteries of artillery. Between them and the anticipated Japanese invading forces there was a space of some three hundred miles. At Kota Baru, Singora and Patani there were twenty-nine infantry battalions and three units of local volunteers. Of the former, just three were British and the remainder either Indian, Australian or Asian. Communications between these various groups were poor, not least because of language differences. Of the Indian battalions only twenty per cent had received even the most basic training.

To cover the defenders there were about fifty or sixty modern aircraft. One hundred and twenty eight aircraft of varying quality were being held in reserve, scattered around Malaya.

Only four battalions of British soldiers were fully acclimatised and jungle trained. These were the Gordons, the Loyals, the Argylls and the Manchesters (who were a machine gun battalion). All four battalions had been retained in Singapore, presumably to defend the island if the Japanese decided to invade. Also retained in Singapore were all the trained artillery personnel and Service Corps units and it was not until the Japanese had obtained a foothold on the mainland of Malaya that it was decided to send the three infantry battalions up country and leave the Manchesters behind to man the machine gun defences of Singapore, the only other machine gun unit there at the time being the 2/22nd Australian battalion.

Of the absolute total of sixty five thousand men under orders on the 7th December 1941, fifteen thousand were British.

The Japanese launched their attack on Malaya with an initial invasion force of fifty thousand infantry men covered by 156 fighter bombers of the Navy 'O' type, followed by 158 tanks and 160 pieces of artillery plus ancillary units.

By the second day of the offensive a further seventy five thousand infantrymen had landed followed by a further influx of fighter planes and artillery.

Apart from the artillery the defenders were equipped with just a basic rifle and ceremonial bayonet. The short steel bayonets had been out of stock since 1940 when a great deal of combat equipment was sent back to England, to replenished losses incurred in the withdrawal from France.

The infantry battalions and other ancillary units which made up Singapore Fortress had been based on the island for more than three years and were practically all known to each other. Just as in England or anywhere else, groups of people become acquainted with similar groups. This was the situation in Fortress at the outbreak of war and having worked together it was anticipated that they would see action together. But this was not to be, and although not immediately obvious there was an effect on morale.

Prior to 7th December all infantry battalions had a detachment from the Royal Corps of Signals attached. These were responsible for the operation of telephone and radio systems, so it was not unusual when on guard duty, for an infantryman to wile away his off duty time sitting in the radio room, where he would hear most if not all conversations being transmitted and received. During the morning of the 19th November 1941 it was noted that quite an interest was being shown in the radio room at Tanglin barracks. The radio operator turned up the volume so that those around could listen in to a battle taking place between a German warship, the Kormorant, and an Australian warship the HMAS Sydney. By the end of the morning both ships had sunk each other. This battle however was not the only important matter travelling across the ether. A Japanese station had begun transmitting messages to its merchant ships and armed services. Included in these messages were three distinct references to possible conflict with Britain and the United States which read as follows:

"International situation tense. When diplomatic relations severed one of the following messages will be transmitted to all services.

(1) Higashi No Kazi Ame (EAST WIND RAIN) Japanese-American relations in question.

(2) Kita No Kazi Kamori (NORTH WIND CLOUDY) Anticipate Soviet Intervention.

(3) Nishi No Kazi Hare (WEST WIND FINE) Commence invasion Malaya Thailand and Philippines''.

The message ended.

This so-called secret message was intercepted by all listening stations around the Pacific and copies were forwarded to the British war office. The response from there read "Take no action"!

The first "Winds" message (West Wind Fine) was transmitted by the Japanese foreign service on 1st December and the same message was repeated at the end of each radio programme until the evening of 6th December, by which time practically every serviceman within Fortress HQ knew the message off by heart.

When the first bombs hit Singapore on 8th December, even though most servicemen and residents anticipated an attack, it still came as a shock.

The Japanese having landed their initial force of fifty thousand infantrymen now began to move forward, followed by a further force of fifty thousand along the coast from Singora down to Kota Baru, meeting very little opposition. The Japanese in full view of all the world had been continually pouring men and equipment into Indo-China since July 1941. A total of 250,000 men were under arms in Indo-China by the beginning of November, as well as numerous divisions at various islands in the Pacific in preparation for the assault on the Philippines and Dutch East Indies.

By midnight of 8th December they had made successful landings in every theatre of their projected advance. By the 9th December every airfield in North Malaya had been bombed out of service. The airfield at Kota Baru was evacuated within four hours of the offensive commencing and all the while that these attacks continued so did the invasion of further troops until well over 150,000 men had entered Malaya with minimum casualties.

On the West side of the peninsula, forces of the 11th Indian Division were making a reconnaissance crossing the border between Malaya and Thailand In the afternoon of 9th Dec they were met with stubborn resistance by what was thought to be Thai military and police, but which in fact were Japanese soldiers dressed in the uniform of Thailand forces. Trying to work round this resistance they encountered the Japanese in full force. Further East, a unit based at Kroh and named Krohforce also crossed the border and, meeting opposition from the Thais, dug in just a short distance inside the border. Both forces however were compelled to withdraw on the morning of the 11th December when they were attacked by larger forces of Japanese infantry and artillery.

Meantime the only two capital ships assigned to the Far East had left Singapore unescorted on 8th December in an effort to drive the Japanese away from Singora. Unfortunately the battleships Prince of Wales and Repulse were observed by Japanese spotter planes and by noon the on 10th December, both ships had been sunk by torpedo bombers. The captain of the Prince of Wales and the Commander in Chief Singapore were both drowned. This catastrophe and the destruction of Pearl Harbour caused some damage to the morale of the men now facing the Japanese. Added to this crushing blow was the order to withdraw towards Kedah.

On 11th December, the Japanese also launched a bombing mission on George Town on the island of Penang causing very many casualties, with the result that there was an immediate exodus.

In the early hours of the 12th the Japanese commenced an assault on Kedah, which was being defended by Indian troops who had only recently been relieved from a sustained delaying action at Jitra and they were ordered to withdraw toward a position North of Alor Star. For two days they held out against intense Japanese suicide attacks and were finally compelled to give ground and fall back a further twenty five miles South of Alor Star.

In the East, Krohcol had been the recipients of heavy machine gun and artillery fire and had also been ordered to retreat and place themselves under the command of 12th Indian Brigade. The British forces who had taken up a position in Kelentan just south of Kota Baru found themselves in the unhappy position of having no road links or communications at all with South Malaya and had to withdraw, having only recently abandoned the airfields at Gong Kedah and Machang just South of Kota Baru. Once the withdrawal sequence commenced the principle task of British forces was negated and on 12th December the force was given orders to retire along the railway line, which was the only possible exit. The withdrawal was completed by the 13th.

On the West coast the Japanese attack on Jitra had reduced the 11th Indian Division to a state where it required urgent relief, but unfortunately there were no reserves available and the situation caused such concern as to trigger a further withdrawal to Gurun, a position half way between Butterworth and Alor Star.

All around the Pacific similar disasters were taking place, all due to the ignorance and muddled thinking of certain individuals who had known of the inadequate state of readiness of the Allied forces. It suited the aims of these people for the Japanese to be seen in the eyes of the world as the aggressors. The ferocity of the Japanese attacks finally caused a slight feeling of apprehension in England. At the same time the Australian government demanded that Australian servicemen should be returned to defend their own country. The British government diverted a Division which was intended for the Middle East toward Singapore. This was the unfortunate 18th Division which arrived in Singapore between 19th and 21st January, unacclimatised and with all their equipment painted in yellow and sand colours for the deserts of Lybia and Egypt, and these had to be left on board the returning ships. The Division itself enjoyed only four weeks of freedom before being taken prisoner.

On 15th December a large Japanese force overwhelmed the 6th Indian Division which was forced to withdraw to the banks of the river Muda on the Southern boundary of Kedah state. On the same day orders were issued to evacuate Penang, a decision which caused great offence to the residents of the island, facilities being offered to the British and Allied nationals first, leaving the local Chinese and Asian community to the mercy of the Japanese.

On the following day the remnants of 11th Indian Division were ordered to withdraw to the Southern border of Province Wellesley to form what was to be called the Krian River line. However, a serious situation developed when the Japanese commenced a forward thrust down the main road. Using three Divisions they quickly captured Kualu Kangsar.

All the British airfields to the North had been captured, but it was still thought essential to maintain a front as far forward as possible in order that the relief forces now anticipated might be landed in safety in an effort to deny the Japanese use of airfields within striking distance of Singapore.

This policy was discussed at the Allied Command Conference held in Singapore on 18th December. The meeting was unaware that the Muda River setback had occurred. The Japanese again pressed home their advantage and a further withdrawal to the South of Perak River was ordered. On the same day the remnants of 6th and 15th Indian Brigades who had suffered tremendous losses were amalgamated to form one Brigade and retire South.

The 9th Indian Division was assigned the duty of securing the airfield at Kuantan and protecting the 11th Indian Division and its communications against attack from the East.

Withdrawal behind the Perak River now became inevitable and on the night of 21/22nd the Divisions fell back. In just sixteen days the Japanese had taken the whole of North Malaya.

On this same day the Japanese commenced an all out assault on all fronts in Malaya, and in the Pacific they invaded the Philippines, Lingayan Gulf and Wake Island, while our great war leader attended a conference in Washington.

Although the Japanese had moved exceedingly swiftly, the military powers in Japan had anticipated a far greater achievement. The retreat behind the Perak River gave the commanders of the Indian Divisions the chance to reorganise and with much needed reinforcements arriving there was a slight lull in the battle.

December 25th was Christmas day, but there was very little Christianity around that year. Rumour had it that the British garrison in Hong Kong had surrendered and morale began to flag, even more so when the rumour was confirmed. As dusk was falling and as each man took up his 'stand-to position', there came the sound of singing from somewhere back in the jungle. At first it was hard to understand what was happening. Then as the wind changed direction, the voices of those men in reserve, plus the sick and wounded could be heard singing the hymn "The day Thou gavest Lord is ended". Many of those men who were singing and those listening had no idea it would be the last hymn they heard.

The Japanese did not recognise Christmas and their artillery commenced to lay down a barrage preparatory to a fresh attack. This was not dissimilar to the tactics used in the First World War: first a softening up by the big guns, followed by mortar fire accompanied by a frontal attack. By the morning of 27th December the remains of the 11th Division, the 6th, 12th, 15th and 28th Brigades had begun another withdrawal. Many men had died since the initial invasion, hundreds had deserted, and it was decided yet again to amalgamate the Brigades and pull back to a position just twenty miles South of Ipoh.

In Singapore many changes in the command structure were taking place. These changes continued through till the middle of January, a matter which did little to improve the morale of the junior officers and indeed some of the senior ones as well. General Sir Henry Pownall had been relieved by Sir Robert Brook Popham as Commander in Chief. Headquarters Eastern Fleet were moving to Batavia in the Dutch East Indies, a move which seemed a bad omen to the men who knew about it, especially when five days later it was learned that Headquarters Eastern Fleet had moved to Ceylon and was operating under India Command. Later General Sir Archibald Wavell was appointed Commander in Chief, which left Admiral Spooner as senior naval officer. Wavell soon transferred his headquarters to Java with Pownall as his second in command. How, the troops wondered, could Wavell possibly lead his men from seven hundred miles away? New Year's Day 1942 found morale at its lowest ebb, even when it was reported that reinforcements were on the way, in the shape of the British 18th Division. It was however another four weeks before they arrived.

An influx of Indian soldiers arrived just in time to witness and join in a further withdrawal. These troops had been despatched direct from towns and villages in India, the most experienced having enlisted just six weeks previously. The War Office promised to send fifty Hurricane fighters and crews by 15th January to give cover against Japanese fighter bombers, who by now ruled the air, but at the same time as the aircraft arrived so did Japanese reinforcements. They now had over 170, 000 men in the North of Malaya.

The planes which arrived in Singapore were never off-loaded, as the men qualified to assemble them had been shipped out to Java and the ship carrying the planes received orders to transfer its cargo to Ceylon.

In the Pacific, the Japanese had taken Manila and Bataan, and in Malaya had bypassed the Indian-held front by landing forces at Telok Anson and across the Perak River. The Japanese gave no respite, always pushing forward seeking out the weakest positions and then throwing masses of men at those points.

On the East coast of Malaya it was the same story. The Japanese first taking Kwantan forcing the 9th Indian brigade to withdraw sustaining very heavy losses, but the losses suffered by the Japanese were also very high.

On 7th January there was a further disaster on the road leading Southwards where 12th and 28th brigades were holding a position astride the road just above the Slim River which forms the boundary between the States of Perak and Selangor. There had been a lull in the fighting. Then suddenly on the morning of 7th January all hell broke loose, dive bombers appearing overhead, tanks to the front and artillery fire dropping accurately among the defenders. Despite gallant opposition the Japanese broke through and although sixty per cent of the defenders were still fighting a rearguard action, orders were given to blow the bridges with subsequent heavy loss of life and many men taken prisoner. The river was in flood as men tried to swim across in full equipment. Others who could not swim decided to try to get away by following the river, hoping to find a way across, but the Japanese were waiting for them. The Argyll and Sutherland Highlanders lost more than fifty per cent of their officers and men in this one battle alone. It was a sadly depleted and demoralised army which tried to reform some miles South of Slim. After this tremendous defeat plans were set in motion for a full scale retreat into Jahore.

In 1938 after the opening of the naval base in Singapore, the Japanese had begun to develop their espionage system, but although known to the British very little was done to counter it. A noticeable influx of Japanese civilians caused no anxiety to the British intelligence services. If it did, there were no obvious signs of counter activity even up to the actual bombing of Singapore on 8th December. The Japanese War Lords had estimated that they would be able to overrun Malaya and Singapore within one hundred days. As the Allies fell back into the state of Jahore they were twenty five days ahead of schedule. When Churchill was asked after the fall of Singapore, why it had happened so easily, he placed the blame squarely on the shoulders of the British officers and fighting men, stating that he was surprised that the Japanese had been victorious. Yet any strategist with just a modicum of intelligence would have been able to tell him that an army without naval or air support is doomed from the start.

The disaster at Slim River had created vast losses not only to the Indian Brigades, but also to the British. The Gordons, the Loyals, East Surreys and Argylls suffered very heavily and the English regiments were amalgamated into what was to be known as the British Battalion. General Wavell made one visit to the front line and from that brief glimpse he was able to assess the whole situation which had so far eluded the previous commanders. Or at least that was how his message back to Singapore Command appeared. With his headquarters in Java he hurriedly issued the order to withdraw into the State of Jahore ordering the 3rd Indian Corps minus what was left of the 9th Indian Division to move immediately and build defences South of a line from Endua, Kluang and Batu Pahat, absorbing the Australian Brigade. Major General Gordon Bennett, with the remainder of the AIF formations plus the 9th Indian Division and the 45th Indian Brigade freshly arrived from India and again untrained in any type of warfare, would be responsible for the North of that line and were also the main buffer to the Japanese advance.

The retreat into Jahore meant the abandonment of the States of Selangor, Negri Sembilan, Mallaca, Kualu Lumpur and all small towns and villages between, thus giving the Japanese vast areas of undefended territory in which to reorganise.

By the middle of January all Indian 3rd Corps had passed through Gordon Bennett's force, carrying out demolition and destruction on all the roads leading Southward, thereby forcing the battalions fighting the rearguard action to disperse into the jungle once their task had been completed. With no knowledge of the country and unable to speak a word of Malay, a large number of these men found themselves behind the Japanese lines, for which they paid the penalty.

On the 14th January in the early afternoon, the Japanese commenced the attack on Gemas. Fortunately the Australians working on their own initiative had prepared an ambush in which the Japanese suffered thousands of casualties, plus losing a large quantity of tanks and artillery, at very little cost to the Aussies. If this kind of tactics had been used from the beginning it is doubtful if the Japanese would have been so successful. Unfortunately this great victory was soon dulled by a series of calamities at Muar River on the Western extremity of the forward line. The Japanese had penetrated an area covered by untrained troops of the 45th Indian Brigade and here, as had occurred in the North, the Indian soldiers threw away their weapons and gave themselves up to the advancing Japanese army, thus exposing the Australian flank and losing the equivalent of one and a half battalions in the process. Communication with the Australians was then lost, allowing the Japanese advance to come within seventy miles of the Southern defence line. It had not at first seemed necessary to withdraw the forward troops but the strength of the Japanese attack at Muar had not been fully appreciated and in spite of efforts to reinforce this sector a further withdrawal was inevitable. As the movement of masses of troops by day would create enormous casualties, it was decided to withdraw under cover of darkness. Once more men without knowledge of the country become separated from their units, eventually being captured or gunned down by the advancing Japanese. The defenders at Muar were in fact cut down in wholesale slaughter and only one thousand men found their way back to the Allied lines, out of a total five thousand .

From 15th January the Australians, with units from the scattered Indian brigades, held up a Division of the Japanese Imperial Guards, thus giving the retreating Allies a much needed respite and allowing their counterparts in the East sector a chance to pull back without further casualties.

The defensive line had already been established by 15th January but there was still no sign of the British 18th Division which had been promised, along with more aircraft. The Indian Divisions were once more reinforced with green recruits straight from India and these same troops were placed immediately to the rear of the front defensive line. The Japanese had now taken over every airfield North of Jahore, enabling them to provide fighter cover for their bombers which were now raiding Singapore three or four times a day and causing devastation not only to the airfields but also the docks and the naval base.

The defence of Singapore was now placed in the hands of three separate commanders all operating under the command of the 3rd Indian Corps. To the East a group under Brigadier Taylor, commander of the Australian 22nd Brigade . In the centre, defending the railway and the main roads were the remainder of the AIF and the remnants of the 9th Indian Division under Major General Gordon Bennett. On the East coast was the 11th Indian Division under Major General Key.

Everything now depended on being able to hold the Japanese long enough to allow reinforcements to arrive, but again as at Muar the Western sector proved the critical one. The Japanese landed a Division down the coast at Batu Pahat and by the evening of the 16th had started to drive a wedge between the Australians and the 11th Indian Division. 11th Division was forced to withdraw its forward Brigade during the night of the 22nd and at the same time the Australians vacated their position, leaving the Japanese in complete command of the main roads East to West. The Japanese were then free to land their forces behind the defensive lines. It became inevitable that a retreat onto Singapore would be the final move and as the Southern-most troops commenced an orderly withdrawal into Singapore, the main body of the 18th British Division arrived in Kepel harbour. After a six week journey which had been climaxed by continual Japanese air strikes, they tumbled ashore … most with nothing but their personal equipment.

During the retreat the 22nd Brigade of the 9th Indian Division became cut off, and out of a full Brigade only one hundred officers and men finally made it to Singapore. Troops from the other Brigades made a safe withdrawal with very few casualties and just after eight o'clock on the morning of 31st January, with a slight mist clinging to the causeway, the last men marched across to the pipes of the Argyll and Sutherland Highlanders. Five minutes later the engineers detonated charges intended to destroy the causeway. The damage created was just a four foot gap in the concrete plus the severance of the main reserve water line running from Jahore to Singapore.

The Battle for Singapore

The arrival of the 18th British Division plus other ancillary units created an embarrassing situation for the quartermaster staffs. There was no where to put them. Singapore island is just twenty miles long and twenty two miles wide. Of this area the city covers five by seven miles, the rest is shrub and woodlands.

When some authors after the war made their bold statements that more than 100, 000 British soldiers were captured by an estimated 30, 000 Japanese, they should have checked their calculators. When the causeway was breached, a total of fifty five thousand Allied fighting soldiers walked into Singapore. The new arrivals included the following regiments: Royal Devon Yeomanry, the Royal Norfolks, the Cambridgeshires, the Beds and Herts, plus companies from a further twenty six regiments, making a total of around 25,000 men bringing the total number on the island to about 80,000 men, many unacclimatised and in a number of cases never having fired a rifle in anger.

Across the causeway waiting to bulldoze their way through were 130,000 Japanese trained infantry men, covered by 200 planes and several battleships and further supported by 150 Tanks plus artillery pieces. It was as well that the Allied forces had no knowledge of the Japanese superiority in numbers and fire power, or there would have been a mass exodus there and then.

The Joker in the pack was General Wavell who sent out a very pertinent message to all commanders, informing them that there was too much movement in the rear areas which was creating moving targets for the Japanese planes. Where, oh where, did he think it possible to hide 80, 000 soldiers and their equipment on an island so small and so vulnerable?

The Japanese had now started bombing the area of Port Moresby in Australia as well as their daily runs over Singapore; their softening up process preparatory to invading from the North. And for four days without a moment of relief they bombed and shelled every inch of the island. I have heard friends talk of the blitz on London and during these four days everyone knew the true meaning of the word Blitzkrieg. Nowhere in Singapore did any building escape the onslaught of these Japanese raids. Most of the new arrivals were placed under canvas. The Cambridgeshires and other units were accommodated on the Bukit Timor race track and concourse, just fifteen miles from the Japanese front line and in continual receipt of their artillery fire. A unit from the 11th Indian Division was camped alongside the botanical gardens and within twenty four hours of their settling in the whole battalion minus ten were completely wiped out. As well as bombing and strafing, the low flying Japanese fighter bombers were now dropping what appeared to be clusters of phosphor bombs which set fire to the tented area. Of the ten who escaped badly burned, only two survived their injuries.

On 7th February a message was circulated from General Percival's headquarters stating emphatically that there would be no surrender. 'Every officer must die at the side of his men' to quote a phrase. The message was supposed to instil a feeling of being British but unfortunately it did not go down very well with those men who had recently arrived on the island. Before the Japanese began their invasion of Singapore further orders were received that all units covering the North East sector should fall back to within five miles of the city. This was seen by most men as an admission that we were not capable of resisting the enemy, and as the Japanese commenced their invasion in the early morning of 8th February they met very little resistance on the North East boundary. The Japanese intelligence had been so thorough that they knew the exact location of each machine gun post along the North and North East coast. The British Defence Chiefs had advised against setting up a defensive position along the West coast as in their opinion the Japanese would never dream of coming that way. So contrary to the British defence commanders' opinions the Japanese invasion came from the North and North West coast. Lights had been rigged up all along the Northern sector, which if switched on would have illuminated the entire causeway and exposed the advancing Japanese who were using any means of transport to get across: rowing boats, small yachts, planks of wood attached to oil drums, while others just swam across. On the causeway itself Japanese engineers had driven a tank into the gap created by the botched demolition and had proceeded to place planks of wood and trees across to form a bridge. Although the Australians had put out scouting patrols and had warned of the Japanese intention no one took the slightest bit of notice at Fort Canning and the lights were never switched on.

By the evening of the 9th the Japanese had obtained a firm foothold and begun to deploy. At this point it was becoming obvious that a number of Indian deserters were in the forefront of the Japanese invasion. This created a dilemma among those men defending, not knowing if the Indians facing them were actually fighting for the Japanese or running away from them. The Japanese tactic now was to use Indian soldiers, plus their own men dressed in Malay civilian dress, to infiltrate the Allied lines and set up nests of snipers which created chaos.

A number of Hurricane fighters, apparently flown from an aircraft carrier, made a brief appearance then flew away. The dispositions on Singapore were divided into three main areas. The Northern area was the responsibility of the 3rd Indian Corps which consisted of the remnants of the Indian Army Divisions plus Major General Beckwith Smith's 18th Division, now under the command of Lt. General Sir L M Heath. The Southern area which included the City of Singapore consisted of the original Fortress troops with most of the fixed defences, the 1st and 2nd

Malay Infantry Brigades, and the Straights Settlement Volunteers, with Major General F Keith Simmons remaining in command. In the Western sector, which was not thought to be the main danger area, were the Australian 44th Infantry under Major General Gordon Bennett. His troops were considered to be the freshest of those who had experienced fighting on the mainland. Anti aircraft was under the command of Brigadier AWG Wildey. Command reserve, which consisted of the 12th Indian Infantry Brigade and a detachment of Chinese irregulars, was placed under command of Lt. Col. Dalley and renamed 'Dalforce'. None of these men carried any arms whatsoever and they were placed under orders of various area commanders.

During the first days, the Japanese artillery fire was returned by Allied artillery pieces but, by the morning of the 9th, most batteries had run out of ammunition. Fierce fighting took place during the Japanese landings that morning. Their casualties were later estimated to be over fifteen thousand killed and more than twenty five thousand wounded. The Allied dead amounted to five thousand with a further nine thousand wounded. The total Japanese invading force consisted of well over 70, 000 men with a further 50, 000 in reserve supported by 150 tanks, 500 aircraft and 170 pieces of artillery. General Wavell had expressed an opinion that there was too much movement in the rear areas. I wonder what remarks he would have made, had he flown over the North coast at the time, and seen more than 200,000 combatants slugging it out with no quarter being asked or given. What further reserves were available were thrown into the cauldron with little regard to their quality and although the Japanese paid very dearly they managed to push a wedge through the West and North coast defences, taking the airfields in the North of the island, then continuing their advance toward Bukit Timor and the heart of Singapore City. The few men left to defend the East coast were ordered to withdraw, leaving the Japanese to invade unopposed on the North East sector, giving access to the islands surrounding Singapore.

On 10th February General Wavell paid his last visit to Singapore and on leaving he issued orders that the island must be defended to the last man, then he returned to his headquarters in Ceylon. His leaving and his parting message did little to sustain morale and certain so-called soldiers decided to follow the Indian pattern and desert. They were not many, but to their comrades who were defending Singapore with their lives, the very existence of these few cowards made them wonder why they were being asked to sacrifice their lives for some foreign island.

By the 11th the Japanese had moved further down the Bukit Timor road capturing the food and ammunition stores plus all petrol reserves. A small team of very brave men were later chosen to infiltrate the Japanese lines and destroy the petrol storage tanks which had previously been ignored when the engineers were destroying materials. Not one of these men returned.

The food situation among the civilians was not so acute, as most of their food was either in the warehouses or on the docks.

On the 12th orders were issued for all forces to withdraw to the city perimeter, a line which included at least one water reservoir. The remaining three or four usable aircraft were ordered to Java and a line of defence was drawn up from Bukit Timor to Paya Lebar, the Australian 22nd Brigade holding the position at Bukit Timor with the British (Fortress and 18th Division) holding the line East to Paya Lebar.

Friday the 13th was indeed an unlucky day. The Japanese bombers attacked almost every hour, with their fighter bombers now in complete command of the air, swooping down and spilling their small bombs and incendiaries like confetti among the now demoralised defenders. The Japanese infantry attacked along a ridge West of Singapore City being defended by the Malay Regiment who held out defiantly, but were finally forced to withdraw leaving behind seventy per cent of their men dead. The Japanese paid very dearly, losing vast numbers in 'head on' attacks. The Allied troops were by now totally exhausted and at a conference of senior commanders it was agreed that the possibility of a counter attack was impossible under the circumstances and all nurses, senior staff, technicians plus surplus officers were ordered to evacuate Singapore. Most of these people were transported aboard small craft including patrol boats, all of them later sunk by the Japanese navy or air force. Among the casualties were Rear Admiral Spooner and Air Vice Marshal Pulford. Two of the small craft, HMS Dragonfly and HMS Firefly, carried nurses. Both were sunk just off a small island close to the East Indies. Around thirty six nurses managed to get ashore where they were then murdered by Japanese soldiers. One Australian nurse, Sister Bullimore, lived to tell the story.

By the 14th the island's water supply was cut off by the Japanese and there remained only forty eight hours' supply in storage tanks. There was enough food to last for several days, but no means of cooking it. A further message came through from General Wavell which said, ÷Your gallant stand is serving a purpose and must continue to the limit of endurance". This was followed by a repeat message from the War Office which stated that all officers were to die at the side of their men. It was impossible for them to do otherwise in these crowded conditions. During the night of the 14/15th, Japanese infantry infiltrated the central sector which was being defended by 130 men, the remnants of the 2nd Battalion Loyals who were extremely well trained and who resisted with all their strength, only giving way after losing a further fifty men. The water situation now became critical, ammunition was in short supply and most of the military food stocks were now in Japanese hands. There were only two alternatives: a counter attack to regain some of the supplies, or capitulation. A counter attack was considered impossible. Even had the men been willing, they were neither fit nor equipped for such a desperate plan. So on the afternoon of 15th February the terms of a surrender were discussed with General Yamashita and a time for a cease fire agreed for 20:30 GMT on the evening of the 15th.

This then was the end of the fighting to defend a far corner of the British Empire. Seventy days of struggle without respite, without proper equipment or naval and air cover and against an enemy far superior numerically. At the time of the surrender it was estimated that there were 65,000 British and Commonwealth service men and women on the island of whom twenty per cent were non combatant. Thirty thousand were British and fifteen thousand Australian.

The Japanese forces comprised 130,000 troops, 150 tanks, 500 planes. A further reserve force of 45,000 men was now freed to return North through Malaya and Thailand to Burma.

The majority of Fortress troops and 11th Indian Division had been completely wiped out. These had all been highly trained units.

Of the 30,000 British survivors, 20,000 had been untrained, unarmed or non-combatants, which gives the lie to Churchill's report that 140,000 British troops had been "overwhelmed" by 30,000 Japanese … a lie for which he never had the guts to apologise.

The Aftermath

The end of hostilities was just the beginning of a further fight for survival as the Japanese issued orders that all prisoners were to make their way to what had once been the Changi garrison, a very large area to the North East of the island. There was no transport provided for the removal of the sick and wounded and it fell upon the men to improvise some mode of transport by using the remains of vehicles which had been damaged in the fighting. Axles and rear chassis were converted into flat waggons on which to place several men with whatever equipment they had. Every man who could walk had to make the journey on foot, a total of about ten miles, which to some men who had fought hard for seventy days without respite now seemed an insurmountable obstacle. Men who pre-invasion had appeared fit and healthy were now demoralised remnants of their former selves, hungry, thirsty and completely beaten physically and mentally. Some refused to move a further inch and as they sat in protest they were either spat on by civilians or beaten by the Japanese and their Indian turncoats. It took forty eight hours to move every man into the Changi area. Meanwhile the Japanese began to round up everyone they considered a threat and this included Chinese women and children. They were given transport as far as the Changi beaches. All of them were secured together by means of rope, string or wire and as they arrived on the beach they were pushed and shoved into a compact bunch and machine gunned to death.

Everyone now realised that what people had been saying about the bestiality of the Japanese was completely true. Their victorious soldiers took whatever they wished from the houses and businesses. Women were raped at gunpoint and then murdered and thrown into the drains or left in their ransacked houses. The lamp posts became festooned with the heads of supposed "criminals", and all Chinese members of the Singapore government and Chambers of Commerce were decapitated and their heads displayed prominently close to the law courts. It had been agreed by General Percival at the meeting with Yamashita that certain British officials including colonial administrators as well as military personnel would remain in Singapore to assist in the handover to the Japanese. Although they had once held high positions in the Singapore government, they were now reduced to menial and degrading tasks, such as cleaning drains and emptying rubbish bins. They were finally transported to Changi civilian prison along with the rest of the European civilians.

The task of cleaning up the sordid and sickening aftermath of war was delegated to British soldiers and gangs of local Chinese and Indian labourers, with instructions that all Allied dead were to be gathered together in groups and buried in shallow graves away from the main roads. No one must remove any personal items or articles of clothing without the express permission of the Japanese soldier in charge. Initially this meant that no one could remove a dog tag, so it was not without risk that one or two men recorded their dead comrades on a piece of scrap paper. Occasionally it was possible to remove something to identify those who were being buried. Eventually the Japanese agreed to allow the removal of dog tags. All Japanese dead were either taken to a point at the side of the road or transported to a small hill at the side of the Ford factory, where the surrender had been signed, and there they were cremated. The ashes of those cremated at the roadside were placed in cardboard boxes. These were then taken to the hill and placed with the other ashes. A total of 23,000 Japanese bodies were recovered within the confines of Singapore Island and a total of nine thousand British and Allied, plus an estimated forty thousand civilian Chinese and Asians. The latter were also cremated en masse, behind the Goodyear tyre factory, after which their ashes pushed into the sea. All round the island where fighting had taken place it was possible to ascertain which units had held the various positions by the unit identification marks. The naval base and to the East had been defended by the East Surreys, the Beds and Herts and Cambridgeshires. Over to the West coast the remains of Australians, Loyals and Malay Regiments were to be found. The carnage and stench caused a number of the workers and indeed the servicemen to react in very surprising ways. One man found a loaded revolver lying by the side of a body. He picked up the gun and without warning started shooting at anyone and everyone including the Japanese guards, one of whom fired back. As the man dropped to the floor, several of the guards started to pump bullet after bullet into his inert body. Some of the workers ran away in fear, the Japanese shouting and firing at their departing backs. Parties of men were now being sent down to various camps, from where they were sent to work removing sand bags and demolishing houses which were in danger of collapsing. Others were sent to the docks to help unload cargo ships which had been deserted along the dockside. Others worked in the hospital, moving wounded British and Allied soldiers out onto the pavement and carrying wounded Japanese soldiers into the now vacated wards. Others had the most odious task of all in removing mines and undischarged ammunition, with the resultant loss of many lives.

Elsewhere in the Pacific the Japanese were advancing. In Burma there were just two British battalions standing in readiness to repel the Japanese, who were now within one hundred and fifty miles of Rangoon, the capital. The Japanese were also now within bombing distance of Australia. The shelling of the California coast by Japanese submarines caused some consternation among the top brass in America and in England and on 24th March Churchill refused point blank to hold an enquiry into the causes of the loss of Singapore. The Japanese moved to within fifty miles of Rangoon, and Singapore Island was full of rumours of a set-up created by Churchill and his intelligence department, with the collusion of Roosevelt, to create a plot which would bring America into the war, a situation which backfired on them, causing the loss of so much territory to the Japanese. In Changi the senior officers were rounded up and taken to various points of the Far East: Formosa, Korea, and even to Japan itself. Divide and conquer was now the Japanese byword as officers were segregated from men. To try to relieve the boredom, schools and debating societies were formed. Some of those involved appeared to have a good knowledge of how the US and British governments had been suckered into believing that Japan was not in any fit state to go to war.

In April the Japanese issued orders that any British or Allied serviceman found outside his respective prison camps "will be shot on sight". Several men gave themselves up from hiding to the Japanese authorities but were executed within days of their surrender.

In Changi the causes of the Japanese successes were discussed, which substantiated some very well known facts. Firstly, the Japanese had a large and very efficient espionage system which had been operating ever since the British government had decided to build a naval base on Singapore. Having assessed the quantity and quality of Singapore's defences, General Yamashita estimated that with just three Divisions he could take the island within one hundred days. This fact was known to the British intelligence services, yet they seemed surprised when in fact it took only seventy days.

Without adequate navy and air force cover the job of defending Singapore was impossible and this fact was well known to the British War Department.

The units used in the defence of Malaya were totally untrained in any form of jungle warfare and without the support of planes or tanks were useless. This is no reflection on the brave men who fought there, it is an indictment against the British government for having known about the impossible situation which existed.

They not only allowed it to happen but had actually gone to some lengths to ensure it happened in order to create the image that Japan was the aggressor.

It had been anticipated that General Percival would have placed a fully trained army in North Malaya in readiness for the Japanese invasion. His Fortress troops would have been able to withstand any direct Japanese invasion of Singapore itself for long enough to pull back these units from the North. As it was he placed untrained soldiers, with no covering support from the ground or the air, in direct opposition to a massive Japanese invasion force. Even when he realised the situation, instead of sending reinforcements immediately, he allowed his front line commanders to withdraw, leaving the Japanese to fan out in all directions. There were very few if any aircraft so it was unnecessary to have bodies of men defending empty airfields. Instead of a defensive air force of 350 fighters and 120 bombers, he only had 150 aircraft available and of these thirty or more were obsolete. The others were no match for the Japanese Navy÷O", which was a well known fact in Whitehall. All down Malaya, troops were being ordered to defend useless airfields instead of being employed in a fighting capacity. The result being that the totally inadequate 11th Indian Division with several battalions of raw recruits was left to try and defend a very extended front line in which many casualties were suffered. The remnants of this Division continued to fight a defensive action all the way down the Malay peninsula until reaching Slim, where it was more or less completely destroyed.

From the initial landings, very few if any concentrations of trained British soldiers had been used. It was as if Percival wished to retain them for his own protection should the occasion arise.

The failure to send fully trained soldiers to the North created a situation where inferior Japanese soldiers were advancing without having to put up a fight. Although Percival was considered to be a well trained staff officer during the First World War, he had little experience of overall command and delegated certain aspects to other staff officers. This later created jealousy within the command, as with Gordon Bennett who was so dissatisfied he left his men and his command and returned to Australia in the middle of the battle for Singapore.

Percival's inability to create a proper defence of Singapore shone out like a neon light to the opposing Japanese. Not being able to distinguish which positions were the more important, he allowed himself to be carried along by his Generals. Instead of him issuing the orders it was the other way round. It was obvious to even the lowest soldier that the Japanese would attack Singapore from the North. All their troop carriers had been despatched to other regions, so there was no way that they could invade from the sea. So massive reinforcements should have been concentrated on the North coast of Singapore, not only to defend but to stand by for a counter attack.

In 1940 and 1941 it was concluded that the Japanese would never try to invade Malaya and indeed it was thought that they would never even consider going to war against the US and Britain. So it was decided that since the Japanese would not attack the US and Britain, there was no sense in establishing any permanent defences around Singapore. When Percival took command, he was told in no uncertain terms that the defence of Singapore would be looked at if and when the need arose. The War Office in England had complete control of all defence finances, so Percival could never have put into operation any plans without their approval. Even when the war was at its height, he was in no position to obtain an increase in pay for the dock workers and labourers. Consequently most of them refused to work for the British. When the Japanese invaded, the war lords in England had to make a decision whether to send support to the Middle East or Singapore. The tossed coin gave the Middle East the verdict and Singapore was left to die. Yet after making this decision, more than fifty thousand British troops were taken prisoner in the Middle East despite having been given the benefit of supplies meant for Singapore.

Areas like Jitra, Krol, Kota Baru, and several other places where it was anticipated that the Japanese would force a landing, were left completely defenceless, even lacking an air raid siren. Then suddenly when the Japanese attacked Malaya and Singapore, Whitehall threw the baby into Percival's lap and said, ÷Here, you are the nearest, get on with it" and although Duff Cooper had the authority and wherewithal to purchase any form of defence and any number of engineers, he did nothing until the Japs were in full control of the North of Malaya.

After the loss of Kedah and Perak, General Heath sent urgent despatches requesting defences to be provided along the main road down the centre of Malaya and at strategic positions, so that his war-weary men could fall back to rest and regain strength. The idea was turned down. The staff officers in the North were pleading with Percival for tank defences to be thrown across the roads, but others working alongside Percival had his ear and the whole idea of tank defences was thrown out as being bad for morale. Not one anti tank obstacle was ever used or even supplied in the whole of the war.

The irritating fact was that, while at training college, Percival's strategy had been to build tank obstacles and defence positions all down the peninsula. However when the war started, the only thing which seemed to be of any importance to him and his immediate staff was the defence of the naval base. There were no ships around to use it and the possibility of it being employed to repair damaged ships was just preposterous. Yet even though the naval base was his one special priority, Percival never bothered arranging any defences along the coast outside it. Consequently the Japanese took it within twenty four hours of their invasion of Singapore.

When the Japanese finally arrived off the North coast of Singapore, they had been fighting non-stop for sixty days and they were stretched to the limit in their line of supply and communications. Although it was suggested that a counter attack was possible along the North Eastern coast of Malaya, the whole idea was cast aside again as probably creating a fall in morale. It seemed that morale issues took precendence over fighting issues. When the 18th Division landed, it provided a unique opportunity to commence a frontal counter attack, but it was considered that the Division was in no fit state physically or mentally to be put into the front line and the idea was dropped.

Unknown to Percival, by mid January the Japanese were running very low on food, fuel and ammunition and it was only after the British vacated Mersing that the Japanese were able to bring supply ships down to the units building up for the attack on Singapore. Had there been just a semblance of air power they could have been stopped.

During Wavell's visit, he had pointed out to Percival that it was essential that defences be built along the North coast. The whole idea seemed to be abhorrent to Percival and his staff and it was not until it was too late that the chief engineer managed to convince Percival that to build defences in the North would not damage the morale of his troops.

The loss of Malaya and Singapore was in no way entirely the fault of General Percival or any of his commanders. The fault lay in the fact that even as far back as 1918, the feasibility of the Japanese starting a war against the West was dismissed. Even when in 1936 the Japanese began to advance their boundaries, it was considered not to be a problem. On the completion of the naval base, in which, incidentally, Churchill had a hand, it was muted that Singapore should be strengthened, with the result that in 1938, a further one thousand men were placed under canvas. This was thought to be sufficient. On the 15th February 1942, when Churchill announced that he had no idea that Singapore had no defences and that it was like sending a ship to sea without a bottom, he was lying through his teeth. He was part of the committee which blueprinted the naval base in 1936.

At the end of hostilities in Singapore, men at Fort Canning and below ground in the control room, were busy destroying all secret documents. There was only one paper shredder, so much of the paper work had to be destroyed by fire, with much of it being blown away across the city by the wind. A number of letters were recovered later to be used as cigarette paper by the prisoners . Among them was a letter from Churchill thanking someone for providing him with an up to date resume on the Singapore defence establishment. The date was November 1941!

Most servicemen have since posed the question, why did he excuse himself over Singapore by stating that he was not aware that it was undefended?

Churchill's assumption was, that once the Japanese had attacked Pearl Harbour, British servicemen in the East would be rushed to America's defence. Neither Churchill or Roosevelt had expected the Japanese to attack Pearl Harbour, Hong Kong, Singapore and the Dutch East Indies simultaneously.

In 1942 and again after the war in Europe, Churchill promised an enquiry concerning the loss of Singapore and Malaya. Even though pressed in later years, he would not agree to any enquiry at all and when invited to attend an enquiry in America he turned it down emphatically stating that he was too busy.

Since the end of the First World War, successive governments had shelved the idea of spending money on the defence of Singapore, Malaya and Hong Kong and it was due to their lack of foresight that not only the Far Eastern territories fell but also British prestige around the World.

After the fall of Singapore the Japanese decided that there were far too many prisoners on the island, so men were despatched to various corners of the Pacific. Only now their numbers had been swelled by the capture of Sumatra and Java as well as Borneo and most of the islands around the Philippines. Men were sent to work in the Japanese mines and shipyards, and to various captured airfields, repairing damaged runways and building new ones. In fact, any task normally done by labourers was handed over to the prisoners. In Singapore work was in progress rebuilding Kallang airport, Seleta and Ne Soom RAF stations and also building new warehouses and repairing bomb damaged ones, plus brick making and a hundred and one other menial tasks including land recovery along the East coast. One peculiarity concerning this was that when the prisoners had finished their stint of earth moving during the day, by night young Japanese recruits would be brought to the site for the purpose of burying the hundreds of Chinese and others, executed by the Kempetai. Today part of the land recovered is named Princess Elizabeth Walk and very few of those who stroll along it enjoying the sunshine and the sea breezes have any knowledge of what lies beneath their feet.

In April 1942, the Japanese called Allied senior officers to a meeting at which they stated that preparations were in hand to build a new prisoner of war camp in Siam (Thailand) and men would be taken by train in groups of three to four hundred. Their job would be to help build the prisoner of war camps. This was the first big Japanese lie, which would eventually lead to many others, although most prisoners knew by now that Japan was the most deceitful nation on earth. In everything they did and in all the words they spoke, the Japanese proved time and again that they could not be trusted to keep even the most basic of promises.

The journey to Thailand to build prisoner of war camps turned out to be a complete falsehood. The prisoners were being sent to build a railway from Bangkok to Rangoon.

In Changi food supplies were running very low and so was morale. At each meal men sat eating and watching each other on the chance that one or other had been served a grain more rice. In many instances it was a case of dog eat dog. Quite a number of prisoners, especially the officers, had managed to hang on to their valuables, while those who had worked on the clear-up of Singapore had (almost to a man) had all their valuables and possessions stolen from them by Japanese soldiers. This situation created envy, and a split was beginning to show in the fellowship which had once existed between officers and men. Anyone who managed to hold on to any form of valuable on completion of the railway, was considered to be either very tight fisted or to have acquired it by unfair means. Such men were leeches, in that they had used up whatever their friends and comrades had to offer, without themselves having shared what they had hidden from the Japanese if such was the case. Such men as these were scum and I take no pleasure in saying that I knew one or two, who survived.

Hundreds volunteered to join the parties going up to Thailand, just to get away from this selfish attitude which had begun to eat into those who had something of value to project.

The trains to Thailand consisted of just one loco and nine or ten metal cattle waggons and into each waggon were squeezed thirty or forty men who in the main at this time were still in a fairly healthy state. For the first few miles the banter was of a jocular manner, but as the sun started to bake the occupants it turned to fear, panic and hatred. Hatred against the Japanese, hatred against their fellow prisoners and hatred against those responsible for having placed them in the position they now found themselves. Occasionally the Japanese guard would allow the doors open, permitting a draft of moving air to penetrate the moving mass and he would occasionally allow individuals to poke their posterior out of the waggon to answer the call of nature. But after one or two days cooped up in this oven, nature took a perverse course and a number of men died and were callously dropped off at the first stop, where their bodies were just as callously thrown into the surrounding jungle. This was the time in most men's lives when they suddenly realised the utter degrading depths to which the Japanese had sunk. Most had read or heard of the treatment meted out to the Jews in Europe and like others had allowed this horror to be erased from their minds because it was not happening to them. However, now it was real and it *was* happening to them and the worst thing was that the humiliation seemed greater than the pain. The British had been brought up in the stiff upper lip school of thought, but now their lips were quivering with hate. Had the great leader Churchill been among those men at that time, he would most certainly have been torn limb from limb. A very large number of British prisoners were Regular soldiers who had seen in action in Palestine and the North West Frontier and they knew a diplomatic double-cross when they saw one, and although they did not know the manner in which it had been accomplished they now knew the means and the end.

As the trains crossed the border between Malaya and Thailand it was noticeable that the locals had very little respect for the Japanese. They occasionally climbed onto the slow moving waggons to barter for articles such as pens, lighters, watches and rings from the prisoners who still remained in possession of such things. Most of the men had lost everything because each day whenever they had been lined up to be counted by the Japanese guards several were relieved of whatever possessions they had.

As the trains moved further into Thailand, the Thais became more daring. Whenever the train stopped they would surreptitiously climb aboard and relieve the sleeping men of everything including the boots which were tied to their feet. War not only brings out the beast in man, it also brings out the greed of self preservation. Any man who had managed to retain anything of value after the fall of Singapore would lose it by bartering, or have it taken from him by the Japanese, the thieving Siamese, or his own thieving mates. So the chances of anyone, apart from real hard nuts, retaining such valuables was non existent.

The first train to arrive at Bampong in the province of Kanchanaburi was on the 1st of July and the people turned out in full to witness the pathetic humiliated bundle of humanity being pushed, beaten and kicked towards a small clearing in the bracken, where they were ordered to line up in order to be counted. As many men came to realise, the ordinary Japanese soldier could not add up. Even simple arithmetic which children of five were capable of in England was a gigantic problem to them. Most soldiers could neither read or write and it was not until we had been prisoners for some considerable time that it was realised that basically they were all illiterate and as one or two put it, they were illegitimate as well. It was always necessary for the guards to have to count the numbers several times before reporting to the next senior soldier, who would then re-check the figures given to him. It mattered not that the British officers in charge had a complete roll and that when placed in four lines it was a simple matter to multiply by four. They insisted in pointing a finger at each person as they shouted out their calculation, ÷Itch, Nee, San√, and at this point had any of the other guards shouted out a message, the one doing the counting lost all concentration and he would need to return to the beginning. In practically all instances this irritating manner of conducting a roll call lasted not less than two hours.

When the guards were satisfied that no one had escaped along the way, the officers or NCOs in charge were instructed to divide the party into working groups, one to commence building accommodation both for the prisoners and the Japanese guards. Others were required to go out and forage for wood, while a further party became cooks. Once the parties had been directed to their specific jobs, along would come one of those slightly more intelligent of the species who would order that "Tu ma cum" indicating that two men were to follow him. Their job would be to carry all the food that could be scrounged or stolen, sometimes at gun point, from the local people. Was it any wonder that very soon the locals retaliated by stealing anything and everything which the Japanese owned, including their rifles and other equipment.

The first and even the second and third attempts at building living accommodation from bamboo and banana leaves was a complete disaster, until one of the brainy Japanese decided that it would be much simpler to employ one of the local men to teach the prisoners how to set about constructing huts to hold parties of two to three hundred prisoners. The guards then hijacked a lorry which they took to a timber yard close to Kanchanaburi where they proceeded to claim all the stocks of wood in the name of the Imperial Japanese Army. Anything which the Japanese required they just took, telling the unfortunate loser to send the bill to the Emperor. The sight of rifles lent emphasis to their demands and it worked every time.

A number of local tradesmen were commandeered into the camp building party and it is not certain if the placing of huts was by accident or intent. They were situated at the lowest point in the area. The latrines etc. had been built at the bottom of a slope and when the rains came all the huts became flooded with water, on top of which rode all the excrement and filth from the latrines. Even after the monsoon, no effort was made to relocate the living accommodation.

Many men had seen death or had been close to it themselves, but when the first death occurred in early May it made everyone suddenly realise that many more of their number were never going to make it home. The prisoners had fallen into a state of apathy making them careless, and not having immediate facilities for hygiene they became vulnerable to any prevalent virus or disease. That coupled with the lack of medicines and qualified medical staff caused a considerable problem to those who had been elected as leaders.

At each and every roll call when the senior officer or NCO announced that a certain number of men were sick and unavailable for work, the Japanese NCO taking the roll call would immediately strike out at the person making this announcement. On occasions this would be followed by the person in charge being taken roughly by the ear and pulled or dragged to where the sick men were laid. He was then ordered to show how a prisoner could be sick when in fact he still had two legs, two arms and two eyes. The sick would then be vocally and physically abused by the Jap NCO until they responded by staggering to the parade ground.

As stated previously, the Japanese who were our guards and mentors were devoid of any normal intelligence. By saying this I do not mean that all Japanese were ignorant, but even among the ones who were intelligent, there were those who used ignorance as a shield against their own lack of understanding and the meaning of humanity.

By the end of July it was common knowledge that as many prisoners as possible were going to be drafted into Thailand to build a railway from Kanchanaburi province to Molmein. Apparently in 1936 there had been a German exploration team looking at the possibility of building such a railway and they had actually gone out and taken levels and sized up the probability. Unfortunately the whole matter was brought to a conclusion when it was realized just how big the task would be. Most of the bench marks, those made from concrete and metal, still remained and it was with the original German plans and drawings that the Japanese engineers decided that by using prisoners of war and forced labour, the proposition would become a reality within twelve months.

Once more there was the difficulty in providing accommodation, so a group of prisoners accompanied by four Thai joiners or carpenters guarded by two or three Japanese soldiers moved forward a week before the working party to build sufficient accommodation for the time being. Once the move to Kanchanaburi town had taken place, the camp they had vacated was immediately occupied by a further batch of prisoners from Singapore. Eventually parties would arrive from Singapore or Malaya, spend seven days in Bampong and then be moved on to Kanchanaburi, Chungkai, Tamakan or one of the freshly built camps along the railway trace.

Prisoners now began to arrive in their thousands and once they had passed through Bampong they were informed which working group they would belong to. There were four main groups, referred to as 1-2-3 and 4 group, each group being divided into battalions, A, B, C etc. Each battalion was assigned a specific task: soil removing, embankment work, bridge building, track laying etc. Others chopped down trees, blasted through rocks or put down the ballast. The setting down of rails was left to whatever fit men were available, plus a number of Japanese who were either training to be engineers or who belonged to the Japanese Railway Regiment.

Civilian labourers were employed collecting soil, clay etc., to build the embankments. By September 1942 no less than 100, 000 labourers and prisoners were working at some point along the railway and by December 1942, 500 were dead.

Christmas that year was celebrated by one or two clerics and chaplains plus several devout Christians. Prayers were said and an attempt was made at singing carols, but the atmosphere and the future outlook gave nothing to the hope of Christianity, but the spirit of Christmas caused the priests and chaplains to approach the Japanese for permission to build a church. The Japanese agreed, providing it was built in the prisoners own time. By the end of January a fine church was completed at Chungkai. It was so soundly built that certain prisoners complained that more attention had been paid to building something which would only be used occasionally, when their own sleeping quarters were in a state of disrepair.

We prisoners had now arrived at a point in our lives when we felt that anything which did not come up to our expectations had been *planned* to cause each of us discomfort, and at a time when things had to be shared between us we watched each other to ensure that no one had even a grain of rice more than we had. We bickered, argued and those with the energy fought with each other, much to the delight of the Japanese. We could not see that we were lowering ourselves to their mentality. Discipline was fast disappearing and it was not until the arrival of several officers from the Regular Army that some form of order and self respect was again established, if only for a short period.

Once these officers arrived at Chungkai and the Japanese saw the difference they made, the commandant ordered that all officers must work alongside the men digging soil, cutting wood etc. The officers refused point blank which resulted in the Japanese commandant ordering his men to bring out their machine guns. The officers were placed just in front of a small hill and were told that they had until mid day to go to work.

That night when the men returned from their given tasks, they expected to see the bodies of the officers awaiting burial. Instead, most of them were either working in the hospital or the cook houses etc. The Japanese commandant had himself capitulated at eleven o'clock that morning and decided that the officers could make their own employment, but they must all find work. This gives a big lie to the film Bridge on The River Kwai. Never at any time have I heard of a man being kept in one of the kennels for more than fourteen days. Any offence which the Japanese thought warranted more than this punishment, the culprit was sent down to Bampong prison. This in no way condones their methods of punishment which could be anything from a slap across the face to many hours of beating with sticks and pick helves.

By the end of February 1943, Chungkai camp had expanded to accommodate fifteen thousand workers, with a separate area within the camp to hold a further five thousand sick. With the large numbers of men now in transit through Chungkai it was obvious to the doctors that a central hospital base should be built in anticipation of the spread of dysentery and malaria which was now rampant.

At the beginning of February a party which had completed its stay in Bampong was required to walk the distance to Kanchanaburi with just two Japanese guards. The opportunity to escape shone like a neon light to a group of four men from the East Surreys ... Privates Croker, Cleaver, Crocker and Dorval ... who decided to take a chance. They surreptitiously made their way to the banks of the river, possibly hoping to either obtain a small boat or to swim across. Whatever was in their minds the four men were captured by Thai villagers and handed over to the Kempetai. The reward was the usual £20 per head. It was intended that the four men should be executed in front of the other prisoners as an example, but due to the pressure from the senior officers at Kanchanaburi their execution took place in semi secrecy just behind what was later to become Chungkai cemetery. My research after the war confirms that all four died on Thursday 4th February 1943. They are buried together in grave 11 A 7-10 at Kanchananaburi. These were the first prisoners to attempt to escape. On 6th March just one month later a party left Chungkai to walk to Dhapong camp, a distance of about twenty two kilometres and were expected to take a day and a half. On the evening of the 6/7th March, four men of the Royal Northumberland Fusiliers quietly slipped into the jungle. They were not missed until morning roll call. The Japanese guard sent word down to the Kempetai office in Bampong and parties of Japanese and Thai police set out to try to locate the four. They had taken refuge beneath a disused Thai hut, but one of the locals had spotted them and informed the police, who in turn informed the Japanese. Just as the posse of Japanese and Thai police were about to surround the hiding place, a young Thai shouted a warning and the group scattered into the jungle. A Thai policeman took aim with his rifle and sent off a shot which hit 3651198 Private Fitzgerald, killing him. The remaining three men continued running not knowing that one of their party had been killed. On 15th March the remaining escapees gave themselves up to the Japanese and were quickly taken to Bampong for trial. They were charged with breaking their parole and found guilty, the sentence being death by firing squad. It was not until a squad of front line soldiers could be sent down from Burma that the execution could take place and this was on the morning of Tuesday 23rd March 1943, at 0800 hrs. Sgt. Reay, Fusilier Kenneally of the Royal Northumberland Fusiliers and Sgt. Joe Kelly of the RAMC, attached to the RNFs remained steadfast to the end. I know because I was in attendance. After the war I checked my dates and figures and found them to be correct. They are buried together at Kanchanaburi in graves 8K28-31.

The execution of these three men had a very quietening effect on the rest of the camp. Morale was as low as it was possible to get. There were those who thought that our officers could have done more to save the men being executed. No one realised that the most senior officers had been removed. Majors and the equivalent ranks were now the senior officers and when one considers that in the Japanese army the lowliest lance corporal can order the execution of a deserter among his own men, what chance did anyone have of reasoning with these trained monkeys. I know that there are those who will cry out at my description of our Japanese mentors and tormentors, but this was the picture they drew of themselves.

The Japanese had no means at their disposal to feed such a vast quantity of men and on many occasions the prisoners were taken into Kanchanaburi and even as far as Bangkok to raid warehouses containing food, mainly rice and vegetables. They also encouraged prisoners to knock over market stalls whenever they were passing. I don't remember any prisoner objecting when it came to picking up the vegetables which spilled onto the ground. We had now descended to our captors' level.

In every camp up and down the line where there were more than one hundred men, a clique would form. Men in these groups would take over any kind of enterprise being formed and would run it for their own gain. The expression dog eat dog was an apt description of some of these racketeers who would sell their own mother into prostitution if it would provide them with a little extra to eat.

Work had commenced on the railway in September 1942. At the time the allocated quota of soil to be moved was set at four cubic metres per man per shift. It did not matter one iota that some men had to carry the soil from maybe a hundred yards away, the quota was still the same. In February/March 1942, the quota was raised to six cubic metres and the shifts shortened to six hours, so that each man would be required to work two six hour shifts in one day and move six cubic metres during each shift. This task would have been difficult for fit men, so the workers used many ingenious devices to make it appear that they had moved the requisite quantity. Lumps of rotting wood, branches of trees, any form of refuse including shovels, spades, picks etc. stolen from the Japanese stores would be used in place of the soil, and finally they resorted to collecting soil from that side of the embankment hidden from their guards.

The bridge builders were similarly pressed. They were required to locate trees for felling, chop them down with the most primitive of tools and then carry them through the jungle. They were not allowed to drag the fallen trees, no explanation was given except to say that it was "Dami Dami". It was not unusual to see groups of anything up to one hundred skeletons with a fifty foot tree probably averaging three foot in diameter, struggling and trying to weave their way between a forest of smaller trees covered in vine and scrub. By the end of the day it was always possible to tell who had been carrying the trees, they all had legs ripped to shreds by the barbs of various plants and deep cuts from having come too close to a bamboo clump.

For the slightest misdemeanour one of the guards would immediately rush at the unfortunate man and commence to deliver blows with first his clenched fist followed by his boot and finally with a lump of wood or the butt of his rifle. In the first few weeks, hundreds of men were hospitalised because of this brutal and savage treatment.

Sick men who could actually sit up to be fed, were considered to be fit enough to be carried out to the sidings or cuttings to break up granite for placing between the railway sleepers, or they would be made to roll up sticks of soil, sand and clay for packing the dynamite or gelignite charges. The system was that pieces of newspaper (a very precious commodity) about ten inches square, would be rolled around a piece of wood similar to a one foot length of a broom handle. One end would be folded over tightly and the wood would be pulled out. The resultant tube would then be filled with a mixture of sand etc. After drilling holes into the rock, a stick of explosive would be pushed down the hole with two thin wires hanging outside. The candles would then be packed into the holes and rammed down. Usually about thirty or forty holes would be packed with explosives. The wires leading from them would then be attached to a dynamo, which when pressed would blow out the rock or granite in all directions. Before blasting a warning, using two pieces of metal being banged together, would sound and the men given just two minutes to vacate the area. Sometimes the Japanese engineer would ignite the charge before everyone had got out of the way, with the tragic result that one or two prisoners would be buried beneath the rock fall. Those buried under large rock falls were left. Others would either be thrown into the river or, carried back to camp for burial if the Jap was in a good mood. One such death was that of Lloyd Bull of the 125 Anti Tank Regiment who was buried by a rock fall deliberately created by Kiyioki Tanaka on 15th January 1943.

About this time, the Japanese top brass were crying out for more speed in finishing the railway, so more pressure was brought to bear on the men. The new work routine consisted of two twelve hour shifts, which in reality meant anything from fourteen to fifteen hours each, with a promised rest day every ten days. Should there be any misdemeanour, a dirty shovel, a missing tool or a broken pick shaft, the rest day would be forfeit for everyone. Occasionally prisoners were, by stealth and cunning, able to acquire food or articles which could be used to ease their predicament. It was an art in itself, being able to return to camp with such plunder hidden from the Japs, when one considers that the only clothing most men wore was a piece of cloth measuring two foot by one foot, to cover their modesty.

If caught with such contraband, the punishment was dire. Three or four Japanese screaming like banshees would fall about the unfortunate victim and using anything hard and heavy they would systematically beat the living daylights out of him. When they had tired of this, the man would be stood to attention outside the guard room or wherever the punishment had taken place, where he would remain until one or other of those responsible would consider that he had been punished enough. In the smaller camps where there were no officers or senior NCOs present, men were left to die where they lay. The Japanese responsible having completed the task in hand would order the party to move on, leaving yet another corpse to rot into eternity.

During rest periods or Tenkos as they were now termed. The Japanese would always disrupt the prisoners' leisure by instituting a search. Everyone had to parade. Even the sick were made to stand, sit or lie down outside their huts, while several Japs tossed their belongings onto the ground, searching for anything of use. One of the Japanese soldiers even accused a doctor of having a radio receiver. In fact it was an instrument designed and manufactured by one of the doctors for use during amputations. The contraption was sent down to Kanchanaburi for inspection, totally disregarding the doctor's offer of a demonstration.

Unfortunately the Japs would occasionally be lucky and, as was the case in Chungkai, locate a radio receiver. The one I refer to was secreted in the bottom of a water bottle and the only means by which it could be operated was by attaching some form of dynamo. The Japanese would not listen to any explanation and the owner was sent to Bampong for trial and subsequently execution.

By April the "speedo" programme had been put into operation. A party of 1,600 men, named F and H force, were mustered in Singapore. They were to be delivered to the Thai border from where they would march all the way to Thanbazayat in Southern Burma, a distance of over 750 miles. Under normal conditions and physical fitness this would still require a great deal of stamina and resilience. The men who started out had neither. The fear of being left to rot in the jungle spurred many of them on, but by journey's end 200 had either died in the jungle or had been found by other prisoners and taken to the nearest camp. Of the remaining 1,400 who arrived at Thanbazayat, only

240 survived the next six months and of them just twenty five returned home two years later.

By June, cholera had hit all camps starting from Molmein in Burma. The rivers were swollen not only with the bodies of prisoners of war, but with people of all nationalites, creeds and colours. They were black and bloated as they were carried along the river Kwai and out to sea.

We had been prisoners for fourteen months when cholera struck and most men had assumed that they had already seen and been a part of every form of humiliation and degradation imaginable. This fresh scourge caused men to weep with fear. For some, cleanliness in attempted avoidance of the disease became a religion. Everything had to be boiled. Cooking and eating utensils were cleaned several times a day. Bathing in the river was banned and all drinking water had to be boiled. Unfortunately, when men are working and losing pints of water in sweat, their thirst becomes unbearable and many inevitably drank water direct from the river, and in most cases they died. The pangs of hunger are not just the rumbling of the stomach, it's much more than that. The stomach walls begin to pulsate and pains similar to indigestion occur, bringing with them the taste of bile which never reaches the gullet. Add to this the sheer frustration of a dry burning throat under a blazing sun which gives no respite and it is easier to understand why these men drank the cholera-infected river water.

The death rate when work on the building of the railway commenced averaged two or three a week in Chungkai. This gradually increased to two a day and finally thirty a day when cholera arrived. Camps lower down the river seemed to have escaped the spread of the disease, except Tamakan where a new base hospital was in process of being built. Kanchanaburi, which was one of the main working camps and was situated at the side of the river, had its quota of deaths and by July 1943 more than 3,500 funerals had taken place. There were exceptions. Tamuan which was the headquarters of 4 POW groups, didn't require a cemetery. Only one man died there and he was shot while trying to escape. All the remaining camps below Tamuan … Darnhai, Pandong and the others … also reported no casualties. Above Chungkai however the disease became rampant and men were dropping like flies sprayed with pesticide.

The scene of death and degradation was similar to a gigantic stage play, being performed in front of a backdrop of Thailand's panoramic views: the hills to the North and North East, with the winding river always within a mile of the railway line. The epidemic did not only strike the prisoners. Every day local people could be seen either bemoaning the death of a relative or attending the cremation of one. Their prayers and chanting throughout the night disturbed the sleep of many and brought pangs of fear to the not so strong.

As is usual in any community or where large numbers of people are thrust together, certain people or names stand out from the rest. Among the Japanese, the most well known and detested name was that of the civilian engineer Kiyioki Tanaka and his henchman Shigayuki Ashimoto. This pair were the most hated and feared men, if they can be called men, along the 350 kilometres of the railway. Their catalogue of crimes was recorded at the end of the war and included the murder of Gunner Lloyd Bull on 15th January 1943 and several more in similar fashion later. Bull, the first prisoner to be murdered in Thailand, was one of the men who had arrived just before Christmas and was suffering from dysentery and malaria. But he was considered fit enough to work on the railway cutting at Chungkai, breaking up large lumps of rock and granite to be used as ballast between the sleepers. Unfortunately Tanaka caught him doing nothing (malaria and dysentery causes tiredness and lethargy). Bull was sent to the top of the rock face where he was required to push or throw loose lumps of rock onto a bogey. The drillers had finished drilling and most of the holes had been filled with explosives with their wires attached to the main detonator wire. Tanaka connected this to the dynamo, a job usually done by one of his assistants. Once he had made the connection he ordered the alarm bell to be sounded. He then climbed to the top of the face, shouting for the men to hurry. Seeing Bull struggling to move clear, Tanaka picked up a long piece of wood, which he used to prod the unfortunate man. Bull lost his footing and began to slither down the side of the cutting. Tanaka then ran down to where the dynamo was situated and instantly pressed the plunger, which brought down tons of rock and granite which fell among the prisoners. When the dust had settled it was realized that Bull was beneath the rubble. As the prisoners ran to try and remove the rocks from him, Tanaka and his henchmen kept them at bay, swinging large iron palings and pieces of wood and shouting at everyone to get back to work. When British officers tried to reason with him, Tanaka just got madder. Thankfully the following day was a rest day and on Saturday 16th January Gunner L Bull was taken direct from the cutting to the cemetery … the tenth man to be buried in the New Year.

Tanaka continued his vicious murdering campaign. In June of the same year he knew that two prisoners were resting inside a deep cave at one of the cuttings near Wampo East. He again deliberately detonated the charges which created an explosion so large that he was reprimanded by the Japanese officer in charge for having risked the lives of his own soldiers. Tanaka was later seen to throw two dead prisoners into the fast flowing river. Not having knowledge of this, the Japanese guard commander assumed that the two men had escaped and a search of the area was conducted. Even when the camp was closed down the Japanese were convinced that two prisoners had managed to get away. After the war, former prisoners told of Tanaka's bestiality and many of them presented evidence against him. Unfortunately, before he could be brought to trial, the British and American governments decided that prosecuting all Japanese war criminals would cost too much money and it was agreed that the 1,876 Japanese prisoners being held in Thailand and Singapore should be set free. Tanaka and his henchman Ashimoto ran for cover in the jungles of Malaya and later worked with the Chinese communists in their fight against the British. They re-emerged from the Thai jungle in January 1990 and were feted as heroes when they returned to their homeland.

One Japanese criminal came to England after the war to investigate the best methods and areas to set up businesses here. His name was Gunso (Sergeant) Saito who was the villain in charge of prisoners on the building of the so-called Bridge on the River Kwai. Saito was a deposed cavalry man who had fought with Yamashita in Malaya. Unfortunately he had also contracted a disease which made him unable to sit on a horse, so he was left behind by the invading forces and given the job of looking after 20,000 prisoners. This was a task he did not accept gracefully, venting his spleen on the poor unfortunates who became his kicking pad. The method of erecting the sub frame which would carry the bridge was done in the old fashioned manner, by erecting a large scaffold from which to lift and drop a very heavy piece of concrete and iron onto the wooden poles to drive them into the ground. The poles were held upright by prisoners pulling on ropes, a scene very similar to the ones depicted in Gulliver's Travels. A Japanese engineer would place himself at the top of the pole which was to be pounded into the ground, and having secured himself by a rope he would start to sing "Itchi ni nasaya" and at the end of the word nasaya, the prisoners had to chorus "One two" then release the heavy lump of rock onto the top of the pole. This would drive the pole about two or three inches into the ground. The whole scenario would be repeated every few minutes until the pole was considered securely embedded. During this performance Saito would strut along finished sections of the bridge and take photographs. Occasionally just for fun as and a means of obtaining an unusual photograph, he would kick one of the prisoners off the structure, taking a snap as the man fell through the air and hit the water.

Another of his traits was seen when anyone committed a minor misdemeanour. He insisted that his guards should punish the culprit by flicking him across the nose with the fingers. The occasional flick on the nose can be painful, but after thirty or forty times the pain becomes excruciating and if any prisoner tried to avoid further punishment in this manner, Saito would resort to his Kendu stick and in practically every instance the poor recipient would finish up in hospital. Another of his favourite punishments was the crucifixion.

The Japanese, like the Germans, assumed that they were the super race and as such all other nationalities, religions and creeds were a joke and if any man committed a serious offence … laugh at one of the guards, be caught scrounging, smoking or skiving … he would be placed on Saito's cross. This was a strong wooden structure which was set in the ground. A man would have his wrists bound to the cross piece, leaving his forearms free. His ankles would also be bound. The cross was built so that the feet of any prisoner fastened to it would always remain on the ground. Buckets of water or sand would placed in the man's hands which were bound in such a manner that it was not possible to release their burden. The punishment lasted for at least one hour and up to as much as eight hours. At first the one hour punishment was accepted as child's play, but as men became weaker and the punishment longer, very few could survive for long. Most of those who suffered in this manner were afterwards transfered to other working parties when they came out of hospital. This was for their own protection. Once a Japanese guard had "marked out" a prisoner, that man's life would be made hell, to the point of death in some instances. Saito was still visiting England up to 1990, a little stooped now, but maintaining the impression that he is as clean as driven snow. But there are those, myself included, who still regard him as a monster.

Work on the railway was now speeded up to the point where the Japanese were making impossible demands on their prisoners. Men were made to work a full twelve hour shift then return to camp and take over duties in the hospital or grave digging, latrine digging and general cleaning chores. The fact that it was now dark meant nothing, the work had to be done or else. A number of the officers devoted all their time to assisting the sick and demoralised prisoners and although they won no recognition from our government after the war, they received, and today still retain, the respect and admiration of all those they tried to help in adversity. Major Cooper, Major Buchan, Major Sykes, W O Thomas, Captain Nash and Lt. Ken Darlow of the Cambridgeshires, the latter giving me the inspiration and the spirit to stay alive. There were many other unsung heroes whose names time has erased from the memory, but there were also those in the camps who gave very little except when requiring a favour in return. One in particular was Lt. M——. A more incompetent, snivelling officer I had never seen in my years of service. His main aim in life was to remain alive and it did not matter whose life he helped destroy or how low he stooped to lick our captors' boots. Suffice it to say that had the trial of war criminals been allowed to continue, a charge against him would most certainly have been presented by me, and he would have found himself in the dock with Tanaka and others like him.

With cholera threatening all the prisoner of war camps, the Japanese were now reluctant to wander about like they had done in the past. This gave a golden opportunity to the prisoners , some of whom broke out and went in search of a local who would buy whatever watches, pens, lighters, rings and other mementos of better days they still had. On most occasions, the money received in exchange for these goods was used to purchase food and medicine and as often as not one or two pints of Siamese whisky. It was sheer gut rot, but many willingly paid what was the equivalent of thirty five pounds a bottle at today's prices. Today in Thailand the same whisky is sold at two pounds a bottle. The impact of this raw spirit upon practically empty bellies was astounding. Small wimpish men would suddenly become Charles Atlas or Samson and the following morning would see the start of a long trail of visits to the hospital with either dysentery or some other deep-seated illness.

Although the Japs called for more speed, and men were being practically worked to death, there were those who still found time, energy and nerve to build and put into operation a secret radio. The one at Chungkai remained in use all through the war without discovery. The method of conveying the news received was handled by a team of officers who, on the pretence of reading the men a story from a book, would provide brief details of the news and then give their opinions as to the possible outcome of certain items. These were the officers who the men could depend upon and to whom they went when things were not going right, and in every instance they were accommodated.

The Japanese started to operate trains from Bangkok up to within three or four miles of the forward working parties. Mostly carrying ballast, lines and sleepers. The first steam trains had whistles similar to those in America and each night as they passed by their weird eerie sound would echo all round, and send the nocturnal inhabitants of the jungle scattering for cover, and those men who were awoken would moan about the disturbance.

In the early days it had been agreed that men who were not working on the railway should be employed building a church. It was constructed in the same manner and with the same materials as the men's living quarters, except that the bamboo was stronger and the palm fronds used for the roofing were worked closer together giving a tighter resistance to the elements. When finished the building could withstand any kind of monsoon, and occasionally when a man's bed space became wet through rain, he would pick up his blanket and go and sleep in the church. That was until someone in authority came along and threw the poor man out.

One of the Japanese guards once commented on the fact that the British spent more time and money worshipping an unknown God than any other nation. In Japan, he explained, many people worshipped outside and where a temple was built, it was built to the memory of someone or some God in particular. It would also be a simple building. Chungkai held a total of fifteen thousand prisoners considered fit to work on the railway. But the total number of men attending Sunday service was little more than one hundred. It seemed to Japanese and prisoners alike a waste that such a large well built structure should only be used just once a week and by so few.

As well as the church, the Japanese allowed the prisoners to construct a theatre. Nature helped in this by providing a large hollow piece of land in a clearing just inside camp. Once the stage had been built it was not unlike a Roman amphitheatre. One of the stalwarts in this venture was a young man whose name I will always remember: Leo Britt. After the war he appeared in a film "The Electric Man" and in my opinion he was a better song and dance man than he was an actor. He and several others would finish their stint on the railway, return to camp and hurriedly scoff their meals, after which it was rehearsals until lights out. Among Leo's productions was the musical extravaganza 'Wonderbar' in which dozens of female impersonators danced and cavorted around the stage in flimsy dresses, causing one or two of the Japanese to think that somehow or other a troupe of females had invaded the camp. Bobby Spong was so impressive in this role I understand that he had a proposal of marriage during the first part of the show. Like everything else which the Japanese cautiously allowed the prisoners to enjoy, it was always subject to cancellation at the least provocation for crimes such as a man not cleaning his shovel when he returned to camp, or a prisoner having the audacity to walk past one of the Japanese soldiers without bowing. So practically all the shows scheduled for a three night run only managed two, which seemed a pity when one considers all the work the artists and stage hands had put into it all.

More prisoners began to pour through Chungkai but now it was noticeable that the influx of Javanese and Dutch was becoming more pronounced. At one stage the Dutch prisoners outnumbered the British and Australians, but they only remained long enough to recuperate from their long journey from the Dutch East Indies, then they were sent up the line.

It was at this time that news began to filter through about other atrocities committed by the Japanese in camps in other countries, also the fate of many of our comrades who had supposedly managed to escape from Singapore. Apparently after the bombing of Tokyo by General Doolittle's men in the early part of the war, the Japanese government had ordered a blackout of the news to its service men. Somehow or other the news leaked out around May/June 1943. The result was that the Japanese on Labuan started to ill-treat anyone who was not Japanese by birth. Prisoners were crucified, being nailed to large trees and left to die and rot in the jungle. Native women were used, abused and then murdered, usually by a bullet in the head. Children suffered a similar fate. The Japanese military have never bothered to conceal the fact that fifty per cent of them were homosexual or bi-sexual. To them people were just commodities and once they had been used, they were destroyed. Of the total number of prisoners sent to Borneo more than seventy five per cent perished, their remains left in the jungle to rot, or thrown into the seas and rivers.

In Thailand the word ''speedo'' was synonymous with death, the guards and engineers using anything to hand to enforce their commands. A vast number of men were by now brainwashed to the level of trained animals, some even to the extent of kowtowing to the guards unnecessarily. The term Jap Happy was given to this type of person. Dignity had diminished long ago, and for some, self respect. It is hard to say this, knowing the suffering which everybody experienced, but it would not be right to try and cover up our own inadequacies and lack of moral fibre.

On the other side of the coin however there were those who distinctly went out of their way to be as unresponsive or aggressive to the Japanese as they possibly could. Very few prisoners of war, being so wrapped up in their own battles, ever knew or heard of the many acts of murder, sabotage and destruction perpetrated by those men who never gave up trying to fight the Japanese from within. Many Japanese guards, officers and engineers went missing, officially reported as deserters when in fact they were no longer alive. I can quote two examples which I witnessed personally plus another in which I was involved, the names of others have gone from my memory. One sentry went missing at Konqueta on the night that one or two prisoners set the Japanese stores alight. It was put down by the authorities that he had deserted in view of his negligence. In fact he had been garroted by one Austen Chamberlain and thrown into the fast moving river after being relieved of his dog tags and the contents of his pockets. Another guard lost his life when a large party of prisoners were being taken by barge from Chungkai to one of the forward camps. The barges were moving by night when the same man, Chamberlain, watched and waited until the guard had begun to relax at the rear of the river barge. Then he struck quickly and positively. After removing everything valuable, he allowed the body to slide into the river and it disappeared seawards. The third case involved a guard who I accidentally killed in a temper. His body was disposed of down one of the large latrines outside the dysentery wards at Chungkai.

With the constant yelling of ''speedo'', the lack of food and medicine and the outbreak of cholera and black water fever, the prisoners now resembled the kind of zombies seen in horror movies today. Everything was as near routine as was possible. Eat, walk, work, walk, eat, sleep. Then repeat the procedure daily until you dropped. There were men there who pre-war were at the peak of their physical fitness. Now they were the pits in physical weakness. While all the time, the railway progressed. June, July, August and September 1943 saw the greatest loss of lives. The Japanese were sticklers for personal cleanliness and it was thought that they might therefore encourage personal hygiene among the prisoners. But their attitude was completely contrary. As soon as a man became ill for any reason he was shunned by the Japanese and in all instances he was not allowed to bathe in the same river which the Japanese drew water from, even though the bathing position was below the watering point. When cholera and black water fever exploded in the camps, the Japanese ordered that in future there would be no burials. Every corpse had to be cremated. But by the same rule, every prisoner who was cremated must have the same six foot grave as those who had been buried. The reason for this was beyond the comprehension of most prisoners. After months of the last post being sounded constantly, the plague came to an abrupt end. No one knows why. The doctors had in many instances put themselves at great risk in tending the sick, while others had actually sacrificed their lives for their patients. Their names live on in the memory or on the scrolls of remembrance though their deeds have long been forgotten.

November 1943 saw the completion of the railway and one would have thought that the Japanese would now relax. But this was not to be. Within hours of the completion of the line, down came the Allied bombers from Burma and elsewhere to blow up what had taken so much blood and sweat to produce. Along with the railway, away went the lives of hundreds more prisoners of war. After each air raid, groups of sick, wounded, weary prisoners were taken out to put back everything which had been knocked down. It was not until January 1944 that the Japanese decided to send groups of men back down country to Kanchanaburi to be kitted out with all manner of shorts and shirts in a myriad of startling colours, before being sent to either Saigon or back to Singapore to begin their journey to the mines and shipyards of Japan.

Occasionally there was a general feeling that the war was almost over, but when this happened, the illusion was swiftly broken by the bullying Japanese engineers, who not having sufficient work to keep their tiny minds occupied, would descend on the nearest prisoner of war camp and insist on hundreds of men being made to walk for miles along the railway line, in order to remove weeds and grass from the side of the embankment. On occasions it would take anything up to four hours to arrive at the chosen spot. Work would be done using bare hands and any piece of wood or metal available. After about six hours without a break, everyone was ordered to return to the main camp, by which time whatever food had been cooked for them had either spoiled or been eaten by their starving comrades.

It was possibly only coincidence that with the completion of the railway, the first Red Cross food parcels began to arrive. Not having any previous knowledge of these much needed gifts, we naturally assumed that six prisoners sharing one parcel was the norm. It was not until word was passed along the line from Bangkok that thousands of these parcels had arrived, that the prisoners realized the Japanese were only handing over one fifth of the number of parcels received. It became a common sight to see Japanese soldiers coming down the line from the Burma front smoking Players, Senior Service and other English and American brands of cigarettes. The same Japanese would occasionally feel sorry for the men working along the railway and throw them bits of chocolate bars, biscuits and occasionally a small container of jam. The Japanese troops were being given the Red Cross parcels meant for the prisoners and we realised then that the Japanese were in a worse condition than ourselves. At this time it was suggested that the fittest prisoners should now band together and formulate a plan to overthrow the guards. The idea took root in Chungkai and gathered momentum. That was until certain officers found out about the scheme and within days most of the fit men had been taken from whatever job they had been assigned to and moved elsewhere. In some cases men were transferred to those groups en route to Japan in place of those already designated, and the possibility of a break-out was smothered. Coincidentally, in November 1943 Mountbatten had accumulated a large amphibious force of more than fifty thousand mixed Allied troops, standing by to invade Burma from the South Western approaches which at the time were defended by just 5,000 Japanese in the rear area and eleven thousand in the forward areas. Mountbatten contacted Churchill for permission to begin the assault on Burma, an attack which would not only relieve the hard-pressed men fighting in Burma but would also cut off the Japanese completely. The reply from Churchill was to the effect that the Americans only required odds of two to one when they went into battle for the Pacific islands and in any event the fifty thousand men under Mountbatten's command were needed for a possible invasion of Europe sometime in the future. The chance of shortening or even perhaps finishing the war in the Pacific had passed.

Meanwhile men in their hundreds were being killed and starved to death only one hundred miles inland from where the amphibious fleet lay at anchor.

Fortunately the prisoners of war had no knowledge of the dispute between Churchill and Mountbatten and they continued to die in ignorance.

With all work on the actual building of the railway now completed, the Japanese allowed their prisoners to try to improve their living conditions, by providing certain areas to be converted into vegetable gardens. Unfortunately they did not supply any seeds for the purpose and the work in clearing the jungle was wasted. Each day parties of prisoners continued to be sent down the line to be kitted out in colourful shirts and shorts in preparation for their journey to Japan. Working parties were made up from those remaining behind and despatched to various sites where they would be required to repair airfields, build roads and mend those which had been bombed. The camp at Chungkai achieved a sinister outline. A moat was built round it and at each corner stood a watch tower, complete with machine gun post. Around all this was bamboo fencing over six foot high at its lowest points. Life inside Chungkai became a miserable existence with the daily routine of roll call, menial work and complete boredom. This was only interrupted by the aftermath of the bombers, when prisoners were made to repair parts of the railway line which had been damaged.

After their usefulness was ended, the Indian, Chinese, and local labour gangs were left to fend for themselves. On a number of occasions, prisoners of war were sent to various camps which had held these native labourers. Here they would be required to dispose of many dead bodies, it being expressed by the Japanese in charge that no evidence should remain. The stench and the sight of so many people left to die of starvation overwhelmed the POWs. So much so that sometimes they themselves died and were disposed of in the same manner as the natives, usually by cremation, or when there were vast numbers, in large pits.

With time on their hands, certain prisoners, especially those nearer to the Burma border, decided that the time was ripe for escaping. Over sixty tried to break free, but on every occasion they were captured and executed, either by firing squad or decapitation.

At Tamuan camp the British officers in charge decided to attempt to bring back a little military discipline and ordered the men to recommence saluting officers and standing to attention when addressing an NCO. The whole idea was preposterous and doomed to failure. Two prisoners were charged with insubordination and while awaiting trial in a hastily constructed guard room they broke loose and climbed over the perimeter fence. They had managed to travel just thirty yards when they were shot down by the Japanese guards.

The Japanese authorities would not hand over the bodies for burial, instead they were sent to Kanchanaburi where they were handed over to the officer in charge of the cemetery with instructions to dispose of them without fuss. No identification accompanied the bodies, which were immediately disposed of in one of the many pre-prepared graves.

At this time the civil prison at Bampong was being used to house POWs, civilian and Japanese criminals. Each cell which would normally hold two men was now required to sleep five or even six, and whenever the prison became overcrowded the matter was resolved by taking what were considered the most troublesome prisoners outside and shooting them. All those who were executed or tortured to death were buried behind the Japanese administration building at Kanchanaburi, which was the headquarters of the Kempetai.

By the end of 1944, thousands of prisoners were moved out of Thailand to other areas. About 3,000 were destined for Japan. Most prisoners who were selected for the trip were given a complete change of clothing comprising shirt, shorts and a pair of Japanese split toe canvas shoes. No account was taken of size, which resulted in a kind of bazaar scene as the men tried to obtain a proper fit. But even this did not solve the problem for many and it was not unusual to see men walking round in these Japanese shoes with the front cut away. The men selected for the move to Japan were also aware of the danger in travelling in a Japanese merchant ship in the Pacific. News had been brought to the camp by a number of American sailors, whose ships had been sunk and who had been picked up by Japanese ships and taken to the nearest port. They told about the battles around the Pacific islands and the many enemy ships being sunk by American submarines. So it was not without some trepidation, that those assigned climbed aboard the train which would take them back to Singapore where they would embark for Japan and the copper mines.

Other men were sent to Singapore and Malaya where they were employed on building and maintaining the airfields, railways and important military installations. Others in Singapore were employed in land reclamation schemes. One party started work on Blaka Mati, now named Pulau Sentosa, where work consisted of building a massive golf course. Today this same course is owned by Japanese, and the cost of membership is so high that very few Europeans could afford to join. Many other Japanese schemes that were commenced during the war became Japanese property afterwards. On the island of Pulau Bukum, which was mostly tree and bush covered, the prisoners were used to destroy as much plant life as possible to make way for a large oil storage depot. Today the island has, I am told, an oil refinery, Japanese financed. All over South East Asia, prisoners and forced labourers were used to create commercial ventures. In Borneo it was very much the same. In Labuan they were used to build a small airfield. When the task was completed only five per cent of the original work force were left alive and this was only because the 1st Australian Corps eliminated 30,000 Japanese defenders and took Labuan on the 10th June. In attempting to hold Borneo the Japanese lost more than fifteen thousand men, the rest were either wounded or taken prisoner. On Labuan itself the Japanese took to the hilly ground above the airstrip, and held out until 23rd June 1945.

At the end of hostilities, it was found that of the 7,000 Allied prisoners who died on Labuan, 3,200 had no known grave. The Japanese commandant, Colonel Suga, destroyed all records appertaining to POWs and their treatment, then committed suicide as the Australian forces moved in to capture him.

Prisoners of war held in Borneo were found in many places including Lutong, Miri and Sambogda. Most prisoners held on these islands were murdered by the Japanese in accordance with the instructions issued by the Japanese War Department.

From the end of the monsoons in September 1944, the RAF commenced its ritual bombing along the railway. This kept the fifteen to twenty thousand prisoners remaining in Thailand very busy, not only repairing the bomb damage, but also by being compelled to remove, carry and store Japanese munitions. At 112 camp there was a large barren hill, with several caves situated around its base, which the Japanese had converted into stores for munitions. Although the distance from the railway was only about two hundred yards, the task of carrying boxes of ammunition and six inch shells was soul destroying even for the fittest of the prisoners, most of whom had worked on the construction of the railway and now resembled skeletons. The Japanese soldiers who escorted the ammunition trains were not used to seeing prisoners of war being used as coolies and they took great delight in humiliating those men who were unable to lift some of the articles being transported to the caves.

Other prisoners were taken to work on the railway which ran from Bangkok to Chungmai, the main junction between Thailand, Burma and Indo China. At this time, thousands of Japanese wounded were being sent down from Burma and at the same time reinforcements were arriving via Indo China, and Chungmai had become a bottleneck which was under constant attack from the RAF. Once more it was hard to understand the mentality of the Japanese. Their soldiers were camped along the streets, sometimes for days. Prisoners were at times compelled to walk along these streets to reach their respective tasks. Occasionally a Japanese soldier fresh from home, would throw a cigarette or a piece of food to them and would laugh at the antics of those prisoners who were not fortunate in catching a ''presento'' as it was termed by the young soldiers. A little further up the road however, the streets were littered with stretchers on which lay the wounded. As the prisoners reached this point, it was not unusual for them to be pelted with bricks and other missiles. The Japanese guards, in most instances, took cover either in the jungle or behind the houses. The worst feature of this, however, was to witness French, German and other civilians of European extraction kow towing and licking the boots of these vile creatures. They were poltroons drawn from the lowest dregs of Europe.

The chances of escape were now the best ever. It was just one hundred and fifty miles to the front line in Burma. On or about the beginning of March 1945, two men from the Royal Artillery, Gunners Holder and Hodgson and a member of the Royal Signals, McHugh, decided to take a chance. The other members of their work party, one hundred in number, each subscribed a little of whatever cash they carried, plus oddments of food, which might last the three men three or four days. They were hoping to hide away on one of the trains which were used to transport the Japanese wounded on the Thai/Burma border. Later everyone assumed that the escape had been successful. I have only recently been informed that the three men never arrived in Burma, let alone England. Apart from the few men who left Singapore just before the capitulation, I have not heard of a successful escape from any of the prison camps. Most escapees died in the jungle or were captured and executed. The Japanese offered a reward of £20 for every escaped prisoner of war and some Thais made a business out of pretending to show friendship to prisoners and offering to take them through the jungle to freedom. They would suggest groups of two or three at a time. Once outside the camp, the prisoners would be taken to a nearby village, where after being supplied with food and drink, they would be told to wait. Their so-called benefactors would then go to the nearest Kempetai officer and lead him to the escapees. The Japanese, took great delight in arranging executions. To them it was an opportunity to display their prowess as warriors or Samurai. There were occasions when the Japanese would order everyone in the vicinity to attend and witness. In Singapore, immediately after capitulation, they conducted such executions in a carnival mood. Wagers were made on which swordsman would make the quickest and cleanest decapitation.

At all camps a record was maintained of each prisoner and the medication he had received from the Japanese, the previous camps he had been at and the time he had spent there. These records were kept by the British officers and NCOs at the instigation of the Japanese. At the camps in Japan, Formosa and the islands close to Japan, prisoners were photographed and numbered. The photographs held at Kinkasaki camp were seized by one of the prisoners (Sergeant Cliff Cookson of the Manchester Regiment) and were offered to the British War Office by him. No one bothered to take up this offer. At the end of hostilities it was found that thirty thousand men were missing believed dead. The lists and the photographs which were kept in each camp would have at least given some indication of where some men had last been seen. But the lists and photographs were totally ignored.

Several men recorded their own lists. I was one of these. Unfortunately mine only contained the names of the three thousand men who I had helped to bury. This list was subsequently handed over to the Commonwealth War Graves Commission. It has never been returned to me!

In Japan and Formosa, where American prisoners were held, certain individuals formed a type of Mafia. The men in charge, with the knowledge of the Japanese, set up a protection racket. Every prisoner was required to donate a percentage of his food ration to these barons. Those failing to toe the line were badly beaten, not only by the American Mafia, but also by the Japanese who supported such activities. Any luxuries such as Red Cross parcels were handed over to these gangsters for distribution, those obtaining anything from the parcels were required to pay these Mafia bosses with part of their rice ration, or some other article of value which they owned. Prisoners working in the copper mines and shipyards suffered a great deal more hardship than others. They worked in shifts which usually lasted sixteen hours out of each twenty four. By the last six months of the war the men had all been reduced to a zombie like routine of, work, sleep, work.

Those who had remained in Singapore were employed in similar manner to other prisoners based close to a large town. Basically they were required to repair bomb damaged airfields and port facilities. The Japanese declared that Syonan, the new name for Singapore, was to become their shining example of the future Asia and many men were used in land reclamation and the rebuilding of the main airport. Discounting the manner in which they went about this transformation, it must be admitted that their thinking was correct, in that the land reclamation and the rebuilding of the airport was completed after the end of hostilities. Tourists and others who today walk along Princess Elizabeth Walk, have no knowledge that the land on which it was built was recovered from the sea and that buried beneath are the remains of many hundred Chinese and other nationals, who were sacrificed in the name of Japanese Imperialism.

Very few people today appreciate how many of Singapore's population went missing during the Japanese occupation. A monument was erected some time after the war when it was estimated that over 500,000 people had vanished. The British losses would give some credence to this, in that of the original 85,000 servicemen and civilians on Singapore in February 1942, less than fifty percent were alive at the end of hostilities and twenty three thousand of those who died have no known grave. The population of Singapore at the outbreak of war was just over two million. So it would be within the bounds of possibility to say that the total number of civilians missing would be nearer nine hundred thousand as opposed to the estimated figure of five hundred thousand.

Singapore is an island measuring roughly twenty by twenty two miles and at the outset of war just half of this area was populated. The rest was jungle and bushland. So it would seem impossible to hide over 500,000 bodies. However, given Japanese ingenuity and well practised skill at disposing of that which they do not wish to be seen, the task was easy. When the prisoners had finished their daily tasks, especially in the area of what is now Princess Elizabeth Walk and along the East coast, the Japanese trainee soldiers and Indian army volunteers would transport the bodies of those who had that day been executed to the workings on the land recovery projects. I can still not understand the attitude of either the Japanese or their allies, the Germans, in wanting to hide the bodies of those they had killed. Nature and the atmosphere would have completed the work for them, instead of which they preferred to bury most, only to find years later that instead of destroying the evidence, nature had actually preserved it.

It is now fifty years since that ignominious day, when after giving their all in the name of the Empire, British and Allied service men and women were allowed to become the slaves of the Japanese, due to the lack of foresight and the muddled thinking of our leaders in England. And still today no one in power has had the courage to admit that these were not mistakes but calculated diplomatic skullduggery.

The naval base and floating dock. At the time it seemed that this floating dock was of more importance than Singapore itself. The structure was built in Britain and towed out to Singapore in 1936. Its overall size can be gauged from the figure in the bottom of the picture.

INSTRUMENT OF SURRENDER

W e, acting by command of and in behalf of the Emperor of Japan, the Japanese Government and the Japanese Imperial General Headquarters, hereby accept the provisions set forth in the declaration issued by the heads of the Governments of the United States, China and Great Britain on 26 July 1945, at Potsdam, and subsequently adhered to by the Union of Soviet Socialist Republics, which four powers are hereafter referred to as the Allied Powers.

We hereby proclaim the unconditional surrender to the Allied Powers of the Japanese Imperial General Headquarters and of all Japanese armed forces and all armed forces under Japanese control wherever situated.

We hereby command all Japanese forces wherever situated and the Japanese people to cease hostilities forthwith, to preserve and save from damage all ships, aircraft, and military and civil property and to comply with all requirements which may be imposed by the Supreme Commander for the Allied Powers or by agencies of the Japanese Government at his direction.

We hereby command the Japanese Imperial General Headquarters to issue at once orders to the Commanders of all Japanese forces and all forces under Japanese control wherever situated to surrender unconditionally themselves and all forces under their control.

We hereby command all civil, military and naval officials to obey and enforce all proclamations, orders and directives deemed by the Supreme Commander for the Allied Powers to be proper to effectuate this surrender and issued by him or under his authority and we direct all such officials to remain at their posts and to continue to perform their non-combatant duties unless specifically relieved by him or under his authority.

We hereby undertake for the Emperor, the Japanese Government and their successors to carry out the provisions of the Potsdam Declaration in good faith, and to issue whatever orders and take whatever action may be required by the Supreme Commander for the Allied Powers or by any other designated representative of the Allied Powers for the purpose of giving effect to that Declaration.

We hereby command the Japanese Imperial Government and the Japanese Imperial General Headquarters at once to liberate all allied prisoners of war and civilian internees now under Japanese control and to provide for their protection, care, maintenance and immediate transportation to places as directed.

The authority of the Emperor and the Japanese Government to rule the state shall be subject to the Supreme Commander for the Allied Powers who will take such steps as he deems proper to effectuate these terms of surrender.

Signed at TOKYO BAY, JAPAN at 0904 I
on the SECOND day of SEPTEMBER, 1945.

重光葵

By Command and in behalf of the Emperor of Japan and the Japanese Government.

梅津美治郎

By Command and in behalf of the Japanese Imperial General Headquarters.

Accepted at TOKYO BAY, JAPAN at 0908 I
on the SECOND day of SEPTEMBER, 1945,
for the United States, Republic of China, United Kingdom and the Union of Soviet Socialist Republics, and in the interests of the other United Nations at war with Japan.

Douglas MacArthur

Supreme Commander for the Allied Powers.

C.W. Nimitz

United States Representative

徐永昌

Republic of China Representative

Bruce Fraser.

United Kingdom Representative

Union of Soviet Socialist Republics Representative

T.A. Blamey

Commonwealth of Australia Representative

Dominion of Canada Representative

Provisional Government of the French Republic Representative

Kingdom of the Netherlands Representative

Leonard M. Isitt

Dominion of New Zealand Representative

The Argylls on patrol. A bren gunner gives cover to a Signals section during running repairs

The evacuation of North Malaya. This evacuation of civilians (including children) created a great deal of ill feeling with the local people because priority was given to Europeans.

The bridge is blown - Heavy Artillery (two limbers, no gun) crossing a ford!

Preparing to blow the bridges at Slim and Muar. This resulted in heavy Allied casualties because both bridges were blown too soon.

Japanese bombers find the Seletar fuel dump.

*A 'General Discussion', Wavell and Percival
outside the Fort Canning Battle Box.*

The first bomb casualty. 7th Dec. 1941.

Preparing to ford a river in Jahore

Further preparations for river crossing

The Loyals on patrol in Jahore

*The Indian Army arrives
in Singapore. January 1942*

Indians securing offshore islands

Indians on patrol

Moving to fixed positions

Waiting for orders

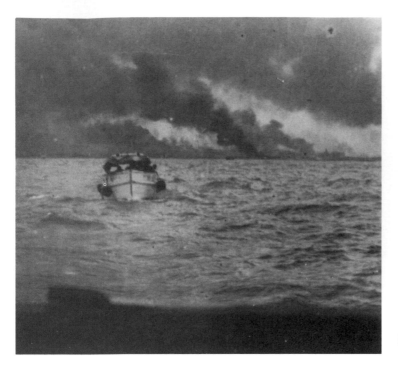

The last of the few.

Singapore, the end as seen from a retiring launch.

Air force on display.

A patched up fighter.

The peace and tranquility of Thailand - a mirage which clouded the future

Chungkai - the doorway to North West Thailand and the first camp to be built on the Death Railway. Today it is a village of discotheques and neon lights.

Return Journey

Returning to Bangkok, I discovered that nothing had changed heat-wise in fifty years, but the people had changed. Now everyone owned a car, lorry, bus or motorcycle, all bearing the names of one Japanese company or other, with streets full to capacity both day and night. The overwhelming stench had not changed however, nor had the numbers of hawkers and Chinese style roadside eating establishments.

Before leaving England, arrangements had been made for a meeting with the Tourist Authority of Thailand (TAT) and it was here within six hours of our landing in Thailand that we met the director of TAT, a Mrs. Sumonta Nakornthab, who in turn introduced her deputy Chalerlap Gachanara. Our meeting was fairly brief, but we managed to convey our requirements to them. Mrs. Nakornthab suggested that we should return the following day, in the meantime she would make the necessary arrangements. Having agreed that TAT would supply transport facilities and a camera team to travel with us to make a video of the tour, providing that two or three Thai news reporters would be allowed to accompany us, the only sticking point was that we were two days away from the Chinese New Year. Because of this the video team would not be available for four or five days. So as not to waste any of our valuable time, it was decided that our party would go on to Singapore to locate the stained glass windows from the garrison church which I had observed being buried during the war.

Most of the moderately priced hotels in Singapore were fully booked and we found ourselves in the Benkoolen Hotel, a name many of the old soldiers from Singapore Fortress will remember with a cynical smile. There had been a bomb crater where the hotel now stood. The Singapore I once knew had changed beyond all recognition, even since my last visit ten years previously. Within an hour of arriving, a deputation from the University and the military had called to meet us to discuss means by which they could assist in locating the stained glass windows. The party included two majors from the Singapore army, two lecturers and a historian from the University.

Although it was ten thirty in the evening, they insisted that we all drive to the spot where I had watched the windows being buried. The journey, although along newly constructed highways, created for me a sense of nostalgia and as we arrived at the spot which had once been the entrance to our jungle camp, I could feel a tingling down my spine and the hairs on the back of my neck began to stiffen. I knew that we were at the right place.

The humid atmosphere hit me as I stepped out of the car and even if the whole area had been covered by a skyscraper building, I would have known that this was the spot. Although there was no moon it was possible to see that, where there had once been a large rubber estate and virgin jungle, there was now a vast flat open area, surrounded by a major road and a housing estate. The following day other interested parties came along to enquire and advise. These included Professor E C T Chew, MA, (Singapore) Ph D (Cantab) Dean, Faculty of Arts and Social Sciences, Kwa Chong Guan, Director the Singapore Social History Department, John Miksic PhD, lecturer, Department of History, National University of Singapore, P J Williams FTC MRRT, technical officer and offshore supervisor for ROV and sonar survey. Plus reporters from the *Mail on Sunday* and the *Sunday Times* and those from local newspapers. With the temperature rising into the eighties under a very hot sun, everyone stood around offering theories, with the occasional cynic doubting that we were in the right place. At three o'clock in the afternoon it was decided to break off, so that the reporter from the *Mail on Sunday* could enquire locally about the possibility of acquiring metal detecting equipment. Although we were on the spot where I saw the windows being buried, the ground was now about fifteen feet higher than it had been in 1981. This was due to the many major roads being built in Singapore. The whole of the area which had once been 'ten milestone camp' was now being used as a dumping ground for surplus road making material. There was a clear view for several hundred yards and although I am still positive of the exact position where the windows were buried, we did not have the equipment we required to locate them. The Singapore Oral History Department had promised that they would supply our team with metal detectors obtained from the Singapore military. Unfortunately, when we made enquiries as to their availability we found that someone at the Hill Street headquarters of the history department had in fact issued orders that the loan of the equipment should be cancelled. It was only the intervention of Peter Woolrich, one of the freelance reporters, which stopped us from returning to Thailand that same day.

Using his influence and money in order to telephone several interested parties, he obtained the assistance of Philip

Williams the manager of Advance Marine, who promised to meet us with his team of trained men and their treasure seeking equipment the following day. Having now been assured that work would begin, I decided to remain in Singapore. In the meantime I was able to revisit the places where I had once lived and survived.

Paya Lebah, which is now an important district in Singapore, was just a small village on the outskirts of the jungle in 1942. The spot where I had set my machine gun up was still there, as were the houses immediately behind, but the wooden house where a school teacher and his daughter were killed by our own bullets had now been replaced by a bus shelter. I walked to the spot where Lew Doughton and I had shot a group of Japanese infiltrating our lines. It was the first time since 14th February 1942, that I had looked down at the ground where they had fallen. I don't know what I was looking for, maybe some sign of what had taken place, but like all the other places in Singapore which endured the fighting, the scars have been obliterated. The Cathay building, once one of the tallest structures in Singapore and one which received a great deal of attention from the Japanese gunners, was now dwarfed by skyscraper buildings and camouflaged by their gigantic shadows.

River Valley Road and Havelock Road camps, which saw so much cruelty and degradation, had been replaced by similar high rise buildings and I wondered if anyone had bothered to remove the many skeletons buried there. The Battle Box at Fort Canning, which had supposedly been sealed by British engineers after they had destroyed all the usable materials, was being reopened that day and I was invited by the American lecturer John Miksic to attend the ceremony. The feeling, as I walked through the Cox Terrace entrance, was like one gets when walking through a graveyard after dark. The last time I had been inside the building was on the night when, with a party from my HQ company, I had escorted General Gordon Bennett across Singapore to the Jardine steps preparatory to his escape from the island. As we walked past the signals ops room and the decoding room, I thought I could hear the voice of Peter Walker the chief wireless operator, but I knew the atmospherics were playing tricks. Peter had died hundreds of miles away on the Death Railway. As we turned right from the command post, the silhouette of two Indian soldiers looked menacingly in my direction, but I knew that no Indian soldier had ever served in the bunkers. These were cardboard cut-outs placed there to give an impression. Although everyone assumed that the bunker had been built specifically for World War Two, it was originally constructed during World War One as a naval operations room, but it was never put to use. Then in 1936, the British War Office expanded and redesigned it to produce what was then a most modern battle box. It was officially opened sometime in 1938. Some evidence still remains of the original building of the 1914/18 period

The following day my small party journeyed to the tenth milestone site, where we were met by historians, engineers and reporters, including Tan Teng Teng a young freelance working for *The Times*. She made up for her small stature by her enthusiastic appetite for work. Although the treasure hunters had brought along metal detectors and sonar equipment, it was not possible to pinpoint the exact position where the windows had been buried. This was mainly due to the many metallic objects and other spoil which had been dumped by the road builders. The steel base from a gas cylinder, the tail fin of a small bomb, the rusting remains of an oil drum were all we found. At the far side of the site stood a large mechanical digger and one or two people had tried without success to induce the driver to dig a large hole in the ground so that the geologists could determine how much spoil had been dumped there. The driver was from Thailand and fortunately for us Teng Teng could speak the language and was able to talk him into digging a hole for us. When he had gone down about eighteen feet, it confirmed that there was on average over fifteen feet of spoil dumped in the area.

Further research would be required, including obtaining a map of the locality circa 1945/60 from which I would be able to point out certain landmarks which would give a fix on the approximate spot, plus any aerial photographs taken between 1945 and 1980. When I had visited the site in 1979 it was more or less as we had left it in 1942, except that most of the rubber trees had been removed. Later aerial photographs supplied by the RAF proved my point. They clearly show the footpath which was opposite the entrance to the camp, and also the position of a Chinese coffee shop. These were the landmarks I had memorised for future use, should we be able to return that way. I was not to know that the windows had not been recovered when the British returned to Singapore after the war.

In the meantime, Peter Woolrich and Philip Williams had managed to contact an Australian team of treasure hunters which had carried specialised equipment which would be able take soundings to a depth of well below twenty feet of earth. Unfortunately, they would not be available for several months and it was decided that members of Singapore University history department in conjunction with the Oral History Department and Singapore museum authorities would try to organise a fund raising event to pay for the Australian team to come to Singapore in search of the windows.

We had now spent four days in Singapore, using up valuable time and money. In order to make our journey worthwhile we visited several places of interest, including Kranji Cemetery. Many people are not aware that this cemetery is built on what was once the largest ammunition dump in the Pacific theatre. Just before the Japanese landed on Singapore, orders were issued for its destruction, but like many similar plans, they were not issued until the last minute. Consequently the job was bungled and only parts of the dump were destroyed. The Japanese decided that they would try to recover the ammunition and prisoners of war were used for this task. The majority of shells and bombs etc. were without detonators, and kept in a separate section of the dump, and apart from one or two accidents quite a large proportion of the hardware was removed, but not the live ammunition and detonators. The Japanese then had the site filled in.

After the war, when the British authorities were selecting a site for the future military airfield, they found that the cemeteries where prisoners of war were buried would be in the way of progress and it was decided that since no one would ever be able to safely build on the ammunition dump site, it might not be a bad idea to transfer the remains of the POWs to this spot. Today a section of the Singapore civil airport is built over the site where the original cemetery stood.

I stood on the edge of what had been the Mandai quarry, where the Japanese had brought us as prisoners to collect the dead bodies of all nationalities. The Japanese soldiers were cremated on the spot and their ashes taken to the so-called Victory Hill at the side of the Ford factory. We had collected the remains of Japanese from all round the island and a total of 25,000 were cremated, their ashes being deposited on the top of Victory Hill, with a large concrete monument built over them. After the war the British government ordered the hill to be destroyed and today it is just a small mound. The monument was broken up and used as hard core for road building.

I revisited places where we had found groups of British and Aussie soldiers who had died during the defence of the island. It was as if it had never happened. The whole of Singapore appeared to be like the phoenix. After rising from the ashes however, it had chosen to draw a curtain over the events of the past.

All through our stay in Singapore I had a feeling that there was not the enthusiasm I had anticipated coming from the present administrators of what had been the garrison church. I attempted at one time to talk to the secretary, George Prior, a one time POW, friend and comrade. Unfortunately, although he was in residence, he preferred not to speak to me on the subject. Slightly disgruntled, I joined the rest of the party for our return to Thailand.

If I thought that we were being cold shouldered in Singapore, I was about to be completely frozen out in Thailand.

When we arrived in Bangkok, as per our previous agreement I called at the offices of the Thai Tourist Authority. My appointment with Mrs. Nakornthab had been arranged for two o'clock in the afternoon. In order to ensure that the meeting was to still go ahead I telephoned her office, only to be told that she was away on leave. I then tried to contact the British Embassy in Thailand to ask for their assistance. I was informed that all the five persons with whom I had been corresponding for the past nine months had left the Embassy and returned home. The feeling I had now was of being kicked in the stomach, first by the TAT and now the British Embassy.

For four days I telephoned for appointments at both places, until finally I was given an interview with one of the military attaches at the British Embassy. He was able to inform me that no-one ever got a satisfactory explanation or reply from TAT and that although the Embassy could not help us in any way, they could recommend a good transport company who would supply us with a mini bus and driver, cheap. My project was being shredded and the whole idea put into jeopardy by just one or two uncaring individuals. Eventually I decided that we would go ahead without the help of any of the so-called establishment or the Thailand Tourist Authority.

We had been given the use of a house by Mr. Chan Kaewkamsaen, a railway employee, and after leaving the heavy portion of our baggage at his house, he and his girl friend took us to Kanchanaburi where we established a base at the Bamboo Hotel.

The name might sound enchanting, but it was far from what it implied. We were given the use of two floating rafts, situated fifty yards from the original wooden bridge on the Kwai. The bridge which gave its name to the film has now been dismantled. Fifty yards further up river stands the original steel bridge which we erected from material brought from Java by the Japs in 1942. Today quite a lot of the steelwork has been replaced and on the Chungkai side of the bridge there are five completely new sections built of Japanese steel. Many of the original excavation holes still remain and, walking along the line, my memory went back to the time when as prisoners we toiled with a chunkel and pick, digging out the soil and carrying it on stretchers made from sacking to where the Japs indicated they wished it to be deposited. Each day as prisoners we had walked the two or three miles from the bridge to Chungkai. Today it seemed to me that the embankment had been lifted higher and, although new sleepers and lines had replaced the old ones, we would occasionally spot the crumbling remains of one of the original sleepers. Nearing the Chungkai cutting I remembered when I had witnessed the execution of the three men from the Northumberland Fusiliers and I retraced my footsteps to the point where they had been so callously murdered. The Thais have erected three spirit houses to replace the crosses they placed there immediately after the shooting. There are no names or anything to indicate where the men were executed. A few yards away is the Chungkai Muslim cemetery. The spirit houses are tended by one or two of the villagers who still remember. The hillside is now covered in creeper and any scars which might have been there have been obliterated by nature. I could not place a floral tribute because we had not intended to come this way. Turning toward what had at one time been the prisoner of war camp, I traced my way to the southern end of the cemetery where the four lads from the East Surreys had been publicly executed. Again there is nothing to indicate that anything out of the ordinary happened here, except the four spirit houses erected by the Thai people so many years ago. The original cemetery has been moved from its position beside the River Kwai to a spot where Chungkai village once stood. Of the camp itself there remains nothing, and with the nettles and brush clawing at my ankles I was I think able to retrace my steps to the point outside the hospital, where in 1943 a certain Japanese soldier was buried down the latrine. I couldn't pray for his soul, because in my mind he hadn't got one.

The Commonwealth War Graves Commission have done a great job in maintaining the cemeteries at both Chungkai and Kanchanaburi. Each day the markers are cleaned and the grass around them cropped. The only interruption comes at the weekend, from the rafts which float down the river with their disco music blaring out from multi loudspeakers. If one wished to visit the cemetery for a few moments of silence and solitude, you would be better picking any other day than Friday, Saturday or Sunday.

We had decided to complete the project no matter what the consequences and for this I must thank my two stalwart friends, Joe Metcalfe for whom we created the title transport director and Phil Cawley our photographer, with myself as trail finder. Without these two helpers I doubt that I would have carried on with the journey. With their support I felt there was no obstacle too big or too awkward that could stand in our way, even though the British Embassy had warned us that there was a possibility we could lose all our equipment, and even possibly land in either jail or be held as hostages. My companions just laughed it off and I thanked God that they had never been in the position when life was just the thickness of a cigarette paper from ending.

Our first two days were somewhat marred by the appearance of a group of ex prisoners of war, come to pay homage to their fallen comrades. We had paid for our tickets to travel on the train which transports tourists along the railway from Kanchanaburi to Nam Tok, a distance of about thirty miles. When the train arrived it was noticeable that the first two carriages were comparatively empty, while the rest of the train was completely full to capacity with many people risking life and limb sitting on the roof. After squeezing on board, Joe, whose curiosity knows no bounds, managed to force his way through the packed passengers to the carriages which were practically empty. As he tried to enter he was stopped by a man dressed in his Sunday best suit and told that these carriages were reserved for a prisoner of war group. After explaining that he was the brother of a POW who had died on this section of the railway, Joe was invited to sit down. All was going quite well until the leader of the party arrived and demanded that Joe leave the carriage at once. The spirit of comradeship which we once knew was coming to the fore once more. "I am telling you to get out of this coach" was the order and Joe was hustled outside into the crowd. (For the benefit of those tourists who paid many pounds for their seats, the price from Bangkok to Nam Tok is about 20 Baht roughly ten pence).

The following day, having heard that the ex POWs were holding a service, we decided to attend in order to swell the ranks. A service was conducted at each cemetery and a eulogy given by the leader of the party, in which he asked everyone to remember the words of the Far Eastern Prisoner Of War Association (FEPOW) "To keep alive the spirit which had kept us alive" and I wondered just how much this domineering little man had learned about comradeship during his incarceration. We quickly boarded our transport and put as much distance between this party and ourselves as possible. I could sense that had I not done so, Joe Metcalfe might well have told this little man exactly what he thought of him. We did not stop until we had reached Tarso to discover that the Thais were busy building a holiday camp on the spot where the POW camp once stood. Below the camp, where once the Japanese quarters had stood, there is now a large cafe disco where on display are photographs of the railway and casings of high explosive bombs which fell into the river below Wampo bridge. On the river there are several floating raft houses and at weekends the air is polluted with the blast of disco music, similar to that at Chungkai.

During our visit a Japanese film company were busy shooting a film, which gave the opportunity for our party to walk across the Wampo bridge. The cave, which I had watched Tanaka blow up with resting prisoners inside, is accentuated by the concrete which was poured to prevent the whole cliff face from collapsing. The second cave has been utilised by the Buddhist monks. What was once a bare cave now holds a statue of Buddha which is supposed to have been there for a hundred and fifty years.

We followed the line through to Hintock, a one time riverside POW camp, now a flourishing town used by drivers of the many heavy goods vehicles transporting sugar beet from the North to the refineries in Bangkok. The only reminder of its previous notoriety is the occasional initial scratched onto a piece of rock jutting from the ground close to where the railway once ran.

After spending a short while here, we elected to travel to Kinsyok which had at one time been one of the largest working camps along the line and which today is well known to the Thai people as a national park. Although we could not speak the Thai language or the Thais speak ours, we managed to deduct from sign language that we should stand at the side of the road and wave the next bus down. The instructions did not include a warning to stand clear once the appropriate signal had been given and it was only the instinct of self preservation which caused us to scramble back from the road as the bus came to a halt just a couple of inches from where our toes had been.

The cost of travel is so cheap that whenever we got on a bus, we paid to go to the end of the journey, allowing us to stop the bus wherever we wanted to. The distance from Hintock to Kinsyok is about twenty miles, which cost just ten pence on the bus, which in this instance took us to the centre of what had at one time been the POW camp.

It was some time before I could decide where we were now standing. This was the centre of a national park and I for one expected to see a hotel, cafe or similar facilities. But, apart from the odd tree trunk seat, there was nothing. As we approached what turned out to be the park offices, we saw a row of Chinese style eating houses. The owner of one directed us to the river side when we asked about sleeping accommodation, and following her directions went down the steep river bank to where there were several floating rafts, similar to the ones we had occupied at Kanchanaburi. The one outstanding difference being that these rafts had no electricity, washing facilities or toilets. It was a case of back to the jungle and back to nature with a vengeance.

After finding the only rafts which could accommodate the three of us, we returned to the eating houses where with more sign language we were able to order a meal. Anyone who visits Thailand, and who like ourselves cannot speak the language but wishes to eat, should ask for Cow Pat. This can be cow pat chicken, cow pat beef etc. and takes the form of fried rice and vegetables flavoured by whatever you have asked for, chicken, beef etc.

We had ordered the only meal we knew by heart, cow pat chicken, when, from the back of the cafe came a screeching noise and when Phil and I went to investigate we found a medium size monkey chained to the upper branches of a tree. The tree looked just as miserable as the monkey sounded. Every leaf and small branch had been snapped off. Seated on the ground close by was an old woman who I was informed was ninety two years of age. While trying to talk to her by sign language and the small smattering of Thai we had picked up, a young girl speaking quite reasonable English introduced the lady as her grandmother, who she told us had been employed by the Japanese as a cook when the railway was being constructed. The grandmother claimed to have helped prisoners of war by stealing tins of sardines and boiled eggs from the Japanese cookhouse which she gave to the prisoners. I suggested that she probably sold whatever she pinched from the Japanese and when my remarks were translated to her, she wanted to bring her hand across my face. In fun, I presume.

After our meal we decided to explore the area, which was now beginning to take shape in my mind. Where once the centre of the POW camps stood there is now a section of small buildings, housing the park wardens and information offices. From here we were able to obtain a small pamphlet explaining where certain places of interest could be found. The most prized exhibit was the remains of what had been the Japanese cookhouse with its eight fire grates. On seeing them my mind flashed back to the days when the Japs placed me in charge of a hundred cows and gave me the title "cowboy". The only other piece of history mentioned was the remains of one of the bridge supports close to the river bank. I walked to the Japanese bath house area, and found it still as it was left. Unfortunately no parks official seemed aware of its significance. Alongside the remains of the bridge support, which is solid concrete, there is also the base of the Japanese radio transmitter and receiver, plus twelve petrified bags of cement which I remember were to be used to make a base for the cookhouse. The railway was completed before the floor could be made. Close by the radio base a concrete bunker still holds what remains of the anti aircraft shells. The site is not all that obvious, but the ammunition dump still remains. Opposite the concrete base of the bridge the ground rises adjacent to the railway embankment. Beneath this mound lie the bodies of a number of prisoners of war and civilian workers who were killed during the air raid on 20th October 1944. There were other places we visited, including the caves, where both the Japanese soldiers and prisoners of war sought shelter during air raids. I sketched a small map showing these places and offered it to the warden in charge, but I had wasted my time, he showed no interest at all. After two days here we decided to move on, and at Philip Cawley's suggestion we decided to go through what remains of the jungle. Unfortunately Joe was only dressed in shorts and he paid the penalty. Every nettle and bamboo thorn tore into his legs, so that after travelling a mere fifty yards we had to stop in order to tend his cuts and bruises, after which he quickly changed into his long trousers. Similar bamboo thorns had been the cause of many men dying during our captivity. After struggling along for what seemed to be about an hour, we found ourselves completely lost. It was noon and the sun was directly overhead, and even though we were walking through the brush we could feel the heat. Finally, as we were about to retrace our footsteps, we saw a young boy who guided us to where the main road cuts through the jungle, and as we stepped out onto the road we were in time to stop a bus heading for Hell Fire Pass. Several helpful hands reached out to assist us with our baggage.

Once seated, we went through the same sign language banter in trying to describe where we wished to go. Within minutes one of the Thai passengers pointed out to us a train which was standing out in an open field. At first sight it appeared like a silhouette, then as we came closer we saw that the whole of the engine and waggons had been painted a rust colour. Nothing on the trains or waggons had been highlighted. There were no numbers or letters and on making enquiries later I was informed that the train and waggons had been placed at this particular point by the Australian Far East POW Association and that the reason for the absence of any highlights was to give the effect which we had seen. It was like a ghost of the past. Just a mile further along the road we got down from the bus and made our way to Hell Fire Pass. During my days as a POW we would only have been able to approach this pass by walking along the railway line or climbing up the rocks from the river below. The Aussie ex POWs, with the assistance of the Australian Embassy and staff, have returned to the pass and rebuilt one of the sections, including parts of the line. The pass cut through seven small mountains which were interconnected by rough intricate bridges, which from below would have resembled a builder's scaffolding. In those days they were known as the pack of cards and cost the lives of more than one thousand civilian and prisoner workers. Also among the rocks are many caves, where several prisoners and others went missing. At the time it was assumed that they had escaped, today we know different. Although the rebuilding of the pass is something to be applauded, I would not recommend a visit to anyone who suffers from heart or respiratory difficulties or who has trouble walking. The present day pass covers about two miles, mostly up or down hill. In the days of its construction, men had to cling to trees and branches for support. To the casual observer it now resembles a small amateurish railway, but it serves as a fitting monument to those who built it.

With a fiery hot sun overhead I was not surprised to hear that one of yesterday's visitors, (the relative of a POW) had died of a heart attack close to where her husband had worked. We resumed our journey as far as Tamaraon point, where the railway line resumes its journey through the jungle along a more permanent base. Here the line has been taken over by villagers as a footpath and boundary between rice paddy fields. The older people, when asked, could remember the trains going through. On arrival at Krai, we ordered our usual meal of cow pat chicken at the local Chinese roadside cafe and it was here I was able to confirm a story I had been told by one of the returning POWs.

Below Krai, and down as far as Brankassi, a massive reservoir has been built which covers the hills and valleys along which the railway ran. Above Brankassi there were a number of small hills, the highest probably about 1,000 feet. Most of these hills contained caves, which had been used by the local people to store rice and other commodities. During the occupation they were used to store various goods including ammunition, and the Japanese had built one or two branch lines leading to the caves to save manhandling. During the night of June 25th 1945, an air raid was in progress. A locomotive standing on the main line had been abandoned and the track had been blown to the South of it. The Japanese as usual had gone into the jungle to escape the bombs. Siamese freedom fighters, with the help of local people, diverted the line by removing parts of the track and relaying them to lead to one of the caves. With the assistance of all hands the engine was manoeuvred into the cave and the track replaced. When the raid was over, everyone went about his usual business. The Japanese must have assumed that the train had continued on its journey, because they never bothered to enquire.

During the building of the Khao Laem Dam in 1985/6, the Australian engineers found the hidden locomotive (number 107) where it had been placed forty years before. The train was removed from the cave and now stands outside a museum in Kanchanaburi. A point to note about it is that the remains of a tree which had grown through the front grill, and needed to be sawn through, have been left entwined through the metalwork.

We decided to return to base and have a rest and clean ourselves, our equipment and clothing. The following day we spent in and around the two cemeteries, where I interviewed some of the visitors. From our conversations I was able to establish that the majority of the tourists had no idea what to expect when they came to Kanchanaburi. Some had half expected to see parts of the camps. Others had no knowledge that the original cemeteries were several hundred yards away or that many of the remains had been brought down from the North.

I decided to visit the site where a local Thai was supposed to have had a dream, in which he was told where the bodies of many victims of the Japanese lay buried. When I called at the local tourist offices I was told that no skeletons had ever been found. Even though I argued with the top man, he was adamant that what I had heard was just a publicity stunt to encourage tourism. As I was leaving the office, a young man pulled me to one side and in perfect English advised me that the boss was lying. He then offered to take me to where the skeletons were being excavated. The place he took me to was the same place behind the jail, where in June 1945 during the big air assault by the Allies, I along with others had been compelled to throw the bodies of air raid victims into one or other of the craters created by the bombs. Among the dead were many British and Aussie prisoners. It was also the same spot where the Kempetai used to bury their torture victims. I was horrified to find evidence of recent excavations, and the remains of a large fire in whose ashes were scattered human remains. When we returned to base, after taking several photographs of the burnt remains of bones and other material, I tried to telephone the British Embassy without success. The man who had taken me to the burial spot came along the following day to advise me that some of the skeletons exhumed were currently resting in black bin bags in the store room of the local museum. On visiting the place the woman proprietor showed me one or two items which had apparently belonged to POWs: an Argyll cap badge and a silver belt buckle, a gold ring and a Swan pen, but she would not allow me to go into the store room to see the black bin bags. I tried once more to alert our Embassy without success, so I wrote a rough letter which I posted on to them. In the meantime I contacted Peter Woolrich, a freelance reporter based in Hong Kong and asked him to investigate. His story appeared in the *Mail on Sunday* on my return to England.

With the knowledge that some people were making money from the remains of POWs, I decided to go as far as possible toward Thanbazayat to where I knew there were more unmarked graves (after the war, I had notified the Commonwealth War Graves Commission where several mass graves were and assumed that they had collected and re-interred the remains).

The following day, leaving our heavy belongings at the raft house, we took the bus to Rin Tin. The old camp and track now forms a small village with much of the railway banking remaining, but no signs of the line itself. After a quick snack, we were able to obtain a lift in a local taxi to Takanoon and Brankasi. These were two of the Japanese storage depots during the war. Today nothing remains except the odd high level footpath which was once part of the railway track. Below Takanoon was Hindato camp site, known by some as Kwiema camp, and as we walked toward the waterfalls and the spring streams it was like walking into a dream, with the smell of the fresh water as it cascaded down from the high hills. Here and there lay rusted pieces of metal which had once supported the pipework carrying water to the camp below, several hundred yards from the hillside. The engineers and other craftsmen had designed and manufactured, from bamboo, a water system which supplied the kitchens, shower houses and the Japanese quarters, but this was the only luxury (if it could be referred to as a luxury) they had, different from the other camps along the line. During our time as prisoners, one or two of the fitter men were able to climb through the cascading water to the top of the hill. Both Phil the photographer and myself tried to reach this spot, for which effort I received a massive abrasion to my left leg and Phil lost his dignity. The intervening years had created a velvet-like moss carpet on the hillside and it was all one could do to remain upright. Down below, our driver was becoming impatient to be on the move. Our next stop was Hindato, but unfortunately all that remains is the name. The site of the camp which became a hell to all those prisoners unfortunate enough to be sent there is now under at least fifteen feet of water and the town of Hindato has been removed to the West side of the giant reservoir.

Our driver introduced us to a Mrs. Pimjai Jongsakul, a young mother of three children who owned several shops in the town plus a large holiday villa on the banks of the reservoir some ten miles up stream. Although she was a very busy person, she still found the time to transport our party up to the villa, where we were allocated a cabin for the sum total of two Baht, just less than one pound sterling. From our cabin we could look out over the vast lake, which now covers Takanoon, Brankasi, and Bangon camps and which gives a clear view of the mountain range which divides Burma and Thailand. Apart from the many Thai people who remember the railway being built, nothing at all remains in Takanoon.

The following day, rising early, Mrs. Jongsakul arrived to transport us to the bus stop in the flourishing new town of Hindato where the last lap of our journey to the Burmese border would start.On the way North we were able to look down from the rough hillside road to the locations of other lesser known camp sites. All that remains of Tamajao at kilo 237 is the built-up bank of the railway, which is now partly used as a jungle track. Tamaran Point 240 kilo, where the jungle and hillside was cut away to make way for the track, is just visible when the bus is taking one of the sharp corners. Looking down from about seven hundred feet it is possible to see the spot where Konquita camp once stood at the edge of the river. The narrow bridging, which at one time was to be the target for destruction by POWs, has been removed and nature has regained that which was formerly hers.

Krikunta and Niki camps have completely disappeared and at this point the river has changed its course so that where the camps originally stood is now the far bank, and inside Burma. Finally we arrived at Sankrai which is the last bus stop before the Burma border. It was just one o'clock and we needed to be ten miles away at Three Pagoda Pass. The site of the POW camp at Sankrai is still visible. The town has become larger, with many buildings housing craftsmen and tradesmen, but one particular area where the cemetery once stood has been left vacant. One of the villagers explained that this piece of land is haunted by the prisoners who were formerly buried there. I tried to explain that there were no spirits and that if there had been spirits of dead prisoners there would be no way that they would wish to harm the people of Sankrai.

The sky was a brilliant blue, without the sign of a cloud and the sweat from our bodies seemed to attract the dust which was being thrown about by a slight breeze. Joe managed to obtain a seat for us on the local bus-cum- taxi, a type of utility van which seated five people on each side and one lucky passenger up front.

We were not so lucky, no-one warned us what the journey would be like as we climbed on board. The distance to Three Pagoda Pass was about ten miles, yet the driver insisted that he could complete the journey in ten minutes. I must admit that he tried, but at what cost. As soon as we left the town he swung off the main highway onto a road which was under construction. Everything was covered with a fine red dust and as the van swept along at speeds of up to forty miles per hour the dust was sucked into the back. No matter what type of protection we tried it was in no way possible to stop it from finding its way into our eyes and nostrils, down the neck and into the scalp. (It took three days to completely remove from our scalps later).

Our arrival at Three Pagoda Pass was greeted with the usual looks of incredulity, more so because we looked and felt so unreal. Our bodies had been covered in this fine red dust, our eyes, nose and ears were full of the stuff and as we began to perspire, the rivulets of sweat created pink lines down our faces. I could not see or even imagine what I looked like to the others, but if I looked anything like them then I must have presented a horrible sight. Joe jumped down from the back of the truck, still clinging to his video camera. He had wrapped a towel round his face as soon as the dust started to pour into the vehicle, but this had not been of any use at all, the stuff found its way into every crevice and I mean every crevice. Phil Cawley busy ensuring that the cameras were in clean and usable condition, had taken no precautions and his hair which had been blowing in the wind looked like the died red hair we see today on certain young people. The vehicle driver directed us to a small general store, where he said we could obtain a drink and something to eat and at the same time wash some of the dust from our faces. But try as we would, the stuff just would not move and after satisfying our thirst and obtaining a plate of the usual cow pat chicken we decided to investigate the area. On asking the driver what time we would need to leave in order to catch a bus back to Kanchanaburi, he grimly shook his head from side to side. ''All bus go till morrow'' was all he would say. It was mid-day and there would be no buses back to Kanchanaburi until the following day. When we asked what time he would be leaving, he looked at his watch and exclaimed two, at the same time shoving two fingers into the air, a gesture which would under normal circumstances have been repeated close to his face. Today however we were once more guests of an Asian nation.

The British Embassy had suggested that we might not get anywhere near to Three Pagoda Pass, and that even if we were so lucky we might easily lose all our equipment and probably our valuables. The reception we received however removed all our fears of anything like muggings or robbery. The younger boys and girls, like most Western youths were too busy trying to impress each other with their motor scooters and small motor cars. The elders were only too keen to walk over and talk to us. One or two I spoke to could remember the Japanese and the building of the railway and pointed to where the line still runs through the pass and on through the border into Burma. As we walked along its bank towards the border we were invited into a small wooden hut which was just inside Burma. This was the military checkpoint, manned by one or two uniformed soldiers and three civilian officials who introduced themselves as the chief customs officer, the immigration officer and the local police chief. The two uniformed men were, I was informed, a colonel and a sergeant of the Burma military forces. Their uniforms might have been handed down by their Japanese associates. Although they were all exceedingly friendly toward us, it was obvious that they were not going to assist us in getting to Thanbazayat. When I tried to involve them in talking about the building of the railway they did not seem at all anxious to discuss it. One of the men, whose father was a Karen who served with the British army in Burma, spoke a little English. It was apparent that his father had lost all faith in the British. He seemed to be saying that the British had made a vow to assist the Karens when the war was over but had not done so. He shrugged his shoulders, "today is same yesterday" he said.

One thing I noted in particular was that several times the men in civilian clothes said the word "two", at the same time putting up two fingers and repeating themselves. Occasionally they said "tomorrow tomorrow two". They were insistent that something was going to happen in "two" … but two what?

It was while we were discussing our prospects that the senior of the uniformed men explained to me that, although I could consider him my friend, he would have no hesitation in shooting me should I try to go past the border and into Burma proper. We had travelled over 300 miles from Bangkok, and Thanbazayat was just sixty yards further along the track, but our chances of getting there were now exceedingly slim.

While Joe continued to talk with them and Phil was managing to take a few photographs, I walked over to talk to one of the locals in order to find if it was at all possible to obtain a guide to take me through to Thanbazayat. The man was quite open in offering me any quantity of Papever (Poppy/Opium), but he suddenly lost his knowledge of English whenever I mentioned "Thanbaya". The locals started to show an interest in us at this point, so we decided to move back into the Pagoda area. For some reason or other, someone has placed two of the metal rail lines in front of the three pagodas, which are about two hundred yards from the actual railway. The point where the railway runs through from Thailand into Burma is well advertised, it is as if they anticipate an influx of tourists. The Burmese signs are in white lettering on a bright blue background, the Thais' are black lettering on a white background.

Standing with our backs to the Pagodas and looking East, we could see military activity taking place on the Dawna Mountain range, which, during our railway building period had been our hope of freedom, always expecting the Allies to come swooping down to release us. The cemetery at Three Pagoda, like others in the North of Thailand has been left undeveloped.

Just when we were about to leave, one of the locals who appeared to have Japanese in his ancestry kept saying Itai, Shikai and pointing toward the mountains.

At the same time he had hold of my arm lightly as if wanting me to go with him, but when we were in sight of our driver it was apparent that he was in a hurry to get away and he released my arm. It was not until we had returned to Kanchanaburi, when I was talking to one of the Thai tourist people, that I learned that the words which the native had used meant "abandoned bodies". I think he was saying that there was a cemetery somewhere toward the mountains, and not being familiar with the language I had missed the chance of probably locating another previously undiscovered burial ground.

Our journey from Three Pagoda back to Sankrai was completed with our heads tightly wrapped in towels to protect us from the dust, so we saw nothing of the countryside at all.

Sankrai can best be described as a left-handed village. A square divided into four equal parts. The dwelling houses and shops, with small businesses are grouped together toward the river side in what I can only describe as the bottom left corner. Above it a further area is taken by the bus company and taxis. A further quarter is cultivated and the fourth area is abandoned land where the prisoner of war camp and the cemetery once stood. A few remaining rail lines can be seen scattered around and at the furthermost end the remains of the Japanese concrete artillery bunkers with odd pieces of junk piled on top. The only bank in town was still open, but when Phil went to cash a travellers cheque he was refused. Phil offered a personal cheque and his Access card, but they were of no use whatsoever. The only currency usable in this area is hard Thai cash. Nothing else is acceptable. So here we were more than three hundred miles away from where we wanted to be and just two hundred Bhat between us. To wait for the bus meant sleeping rough in the fields or jungle, because there were no hotels or rafts in this area and from what we could see there were just one or two small eating houses. Across from the bus station there was a building with the sign 'Transport Office'. I wandered over and went inside in the hope that someone could speak English and be able to help us. My luck was well and truly in. A young Thai girl behind the counter spoke very good English indeed and after telling her my troubles she pointed outside and said "Find the monk, he will help you" At first I thought she was having a joke at my expense, because everyone in the place started to laugh. Once outside however I quickly spotted a Saffron-robed monk to whom I introduced myself before starting to explain my problem. In even better English, he raised his arm and told me to slow down, "My English is good, but not so fast". The monk was Father P.S.Setapan, a superior of the temple at Kanchanaburi, Wat Phrathaendongrang. After telling him of our problem he suggested that we take a seat in the eating house and enjoy a cold drink, while he went and made some arrangements for us.

After gathering our equipment together we sat waiting in anticipation. Within thirty minutes the good father was back to tell us that for three hundred Bhat, one of the local men would drive us to Kanchanaburi. When we explained that we only had two hundred. He said not to worry, he would find someone to make up the difference. It was very shortly after that he came to direct us to a Toyota utility van, the type with a canvas covering the rear section. Usually the rear area would seat five people comfortably, but when we arrived there were already five young Thais in it, so it was necessary to drop the tail board, which would allow Phil and myself to balance on the back few inches, while Joe being the gentleman that he always is, climbed over the Thais and squeezed himself between them and the back of the driver's cab. In the front with the driver was Setapan and one of the novices. As soon as we were all aboard, the driver took us round to the local temple, where Setapan and his novice went inside to eat a meal. The monks must not eat after sundown or before noon, so we had to wait while they ate, said their prayers and completed their ablutions. All the time the sun was belting down and our party of travellers were beginning to sweat profusely. One would have imagined that being on the tail board I would be cooler, but with the sun shining directly down the only consolation was that the sweat dried on my face before it could travel down my neck.

Once the monk and his novice had joined us, the driver lost no time in pushing the vehicle from twenty miles per hour up to sixty and seventy. Sankrai is over two thousand five hundred feet above sea level, Takanoon and Hindato are about five hundred feet, so that as well as speeding along the mainly empty roads at well over the normal speed, we were dropping hundreds of feet as we turned every corner. With one hand clinging to the roof and one foot behind the chain which held the tail gate, Phil and I held on like grim death. As a young man, I might have appreciated the journey and the hairpin bends, but at seventy one years of age the muscles and bones do not bend so readily to the needs, and when we finally took a break after three hours it was all that I could do to straighten the leg which I had placed behind the chain. Phil was many years younger and his limbs more pliable, while Joe was situated in the best position of all. We took five minutes to answer the call of nature and then with the sun dipping behind the hills we recommenced our nightmare journey. The Thais who were travelling with us were a group of singers, and like pop groups everywhere they assumed that the world owed them a living. They began to push themselves into a sleeping position, one with his foot practically under my chin and it was all that I could do to use my loose hand and arm to pry his foot away. Fortunately one of the females in the group seemed a little more humane and she belted the sleeping man with her slipper. Although it caused the youth to wake, his reaction was to kick out and he very nearly kicked me out of the waggon. It took just six hours from Sankrai to Kanchanaburi, a total of three hundred odd kilometres, about one hundred and ninety miles. Once we were back in Kanchanaburi, we felt easier and much safer.

The following day was declared a rest day, so that we could apply soap and water to our clothing and ourselves. Unfortunately the level of the river had dropped during the night. This is a common occurrence and is created by the water supply being cut off by the dam operators to the North.

Having some time to spare, it was decided that we would look further into the matter of a certain merchant employing labourers to dig up the skeletons of those who had either died during the air raids on the 24th June 1945 or who had died a miserable death at the hands of the Japanese police. The area we visited is just to the rear and to the right of the present day Kanchanaburi prison. This was the spot where in June 1945, while crossing over Kanchanaburi en route to Uttaradit, the party I was with were caught up in the biggest air raid we had seen so far. When it was all over, pushed kicked and cajoled by our Japanese guards, we were made to collect the victims of the air raid. These included POWs and civilians, also one or two Japanese. The Japanese were not interested in race creed or religion. If the body was not walking about it had to be thrown into the holes created by the bombs. At the time I was informed we buried over 1,200 in this manner. Today very little can be found and we are continually being told officially that there were only Asians in the graves. When one considers that at this time the population of Kanchanaburi was just 1,300 people and the POWs numbered about 10,000 in camps nearby, I wonder how the skeletons recovered can possibly be all Asians.

After being assured by the local Thais that the skeletons which had been removed included those of British and Allied prisoners, we made our way to confront the merchant who was about to use the remains in his macabre exhibition. At first his wife freely conceded that the skeletons were indeed those of Allied prisoners of war, but when we were joined by news reporters she changed her story, saying that they were all Asian soldiers or Chinese coolies. Today the ground remains as it was left by the grave robbers, including partly dug holes. In the centre, a pile of black and grey ash, the remains of over 700 skeletons which were incinerated so that they could not be identified. Skeletons which the Allied governments had suggested should receive a decent burial had been handed over to a religious group, who, although with some reverence, decided that the simplest and quickest way would be to incinerate the lot. In this way any argument as to whose remains they had been would die in the dust which remained.

Our visit to this place had put a damper on our spirits, but it did not deter us from visiting individual camp sites along the line each day. The camps below Kanchanaburi have long since become absorbed into a vast metropolitan state. Above Kanchanaburi there are still some signs of our previous occupancy as far as Nam Tok, but from there very little remains except in several areas where the railway bankings and cuttings have found a better use. There are still many places boasting pieces of the metal lines and broken down carriages or waggons, and some where the pieces of land which once held the murdered bodies of British and Allied service men still remain untouched, mainly through fear of seeing ghosts. I like to think that it is the Thai way of showing a form of respect.

Looking back before leaving Kanchanaburi it was hard to imagine that along the track we had travelled more than 150,000 human lives had been sacrificed. Yet the Japanese government had the audacity to erect a memorial to the engineer who was responsible for its construction.

Burma/Siam Railway Criminals

The following is a selection of some of the more widely known Japanese war criminals who were tried by the War Crimes Tribunal Committee. Almost all those who worked on the construction of the Burma/Siam railway would be familiar with the names of these characters and their sadistic tendencies. Many more were tried and subsequently sentenced, while many others were set free by the committee.

There is insufficient space to list all the criminals, so if the names of the ones who helped to make your life Hell do not appear, don't be disappointed. They probably swung in the breeze just as easily as the others.

	Nickname	Unit/Prison Camp	Sentence
Capt. Daimon.	Jack Diamond	Kanu, Wampo, Tarso, Niki.	10 Yrs Imp.
Col. Ishii.		All Railways.	Death by Hanging.
Col. Nakanura.		All Railways.	Death by Hanging.
Korean Fumimoto.		Krai Krai, San Krai.	Death by Hanging.
Korean Iwaya.	The Mad Mongrel	All POW Camps in Thailand.	Death by Hanging.
Korean Kumdioji.	The Bombay Duck	All POW Camps in Thailand.	15 Yrs Imp.
Korean Matoyama.	The Black Prince	All POW Camps in Thailand.	Death by Hanging.
Korean Matsumoto.	The Silver Bullet	All POW Camps in Thailand.	Life Imp.
Korean Minaka.	The Singing Master	All POW Camps in Thailand.	Life Imp.
Korean Morimoto.	The Mad Bugler	All POW Camps in Thailand.	Life Imp.
Korean Takavama.		Most Northern Camps.	Death by Hanging.
Korean Takemino.	Efficiency	Non Pladuk, Bangkok, Uban.	9 Yrs Imp.
Korean Takemoto.		Chungkai.	2 Yrs Imp.
Korean Tokuama.	Donald Duck	All POW Camps in Thailand.	Death by Hanging.
Korean Tomotama.		All POW Camps in Thailand.	10 Yrs Imp.
Lt. Col. Yanagita.		All Railways.	20 Yrs Imp.
Lt. Isuki.	The Kanu Kid	All POW Camps in Thailand.	Death by Hanging.
Lt. Kokuba.		211, Konquita, Sankri.	Death by Hanging.
Lt. Nobusawa.	The Horse Doctor	Chungkai, Niki, 211.	Death by Hanging.
Maj. Chida.		All Railways.	10 Yrs Imp.
Maj. Gen. Isheda.		All Railways.	10 Yrs Imp.
S/Maj. Eda.		Northern Camps.	Death by Hanging.
S/Maj. Hiramatsu.	The Tiger	All POW Camps in Thailand.	Death by Hanging.
Sgt. Norro.	Baldy	Kanu, Wampo, Tarso, Niki.	15 Yrs Imp.
Sgt. Okada.	Doctor Death	Kanu, Hintock, Kinsyok.	10 Yrs Imp.
Sgt. Shimdjo.		Kanburi Comm Officers Camp.	4 Yrs Imp
Sgt. Terrakoshi.		Most Northern Camps.	Death by Hanging.
Lt. Takasakai.	The Frog	Tamakan, Kanchanaburi.	Death by Hanging.
Korean Kanoshiro.	The Undertaker	Nakon Nyok, Non Pladuk.	Death by Hanging.
Maj. Mizutani.		Cdr of No. 5 POW Group.	Death by Hanging.
Maj. Noguchi.		No. 2 I/C No. 5 POW Group.	Death by Hanging.
Capt. Torumoto.		No. 3 I/C No. 5 POW Group.	Life Imp.
Lt. Osato.		Chungkai.	3 Yrs Imp.
Korean Ozawa.		Chungkai, Tamakan.	4 Yrs Imp.
Korean Hatayashi.		131 Kilo Songkrai.	Death by Hanging.

Korean Hosumi.		131 Kilo, Songkrai.	Death by Hanging.
Korean Akawa.		131 Kilo, Songkrai.	Death by Hanging.
Korean Otsuki.		131 Kilo, Songkrai.	18 Yrs Imp.
Capt. Suzuki.	The Godfather	Tonchan.	Death by Hanging.
Sgt. Yamamoto.		Tanchan and Southern Camps.	Death by Hanging.
Korean Chiba.		Tanchan, Tamakan.	Death by Hanging.
Col. Sugasawa.	The Admiral	All POW Camps.	12 Yrs Imp.
Korean Takemoto.	The White Slug	Chungkai.	2 Yrs Imp.
Sgt. Sukano.		Chungkai.	5 Yrs Imp.

The following were implicated in the torture and murder of British POWs at Kanburi/Chungkai:

Maj. Ohida.	Kempetai.	9 Yrs Imp.
Capt. Kamai.	Kempetai.	Death by Hanging.
S/M. Iijima.	Kempetai.	Death by Hanging.
S/M. Urikawa.	Kempetai.	Life Imp.
Sgt. Watanaba.	Kempetai.	Life Imp.

Lt General Fukuei, the military governor of Singapore was taken onto the beach at Changi and executed by Australian troops on the 16th August 1945, without trial, for his part in the execution of Allied prisoners of war and thousands of Chinese civilians between February 15th 1942 and July 25th 1945.

Sgt Okayama, one of the Changi prison officers who turned a blind eye, got 7 Yrs Imp.

S/M Toyod, one of the prison officers who assisted in executions, was hanged.

Sgt Kawamoto was hanged for crimes commited in Hong Kong and Singapore.

As was Lt Ina Uyi.

The foregoing are just a few of the Japanese war criminals who were captured and made to pay the penalty. A further 1,760 known criminals were released on the orders of General MacArthur with the excuse that to provide witnesses at their trails would prove too costly. All Allied justice departments were advised to do likewise.

(*Author's note*: Most prisoners of war camp guards were of Korean origin, their officers and NCOs being Japanese. Korea had been annexed by Japan in 1910 and was a part of the Japanese Empire until the end of World War Two. Hence its male citizens were conscripted into the Imperial Japanese Army.)

St. George's Church, originally built as the garrison church at Tanglin.

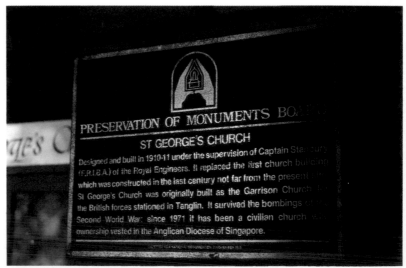

Stained glass window which replaced those buried in Feb. 1942.

In search of the lost stained glass windows, Jan. 1992

Mr. Chan Kaewkamsaen our Thai provider who gave our party food, accomodation, transport and every good wish possible.

Setapan, The Karen monk who came to our assistance when we were in need.

The Gheko. A true native of Thailand. Many POWs will remeber his rude calls in the late evening.
TUT YU! TUT YU!

The site of the original Kwai Bridge seen from Kanchanaburi

An original locomotive used by the Japanese.

The remains of the sidings at Kanchanaburi

The banks of the River Kwai at the site of the orig

...den bridge destroyed by Allied bombers June 24th 1945.

Original cattle waggons used for transporting prisoners of war.

The ghostly appearance of a train which was deposited in a field several hundred yards from the Death Railway.

Children of Thailand today ...

... in the land of smiles!

The cutting at Chungkai. This took eight weeks to complete and cost in excess of 100 lives, most of them murdered by the Korean guards.

Nakompaton.

The common hibiscus of Thailand

Opposite: *Sunset over the lake which now covers Brankasi, Hindato and Takanoon.*

The waterfalls at Kinsyok used by the Japanese as a bathing area. The British POW camps were situated lower down the stream.

JAPANESE TROOP STOVE IN WORLD WAR II
DURING WORLD WAR II JAPAN MOVED ITS ARMED
FORCES IN TO THAILAND IN THE YEAR 1941 THE
JAPANESE'S ULTIMATE GOAL WAS TO MOVE
THEIR TROOPS IN TO BURMA THEREFORE THEY
CONSTRUCTED INFAMOUS DEATH RAILWAY
TO TRANSPORT MASSIVE AMOUNTS OF
TROOPS AND AMMUNITIONS THROUGH THAILAND
IN TO BURMA SECURING THE SAI YOK DISTRICT
WAS IMPERATIVE TO THE JAPANESE'S OVERALL
STRATEGY SAI YOK DISTRICT WAS ALSO SUITABLE
FOR RESOURCE EXPLOITION; FOOD THE DENSE
FOREST COVER PROVIDED EXCELLENT COVER
FROM ENEMY ATTACKS, AND TODAY ONE
CAN STILL SEE IN THE EARTH THE REMNANTS
OF THE STOVES THE ARMY BUILT TO FEED
THEIR TROOPS.

A misleading sign! This was actually for the POWs not the Japanese army.

The Japanese cookhouse which was situated astride the freshwater stream at Kinsyok.

The original prison camp area at Kinsyok.

More tourist exhibits. Such museums are now a flourishing tourist attraction in the Kanchanaburi area.

The cuttings at Chungkai. The first was completed in March 1943.

These roads, once jungle paths, along which the prisoners of F&H Force were force marched through Thailand to Burma in 1943, have been opened up to reveal the wonderful scenery which had been obscured at the of time the POWs' predicament.

Two of the stations still in operation along the railway were once POW camps above Takarin camp.

Wampo South Camp.

The grave robbers' site at Kanchanaburi.

Opposite page: *One of the original trains which the Japanese imported from the Dutch East Indies.*

The scaffolding beneath Wampo. Renewed beams but the same structure.

The bridges at Wampo, today a tourist attraction and often used by Japanesefilmcompanies.Their history books do not record any of this...

... but they still glorify it in their films!

Looking down from the Kwai Bridge.

Opposite: *The view of the bridge from the train.*

The author crossing the Kwai Bridge on foot.

More of Hell Fire Pass, in which the Australian POWs have now placed a memorial, and ..

.. the infamous drillholes in the rock face!

The lines lead to nowhere at the Pack Of Cards bridge in Hell Fire Pass.

The Kwai at Kinsyok. This scene is as it was in 1943. A place where any prisoner fortunate enough to be able to sit and rest was able to admire the beauty of Thailand.

The pathway leading to the bridge at Kinsyok, again nothing has changed in 50 years.

A young girl waits for the school bus, Kinsyok National Park.

Japanese bath houses, like this one, were built across streams.

Inside our floating raft house.

Trains and waggons. A tourist exhibition at Kanchanaburi with rolling stock from manufacturers as far apart as Glasgow and Java.

Spring floods on the Kwai controlled by the dams and reservoirs at Brankasi.

On top of the railway banking at Kuishi. The trees have now grown through where trains once passed by.

The remains of a bridge above Kinsyok, close by and still intact are the remnants of a Japanese ammunition dump.

End of the line at Matona. All that remains of an era.

Number Two cutting at Chungkai. It was from the top of these rocks that Kiyioki Tanaka blew away Gnr. Lloyd Bull of 125 Anti Tank Regiment on the morning of 13th Jan. 1943.

In the early hours of March 7th 1943 four men decided to escape from the Japanese. Sgt. Edward Reay, Fusilier Timothy Kenneally, Sgt. Francis Kelly and Pte. Patrick Fitzgerald. The next evening the group were spotted by the Thai Police and Pte. Fitzgerald shot dead in the back whilst running for cover. The remaining three remained at large until, thirsty and hungry, they surrendered on March 19th. After a hasty trial they were sentenced to death by firing squad. On March 23rd they were executed here, today marked by a spirit house erected by the local people.

The riverside at Matona, where, whenever the Japs would allow it, prisoners could relax and bathe.

A train passes precariously round the bend at Wampo Scaffold.

The Kwai Bridge at night. At weekends during the tourist season a firework display with sound effects takes place here.

Opposite page: *Dawn on the Kwai.*

A train, being filmed by a Japanese crew, passes across Wampo.

One of the approaches to Hell Fire Pass recreated by the Australian POWs Association between 1990 and 1992.

We discover more rolling stock remains!

The woods at Kinsyok, now stripped of all bamboo and open to the public for recreation.

Scenes at Hell Fire Pass: The railway passes through this junction which is several hundred feet above the river and cost in excess of 500 Allied POWs and civilian forced labour lives.

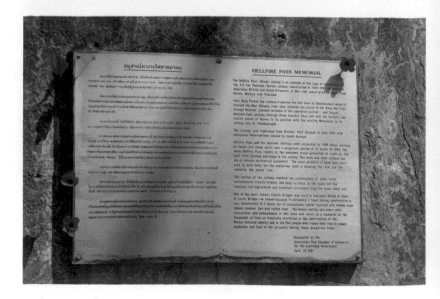

Early morning at Hell Fire Pass.

From Here To Eternity!

The Waterfalls at Hindato. The only change is the disappearance of all the tunnels, drains and piping manufactured by the POWs for their captors' use.

The caves at Matona. The only change is the wear and tear caused by visiting tourists.

Top Left:*The Thai notice above states that the Wampo Bridge was completed in 17 days. Actually it took four months, after which it was knocked out several times by Allied bombers.*

Above: *The concrete shores up the cave which was blown up by Kiyioki Tanaka killing at least two prisoners trapped inside.*

Right: *Our hostess at Takanoon, Mrs. Pimjai Jongsakul.*

Opposite: *Dawn on the Khao Laem Reservoir which now covers Hindato, Brunkasi and Konquita.*

The site of the original cemetery at Sankrai remains deserted. The locals claim that they sometimes hear the voices of the men who are buried there.

Previous pages: *Floating homes on Khao Laem Reservoir.*

A view of the Dawna Hills above San Krai.

The main road, once a jungle track which the weary prisoners took through Three Pagoda Pass into Burma.

The red dust roads leading from Krai to the Burma border.

Previous pages:*The Three Pagodas which straddle the road leading to Burma, once a welcome sight to those POWs struggling the last few miles through the now diminished jungle of North Thailand. Today, as well as serving religious functions they are a meeting place for young people of the village.*

Joe and I pose for a photograph on the main highway leading from Three Pagoda Pass via the Dawna Hills.

Notice for the tourists to observe when entering Burma legally.

The remains of the railway at the Burma border. The line at this point has been converted into a footpath as far as Chingara and Pakatonsu.

Looking back toward Krai, the jungle and undergrowth now cleared.

Looking into Burma from the Three Pagoda site. Rails and rolling stock still remain where left when the Japanese were defeated.

The border checkpoint at Chingara. The old railway banking is now the main highway into Burma.

One of the cuttings at Nikiniki

A further shot of the Pagodas

The River Kwai at Takarin.

A modern train approaches the Chung Kai cutting.

The modern Burmese equivalent of the Three Pagodas.

A train cautiously travels along the Wampo Stretch.

Examining the high explosive casings used in the bombing of bridges and recently recovered from the River Kwai.

The camps at Arhill and Wampo are being converted into accomodation for tourists. The local businessmen and Japanese intend to illuminate the bridge and provide firework displays imitating the bombing raids over the Wampo.

Roll Of Honour

Royal Navy

GENERAL
ADKINS, Wrtr, Francis J, D/MX67643
AHERN, Stkr, Patrick, D/KX96816
ANDREWES, Ord Smn, Dennis E, D/JX166573
ANGUS, Stkr, William C, D/KX130605
ANKERS, Stkr, Vincent C, D/KX99202
ANNIS, Stkr Po, Thomas, D/K64304
ANSTEY, Boy, Peter R, D/JX164040
ANTON, Ab, Sydney, D/JX194995
ASHTON, Ab, John J, D/J39383
ASHWORTH, Smn, Jack, D/SSX29264
ASHWORTH, Sk Brth, Eric R, D/X7799
ATKEY, Mr Com Sup Off, J W H
AYRES, Stkr, Charles, D/KX94696
BACK, Stkr Po, Cecil R, D/K62597
BAILEY, Stkr Po, Walter G, D/KX83587
BAIN, Stkr Po, Donald, D/KX81941
BARLOW, Stkr, Ernest, D/KX128068
BARNES, Stkr, Norman, D/KX114886
BARNETT, Stkr, Charles A, D/KX96149
BARRON, Po Cook, William, D/MX48074
BARWIS, Chf Po, Harry L, D/M26640
BAXTER, Ab, Cyril, D/SSX29265
BENNETT, Eng Art, Arthur C, D/MX53080
BENNETT, Sub Lt, P L
BENNETTS, Plmbr, Leslie A, D/MX74276
BENSON, Ab, Clifford, D/SSX28212
BERRY, Stkr, Kenneth P, D/JX157619
BICK, Ab, Herbert G, D/JX195026
BILLINGS, Dvr, Ernest Albert, T/233016
BLAIR, Lt, C T
BOLTON, Stkr Po, William T, D/KX80192
BOND, Boy, Thomas, D/JX175859
BORD, Po, Frederick V, D/JX139648
BOWDEN, Mrn, Eric S J, PLY/X100188
BOWER, Stkr, Frank, D/JX219984
BOYD, Ord Smn, John M, D/JX159301
BOYDE, Eng Art, John, D/MX60265
BOYNE, Ord Art, Peter, D/MX72686
BRABANT, Stkr, John H, D/KX96139
BRACKEN, Eng Art, Richard, D/MX74089
BREWER, Mtr W Mech, A J
BRITTAIN, Eng Art, Frederick J, D/MX55505
BROMHAM, Po Cook, Cecil R, D/MX50788
BROOKS, Marine, Frederick, PLY/X100125
BROS, Midi, A C R
BROWN, Stkr, Vivian T, D/KX129407
BROWN, Ab, Robert, D/JX154199
BROWN, Eng Art, Percy, D/236
BROWN, Chf Eng Art, Herbert W, D/MX37214
BURROWS, Stkr, Arthur J, D/KX82672
BUSH, Mrn, Robert A, PLY/X5811
BUTLER, Stkr, John, P/KX109256
CADMAN, Stkr, William L, D/KX81249

CAIRNS, Stkr, Cyril, D/KX115277
CAMERON, Chf Stkr, Hugh, D/K60485
CAMPBELL, Mstr, H J E,
CANTY, Stkr, John D, D/KX114776
CAPPER, Stkr, Cyril, D/KX102769
CARRATT, Stkr, Kenneth C, D/KX102943
CAVANAGH, Surg Lt, W.G,
CAVELL, Mr Com Elec, A F,
CAWDREY, Stkr, Ronald, D/KX121021
CAWTE, Po, Harry W, D/M40132
CHAFER, Teleg, Ronald S, D/JX169763
CHAMBERS, Cpl, William R, PLY/X2212
CHAPMAN, Air Mech, Charles E, FAA/FX77082
CHARD, Stkr, Alcwyn M, D/KX115032
CHESTER, Teleg, Leonard, D/JX169768
CHINN, Stkr, Charles L, D/KX121003
CHRISTMAS, Ord Smn, Raymond W, D/JX1633202
CLEAVES, Ab, Thomas H, D/JX172552
CLEMENTS, Gnr, John Graham, 1438759
CLOUGH, Ordnce Art, Leonard, D/MX73057
COBBE, Lt Com, C H,
COE, Ord Smn, Herbert W, P/JX274261
COLLINS, Sub Cmdr, Walter,
CONLAN, Teleg, Charles E, D/JX169681
COOKSON, Ab, Richard, D/JX153141
COOPER, Ab, James V, D/JX137318
COTTLE, Cook, Cecil R F, D/MX73748
COUGHLAN, Stkr Po, Jeremiah, D/K66230
COWAN, Ord Smn, David, P/UD/X1415
COWAN, Stkr, Charles, D/KX85825
CRADDOCK, Stkr, William, D/KX105372
CRAFT, Stkr, John W, D/KX102859
CROSS, Marine, Walter S, PLY/X100425
CROWSON, Mech, Harry, D/KX80066
CUMMINS, Mstr Arms, Charles H, D/M39786
DALPUGET, Ord Smn, Jack P, D/JX238482
DALY, Stkr Po, Dennis, D/KX81411
DALY, Po, Arthur W, D/JX134224
DANIELS, Shpwrgt, Walter F, D/MX50044
DAVIES, Ab, Robert, D/JX188785
DAVIES, Midi, R I,
DAY, Mr W Mech, T W,
DEACON, Ord Smn, William T, D/JX227709
DEACON, Stkr Po, Herbert K, D/K62473
DEEMER, Ab, Harold A J, C/SSX29173
DENNEHY, Stkr, Thomas, D/KX96141
DEWHIRST, Ab, Henry, D/SSX29449
DIXON, Stkr, Bruce E, D/KX115202
DOBSON, Ord Smn, Reginald, D/JX238575
DONNITHORNE, Stkr, Francis, D/KX96136
DONOVAN, Ab, Timothy F, D/JX153610
DOOLAN, Ab, Andrew, D/SSX32880
DOUGLAS, Cook, Wilfred, D/MX63150
DOWNIE, Boy, Daniel D, D/JX184609
DOWRICK, Boy, Frederick E, D/JX77226
DUFFIN, Stkr Po, Patrick, D/KX77364
DUFFY, Stkr, Patrick J, D/KX120357

DUNN, Stkr, William A, D/KX115201
DUNNE, Stkr, William J, D/KX91821
DURNELL, Ab, Norman F, D/JX154235
EASTERBROOK, Stkr Po, Randolph W, D/K63104
EDWARDS, Ord Smn, Walter W, P/JX257635
EDWARDS, Ord Smn, John G R, P/JX274428
EGGLESTON, Ord Smn, Douglas, D/JX166602
EKE, Cook, James R, D/MX72721
EVANS, Ord Smn, Reginald W, D/JX166583
EVANS, Stkr, Francis, D/KX102760
EVANS, Stkr, Frederick, D/KX81735
EVENS, Stkr, Francis W, D/KX93429
EWEN, Ab, William, D/SSX29434
EXETER, Stkr, Douglas L, D/KX99227
FAIRCHILD, Cook, Rowland, D/MX53413
FAIRFOUL, Ab, Sidney, D/SSX24333
FAIRHURST, Smn, Stanley, D/JX269371
FARLEY, Stkr Po, Thomas, D/KX83419
FARLEY, Stkr Po, William G, D/K65731
FENTON, Po, Elba, D/J99965
FEWINGS, Chf Elec Art, Reginald A, D/M38500
FISH, Stkr, Wilfred, D/KX120504
FLETCHER, Smn, Neville, D/JX272231
FLINT, Smn, Eric M, D/JX199935
FOSTER, Plmbr, Henry C A, D/MX54943
FOSTER, Ab, Leonard N, D/JX213499
FOX, Mrn, Jack, PLY/X100128
FOY, Ord Smn, Charles J, C/JX238138
FRANCIS, Ab, Leighton R, D/SSX21548
FRANKLIN, Stkr, Henry S, D/KX115283
FROMENT, Stkr, Lewis G S, D/KX97948
FROST, Pntr, Charles, D/MX45136
FUDGE, Cook, William F K, D/MX64898
FULTON, Ab, Leslie J, D/JX143972
FURNESS, Stkr, Edward, D/KX105995
GALBRAITH,Ord Smn, Roy W T, D/JX272255
GALVIN, Stkr, Wilfred S, D/KX120511
GARDNER, Ord Smn, Leonard, P/JX272521
GARDNER, Po, George R, D/JX136303
GARNER, Stkr, Walter E, D/KX82865
GARNSWORTHY, Po Cook, Sydney, D/M38151
GARRARD, Eng Art, Eric, C/MX76795
GEDDES, Eng Art, Lawrence, D/MX72671
GERMAINE, Smn, Harry J, D/JX175692
GIBBS, Boy, George E, D/JX181926
GIBBS, Mrn, Edward G, PLY/X2538
GIFFORD, Lt, J R,
GILCHRIST, Ab, Alexander, D/JX185171
GILLESPIE, Ord Smn, Charles, P/JX284362
GIRVAN, Stkr, Edward J, D/KX93500
GOLBY, Mrn, Frederick T A, PLY/X3197
GOODMAN, Boy, Herbert G, D/JX177491
GOODRUM, Ab, Arnold H, C/JX157787
GORDON, Ab, Reginald, D/JX206089
GORDON, Stkr, Isaac A, D/K109129
GOSLING, Stkr, Thomas H, D/KX105349
HATHERALL, Sgmn, Percival G, D/SSX32982
HAWKE, Writer, Fred K D, D/MX63500
HAWKINS, Midi, J M,
HAYS, Stwd, George, D/LX24069
HEATH, Po, Francis M, D/J99530
HEMINGWAY, Sup Asst, John H, D/MX67599
HEVERON, Ab, Frank, D/JX213553

HEYWOOD, Ab, Harry, D/SSX17618
HICKS, Ab, Jack, D/JX144357
HIGGINBOTHAM, Mrn, James, PLY/X100325
HINDER,Stkr Po,Arthur S,D/K12467
HOBSON, Stkr, Tom D, D/KX97063
HOCKNEY, Mrn, Kenneth, PLY/X100721
HOLDEN, Boy, (k/n), D/JX166606
HOLLOWAY, Teleg, Donald M, D/JX162945
HOLMES, Ab, John W, D/JX213540
HOLSGROVE, Boy, James, D/JX180639
HOMER, Stkr, William, D/KX111897
HORLEY, Po, (k/n), D/JX158721
HORRIGAN, Cook, Patrick A, C/MX52076
HORTON, Ab, William, D/JX200535
HOTCHKISS, Elec Art, (k/n), C/MX76240
HOWELL, Yeo Sigs, Ronald S, D/JX129115
HUGHES, Po, Verdon, D/J42301
HUGHES, Coder, Davis W B, D/JX220474
HUNTING, Lt, R A,
RYDER, Eng Art, Arthur, D/MX55103
ILES, Stkr, Rex G, D/SKX76
JACKS, Cook, Albert, D/MX60988
JACKSON, Shpwrgt, J E,
JACKSON, Ab, Ernest V, D/JX154726
JACQUISS,Cmmander,B.,
JAGO, Shpwrgt, Leslie M, D/MX70132
JAYES, Stwd, Alwyn, D/LX25182
JEANS, Ab, Robson S, D/JX171618
JEANS, Sgmn, Wilfred C, D/JX208140
JEFFREY, Ab, William H, D/J22449
JENKINS, Smn, Harold, D/JX221167
JOHNS, Stkr, Alfred G, D/KX87665
JOHNSON, Boy, Joseph T, D/JX175870
JOHNSON, Gnr, Harold Clifford Alwyn, 872658
JONES, Mrn, Stanley, PLY/X100181
JONES, Mrn, Harry, PLY/X100118
JONES, Sgmn, Ronald A, D/JX223262
JONES, Sig Boy, John, D/JX170295
KEELER, Mrn, Murth B, PLY/X100133
KENT, Ab, Leonard D, D/JX186887
KERSHAW, Wrmn, John F, D/MX68901
KINDER, Midi, R,
KING, Ab, Arthur L, D/JX213552
KNIGHT, Jnr, Frederick, D/MX53342
LACEY, Mrn, William, PLY/X100426
LANG, Eng Cmdr, H,
LANG, Stkr, Joseph, D/KX115852
LEAR, Sup Asst, George R, D/X173
LONG, Stkr, Andrew, D/KX129220
LOVING, Elec Art, William J L, D/MX60227
LOWTHER, Shpwrgt, James, D/M19901
LYNCH, Boy, Michael F, D/JX183682
MADEN, Mrn, Walter, PLY/X100121
MAGAHY, Po, Thomas J, D/JX133634
MANLEY, Stkr, Jeremiah, D/K24622
MARSHALL, Eng Art, Leslie, D/SMX84
MARSHALL, Stkr, George, D/KX128324
MARTIN, Smn, Francis J, D/JX255952
MARTLEW, Ab, Victor, D/SSX27896
MASTERS, Smn, William F C, D/JX238722
MATTHEWS, Slmkr, Robert, D/J52460
McBRIDE, Smn, Patrick J, D/JX238753
McCAMERON, Stwd, William C, D/LX25488

McCLINTOCK, Boy, Robert, D/JX180543

McCULLAUGH, Sgmn, (k/n), D/JX172327

McEVAN, Teleg, John M D, D/SSX31341

McGRATH, Marine, Charles G, PLY/X100182

McGREGOR, Cpl, Leonard, PLY/X785

McGREGOR, Stwd, Robert, C/LX22480

McGUINNESS, Boy, James E, D/JX184573

McKENZIE, Ab, John B, D/SSX20261

McKENZIE, Boy, John, D/JX180679

McNELIS, Ab, James, D/MDX2301

McSPARRON, Po, John R, D/JX141250

METTRICK, Ab, Jack, D/JX213528

MILLS, Stkr, Arthur, D/KX132967

MITCHELL, Ab, John, D/JX212002

MOFFAT, Smn, Thomas C, D/JX27237

MONK, Stkr, Thomas, D/K20885

MORGAN, Jnr, Kenneth, D/MX70638

MUNDY, Ab, Arthur A, D/JX213490

NEWBERY, Sur Cmdr, D A,

NEWLAND, Stkr, Reginald, D/KX115045

NOON, Smn, John E, D/JX238283

NORSWORTHY, Stkr, John T, D/KX114866

NYE, Stwd, Joseph A, P/LX22462

O'GRADY, Stkr, James, D/KX94347

OFFEN, Stwd, Ernest R, C/LX25333

OWEN, Po, Goronwy W, D/JX136455

OWEN, Boy, Edward, D/JX180616

PAGE, Sub Lt, W R D,

PARKER, Stwd, John S, C/LX22847

PARKINSON, Smn, Eric H, D/JX286187

PARRY, Ab, Colin, D/SSX27358

PARSONAGE, Stkr, William, D/KX122338

PARSONS, Air Mec, Kenneth J, FAA/FX76341

PASCOE, Elec Art, Donald, D/MX62520

PASSMAN, Ord Art, James, D/MX68279

PERRY, Eng, S H,

PILKINGTON, Ab, Norman, D/JX219922

PLATT, Boy, Kenneth, D/JX180591

POPE, Stkr Po, Sydney H P, D/K65853

PORTER, Teleg, Henry W, D/JX155258

POTTER, Ab, James W, D/SSX24861

POXON, Coder, William H, D/JX216187

PRICE, Marine, David E, PLY/22003

PROCTER, Ab, Herbert, D/JX213626

PROCTOR, Stwd, Henry G, D/LX26380

PROFFITT, Marine, Bert, PLY/X2676

PUDIFOOT, Gnr, C W,

RANDLES, Po, Charles L, D/MX51172

RANKIN, Stkr, Albert, D/KX126888

RAY, Cpl, Herbert, CH/X1478

RAYNER, Stkr, Jack, D/KX117603

REED, Stwd, Ronald W, D/LX24445

REYNOLDS, Boy, Alexander R, D/JX183660

RICE, Marine, William J H, PLY/X100348

RICE, Ab, John F, P/JX213723

RICHARDS, Shpwrgt, Thomas J R, D/M3318

RICHARDS, Stwd, Fredk H, D/L11222

RIDGEWAY, Samuel J, Stkr, D/K58486

ROBERTS, Stkr, William L, D/JX220009

ROBERTS, Stkr, John L, D/KX105946

ROBINSON, Ab, Albert, D/SSX19772

ROGERS,Era 2nd Cl,Joseph Thomas,P/MX50729

ROPE, Stwd, Walter E, C/LX27001

ROWE, Lt, E R,

ROWE, Ab, Percy J, D/JX128324

RUTHERFORD, Stwd, William E, D/LX22262

SANSUM,Ab,Leslie George Arthur,C/JX699557

SCOTT, Marine, Herbert G S, PLY/21635

SCOTT, Eng Art, Howard B, P/MX79521

SEARLE, Eng Art, Richard W J, D/MX49526

SHARLAND, Stkr Po, William J, D/KX57937

SHAW, Boy, Alexander, D/JX180678

SHEEN, Po, William J, D/JX141174

SHEPHERD, Mrn, Thomas S, PLY/X2346

SHERIDAN, Smn, Stephen, D/MDX1995

SHIMMIN, Stkr, Richard, D/KX108681

SLY, Cook, Fredk J, D/MX66608

SMITH, Mrn, Alexander, PLY/X3817

SMITH, Stkr, Walter, D/KX110083

SMITH, Ab, Samuel, D/SSX21390

SMITH, Ab, Samuel, D/JX198146

SMITH, Boy, John, D/JX166841

SOUTHARD, Ab, Victor, D/J30705

SPENCE, Stkr, Mervyn C, D/KX111623

SPENCER, Po, John S, D/J103707

SPOONER,Vice Admrl (DSO),Ernest John,

SPRUCE, Boy, Stanley G, D/JX177297

STAPLETON, Boy, Gilbert, PLY/X3794

STEELE, Eng Art, John H, P/MX79494

STEVENS, Stkr, Arthur J, P/KX130591

STEWARD, Stwd, Dudley C, C/LX27854

STEWART, Stkr, William, D/KX126893

STOCKBRIDGE, Stkr, William F, D/KX127888

SUGDEN, Stkr, Horace T J, D/KX83968

SYMONS, Eng Art, Harry R, D/M6288

TAMES, Stkr, Walter F, D/KX108406

TATTON, Smn, Christopher, D/JX285167

THOMPSON, Wrmn, Eric, D/MX71532

THORNHILL, Elec Art, Edward J, D/MX70457

THYER, Chf Mech, Leslie M, D/K17277

TRAYNOR, Stkr, William E, D/KX128239

TRUSCOTT, Stkr, Charles E, D/KX118204

VINCENT, Stkr, Leonard A, D/KX111650

WALLACE, Eng Art, Ernest M, D/192ED

WALTERS, Ab, Roy M, D/JX213068

WALTON, Stkr, James K, D/KX81727

WARD, Com Ord Off, H G,

WATSON, Paymstr Midi, J L C,

WEAVER, Boy, John H, D/JX166625

WEBB, Paymstr Com, L V,

WEEKS, Stkr, Henry T C, D/K18004

WESTLAKE, Ord Art, William H F, D/MX46253

WHEATON, Pntr, Horace, D/MX45571

WIDDECOMBE, Shpwrgt, Jack, D/MK51878

WIDDICOMBE, Elec Art, Leonard C, D/M36732

WILKINSON, Chf Stkr, Sydney, D/K63595

WILKINSON, Smn, Paul L, D/JX170159

WILLIAMS, Stkr, William G H, D/KX88646

WILLIAMS, Stwd, William C, C/LX24415

WILLIAMS, Ab, Robert, D/JX192081

WILLIAMS, Stkr, James H, D/K18846

WILLIAMS, Cook, Ernest R, D/MX80606

WILSON, Ab, Ernest, D/JX213037

WINGFIELD, Chf Elec Art, Basil F P B, D/MX47709

WINSTANLEY, Stkr, John C, D/KX88140

WINTER, Mrn, Douglas, PLY/X2804

WITHERS, Ab, Stanley C, D/JX190360
WOOD, Lt, L F,
WOOD, Stkr, William, D/KX90391
WOOLLONS, Chf Shpwrgt, Leonard J, D/M35168
WRIGHT, Stkr, Stanley, D/KX111655
WYATT, Bdmn, Harold W W, RMB/X730
YARWOOD, Boy, Colin, D/JX162075
YOUNG, Ab, William G, D/J100418
YOUNG, Boy, Robert E, D/JX166632
YOUNG, Boy, James, D/JX166629

HMS VICTORY (VR)
DYASON,Lt,Richard Christopher Cornwall,

HMS INDOMITABLE (VR)
DEARNLEY,Sub Lt,Brian Palmer,

HMS PRINCE OF WALES (VR)
ARMITAGE,Lt,Benjamin Hodes,

HM HOSPITAL SHIP GERUSALEMME
FREEMAN,P/o,Thomas Herick,C/NX2542
WILSON,Eng,Commdr George Dearnley,

HMML193
POLLITT,Ab,Sydney,P/SX395557

HMML 310
FLOWER,A.B.,Robert William,C/JX204280
GIBSON,Ab,Bert,C/JX198996
LITTLE,Sto 2nd Cl,John,D/KX11334
TOWNEND,Sto,Edwin Richard,C/KX127382

HMLST 50
GWYNN,Ab,George William,C/JX238903
PRICE,Sgmn,Edward Anthony,C/JX308179

HMLST 117
NICHOLAS,Ab,Donald,D/JX563795

HMML 193
NASH,Sto 1st Cl,Donald Leslie,C/KX171963

HMLST 235
BROCKLESBY,Po,Mornington Broughton,C/MX12644

HMLST 293
PENNINGTON,Ab,Robert James,D/JX363216

HMLST 373
LING,Ab,Peter Anthony,C/JX376638

HMLST 382
BROWN,Ab,Albert,C/JX408719

HMLST 413 (VR)
CHARLWOOD,Sub Lt,John Vernon,

HMLST 489
ELLIOTT,Ab,Alexander,C/JX372782

HMLST 682
DONNELLY,Mrn,Robert,PO/X122866

HMLST 3008
SMITH,Sub Lt,Harold Russell,

HMLST 3020
MAWHINNEY,Sto 1 Cl,Hugh,C/KX171958

HMLST 3402
THEXTON,Po,George Raymond,C/NX321

HMLST Q1
SUNTER,Po,John Scot,C/MX663153

HM MINESWEEPER 2203
HATCH,Cook,Albert,LT/MX534915

HMS ABERDARE
MELDRUM,Ab,Samuel Montgomery,P/SSX20204

HMS ABINGDON
GIRVAN,Ab,John Maccallum,P/SSX21867

HMS ALDGATE
HAVELOCK,Ab,William,C/J80251

HMS ALUNIA
GIBSON,Ldng Sto,Thomas .B,D/KX158085
ROOKE,Sto 1st Cl,Douglas George Alfred,D/KX601107

HMS ANSON
DENT,Sgmn,James Lancelot,D/JX581828,

HMS BELFAST
LONG,Cpo,Tel Alfred Martin,P/J111691

HMS BERMUDA (RM)
HEPPELL,Mrn,Redvers Gordon,PLY/X4420

HMS BRAGANZA
CARR,Coder,Ernest Geoffrey Francis,D/JX733998

HMS CAESAR
BARRY,Ldg Sea,Vincent,D/SSX19894

HMS CAMPERDOWN
McCONNELL,Ab,Patrick,D/JX286780

HMS CAPETOWN
MARTIN,Ab,Hubert Beans,D/J102607

HMS CAVALIER
SPIERS,Sto,Peter Frank,P/KX726053

HMS CHINKARA (RM)
MELLOR,L/Cpl,Ernest William Benn,CH/X113915

HMS CICALA
DOWLING, Sto, Maurice, P/SS117816
GRIFFITH, Supas, Robert Thomas, D/MX55858
MEARS, Ldg Smn, Albert Edgar, D/JX141563
NEILL, Ab, Ernest Robert, D/SSX14813
YARWOOD, Ldg Tel, Colin, P/WRX617

HMS COMUS
SPENCER,Ldg Smn,Joseph,P/JX801593

HMS COPRA
KETLEY,Marine,Robert James,CH/X116222
PAGETT,Tw,Albert F.,P/LX726467

HMS COPRA (VR)
CLARK,Sub Lt,Charles Henry,

HMS CORNFLOWER (VR)
ROGERS,Wo,J.,105

HMS DUNCANSBY HEAD
ALDER,Stew,Sydney J,P/LX22276

HMS DURBAN
BROCKHURST,A B.,Albert James,R/SSX19364
HOBBS,Ldg Seaman,Albert Edward,P/J98051
WALKER,Ord Smn,Henry Joseph,C/JX168221

HMS EAGLE
MOORE,Ab,Harry,P/J68989
ROBINSON,Ord Sgmn,Edward,P/JX155156

HMS ENCOUNTER
WOOD,Sto 1st Cls,Henry Robert,C/K52154

HMS EXETER
ANDREWS, Era, William Lewis, D/M34376
JEFFS, Ab, Harold Tom F, D/SSX20620
McGOWAN, Sto, Edward, D/KX111367
PHILLIPS, Yeo Of Sigs, William Thomas, D/JX140180
SOPER, Ch Era, George Sydney Norman, D/MX51596
WEST, Ch Era, Albert E., D/MX37662
WILLIAMS, Ab, Victor George, P/JX236353

HMS FAREHAM
DONNELLY,Ldg Smn,William,D/JX126358

HMS FORMIDABLE
STRADWICK,Sub Lt,Walter Thomas,

HMS FORMIDABLE (VR)
MAITLAND,Sub Lt,Leslie Alan,

HMS GOLDEN HIND
CHURCHOUSE,Sub Lt,Geoffrey Keith,

HMS GRASSHOPPER
BETTERIDGE,Ord Seamn,Thomas,C/JX262283

HMS HARTLAND POINT
BURNS,Sto 1st Cl,Robert,D/KX/154462
WOODCOCK,Ab,Frederick Raymond,P/JX711585

HMS HIGHFLYER
COOMES,A/b,Roy Norman,P/JX626323
TAYLOR,Mrn,John Patrick,PO/X118041

HMS HONG KONG
BELL,Ab,Norman Mcleod,D/JX19422

HMS ILLUSTRIOUS
NEWTON,Sub Lt,Sidney,

HMS IMPLACABLE
BEDORE,Sub Lt,Glen Emerson,
DOY,Sub Lt,Neville George,

HMS INDEFATIGABLE
BONASS,Sub Lt,John Francis Joseph Andrew,
HOCKLEY,Sub Lt,Fred,
HMS INDOMITABLE
BARNETT,Sub Lt,Sidney Charles,
JENNER,Po,Air Kenneth William,FX90676

HMS INDOMITABLE (VR)
FARMELO,Sub Lt,Christopher Bertram,

HMS KELANA (VR)
PAGE,Sub Lt,Roy Arthur,

HMS LANDSWELL
ATHERTON,Sto 1st Class,Harry,C/KX1771743
CHANCELLOR,Ldg Rad Mech,Thomas Edwin,P/MX116079
CHANDLER,Ld Stew,Percival Alfred,LT/LX27749

HMS LANKA
JONES,E R A,Barrie,D/MX508696
MAXWELL,Maj,John,
SMITH,Sba,Michael,D/MX558102
SMITH,C/Sjt,Ernest Charles,EX/SR8111

HMS LOCH LOMOND
GALPIN,Ab,James Alfred,C/JX20201

HMS LOCK ECK
O'DONNELL,Ab,Malcolm Smith,P/JX708945

HMS MOTH
GAY,Sup Ass,Harry,C/MX58799,

HMS NELSON (RM)
MILLIKEN,Maj,Frank Andrew,

HMS ODYSSEY
LINDOP,Lt Cmdr,Richard Heane,

HMS OPHIR
GIVEN,Sba,Charles N,D/MX93843

HMS PEMBROKE 11
WELLS,Ab,Arthur William Cement,C/JX299677
WHITE,Ab,Edward Charles Peter,C/JX259190

HMS PETEREL
DUNBAR,Sto,James,C/KX87890
LIDINGTON,Ldg Tel,William H,P/J80117

HMS PHEASANT
WILLETT,Lt,Francis Wiliam,

HMS PLUCKY
CLAY,Ab,Terence,P/JX514844

HMS PLYM
PAINE,Sto,Frederick George,D/KX155772

HMS PRESIDENT
BLAIR,Ab,Frederick,D/JX267052

HMS PRINCE OF WALES
BACK, Mrn, Percy George Edward, PLY/X21505
BROWN, Cpl, John, LY/X2140
DALLEY, Mrn, George Alexanda, PLY/X3821
DEMPSEY, A B, Joseph, D/JX179621
FORTUNE, Cpo, John Park D/j, 105059
HANNAFORD, Mrn, Frederick Joseph George, PLY/20209
HARRIS, Sto 1st Cl, Wilfred, D/KX95750
HIGGINS, Mrn, Douglas Ewart, PLY/X2002
HULL,A/b,Richard,D/JX1967666
KIRKPATRICK, Ldg Smn, David, D/JX218782
LIBBY, Sto 1st Cl, Frederick Thomas, D/KX105371
MILLS, Mrn, David Henry, PLY/X100120
MURFIN,Cpl,Francis Sidney,PLY/X2233
NANKIVELL, Sto 1 Cls, Cecil, D/SS125658
PAGET, Po, Frederick Charles, D/JX136130
PAILEY, Po, John Horace (DSM), D/J105980
SHORE, Ab, Robert, D/JX141486
TAYLOR, Ld Sto, George Edward, D/KX92436
THOMPSON,Cpl,Lionel Charles,PLY/X1521
TINCKNELL, Marine, Francis Herbert Jack, PLY/X100103
VARTY, Mrn, Richard, PLY/X2518
WALKLEY, Sto, Thomas A, D/KX112364
WILIAMS, Era, John Philip Moss, D/M52566

HMS PURSUER
OSBORNE,S/mn,Albert Dacre,LT/JX372636

HMS REDSTART
THOMAS,Ab,Ivor Edward,P/SSX28641
ELDRIDGE,Ab,Harry Norman P.J,110399

HMS REPULSE
ANDERSON, Lt John, C/JX159287
ANTHONY, Marine, Kenneth, PLY/X3773
BLAIR, Lt (e), Cyril Tom,
BREMRIDGE, Mid'n, James Philip Henry,
BUCKLEY, Cpl, Victor, PLY/X2099
ELLIOT, Marine, David Mons Lorain, PLY/X101537
HORNBY, Sjt, Edward, PLY/X1301
JEANS, Ab, Robson Scott, D/JX171618
LOVING, El Art, David William John Llewellyn, D/MX60227
MILL, Marine, Keith Clifford, PLY/X3180
NEWLAN, Sto 2 Cls, James Reginald, D/KX115945
NUGUS, Marine, Philip Charles Henry, PLY/X3177
SHARLAND, Po, William John, D/K57937
SMITH, Po, William, D/JX151875
SULLY, Mrn, S.T.W., PLY/X3775

HMS ROBIN
GEORGE,Eng,Frederick Charles Granville,

HMS ROYAL SULTAN
McAFEE,Sto 1st Clss,James George,D/KX138902

HMS SCORPION
CUMMING,Ord Smn,Henry James,D/JX191162

HMS SIANG WO
GALBRAITH,Lt Comdr,John Archibald,

HMS SIMBANG (RM)
GRIFFIN,Mrn,Donald Frank,CH/X113236
WALMSLEY,Ldg Mech,Cyril Billington,L/FX682925
WALMSLEY,Ld Mcch,Cyril Billington,L/FX682925
TWELLS,Sto,Harold,P/KX178158

HMS STRONGHOLD
CRAWFORD,Sto,George William,C/KX107328

HMS SULTAN
BROWN, Mrn, Cyril Charles John, PLY/X2584
BURBIDGE, Sto 1st Cls, Robert William, D/KX113261
CAIRNS, Marine, Frederick Henry, CH/X2175
CHATFIELD, Ab, Alfred Charles, P/JX276477
DARWALL, Lt, John Evelyn Desmond,
DAVIDSON, Ordnce Articfr, David, P/MX52321
FRAMPTON, Commdr, Pendarvis Lister,
GATWARD, Lt, Edgar Hulme,
GIFFIN, Sto, George Arthur, R/KX110177
GLOVER, Ab, William Charles, D/J88112
HAWKINS, Ab, Denis Levi, P/JX159915
HOLLAND, Mrn, Arnold, PLY/X219
JOHNSON, Ab, James Burt Openshaw, D/JX188535
JONES, Sto 1sr Cl, John, C/KX104964
KEELING, Po, Ralph, D/JX135907
KESSACK, Ab, William, C/JX376307
LE MESURIER, Lt, John Laurens,
LEE, Rad Mech, Stanley Terence, P/MX517462
MILN, Sur Lt, David Anderson,
PEARSON, B, Ernest James, D/JX198445
PECOVER, W/o, George James,
ROBINSON, Ab, Alfred Ernest, C/JX192363
RUSSELL, Ab, James Edward, P/LX215074
RYAN, Ab, Thomas, D/JX172380
SCAMMELL, Sto, Leonard Stanley, D/KX126814
STEPHENS, Po, Maurice F, P/MX503865
SURTES, Yeo Sigs, Robert, C/JX138690
TAYLOR, Wrmn, Stanley, D/MX70683
TAYLOR, Era, Clifford Bem, DM/22029
THOMAS, Ab, Idris, R/JX219786
TURNER, Ch Sto, Abraham, P/K43828
TWEEDALE, Teleg, Raph Allan, P/JX252040
WATSON, Ab, Percy C/j, 41288
WRIGHT, Cpl, David, PLY/X4319

HMS SUSSEX
BUCHANAN,Ord,Seamn William,C/JX788467

HMS TAMAR (RM)
ALLISON, Cpo, John, D/MX45771
ANDERSON, Po Tel, Thomas Albert, C/JX144913
ANDREWS, Cpo, William Henry Austin, D/J43976
ASHTON, Ldg Tel, Cyril Richard, C/SSX20134
BAILEY, Bmskp, Stanford Arthur,
BATER, Spcpo, Harold Charles, D/M37318
BULL, Ab, Francis Charles, D/JX165781
BURFORD, Teleg, Frederick James, P/JX201141
BURROWS, Ab, Kenneth George, P/J102981
CASSIDY, Jnr, John Mcferran, P/UDX1320
CHAMBERS, Ab, James L, C/SSX28512

CHISWELL, Shipwt, Reginald Clarence George, D/M28197
DOWSETT, Po, Samuel, C/JX156068
DYKE, Era 2nd Cl, Leslie Edward, C/M39586
EDGE, Ch/art, Ellis Taylor, P/M6033
FIELDHOUSE, Po, John Thomas, P/KX93901
HEWETT, Marine, Edward Tucker, CH/X458
HORDER, Mot Mech, Douglas George, P/MX67988
HUMPHREY, Ab, Bert De'arcy Langford, P/J42027
IRELAND, Writer, Michael Norman, P/MX70045
JACQUES, Sgmn, John M, P/JX205696
JEFFS, Ch Era, Sydney Hill, C/MX46760
MATHESON, Mtr Mech, Donald, P/MX64555
MAXTED, Ldg Tel, Richard, C/JX140591
PRICE, Sgmn, Walter, D/JX235643
SCALLY, Writer, Dennis Frederick Joseph, P/MX80371
SMART, Po Sto, Stanley G., D/KX81418
SMITH, Ab, Edwin Leslie George, P/J28740
STARE, Telgft, George Christopher, P/SSX31692
STEWART, Ab, Donald, D/JX146752
STOKES, Ab, David, P/J34983
SYMONS, Yeo Of Sigs, Robert Charles, D/JX147813
TAYLOR, Wrnt Eng, Arthur William Francis,
THOMAS, Sba, Gwynfor, P/MX64986
TODD, Cpo, James, D/JX149160
VARNEY, Ab, Harry, P/J18390
WALL, Sjt, T.M., PLY/X22054
WATTS, Po, Thomas, P/J14612
WILLIAMS, Ch Era, George A, D/M37680

HMS TENEDOS
JENNINGS,Ab,James Henry,R/JX142296

HMS TERN
CHILDS, Po, George M, C/JX147246
DOW LDG, Sto, Robert, C/KX90980
PAYNE, Ab, Ernest William, C/J94361
POLLITT, Ldg Sto, Robert Henry, P/KX83981
PRICE, Ldg Sto, Ernest, C/KX81053
SKINNER, Po, Sidney Albert, C/JX132691

HMS TERROR
BROWN,Era 4th Cl,Frederick,P/MX716139
FYNN,Stkr 1 Cls,William Leonard,C/KX598460
GASCOIGNE,Sto Po,William John Slater,DK/56982

HMS TEVIOT BANK
FRYER,Lg/smn,Leslie James,C/J109746

HMS THRACIAN
ADAMS, Po, Leonard George, D/JX130985
BURGIN, Ab, Ernest, D/SSX20669
DAVIES, Ab, Henry, D/JX153156
DUFFY, Po, John, D/JX134983
GARDINER, Sto, Leslie John, D/K56061
MORGAN, Sto 1sr Cl, Melville M, C/KX105321
SCHOFIELD, Ab, Ralph, D/SSX19755

HMS TRAMP
HOOKER,Ab,James,P/SSX21736

HMS VICTORIOUS
HILL,Sub Lt,Eric,

Merchant Naval Service

MV DALHOUSIE MN
LLEWELYN, Ch Off, Edward

MV HARPA MN
BOYACK, 5 Eng, Thomas B
MV HAURAKI MN
HOLLAND, Gmn, Wiliam
HUGHES, Ot Mech, Lewis

MV PATELLA BCM MN
BARBER, Mast, Robert Malcolm
CORRADINE, Eng Off, Frank
LOWE, 5th Eng, Stuart Owen

SS AUST MN
OWEN, Frmn, Robert

SS BEN NEVIS MN
HARLAND, Ab, Edward Valentine
LAURENSON, Ab, Anthony

SS DALHOUSIE MN
BROWN, 3rd Off, Robert Millar

SS EMPRESS OF ASIA
ELWORTHY, Pntymn, Douglas Richard
TOWERS, Deck Boy, James Joseph

SS GEMSTONE MN
CLEMENTS, Ab, James F
MANNING, Ab, Darnley
PHILLIPS, Btsn, Caleb

SS GLOUCESTER CASTLE MN
ANDREWS, Watchman, Arthur Ernest
MACMAHON, Ass, Stew John

SS HARPA MN
GRANT, Ch Eng, Alexander Hope Gordon
VANVUUREN, 4th Eng,
WIDDAS, Ch Eng, Gordon
WOODBRIDGE, 3rd Eng, H.J.

SS KAIPING MN
STRUTH, Mstr, James Barker

SS KATHLEEN MOLLER MN
MASON, Mstr, Cecil

SS KIRKPOOL MN
KENNINGTON Albert Master

SS LARGS BAY MN
CARBRY, Firman, James Aloysius

SS LYLEPARK MN
ARCHER, Ab, Horace Frederick

SS MARIE MOLLER MN
CRAFTER, Ch Eng, Ernest Richard (DASC)

SS OSCAR11 MN
PALMER, Master, Walter Howard.

SS WELLPARK MN
FERGUSON, 3rd Off, Leonard

MAIN, 3rd Off, John Mcpherson

SS WILLESDEN MN
DONALDSON, Ab, John
JAMES, Fireman, Joe
MENDI, Grsr, Joe
RUNCIE, 3rd Off, Alex
WILLIAMS, Donk/mn, Alfred

Army

ADJUTANT QUARTER MASTER GENERAL
MALAY COMMAND
AMPHLETT, Lt Col,Baron William John,27657

ARGYLL & SUTHERLAND HIGHLANDERS
ADAM, Pte, Thomas Stevenson, 3323207
ADAMSON, Sjt, David Young, 2979216
AIREY, Pte, Raymond, 3322720
ALLAN, Pte, John, 3130917
ALLAN, Pte, Andrew Davidson, 3322690
ALSTON, Sjt, James Brown, 2984051
ANDERSON, Cpl, Robert William, 2979594
ANDERSON, Pte, James, 3128682
ANTHONY, L/Cpl, George, 2568846
ASHCROFT, Pte, William John, 2982162
ATKINSON, Pte, Robert Walter, 860443
ATKINSON, Pte, Myles Thompson, 2986034
BAIN, Cpl, John, 2977098
BAIRD, Cpl, Robert, 2979717
BAIRD, Pte, Alexander, 2982021
BALLANTYNE, L/Cpl, Rchibald, 3320465
BANCROFT, Lt, Geoffrey, 204892
BARTLEY, Bdmn, Raymond, 3130487
BAXTER, Sjt, Ronald Joseph, 3321646
BAXTER, Pte, James, 1979910
BEATTIE, Sjt, Robert Graham, 2979179
BECKETT, Cap, Ranald High Colin, 74361
BELL, Pte, John William, 2982066
BELLETT, Pte, George Singleton, 13029025
BELLIS, Pte, Robert, 3322730
BELLIS, Pte, George James Daniel, 3128486
BENNETT, Pte, Arthur, 2989711
BENNY, Pte, Hugh Kelso, 2979605
BENTLEY, Cpl, Aubrey Gordon, 2572163
BERTOLINI, Pte, John, 2987779
BICKER, Sjt, William, 2979488
BIGGARSTAFF, Csm, Alexander, 2971522
BIRKMYRE, Pte, David, 2977421
BLACK, Pte, William, 2984349
BLACKWOOD, Capt, Frederick Michael Ponsonby, 74706
BLATHERWICK, Pte, Sanley, 4981095
BONAR, Cpl, Edward Campbell, 2978796
BOYD, Cpl, Hector, 2981618
BRANDON, Bdsmn, Charles Eric, 2979482
BRANSON, Pte, Henry James, 13021189
BROWN, Sjt, Thomas, 7009563
BROWN, Pte, David, 2979723
BROWN, Pte, Robert Nightingale, 2977260
BROWN, Pte, Joseph, 3322737
BUCKLEY, Pte, Robert, 3322739
BURKE, Pte, Thomas, 3324879
BURNETT, Pte, James Fairley, 3324880
BURNS, Pte, Thomas, 3132410
BURROWS, L/Cpl, Stanley Thomas, 3321661
CAIN, Pte, Robert, 2989044
CALDERWOOD, Sjt, James, 2979504
CALDWELL, Pte, Robert William, 3132837
CALLAND, Pte, Jack, 3322743
CAMERON, Pte, Samuel, 2980572
CAMPBELL, L/Cpl, Duncan, 2979560
CAMPBELL, Pte, John Boyle, 2976016
CAMPBELL, Pte, William, 3323216
CAMPBELL, Pte, Henry Cunningham, 2986248
CAMPBELL, Pte, Harold, 2979195
CANNON, Pte, Thomasd, 2981967
CARLETON, Pte, Robert Mcnair, 2989050

CARSON, Pte, James Nash, 3323218
CATLING, Pte, John, 3321669
CHILD, L/Cpl, John Joseph, 2979837
CHRISTIE, Pte, Peter Watson, 3323405
CLARK, Pte, Richard, 3132838
CLARK, L/Cpl, Hector Cameron, 2983517
CLARK, L/Cpl, Bernard, 3322698
CLARKE, Pte, Frederick, 2979730
CLASPER, Pte, Henry, 3322763
COCHRAN, Pte, William, 2979983
COCHRANE, Pte, George Gordon, 2979739
COLE, Lt, Walter, 225875
COLLISTON, 2/, John Joseph, 190254
CONLON, Cpl, James, 2029585
CONNELL, Pte, Arthur William, 3322766
CONNELLY, Pte, George, 3323221
COOPER, Pte, Charles Henry, 2982011
CORR, Pte, Peter, 3323224
CRONE, Pte, John Smith, 2031458
CRONIN, Pte, John, 2990948
CROUTH, C/Sjt, Frederick, 2979854
CROZIER, Pte, William, 2982047
CRUICKSHANK, Pte, James, 2984527
CUNNINGHAM, Pte, Alexander, 2979993
CURLEY, Pte, Thomas, 3322772
CURRIE, Pte, Robert, 2989476
DALY, Pte, William, 2979724
DARBY, Pte, William, 2979629
DARROCK, Sjt, Albert Dcm, 2980642
DAVENPORT, Pte, Duncan, 2986637
DAVIDSON, Pte, John, 3132101
DAVIDSON, Pte, Francis Burnett, 2979925
DAY, Pte, Albert Hogarth, 2973393
DEMPSEY, Pte, Robert, 2967616
DEVLIN, Pte, Neil Kirkwood, 2982027
DICKIE, Cpl, John, 2979294
DITCHAM, Cqms, James Frederick, 7257924
DOCHERTY, Pte, Robert, 2982155
DOCHERTY, Pte, John, 2982044
DOHERTY, Cpl, William, 2979966
DONNELLY, Pte, Edward, 2979747
DORAN, Pte, John, 2979587
DUFF, Cpl, John, 2975231
DUFFIELD, L/Cpl, George Thomas, 3322778
DUFFY, Pte, Joseph, 2986095
DUNBAR, Pte, Ronald Jeffries, 3322779
EASTHAM, Pte, Robert, 3855072
ECKFORD, Pte, William, 2982105
EDGAR, Pte, Robert, 3323228
ELLIOT, Pte, Alexander, 3053290
ELLIOTT, Pte, William E, 3321544
EMBLETON, Pte, John, 2979243
ETHERINGTON, Pte, Frederick, 3322782
EVANS, Pte, William James, 3132866
EVANS, Pte, Harry Phillip, 3322783
FAIRLESS, Pte, Walter Harold, 2982014
FARRELL, Pte, William, 6459446
FEENIE, Pte, William Murphy, 2989492
FEIGHAN, Pte, Michael, 2982225
FERGUSON, Pte, James Gray Rodger, 2191594
FERRY, Pte, Thomas Davis, 2979883
FITZPATRICK, Pte, John Joseph, 2979743
FLETCHER, Pte, Archibald Mcdonald, 2979378
FLETCHER, Pte, Donald, 2978776
FORSTER, Pte, Allan, 2989009
FOTHERINGHAM, Pte, William, 2982076
FOTHERINGHAM, Pte, Alexander, 2975232
FRASER, Pte, William, 2982090
FRASER, Pte, Donald, 2979638
GARTLAND, Pye, Owen, 3322787

GEE, Pte, Thomas Kenneth, 3320201
GENTLE, Cpl, Charles, 2979365
GIBSOBN, Pte, Richard, 2979074
GIBSON, Pte, James Mcrae, 2982987
GIBSON, Pte, Gordon, 3322788
GIBSON, Pte, Ernest, 2979453
GIBSON, Pte, David, 2985986
GILBERT, Pte, William Hardman, 3322789
GILFILLAN, Pte, George, 2986046
GILLIES, L/Cpl, Robert Lusk, 29797052
GISPERT, Lt, Albert Stephan Ignatius, 371854
GOLDIE, Pte, James Clark Ogilvie, 2990009
GRAHAM, Pte, John, 2979869
GRAHAM, Pte, William, 2990345
GRAHAM, Pte, Robert, 2990015
GRAHAM, Pte, Jack, 3322790
GRAY, Pte, William Hailstone, 2979535
GRAY, Pte, Christopher, 2979856
GREENAN, L/Cpl, William, 2979847
GREIG, Cpl, James Russell, 2979680
GREWAR, Pte, Andrew Stewart, 2979280
GRIEVES, Cpl, Thomas, 3322792
GROOM, Pte, William Henry, 2979769
GWYNNE, Pte, John, 2979264
HADDOCK, L/Cpl, Arthur, 2988091
HADDON, Pte, Stanley, 3322795
HAGGART, L/Sjt, James, 2979668
HALFPENNY, Pte, Thomas, 3322796
HALL, Pte, Stephen, 29890118
HAMILTON, Sjt, Robert, 2979694
HAMILTON, Sjt, Andrew, 2979289
HARBRON,Pte,William Allen,3322799
HARCOURT, Pte, John, 2979998
HARDIE, Sjt, James, 2979749
HARDIE, Pte, Albert, 2979976
HARDY, Pte, Frederick, 3325356
HARKINS, Pte, James Anderson Mm, 2989508
HARRISON, Pte, John William, 3131443
HARTFORD, Pte, Patrick, 2979655
HASTINGS, Pte, John, 3322803
HAWTHORN, Pte, Hartford, 3322804
HAYES, Cpl, George Albert, 4268688
HENDERSON, Pte, Ralph Forster, 3053016
HIRD, Pte, Eric Lambert, 2979836
HISLOP, Pte, William, 2980882
HOLMES, Pte, Peter, 2981610
HOLMES, Pte, Daniel, 2978069
HOOKEY, Sjt, Victor, 2978675
HUGHES, L/Cpl, Robert, 2968584
HUNTER, Pte, William, 2819674
HYLAN, Cpl, Sydney Edward, 2979462
INNES, Pte, Alexnder, 2986059
JACKMAN, Cpl, Albert, 2979922
JACKSON, Pte, Harold, 332280
JAMES, Pte, Walter, 4622902
JAMIESON, Pte, George, 2979802
JOHNSON, Pte, Lawrence William, 3322823
JOHNSON, Sjt, Donald Vivian, 2975608
JOHNSTONE, Pte, Hugh Osborne, 2985292
KEENAN, Pte, Charles, 2979825
KELLOCK, Pte, David, 2979514
KENNEDY, L/Cpl, Thomas, 2984609
KERR, Pte, Dennis, 2989869
LAIDLER, Pte, John Bell, 2981100
LEE, Pte, Charles, 3322831
LEES, L/Cpl, James, 3324835
LEWIS, Pte, John Edward, 13021734
LIDDLE, Pte, James Campbell, 2979221
LINN, Pte, William, 2986052
LOVE, Psm, James, 2979352

MACARTHUR, Pte, James Neil, 2979951
MACINNES, Pte, Alexander, 2986501
MACINNES, 2/lt, John, 187155
MACKELLAR, Maj, James Oliphant, 118022
MACLEOD, Pte, Alexander, 2982102
MACNEIL, Pte, Richard Peacock, 2982002
MACPHERSON, Pte, John, 3323251
MARSHAL, L/Cpl, James, 2978565
MARSHALL, Ptc, David, 2990102
MARTIN, Pte, John, 2992064
MARTIN, Pte, Archibald, 3322716
MAUGHAN, Pte, George, 3322838
McARDLE, Pte, Michael, 2979810
McAULEY, Pte, Daniel, 2982068
McCAL, L/Cpl, James, 2985491
McCALLUM, Pte, Gerald, 2980481
McCUAIG, Pte, James, 2982083
McDINE, Csm, Archibald Frederick, 2972296
McGHEE, Pte, Robert, 2990876
McGIBBON, L/Cpl, Duncan, 2984100
McGILLIVRAY, Pte, Alistair, 2875111
McGOWAN, Pte, William Tennyson, 3326907
McGRATH, Pte, Danial John, 3308928
McHUGH, Pte, William, 2987929
McKELL, L/Cpl, Jonathan, 2979722
McKIE, Sjt, Thomas, 2979188
McKNIGHT, Pte, William James, 2979756
McKNIGHT, Pte, James Hughes, 2986112
McLACHLAN, Pte, William, 2979908
McLACHLAN, Pte, Richard, 3326707
McLARDIE, L/Cpl, Robert, 2981666
McLAUGHLIN, Pte, Francis, 3326708
McLEAN, Pte, James Dewar, 3318459
McLEAN, 2/lt, Kenneth, 193888
McLEAN, Pte, John Currie, 2982022
McLEAN, Pte, John, 2985962
McLEOD, Drmr, Edward, 2982017
McMENEMY, Piper, Charles, 2979693
McMILLAN, Pte, John, 2992030
McMILLAN, Pte, Alexander Mcdougal, 2985819
McMURREY, Pte, John Brown, 2979732
McNAIRNEY, Pte, Thomas, 3324741
McNICOL, Pte, Daniel, 2977810
McNIVEN, L/Cpl, John Alexander, 2982058
McPARLAND, Pte, Edward, 2979850
McQUEEN, Pte, Robert, 2979579
McSHANE, Pte, Duncan, 1981599
McVEY, Pte, William, 2987350
METCALFE, Pte, Alfred, 2989071
MILES, Pte, Benjamin Lambert, 2979949
MILNE, Pte, Alexandr, 2979914
MKERNON, Pte, Thomas, 3130864
MNEISH, Pte, Mark Doran, 3323250
MONK, Pte, Patrick, 2979852
MONTGOMERY, Pte, William Dick, 2984381
MORETON, Pte, George, 2979965
MORRICE, Pte, Stephen, 3321262
MORRIS, Cpl, Douglas, 3318447
MORRISON, Spr, Thomas Nelson Lucas, 1874946
MOWAT, Pte, William, 2979632
MOYES, C/Sjt, Archibald David, 2981025
MUCHAN, Pte, Joseph, 2979712
MUNRO, Pte, Neil Boyle, 2980831
MUNRO, L/Cpl, Charles, 2979781
MURRAY, Pte, Patrick, 3130745
MURRAY, Pte, James, 2974761'
MURRAY, Pte, Allan, 2980559
NAPIER, Lt, Donald Graham, 98583
NEAGLE, Pte, William, 2974092
NEWTON, Pte, Anthony, 3322852

O'BRIEN, Pte, Francis, 3324793
O'CALLAGHAN, 2/lt, John, 265384
O'NEIL, L/Cpl, Robert, 3310709
O'NEILL, Pte, George, 2068567
ORR, 2/t, Robert Alexander, 177904
ORR, Pte, Hugh, 2990126
PARKINSON, Pte, Thomas, 3322855
PARRY, Sjt, Robert, 2976637
PARRY, Pte, Charles, 3322856
PATERSON, L/Cpl, George Thompson, 2979817
PATERSON, Pte, Robert Mcintyre, 2978259
PATTISON, Pte, James, 2146942
PEDDER, Cpl, William Somerville, 2979261
PEDDIE, Pte, James, 2979423
PENDREIGH, Pte, William, 2987012
PHILLIPS, Pte, John, 807088
PORTER, Csm, Alexander Scobie, 2974400
PROW, Pte, Walter, 297845
PURVES, Sjt, Thomas (MM), 2974492
RALSTON, Pte, James, 2985536
RAMSAY, Pte, James Rintoul, 2979990
REID, Pte, Robert, 2816681
RENNIE, Cpl, Angus, 2979984
RENTON, Cpl, Wilfred Cavell, 3322869
RICHARDSON, Pte, William, 3322872
RICHARDSON, Cpl, William, 3322871
RITCHIE, L/Cpl, George, 2979204
ROBERTSON, Lt Col, Lindsey Buchanan, 19305
ROBERTSON, Pte, James, 2985950
ROBERTSON, Pte, Peter, 3326745
ROBSON, Pte, Norman Baird, 3322876
ROBSON, Pte, George Bell, 3319046
RODGER, Pte, Peter, 2979989
RODGERS, Pte, George Arthur, 2978521
RODHAM, Cpl, Archibald Stewart, 2978048
RONALD, Cpl, Alexander, 2983952
ROSS, Cpl, Arthur, 2978768
RUMBOLD, Pte, John Henry, 2992389
RUSSELL, Pte, David, 801743
RUSSELL, Pte, John, 2979806
RUTTER, Pte, Sydney, 3322879
SCANLAN, L/Cpl, Edward, 2979681
SCOTT, Pte, Hugh, 3323262
SCOTT, Pte, Andrew, 2979980
SCOTT, Pte, James, 2979896
SHANKS, Pte, William Paterson, 2979863
SHEEKEY, Pte, John, 2983577
SHELDON, Pte, Thomas, 3322881
SHIACH, Lt, David Gordon, 137942
SHINGLER, Pte, Frank, 2990757
SIMPSON, Pte, Donald, 297134
SLOAN, Psm, Hugh Cairn Duff, 2979692
SMITH, Sjt, Norman Henry, 3319055
SMITH, Pte, George, 2979771
SMITH, Pte, William Allan, 2982034
SMITH, Sjt, Robert, 2979182
SMITH, Pte, Peter Neilson, 2568849
SMITH, L/Cpl, John, 2979459
SMITH, Pte, James Black Glenesk, 2990167
SMITH, L/Cpl, John, 2979459
SNADDON, Pte, John Mitchell, 2982004
SOMERVILLE, Pte, James, 2974437
STEELE, C/Sjt, Ronald, 4124675
STEVEN, Pte, David, 2979853
STEVENSON, Pte, William, 2979567
STEVENSON, Pte, William, 2987224
STEWART, L/Cpl, Patrick, 2979752
STEWART, Lt, Alexander Balfour, 137943
STEWART, Lt, Neil, 67574
STEWART, Pte, James, 2979263

SUTHERLAND, Sjt, George, 5567203
TAYLOR, 2/lt, George Donald, 279794
TAYLOR, Pte, Reginald Edward (MM), 2966508
TENNANT, Pte, Thomas Joseph, 3322898
THOMPSON, L/Cpl, Joseph, 2986576
THOMPSON, Pte, Samuel, 2981450
THOMPSON, Cpl, Robert, 2979555
THOMPSON, Piper, Robert, 2977308
THOMSON, Pte, James, 2979831
TINDALL, Pte, Dennis, 3322904
TODD, Pte, John, 2978030
TRAIL, Pte, George, 2979849
TRENCH, Pte, John Percival, 3322905
TURNER, Caps, Timothy, 175540
WAKENSHAW, Pte, Thomas Edward, 3322908
WALFORD, Pte, Walter, 3322909
WALKER, Pte, James, 2976557
WALKER, Pte, Alexander Campbell, 332700
WARDLE, L/Cpl, Henry, 3318945
WARNER, Pte, Joseph Albert, 2978966
WATSON, Pte, Edward Starr, 3322913
WATT, Cpl, James, 2977566
WATT, L/Cpl, George, 2979971
WESTHEAD, Pte, Edward, 2970010
WHITE, Cpl, Harry Ezra, 2982098
WILKIE, Lt, Arthur Digbie, 113423
WILLIAMSON, Pte, James, 2979038
WILSON, Pte, Charles William, 3322920
WILSON, Bdsmn, David, 2979166
WILSON, L/Cpl, Samuel Douglas, 2982154
WYNN, Pte, Albert Heffie, 2982032
YOUNG, Sjt, James, 2977548

ARMY CATERING CORPS
BARBER, Pte, Alfred Thomas, 10630599
BOURNE, Pte, Walter Joseph, 10630007
BURDEN, Sjt, Charles Walter, 5933116
CARTER, Pte, Harry, 10631243
CLUCAS, Pte, Stanley, 10631920
COSGROVE, Pte, William James, 10630241
CROW, Pte, William Stanley, 10630780
CUMMINGS, Cpl, John, 3855799
DANIELS, Pte, Peter, 10631347
DYBLE, Pte, Charles Edward, 5774681
EDGE, Cpl, Thomas William, 40970747
GOOCH, Sjt, George Harold Albert, 5827343
GOODLIFF, Pte, Kenneth Edward, 1107747
GRIFFITHS, Pte, Leslie George, 10630017
HIBBITT, Gnr, Stanley, 5932888
HODGES, Pte, Frederick, 4805361
HOULDSWORTH, Sjt, James Howitt, 7627524
KING, Pte, Alfred, 4807306
LEWIS, Pte, Thomas Ronald John, 10631902
McMEEKIN, Pte, William Gable, 241080
PARSONS, Pte, Sidney, 1063190
POINTER, Pte, Lyndo Cecil, 5778260
RAVDEN, Pte, Conrad, 6020994
RENNIE, Pte, Alexander, 14364524
ROWNEY, Cpl, James, 5828598
SADLER, Pte, John Thomas, 2120175
SCARLETT, Pte, Albert, 4756468
SMITH, Sjt, Walter, 5945931
SMITH, Cpl, Geoorge Edward, 4274102
SQUIRES, Pte, John Daniel, 5827790
WINSBURY, Pte, Ronald Victor, 5730254
WOOD, Sjt, William, 5946198
WOOLNER, Pte, William, 5824779

BEDFORDSHIRE & HERTFORDSHIRE REGIMENT
ABSON, Pte, James William, 5950963

AINSWORTH, Sjt, Francis Ernest, 5950225
ANGELL, Pte, Leslie Victor, 5951842
ANGELL, Pte, David Morrison, 5952585
AUGER, Pte, Donald Henry, 5956214
AUSTIN, Pte, Albert James, 5950688
AVEY, L/Cpl, Eric Leslie, 5951963
BAGSHAW, C/Sjt, Henry Arthur, 5952756
BALL, Pte, Kenneth Owen, 2210825
BAMBRIDGE, Pte, Albert Stanley, 5950134
BAMSEY, Pte, Philip Henry, 5956170
BARDEL, L/Cpl, Arthur Henry, 5953335
BARKER, Pte, Frederick Horace, 5950218
BARKER, Pte, Frederick Arthur, 5949335
BARNARD, Pte, Stanley Charles, 5945846
BARTLETT, Pte, Alex, 5951312
BEADLE, Pte, James George, 5958718
BELL, Pte, Arthur Herbert, 5952687
BIGGS, L/Cpl, Edward Cornelius, 5951821
BIGGS, Pte, Robert Dobson, 5933195
BILLING, Pte, Edward Michael, 5949374
BIRCH, Pte, Charles Arthur, 5952696
BIVANS, Pte, Robert Storey, 5950368
BLOSS, Sjt, George, 5946345
BLOUNT, Pte, Edgar Oswald, 5949518
BLOXHA, Pte, Jack Albert, 5956226
BLYTH, Pte, Reginald George, 5952598
BOND, Pte, John, 5952560
BOZIER, Pte, William David, 5956240
BRACE, Pte, Henry Terance, 5951917
BRANT, Pte, Alfred John, 5959184
BRAY, Pte, Frederick James, 5956235
BRAYSHER, Pte, Albert Frederick, 5956849
BRIGHTMAN, Pte, Arthur Charles, 5952642
BRUCE, Pte, Edward Ernest Henry (MID), 5952603
BURCH, Pte, James Oliver Robert, 5951789
BURNAGE, Pte, Sidney George, 5951948
BURNS, Pte, William Parker, 5952703
BURS, Pte, Thomas Arthur, 5952179
BUSH, Pte, James John, 5951971
CALLEWAERT, Pte, Albert Louis, 5951972
CANNON, Pte, Harry Morgan, 5956256
CARRUTHERS, Pte, Leslie Gordon, 5952707
CARTER, Pte, John Douglas Haig, 5950867
CATLIN, Pte, Horace Arthur, 5955758
CATO, Pte, Frederick George Bert, 5952182
CATTERALL, Pte, John, 5952645
CATTERALL, Pte, Albert, 5956862
CAWTHORNE, Pte, Maurice, 5952722
CHAMBERLAIN, Pte, Ernest John, 5955761
CHAMBERS, Pte, Arthur Edward, 5953208
CHAMMINGS, Pte, George Harold, 6024272
CHERRY, Pte, Frank Dennis, 5951349
CHORLTON, Pte, Geoffrey, 5955225
CLARK, Pte, Herbert Charles, 5950056
CLARK, L/Cpl, Reginald, 5951193
CLARKE, Pte, Sidney Melville, 5956259
CLARKE, Pte, Frederick William Henry, 5950198
CLARKE, Pte, John Herbert, 5953024
COATH, Cpl, Reginald France, 5953025
COCKBURN, Pte, Francis William, 5950050
COLE, Pte, Walter Henry, 5952616
COLE, Pte, Ephraim, 5956609
COLLIER, Pte, James, 5955776
COLLINGRIDGE, L/Sjt, Ralph Frederick, 5947372
COLLINS, Pte, Joshua Louis, 5955777
COLLISON, Pte, Dennis Jack, 5955778
COOK, Pte, Alfred, 5950460
COOMBS, Pte, Stanley Herbert, 5953030
COOPER, Pte, Sydney George, 5956613
COX, Pte, Robert Henry, 5953032

COX, Pte, Reginald Thomas, 5951976
COX, Pte, Herbert Walter, 6004971
CRANE, Pte, Leslie Kenneth, 5950719
CRAWLEY, Pte, Albert Edward, 5951900
CRAWLEY, Pte, Francis William, 5952518
CRAWLEY, Pte, Lloyd George, 5951123
CRAXFORD, Pte, William George, 5951977
CROSS, Pte, Albert Edward, 5950980
DARCH, Pte, Arthur, 5953037
DAVIES, Pte, Frank Percy, 5950521
DEAN, Pte, Harry H.C., 5956263
DENTON, Pte, Angus MACdonald, 5956619
DIMMOCK, Pte, John Frederick, 5950551
DINES, Pte, Albert Edward, 5955494
DIPROSE, Pte, Percy Douglas, 5952710
DONOVAN, Pte, Philip James, 5950041
DUNBABIN, Pte, James, 5956262
DUNHAM, Pte, Oliver Charles, 5951044
EDWARDS, Pte, Frank Walter, 5953045
EMERTON, Pte, Herbert, 5951983
EVANS, Pte, Stanley, 5951363
FAGG, Pte, William Patrick, 5955547
FAIRMAN, Pte, Basil Lionel, 5989739
FARINGTON, Pte, Ernest Leonard, 5953050
FARMER, Pte, Arthur Eric, 5949162
FARNHAM, Pte, Harold.J., 5956269
FAUGNAN, Pte, Thomas, 5953051
FENSOME, Pte, Claude, 5955321
FINEGAN, Pte, Leslie Frederick, 5953052
FISHER, Pte, Harry John, 5951092
FLOYD, Pte, Joseph Edward, 5955645
FOLEY, Pte, Henry Charles, 5950973
FORD, Pte, John, 5955554
FRANKLIN, Pte, John Daniel, 5953055
FREE, Pte, Leonard, 5955557
FREEMAN, Pte, Philip John, 5956273
FREEMAN, Pte, Jack, 5956968
FULFORD, Pte, Ernest John, 5950602
FULLER, Pte, Almond Herbert, 5956270
GAME, Pte, Joseph, 5951987
GARDNER, Pte, John Thomas, 5949707
GAYLER, Cpl, Edward Frederick, 5951112
GEARY, Pte, Leonard, 5955559
GEEVES, Pte, Harold Frank, 5953058
GEORGE, Cpl, Frederick, 5955560
GILCHRIST, Pte, David James, 5952926
GILFILLAN, Pte, Albert, 5950596
GOMME, Pte, John Edward, 5956283
GOOCH, Pte, Granville Stewart, 5950172
GOODE, Pte, Leslie George, 595564
GOODE, Pte, Leonard Francis, 5950332
GOODWIN, Cpl, Charles William, 5945810
GOODY, Pte, Reginald, 5960329
GRAY, Cpl, Ronald, 5950488
GRAY, L/Cpl, Ralph Ford, 5951682
GREEN, Cpl, Cyril, 5953352
GURNEY, Pte, Leonard Ralph, 5955570
GURNEY, Pte, Francis George, 5951376
HALE, Pte, Frederick George, 5951764
HALL, Pte, Reginald William, 5950230
HALL, 2/lt, Frank, 156326
HAND, Pte, Walter Frederick William, 5956299
HANLON, Pte, Patrick, 5950453
HARPER, Pte, Ronald Alexander, 5951991
HARRIS, O Pte, Walter Colin, 5950327
HARRIS, Pte, Leonard Henry, 5953071
HARVEY, Pte, Charles Henry, 5950975
HAWES, Cpl, Horace Edgar, 5950421
HAYES, Pte, Philip Radford, 5956293
HAYSMAN, Pte, Donald, 5955578

HEALEY, Pte, Thomas Francis, 5949809
HEDLEY, Cpl, Joseph, 5951384
HEWITT, Pte, William Frank, 5956982
HIGH, Pte, Harold William Struthers, 5951830
HOLDEN, Pte, Jack Percy, 5955585
HOLLIER, Pte, Francis Edward, 5951387
HOLLIMAN, Pte, Ernest Charles, 5959068
HOLLYLEE, Cpl, Arthur Frederick, 5951315
HORNETT, Cpl, James Benjamin, 5951995
HORNSBY, Cpl, Leslie Charles, 5949698
HOWARD, Pte, Arthur Leonard, 5955273
HULL, Pte, Jack, 5956291
HUMPHREY, Pte, Frederick William, 5951388
HUMPHREYS, Pte, Andrew, 5950575
INGRAM, Pte, Robert William, 5949245
IRONS, Pte, William Charles Alfred, 5953090
IVES, Pte, Raymond Henry, 5955606
IZZARD, Pte, Cecil William, 5949582
JACKSON, Lt, Donald Harry, 113468
JARVIS, Pte, Robert, 5956643
JENKINS, Pte, Ernest Cairo, 5951998
JOHNSON, Pte, Alfred, 5950957
JOHNSON, Sjt, Arthur Charles Frederick, 5952942
JONES, Pte, Alfred William, 5953644
KNIGHT, L/Cpl, Albert Ernest, 5951392
KNIGHT, Pte, Dennis Frederick, 5955139
LANE, Pte, Charles Thomas, 5952653
LANE, Pte, Alfred George, 5949684
LANGSTON, Sjt, Frederick Arthur, 5946227
LARGE, Pte, George Edward, 5950136
LAWRENCE, Pte, Victor Albert, 5954689
LEE, Pte, Thomas John, 5953106
LEWIN, Cpl, John, 5952004
LOSS, Pte, Horace, 5959012
MADDAMS, Pte, Percy Richard, 5955490
MANNALL, Pte, Albert Leslie, 5950591
MAPLEY, Gnr, Jack William, 5950730
MARKS, Pte, George Edward, 5959250
MARTIN, Pte, Leonard, 5950987
MARTIN, Pte, Percy Robert, 5953113
MAYNE, Pte, Frank, 5942925
MILLS, Pte, Harry, 5959684
MILTON, Pte, Henry William, 5955144
MOORBY, Pte, Albert Charles, 5950944
MUMFORD, Pte, Sidney Claude, 5822243
NASH, Pte, John James, 5951398
NEWELL, Pte, Edgar Herbert, 5959689
NORMAN, L/Cpl, Gerald Herbert, 5952006
NORTON, Pte, Thomas William, 5953124
O'CONNOR, Pte, Patrick Bernard, 5950607
O'DEL, L/Cpl, Eric George, 5949716
ONOIONE, Pte, Frederick, 5950468
OWEN, Sjt, Leonard, 5947386
PAGE, Pte, Albert Charles, 5952654
PARKER, Pte, Victor George, 5951254
PARROTT, Cpl, Leslie Joseph, 5950109
PATTERSON, Pte, Kenneth, 5953129
PAYNE, Pte, Stanley John, 5952345
PEASNELL, Pte, William Wickham Frederick, 5951403
PERKINS, Pte, Frederick W, 5947537
PERRY, Pte, Malcolm Alan, 5950095
PERRYMAN, L/Sjt, Ernest, 5951407
PETTIT, Pte, Edmund John, 5949064
PHAIR, Pte, Sidney Alfred, 5950016
PHILLIPS, Pte, Kenneth William, 5953131
PLUM, Pte, Albert George Horace James, 5950318
POPE, Pte, David George, 5955317
PRIOR, Pte, Joseph George, 5950196
PURSER, Pte, Frank Arthur, 2201226
PYCOCK, Sjt, Alfred Leslie, 5950736

QUANTRELL, Pte, Walter Henry, 5947770
QUENBY, L/Cpl, Richard, 5950023
RABONE, Pte, Thomas, 5956692
RACKLEY, Pte, Ernest Arthur Cyril, 5952010
RAINBIRD, Pte, Leslie Ernest, 5950117
RAYMENT, Pte, Harold Edward, 5952550
RICHARDSON, Pte, William Dennis, 5952012
RICHARDSON, Cqms, Stephen Lionel, 5946061
ROBERTS, Pte, Joseph William, 5950954
ROBINSON, Cpl, Ernest Alfred, 5948397
ROBINSON, L/Cpl, Wardle Hunter, 5951409
ROBINSON, Pte, Frederick Joseph, 5947992
ROGERS, Cpl, Norman Cecil Owen, 5950175
ROLPH, Pte, Edward Samuel, 5945933
ROLPH, Pte, Douglas Frederick, 5989149
SAUNDERS, Pte, Charles, 5951943
SAVAGE, Pte, James Henry, 5949707
SCHOLES, Pte, Jack, 329890
SCRUTTON, Pte, Donald Frank, 5951961
SEAR, Pte, James Theodore, 5953151
SEL, L/Cpl, Frederick William, 5952485
SLADEN, Capt, Ugh Frederick Lambart, 95259
SLINGO, Pte, Frank Edward, 5944178
SMITH, Pte, William Finlay George, 6024448
SMITH, Pte, John William, 5952950
SMITH, L/L/Cpl, Ernest James, 5956377
SMITH, Pte, Ralph Charles Sidney, 5953160
SMITH, Pte, John William, 5952950
SMITH, Pte, John, 5951935
SMY, Pte, Walter George, 5951937
SPAVINS, Pte, Ronald Ernest, 5951415
STAR, 2/lt, Glyn Whinthorpe, 164528
STEPHENSON, Pte, George, 5955748
STOKES, Pte, Frederick Charles, 5952018
STONTON, Pte, Frank Ernest, 5952285
TAYLOR, Pte, Ronald, 5950343
THEWLES, Lt, William Edmond, 89982
THODY, Cpl, John Thomas, 5952663
THOMPSON, Sjt, William Henry, 5947983
THRUSSELL, Capt, Stanley Hector, 117082
THURSTON, Pte, Arthur John, 5946540
TIMPSON, Pte, Reginald James, 5951723
TOBIN, Pte, James Francis, 5960212
TOMLINSON, Pte, Francis Edward, 5953170
TURNEY, Pte, Edgar Harold, 5953172
WADE, Pte, Ronald Joseph, 5346830
WALKER, Pte, Geoffrey William, 5952667
WATTS, Pte, Thomas George, 5950170
WELHAM, Sjt, Robert Ernest, 5946692
WELLS, Maj, Thomas Capper, 63949
WHITBREAD, Pte, Henry John, 5944175
WHITE, Pte, Walter, 5952635
WHITE, Pte, Sidney, 5952577
WHITEHEAD, Pte, Stanley Gordon Richard, 5951416
WICKENS, Pte, Charles, 5953184
WILDER, Pte, John George, 5955651
WILDMAN, Pte, Maurice Arthur, 5951421
WILES, Pte, Edward Claud, 5950044
WILLETT, Pte, Arthur Daniel, 5955656
WILLEY, Pte, Stanley, 5953196
WILLIAMS, Pte, Richard Ernest, 5955661
WILLIAMS, Pte, Albert Walter, 5952302
WILLIAMS, Pte, George, 5955659
WILLOUGHBY, Pte, Albert William, 5956749
WILLSHER, Pte, Thomas Hnery, 5955166
WILSON, Pte, Gerald Edmund Peter, 5952669
WILSON, Pte, Henry, 5955670
WILTON, Cpl, Lawrence, 5951422
WINFIELD, Pte, Eric Walter, 5951256
WINSTANLEY, Pte, John Edmund Peter, 5955679

WINTER, Pte, Henry William, 5955682
WINUP, Pte, Thomas, 5955678
WORSTER, Pte, Frederick Henry, 5955695
WRIGHT, Sjt, William, 5946307
WRIGHT, Pte, Reuben Albert, 5947588
YIRRELL, Pte, Bertram Robert, 5955705
YORK, Cpl, David L George, 5952672
YOUNG, Cpl, Richard, 5956407
YOUNG, Pte, Benjamin Frank, 5959743
YOUNG, Pte, Owen Arthur, 5953194

BLACK WATCH REGIMENT
EDNIE,Sub Cndr,James,2750057
JONES,Maj,F.,314355

BRITISH SPECIAL FORCES
GORDON,Capt,Roderick
REGAN,Capt,E.
WRIGHT,Capt,Herbert Charles

BORDER REGIMENT
PONTON,Sjt,Clarence Sidney,3597112
MONAN,Pte,John,3596802
NEW,Sjt,Jack,3606747

CAMBRIDGESHIRE REGIMENT
1 BATTALION
ANDERS,Pte,Norman,5827486
ANDREWS,Pte,Cyril,2933303
ANGEL,L/Cpl,Alexander,5933249
ASHMAN,Cpl,Stanley Geoffrey,5832444
AUSTIN,Sjt,Reginald George Cecil,5933178
AUSTIN,Pte,Vernon Clifford,5832447
AVERY,Pte,Frederick William,6018844
BABER,Lt,Anthony Hugh,140668
BACON,Pte,Leslie Bernard,5833215
BAILEY,Pte,Eddie,5834028
BAKER,Pte,William,5830861
BAKER,L/Cpl,Eric Gordon,5933206
BALDWIN,Pte,Arthur William,5933345
BARBER,Pte,Kenneth Charles,5827319
BARFORD,Pte,Sidney William,5833765
BARLOW,Pte,Arthur Charles,5823535
BATCHELER,Pte,Arthur George,6019489
BATEMAN,Pte,Horace Frederick,5933522
BAXTER,Pte,Albert Edward,5831163
BEARD,Pte,Ernest Albert,6028781
BELL,Pte,Richard Lionel,5932549
BENNETT,Pte,Franklin James,5932687
BETSON,Pte,Harry Walter,593239
BIGGS,Pte,Sidney George,5933200
BIGMORE,Lt,John,145394
BLACKMAN,Pte,John Henry,6018661
BRADFORD,Pte,Charles Victor,5836514
BROWN,Pte,Sidney Herbert Anthony,6019089
BROWN,Pte,Edmund John,5831167
BROWNE,Pte,Albert Wilfred Edward,5933565
BUNCE,L/Cpl,Charles Ernest,5832498
BURGE,Pte,James Henry,6019362
BURRELL,Sjt,Leonard George,6020827
BURROWS,Pte,Albert Erthur,6020335
BUSSEY,L/Cpl,Alec George,5832504
BUTCHER,Sjt,Frederick Ernest Charles,5933377
BUTLER,Pte,Maurice Henry,5832941
CADE,Pte,Harold Ronald Hill,5933453
CANN,Pte,Reginald,5933320
CANT,Csm,Alfred,5823144
CARLETON,Pte,Arthur William,5932864
CARTER,Pte,Arthur Edward,5931752
CARTER,L/Cpl,John,6019360

CARTER,Pte,Charles Raymond,5933312
CASTLE,Pte,R.F.J.,5959192
CATHERSIDES,Pte,George William,6019316
CHAMBERS,Pte,Berie Charles,6019093
CHAPMAN,Pte,Claude Alfred,5836250
CHAPMAN,Pte,Peter,5836251
CHURCH,Pte,Kenneth Sidney James,5827913
CLARK,2/lt,William Henry,197126
CLARK,Pte,Edward Phelps,6018692
CLARK,Pte,Jack,5832524
CLARK,Pte,Albert,5933436
CLARKE,Pte,John Alfred,5832527
COCKERTON,Sjt,John Harry,5932914
CODLING,Pte,Thomas Edward,5832534
COHAM,Pte,Arscott,6019063
COLE,Pte,Ernest Harry,5933318
COLEBY,Pte,Arthur Hector,1803927
COLLINS,Pte,Charles James,5831740
COOK,Pte,Walter,5933278
COOMES,Pte,Reginald,6018876
COOPER,Pte,Alfred John,6028811
COOTE,Pte,Charles Victor,5832401
CORNWELL,Pte,Willie George,5933481
COUSINS,Pte,Harold Robert,5830341
COWLING,Pte,William John,6020843
CRABB,Pte,Christopher Alfred,5933786
CRAGG,Pte,Wilfred,6013855
CULLIFORD,Pte,Arthur Stanley,6020849
CUNNINGHAM,Pte,James Henry,5830343
CUSTERSON,Pte,Norman Charles,5933218
CUTTING,L/Cpl,Ernest Phillip,5832552
DARLOW,Lt,Kenneth Owen,134198
DAY,Cpl,George Daniel,5823645
DEFEW,L/Sjt,Reginald Edmund,5832558
DESBOROUGH,Cpl,Douglas Arthur,5933216
DREW,Pte,John Henry,5828930
EARP,Pte,John Henry,4805336
EDGLEY,Pte,Alfred,5932931
EDWARDS,Pte,Maurice Francis,5933141
ELDRED,Pte,Ernest John,5832572
ELMER,Pte,Sidney John Herbert,5832576
ELVIDGE,Pte,Gordon Frank,5832577
EUSDEN,Sjt,Harold James,5932258
EYLAND,Sjt,Kenneth Robert,6020863
FAIRCLIFF,Pte,William,5932727
FIDDAMAN,Pte,Reginald Thomas,5833690
FITZPATRICK,Pte,Thomas James,5933430
FORSDIKE,Pte,Reginald Harry,5833565
FORTUNE,Pte,Eric James,6921090
FREEMAN,Pte,Henry,6019104
FRENCH,Pte,Harold Edward,5933185
FULLER,Pte,Frederick William,5832598
FULLER,Pte,Reginald,5932654
FUSSEY,Pte,Richard William,5933317
GADSBY,Pte,Cyril Frank,5832599
GARNER,Pte,Charles,6020874
GARNER,Pte,Alfred Charles,5827518
GATES,Pte,Douglas Graham,5933156
GIBBONS,Pte,Frederick George Harry,6020878
GIBBS,Pte,Cecil John,5832298
GIL,L/Cpl,Charles Henry,5824245
GLADWELL,Sjt,Arthur John,593322
GODDARD,Pte,Gerald,5827286
GORHAM,Pte,Frederick Charles,5834374
GRACE,Pte,Henry,5833574
GRANT,L/Cpl,Frederick Arthur,5832618
GREEN,Cqms,William Charles,5931516
HALE,Pte,Harry,5836037
HALES,Pte,John William,6019108
HALL,Pte,Ernest John,5827496

HARD,Pte,Douglas George,5828901
HARDY,Pte,William Harold,5933114
HARROLD,Pte,Clarence Henry,6019111
HARVEY,Pte,Reginald Richard William,6019449
HASKINS,Cpl,James Archie Phelps,5933079
HAWKINS,Pte,Edward Leonard,6020896
HAYLOCK,Pte,Edward Victor John,5933427
HAYNES,Pte,Leonard Herbert,5933204
HAYNES,Pte,Leonard Herbert,5933204
HAYWARD,Pte,William Douglas,5828919
HAZELL,Pte,Alan Wentworth,5933308
HAZELL,Pte,John William,6019389
HEFFER,Pte,Arthur George,5933192
HENSBY,Pte,Arthur John,5829893
HIGH,Pte,Alfred John,5933146
HINES,Pte,Charles Alfred,6019391
HITCH,Pte,Edwin John,5933699
HITCH,Pte,Edwin John,5933699
HOCKEY,Capt,Frank Spencer,79055
HOLDER,Pte,Charles Allan,5933435
HOLMES,Pte,Albert William,6028817
HOLYHEAD,Sjt,William,5830805
HONEYBUN,Pte,William George,5932570
HORTON,Pte,Harry,5830768
HOWARD,L/Cpl,Paul Arthur,6018796
HOWE,Pte,Herbert,5830398
HOWLETT,L/Cpl,Edward John,6019464
HUGGET,Pte,Arthur John,5835987
HUNT,Pte,Robert Algar,5933373
HUNT,Pte,Albert Edward,6020910
INWARDS,Pte,Harold,5831213
JACOBS,Pte,Leslie Robert,5933766
JAKES,Pte,George Walter James,55933691
JAMES,Pte,Basil,5830872
JENKINSON,Pte,Stanley,5830405
JOLLEY,Sjt,John Arthur,5933199
JORDON,Pte,Albert Leslie,6020922
KERRY,Pte,Walter Frederick,5932743
KIDD,R/s/m,John,5821508
KIDMAN,Pte,Arthur Mitchell,593322
KING,Pte,Charles Robert,5833717
KIRKPATRICK,Pte,Greig James,5933202
KNIGHT,Pte,Herbert Basil,5933450
KNIGHT,L/Sjt,Eric,5830969
LAMBETH,Pte,Albert Ernest,5832687
LAMMIN,Pte,Charles Henry,6020935
LANE,Pte,Arthur Cyril,6028766
LEWIS,Pte,George,6028641
LONG,Pte,Harry George,6019122
MALSTER,Pte,John,5833838
MAPPLEDORAM,Cpl,Herbert,5933601
MARLOW,Pte,Alfred John,5835594
MARSHALL,Pte,Alan Raymond,5828898
MARTIN,Pte,Archibald Derrick,5933325
MILES,Pte,Henry Charles,6028768
MILES,Cpl,Douglas George,5933152
MILLS,Pte,Frederick William,5836430
MOORE,Pte,Cyril John,6023019
MORTLOCK,Pte,Alexander Sidney,5932165
MOSELEY,Cpl,Gordon Peace,5932689
MOULE,Pte,Henry Alfred Thomas,5933503
NEVILLE,Pte,Edmund Charles,5829992
NEW,L/Cpl,Frederick William,6019410
NEWBURY,Pte,William James,6019342
NEWMAN,Cpl,Frederick John,5931744
NEWSON,Capt,Jack Frank,124559
NEWTON,Pte,Stanley,5824645
NICHOLLS,Pte,Thomas George,5933561
NICKEL,Pte,Jack Edward,5933611
NORTON,L/Cpl,Reginald,5933336

NUNN,Cpl,Benjamin Charles,5879974
O'BRIEN,L/Cpl,John,6020968
OSBORNE,Pte,Leslie George,6019412
PAGE,L/Cpl,Horace Obed,5932799
PALMER,Sjt,Jack,5825689
PALMER,Pte,Eric William,5836264
PARR,Pte,Walter Frederick,5932625
PARSON,Pte,Eric Robert,5831654
PATRICK,Pte,Alec Bromley,6019310
PATTERSON,Pte,James,6028622
PATTLE,Cpl,Henry Tee,5948798
PAUL,Pte,Alfred Russel,5827869
PAYNE,Pte,Ronald Robert Owen,5932755
PEACH,Pte,Stanley Frederick,5836413
PERROTT,Pte,Arthur Laslie,5830465
PETO,Pte,Fredeick,6018836
PETTICAN,Pte,Albert Victor,3835569
PICTON,Pte,Stanley,5833625
PIKE,L/Sjt,Albert John,6019132
PILCHER,L/Cpl,Victor,5933180
PIPE,Pte,Alfred George,5835530
PLUMB,Pte,Robert George,5933102
PORTER,Cpl,Ernest,5932802
POTKINS,Pte,Philip Frederick,5836134
PRIDE,Pte,William Arthur,6028911
RAMSCAR,Pte,James Edward,6019448
RANDLE,Pte,Leonard William,5832219
REDFERN,Pte,Bernard,6018580
REEVE,L/Sjt,William Henry,6020997
RICE,Pte,John William,5932777
RIDDALL,Pte,Charles Douglas,6019418
RITCHIE,Pte,Douglas Alfred,6019346
RIVERS,L/Cpl,Bertram Albert,5830790
ROBINSON,Pte,Jack,5827748
ROSE,Pte,Philip,6019444
ROUMANIA,Pte,Abraham,6028772
RUSE,Cpl,Bernard Henry,5933708
RUSHBROOK,Pte,Edwin,5933526
RUST,Pte,Maurice Charles,5833347
RUTTERFORD,Pte,Stanley Oliver,5933356
SAMPLE,Pte,Peter Weston,7891426
SAYER,L/Cpl,George Arthur,5933052
SCOTCHER,Pte,William Herbert,5831570
SCOTT,Pte,Sidney,5833644
SEAMARK,Pte,Frederick Charles,5933830
SIMPER,Pte,John Arthur,5827625
SIMS,Pte,John Thomas,6028774
SINGLETON,Pte,Joseph Wilfred,6028971
SMITH,Pte,Sidney George,5830692
SMITH,Pte,Ronald Francis Samson,6020082
SPALDING,Cpl,George A,5828904
STAGG,Pte,George,5932638
STEARN,Pte,George Lester John,5933423
STOCK,Pte,Ernest Edward,5933186
STONEHAM,Pte,Robert Alfred,6019463
STUBBERFIELD,Cpl,Ronald Frederick,6021034
STURT,Pte,Herbert Henry,5824240
SWANN,Pte,Charles William,5933370
TAYLOR,Lt,Orton Sidney,72543
TAYLOR,Pte,Ernest John,6028688
THAXTER,Pte,Christopher Harry,5932803
THOMPSON,Pte,George William,5833660
THOMPSON,Pte,Alec George,5827755
THOMPSON,Pte,Frederick William,6019487
THURGOOD,Pte,Frank John,5933078
TIMBRELL,Pte,Edward George,6028777
TINKLER,Pte,Owen,5827756
TOFTS,Sjt,Sidney Alfred,5933276
TUCKETT,Pte,Neville,6018901
TWINN,Pte,Charles Henry,T/71373

UNWIN,Pte,Sidney John,5933281
VENN,Pte,Vincent Stanley,5830532
WADE,Sjt,William,5932683
WAKEFIELD,Pte,Reginald William,5828912
WALKER,Pte,James Alfred Pratt,5832842
WALLACE,Pte,William Henry,6019309
WALLIS,Pte,Kenneth James,5933310
WATLING,Cqms,Herbert,5825850
WATTS,Pte,Rovbert Andrew,5933842
WATTS,Pte,Arthur Leslie,5836425
WATTS,Pte,Reginald Charles,6029064
WEATHERHILL,Pte,Walter Ernest,13020461
WELCH,Pte,Wiliam Henry,5830846
WELLING,Cpl,Walter William Sidney,6019435
WESTMORELAND,Pte,Eric,5833672
WESTON,L/Cpl,Herbert Edward,6028840
WHINNEY,Pte,Benjamin John,5834837
WHITELEY,Pte,Samuel Wilfred,5933027
WILLCOX,Pte,Harold Morgan,5833208
WILLIAMS,L/Cpl,Richard Henry,5933407
WILLIS,Pte,Henry George William,5828890
WILSON,Pte,George,5833677
WILSON,Sjt,Victor William,5828907
WILSON,Pte,William,5932641
WILSON,Pte,Eric Arthur,5827760
WISEMAN,Pte,Archibald Henry,5932678
WOOD,L/Cpl,William George,5827494
WORSLEY,Pte,George William,5832341
WRIGHT,Pte,George,5933266
WRIGHT,Pte,Maurice Harry,5933274
WRIGHT,Pte,Thomas Arthur,5933267

CAMBRIDGESHIRE REGIMENT
2 BATTALION
ABRAHAM, Cpl, George Frederick, 5828856
ALLGOOD, Pte, Donald, 5933499
ALLISTON, Pte, Augustino, 810994
ALNUTT, Pte, Frederick George Mathews, 5833498
ANSELL, Pte, Noah, 5832439
ARMSTRONG, Pte, Albert Edward, 5933891
ARNOLD, Pte, Richard, 5828849
ASPLIN, Pte, Charles Harry, 5832911
AUKER, Pte, Leslie Wilfred Thomas, 5832445
AYLOTT, Pte, Edward John, 5828883
BAKER, Pte, George William, 5833216
BALDWIN, Pte, Roy Thomas, 5833680
BARRETT, Pte, Arthur Alfred, 5933572
BARTON, Pte, Herbert John, 5833510
BAXTER, Pte, Charles Henry, 5829685
BAXTER, Pte, George, 5833770
BEDFORD, L/Cpl, Jack, 5882886
BEDFORD, Pte, Sidney, 5827413
BELL, Pte, Jackson, 5833771
BENNETT, Pte, Albert Dennis, 5933613
BENSLEY, Pte, Charles Verdan, 5932918
BENSLEY, Cpl, Bert, 5933894
BILEY, Pte, Jack, 5831140
BIRD, Pte, Daniel Albert, 5832477
BISHOP, Pte, William Edward Thomas, 6018965
BLOCK, Pte, Robert Stanley, 5831079
BLOOMFIELD, Pte, Charles Henry, 5933123
BLOWS, Pte, Albert Edward, 5830164
BLUNDEN, Pte, George Percy, 2926658
BREMNER, Pte, James, 5832489
BRIARS, Pte, Ronald Albert, 5833520
BRITTON, Pte, Arnold, 5933727
BROWN, Pte, William, 5833524
BROWN, Pte, Arthur William, 5932903
BROWN, Pte, William Henry, 5933490
BRUCE, Pte, George James, 5833526

BRUNDISH, Pte, Donald Eustace, 5829675
BUCK, Pte, George Arthur, 5832495
BUCKLE, Pte, Harry James, 5831132
BUNKALL, Pte, John Allen, 5775494
BUNNING, Cpl, Stanley Traylen, 5933875
BURBRIDGE, Pte, James William, 5933569
BURDER, Pte, Robert George, 5833779
BURKETT, L/Sjt, George Alfred, 5933705
BURLES, Pte, Archibald Albert, 5828820
BURRELL, Pte, Walter Edward, 5933591
BURRIDGE, Pte, Edward Alfred James, 5831147
BURROUGHS, Pte, George Ralph, 5831168
BURTON, Pte, James Henry, 5932674
BUTLER, Pte, Leonard Frank, 6013892
BUTTLE, Pte, Clifford William, 5831149
BYATT, Pte, Harold .A., 5836249
BYFORD, Pte, Victor William, 5827585
BYRNE, Pte, Vincent, 5836289
CALDECOAT, Pte, Ernest George, 5933558
CAMP, Pte, William David, 5835466
CARROLL, Pte, Thomas, 13020076
CARTER, Pte, Alfred Roland, 5933760
CATCHPOLE, Pte, Alfred Edward, 6204699
CHAMBERS, Pte, Leslie Charles, 5832948
CHESTER, Pte, Walter, 5933187
CHIVERS, Lt, Hugh John, 90415
CLARY, Sjt, Cecil Francis, 5933560
CLAYTON, Pte, Bertram, 5835470
CLOVES, Pte, George Ernest, 6020838
CONE, Pte, Percy, 5932493
CORNISH, Pte, Ernest George, 5831159
COX, Pte, John Edward, 5933684
COX, Pte, Leslie George, 5932982
COX, Pte, Sidney Ronald, 5933512
CROWSON, Pte, Christopher William, 5933728
CROWSON, Pte, Ronald, 5933738
CUDWORTH, Cpl, Leslie Charles, 5827926
CURTIS, Pte, George Arthur, 5933072
CUTLACK, Capt, Cecil William Robin, 78249
DALE, Pte, John Thomas, 5933042
DANNATT, L/Cpl, Kenneth Edward, 5933677
DAVIES, Pte, Robert Griffith, 5933768
DAWSON, Pte, Ronald Ash, 5933817
DENTON, Pte, Walter William, 5834256
DERSLEY, Pte, Charles Harry, 5831108
DIXON, Sjt, Herbert Thomas, 5933669
DOUTHWAITE, Lt, Arthur James Percy, 124451
DUDMAN, Pte, Herbert, 6028783
DUGGAN, Pte, Charles Albert, 5830936
DUMPLETON, L/Cpl, John Stephen, 5831195
DUNLOP, L/Sjt, James Gordon, 5933752
DURRANT, Qms, Edward, 5819377
EASTWOOD, Pte, George Douglas, 5831035
ELL, L/Cpl, Gordon Hubert, 5828844
ELLIOT, Pte, Robert, 4803638
ELSAGOOD, Pte, George Henry Richard, 5932821
ENNION, Capt, Thomas Richard, 90445
EVERARD, Sjt, John William, 5933819
FISHER, Pte, Donald, 5933486
FOSTER, Pte, Thomas, 5829955
FOULGER, Pte, Neville, 5836252
FOUNTAIN, Pte, Frederick, 5835493
FRANCIS, Pte, Russell Bernard, 5827947
FROST, Pte, Cyril Thomas, 5832990
FRUSHER, Cpl, Gerald, 5933737
FULBROOK, Pte, Edwin James, 5830195
FULLER, Pte, Thomas, 5835494
GALE, Pte, John Francis Nelson, 5831036
GARDINER, Pte, John, 6028732
GARN, Cpl, James Gordon, 5831197

GASTER, Pte, Edward George, 6023673
GATHERCOLE, L/Cpl, Wilfred, 5827519
GIBBS, Pte, Douglas Albert, 5933753
GILBERT, Pte, Stanley, 5933065
GINGER, Pte, Stanley George, 5833931
GLASSCOCK, Pte, Harold James, 5830567
GODFREY, L/Cpl, Reginald Charles, 5833571
GOLDER, Pte, Edward Frank, 5833933
GOLDSMITH, Cpl, Bernard Roy Edward, 5830618
GOOCH, Cpl, Gordon Douglas, 5830375
GOODALL, Pte, Horace Leslie, 5933858
GORRINGE, Pte, Ernest Henry, 6019212
GOSS, Pte, Percy William, 5828841
GOWER, Pte, Dick Thomas, 7568934
GRAHAM, Pte, Joseph, 5933905
GRAY, Pte, Percy Cecil, 5833274
GREAVES, Pte, Arthur Charles, 5933859
GREEN, Pte, Clifford George, 5828811
GREEN, Pte, James William, 5831199
GREEN, Pte, Roland, 5933473
GREGORY, Pte, Cuthbert, 5827529
GREGORY, Pte, Alan Charles, 5827275
GROOM, 2/lt, Basil Raf, 164500
GROOM, Pte, Stanley William, 5828535
GROUNDS, Capt, Frederick Ambrose, 79053
HACKETT, Pte, James, 5833440
HALL, Pte, Horace, 5775555
HAMMOND, Pte, Thomas Sylvester, 5933599
HAMMOND, Pte, Arthur, 5933765
HAMMOND, Pte, Ronald, 5833579
HAMMOND, Pte, Victor Reginald, 5830380
HANSFORD, Pte, Frederick Lewis Wilson, 6028675
HARDWICK, Pte, Philip Clarence Brown, 5831101
HARLOCK, Pte, Thomas, 5833580
HARNWEL, L/Cpl, Kenneth Charles, 5933552
HARRIS, Pte, Thomas Wlliam, 5831787
HARRIS, Pte, Clifford Roland, 5827356
HARRISON, Pte, Charles Frederick, 5832634
HARRISON, Pte, Thomas Freeman, 5830796
HART, Pte, Leslie John, 5829997
HART, Pte, Leslie Frank, 5832636
HARVEY, Pte, Victor Albert, 5827650
HAWKINS, Pte, Ronald Booth, 5833586
HAWKINS,L/Cpl,Henry Gordon,5933414
HAYLOCK, Pte, Frank William, 5933460
HAYNES, Pte, George, 5833288
HENGEST, Pte, Carl Frederick George Alexander, 6019218
HEWITT, Pte, John Edward, 5823597
HOBBS, Pte, Owen Charles, 5932988
HODGES, Pte, John William, 5835501
HODSON, Pte, Bernard Thomas, 5829998
HOLLOWAY, Pte, Stanley Bernard, 5832146
HOOPER, Pte, Colin Paul, 5830395
HOPSON, Pte, William Reginald, 5830767
HORNSBY, L/Cpl, Harry, 5833591
HOUGHTON, Pte, Albert Edward, 5832655
HOWARD, Pte, Leslie Thomas, 5832656
HOWARD, Pte, Leslie Frederick, 5833592
HOWE, Pte, George Alexander, 5831282
HOWE, Cpl, John Henry, 5933506
HULYER, Pte, Ernest George, 5836258
HYAM, Pte, Raymond Bertie, 5933821
HYAM, Pte, Gordon Victor, 5933854
JACKSON, Pte, Harry, 5835120
JAMES, Pte, John Thomas, 5831007
JANSEN, Pte, Frederick Albert, 5831214
JEEPS, Pte, Laurence, 5933761
JEFFERSON, Pte, Archie, 5933457
JEFFREY, Pte, Reginald George, 885427
JOHNSON, Pte, Edward, 6026945

JONES, Pte, Edwin Horace, 5830963
JUGG, Pte, Harold William, 5933590
KERRIDGE, Cpl, Horace, 5933701
KNIGHTS, Pte, Alan Maurice, 5832162
KNOLL, Pte, Ronald Ernest, 5828889
LAWSON, Pte, Wilfred George, 5830973
LONG, Cpl, Herbert James, 5933546
LUFF, Pte, Aubrey, 5933084
MADELEY, Pte, John Norman, 3833836
MAIDWELL, Pte, Frank, 5833046
MALLION, Pte, Leslie Charles, 5831015
MALONEY, Pte, Edward, 6026975
MANN, Pte, Jack, 114535
MANNING, Pte, Bertie Albert, 5831017
MANSFIELD, Pte, Harry Jack Thomas, 5827550
MARKHAM, Pte, George Alexander, 6018234
MARKWELL, Pte, Edward George, 5831651
MARRIOTT, Capt, Christopher Aniel Wynn, 91017
MARSH, Pte, Arthur, 5830661
MARSHALL, Pte, Reginald George, 5833610
MARTIN, Pte, William Alec Jesse, 5824683
MARTIN, L/Cpl, Wilfred Arthur, 5828816
MARTIN, Pte, Ernest Henry, 5933772
MASON, Pte, Felix Oswald Sydney, 5775495
MASON, Pte, Raymond Oswald, 5827729
MAYLE, Pte, Charles, 5932521
McGLYNN, Pte, John, 3833454
MEWS, Pte, Sidney, 5933741
MICKLEBURGH, Pte, Sidney Jack, 5831053
MITCHELL, Pte, William Ernest, 6027022
MORRIS, Pte, Alfred Bernard, 5828824
MORTLOCK, Pte, Victor Sidney, 5831260
MOWER, Pte, Reginald Stanley, 5827651
MUFFETT, Pte, Arthur Henry, 5933906
NEWMAN, Pte, Sidney, 6028683
NICE, L/Cpl, Leonard Vincent, 5933417
NICHOLS, Pte, Ernest William, 5933723
NIGHTINGALE, Pte, Charles Stanley, 5932828
NUNN, Pte, Albert Edwin, 5933391
O'HANRAHAN, Pte, Bernard Joseph, 5830452
OSBORN, Pte, Harold Charles, 5831262
PAGE, Pte, George Thomas, 6914090
PALMER, Pte, George Edward, 5830242
PARISH, Cpl, Arthur, 5823596
PAYNE, Pte, Arthur, 5835527
PEACOCK, Pte, Lawrence Arthur, 5833623
PEACOCK, Pte, George Harold, 5830978
PEARCE, Pte, Leonard Stanley, 5828233
PEARCE, Pte, John William, 5824604
PEARL, Pte, George Robert, 5832745
PEARSON, Pte, William David, 5932343
PECK, Pte, Hermond Philip, 5830461
PEE, L/Cpl, Jesse Reginald, 5931844
PHILLIPS, Pte, James, 6028707
PIDDOCK, Pte, Douglas, 13021488
PIKETT, Pte, Herbert Alfred, 5932374
PLUCK, Pte, Arthur Douglas, 5830982
PORTER, Sjt, Charles Alec, 5933070
POTTER, Pte, Charles, 5831296
POTTER, Pte, Roy Anthony Haigh, 5829463
POUNTNEY, Pte, Oward Owen, 5833629
PRESTON, L/Sjt, William Charles Harry, 5933598
RACKHAM, Pte, Tony George, 882215
RADFORD, Pte, Stephen Henry, 5833097
RANSOME, Sjt, Frederick Douglas, 5830476
RASBARY, Pte, Alfred George, 5833637
RASBARY, Pte, Alfred George, 5833637
READ, Cpl, John Joseph Henry, 5824888
REEVES, Pte, Lloyd Gordon, 5828821
RICHARDSON, Pte, John Francis, 593399

RICHER, Pte, George William, 5832771
RIDGEON, Pte, Reginald Charles, 5830481
RIDGEWELL, Pte, William Harry, 5933458
RISBY, Pte, George Charles, 5828528
ROBERTS, Pte, Alfred George Sidney, 5833462
ROBINSON, Pte, James Henry, 5833702
ROBINSON, Pte, Maurice Frederick, 5827865
ROGERS, Pte, Sidney, 5827806
ROGERS, Pte, Percy Samuel, 5823682
ROGERS, Pte, Herbert John, 5828783
ROLLINGS, Pte, Thomas Maurice, 5827561
ROPER, Pte, David Richie, 756508
ROSE, Pte, Joseph Leonard, 5830795
ROSE, Pte, Carl, 5832781
ROWELL, Pte, Frederick, 5833109
RUNHAM, L/Cpl, Gordon Henry, 3933259
RUTTER, Lt, Dudley Leicester, 74455
RUTTERFORD, Pte, Henry Victor, 5933505
SANDERS, Pte, Ivor Aubrey, 5827814
SARGENT, Pte, Alec George, 5830993
SAVAGE, Pte, Richard Edward, 6019265
SEAGER, Pte, Stanley, 5826642
SEELEY, Pte, Edgar, 5831233
SELLS, Csm, Ernest, 5931331
SELLS, Csm, James Simion, 5932331
SHARPE, Pte, Harry Kilsby, 5933642
SHARPE, Pte, George Ernest, 5933633
SHELCOTT, Pte, Alfred George, 5831234
SHELDRICK, Pte, Wilfred Edwin, 5828785
SINDEN, Pte, Charles Frank, 5933397
SIZER, Pte, Harold Joseph Fred, 5836240
SMEE, Pte, William John, 5835583
SMITH, Pte, Thomas Albert, 5832807
SMITH, Sjt, Robert John, 5826116
SMITH, Pte, Percy Robert, 6024446
SMITH, L/Sjt, Frank, 5932071
SMITH, Pte, George, 5837627
SMITH, Pte, Sanley, 5830623
SMITH, Pte, Ronald Archer, 5933574
SMITH, Pte, John James, 5933589
SMITH, Pte, James Gilbert, 6028627
SNEESBY, Pte, Ernest Allen, 5828753
SNEESBY, Pte, John Anthony, 5832811
SNOW, Cpl, Richard James, 5829996
SOUSTER, Pte, John William, 6029181
SOUTHERILL, Pte, William, 5933720
SPEED, Pte, Frederick William, 5828959
SPINKS, L/Sjt, Ralph William, 5933171
SPRIGGS, Pte, Leslie John Edward, 5833706
STAFFORD, Pte, Joseph, 5831029
STANFORD, Pte, John Robert, 5933855
STEPHEN, Maj, Alfred Bodger Grant, 32392
STIFF, Pte, Charles Kitchener, 5831241
STILL, Pte, Horace Charles, 5831124
STIMPSON, Pte, George Morris, 5933540
STRAIGHT, Pte, Henry Thomas, 6019277
SUMMERS, Pte, William Charles, 5831305
SWAIN, Pte, Cecil Charles, 5933491
TAYLOR, Pte, George William, 5831307
TAYLOR, Pte, Walter, 6023246
TAYLOR, Pte, Reginald George, 5831244
TAYLOR, Pte, Norman William, 5933870
THOMPSON, Pte, Arthur Joseph, 6028658
THORNE, Lt Col, Gordon Calthrop Dso, 13944
THORNER, Pte, Percival James, 6026934
THORP, Pte, John Philip, 5835298
THORPE, Pte, David Ernest, 5831246
TINGEY, Pte, Harry Joseph, 5933419
TODD, Cpl, George Roland, 5828758
TODD, Pte, Archibald, 5833372

TRICKER, Pte, Leslie, 5827794
TROTMAN, Pte, William Robert, 6013883
TUCK, Pte, John, 6028567
TUCK, Pte, Arthur James, 5933902
TUCK, Cpl, Alfred Harry, 5932842
VENNELL, L/Cpl, Victor Henry, 5827690
WADLOW, Sjt, Jack Raymond, 5932302
WALKER, Pte, John William, 5824889
WALKER, Pte, Percy Edward, 5933498
WANT, L/Cpl, John Thomas, 5830537
WARREN, Pte, Alfred Jack, 5830538
WATCHEM, Pte, Albert William, 5527809
WEAVER, Pte, Frederick Bernard, 5828766
WEBB, Pte, Cyril Henry Walter, 5831250
WELHAM, Pte, Jack, 5933625
WELLS, L/Cpl, Herbert, 3933696
WENN, L/Sjt, George William, 5933583
WENTWORTH, Pte, William Frederick, 5827505
WESLEY, Pte, Frederick Charles, 5933159
WESTWOOD, Pte, John James, 5835557
WHITE, Pte, Douglas Joseph, 5831312
WHITE, Pte, Abraham Basil John, 5834834
WHITE, Pte, Charles Samuel, 5831128
WHITEFIELD, Pte, Dennis Eric, 5831247
WHITEHOUSE, Pte, Robert Henry, 5831032
WHITING, Pte, John William, 5831314
WILLIAMS, Pte, James Stephen, 5933404
WILLIAMS, Pte, Albert, 5933763
WILLIAMS, Pte, George, 5830706
WILLIAMSON, Pte, Leonard George, 5835303
WILLIS, Pte, Walter Reginald, 5833888
WILLSON, Pte, Kenneth James, 5933352
WILSON, Pte, Francis Victor, 5827782
WILSON, Capt, Eric Owen, 90556.
WOOD, Pte, William James, 5530551
WOODARD, Pte, Stanley Ernest, 5834842
WOODBRIDGE, Pte, Albert James, 5825739
WOODS, Pte, Frederick James, 5832867
WOODWARD, L/Cpl, Roy, 5933769
WOOLLARD, L/Cpl, Thomas Charles, 5828965
WORSLEY, 2/lt, Paul Reginald Carmichael, 164487
WRIGHT, Pte, Herbert, 5836271
WRIGHT, Sjt, Harry George, 5825417
WRIGHT, Pte, Frederick Charles, 5832873
WULBERN, Pte, Stanley James, 5828774
YOUD, Pte, Frank William, 5933861
YOUNG, Pte, Percy Norman, 5835588

CAMBRIDGESHIRE REGIMENT
4 BATTALION
NICHOLLS,Cpl,Gerald,5774671

CAMBRIDGESHIRE REGIMENT
6 BATTALION
APPER,Pte,Harold Joseph,5771527
SUNMAN,Pte,Leslie Albert,5779672

CAMERON HIGHLANDERS
IANNETTA,Pte,Anthony,19091361
McINTOSH,Rflmn,Hector,3253615
SKAKLE,Pte,A.,14819257

CAMERONIANS
ASQUITH, Rfmn, Wilfred, 1802303
CARMICHAEL, Rfn, John Brown, 3252335
CHIVERS, Rfmn, Thomas Bernard William, 14727753
FENTON, Rfmn, John, 1805696
REDDICK, Cpl, John Muir, 3309518

COLDSTREAM GUARDS
CALVERT,Sjt,Albert Lancelot,2653362

CORNWAL LIGHTINFANTRY
O'NIEL,Sjt,Terence Michael George,5445092

CORPS OF ROYAL ENGINEERS
ADDINGTON,Spr,William Edward,1873985
ADKINS,Spr,Frederick Edwin John,1907896
AINSWORTH,Dvr,John,2147201
ALLEN,Spr,Ernest John,1096946
ALLIBONE,L/Sjt,Ernest Cyril,186726
ALLIN,Dvr,Ernest George,2076211
ALLISTON,Sjt,Bramwell Herbert,1671799
ANDERSON,Spr,George Victor,1872454
ANDREWS,L/Sjt,John Charles,2094163
ANGELL,Spr,John,2090385
ARBER,Dvr,Stanley Edward,2070850
ARMSTRONG,Spr,Walter,2000617
ARMSTRONG,L/Cpl,Kenneth John Francis,1870413
ARTER,Spr,William Sidney,2038812
ASHLEY,Dvr,George Asrthur,2078641
ASHLEY,L/Sjt,George Edward,1867407
ASKHAM,Spr,Percy George,2017778
ATKIN,Dvr,Aubray Cyril William,2005896
AXFORD,Dvr,Henry Edward,2115059
BADGER,Lt,James Spencer,111255
BALDWIN,Sr,Henry Bert,2013604
BAMFORTH,Dvr,Leslie,2115792
BAMMANT,Dvr,Albert Gordon,2076213
BARLOW,Spr,George Alfred,1873296
BARRET,Spr,Colin Leslie,1872929
BASHAM,Spr,William James,5671162
BASLLARD,Spr,Clifford,3855038
BASSETT,Spr,Jack,2130404
BATE,Maj,John Eglington,63047
BATES,Spr,Arthur John,1888782
BAVISTER,Spr,Robert,2069996
BEAMENT,Qms,George Robert,1865764
BEARDSLEY,L/Cpl,Samuel,4982972
BEARDSWORTH,L/Cpl,Eric,1872983
BEARNE,Spr,Leslie Charles,841625
BECK,Spr,Sidney Robert,2032997
BEE,Dvr,Claude Howard,1890012
BELCHAM,Maj,Douglas Francis,140451
BESANT,Spr,William James,1874050
BEVAN,Lt,William James,178402
BIRD,Spr,Harold Benjamin,2120193
BOAKES,L/Cpl,Sidney Ronald,1872959
BODDY,Sjt,Frederick George,1874283
BRADBURN,Dvr,Arthur,1927511
BRANCH,Sjt,Alfred Bert,2070769
BRANSON,Dvr,John Henry,2012930
BRETT,Spr,Percy Henry,2018270
BROWN,Cpl,John Richard,1871526
BROWN,Spr,Eric,209744
BROWN,Dvr,Horace Edgar,2075868
BROWN,Spr,Walter Frank,1874815
BROWN,Dvr,Horace Edgar,2075868
BROWNLIE,2/lt,William,225146
BRUSHETT,Spr,Merton,1894355
BUCK,Spr,James,1922093
BUCKLEY,2/lt,A.B.,370404
BULLOCK,Spr,Charles William,2090352
BURNETT,Spr,Alan Frederick,2191935
BURT,Cpl,Joseph Hercules,11863434
BURTON,Cpl,Henry Ronald,1984111
BURY,Spr,Leonard Joseph,1871935
BUSSEY,Spr,Reginald William,2017783
BUTCHER,Qms,James Arthur,1866444

BUTLER,Cpl,Edward Amelius During,1866889
CAMERON,Sdpr,Leonard John,5183097
CAMPBELL,S/Sjt,William Simpson,1867026
CANE,Cpl,Ronald Arthur Hale,1869471
CANTWELL,Capt,Qm Jammes Joseph (MBE MM),205504
CARDING,Spr,Henry,1897638
CARTER,L/Cpl,Thomas,1874621
CARTWRIGHT,Spr,Leonard Thomas,1871923
CHAPMAN,Spr,Samuel Raymund,14322308
CHAPMAN,Spr,Joseph Anthony Patrick,2030565
CLARK,Spr,Charles Edward,2039161
CLARKE,Lt,Ernest Norval John,306213
CLARKE,Dvr,Geoffrey Harold,1892404
CLAY,Spr,Leslie George,1890157
CLEMENTS,Dvr,Arthur Wilton,2003246
CLEMENTS,Dvr,Arthur Wilton,2003246
COCHRANE,2/lt,Henry Goudoeder,223258
COKER,Spr,Jack William,2093204
COOK,Cpl,Peter Buchanan,1947281
COOLING,Spr,Ernest Herbert,1440248
COOMBES,Cpl,James Franklin,1873200
COOPER,Csm,Cecil Percival,1869076
COOPER,Dvr,William Henry,2003402
CORRIE,Maj,Noel Howard Yatt,56625
COTTINGHAM,L/Sjt,Leonard Ernest,1870895
CRADDOCK,L/Sjt,James Edwin,19892367
CREDLAND,Spr,Leslie Charles,1871864
CRILLEY,Spr,William,2013046
CROCKER,Cpl,Norman Charles,2033616
CROSSAN,Spr,Harold,1875331
CROSSKEY,L/Cpl,Frederick Victor,1890565
CUND,Spr,Henry George,2125462
CUNDY,Spr,James Douglas,1873843
CUNNINGHAM,Cpl,James Albert,1870394
CUNNINGHAM,Spr,Anthony,2090476
CURAN,Cpl,John Patrick,1873311
CURRY,S/Sjt,William,1861266
CURTIS,Spr,Harry Stephen,2009984
CUTLER,Cpl,Arthur Alexander,1928119
DANT,Spr,John Edward Robert,2070120
DAUBNEY,Spr,Dennis,1871052
DAVIES,L/Sjt,John,2068966
DAVIES,S/Sjt,Richard Desmond,1867338
DAY,L/Sjt,Frederick John,2068694
DAY,L/Cpl,Reuben John,1874426
DENGATE,L/Sjt,John,1869211
DEXTER,Spr,David Cameron,1074684
DIXON,Dvr,Eric Christopher,2073161
DONCASTER,Spr,James Robert,2092574
DOUCE,Dvr,Richard Dennis,14724942
DOWNIE,Capt,Desmond John Fairbairn,255901
DOWNING,Spr,George Frederick,2066977
DUNHAM,L/Cpl,Ernest,2091246
DYASON,L/Cpl,Frederick Hart,2318902
DYER,Spr,Gilbert Charles,1874151
DYER,Bsm,Charles Henry,828358
DYNE,Cpl,Charles Forbes,2075873
EADIE,Spr,Thomas,1986097
EAST,Spr,Leonard,2072258
EASTER,Sjt,Frank,1892407
EASTER,Spr,Stanley William,2124419
EASTMEAD,Cqms,Cyril George,1862341
ECCOTT,Spr,Ronald William,5497719
EDWARDS,Csm,Charles William,2217719
EHTERIDGE,Sjt,Thomas,1892385
ELLENDER,Qms,William Hubert,1863600
ELLENDER,Qms,William Hubert,1863600
ELLIOTT,Dvr,Herbert,2115859
ELLIS,Spor,Sydney Frederick,2035085
EMMETT,Spr,George,1874037

ENGLEFIELD,Spr,David George,1873537
EVANS,Spr,George Alfed,14254526
EXCELL,Lt,John Ernest,160066
FAWCETT,Spr,John Robert,1871744
FINCH,Spr,Albert Anton,1873766
FISK,Dvr,Edwin William,2003407
FLACK,Dvr,Walter Alfred,2090332
FLOWER,Sjt,Charles Frederick,1866674
FOOKS,Spr,Frederick John,1872958
FORD,Csm,William Benjamin,1862781
FORD,Qms,Albert Edward,1865943
FORD,Qms,John Richard William,1866422
FORTH,Spr,Albert,2057662
FOSTER,Dvr,George Monty,T/155605
FOSTER,Spr,Donald,1869578
FOUNTAIN,Spr,Alfred Morris,2014599
FOX,Capt,Henry Leslie,157155
FRASER,L/Cpl,John,1871603
FREEMAN,Cqms,Frank Ernest Mm,1849962
FROSDICK,Dvr,Ronald Gibson,2076215
FURSE,Lt,William Edmund,98880
FURZE,Dvr,Dennis James,2076232
GALES,Csm,Christopher,1859679
GARDNER,L/Cpl,Frederick Henry,1872723
GARNER,Spr,Denis Eric,2002299
GEE,Spr,Terence Eugene,1873618
GEEN,Lt,Garnet Harry Cecil,137180
GERRARD,Spr,Donald,1897668
GIBSON,Spr,John Bamborough,1923252
GIL,L/Cpl,Walter,14620448
GILES,Spr,George Thomas,1871281
GILMOUR,Spr,George,1874644
GILMOUR,2/lt,Alexander,162103
GILZEAN,Spr,John Atkinson,1869008
GLENISTER,Lt,Peter Reginald,91851
GLOSSOP,Lt,Norman Oscar,130891
GLOVER,Spr,Neild Macdonald,1880690
GLOVER,Spr,Ernest,1873397
GOOCH,Spr,Harold,1892410
GOODGER,Spr,Robert,1870838
GOODWIN,Cpl,Edwin John William,1862204
GOULD,Capt,Arthur,113834
GOULD,Spr,George Patterson,4267366
GOULSTONE,L/Sjt,Frederick Albert,1871382
GRAHAM,Spr,Rodie Norman Inchie,1873846
GRANT,Cpl,George Yeoman,1865711
GRANT,Cpl,Donald Joseph,1874312
GRAPES,Sjt,William Harold,1874647
GREEN,Cpl,Owen Robert Vincent,2091250
GREEN,Spr,Alexander Robert,2070107
GRICE,Dvr,Neville Francis,2002914
GROVES,Spr,William George,1873932
GUNTRIP,Dvr,Percy Gordon,2070427
HAIGH,Spr,Douglas Harold,1874514
HAIME,Spr,Stanley James,1877212
HAL,L/Cpl,William Walter,2091267
HALLS,Spr,Joseph Albert,2009993
HANN,L/Cpl,Reginald Valentine,1873276
HANNINGTON,Lt,James Rigby,170521
HARDING,Cpl,Raymond Geoffrey Selwyn,1872855
HARDWICK,Spr,Ronald,1871082
HARDY,Cpl,Cyril Thomas,1871443
HARRAN,Spr,James Patrick,1870533
HARRIS,Spr,Gerald Mark,1874487
HARRISON,L/Cpl,Edward William,5828522
HARRISON,Sjt,Thomas James,1882087
HARRISON,Spr,James Alfred,2111363
HARRISON,Spr,Harold,1874428
HART,Sjt,Edward Walter,1868520
HARVEY,Spr,Eddy George,1872868

HATTON,Sjt,Sydney,533823
HATTON,L/Cpl,Ronald Charles,2075595
HAWORTH,L/Sjt,Albert Edward,1924556
HAYLOCK,Spr,Henry Gratton,1888627
HAYWOOD,Spr,Albert Arthur,1872854
HEALEY,Spr,John William,1875454
HEATH,Wo/2,Charles Richard,1862139
HEATH,Spr,Albert Edward,1874413
HELLYN,Spr,Ernest,1872722
HIGHAM,Spr,Joseph Patrick,1875766
HILL,Sjt,John Thomas Taylor,14441120
HITCHEN,Spr,George Major,4746299
HITE,Spr,Thomas Payne,20911748
HOBBS,Qms,Frank William,1860696
HOGARTH,Cpl,David,2032596
HOLLINS,Sjt,Cecil Edward M,1865979
HOLTAWAY,Spr,Rhtur Frederick,1892413
HOWARD,Spr,George Edward,2017791
HOWARD,Dvr,Stanley John,2003168
HUBBARD,Cpl,Arthur Frederick,1862751
HUDSON,Spr,Edward,2013227
HUGHES,Spr,William Frederick,852924
HUNTER,Spr,Sidney,1872779
HUNTER,Capt,Alexander,213614
HUTCHINS,Spr,David William,1870889
HUXTABLE,Maj,Charles John,120702
HYAMSON,Lt,Theodore David,132095
INGLETON,Spr,Roy Franklin,1877209
INNES,Maj,Leslie Walrond,22631
JAMES,Cpl,Charles Alfred,1871324
JARROLD,Cpl,Leonard Hubert,1871677
JARVIS,Spr,Harry,2128766
JELLINGS,L/Cpl,John,2070119
JENKINS,Spr,Frederick,1877283
JERMY,Dvr,Eric Walter,2076986
JICKELLS,L/Cpl,Harold George,2003410
JOHN,Spr,Frank,134277
JOHNSON,Spr,Douglas,2072995
JOHNSTON,Spr,Norman Robert,1873558
JOHNSTON,Spr,Jack,1906915
JONES,Spr,E.,1948385
JONES,Spr,John Henry,1873171
JONES,Spr,Victor Harold,5496607
JORDAN,Wo/1,Leonard Arthur,1859184
JORDON,L/Sjt,Thomas Stephen,1863812
JOY,Spr,Bertram,1873292
KENNEDY,Spr,James Sharp,2118659
KENT,Spr,Henry,2033393
KERR,Spr,Mathew,2001931
KING,Spr,Frank William,2017793
KNAGGS,Maj,Charles Michael,273533
KNIGHT,Qms,John Charles,1867775
KNOWLES,Spr,George Leonard,1888813
LANGLEY,Dvr,James William,2003203
LAWRIE,L/Cpl,John Scott,1888848
LEVEY,L/Cpl,Frederick George Thomas,5569110
LUCAS,Spr,Albert Charles,1873470
LUDMAN,Spr,Stuart Alfred,2072250
LUMKIN,L/Cpl,Eric William,2078659
LUMLEY,Capt,Derrick Bernard,334963
LUSH,Spr,Cyril Edward,1869296
MANSFIELD,Spr,William John,2016081
MANTON,Spr,Peter,2076974
MARKS,Spr,Raymond John,2144841
MARROITT,Csm,Ronald Charles,14834313
MARSHALL,L/Cpl,Alfred George,2005477
MARSHALL,Spr,William Johnson,1877067
MARSHALL,Cqms,Alfred,1863370
MARSHMAN,Dvr,Gilbert Nathaniel,2011967
MARTINS,Spr,Frederick,2076234

MASKELL,Dvr,Victor,2003073
MASKELL,Spr,Frederick Thomas,1872285
McDADE,Cpl,Edward Albert,2027396
MEEK,Cpl,John Henry,1871978
MEGSON,Qms,Frank Cyril,1866583
MERCER,Spr,Ernest Henry,1906872
MERRIFIELD,Spr,Victor Bert Wood,1877207
MIDDLETON,Pl,Frederick Daniel,1869164
MILK,Sjt,George Edward,2077949
MINNS,Cpl,Leonard Harold,1867157
MOORE,Spr,Richard Thomas,1872424
MOORE,Spr,Percival Albert,5931853
MOORE,Maj,Denis Dixon,49890
MOORE,Spr,Fred,1874085
MORETON,Qms,Sydney William,1862892
MORGAN,L/Cpl,John,1874158
MORLEY,L/Cpl,Albert Jesse William Gerald,1868253
MORRIS,Spr,James Stuart,1874306
MORRIS,Lt,Edward Henry,272464
MORRIS,Cpl,Leslie Carrine Brinton,1862708
MORTON,Spr,John Irving,2138872
MORTON,Spr,Eric,1874736
MULLINS,Spr,Reginald Richard,1874852
MURGETT,Spr,Arthur William,2075596
MURPHY,Spr,John,14319458
MURRAY,Spr,Robert Paton,1874335
NAIRN,Spr,William,1873048
NASH,Capt,Thomas Wilfred,56620
NEUBRONNER,S/Sjt,Robert Louis,1931957
NEVELL,Capt,Alan Andrew,132086
NEWBY,Spr,Norman Harold,1875419
NEWMAN,Spr,Owen Gilbert,2009982
NEWMAN,L/Cpl,Hrbert,1871198
NEWMAN,L/Sjt,Peter Frederick,14663127
NICHOLSON,Spr,William Thomas,2134718
NICOL,Spr,William,2130415
NOBLE,Spr,Eric Arthur,1871124
NORTH,Sjt,James,2338672
NOWILL,Spr,Donald,187165
NUNN,L/Cpl,Alderman James,2037561
O'BRIEN,Dvr,William Charles,2078637
O'CONNOR,Rsm,Christopher Michael,15000066
O'ROURKE,Spr,Francis John Lawrence,214649
ORCHARD,Spr,George William,2138555
OWENS,Spr,William,2135256
PALMER,Lt Col,George Archdale,18178
PARR,Spr,Arthur William,1910839
PASS,Spr,Ronald Victor,1872651
PAYNE,Spr,Sidney,1991421
PAYNE,L/Sjt,Arthur Alfred George,5667668
PEARCE,Spr,Lewin James Raymond,1873684
PEARCY,Capt,Cecil Lienel,113839
PEMBERTON,L/Cpl,George,1871779
PENFOLD,L/Cpl,Julian,1873483
PERRIMAN,Spr,George Raymond,1924664
PETTIT,Spr,Charles Thomas,2138565
PETTY,L/Sjt,Ernest John,1867269
PHILLIPS,Lt,William Harold,337673
PICKERSGILL,Capt,Cecil Douglas,56815
PLANT,Spr,Joseph William,1872984
PLATTEN,Dvr,Reginald,2003075
POULTER,Dvr,Cyril George,2077086
POULTON,Spr,Joseph William,5881408
POYSER,Lt,Stuart Vernon,145287
PRICE,Spr,Gilbert Riley,2036272
PRICE,Spr,Leslie Donald,1874021
PRIVETT,Cpl,Ernest James,2040996
PRYKE,Spr,Harry Robert,1890845
PUGH,Sjt,Edwin Baldwyn,2068017
PURFIL,L/Cpl,Henry,2309659

RAMPTON,Spr,Albert Edward,14895131
RANSON,L/Cpl,George Victor,2031849
READ,Spr,Alfred Bernard,1907144
REDMAN,Cpl,Frederick James,1869221
REED,L/Cpl,Edward John,1873223
REEVES,L/Cpl,Jack Norman,1872843
REGELOUS,Spr,P.W.,14586178
REGLER,Spr,Robert Sidney James,1873308
REILLY,Spr,Patrick Joseph,2000602
RENNIE,Spr,John Nowell,2011028
RESTALL,Rsm,Leonard James,1859635
REYNOLDS,Dvr,Herbert,1890017
REYNOLDS,Spr,Percy Robert,1871637
RHIND,Spr,Alexander Moray Martin,1873073
RICHARDS,Lt,Rupert Geoffrey,12982
RICHARDS,Spr,Richard Edward,1871085
ROBERTS,L/Cpl,Jack,1873422
ROBERTS,Spr,Hugh,14664647
ROBERTS,Cpl,Ernest Hugh Owen,1867718
ROBINSHAW,Spr,Harry,2128099
ROBINSON,Spr,Spencer,1871729
ROBISON,W/o,1 Thomas William Brydon,1854825
ROCKETT,Spr,Harry Major,2090370
ROGERS,Spr,James,1478166
ROOCROFT,Spr,James,1873522
ROONEY,Spr,Lelsie Michael,2078654
ROSS,Spr,Horace Alfred,6203372
ROWLAND,Dvr,Thomas Joseph Hamilton,2003061
ROWLAND,Capt,Thomas Denys Stafford,264569
ROWLANDS,Spr,Fred Forsyth,1860929
RUDKIN,Dvr,Victor Frederick,2003421
RUSHBROOK,Spr,Melvin Clive,2075845
SALMON,L/Cpl,Alfred George Thomas,1865168
SAUNDERS,Dvr,Peter,2003422
SAY,Spr,Victor Harold,1991320
SAYER,Pte,Edward Herbert,2033503
SCOTT,Spr,Clifford,1874122
SEAGROVE,Spr,Sydney,1917524
SEAMAN,L/Cpl,Neville Walter William,2090372
SECKER,L/Sjt,Walter Edward,2046145
SEWEL,Spr,Kenneth,14763021
SHARMAN,Spr,Roland George,2002317
SHAW,Spr,Horace,2016091
SHENTON,Csm,Horace,1894042
SHEPHERD,Spr,Cyril,1873238
SHERWIN,Spr,Frederck Norman,2120396
SHERWOOD,Spr,Bernard Thomas,1892395
SHEWARD,Spr,George Harold,2012913
SMITH,S/Sjt,Norie Lionel,1877106
SMITH,Spr,George Henry,2120086
SMITH,Spr,Frank,2017807
SMITH,L/pl,Ernest Charles,1870514
SMITH,Spr,Reginald Thomas,1922876
SMITH,Spr,Austen,1872594
SMITH,Sjt,Sidney Arthur,2031034
SMITH,Spr,Malcolm,1909687
SOARS,Spr,William Henry,1873978
SOLOMON,Maj,David Bowen,185536
SOUTHALL,Spr,Alec,1892396
STANLEY,L/Cpl,Albert,1873539
STAVELEY,Dvr,Esse James Carroll,2025966
STEPHENSON,Spr,Adam,2120397
STEWARDSON,Spr,Ernest,2120080
STILL,L/Cpl,Frank Norman,2071046
STODDART,Spr,Bertram James,2120205
STONE,Spr,Edward Ronald,1574428
SUTHERLAND,Sjt,John Flett,1871274
SWEATENHAM,L/pl,Leonard Frank,1905689
TALLON,Spr,John,1874081
TATE,Sjt,Thomas William,14768103

TAYLOR,L/Cpl,Sydney George,1872802
TAYLOR,Csm,Frank Ernest,1861989
TAYLOR,Cpl,Guy Ralph,1874436
THETFORD,Spr,John Wesley,2068016
THORNTON,Spr,Albert Kenneth,1877435
TIBBS,L/Cpl,John Francis Charles,2031740
TICE,Spr,Raymond,2037163
TITTERTON,Spr,Edwin Vernon,2116373
TOLL,Dvr,Arthur George,2003426
TURNER,Spr,George,991478
URQUHART,2/lt,David Ranulf Delme,198968
VARCOE,Lt,Thomas Henry,288210
WALKER,Spr,Ralph Townsend,6398396
WALKER,Spr,James Charles William,2070822
WALLER,Spr,Herbert,2117302
WALTON,Sjt,Isaac Elliott,14544426
WATSON,Capt,J.L.,250229
WAYLING,Spr,Jack,1922002
WELLS,Spr,John Raymond,1873117
WELSH,Sjt,Bertie George,1863567
WEST,Spr,Ronald,1872561
WHEADON,Spr,Sidney Charles,1871566
WHISKER,L/Cpl,Thomas Harvey,2090376
WHITE,Spr,Arthur Leslie,1893967
WHITTAKER,Spr,Albert Victor,834193
WILKES,Spr,T.,14766899
WILKINSON,Maj,Michael Thomas Lean,31618
WILLETTS,Spr,George,1892360
WILLIAMS,Spr,Thomas,1922860
WILLIAMS,Spr,Percival Leonard,1874254
WILLIAMS,Lt,Neil Benjamin,139045
WILLIAMS,Spr,Charles James,1872782
WILLIAMSON,Spr,Charles,2094455
WILLMOTT,Spr,Leslie George,1906464
WILSON,Dvr,Frank,2090383
WILSON,Qms,George Francis Edward,1862768
WOOD,Sjt,William Claude Renchley,1870077
WOODS,L/Cpl,Herbert George,1874004
WRIGHT,Dvr,Reginald,2017831
WRIGHT,Lt,Edward David,343416
WYNNE,2/lt,Alfred John,64021
YORK,Spr,Dennis George,1922868

CORPS OF ROYAL ENGINEERS
BOMB DISPOSAL
EASON, Sjt, Charles Edward, 1859936
FIDLER, Spr, Albert, 1873445
GREEN, L/Sjt, Allan James, 1867621
GYMER, Spr, Eric, 1874829
JONES,Spr,Albert Eric Mathew,1871739
McCABE,L/Cpl,John,1871419
MACMULLEN, Spr, John, 2034523
McGUINESS, Spr, Danial Victor, 3710671
METCALFE, Spr, Ronald Arthur, 1877456
PILBEAM, Spr, Charles Arthur, 1874091
POTTER, Spr, Austin Charles Edward, 1874307
REHBIEN, Spr, John, 1875168
THARME, Spr, George Henry William, 1874751
WRIGHT, Spr, Laurence Walter, 1871009

CORPS OF ROYAL ENGINEERS
2 SPECIAL BOAT
JOHNS,Capt,William Edward Field,241202

CORPS OF ROYAL ENGINEERS
251 COMPANY
GOODLIFFE, Sjt, Sydney Arthur, 2078671
HOLMAN, Spr, Leslie, 2017789
JONES, Spr, Ernest William, 2120218
SUTTON, Spr, Frederick Bertram, 2017829

VINCENT, Dvr, Leslie Ivor, 2079894

CORPS OF ROYAL ENGINEERS
560 COMPANY
COOKE,Cpl,Kenneth Francis,2002911
SMITH,Spr,William Francis,1903051
SMITH,Spr,Alexander,2130447
WALKER,Spr,John Frank,2120373
WILKINSON,Dvr,Charles Thomas,2115119

CORPS OF ROYAL ENGINEERS
FORTESS
BANTIN, Spr, George Reginald, 2046520
CAMERON, Spr, Robert, 2877517
CAMPBELL, Sjt, Thomas, 1863134
CROSSE,Spr,Percy Frederick,1871401
FOOKES,Csm,Maurice Ernest,1867411
FUNNELL,Spr,Ronald,1871938
FURNESS, Spr, Arthur, 1870067
GUNNELL, L/Cpl, John Jordon Henry, 1867067
HANNAH, Spr, Richard Clement, 1873672
McDERMOTT,Spr,W.T,14694553
SMITH, Cpl, George Smedley, 1874285
SOTHERN, Sjt, John Frances Stanley, 1670034
SPATCHETT, Spr, David Victor, 1874767
STIFF,Spr,John Richard,1873707
STOCK,Spr,Cyril Francis,6010173
SWINDON,Spr,Richard,2029528
THOMPSON, L/Sjt, Mathew, 1864493
WARD, L/Cpl, Frank Harold, 1874422
WATHEN, L/Cpl, Stanley George, 1873241

CORPS OF ROYAL ENGINEERS
159 RAILWAY COMPANY
WELLSTED,Dvr,Edward Cyril,1893365

CORPS OF ROYAL MILITARY POLICE
BALL, Cqms, Francis John A, 7686041
BISH, L/Cpl, Maurice, 897641
BRIGGS, L/Cpl, David Ronald, 14830720
BUSWELL,Spr,Jack Goodrich,977
CAMPBELL, Pte, Frank, 2979442
CRETSOR, Rsm, Robert, 400728
CROSSE,Capt,Edward Castlemain,152
DANCE, L/Cpl, Robert George, 2574422
DAVIES, L/Cpl, Joseph, 7690413
DAVIES, Cpl, Caradwig Morgan, 3954983
EVANS, Pte, David William, 13621
FALKNER, Cpl, William Leonard John, 7685737
FEATHERSTONE, Cpl, Arthur Ernest, 1071050
FENN, Cpl, Donald Hugh, 7686994
FENNELL, L/Cpl, Robert Richard, 13300
FINLAY,Cpl,Frank Noble,13189
FOSTER, L/Cpl, Derek Levermore, 7690109
FRASER,Pte,Henry,13105
GRUNDY, L/Cpl, James, 3855223
HARRISON, L/Cpl, Thomas, 7688560
HARVEY,Pte,John Edward,12538
HODGESON, Sjt, Edward Cartner, 3593342
HORNBLOW, L/pl, William Percy, 7690108
HUTSON, L/Cpl, Cyril Mons, 7933672
JENNINGS,Capt,Harold Godfrey,
KEELTY, L/Cpl, John Patrick, 5618165
KETTLEWELL, L/Cpl, Charles Lloyd, 7688565
LAWRENCE, L/Cpl, Bernard Charles, 7687275
McLEW, Sjt, Donald, 2693210
MILES, Sjt, Frank W, 2655414
MONAGHAN, L/Cpl, Richard Hamilton, 2829792
NOBLE,Spr,Andrew Mitchell,845
OLDHAM, L/Cpl, James Charles, 3526857

ONLEY,Cpl,Stanley Thomas,13227
OSBORN,Cpl,Albert William,445
PARK,Pte,Herbert Hugh,152
PARKER, Cpl, Edward John, 299522
PINDER, L/Cpl, Edward, 3861991
POOLE, L/Cpl, Arthur, 7687457
QUEEN, Cpl, Joseph, 2655729
ROSSITER, Cpl, Thomas Anthony, 850819
SANDS,Lt,Norman Herbert,956
SANG, L/Cpl, William Walker, 2876493
SHIRRAN,Spr,Andrew,924
SHRIMPTON, L/Cpl, Henry Ronald, 5727489
SIDFORD,L/Cpl,Stephen William,758
SIMMS, Cpl, Arthur, 3854734
SPEDDINGS,L/Cpl,Lawrence,7688666
STOCKS, Cpl, Arthur James, 7688069
TACCHI,Lt,George Clifford,
TEGGARTY, Cpl, William, 1068381
TILLOTSON, L/Cpl, Harold, 3854686
TIMM, Cqms, James, 6145
TOVEY, Cpl, George Henry, 5252779
VEALE, L/Cpl, Adrien Clarence, 2656792
VEALE, L/Cpl, Adrian Clarence, 2656702
WAKEFORD, L/Cpl, Guy William Stanley, 7689987
WARD, S/Sjt, Thomas Richard, 2607974
WILLIAMS,L/Cpl,Douglas Llewelyn,851381
WILSON, Sjt, Sydney William, 2610402

DEVONSHIRE REGIMENT
TREGEA,Pte,George Henry,5630912
WALKER,Sjt,Sidney Ernest,5731183

DORSETSHIRE REGIMENT
BOX,Pte,Geoffrey Alan,14847018
CARROLL,Pte,D.,19001483
HEWISON,L/Cpl,K,14986513
KINMAN,Pte,J,4843083
REID,Maj,John,18131

DUKE OF CORNWALL LIGHT INFANTRY
TOMS,Sjt,Leonard,2656451

DUKE OF WELLINGTONS
CHISHOLME,Sjt,Herbert Reginald,4621457
ROCHE,Pte,P.B.,19125910
STRINGFELLOW,Sjt,Jack,4613455

DURHAM LIGHT INFANTRY
BARRATT,Pte,George Leslie,14894936
BARRETT,Pte,L.,14927286
DEAR,Pte,John William,14473487
McGREGOR,Pte,Duncan Roy,14835773

EAST SURREY REGIMENT
ABERY, Sjt, Martin Robert James, 6139192
ABRAHAMS, Pte, Robert William, 6147287
ALEXANDER, Pte, Douglas, 6142870
ALLEN,Pte,Donald Wiliam,6142872
ANDERSON, Pte, Stanley Albert, 6142274
ANDERSON, Pte, Leonard, 6141474
ARLETT, Pte, William Harold Walter, 6141108
ARNOLD, Pte, Harold William, 6142271
ARNOLD, Bdsmn, James Wiliam, 6141277
ATKINS, Pte, Frederick, 6141606
AUSTIN, Cpl, C.B., 6141875
AYRES, Pte, Alan Roskell, 6140619
BAGNARO, Pte, D., 6147296
BALL, Pte, Sidney Hawkins, 6140698
BALLARD, Pte, Charles Harry, 6141422
BANNATYNE, Pte, Thomas, 6147301

BARLING, L/Cpl, Frederick William J, 6194618
BARTRAM, Cpl, James, 6143528
BATT, Pte, W.A., 6147306
BECKESS, Pte, Charles Henry, 6137211
BECKETT, Pte, Edward William, 6141815
BEESLEY, Pte, Stanley Herbert William, 6147308
BELHAM, Cpl, John Charles, 6515929
BERKELEY, L/Cpl, Ernest Harry, 6142252
BEVAN, Pte, William Charles, 6147310
BINGHAM, Lt, Leslie Paget Birkett, 156467
BLACKMAN, Pte, John Alfred, 6138700
BLACKMAN, Pte, Arry Edwin, 6141461
BLAKE, L/Cpl, Frederick William, 6141066
BOBE, Lt, Raymond Hellier Victor, 99784
BOOKER, L/Cpl, David William, 6150586
BOYCE, Cpl, Douglas William, 6142351
BRIGHTMAN, Cpl, Douglas, 6141472
BROOM, Pte, George William, 870273
BROWN, Pte, John Alfred, 6142675
BROWN, Pte, John, 6142319
BROWN, Pte, Frederick, 6619782
BROWN, Cpl, Charles Henry, 6141393
BROWN, Pte, Albert William, 6147323
BRUMBY, Pte, Alfred James, 6141007
BUCKLE, Drmr, Victor Clive, 6141413
BUDGE, Pte, Wlifred Clarence, 6103394
BULLARD, Csm, Frederick Michael Joseph, 6137399
BURGESS, Sjt, Frederick Lewis, 7334154
BURKETT, Pte, Thomas Francis William, 6147326
BURROWS, Pte, John Henry, 6145189
CANT, L/Cpl, Alfred Edward, 6147329
CARR, Pte, Ernest Albert, 6142632
CARTER, L/Cpl, Alfred, 6141030
CASON, Csm, George Edwrad, 6137002
CAST, Sjt, John William, 6140616
CHAPMAN, Pte, Beverley Frank James, 6459440
CHASTON, Pte, Robert Henry, 6142215
CHENNELL, Pte, John Charles, 6143280
CLARK, Psm, Thomas, 6136352
CLARK, Pte, James, 6141872
CLEARY, Sjt, Maurice Stanley, 6140983
CLEAVER, Pte, Ernest James, 6140958
CONSTABLE, Pte, Henry James, 5638
COOKE, Pte, Alfred Philip, 6142764
COOMBES, Pte, Derek Reginald, 6141002
COOPER, Cpl, Esau Alfred, 6141884
COOPER, Cpl, Sydney George, 6200456
COOPER, Pte, H.W., 6147346
CORBETT, Pte, John, 6143100
CORLETT, Pte, John, 6136702
COTTLE, Pte, Kenneth Arthur Henry, 6103396
CRAIG, Cpl, John Henry, 6140934
CRAIG, Pte, Frederick Thomas, 6142876
CROKER, Pte, John, 6141853
CUDD, Pte, George William, 6458150
DANIELS, Pte, Robert, 6141898
DARBY, Pte, Harold, 6144875
DAVIES, Pte, Thomas Gwyn, 6141334
DAVIS, Pte, Ronald Charles, 6142258
DEADMAN, L/Sjt, Ronald Richard, 6140095
DEAKIN, Pte, Horace John, 6141318
DEDMAN, Pte, Robert Arthur, 6142607
DOBSON, Pte, William John, 6140973
DONALDSON, L/Cpl, Charles Alexander, 6141079
DORVAL, Pte, Norman Maurice, 6142762
DOUGHERTY, Pte, William George, 2045710
DOWLING, Maj, Francis Barre Beresford (MC), 15148
DRISCOLL, Pte, Jame Edward, 6147747
DUFFY, Pte, Cyril, 6147748
DYE, Pte, Sydney, 6144826

DYNE, Pte, Francis, 6140933
EDGSON, Pte, Victory Charles, 6142265
EDMONSON, Lt, Maurice Gilbert Devereaux, 164275
ETCHES, Pte, Henry Frederick, 6146373
EVANS, Pte, Douglas Frank, 6141480
FENNELL, Pte, Alec Frederick, 6147366
FIELD, Pte, William Melville, 6141780
FITZPATRICK, Pte, Bernard, 7370687
FLUIN, Pte, Harry William, 6141042
FOLEY, Csm, John Henry Rathborn, 7211462
FOULGER, Pte, Stanley Edward, 6141171
FOYSTER, Drmr, Alfred, 6141371
FREELAND, Pte, Albert George, 6142817
FREEMAN, Pte, Henry, 6141043
FRIDAY, Sjt, Clement Frank, 6142234
GADD, Pte, Ronald Gordon Victor, 6142281
GADSDEN, Pte, Leonard Arthur, 6147786
GARRARD, L/Cpl, Vivian George, 6141882
GEORGE, Sjt, Harold, 6137187
GOSILING, Pte, Eric Alton, 6142642
GOVE, Pte, George, 6141808
GRAY, Cpl, James Stanton, 6137250
GRAY, Pte, James Arthur, 6141012
GREENWOOD, Pte, George Henry, 6147754
GRENAWAY, Pte, William, 6142202
GRINTER, Pte, Norman James, 6096596
GUNN, L/Sjt, John Henry, 6141447
HALL, Sjt, William Frederick, 6139858
HALL, Pte, James, 6140992
HARDY, Pte, Geoge William, 6147788
HARRIS, Pte, Albert John, 6141427
HARRISON, Pte, Robert, 6141804
HARVEY, Pte, John Herbert, 6141478
HASTELL, Sjt, James Edward, 6141876
HATT, Pte, Edwin Ronald, 6149831
HAWKINS, Cpl, Richard Edwin Nowell, 6142270
HAYES, Pte, Albert Frederick, 858445
HEATH, L/pl, John, 2032257
HECKETT, Pte, Victor Alfred, 6141458
HEFFERMAN, Pte, Edwin Stephen, 6140960
HENTY, Cpl, George, 6140929
HEWITT, Pte, William, 6142451
HICKEY, Pte, Leonard William, 6140987
HILLER, Cpl, Albert William, 6140646
HOBBS, Pte, Sidney, 6141465
HOLLIDAY, Pte, Charles Robert, 6142633
HOLLOWAY, Pte, Arthur, 6147393
HOLMAN, Pte, Stanley John, 6142256
HOLMES, Pte, Reginald Alfred, 6142244
HOOKEY, Pte, Edward George, 6141078
HORNSEY, Pte, Wilfred, 6147396
HORWOOD, Pte, Edward Oscar, 6140307
HOWES, Pte, Henry, 6144881
HOWLETT, Pte, Christopher James, 5949181
HUBBARD, Pte, J.A., 6142686
HUMPHREYS, Cpl, Frederick John, 6142224
HUNT, Pte, Frank Norman, 6141550
HUNT, Cpl, Albert, 6142634
HUNT, Pte, Arthur V., 3854785
HUZZEY, Pte, Peter, 6142860
JEFFERY, Pte, Ronald, 6141294
JEFFRA, Pte, Arthur George, 879000
JENKINS, Gnr, Evan Gwyn, 6147404
JENKINS, Pte, William Lawrence, 6140878
JENKINS, Pte, Donald, 6141300
JENN, Pte, Ernest William Leonard, 6140955
JENNINGS, Pte, Leonard George, 6139085
JOHNSON, Pte, Thomas Edward, 6141468
JOHNSON, Pte, Eric Fred Bradbury, 6141070
KERRICH, Capt, John Arthur, 71149

KING, Pte, Thomas Frederick, 6147410
LEACH, Pte, Henry Stephen, 6150595
LEONARD, Pte, Henry Edward, 6141356
LOCK, Pte, Creswick Thomas, 6146680
LONG, L/Cpl, Roland Frederick, 6143296
LUNNY, Pte, Samuel, 6142898
MANLEY, Band Mastr, Ernest Edward,
MARDLIN, Pte, Donald John Henry, 6141459
MARSH, Pte, Edward Albert, 6140735
MARMAN, Pte, Thomas Edward, 6141001
MASON, Cpl, Maurice Victor, 6142805
MATHEWS, Pte, J, 6141423
MAY, Pte, Albert Edward, 6143337
MAYAERS, 2/lt, Walter Knight, 180184
MAYNARD, Cpl, Jesse Edward, 6139969
McLEARY, Pte, John Mcdonald, 6140746
MEDDINGS, Pte, Thomas Robert, 6141901
MEDDLE, Sjt, Henry Charles, 6141409
MERRY, Pte, Leslie Alexander, 6141349
MILLER, Pte, Harry Walter, 6140690
MILNER, Cpl, Lewis James, 6142600
MINIHANE, Pte, John, 6142219
MITCHELL, Pte, John Sidney, 6141321
MITCHELL, L/Cpl, George, 6141811
MITCHELL, L/Cpl, Douglas Albert, 6142621
MOORE, Cpl, Reginald Albert, 6141867
MORDECAI, Cpl, George Henry, 6140591
MORRIS, Pte, Alfred George, 6147442
MORTON, Pte, H.G., 6145202
MUSGRAVE, L/Cpl, Albert, 6142221
NOAD, Pte, Percy, 6141344
NOBBS, Pte, C.G., 6145178
NUNN, Cpl, Leonard George James, 6895878
NUTHALL, L/Cpl, A., 6141717
OSBORN, C/Sjt, Valentine Thomas, 6137516
PAGET, Pte, Arthur James, 6140627
PARDOE, Pte, Leslie Wilfred (MM), 6140871
PARKER, Pte, Stephen, 6142287
PARR, Pte, Albert William Frederick, 6139395
PAU, L/Cpl, W.G., 6140626
PAYNE, Pte, Arthur William, 6141338
PEARCE, Pte, William Walter, 6142361
PEEL, Pte, Stanley Robert, 2043233
PENFOLD, Pte, George, 6138702
PERKINS, Sjt, William Jeffrey Millar, 6141466
POPE, Pte, Raymond Godfrey, 6141364
POTTER, Sjt, George Henry, 6141496
PRITCHARD, Pte, Leonard Francis, 6145435
PUGH, Pte, John Owen, 61474682
RANCE, Pte, Leonard Wilfred, 6143679
READ, Pte, Harry Albert, 6134642
REEVES, L/Cpl, Charles George, 6147473
REYNOLDS, Cpl, John William George, 6140314
RICHARDSON, Pte, Charles, 6140498
RIDDLE, Cpl, Oswald Robert, 6141745
ROBERTSON, Pte, Harold Stanley Hay, 6140985
ROBINSON, Cpl, Albert Alfred Francis, 6147480
ROCHE, Sjt, Sidney William, 6134726
ROGERS, Cpl, Thomas William Mark, 6286551
ROWLANDS, Pte, Edwin George, 685228
RUDD, Sjt, Albert Edward George, 6141054
RUSSELL, Pte, Edward John, 6141405
RUSSELL, Pte, Stanley Albert Spicer, 6141385
RUSSELL, 2/lt, Henry Neville Dashwood, 42136
SALTER, Pte, Joseph Alexander, 867043
SAMPSON, Pte, T.W., 6141093
SAMUELS, L/Cpl, Eric, 6141387
SANDERS, L/Cpl, Stanley Thomas, 6140481
SEAR, Lt, Leonard Alfred, 164279
SEATON, L/Cpl, William James Alexander, 6140921

SEYMOUR, Pte, Sidney Charles John, 6147489
SEYMOUR, Pte, L.W.J., 6140616
SEYMOUR, Pte, Sidney Charles John, 6147489
SHARP, Pte, William Walter Charles, 6140803
SHAW, Pte, William, 6147767
SHEMMINGS, Csm, Robert Patrick, 6137261
SHEPHERD, Pte, Robert George, 6144803
SHEPHERD, Pte, Albert Gordon, 6141380
SHERFIELD, Pte, Bertram Harry, 6141873
SHORT, Pte, Samuel William, 6147492
SHRIMPTON, Pte, Arthur Frank Halton, 6141847
SINCLAIR, Pte, John Daniel, 6147495
SLADE, Pte, Alfred, 6147496
SMITH, Pte, Leslie Percy Patrick Arthur Sidney, 6140833
SMITH, Pte, Tom, 6141833
SMITH, Lt, Dennis Keith, 99739
SMITH, Pte, Albert Ernest, 6142639
SMITH, Pte, Kenneth Henry, 7687734
SMITH, Pte, Frederick William, 6142289
SNOWDEN, Pte, Harry, 6141839
SPENCER, Pte, Reginald Clarence, 6141464
STALLWOOD, Pte, Frank Henry, 6142233
STANFORD, Pte, John Harry, 6144898
STAPLEHURST, L/Cpl, Arthur, 5496402
STEEL, Pte, Arthur Louis, 6147502
STEPHENS, Pte, Albert, 6103348
STILES, Pte, Charles, 6139787
STOCK, Pte, Oliver George, 6140901
STONE, Pte, Arthur Robert Henry, 6150263
STREET, Pte, George Robert, 6085830
STRONG, Pte, Reginald John, 6854260
SWAIN, Pte, Ronald Sidney, 6147505
SWANSBURY, Pte, Kenneth Thomas, 2048258
TAME, Pte, Henry William, 6147507
THOMPSON, Pte, David, 61055
THOMSON, Pte, Joseph George, 6139757
TONNISON, L/Cpl, Frederick, 6012355
TOOTH, Pte, Richard Maurice, 6103356
TURNER, Pte, Herbert Sidney, 6140689
UPHOLD, Pte, Harold Eric, 6140482
VAUGHAN, C/Sjt, John Francis, 6136676
VINCENT, Pte, Reginald Amos, 6142273
WALL, Pte, Cyril Leonard Herbert, 6141358
WARN, Pte, Cecil Fred Cole, 6141417
WARREN, Pte, James William, 6142268
WATERS, Pte, Harold, 4140961
WEBLEY, Pte, Ronald Arthur, 6142247
WEBSTER, Pte, Alfred Thomas Joseph, 6144089
WELLS, L/Cpl, Frank, 6140963
WHEELER, Pte, Ronald Anthony, 6142656
WHITTALL, Pte, Jack Charleton Frederick, 6140240
WILDMAN, C/Sjt, Victor Edward, 6539104
WILKS, Pte, Kenneth Albert, 837452
WILLIAMS, Pte, George, 6147543
WILLIAMS, Pte, Francis Alfred, 6150598
WILLINGALE, Pte, George William Charles, 6147537
WILMHURST, Pte, Ronald Geoffrey, 6142631
WILSON, Sjt, Harry Frank, 2027958
WILSON, Pte, George, 6140474
WILSON, L/Cpl, Frederick Alfred Robert, 6149703
WILSON, Pte, Henry George Thomas, 6142275
WOODS, Pte, John, 6142206
WOOLLARD, Pte, Ronald Leslie, 6141363
WOOLLARD, L/Cpl, Edward John, 6139791
WRIGHT, Pte, Samuel Wilson, 6142681
YEWINGS, L/Cpl, Charles William, 6142253
YOUNG, Cpl, Francis Murdo, 6146021
YOUNG, L/Cpl, Leslie Lionel, 6142857

EAST YORKSHIRE REGIMENT
BULMER, Cpt, John, 126073

ESSEX REGIMENT
DAVISON, Lt, Peter Douglas, 331870
SNOXELL, Sjt, H.F.W., 6011070

GLOUCESTERSHIRE REGIMENT
LIVERSIDGE, Capt, Alan John, 105530
RICHARDSON, Cpl, David John, 14403062
WATSON, L/Cpl, Eric Edward, 14759585

GORDON HIGHLANDERS
ADAMS, Pte, George, 2876456
ADAMSON, Pte, Wiliam Alexander, 3318953
AITKIN, Cpl, Victor, 2867159
AITKIN, Pte, Alexander, 2876833
ALEXANDER, Pte, William, 2876167
ALLAN, Pte, James, 876278
ANDERSON, Pte, Francis, 2879194
ANDERSON, L/Cpl, Harry, 2880438
ANDERSON, Pte, Lewis Robert, 2879103
ANDERSON, Pte, Alexander Macdonald, 2885220
ANDREWS, Pte, Raymond .A.B, 2889835
ANGUS, Pte, John, 2876378
ANNAND, Pte, Andrew, 2874878
ARMOUR, Pte, George, 2879048
ATKINSON, L/Cpl, Norman, 2876783
BARCLAY, Pte, James Alexander, 2877049
BARR, Pte, James, 2879494
BARRON, Pte, James Roy, 5437421
BARRRIE, Pte, James William, 2889909
BASKETT, Pte, James Henry, 2879118
BEANGE, Pte, Alexander, 2876170
BENT, Sjt, Percival, 2865598
BIRSE, Pte, Robert, 2880272
BISSETT, Pte, Alexander Wallce, 2879129
BOWLEY, Pte, Stanley, 2889838
BRANDER, Pte, George, 2868950
BROOKS, Pte, James, 2876534
BROWN, Sjt, Percival William, 2876136
BROWN, Pte, Henry, 2874894
BROWN, L/Cpl, John, 2876664
BROWNLIE, Pte, James, 2876766
BRUCE, Pte, James Alexander, 2876430
BRUCE, Pte, James, 2877915
BRUCE, Pte, Frank, 2876310
BUCHAN, Pte, Henry James, 2876281
BUCHAN, Pte, John, 2927429
BUCHANAN, Pte, Charles, 3312672
BURNETT, Sjt, James, 2874727
BURR, Pte, John Lundie Michie, 2885019
BYRNE, L/Sjt, Horace James, 2874232
CAMERON, Pte, John, 2876892
CAMPBELL, Pte, Robert William Baillie, 2889830
CAMPBELL, Pte, John, 2884170
CAMPBELL, L/Cpl, Gordon, 2876951
CAMPBELL, Pte, Henry Masterton, 2879498
CARROLL, Bnd Sjt, Francis Noel, 3050201
CASS, Pte, Thomas, 3184402
CASSERLY, L/Cpl, John, 3322148
CASSIE, Pte, George William, 2876173
CASSIE, L/Cpl, Webster, 2876268
CHALMERS, L/Cpl, William, 1664943
CHALMERS, Pte, Harry, 2876941
CHALMERS, L/Cpl, James Smith, 2876387
CHARLES, Pte, Thomas Hayward, 2876549
CHARLES, Pte, Edward Douglas, 2876613
CHISHOLM, Pte, James, 2877911
CHRISTIE, L/Cpl, William, 2876314

CHRISTIE, Pte, John William, 2875173
CHRISTIE, Pte, George, 2876346
CHUTER, L/Cpl, Frederick Henry, 6013954
CLARKE, Pte, Edward George, 2889362
CLYNE, Pte, George, 2878924
COCKIE, Pte, Edward, 187266
CODD, Pte, James, 2889844
CONSTABLE, Pte, Charles Edward, 2885805
COOPER, Pte, John Watson, 2877306
COOPER, Pte, Roy, 2876517
COPELAND, Pte, Andrew Mcbride, 3318883
COWIE, Pte, Alexander, 2875884
COWIE, Pte, Arthur John, 2876224
CROOKSHANKS, Bdmn, John, 2877424
DAVIDSON, Cpl, William, 2875673
DAWSON, Pte, James, 2875907
DAWSON, Sjt, Alxander, 2876408
DAWSON, L/Cpl, William, 2875944
DEVINE, L/Cpl, James, 2888242
DICKIE, Pte, David, 2876359
DOCHERTY, Pte, James Joseph, 2885195
DUNCAN, Pte, Thomas, 2872737
DUNCAN, Pte, Alexander Mcintosh, 2871017
DURNO, Pte, Alexander, 2876738
EDWARDS, L/Sjt, Ernest Joseph, 2876670
ELDER, Pte, Allan, 2876877
ELDER, Pte, Henry, 2876671
ELLIOT, Pte, Kenneth Ivor, 2875364
ELLIOT, Cpl, George, 406004
ENGLISH, Pte, Charles, 2876675
ESSLEMONT, Pte, John C., 2877448
FALLON, Pte, Patrick, 2876590
FARQUHAR, Pte, Alexander, 2879177
FERGUSON, L/Cpl, Alexander Gillespie, 2883876
FINDLAY, Pte, Alexander, 2876295
FINNNIE, Pte, Robert, 2876182
FORBES, Pte, James, 2876466
FORBES, Pte, Robert, 288904
FORSYTH, Cpl, Albert, 2876402
FORSYTH, Pte, Simon, 2876183
FRASER, Pte, Stanley Wilson, 2876424
FRASER, L/Cpl, Laurence, 2878251
FRASER, L/Sjt, Henry Albert, 2876343
FRASER, L/Cpl, Gordon Wilson, 2876635
FRASER, Pte, Samuel, 2876545
FRIEL, Pte, Edward, 2883879
GALLAGHER, Pte, David Bryce, 2876625
GIBB, Sjt, Kenneth Mcrae, 2876221
GIBB, Pte, Charles, 2876265
GIBB, Pte, Alexander, 2875351
GIBB, Pte, John, 2874771
GIBBS, Pte, Robert Alfred, 2880946
GIBSON, Pte, William Henry, 2871179
GIFFORD, Pte, Harold, 2876841
GILCHRIST, Pte, Alexander, 2979907
GLENNIE, Pte, Peter, 2876184
GORDON, Pte, Ronald, 2879187
GORDON, Pte, Hamish, 2979473
GORDON, Pte, George Alexander, 2876400
GOWLING, Pte, Albert, 3055031
GRAHAM, Pte, Alexander, 2889054
GRANT, Pte, Alexander, 2876355
GRANT, Pte, Robert, 2876872
GRANT, Pte, Anthony Kray, 2879039
GRAY, Pte, George Simpson, 2876287
GREEVES, Cqms, Harold, 2865694
GRIEVE, Pte, Sydney, 2876495
GRIFFIN, Pte, Michael, 3322234
HALL, Pte, Norman, 2876353
HAMILTON, Cpl, Thomas Lawrie, 2876694

HARPER, Pte, Thomas, P/2883893
HARROLD, Cpl, James, 2876332
HARTER, Capt, Michael William, 66174
HAY, Pte, James, 2876237
HENDERSON, Pte, Douglas James Valentine, 2875951
HEPBURN, Pte, Jonathan, 2878244
HEPBURN, L/Sjt, Archibald, 29875872
HILL, Pte, William, 2876410
HORNE, Pte, Alexander, 2077856
HOWIE, Pte, Charles Bain, 2876363
HUGHES, Pte, Patrick Peter, 2883941
HUNTER, Pte, William Brown, 287681
HUNTER, Cpl, Thomas, 2876316
HUTCHISON, Pte, Ronald Roberts, 2889828
IMRAY, L/Cpl, James, 2876622
INGRAM, Pte, Robert, 2876185
INGRAM, Pte, James Barclay, 2876257
INNES, Pte, James, 2876415
IRVINE, Pte, Robert Laurence, 2879052
IRVINE, Lt, Robert Hugh, 113410
JAFFREY, Pte, Robert Ingram, 2876509
JAMIESON, Pte, Andrew John, 2876448
JOHNSTON, Pte, John, 2876619
JOHNSTON, Pte, Robert, 2876371
JOHNSTONE, Pte, David, 2876713
KENN, Pte, Robert Stewart William, 2880747
KENNEDY, Pte, William, 2875904
KENNEDY, Pte, John George, 2875549
KNIGHT, Sjt, Frank, 2874564
KNOX, Pte, Henry Crighton, 2875846
KNOX, Cpl, Andrew, 556229
KNOX, Pte, Henry Crighton, 2875846
KNOX, Cpl, Andrew, 556229
LEE, L/Cpl, David, 2877496
LEIPER, Pte, William Henry, 2876784
LYON,Lt Col,Ivan (DSO MBE),66175
MACDONALD, Pte, Alexander, 2874280
MACKIE, Pte, William, 2879250
MACKINNON, Sjt, Robert Joseph, 2873837
MACLEAN, Pte, Simon Alexander, 2873074
MAIR, Pte, George Reid, 2876564
MALCOLM, Pte, James Alexander, 2878815
MASSIE, Pte, James, 2869598
MASSON, Pte, James Donaldson, 2876725
MATHERS, Pte, James Alexander, 2876526
MATHERS, Pte, William, 2873793
McARTHUR, Pte, Robert, 7575045
McBETH, Pte, Hugh, 2885088
McDOUGALL, Pte, William, 2746656
McINTOSH, Pte, James, 2876496
McKAY, L/Cpl, Stephen, 2875660
McKAY, Pte, William, 2878442
McKEAN, Pte, Frederick, 2879190
McKENZIE, L/Sjt, John, 2876595
McLEISH, Pte, Frank Watson, 2879002
McLEOD,Pte,Harry,2875021
McLEOD, Pte, Hector, 2876758
McLEOD, Cpl, Alexander S B, 1661787
McNALLY, Pte, John, 7681724
MENNIE, Pte, James, 2875778
MENNIE, Pte, William Milne, 2876853
MENZIES, Pte, Achibald, 2876810
MIDDLETON, Sjt, William Pollock, 2875856
MILLAR, Pte, Thomas, 2876698
MILNE, Pte, Harold, 2878400
MILNE, Pte, Richard Henry, 1871941
MILNE, Sjt, Charles, 2866704
MILTON, Sjt, James, 2875801
MITCHELL, Pte, George, 2876385
MITCHELL, Pte, James, 2876391

MOGGACH, Pte, John Alexander, 2876488
MOIR, Pte, John, 2876305
MOIR, Pte, James Alexander, 2869425
MOIR, Pte, Alexander Mclean, 2876190
MONRO, Capt, John Garside, 77690
MORGAN, Pte, Arthur, 2876361
MORISON, Pte, Gilbert J.A., 2876907
MORRISON, Pte, Charles, 2879155
MORTON, L/Cpl, Charles James Hird, 3308703
MURDOCH, Sjt, James, 2872442
MURPHY, Pte, James, 2877304
MURRAY, Pte, John, 2876056
MURRAY, Csm, Edward Scorgie, 2870500
NAPPIER, Pte, James Burr, 2876793
NESS, Pte, Donald, 2876503
O'NEILL, Pte, Joseph, 2876469
ORMISTON, Cpl, James Joseph Brown, 2876612
OSBORNE, L/Cpl, Wiliam, 2876483
PALMER, Pte, Richard, 2876570
PARLEY, L/Cpl, Alexander, 2874254
PAYNE, L/Cpl, Jack, 2876228
PENMAN, Pte, Thomas, 2876968
PETERKIN, Qms, James Moir, 2871383
PETRIE, Pte, William Mcgregor, 2878085
PETRIE, Pte, Kenneth George, 2884113
PETRIE, Pte, Hugh Simpson, 2872962
QUIRI, L/Cpl, William George, 2875986
RANKIN, L/Cpl, George, 2879991
RATTRAY, Pte, Alexander, 2875543
REID, Pte, George, 2876868
RIDDELL, Pte, George, 2876511
RIDDOCH, Pte, Lexander Rumcie, 2876274
RITCHIE, Pte, James Scott Rogie, 2876263
ROBERTS, Pte, Pecy Marshall, 2873087
ROBERTS, Lt, George, 186375
ROBERTSON, L/Cpl, Thomas Davidson Gray, 2884617
ROBERTSON, Pte, John, 2876253
ROBERTSON, Pte, James, 2884060
ROSE, Pte, William, 2876376
ROSS, Pte, Alexander, 2876875
ROSS, Cpl, Peter, 2876279
RUSSELL, Lt, John Anthony Peregrine, 130751
SANGSTER, L/Cpl, John, 2877014
SCOTT, L/pl, Roy Stewart, 2879196
SCROGGIE, Pte, George, 2875608
SEY, Sjt, John, 2876336
SHAW, L/Cpl, Percy, 6978297
SHEARER, Pte, Duncan, 2876273
SHEILDS, Pte, William, 3322882
SHIRRAN, Sjt, Henry, 2876219
SIMPSON, Pte, William, 2876347
SIMPSON, Pte, Norman, 2876405
SIMPSON, Pte, Joshua, 2879144
SIMPSON, L/Cpl, Alexander, 2885796
SIMPSON, C/Sjt, William, 2875477
SIVEWRIGHT, Pte, Alexander, 2874740
SKENE, Sjt, Thomas, 2876335
SMITH, Cpl, John Alexander, 2876272
SMITH, Pte, James, 2871379
SMITH, L/Cpl, Gordon Elton, 2888677
SMITH, Pte, James, 2889893
SMITH, Pte, George, 2875895
SPENCE, Psm, Robert Ross, 2872799
SPENCE, Cpl, William Alexander, 2876155
STEVENSON, Pte, Harry West, 844254
STEWART, Pte, John F, 2880733
STEWART, Lt, Vincent Irvine Derek, 189550
STOLWORTHY, L/Cpl, John Henry, 2879041
STOPPER, Pte, George Leslie, 2885707
STRACHEN, Pte, John Cullen, 2885773

STUART, Pte, Douglas Haig, 2876598
STUART, Pte, Alexander, 2882540
SUMMERS, Pte, Gordon Wiseman, 2879466
SUTHERLAND, Cpl, David, 2888468
TAYLOR, L/Cpl, Edward William, 406008
TAYLOR, Pye, Robert Brander, 2876657
TAYLOR, Pte, John Davidson, 2874983
TAYLOR, L/Sjt, Douglas John, 825497
TELFORD, Pte, John, 2883944
TENNANT, Pte, Charles, 2876366
THAIN, Pte, John Charles Lyon, 2876358
THOMPSON, Pte, James, 2876636
THOMPSON, Pte, Mathew George, 2876729
THOMSON, Pte, John, 3322299
THORBURN, Pte, John, 2888390
TOPP, C/jt, Edward Frederick, 2873868
TRUSSELL, Pte, Leslie Edes Dudley Ernest, 2876318
TURNBULL, Pte, William, 2879081
VARLEY, Pte, Joseph Henry, 4271739
WALKER, Pte, John, 3322303
WALKER, Pte, Joseph Patterson, 2885713
WALKER, Pte, George, 2876241
WALKER, Bdmn, Charles Morton, 2873378
WALLACE, Pte, John Murray Napier, 2876354
WATSON, Pte, Duncan, 2879141
WATSON, Pte, Thomas Postlethwaite, 2883948
WATT, Cpl, George Delgarno, 2875970
WATT, Pte, Alexander, 2876645
WATT, Pte, John, 2876393
WEST, Pte, Frank Cassie, 2876204
WHARMBY, L/Cpl, Stanley, 2886915
WHEATLEY, Pte, Arnold, 2884776
WHITE, Pte, Andrew James, 2879060
WHYTE, Pte, Henry, 2876205
WILL, Pte, Robert Charles, 2883814
WILLIAMSON, Pte, Andrew Charles, 2879056
WILLOX, Pte, Robert William, 2883815
WILSON, Pte, James, 3322309
WILSON, Pte, George Angus, 7887495
WILSON, Pte, Thomas, 2876609
WILSON, Pte, James, 2873692
WILSON, Pte, Alexander, 2876502
WILSON, Pte, John, 2889825
WINTON, Csm, Andrew, 2872532
WISEMAN, Pte, Robert, 2876580
WITTY, L/Cpl, Frederick, 2876737
WOOD, Pte, Alexander, 2879027
WOOD, Pte, Peter, 2883945
WOOD, L/Cpl, Alexander Wilson, 875116
WOOD, Pte, John William, 3322258
WOOD, Pte, William, 2876883
WYNN, Pte, George, 2879128

GREEN HOWARDS
ANKRETT, Pte, Frank, 1427540
MOAT, Maj, John Henry Frothingham, 44113

HAMPSHIRE REGIMENT
ARMSTRONG, Lt, Richard George De Ligny, 279562
WILSON, Pte, Aubrey Leslie, 14887601

INTELLIGENCE CORPS
CAUVIN, Capt, Louis Patrick Trevelyan, 359541
CROOK, Lt, Francis John Fielding (DSO), 59631
DOBSON, L/Cpl, William, 4857762
ELIS, L/Cpl, Herbert, 4857838
HAMILTON, Lt, Laurence Bulmer, 216932
HARRIS, Cpl, John Edward, 1470402
HERBERT, Pte, Frederick Peter, 6769454
HICKEY, L/Cpl, James, 3527490

HURST, L/Cpl, William Ernest John, 6141910
JAMIESON, Pte, John, 2871098
MACRAILD, Csm, Alexander, 2980532
MALCOLM, Lt, Coert Grobbelaar, 225143
NASH, Pte, Lewis Willoughby, 4856897
NUNN, Sjt, Kohn Brabant, 7689646
RIGBY, L/Cpl, John, 3858774
ROBERTS, Sjt, Leonard Thomas, 10350723
RUSSELL, Lt, M.L., 245542
SHAW, L/Cpl, William Avelyn, 981677
SMITH, L/Cpl, James Orr, 14920160
SPENCER, Csm, Geoffrey Gordon Joseph, 14690150
STRINGFELLOW, L/Cpl, William, 3855662
WATT, Sjt, Ian James, 14258444
WESSELL, L/Cpl, Frank, 4856590
WRIGHT,Csm,John William,2608701

KING'S OWN HUSSARS
ALTON, Tpr, George, 554863
BARSON, Tpr, William James, 552028
BENNETT, Tpr, Ellis, 7931567
BUCK, Cpl, Edwin Norman, 392206
BUTLER, Tpr, Ralph David, 554363
CALLAGHAN, Tpr, Charles, 7905199
CARTER, Tpr, Sidney Albert, 553865
CHAMPION, Tpr, Henry John William, 6202223
CLARKE, Tpr, Thomas John, 3974063
CLARKE, Sjt, David Stephen, 861493
DERRICK, Tpr, Victor Norman, 319806
DUNNING, Tpr, Norman, 7933280
EDWARDS, Tpr, Frederick Ernest, 4913355
FARMER, Sjt, Albert, 550681
GILMOUR, Tpr, John, 7901289
HARRISON, Tpr, Victor, 7894665
HUSTWICK,Tpr,Thomas Simpson,7877969
JARVIS, Cpl, Frank William, 554343
MACLACHLAN, Tpr, Robert, 7899119
MARRIOTT, Tpr, Edgar Henry, 3385975
MARTIN, Tpr, Henry Sylvester, 554672
MORRIS, Cpl, George Frederick, 552648
PAGE, Tpr, Ernest Joseph, 7932239
PERRY, Tpr, William, 5248434
POWELL, Gnr, George, 405502
PREECE, Cpl, George James, 402661
PRITCHARD, Tpr, Wilfred, 7890060
READ, Tpr, Frank Lewis, 7904100
ROBERTS,Tpr,Rufus John,7901910
SCOTT,L /Sjt, George, 553981
SIMMONS,L/Cpl,William,553172
SMITH, Tpr, Henry John, 7901787
SPONG, Tpr, Reginald William, 558462
STANFORD, Cpl, William Leslie James, 553192
STIGANT, Cpl, Edward William Charles, 543906
TURNER, Tpr, Walter Dyson, 3527946
WATERS,Tpr,Benjamin Raymond,7901752
WILLIAMS, Cpl, Ernest Charles, 405133
WILLIAMS, Tpr, Ernold, 7899863
WILLIAMSON, Tpr, Kenneth, 553616

KING'S OWN SCOTTISH BORDER REGIMENT
DICKSON,Cpl,Robert,552316
EMERY,Sjt,Alfred William John,553240
JONES,Sjt,William Frederick,6140422

KING'S SHORPSHIRE LIGHT INFANTRY
RODGERS,Capt,Geoffrey Wilson,107450

LOYAL REGIMENT
2 BATTALION
ADAMS, L/Cpl, John William, 3855160

ADKINS, Pte, Richard Edward, 3855527
ALDRIDGE, Pte, Patrick, 3856402
ANKERS, L/Cpl, John Ashley, 3862931
ANSELL, Pte, John, 3865694
ASHWORTH, L/Cpl, Clifford, 385733
ASTOR, Cpl, Joseph, 3859625
ATHERTON, Pte, Thomas Hodson, 3858464
ATKINSON, Pte, Edwin, 3859783
ATKINSON,Lt,James Dennis,346471
BAILEY, Cpl, Ronald John Bertie, 3860027
BAINES, Pte, James, 3861852
BAKER, Pte, Edward Thomas, 3856899
BAKER, Pte, David Sydney, 3856906
BAKER, Capt, James, 150542
BARKER, Pte, George William, 3854749
BARNES, Pte, Fred, 3858473
BARNETT, Pte, John, 3856871
BARRY, Pte, Thomas, 3856001
BAXTER, Pte, Robert, 3856065
BEDFORD, Pte, Harold, 3854719
BEL, L/Cpl, William Tyler, 3854927
BELLINGALL, L/Cpl, Richard, 3853430
BENSON, Pte, William, 3855972
BIRD, Pte, Thomas, 3854665
BIRTWHISTLE, L/Cpl, Robert, 3857408
BLACKLEDGE, Pte, Alfred, 3859507
BLACKLEY, Pte, Hugh, 3853460
BOAST, Pte, Ashby James, 3856285
BODEN, L/Cpl, Geoffrey, 3659188
BOND, Pte, Francis Robert, 2946559
BOUNDS, L/Cpl, Cyril, 3854798
BRANNAGHAN, Cpl, Henry, 3380919
BROOKS, Pte, Wilbraham Ernest, 3856366
BROPHY, Pte, Lawrence, 3855780
BROWN, Pte, James, 3857622
BUCK, Pte, Thomas, 6399400
BURCHETT, Tpr, R.W., 14789216
BURDON, L/Cpl, Frank, 3854833
BURNS, Pte, Edward Francis, 3860962
BURTONWOOD, Pte, David, 3857643
BUSBY, Cpl, Alfred, 3854683
BYRNE, Cpl, John Thomas, 3855244
BYRNE, Pte, Francis, 3854772
BYRON, Pte, Robert, 3856206
CANBY, L/Sjt, Sylvester, 3855004
CARDWELL, L/pl, Stephen, 3858130
CARROLL, Sjt, James, 3854743
CARTER, Pte, John, 3858839
CASSIDY, Pte, Thomas, 3858895
CHAINEY, Pte, Reginald John, 3855746
CHANTLER, Pte, James Joseph, 3856344
CHARNOCK, L/Cpl, Charles, 3852850
CHATWIN, L/Cpl, Martin Robert Frank, 6977985
CHESTER, Pte, Robert, 3858075
CHISLETT, Pte, George .T.W., 5947349
CLEATOR, Lt, Arthur Bertram, 129633
COBLEY, Lt Col, Frank Reginald Newnum, 52989
COLE, Pte, Clifford, 3853925
COLLINS, Pte, Bert, 3856642
CONNOLLY, Pte, Lawrence, 3855217
CONSTABLE, Pte, Roy, 3387802
COOK, Pte, James Edward, 3857566
COOK, Pte, Arthur, 3853628
CORFE,Pte,John,3860659
COSTELLO, Pte, James, 3856054
COWELL, Pte, Norman Alfred, 3857416
COWELL, Pte, Fred, 3855962
COYNE, Pte, Arthur, 3859434
CRANSHAW, L/Cpl, Stanley, 3855730
CRANSHAW, Pte, Norman, 3852529

CRATHERN, Pte, John Henry, 3855136
CROSSLEY, Sjt, Joseph, 3855227
CROSTON, Pte, James Wilfred, 3855794
CUCKLOW, Bdsmn, Frank Alfred, 3855389
CULLEN, Pte, Thomas, 3854670
DAVIDSON, Cpl, Terence, 3526194
DAWSON, Cpl, Walter Langley, 3854153
DEAN, Pte, Stanley, 3857682
DERBYSHIRE, Pte, Frank, 3855711
DICKER, Pte, Sidney John, 3854699
DICKINSON, L/Cpl, Alexander, 3854774
DIXON, Pte, Harry, 3860284
DYMOND, Pte, Thomas Gordon, 3855002
ECKERSLEY, Pte, Harry, 3858514
EDGE, Rsm, Francis, 3850247
EDWARDS, Pte, Charles Alexander, 3855185
ELLINGHAM, Pte, Cornelius, 3854756
ELLIS, Cpl, Samuel Leonard, 4912782
FALLOVER, Pte, Thomas Henry, 3854617
FAWCETT, Pte, Harry, 3856701
FIELDING, Pte, William, 3855353
FILDES, Pte, Norman, 3855665
FINLEY, Pte, William, 813988
FINNEY, L/Cpl, Fred, 3854708
FISHWICK, Pte, Harold Henry, 3861326
FORD, Pte, Frederick Thomas, 3854718
FOSTER, Pte, John, 3855981
FOWLER, Pte, John, 3855195
GALVIN, Pte, John, 3523297
GARSDEN, Pte, Joseph, 3854148
GAVEN, Pte, James, 3855736
GENTLES, Cpl, Clarence Mercian, 3854358
GILBERT, L/Cpl, Alfred, 3858527
GOOD, L/Cpl, George Joseph, 3855539
GOODIER, Pte, Robert, 3855008
GOUDA, 2/lt, Arnold Albert, 186370
GREEN, Pte, Samuel Edwin, 3857674
GREEN, Pte, James, 3858850
GREENWOOD, Pte, James, 3860665
GRIERSON, Pte, William Eric, 3855093
GRIFFITHS, Pte, Trevor, 3961711
HAIGHTON, Pte, George Edward, 3855731
HALL, Pte, Robert, 3855407
HALLHEAD, Pte, Thomas, 3854414
HALPIN, Pte, James Patrick, 3856503
HAMER, L/Sjt, George Samuel, 3855376
HARGREAVES, Pte, Stanley, 3858539
HARRADEN, Pte, Gilbert, 3856378
HARRISON, L/Cpl, Benjamin, 3855642
HART, Pte, Richard, 3857543
HARTLEY, Cpl, Andrew, 3385394
HASLAM, Pte, Frederick, 820353
HAWKEN, Pte, Ralph, 3865646
HAYCROFT, Sjt, Cecil, 3855145
HAYWARD, Pte, William John, 3855401
HEARN, Rqms, Alfred, 3847069
HENDRY, Pte, James, 873325
HENRICK, Cqms, Thomas Francis James, 3852751
HERBERT, Pte, James Horace Victor, 3855965
HIBBERT, Pte, Walter, 3856687
HIGSON, Pte, Thomas, 3854969
HOLCROFT, Pte, Joseph Henry, 3856322
HOLDEN, Cpl, Gerald, 3384885
HOLT, Pte, Philip, 3858825
HOWARD, Pte, Frederick Joseph, 3854737
HOWELL, Trp, Thomas, 14406788
HOYES, Pte, James, 3856353
HULME, Pte, Samuel, 3855303
HUNT, Pte, Wiliam, 3855388
HUYTON, Drmr, George, 3855954

JACKSON, Pte, John, 3855979
JACKSON, Drmr, John, 3852226
JACKSON, Pte, James, 3848668
JAMES, Pte, Jonathan William, 3851046
JOHNSTON, Pte, Walter, 3854655
JONES, Pte, Thomas, 3856488
JONES, Pte, Richard George, 3861987
JORDON, Pte, Arthur, 3854953
JOWETT, Rsm, Philip George, 3855424
KELLY, Bdsmn, Douglas John, 3855765
KNOWLES, Pte, Francis, 3860029
LANE, Pte, Henry James, 3855958
LANE, L/Cpl, Daniel, 3958348
LINDSELL, Pte, Stanley Ernest, 3854738
LODGE, Pte, Herbert, 3855485
LONGWORTH, Pte, David, 3855116
MANSLEY, Pte, Fred, 3856190
MARLOW, Pte, Alban, 3854935
MARTIN, Pte, James David, 3856371
MASHITER, Pte, Joseph William, 3853546
METCALF, Pte, James Albert, 3853934
METCALFE, Pte, William Hampshire, 3446355
MILLS, Pte, Frederick Thomas, 3855551
MONAGHAN, Pte, John, 3851473
MOORCROFT, Pte, Thomas, 3858580
MORELAND, Cpl, Thomas Stafford, 3850221
MORGAN, Pte, Harold, 3856722
MORRIS, Pte, William, 3857053
MORRIS, Pte, Harry, 3530508
MORRIS, L/Cpl, Albert, 3855330
MURDOCH, Lt, Thomas Moore, 164282
MURPHY, Pte, Thomas, 3854741
MURPHY, Pte, John, 3851664
NAYLOR, Pte, Albert, 3855161
NEARY, Pte, Wilfred, 3853627
NEILD, Pte, Leslie, 3855007
NIGHTINGALE, Pte, Frederick, 3856388
O'BRIEN, Pte, Michael, 3854559
O'BRIEN, Pte, John, 3855766
O'TOOLE, Pte, Richard, 3854093
OSBORNE, Pte, Samuel, 3855549
OSBOURNE, L/Cpl, Phillip, 3854712
OULTON, Pte, Frank, 839838
PARKER, Pte, John James, 3855501
PARKINSON, Pte, Frank Clifford, 3856612
PARKINSON, Pte, Norman, 3859455
PARSISSON, Pte, John, 3856611
PATCHETT, Cpl, John Walter, 3855535
PENDLEBURY, Pte, Vincent Horace, 3855420
PENNINGTON, Pte, Edward, 3856207
PIDDOCK, Pte, George, 3855112
PIGOTT, Lt, Roger Burton, 130072
PLACE, Pte, John Albert, 3856583
PLACE, Pte, James, 3855051
POMFRET, Pte, Eric, 836007
PORTER, Cpl, William, 3855317
POSTLETHWAITE, Pte, Frederick Wallace, 3858594
POXON, Pte, Ernest, 3856678
PRATT, Pte, Robert James, 3856751
PRICE, Pte, Albert Edward, 3858840
PRICE, Pte, Jack, 3527695
PRITCHARD, Pte, Peter, 3856767
PROBIN, Pte, Thomas, 2056022
PRYLE, Pte, Harold, 3856914
PRYOR, L/Cpl, James, 3854706
PULLIBLANK, Capt, Richard Aldwyn, 50954
RADLEY, Pte, Harold, 3856636
RAVEN, Maj, John Arnold, 36757
RAVENSCROFT, Pte, Cyril, 3861626
REILLY, Pte, Bernard, 4745929

RILEY, Pte, William, 3858975
RIMMER, Pte, Ronald, 3859599
ROADES, Csm, John, 6189306
ROBERTS, Pte, Harold, 3723437
ROBERTS, Cpl, Frederick, 3855727
ROBERTS, Pte, Mark, 3855363
ROBINSON, Pte, Nathom, 3858601
ROTHWELL, Pte, James, 3856693
ROYLE, Cpl, John, 3855395
RUMFITT, Pte, Edward, 3859295
RUSH, Cpl, Philip, 3854640
SADLER, Csm, William Charles, 3850712
SHARPLES, Pte, William Stanley, 3855000
SHAW, Pte, Joseph, 3856933
SHAW, Pte, James, 3859525
SHELDON, Pte, Ronald, 3856856
SHENTON, Pte, Harold, 3854722
SHEPHERD, Pte, Henry, 3855956
SHIELD, Pte, John Reginald, 3855063
SHIPPERBOTTOM, L/Cpl, Reuben Gorton, 3854771
SHOWELL, L/Sjt, Thomas, 3855834
SKELDON, Pte, Alfred, 3856489
SKINNER, Bdsmn, John Kenneth, 3854858
SLOAN, Pte, Hugh Ypres, 3855668
SLOANE, Pte, Frederick, 3857677
SMETHURST, Pte, Robert, 3855387
SMITH, Pte, Henry, 3856894
SMITH, L/Cpl, Henry, 3535104
SMITH, Pte, Richard, 3861723
SMITHIES, Pte, Archbell, 3858617
SMYTH, Pte, Samuel, 3856526
SOUTHERN, Pte, Ronald, 3856350
SPALDING, Pte, Fred, 3856093
STANNARD, Pte, Henry, 3857220
STAPLES, Pte, James, 3856912
STEVENSON, Pte, Joseph William, 3855113
STOPPFORTH, Pte, Walter, 3857295
SUMNER, Pte, Joseph Edward, 3854175
TAFT, Pte, Albert, 3856492
TASKER, Pte, Norman, 3859385
TAYLOR, Sjt, Edward, 3849831
TAYLOR, Pte, Robert, 3854830
TAYLOR, Pte, Walter Leonard, 3854747
TAYLOR, Pte, Edward James, 3856703
THOMAS, Cpl, William Henry, 3854646
THOMAS, Pte, Gwilym, 3852211
THOMPSON, Pte, James Richard, 3855682
THOMPSON, L/Cpl, Fred Lonsdale, 3859129
TIMBRELL, Pte, Cyril, 3856625
TOOTHILL, Pte, Colin, 3855209
TOPPING, Cpl, John James, 3858312
TORR, 2/lt, Philip Wood, 156642
TOWNSON, Pte, Tom, 3849773
TRIVETT, Pte, George Herbert, 3855151
TULLY, Pte, Henry, 3855025
TURNER, Cpl, Harold, 3853110
URMSTON, L/Cpl, John Joseph, 3858908
VINCENT, Cpl, Henry Peter, 3855692
WALKER, L/Cpl, George, 3855171
WALKER, Pte, Horace James, 3859564
WALL, Pte, Thomas William, 3854711
WALSH, Pte, Leonard, 3855502
WEBSTER, Pte, Frank, 3856939
WELLS, Sjt, Stanley, 3854915
WELSH, Pte, Robert, 3855480
WESTHEAD, Pte, Thomas, 3854291
WHITAKER, Pte, Cyril Yates, 3855863
WHITE, Pte, Jack, 3856422
WHITEING, Capt, John Francis (MC), 63609
WHITTAKER, Pte, Harry, 3857615

WILKINSON, Pte, Samuel, 3855547
WILKINSON, Pte, Edward, 3854938
WILLIAMS, Pte, John, 3854751
WILLOCK, Pte, John, 3855495
WILSHER, Pte, James George, 3855204
WILSON, Pte, Edward Kenneth, 3856566
WITHERS, Lt, Gerald Guy, 126443
WOODHEAD, Pte, William, 3855713
WORTHINGTON, Pte, William, 3856302
WRIGHT, Pte, Douglas George, 3855886
YATES, Pte, Thomas, 3535152
YATES, Pte, George William, 3849800
YATES, Pte, Albert, 3859509

LOYAL REGIMENT
5 BATTALION
AARON, Tpr, Abraham, 4133199
ADCOCK, Cpl, Herbert, 5772198
AINSCOUGH, Tpr, James, 3857074
ALLEN, Tpr, Albert, 3859193
ASTLEY, Tpr, Harold, 3859194
BAGSHAW, Tpr, Richard, 3859199
BAILEY, Tpr, Albert, 4133535
BAILEY, Tpr, Fredrick W., 3861786
BAKER, Tpr, Leslie, 4133249
BARNES, Trpr, Frederick, 3855807
BENNETT, Tpr, Cyril, 3859203
BIRCHALL, Tpr, Frederick, 6918591
BIRCHALL, L/Cpl, Edwards, 3856261
BOOTH, Trpr, William, 4133444
BOURNE, L/sgt, Jack, 3858362
BRACEGIRDLE, L/Cpl, L, 3857709
BROKSBANK, Tpr, Alan, 3838375
BROWN, Tpr, Thomas, 3859202
BROWN, Tpr, George, 4133231
BRYAN, Tpr, James Henry, 3856743
BURROWS, Cpl, William Frederick, 6915268
BURROWS, Tpr, Wilfred, 3449993
BUSBY, Tpr, Francis George, 6194786
BUTTERWORTH, L/pl, James Arnold, 4132875
CALDERLEY, Tpr, Joseph, 3857157
CALVER, Sjt, Leonard John, 5775170
CAMPBELL, Trpr, Charles, 4133286
CARR, Tpr, Edward, 3857355
CHECKETTS, Trpr, Joseph, 4133253
CHEESEBOROUGH, Tpr, Alfred, 3521006
CLARK, Tpr, Eric, 3857724
CLULEY, Tpr, Gordon Anthony, 6915050
COOKE, Tpr, Joseph, 4133233
DAVIS, Sjt, Bertie Albert, 4796850
DEARDEN, Tpr, John, 4132744
DENYER, Tpr, William Charles, 6918688
DIXON, Capt, Richard Wickham, 69985
DUNNING, Tpr, George Edward, 3859176
EDEN, Tpr, George, 3859227
EMMOTT, Tpr, Douglas, 3859125
FALLOWES, Tpr, Raymond Victor, 6918712
FEASEY, Tpr, Demnis Thomas, 6918314
FISHWICK, Tpr, Joseph Henry, 3859232
FOSTER, Tpr, Richard, 3865414
FOSTER, L/Cpl, Graham, 4972672
FRANCIS, Tpr, William Henry, 413293
GEARY, Trpr, Walter William, 3859245
GIBBONS, Tpr, Alfred Charles George, 6914847
GILDERT, Tpr, John, 3858028
GORTON, Cpl, Peter Bristowe, 6914849
GRANT, Sjt, William Charles Henry, 3851935
GREGORY, Trpr, Edwin, 2856089
GRIFFITHS, Tpr, Wilmer John David, 3859151
GULLIVER, Tpr, William N.J., 3859238

HALFPENNY, Tpr, Frederick, 3534133
HALLETT, Cpl, Leslie, 6914855
HANSON, Tpr, Arnold, 3859259
HARTLEY, L/Cpl, Sidney Stuart, 4978672
HARTSHORN, Tpe, Jesse Fletcher, 3859251
HAYNES, Tpr, Norman, 3857326
HAYSTON,Cpl,John,3857664
HENDERSON,Tpr,Robert George,14282388
HICKLEY,Tpr,Harold,3534150
HILL,Lt,Bernard Leslie,130134
HODGSON, Tpr, John, 3710938
HOLDING, Tpr, Ernest Henry Thomas, 6918753
HOLLICK, Lt, John Aubrey, 117961
HOLLINWORTH, Tpr, William, 3850997
HOLT, Trpr, William, 3857572
HOOPER, Tpr, Ronald, 3858377
HOPE, Tpr, Herbert, 3855855
INMAN, Tpr, Victor George, 6914662
JACKSON, Cpl, Eric, 3856391
JOHNSON, L/Cpl, Arthur Thomas, 5773790
KNOWLES, Cpl, Donald, 3858366
LANDER, Tpr, Ronald Sidney Charles, 6348451
LATHAM, Tpr, James, 4133212
LIVER, Tpr, William, 3859160
LOBB, Tpr, Ernest Bertram, 3859270
LOYE, L/Cpl, Robert Arthur, 6916782
LUBY, Tpr, John, 3856499
MARSHALL, Tpr, Charles Henry, 4132113
MASTERS, Tpr, Sidney Francis, 4133370
MAYOR, Tpr, Bert, 3859101
McCARTHY, Cpl, Ralph, 3856842
McLOUGHLIN, Tpr, John, 3859276
MERRILL, Tpr, Charles, 3856097
MILLER, Tpr, Stanley, 3852860
MORAN, Tpr, Patrick, 3865276
MUNCASTER, Tpr, Charles Benjamin, 3858370
NEWTON, Trpr, John, 3857290
NOLAN, Tpr, Joseph, 4133268
OGDEN, Tpr, Jonathan, 3646201
PALMER, Tpr, Alfred Joseph, 2058842
PARKER, Tpr, Wiliam, 3857151
PARTINGTON, Spr, Lewis Hodgkiss, 3857135
POLITTT, Tpr, Frank, 3857265
POPPLEWELL, Tpr, Richard Cecil, 4133218
PRICE, Tpr, Walter, 3855199
RAE, Tpr, Louis, 3854901
RANDALL, Maj, Frederick Jones, 63895
REID, Tpr, James, 3859291
RICHARDS, Tpr, Harry Leonard, 6467382
RIDING, Trpr, John Francis, 3859184
RILEY, Tpr, Norman Horace, 3855120
RIVINGTON, Tpr, John Douglas, 3859119
ROBBINS, Sjt, Edward, 3856746
ROBINS, Cpl, Francis Henry, 4267806
ROTHWELL, Tpr, Richard, 3856088
ROWLANDS, Trpr, Albert Hewitt, 4133459
RUSHTON, Tpr, Arnold, 3855827
SALTER, Trpr, Arthur, 4133411
SCHOFIELD, L/Cpl, William, 3859301
SCHOFIELD, Csm, Tom, 3851687
SCOTT, Tpr, Hary Bertram Thomas, 6917533
SHAW, Tpr, Alert Edward, 3859178
SHAW, Cpl, Frank, 3859315
SHEPHERD, Tpr, Robert, 3855617
SIMISTER, Tpr, John Edwin, 4133613
SMITH, Tpr, Jack, 3859296
SMITH, Tpr, Frank, 4133301
SMITH, L/Cpl, Robert William, 6917998
SMITH, Tpr, Frank Edward, 4133560
SNEDDON, Tpr, Thomas, 3129125

SPALDING, Tpr, Harold Norman, 3859313
SPENCER, Tpr, Harry, 3859303
STAINBANK, Tpr, Charles, 3857244
STANIFORTH, Tpr, Edmund, 4132871
STEELE, Tpr, Henry Albert Turngrove, 3857294
STEVENSON, Tpr, Norman Sullivan, 3859106
STEWART, Tpr, William Douglas, 5051068
STRELLEY, Lt, Charles Douglas S, 184650
STRETCH, Tpr, John, 3856747
STUBBS, Cpl, Robert Langhorn, 5950934
SUTTON, Tpr, Robert, 771763
SWINDELLS, Lt, Francis George, 117962
TAYLOR, Tpr, James Morris, 3859321
THOMAS, Tpr, John David, 3854922
TONG, Tpr, Robert, 3856038
TWATT, Tpr, James, 2932522
TYRER, Sjt, Ernest, 828192
WELLS, Tpr, Dennis Charles, 6346652
WINCHESTER, Tpr, Frederick Howard, 3859174
WOLFENDALE, L/Cpl, Joseph, 3856128
WOLFENDEN, Tpr, James, 3864610
WOODS, Sjt, Arthur James, 3902746
WOOLFORD, Tpr, Frederick John, 6914757
WORRALL, Tpr, Thomas, 3864838
WRIGHT, Tpr, Richard Henry, 3856820
WYSE, Lt, John Malin, 137215

MANCHESTER REGIMENT
ANDERSON, Pte, Arthur, 3529611
BAILEY, Pte, Harry, 3531207
BALL, Pte, Lawrence Bradman, 3534126
BAMFORTH, Pte, Herbert, 3529822
BARRY, Pte, William, 3529530
BARSTOW, Pte, Joseph, 3533911
BEBBINGTON, Sjt, William Yarwood (DCM), 3525822
BECKETT, Pte, James, 3529831
BELL, Pte, William, 3524382
BENNETT, Pte, Samuel Alexander, 2034499
BIMSON, Pte, George, 3526058
BLAKELEY, L/pl, Walter, 3527273
BOARDMAN, L/Cpl, Ernest, 3526098
BOLTON, Pte, John Bernard, 3529726
BOURNE, Pte, Frank, 3530230
BOYNE, L/pl, Patrick, 3257514
BRADFORD, Pte, Walter Francis, 4800131
BROCKLEY, Pte, Charles, 3527523
BROOKS, Pte, Harold, 3535952
BRUNT, Pte, Richard, 3525130
BYERS, Pte, Thomas William, 3528784
CHATTERLEY, L/Cpl, Joseph Simpson, 3523473
CHRISTIAN, Pte, James, 3524474
CLARKE, L/Cpl, Norman Eric, 3534723
CLARKE, Pte, Robert Vernon, 3532996
CLAYTON, Pte, Edward, 3534727
CLEGG, L/Cpl, James William, 3534738
COAN, Pte, James John, 3535648
COLLINS, Pte, David John, 3530377
CONNOR, Pte, John Joseph, 3534735
COOGAN, L/Sjt, James Joseph, 3525478
COOPER, Pte, Alfred, 3534715
COOPER, Maj, Geoffrey Danvers, 18843
CREESE, Pte, Mervyn, 3526175
CREIGHTON, Pte, Samuel, 3527593
CRICHTON, Pte, Ralph, 3528102
CROMPTON, Pte, Harold, 3534653
CRONSHAW, Pte, John, 3527531
CROOKES, Pte, Thomas Henry, 3533842
CROWTHER, Pte, Fred, 3528299
DANIELS, Pte, Ronald Leonard, 3534710
DAVIES, Pte, Joseph Edgar, 3530313

DAWSON, Pte, Albert Stanley, 3525595
DERMOTT, Cpl, Cyril, 3528806
DIAMOND, Pte, Walter George, 3770001
DICKINSON, Pte, Norman, 928992
DODD, Pte, James Henry, 3526533
DODD, Cpl, Henry, 3526413
DOOLEY, Sjt, James William, 3525853
DOUGLASS, Maj, William James, 40663
DOYLE, Csm, John, 3518059
DURWARD, C/Sjt, Quentin Longshaw, 3518143
DYSON, Lt/col, George St John Armitage (MC), 8409
EDWARDS, Pte, George, 3527281
EDWARDS, L/Cpl, Albert, 3535877
EVANS, Pte, Thomas, 3529234
EVANS, Pte, Richard, 3534725
EVERETT, Csm, Edward, 4605008
FALLOWS, Pte, Ernest Ben, 3534659
FARNELL, L/pl, Norman, 3524258
FELLOWES, C/Sjt, Herbert Frank, 724269
FENNER, Pte, Leslie, 3534006
FENSOME, Cpl, Ronald James, 3526518
FLANAGAN, Pte, John, 3529689
FLETCHER, Pte, Selwyn, 3528035
FLUCK, Pte, John Thomas, 3526649
FOOTE, Cpl, Thomas, 3527020
FORBES, Pte, Ernest, 3526387
FOULKES, Pte, Reginald Ewart, 3526096
FOX, Pte, James Herbert, 3534058
FREER, Cpl, Thomas, 3446742
GEORGE, Pte, Harold, 3529569
GERRARD, L/Cpl, George, 3533723
GLASS, Pte, George Edgar, 3526486
GRANT, Pte, Donald, 3528818
GREENHALGH, L/Cpl, Ernest, 3534700
GRIFFITHS, Pte, Thomas, 3535929
HAKE, L/Cpl, Stanley Arthur, 3523133
HAL, L/Cpl, Albert, 3530911
HALL, Pte, Staney, 3526624
HALLIWELL, L/Cpl, John, 3522539
HAMILTON, Pte, Harvey, 3534044
HANKINSON, Pte, George, 3528829
HARKISS, Pte, Elmer Cecil, 3528162
HARPER, Pte, Wilfred, 3528082
HARRIS, Pte, Frederick George, 3527653
HARRISON, Pte, Peter, 3525825
HARRISON, Pte, George Edward, 3534108
HARRISON, Csm, William, 3524539
HARVEY, Pte, Leonard Tournal, 56921
HAUGHTON, Pte, William, 3515086
HEALEY, Pte, Thomas Bernard, 3526592
HEALEY, L/Cpl, Reuben, 3532874
HEFFERAN, Pte, John Stanley, 3526696
HENNIKER, Pte, James, 3528585
HENSMAN, L/Cpl, Arthur Charles, 3523737
HEPWORTH, L/Cpl, Sidney, 3526054
HEWKIN, Pte, Frank Wandsworth, 3529515
HICKEY, Pte, Patrick, 3529437
HOGG, Boy, Alfred, 3534748
HOLLAND, Pte, Norman, 3533023
HOUGH, Pte, George Arthur, 3527674
HOUGHTON, L/pl, William, 3532931
HOULDSWORTH, Pte, George, 6210430
HOWE, Lt, Dudley Melville, 121943
HOWE, Pte, Ronald, 3529690
HOWLEY, Pte, Richard Henry, 3527701
HUDSON, Pte, Arthur, 3529455
HUGHES, Pte, Alfred, 3529664
HUGHES, Pte, Frank, 3530315
HUGHES, Pte, Felix, 3527515
JACKSON, L/Cpl, John, 352807

JAGGERS, Pte, Horace, 3529614
JAY, Pte, Frank William, 3527464
JEFFERS, Pte, Mathew, 3529602
JENNINGS, Pte, Harold, 3534824
JOHNSON, Pte, A.E.J., 3529054
JOHNSON, Pte, William, 3526467
JONES, Pte, Andrew, 3528449
JONES, L/Cpl, John Henry, 3533976
JONES, Pte, Albert Lloyd, 3534648
KEATING, Sjt, James, 3523252
KELLY, Pte, Thomas Edward, 3533758
KELLY, Pte, John, 3529769
KERSHAW, Pte, Vincent, 3533371
KINCHIN, Pte, Norman, 3525962
KIRK, Pte, Joseph, 3534643
LADLEY, Pte, James, 3533764
LALLEY, Pte, Thomas Patrtick, 3523862
LAMBERT, Pte, William, 3535646
LATHAM, Pte, Ralph, 3534641
LATHAM, L/Cpl, Fred, 3527467
LEE, Pte, Henry, 3526284
LEE, Pte, Henry, 3526284
LEWIS, Csm, Frederick, 3521326
LINDSAY, Pte, Gladstone, 3534663
LLOYD, Pte, John, 3524312
LOVE, Sjt, Cyril, 3527527
LOW, Lt, David William, 129560
LUCAS, Pte, Thomas, 3530192
LUCOCK, Pte, Kenneth Claude, 832836
LUDBROOK, Pte, Edward Ellis, 3528565
MAHON, L/Cpl, Joseph Edward, 3534642
MALCOLM, Pte, Robert Edward John, 3526952
MALONE, Pte, Peter, 3535938
MARTIN, Boy, James Walter, 3536562
MASKERY, L/Cpl, Joseph, 3525898
MASON, Pte, Frank, 3527186
McCLURG, Cpl, Wiliam Daniel, 3526949
McKINLEY, Pte, Francis, 3535939
MEREDITH, Sjt, Ernest, 3511718
MIDDLETON, L/Cpl, William, 3529147
MILBURN, Pte, John, 3526684
MILLWARD, Pte, George, 3526710
MITCHELL, L/Cpl, Donald, 3528870
MITCHELL, Pte, Joseph, 3528935
MOORBY, Pte, Harold, 3534661
MORRISAY, Pte, James, 3526771
MOULD, Pte, John, 3534696
MURPHY, Pte, Maurice Joseph, 3529695
MYERSCOUGH, Csm, Arthur Frank, 3524843
MYLCHREEST, Sjt, John Alfred Denzil, 3525476
MYNETT, Pte, John William, 3534742
NOBLE, Sjt, Leslie, 3526838
NOLAN, Sjt, Patrick Peter, 3526623
NUTTALL, Pte, Arthur, 3526120
O'NEILL, Pte, Vincent, 3529495
OLSSON, L/Cpl, Richard, 3253990
ONLEY, Pte, Thomas, 3532450
OPENSHAW, L/Sjt, Arthur Stanard, 3524069
ORME, Pte, Samuel, 3525775
OWEN, L/Cpl, Thomas, 3525959
PARR, Pte, Richard, 3534686
PEMBERTON, Pte, Francis, 3529435
POWELL, Sjt, William, 3526097
PRUDEN, Pte, Raymond, 3527580
PRYCE, Pte, George Edward, 3527643
QUINN, Lt Qm, Thomas (MM), 89781
REEVES, Bsmn, Harry Vincent, 3528632
RIDGWAY, Pte, Henry Vincent, 3532875
RILEY, Pte, James, 2568332
ROBE, Pte, John Robert, 3534689

ROBERTS, Pte, William Anthony, 3530225
ROBERTS, Pte, Herbert, 3525943
ROBINSON, Sjt, Albert, 3442837
ROGERS, Pte, Aaron, 3530087
ROGERSON, Pte, Charles, 3529473
ROGERSON, Pte, John, 3534683
ROWBOTHAM, Pte, John William, 3520107
RUSHTON, Pte, Nicholas, 3533928
RYAN, Pte, John, 3527266
SCHOFIELD, Pte, Ernest, 3528781
SCOTT, Pte, Bernard Patrick Joseph, 3533997
SHAW, Pte, John, 3527746
SIGLEY, Pte, Harold, 3536002
SILCOCK, Pte, Harry, 3528096
SMITH, Pte, George Edward, 3526125
SMITH, Pte, Arthur, 3534640
SODERBERG, Pte, Charles Edgar, 3534665
SPENCER, Sjt, Arthur, 3525760
SPURLING, Pte, William, 3535743
STEELE, Pte, Leslie Arnold, 3529123
STEWART, Pte, Bernard, 3529329
STILWELL, L/Sjt, Sidney William George, 3526908
STONES, Pte, James Alfred, 3535946
STRAUGHAIR, Pte, Robert William, 3528874
STURCH, Rsm, Albert, 3514765
SZARKOW, L/Cpl, Alexander, 3533802
TAYLOR, L/Cpl, David, 3527507
TAYLOR, Pte, Cecil, 3523626
TAYLOR, Pte, Arthur, 3527601
TAYLOR, Pte, Fred, 3531715
TAYLOR, Pte, Samuel, 3527536
TAYLOR, L/Cpl, James, 3527543
THOMAS, Maj, Frederick John Herbert, 186250
THOMAS, Pte, Alfred Leonard, 3530383
THOMPSON, L/Cpl, John Christopher, 3527473
TRUEMAN, Pte, Norman John, 3527492
VAUGHAN, Pte, James, 3527115
WALFORD, Pte, John Albert, 3534731
WALKER, Pte, Charles, 3529183
WALKER, Pte, John, 3526919
WALLACE, Bdsmn, George, 3527237
WALLER, Pte, Hargrave, 3534679
WALTON, Pte, John, 3529793
WARD, Cpl, Herbert, 3519394
WARREN, Sjt, Harold, 3525376
WATSON, Pte, Robert, 3529720
WAUGH, Pte, James Kenneth, 3528090
WEBSTER, L/Cpl, Bertie, 3526583
WHITE, L/Cpl, Kenneth William Francis, 3533697
WIGGETT, Pte, James, 3526565
WILKES, L/Cpl, Stanley, 3527645
WILSON, Pte, John Henry, 3536005
WILSON, Pte, Squire, 1528349
WINDSOR, Sjt, Stanley, 3517970
WOODBURY, Pte, Joseph, 3528288
WOODHOUSE, Pte, William Henry, 3535975
WOODWARD, Pte, John, 3527662
WREN, Pte, William, 3528919
YARWOOD, Pte, Robert, 3534709
YOUNG, Pte, Herbert, 3534064
YOXALL, Drmr, Peter, 3528152

SEC INT MANCH
SMITH,S/Sjt,Joseph,3525904

MIDDLESEX REGIMENT
ALLAWAY,Pte,Lonard James,4030955
BENNETT, Pte, Thomas Wilfred, 6203600
BETTS, Sjt, Charles, 5769666
BINDON, Pte, Frank James, 6201249

BUNKER, Pte, John Sidney, 6207610
CASTLE, Sjt, Thomas Richad Montague, 6197065
CHEESEWRIGHT, Lt, Cyril F, 149468
CLARK,Maj,Sidney John,261
COHEN, Pte, Norman, 6203958
COLOCOTT, Pte, Thomas Lionel, 6207656
COX, Cpl, William Thomas, 6199136
DAVIS, L/Sjt, Victor Charles, 6203244
DAVIS, Cpl, Frederick James, 6194972
DIXON, Pte, Aaron Hedley, 6210892
EATON, Pte, Walter T., 836184
ELLIOTT, Pte, Harry George, 6213488
FARR, Pte, George Harold, 6202933
FERRISS, Pte, Stanley Richard, 6201181
FOX, Sjt, William Robert, 5989045
FUNNELL, Pte, John, 6202119
GARDNER, Pte, George Albert, 6201661
GIBBS, L/Cpl, Arthur Henry, 6202707
GOLDSMITH, Pte, Frederick Ernest, 6723293
GRAFTON, Pte, Ernest Charles, 6202775
GRAY, Pte, George John, 6202108
GUDGEON, Capt, Henry Noel Clifton, 64627
GUNN, Pte, Laurence Frederick, 6213499
HARRISON, Pte, Edward, 6202330
HARVEY, Pte, John Baptiste Clifton, 6200684
HUGGETT, Pte, John, 6213513
HUGHES, L/Cpl, Leonard, 6207586
JONES, Pte, John, 6198827
JONES, Pte, Harry George, 6202789
LAMB, Pte, Joseph Patrick, 6210636
LINTON, L/Cpl, Victor Joseph Francis, 6200987
LOMBARY, Pte, Marcel Philyp, 6202791
MATHEWS, Pte, Thomas, 6212893
MEAKIN, Cpl, Frank, 6207916
MILLER, Pte, Charles Alfred, 6202863
NIX, Bdsmn, Kenneth Roy, 6202380
PAINTING, Cpl, Robert, 6200827
PARKER, Pte, James Ernest, 6202344
PEGG, Pte, Charles Walter, 6212991
PINNOCK, Pte, William Jacks, 6201233
RANSON, Pte, Eric, 6200793
REEVES, Cpl, Ronald, 6201116
ROOT, Pte, Alfred Edward, 6203948
SACH, Pte, George Henry, 6198387
SANDELL, Pte, Alfred Albert, 6213002
SEARLE, Pte, Alfred Edward, 6214365
SHEEHAN, Pte, Maurice, 6202103
SLANN, Pte, Frederick Allan, 6210552
STEWART,Lt Col, Henry William Motcrieff (OBE MC CDG), 9005
STURGES, Pte, Albert, 6202743
SULLIVAN, Pte, William, 6213591
TIBBLE, Csm, William Ernest Joseph, 6194081
TOOMBS, Pte, Joseph Henry, 6208218
WEBSTER, Pte, George Alfred, 6201926
WILDERSPIN, L/Cpl, Harry Albert, 6201867
WILLSON, Bdsmn, Donald George, 6201222

NORTHAMTONSHIRE REGIMENT
BARROW,Capt,Bryan Palliser,117681
BEADLE,Pte,H W,14752854
HARPER,Pte,John,11426760
HARRINGTON,Pte,J A,14719966
HOFMAN,Capt,Ralph Augustus,74675
MILLS,Lt,Walter Wakefield,320413
PHILPOT,Pte,G C,14808580

NORTH STAFFORDSHIRE REGIMENT
BETTON, Pte, Harold, 5048419
CLARKE, Pte, Wilfred, 5048067
MELLOR, Pte, James, 5048057

WOOD,Sjt,Kenneth Douglas,5058090

PARACHUTE REGIMENT
BROWN,Pte,Frederick Fellows,14990105
CHOPPING,Pte,William Robert,6207651
DINSMORE,Pte,James,14417305
DUNKERLEY,Pte,Jack,14827900
HAMMICK,Lt,Roger Alexander,249848
HUNTER,Pte,Douglas,14445912
KEAN,Sjt,Albert Melville,4469953
LE CLARE,Sjt,Charles Henry,6139525
LEE,Pte,Colin,14771043
MITCHELL,Sjt,Morley William Mm,5511499
NUTTALL,Pte,Reginald,14427563
SEAL,Maj,M.T.F.,164935
SMALL,Pte,William Frew,7953245
SMITH,Lt,Bernard Francis,326561
TAYLOR,Sjt,Roy Charles,14497534
WARREN,Lt,Robert Stanley,335192

PIONEER CORPS
CLARE, Pte, Joseph, 13087216
EVANS, Sjt, John Herbert, 4191806
FISHWICK, Pte, William, 13062006
FLETCHER, Pte, Reginald, 4196101
GOODWARD, Lt, John Sidney, 227123
GRAY, Cpl, John, 13051122
HIBBERT, Sjt, John, 13062037
HOWARD, Pte, Charles, 13056495
KEELAN, Pte, George Ambrose, 13100370
MARSDEN, Pte, Benjamin, 13056787
MILLER, Pte, William, 13056412
MITCHEL, L/Cpl, Frank, 13056355
QUARMBY, Pte, Harry, 13062041
SMITH, Capt, Charles Franklin, 233670
WEBSTER, Pte, William Henry, 13056966

QUEEN ALEXANDRA'S IMPERIAL
MILITARY NURSING SERVICE
AYERS, Sister, Eileen Norah, 206581
BLACK, Sister, Charlotte Florence, 206670
CARROLL, Sister, Edith Katherine, 206070
CLEWETT, Sister, Catharine Hilda, 208176
COOPER, Sister, Mary, 206892
COWARD, Sister, Laura, 206068
DUNLOP, Sister, Doreen Violet, 363771
FINLEY, Sister, Margaret Aven, 206153
FOWLER, Sister, Marjorie Helen Taylor, 206752
HERVEY-MURRAY, Sister, Agnes Joan, 208739
HODGSON, Sister, Marjorie Aizlewood, 206211
JONES, Sister, Mavis Joy, 313979
MONTGOMERY, Sister, Helen Louise, 206325
MUIR, Sister, Anne Wilson, 208738
PEDLOW, Sister, Edith Doreen, 206391
RUSSELL, Matron, Winifred, 208018
SULLIVAN, Sister, Nancy, 366317
SYMONDS, Sister, Lorna Sybil, 209317
TOMBS, Sister, Dorothy Helen, 206488
WELLS, Sister, Brenda Irene, 206534
WEST, Matron, Cicely Lucy Mary, 206503
WRIGHT, Sister, Irene, 209440

QUEEN'S OWN CAMERON HIGHLANDERS
PALMER,Pte,Ronald Charles,14989358
BOYD,Cpl,John Farmer,14820739

QUEEN'S ROYAL REGIMENT
CLIFTON,Lt,Alan Edward,350792
FITZGERALD, Pte, James, 3782746
FORESTER,L/Cpl,William Alfred Ernest,14496226

LITHERLAND, Pte, John, 14820220
RICHARDSON, Pte, J., 14183669
WALLS, Pte, A.V., 14803140

RECONNAISSANCE CORPS
FITZGERALD,Lt,Thomas Edward,137213

ROYAL ARMOURED CORPS
CHRISTIAN,Tpr,Arthur,7915979
CORCORAN,Lt,Thomas Albert,315269
FRENCH,L/Sjt,Charles Henry,7884539

ROYAL ARMY CHAPLAINS' DEPARTMENT
CHALKE,Rev'd,Richard Cradocke,139815
CHAMBERS,Rev'd,Gilbert John Marion
DEAN,Rev,John Oswald,52744
RAWSTHORNE,The Rev,Peter,99438,
SMITH,Rev,Henry,135499
SHORT,(The Rev),John Harold,139505
WANLESS,Rev,John Thirwell,77336

ROYAL ARMY DENTAL CORPS
BAIRSTOW, Pte, Ronald William, 7538134
BROWN, Capt, John Green, 135340
CARDWELL, Capt, Ernest Colin, 120229
MAPLESDEN, Pte, Victor Joseph Lloyd, 7538056
WALKER, Capt, William, 118396
WALKER, S/Sjt, Sydney, 7536231

ROYAL ARMY EDUCATIONAL CORPS
MARTIN, W/o 1, David, 1862349
NEVILLE, Sjt, Cecil Charles, 134367
ROYDS, Sjt, Edward Middleton, 7677864
TIMBERS, Capt, Arthur Robert, 143937

ROYAL ARMY MEDICAL CORPS
ADAMS, Pte, Roger, 7394281
AHIM, Pte, Horace Stanislause, 7532501
ALDRIDGE, Pte, Henry John, 1051394
ALDRIDGE, Capt, Bernard Henry Mooring, 133194
ALLAN, Capt, George Ferguson, 128562
ALLARDICE, Capt, Ansome Mcnamara, 633664
ANDREE, Pte, Anthony Wilfred, 7532580
ANDREWS, Pte, Adolphus Henry, 7518322
ANDREWS, Pte, Joseph Frederick, 7368802
ASHWORTH, Pte, Charles, 7394190
AUSTIN, Pte, Douglas, 7344041
BANTOCK, Pte, Alfred, 7258779
BARROW, Pte, Jack Edward, 7517037
BARTHOLOMEW, Pte, L.H., 7532692
BEAUMONT, Pte, Eric, 7374103
BELTON, Pte, A. R., 7374104
BIGNELL, Pte, Arthur E. V., 7347978
BOULTON, Pte, Richard Arthur, 7368910
BOWGEN, Pte, Stephen Robin, 7372857
BRADLEY, Cpl, Stanley, 7262602
BRECK, Pte, Albert Henry, 7391326
BROWN, Pte, Aldred Alfred, 7387472
BROWN, L/Cpl, Jack Robinson, 7532518
BROWN, Pte, William T, 7262686
BRUTON, Cpl, John, 7261480
BUNNEY, Pte, John Edward, 7521109
BURNETT, Cpl, James Smith, 7262350
BURTON,Colonel,Charles Frank (MC),8617
BUTLER, Pte, Kenneth Robert, 7517540
BUTTERWORTH, Pte, Norman, 7374117
CAMPBELL, Capt, Charles Freebairn, 122826
CARAPIET, Pte, George, 7532686
CLARKE, Pte, Reginald A., 7368806
COLLETT, Pte, William Joseph, 7535348

COLLINS, Pte, Arthur George, 3795756
COPPERWHEAT, Pte, Harry John, 7372877
CRABTREE, Pte, James Henry, 7396732
CURRY, Pte, James Christopher, 7321364
DANIELS, Capt, Frank Lancelot Kenneth, 111986
DAVIDSON, Pte, Robert, 7365292
DE CRUZ, Pte, Stanley, 7532565
DEALTRY, Cpl, Frederick Leonard, 7343534
DEAN, Cpl, Reginald A.,
DIVER, Capt, John, 112639
DOWNS, Pte, James W, 7263665
DUTTON, Pte, James H.,
EASTWOOD, Capt, Alfred Kenneth, 175665
EDNEY, Pte, Howard William, 7265608
EDWARDS, Pte, Horace, 4838601
ENTWISTLE,Pte,Edward,7389717
EVANS,Pte,David John,14852840
EVANS, Sgt, W. P., 7518179
FOX,Pte,Maurice,7532623
GALOONG, Pte, H, 7532742
GOODSALVE, Pte, Frederick George, 7368588
GORDON, Cpl, Thomas, 7262343
GORDON, Pte, Robert J, 7518982
GORONWY, Capt, John Wayne, 183683
GRAY, Pte, William Louis, 7532630
GREEN, Pte, Philip Randolph, 7394548
GREY, Pte, Stephen Charles, 7253737
GRIFFITHS, Pte, Ivor James, 7516384
HARRIS, Pte, Herbert Leslie, 7516390
HARTERY, Sjt, John, 7249743
HAYES, Pte, Lloyd Frederick, 7538777
HAYWARD, Pte, Reginald Samuel John, 7521581
HENSON, Pte, Joseph Sydney, 7532538
HILL, Pte, Frank, 7374184
HILLARD, Pte, Leslie George, 2575532
HOARE, L/Cpl, Reginald S., 7368906
HOLLAND, Pte, Clifford Harold, 7383317
HOPPER, Cpl, Joseph, 7260165
HOULT, Pte, Joseph, 7356301
INNES, Pte, J A, 7532596
IRVINE, Lt, Donald Ferguson, 223811
ISAAC, Cpl, Idris Wen, 7519883
JACKSON, Pte, Leslie Bell, 7385352
JAMES, Sjt, George Thomas Percy, 7258894
JACQUES, Sgt, Wilfred, 4033251
KELLY, Sjt, Francis Joseph, 7259593
LAY, Pte, Arthur Charles, 7368890
LEWIS, L/Cpl, Jack Valentine, 7262366
LEWIS, Pte, Kenneth Everett, 7520901
LEWIS, Pte, Gordon Ashby, 7522629
LEWIS, Pte, R, 7372833
LLOYD, Pte, Hugh, 7362254
LONG, Pte, Leslie B., 7368819
LOYNES, Pte, Alfred Frederick, 7365046
MALLON, Pte, John, 7392143
MARKS, Pte, John, 7538096
MARSTON, Cpl, Herbert Hill, 4911630
MATTTIMORE, Cpl, Joseph, 7359080
MAXWELL, Lt Qm, Andrew, 154192
McCARTNEY, Pte, John Morley, 7385533
McDONOUGH, Cpl, Patrick Frederick, 7261975
McEWEN, Cpl, James Bisset, 7516689
McGARVIE, Pte, Edward, 7393195
MELLOR, Pte, G. E. T., 7374095
MENGES, Pte, William Richard, 7395384
MINIFIE, Pte, Ronald George, 7366735
MINJOOT, Pte, Daniel Anthony, 7532577
MINNS, Pte, Stephen Vincent, 7263436
MITCHEL, L/Cpl, Hugh Reginald, 7520621
MOSELEY, Pte, Alfred Eric, 7383142

MOYNIHAN, Maj, Charles Arthur, 73568
MURPHY, Lt, Col Thomas Kiely, 75583
MURPHY, Cpl, Joseph, 7009425
MURPHY, Pte, Wilfred, 7364291
NEAVES, Pte, Percy John, 7372907
NEILL, Sjt, Alexander, 7263142
NEWMAN, Pte, Reginald Henry, 7373276
NICHOLLS, Pte, Douglas Stanley, 7382641
NONIS, Pte, Frank, 7532636
NORMAN, Pte, L., 7374029
OLDHAM, Cpl, Norman, 7380723
OLIVER, Pte, George, 7265002
OLIVER, Pte, Edward Robert, 7372476
ONSLOW, Pte, Frank Henry, 7392656
OSTEL, L/Cpl, Anthony, 7260957
PARKINSON, Capt, Roylance Lynton, 111779
PEREIRA, Pte, Percy Ethridge, 7532588
PHILLIP, Pte, Maurice Arthur, 7344039
PICKERING, Sjt, John Arthur, 7261267
PIERCE, Pte, Stanley William, 7382057
PINTO, Pte, L F, 75324598
PUDNEY, Pte, Eric E., 7368826
QUIGLEY, Pte, Francis, 7264226
RAEBURN, Pte, Albert, 7532599
RAPLEY, Pte, Arthur William, 7384398
RICHARDSON, Pte, Victor Sydney Miles, 7383018
RITCHIE, Pte, Glenalvon Edwin, 7263686
ROBERTS, Pte, Donald, 7368241
ROBERTSHAW, Pte, Wiliam, 7261879
ROBERTSON, Pte, Ernest Alexander, 7392223
ROBINSON, Pte, Charles, 7365033
ROBINSON, Pte, Frank, 7522046
ROBSON, Cpat, Cedric Rowntree, 122820
RODGER, Pte, Robert, 7347843
ROE, S/Sjt, James Gilbert, 7253458
ROGERS, Lt, Geoffrey, 223350
ROGERS, Pte, Henry Harold, 7379467
ROSE, Pte, Harry, 7521340
ROSE, Pte, Roy H., 7395430
ROSS, L/Sjt, Henry James G, 7263015
SAGGERS, Pte, William J.,
SALISBURY, W/o 1, William Alan, 14299122
SCHOFIELD, Capt, John Varley, 131357
SCOTT, Sjt, Thomas, 7262038
SELBY, L/Cpl, Bertram Arthur, 7376301
SHAFFREY, Sjt, James Patrick, 7258526
SHARMAN, Pte, Kenneth Leslie, 7372727
SHEDDEN, Pte, Prince Edward, 7531746
SHERER, Pte, Leonard, 7376254
SHERRIF, Sjt, Thomas, 7261918
SIDDALL, Pte, Dennis, 7521896
SILKE, Pte, Harold William, 7262514
SINCLAIR, Pte, Edward William, 7263182
SMITH, Cpl, Ray, 7263277
SPENCER, Pte, Richard, 7264550
SQUIRES, Maj, Seth Kenneth, 221606
STANLEY, Pte, William Thomas Clement, 7532525
STEEL, L/Cpl, William, 7374061
STOKER, Pte, Andrew Leslie Wallace, 7519979
STRINGER, L/Cpl, Stringer, Douglas N.,
SUMMERSGILL, Sjt, Jack, 7263250
SUNDERLAND, Sjt, Cyril John, 7354270
SUTHERLAND, Capt, Arthur Wemyss Gordon, 106132
SWEENEY, Pte, Randolph Michael, 7887203
TAY, Pte, Joseph Mathias, 7524475
TETLEY, Pte, Denis, 7365614
THESIERA, Pte, Martin John, 7532609
THOMAS, Pte, Rhys, 7372578
THOMPSON, Capt, Humphrey Barron, 128238
THORPE, Lt Qm, Roland Henry, 154216

THORPE, Dvr, Albert, T/157214
TYNER, Sjt, William Charles, 6630623
UNDERHILL, L/Cpl, Harry, 6400858
UNDERWOOD, Pte, Roy Sidney, 7535272
UNGLESS, Pte, Robert Joseph, 7368909
VASSALL CALDER, Maj, Clarence Alexander, 94076
VEALE, Pte, Percy Henry, 14398391
WALKER, Pte, James Campbell, 7263486
WATTS, Pte, Wilfred Walter, 7521383
WESTON, Lt, William Frederick Jayne, 195116
WHITLEY, Pte, Jack, 7374338
WILKINS, Cpl, Fernley, 7258688
WILLIAMS, Cpl, George, 7262160
WILLIAMS, Pte, Charles James, 7521282
WILLIAMS, Pte, Gwyn Raymond, 7365750
WILLIAMS, Pte, Amos Alfred, 7521439
WILLIS, Pte, Percy Edward, 7372031
WILSON, Pte, James Tweedly, 7538277
WING, Pte, James Frederick, 7383091
WOOD, L/Sjt, Frank, 7263480
WOOLNOUGH, Sjt, Ernest Robert James, 7372696
YOUNG, Pte, Robert John, 7262898
YOUNGS, Pte, John Hedley Norcup, 7372701

ROYAL ARMY ORDNANCE CORPS
ADAMSON, L/cpl, Geoffrey Francis, 1513413
ADAMSON, Pte, Geoffrey, 7648640
ADAMSON, Pte, George Douglas, 7628472
ADLINGTON, Sqms, Robert James, 7587596
ALEXANDER, Cpl, William, 7610304
ALLOTT, Pte, Edgar, 10542255
ANDERSON, Pte, William Lipscomb, 7639519
ANDERSON, Pte, Peter, 10539894
ANDERSON, Pte, David, 3322963
ARKLE ARM, Sjt, Francis, 7589916
ARMITAGE, Pte, Harold, 7630164
ARMSTRONG, Pte, Thomas Kennedy, 1578879
ASHARD, Cpl, Harry Peter, 7647055
ASHDOWN, Pte, Trayton, 7648239
ASHWORTH, Cpl, Roland, 7648551
ASPINWALL, L/cpl, Joseph, 7594456
ATKINS, Pte, Arnold Wilson, 7646745
AXFORD, Pte, George William James, 2035354
BACON, Sjt, Rnest Ivor, 1069547
BAILEY, Sjt, Leonard, 7616877
BAILEY, Pte, Ronald Arthur, 7625574
BAKER, Pte, Hugh, 7653771
BALDWIN, Pte, Samual Robert, 937671
BANNATYNE, Pte, George Renton, 7645434
BARNETT, Pte, Cyril Henry John, 7636387
BARRY, Pte, James, 3386082
BARRY, Pte, William Edgar, 7649437
BARTER, Pte, Walter James, 7626831
BARTHOLOMEW, Sqms, Thomas Frederick, 7611767
BATE, Cpl, Joseph Michael, 7648761
BATESON, Pte, Norman Hector, 19541113
BENTLEY, Pte, James Samual, 7642975
BENTON, Pte, Cyril, 2088880
BEXFIELD, Pte, Frederick George, 6025672
BIBBY, Pte, Arthur James, 1572468
BILLSON, Cpl, Jack William, 7586131
BIRNIE, Cpl, James, 7620965
BISS, Maj, William Charles, 119116
BLAND, Pte, Arthur Samual, 7647899
BLEMINGS, Pte, Thomas, 6723410
BLYTHEN, Pte, Ralph, 7640369
BONNER, Pte, Ivor Edwin, 7634202
BOOTH, Pte, Ronald Basil John, 7645338
BOURKE, Sjt, Patrick Joseph, 14943895

BRAGGER, Pte, Edward, 7603150
BRIDGE, Pte, Harry, 10532748
BRIGHT, Pte, Edward Henry, 5444206
BRINDLEY, Pte, Roy, 14111561
BROWN, Pte, John Gow, 7610558
BROWN, Pte, John, 7636612
BROWN, Pte, Reginald Samual, 4864834
BROWNE, Pte, Philip Willoughby, 7598743
BROWNE, Capt, Francis John, 36439
BROWNE, Pte, Stanley William, 7635209
BROZYNA, Maj, Harold Lenton, 63647
BRUNT, S/sjt, Richard Allen, 76298566
BRYDSON, Pte, Dixon Black, 10530143
BULMER, Pte, Ronald, 7597659
BURGESS, Pte, James, 7636614
BURGESS, Pte, Frederick William, (K/N)
BURTON, Pte, Andrew, 5043437
BURTON-PHILLIPSON, Pte, Walter Kenneth, 7653268
BUTLER, Pte, William, 1578691
BYRNE, Pte, Edward, 4124448
CAHILL, S/sjt, John Charles, 7588646
CANE, Sjt, John Ernest, 7624732
CARLEY, Sjt, Noah, 7600359
CARR, Sjt, Walter James, 7581246
CARRUTHERS, L/cpl, Ernest David, 7618243
CARSLAW, Pte, George Baird, 10538420
CHOULARTON, Pte, George Frederick, 7613779
CLARK, Pte, Thomas, 7646560
CLAXTON, Pte, John Alfred, 10554999
COLE, Arm Sjt, Victor George Alexander, 7584492
COLLACOTT, Pte, Ronald Alfred, 5123818
COLLIER, Pte, Henry David, 10531274
COLLINS, Sjt, Reginald George, 7647131
COLLINS, Qms, Reginald Philip, 7587007
COOPER, Pte, Raymond Hilary, 7607793
COOPER, Pte, Clifford, 7633120
CORKERY, Pte, Vincent Joseph, 7636929
COUSINS, Pte, John William, 4757313
COX, Sjt, Clifford, 7610233
COX, Sqms, Francis William, 7628296
CRACKNELL, Pte, George Edward, 4537847
CRANMER, Cpl, Daniel, 7605348
CRATRE, L/cpl, Ronald Ward, 2640280
CROCKETT, Sjt, Arthur James, 24200404
CROSS, Sqms, Dennis Arthur, 7636071
CUNNINGHAM, Pte, Harry, 4626516
DANIELS, Pte, James Frederick, 10556812
DAWES, Pte, George William, 4757061
DICKINSON, Pte, Ronald, 7592691
DOBBS, Pte, Herbert William, 7643018
DONALD, S/sjt, Michael John, 5122445
DORIAN, Sjt, William Charles, 7635620
DOWER, Pte, John, 7647171
DRURY, L/Cpl, Harold, 7596785
DREW, W/o, George Albert, 760478
DUNNETT, L/Cpl, John, 7641419
EDWARDS, L/cpl, John Wilfred, 7631328
EDWARDS, Cpl, William, 7631141
ELDRIDGE, Pte, Ronald James, 10531809
ELLIS, Pte, Edward, 7629220
ELLISON, Pte, John William, 10534512
ELMS, Pte, Arthur Charles, 7649501
EMERY, Cpl, Harry Marshall, 10532593
ENTWISTLE, Pte, William, 7608356
ERRIDGE, Pte, Charles George Benjamin, 7602230
ESSAM, Sjt, Edward James, 10573176
FARQUHARSON, Arm Qms, David, 1069165
FENNER, Pte, James Ernest, 1572487
FIELD, Pte, Harold Charles, 1600707
FIELDHOUSE, Lt Col, Harry (OBE), 85126

FIELDING, Pte, Harold Hawoath, 7647349
FIELLDING, Pte, Thomas Leonard, 10532054
FILLARY, Qms, Frank, 7633742
FISHER, Cpl, Arthur Thomas, 7608599
FITZGERALD, Pte, Patrick, 3651198
FLACK, Pte, George Edward, 7649507
FLETCHER, Pte, Leslie, 10532128
FLETCHER, Pte, Ernest, 7615822
FLETCHER, Pte, Eric, 7591250
FLINT, Pte, Albert, 1578955
FORD, Lt, William, 216791
FORD, L/cpl, Harry George, 5441620
FORREST, Pte, George, 7624215
FOSTER, Pte, Roy Cromwell Secondus, 7608608
FRAMPTON, Pte, Archibald, 7633465
FRANCIS, Sjt, Dennis Wynn, 3911845
FRENCH, Pte, Ernest William, 7611350
FRICKER, Pte, Frederick William, 1751219
FROGGATT, Pte, Ernest, 7597057
FUREY, Pte, Eric John, 7649141
GALBRAITH, L/cpl, John William Mcbain, 7619640
GARBETT, Pte, Frank Raymond, 1053153
GIBSON, Pte, Clifford, 7602906
GILLARD, S/sjt, Harold Hall, 7586888
GODDARD, Sjt, John Alfred, 7594471
GOLDFINCH, Lt, Edward William, 202700
GOODMAN, Pte, James Leonard, 7635100
GOUGH, Pte, Eric Wiliam, 5569221
GRAY, Pte, John Waugh, 7599226
GREAVES, S/sjt, Robert Johnson, 1981705
GREEEN, L/cpl, Donald John, 7637158
GREENAN, L/cpl, Bernard, 7642209
GRIGGS, Pte, Joseph William, 7656400
GRINDLEY, Pte, William, 7629451
GROOM, Pte, Thomas, 3782380
GUY, Pte, James William, 7649295
HAMMOND, Pte, Arthur Edmund Lilleyman, 7635383
HANDLEY, Pte, Francis William, 1579007
HANNAFORD, Pte, Francis Charles, 1578856
HARDING, Pte, John Edward, 7637998
HARDING, Pte, Alfred Henry, 5730227
HARDY, Pte, Thomas Dennis, 7619436
HARRIS, Pte, Frederick Charles, 1579102
HARRISON, Sjt, Harry, 7635675
HAVINDEN, Pte, Frederick William, 7655697
HAWKE, Pte, Edward George, 10531845
HAYES, Lt Col, Frederick Gerald, 127468
HAYTER, Pte, George, 7648481
HEATH, Sqms, William Frank, 7624249
HEELIS, Sjt, Sydney Lawson, 7635858
HELLABY, Pte, Arthur Herbert, 7655266
HENSON, Pte, Henry George, 7610445
HEPWORTH, Pte, Philip Mathew, 7641808
HERBERT, Pte, Ronald Alan Henry, 10531849
HERDMAN, Pte, Maurice, 10545251
HICKEY, Lt, Vivian Wilfred Michael, 205997
HILL, S/sjt, William, 7587636
HILL, Pte, Cyril, 7637702
HILL, Pte, Frederick Robert, 7628581
HILLMAN, Pte, Albert James, 10547436
HIPWELL, Pte, Vcitor James, 7664132
HODGSON, S/sjt, Thomas, 7610705
HOLDER, Pte, Horace Graham, 10543182
HOLLICK, Pte, William Edward, 10551406
HOLLICK, Pte, Henry Thomas, 7651459
HOLLIS, Pte, Douglas Harrington, 7603834
HOLLOWOOD, Sjt, Eric Emsley, 7593656
HOOD, Pte, Kenneth Ernest, 7642413
HORTON, Pte, Clifford Solomon, 7650192
HOWLETT, Pte, Arthur Leslie, 10531399

HUDSON, Pte, William Thomas, 10531859
HUDSON, Pte, Norman, 7648738
HUGHES, Pte, David Morris, 7643901
HURRELL, Sjt, Robert George, 5768950
HUTCHISON, Pte, Peter Bolan, 2191302
IVES, Lt Col, Augustus Harry, 70684
JACKSON, Pte, John Cunningham, 5345466
JACKSON, S/sjt, William, 7611320
JAMES, Pte, John Frederick, 7607558
JAYCOCK, Pte, Albert George, 14905139
JEFFREY, Pte, Samual, 622468
JENKINS, (k/n), Elwyn William, 7612436
JERVIS, Pte, George, 7643273
JOHN, Pte, Aneurin, 7630316
JONES, Pte, Hugh Cory, 7648537
JONES, Pte, Enoch, 7584645
JONES, Pte, Wilfred, 10541104
KAVANAGH, Pte, Bernard, 7618208
KEIG, Pte, William Edmund, 10532469
KEIGHT, Gnr, Kenneth Edmund, 7611179
KILMISTER, Pte, Bernard George Cedric, 7612089
KING, W/o 1, Ronald, 10588634
LAMBERT, Sqms, Harry, 7609464
LAMBERT, Capt, Cecil Elsbury, 97334
LAW, Capt, William Templeton, 128070
LINES, Lt, William Arnold Augustus, 230137
LONG, Pte, Frederick Arthur, 7650399
LORD, Pte, Ernest, 7654985
LORD, Pte, George Kershaw, 3446249
LOUGH, Pte, John Sinclair, 10546426
MADEN, Pte, James Raymond, 7622553
MAGUIRE, Pte, David, 10540510
MANKTELOW, Sjt, William Charles, 6978172
MANNING, Pte, David William, 10558775
MAPP, Sjt, John Walter, 7617331
MARKS, Sjt, Gordon, 7599298
MARKSON, Pte, Norman Gilbert, 10541985
MARR, Pte, Michael F., 10553997
MARSHALL, Wo/1, Harold, 7586836
MARSHALL, Pte, Ralph, 7633885
MARSHALL, Pte, James John, 3459050
MARTIN, Pte, John Francis, 3064219
MARTIN, Pte, James, 7635427
MARTIN, Pte, Ernest William, 7646710
MASON, Cpl, Alfred Charles, 7595807
MATTHEWS, Pte, Sidney Albert, 1518125
MAWER, Pte, Raymond Salter, 7648405
MAYTUM, Pte, Alfred Harwood, 10546148
MCCURLEY, Pte, William, 7637115
MCSWAN, Pte, Donald, 10548548
MENNIS, Pte, Charles Walter, 5443593
METCALF, Sjt, Arthur James, 14377513
MILLAR, Pte, James Wylie, 3064549
MONAGHAN, Pte, Philip Henry, 7620859
MOON, Pte, Wiliam Edward, 7655747
MORGAN, L/cpl, Harry, 7648049
MORRIS, Pte, Albert Owen, 7590288
MORROW, Pte, Frederick John, 7640662
MOUNTAIN, Wo/1, Peter, 7611259
MOYES, Wo/1, Sidney Charles, 7585755
MURFITT, Pte, George Harold, 10556128
NEEDHAM, Pte, William, 157522
NEWSOME, Pte, Charles Timothy, 14175316
NEWTON, Pte, Charles, 7615853
NORTH, Pte, George Edward, 7646915
NORTHROPE, Cpl, Geoffrey Pattinson, 7649107
NOYCE, Sjt, Henry Charles, 7591472
OATES, S/sjt, Arthur Thomas, 7607954
OLDHAM, Pte, Wilmot Barrett, 3450739
ORTIGER, Maj, Henry, 64808

OSCROFT, Pte, Cyril Parker, 10555508
PAGE, L/cpl, Harold James Cedric, 7648416
PANNELL, L/cpl, Alfred Herbert, 921984
PARKER, Cpl, Albert George Walter, 14082282
PARKER, Pte, Charles Edgar, 10544719
PARR, Pte, John Henry, 7620394
PARROTT, Cpl, Frank Henry, 5723590
PARTRIDGE, Qms, Lifford John, 7602122
PASSMORE, Pte, Alfred John, 7629126
PAYNE, Pte, Norman Ashley, 10531905
PEARCE, Pte, George Harold, 7636390
PEARCE, Sqms, Frank, 7610575
PEARCE, Pte, Albert John, 6033482
PEARSON, Pte, George, 7613835
PEEL, Pte, John, 10537214
PEERS, Pte, Frederick George, 7639241
PERRY, Pte, Stanley Richard, 7640185
PERRY, L/cpl, Philip Henry, 7618225
PESTELL, Pte, Robert Frederick, 7649975
PETHERWICK, Pte, John Ernest, 7649009
PHILLIPS, S/sjt, Leslie Alan, 7585472
PHIPPS, Pte, George Victor, 7636112
PICKLES, L/cpl, Maurice, 7610360
PILLING, Pte, Arthur Donald, 7563060
PITTS, Pte, John Henry, 6399399
PRATT, Pte, James Hunter, 7615318
PRICE, Pte, Rex Percy Woodville, 7630908
PRITCHARD, L/cpl, John Richard, 7628511
QUINCEY, Pte, Arthur Leslie, 7611888
RADFORD, 2/lt, Albert Stanley, 189762
RAINE, Sjt, Thomas Hnery, 7637550
READ, S/sjt, William Herbert, 732662
REANEY, Cpl, Edward, 7639423
REGAN, Pte, Patrick, 1630745
REID, Pte, William, 7632372
RICHARDSON, L/cpl, Jasper Edward, 7628717
RICHMOND, Pte, Edmund Southgate, 7635796
RIDLER-DUTTON, Sqms, George Archibald, 7625949
RILEY, L/cpl, William Robert, 7648090
ROBERTS, Pte, Ivor Llewelyn Cross, 7600713
ROBERTS, L/cpl, Irvin Mercer, 7611016
ROBINSON, Sjt, Luther Gordon, 7587634
RODWELL, Pte, Herbert, 7625422
RUSHWORTH, Pte, Norman, 7596159
SAUNDERS, Sjt, Percy Kitchener, 7624351
SAUNDERS, Pte, Ronald Henry, 7599476
SAVAGE, Pte, Frederick L., 7634069
SCHOFIELD, L/cpl, Harold, 7642173
SEARLE, Pte, Kenneth Leslie George, 7625276
SELLS, Pte, George Ernest, 7617183
SHALES, Pte, Douglas Arthur, 7619903
SHANNON, Lt, Hugh Gorddard, 223275
SHAW, Pte, Gerald Frank, 7649992
SHAW, Pte, Albert, 10541336
SHEEN, L/cpl, Frederick Cawood, 7648434
SHERWOOD, Pte, William Edward, 7638888
SILCOCK, Pte, James, 14177838
SIMMONS, Cpl, George Luck, 56862
SIMPSON, Pte, Charles Albert, 7615901
SKIMMING, Sjt, Archibald, 7634180
SMITH, Pte, Thomas Rowland, 7643604
SMITH, Pte, Percy, 7638929
SMITH, Cpl, James, 7625541
SMITH, Pte, Frederick, 7630018
SMITH, Pte, Ronald Alexander, 1759051
SMITH, Sjt, Harry, 7393682
SMITH, Pte, Maldwyn Ernest, 7616501
SNOWDON, Sjt, Hillip Simpson, 7594276
SPONG, Pte, Robert Albert, 7655196
SPURGE, Pte, Charles Edward Douglas, 7627766

ST CLAIR, Pte, Claude Evelyn Edgar, 7639972
STANLEY, W/o, 1 George Herbert, 7583070
STARKISS, Pte, Richard Oliver, 7650004
STEPHENSON, Pte, Joseph Stanley, 10556291
STREETS, Pte, John Alfred, 7634700
SUTCLIFFE, Pte, George James, 7614790
SWAIN, Pte, William James Heald, 7631332
SWEETING, Pte, Alfred Joseph, 10541432
SWORDER, Pl, Leslie John Dupont, 7636372
TAGG, Sjt, Ronald James, 839219
TAKLE, Pte, Sidney Lennard, 4626315
TAYLOR, S/jt, Alfred George, 7635903
TAYLOR, Pte, Arthur, 10553172
TEMPLETON, Pte, William Gibson, 10550180
TENNANT, L/cpl, John, 7624382
TERRY, Lt, Stanley Gordon, 185922
THOMPSON, L/cpl, John Sherroffs, 7626702
THORPE, Sqms, Benjamin Arthur, 7588160
THRIFT, Gnr, Leslie Rowland, 10531950
TIDMARSH, Pte, Leonard Willie Alan, 1055449
TINDLEY, Pte, Alfred Charles, 10542236
TINKLER, Pte, Francis Henry, 7622166
TODD, Pte, Henry James, 10531621
TOMKINS, Pte, Robert Alex, 7648456
TOMPSETT, L/Cpl, Herbert William, 2366407
TOWNEND, Pte, Frank, 7612783
TRASK, Pte, Robert Geoffrey, 1055171
TROUT, Pte, Richard, 7600994
TRUE, Sub Cmmdr, George Biddle, 6136327
TURNER, Pte, Henry Duff, 7636788
TURNER, L/sjt, Frank, 7585785
TYLER, Pte, Sidney John, 7619882
VESEY, Pte, Henry Austin, 7642127
VICKERS, Cpl, Robert Hayward, 7621965
VICKERS, Pte, Robert Hayward, 7621965
VOSS, Pte, Charles Alfred, 7647522
WALE, Pte, Lawrence Clifford, 10541349
WALKER, Arm Sjt, Percival Francis Joseph, (K/N)
WALKER, L/cpl, John Joseph, 7595163
WALL, Pte, Geoffrey William, 7621391
WALLIS, L/sjt, George Frank, 7648638
WALTON, Pte, Harold Alfred, 2581162
WAPLINGTON, Cpl, Henry Pearson, 7640044
WARHURST, L/cpl, Clifford Hamilton, 7599001
WARING, Pte, Leonard, 4467438
WATCHMAN, Pte, Alec Craig, 7649204
WATSON, Pte, Harold Francis, 10531955
WATSON, Cpl, Arthur John, 7634191
WEBB, Pte, Leslie Ernest, 7643957
WEBB, S/sjt, George William, 7643973
WEEKS, Pte, Reginald Thomas, 7618753
WEST, Pte, Owen Peter, 10555173
WHATELY, Maj, William Levinge, 71522
WHEELER, 2/lt, Colin Bain (MC DCM MM), 82773
WHITBY, Pte, Bernard Edward, 7649826
WHITTAKER, Pte, Harold, 10547532
WIGLEY, Sub Cmdr, John Ernest, 7587136
WILKINSON, Pte, Bert, 7642238
WILLIAMS, Pte, Robert Reginald, 7637321
WILLIAMS, Pte, William Alfred, 10534452
WILLIAMS, Pte, Frank, 7633090
WILSON, Cpl, Kenneth Frederick, 7594518
WINTER, Pte, Edward John, 7625862
WINTER, Cpl, Henry Watson, 7591189
WINTER, Pte, Sydney Henry, 10531662
WINTER, Pte, George Donald, 7607948
WITHEY, Pte, Leslie, 7648699
WOOD, Pte, Percy Douglas, 7629277
WOOD, Pte, John William, 7649831
WOODHEAD, Pte, John Watkin, 10538482

WRIGHT, Pte, Robert, 7592856

ROYAL ARMY VETERINARY CORPS
ORR,Lt Col,William,333010

ROYAL BERKSHIRE REGIMENT
ANDERSON, L/Cpl, William Arthur, 5336085
BAMPTON,Cpl,Joseph,5349806
BARBER, Cpl, Ronald Owen, 5349737
EVERIT,Sjt,Laurence William,5334914
JOHNSON, Sjt, Frederick George, 5336091
MOLE, Capt, Wallace, 200310
NILSON,Pte,Victor Francis,5349526
RICE,Sjt,Thomas Arthur,5334906
THEODORE, Sjt, Desmond Anthony, 5349493
WALLACE,Sjt,George William,5334661

ROYAL CORPS OF SIGNALS
ABERDEIN,Sgmn,John Eric,2344407
ADAMS,Sgmn,Geoffrey Lane,2582098
AITKEN,2/lt,Alexander James,145788
ALDEN,Sgmn,Dennis Victor,2366657
ALDERMAN,Sgmn,John Hart,2580601
ALEXANDER,Dvr,James Main,2337884
ALEXANDER,Sgmn,Benjamin Ernest,2328401
ALLAN,Sgmn,David Andrew,2341514
ALLEN,Sgmn,Wiliam J,2324132
ALLEN,Dvr,Joseph,2356248
ALMOND,Sgmn,Alfred,2360239
ANDERSON,Cpl,Thomas,2576020
ANDERSON,Dvr,James,2341704
ANDREWS,L/Cpl,Alfred,2360240
ANSELL,Dvr,Cecil Edwin,2371318
ANSETT,Smgn,Walter George,2323443
ANTHONY,Cpl,Bruce Edwin Arnold,2335321
ARMITAGE,Sgmn,Harry,2311154
ARNOLD,Dvr,William,2323853
ARNOLD,Sgmn,Royston Stanway,2319349
ARNOTT,L/Sjt,John,2327031
ARUNDALE,Sgmn,Jack Stuart,2343236
ARUNDEL,Sgmn,James Francis,2356642
ASHWORTH,Cpl,Edgar,2341364
ATFIELD,Sgmn,Edward Dudley,2348115
AVONS,Sgmn,Joh Michael,2363023
BADDELEY,Csm,John,2312772
BAILEY,Sgmn,Lewis Jackson,2597280
BAILEY,Sgmn,Archibald James,2357018
BAKER,Dvr,George Alfred,2366664
BAL,L/Cpl,Tom Baxenden,2329912
BALL,L/Sjt,William Lionel,2342877
BAMFORD,Dvr,Robert,2350143
BAMFORD,Sgmn,William,2593526
BAMFORD,Sgmn,Ernest.L,2360379
BANKS,Sgmn,Gordon,2597372
BARKER,Sgmn,Alfred Henry,2324697
BARKER,L/Cpl,Cecil George,2328918
BARLOW,Capt,Richard George,117760
BARR,L/Cpl,Sidney Arthur,2366368
BARTON,Sgmn,James Conrade Samuel Milliner,2325367
BARTON,L/Cpl,William,3773413
BASNETT,Sgmn,Robert Campbell,2569251
BATEMAN,Cpl,Frederick James,2333445
BATTY,L/Sjt,George,2579174
BEALES,Sgmn,Ronald,2358535
BECK,L/jt,John Thomas,1313139
BECK,Sgmn,Russell George,2336015
BEDFORD,Sgmn,Edgar,2336035
BELGIAN,Sgmn,Walter,2593740
BELL,Sjt,George,2337886
BELLIS,L/Sjt,Reginald John,2315272

BENNETT,Sgmn,Sidney,2323504
BENNETT,Sgmn,Sydney Edward,2336983
BENNINGTON,Csm,Lorenzo,2321693
BENTON,C/pl,Horace Douglas,2331665
BERRY,Cpl,William Edward,545843
BEXTON,Sgmn,Donald Robert,2358222
BLACKBURN,Sgmn,William Stanley,2580987
BLACKMAN,Sgmn,Robert Ernest,2323414
BLACKWELL,Sgmn,Arthur Henry James,2338411
BLANCHARD,Sgmn,Alfred Ernest,2350745
BLAND,Sgmn,William George,2348120
BORGEN,Sgmn,Axel James,2593674
BOYD,Cpl,Walter James,2333392
BRADLEY,Sgmn,William Alan,2358200
BRIDGE,Sgmn,Reginald,2331683
BRIDGE,Sgmn,Jim,2587219
BRIERLY,L/pl,Frank,2347990
BROOKS,Sgmn,Herbert,2344248
BROUGH, Sgmn, George Arthur, 2584399
BROUGHTON,Dvr,Maurice Edward,2351861
BROWN,Sgmn,Walter Cockerham,2589762
BROWN,Sgmn,John Edward,2351225
BROWN,2/lt,Sutherland,225871
BROWNE,Sgmn,Leon Melbourne,2752421
BUCKLAND,Sjt,Sidney Henry,2346584
BUNDY,Sjt,Cecil,2319902
BUNTING,Sgmn,Frederick,2353880
BUNTING,L/Cpl,Dennis William,2335222
BURCHETT,L/Cpl,Cecil Thomas William,2325003
BURDITT,Sgmn,Roland,2346149
BURGESS,L/Cpl,E.J.,14969368
BURGESS,Dvr,Edward John,2350382
BURKITT,Sgmn,Charles,2356663
BURNELL,L/Cpl,Stanley Charles,2345583
BURROWS,Cpl,John Frederick,2565527
BURTON,Sgmn,Thomas William Alexander,2595043
BUTLER,Dvr,J.,2351995
BUTTON,Sgmn,Walter,2325425
CADDY,Sgmn,William Metford,5672704
CALDWELL,Sgmn,Joseph,2359430
CAMPBELL,Sgmn,Colin Whitton,2695219
CAMPBELL,Dvr,Alexander,2583962
CAPPER,Sgmn,Jack,2342708
CARR,Sgmn,John Richard,2366826
CARRUTHERS,Sgmn,John,2359437
CARTWRIGHT,Sgmn,Norman,2344315
CASSIDY,Sgmn,Michael John,2328716
CAWTHREY,Sgmn,Jack,2349561
CENCT,Sgmn,Alfredo Petro Angelo,5675308
CHADWICK,Sgmn,George Kenneth,2360898
CHARLISH,Sgmn,Arthur William Lloyd,2325035
CHEW,Sgmn,Edward John,2349443
CHILDS,Sgmn,William Robert,2325725
CHILDS,L/Cpl,Alan Henry,2366677
CHILTON,L/Cpl,Albert Benjamin,2360263
CHITTY,L/Cpl,Albert William,2358015
CLARK,Dvr,Charles Percy,2371500
CLARK,Sgmn,Alfred Charles Bridgman,2341308
CLARKE,Cpl,William Arthur,2578462
CLARKE,Cpl,Percy William,2323131
CLEMISHAW,Sqmn,Walter Raymond,2591561
CLEMSON,Sgmn,Hedworth,5883486
CLIVE,Sgmn,William Robert,2337521
COATES,Stmn,Ernest,2330292
COATHUPE,L/Cpl,Cecil Stanley,2340555
COCKRILL,L/Cpl,Leonard Raymond,2522840
COFFIN,Sgmn,Ernest,2365045
COKER,Sgmn,William Henry,11056346
COLENTZO,Sgmn,Seymour,2350393
COLLIER,L/Cpl,John,2347998

COLLINGS,Sjt,Samuel,555240
COLLINS,Sgmn,Albert James Benjamin,2592669
COLWILL,Dvr,Leslie James,2347197
COMBSTOCK,Dvr,Willliam Henry,7869394
CONDUIT,Sgmn,Percival Frank,5569479
CONLEY,Sgmn,John,3129355
CONROY,Sjt,Patrick,2312826
COOK,Cpl,William Charles,2361905
COOPER-GREGORY,Sgmn,Edward,2594199
CORBYN,Dvr,Stephen Alfred Edmund,11056364
CORMACK,Dvr,J,14934158
CORNISH,Sgmn,Robert William John,2336990
COTTON,Sgmn,Harry,6028728
COTTON,Sgmn,Douglas George,2335965
COWE,L/Cpl,John,3194819
COWEN,Sgmn,Harold,2320201
CRABTREE,Sigmn,Walter Edward,2336077
CRAFT,Cpl,George Thomas,2333954
CRAIG,Sgmn,Tom Dixon,2358215
CRAIG,Sgmn,Oel,2589939
CRIGHTON,Sgmn,Robert,2593481
CROSSLAND,Sgmn,Kenneth,2346042
CROSTON,L/Cpl,Charles Trevor,2322439
CRUMP,Sgmn,Edwin Herbert,5381830
CUNNINGHAM,Sjt,Edward,4530985
CURTIS,Sgmn,Harold,2356670
CURTIS,Sgm0,Edward Alfred,2580951
DACKHAM,L/Cpl,Ernest Edward,2324209
DALLOW,Dvr,Albert,2328931
DAVEY,L/Sjt,James Reginald,2341152
DAVEY,Sgmn,Leslie Edward,2343012
DAVIES,Cpl,Basil,2348575
DAVIS,Sgmn,James Leslie,867873
DAVIS,Sgmn,Edwin,2346323
DAWES,Sgmn,Allen,849546
DENNISON,Sgmn,Frederick Albert,2364113
DENNISON,Sgmn,Aubrey Cecil,6214464
DICKSON,Sgmn,Albert,2343074
DIGSBY,Sgmn,John James,2357678
DINNEEN,L/Cpl,Edmund,2326544
DITCHFIELD,L/Cpl,Norman,2581714
DIXON,Sgmn,Ronald James,14887768
DODD,Dvr,George,2340511
DOOGAN,Dvr,William Richard,2362220
DORKINS,Cpl,Horace George,2338377
DOWNEY,Dvr,George Fenwick,4270308
DOY,L/Cpl,Donald Hillier,2589735
DOY,Cpl,Leonard Charles,2593122
DRIVER,Dvr,Claude William,2592234
DUMPLETON,Sgmn,Cyril James,2336718
DURWARD,Sgmn,James Gordon,2341528
EARNSHAW,Cpl,Jack Kenneth Sunderland,2582792
EARNSHAW,Sgmn,Tom Edwin,2349756
EDGAR,Sgmn,Thomas Samuel,2340519
EDINGTON,Sgmn,Kenneth,2351634
EDMONDSON,Sgmn,Robert,2351273
EDWARDS,Cqms,Thomas Kenneth,2584203
EDWARDS,L/gt,Sydney Edward,2571825
ELIS,L/sgt,Alexander Claude Richard,2568715
ELKINS,Sgmn,Lional Edwin,2360930
ELLERY,Cpl,William,2342207
ELLIS,L/Cpl,John Charles Howard,2585312
ELLISON,Dvr,Sydney,2337773
ELVIDGE,Dvr,John William,2346156
ELWELL,Dvr,Francis Kenneth,2359056
ELWICK,Cpl,Francis George,2579302
EMMETTT,Dvr,William George,2335973
EVANS,Cpl,Stanley Lewis,2322442
EVANS,Dvr,Harold,2581797
EVENETT,Sgmn,Alan George,2330259

EVENING,Sgmn,John Robert,2345388
EVIDENT,Sgmn,William,2364722
FABIANI,Sgmn,Ferninando Antonio,3133441
FARR,Sgmn,Vernon Clifford,2580051
FARROW,Sjt,Harold William,2386997
FAULKNER,L/Cpl,Leslie William,2340921
FAUNCH,Sgmn,Stanley Ernest Walton,2597471
FIELDHOUSE,Sgmn,Stanley,2353991
FINCH,Sgmn,Frederick John,2341177
FINDLEY,Dvr,James Railton Campbell,2357144
FISHER,Dvr,Frank Alfred,2589218
FLAHERTY,Dvr,Harry,2356677
FLEMING,Dvr,Edward George,2344001
FORD,Sgmn,Laurance Reginald,2331261
FORREST,Dvr,William Sylvester,2357926
FOSTER,Dvr,Frederick Horace,2579156
FOTHERINGHAM,Sgmn,Robert,2336729
FOWLER,Dvr,John Charles,2335796
FOX,Sgmn,Charles Nevil Worton,2591054
FOXON,Sgmn,Douglas,2348152
FRANKLIN,Dvr,Jacob,2342210
FRASER,Sgmn,Alexander,2361522
FROBISHER,Dvr,Eward Francis Henry Frederick,2346912
FROST,L/Cpl,Walter Reuben,23126650
FROST,L/Cpl,John Richard,2364733
FULLARTON,Sigmn,Alexander Frederick,2366953
GADD,Sgmn,James Henry,4625897
GALBRAITH,Sgmn,Dougal Mctavish,2583951
GAMBLE,Sjt,Claude David,2322444
GARBUTT,L/Cpl,Frank Chalders,2341277
GARDINER,Cpl,Robert John,2351824
GARDNER,Sgmn,Victor,2346339
GARMAN,Sgmn,Leslie Walter,2336267
GARNETT,Sgmn,George Francis,2343304
GASSON,L/Cpl,John,5197851
GATFORD,Sjt,John Albert William,2319851
GATHERCOLE,Sgmn,Frederick John,2341339
GAUSDEN,Pl,Alfred Peter,2342213
GAW,Sgmn,Tephen,2358280
GEIGER,Sgmn,Arthur George Bernard,2586614
GEORGE,L/Sjt,Cyril,2583092
GHEY,Sjt,Geoffrey Owen,2565876
GILBERT,L/Cpl,Ronald Arthur,2325023
GILBERT,Sgmn,John Gordon,2336708
GILL,L/Cpl,John Richard,3128805
GLASSETT,Dvr,Ernest,2349993
GLOVER,L/Sjt,Victor Tom,2351310
GLOVER,Dvr,Robert Henry,2370913
GODDARD,Sgmn,Samuel,2587171
GOOD,Dvr,Francis,2341583
GRAHAM,Sjt,Andrew,2326186
GRANT,Sgmn,Malcolm Andrew,2361470
GRANT,Dvr,James,2338575
GRANT,Sgmn,Ronald,2368814
GRANT,Sgmn,Graeme Ian,2336188
GRAY,Sgmn,Robert Frederick,2365551
GRAY,L/Cpl,James,2335596
GRAY,Sgmn,Albert Arthur,2343206
GRAY,Sgmn,William,2355308
GRAYSTON,Sgmn,William Charles,2364016
GREENFIELD,Sgmn,George,2575199
GREENWOOD,Sgmn,Lewis Renshaw,2329014
GRIERSON,Sgmn,John Archibald,2327032
GRIFFIN,L/Cpl,George,3307920
GRIFFIN,Sgmn,Henry Daniel,2345217
GRIMES,Dvr,Wilfred,2592881
GROVE,L/Cpl,Norman,2324059
GROVES,Sgmn,Frederick Joseph,2337006
GUNSON,Sgmn,George Rothery,2343782
HALL,Sgmn,Kenneth Arthur,2338349

HALL,Dvr,Arthur,2347199
HALLAM,Capt,Richard Henry,155605
HALPIN,Sgmn,Eric,2327565
HAMILTON,Sgmn,David Swan,2321409
HAMPSON,Sgmn,Harold,2326825
HAMPTON,Sgmn,George William,2355707
HANCOCK,Dvr,William,2317493
HARDY,Sgmn,James Ernest,2333160
HARRIES,Sgmn,William Islwyn,2336165
HARRIS,Sgmn,Leslie Fred Arthur,2328389
HARRISON,L/Cpl,Ernest George,2584864
HARRISON,L/Cpl,Elliot Norton,2359063
HARRISON,L/Cpl,Leslie William James,2365626
HARROD,Cqms,George Arthur,2323067
HARROLD,Cpl,Joseph Gordon,2313178
HART,Sgmn,Harold,2590642
HART,Rsm,Robert Charles William,2314313
HARVEY,Cpl,William Charles Logan,2315737
HARVEY,Lt Qm,Charles Ernest,130700
HASSALL,Sgmn,Lawrence Stuart,2337145
HATHAWAY,L/Cpl,John James,2584452
HAWKES,Csm,John Burdis,1859707
HAYES,Sgmn,Walter,2351836
HEAP,Cpl,Albert Attwell,2322413
HEBB,Dvr,Francis Wiliam,2317641
HENDERSON,Sgmn,Robert Malcolm Beattie,2358192
HENNESSEY,Cpl,George Thoas,2360972
HENRY,Sgmn,Albert Francis,2580454
HESP,Sigmn,Ernest,2368405
HICKSON,Sgmn,Reginald Frank,2350894
HIGGINS,Sgmn,John Francis,2366208
HIGSON,Sgmn,Norman Cyril,2594948
HILL,L/Cpl,Reginald Harry,2335781
HILL,Sgmn,John,23251736
HILL,Csm,James Mertin,792008
HILL,Dvr,Frederick Samuel,2365632
HILL,L/Cpl,Bernard,2339424
HILL,L/Cpl,Reginald Harry,2335781
HILLS,L/Cpl,William Charles,2325726
HIPPLE,L/Cpl,Vincent,2356970
HOARE,Dvr,John Edward,2342223
HOBBS,Sgmn,Ronald Day,2334359
HOBSON,Sigmn,George,2587089
HODGE,Dvr,John Gaselee,2346269
HODGES,Sgmn,Charles Harison,851302
HODGSON,L/Sjt,Will,4745737
HODGSON,Sgmn,Thomas William,2348770
HODGSON,Sgmnm,Roy,2369914
HOLMES,Dvr,Leslie Edward,2363766
HOLMES,Cpl,James Lowrey Elliott,2325161
HOLMES,Sgmn,Bernard Stanley,2575125
HOLWAY,Cpl,Sydney Ross,14589902
HOOPER,Signm,Arthur William Gilbert,2355638
HOPE,Sjt,Bernard,2324487
HORSEFIELD,Sgmn,Sidney,2348772
HORSMAN,Sjt,Harry,2320387
HOUGH,Sgmn,William Henry,2321627
HOUGHTON,Dvr,James,2359679
HOWARD,Sgmn,Charles,2350411
HOWARD,Lt,John Milman,308146
HUDSON,Sgmn,Fred,2328944
HUGHES,S/jt,James,4445064
HUGHES,L/Cpl,Griffith Charles,2334960
HULL,Dvr,Frederick,2586683
HUMPHREYS,L/Cpl,John Harry,2357584
HUMPHRYS,Maj,Stephen Gordon,41149
HUNT,Sgmn,Alec,2589954
HUNT,Sgmn,James,2597715
HUTSON,Dvr,Robert,2371489
HYDE,Cpl,Douglas,2328043

HYDE,Sgmn,George,2351640
INGLIS,Sgmn,Hector,2341571
IRWIN,Sgmn,William George,2341232
JACKSON,Dvr,Joseph,2336309
JAMES,Sgmn,Edward Robert,2367227
JAMES,Sgmn,Cyril Walter,2332662
JAMIESON,Sgmn,Percival William,2319769
JAQUET,Sgmn,Edwin Dennis,2337270
JARRETT,Cpl,Ronald David,2353496
JEFFREY,Dvr,Frederick George,2365873
JEFFREY,L/Cpl,Stanley William,2335643
JENNINGS,L/Cpl,Joseph,3597099
JENNINGS,Sign,Reginald Edmund,2330083
JONES,Sgmn,Elfed,2336678
JONES,L/Cpl,David Elwyn,2595146
JONES,Sgmn,James Robert,2341465
JONES,Rsm,Ivor Edward,2580161
JONES,Sgmn,William Douglas,2341889
JONES,Sgmn,William Henry,2592305
JONES,Dvr,Frederick George,2357589
JONES,Cqms,William,2313952
JUDGE,Dvr,William Walter,2346801
KAY,Sgmn,James,2326356
KELLY,Sjt,James,7009112
KENDRICK,Sgmn,Bernard Samuel,2337149
KENNARD,L/jt,Harold Leslie,768835
KERR,Sgmn,John,2346177
KERR,Sgmn,William,2318128
KEY,Sgmn,Peter,2595680
KIERNAN,Sgmn,James Alfred,2578444
KING,Igmn,Ronald Percy,5498742
KITCHINGMAN,Sgmn,Cyril,2338670
LAKER,Cpl,Leslie Reginald,2325314
LAMBERT,Sgmn,John Leslie,2366696
LANDRAY,Sgmn,George William Henry,2592711
LAWRENSON,Cqms,George,2310810
LAWSON,Sigmn,Alexander,2341752
LAWTON,Sgmn,Albert,2324220
LEGGETT,Sgmn,Horace Henry George,2590922
LEITH,Smgn,John William Horace,2335834
LEITH,Sgmn,Harry Lauder,2319998
LESTER,Sgmn,Herbert,2365654
LEWIN,Cpl,Russell George,5883252
LEY,Sgmn,Wilfred Martin,2345060
LINLEY,Sgmn,William Alfred,2358207
LITHAUER,L/pl,Ronald Louis,2325527
LOMAS,Sgmn,Arthur Jack,2344426
LORD,Sgmn,Harold,2353654
LOWES,L/Cpl,Leslie,2360316
LUDBROOK,L/Cpl,William Frederick,2560297
LUMB,Sgmn,Harry Dixon,4323625
LYNCH,Sgmn,Albert,2345170
LYNN,Sgmn,Thomas Edward,2357597
LYON,Sjt,John,2561251
MACDOBALD,Sgmn,Ian Lyon,2365373
MACFARLANE,Sgmn,George Halket,2582143
MACFIE,Sgmn,Alistair Bruce,2343377
MACPHERSON,Dvr,Ian,2580832
MAINPRIZE,Capt,James Leonard,105553
MANAGHAN,L/Cpl,Ernest Christopher,2319563
MANNING,Sgmn,Alfred Arthur,2365663
MANNION,Dvr,Joseph Neville,2370553
MANSON,Sgmn,William Jack Andrew,2327367
MANSON,Sgmn,Andrew William,2589157
MARSDEN,Sgmn,Alfred,2325758
MARSH,Sgmn,Walter Leslie,601577
MARSHALL,Sgmn,Charles Frederick,2345268
MARSHALL,Sgmn,Charles John,2586371
MARSTON,Sjt,H.V.K.,14854337
MARTIN,Sgmn,Robert,2357964

MARTIN,L/Cpl,Charles John,2319256
MARTIN,Sgmn,Harold Albert,3914711
MARTINDALE,Sgmn,Joseph Leo,2340500
MASON,Sgmn,Harold,2587082
MATHEWS,Sgmn,Ernest Leonard,2582572
MATTHEWS,Sgmn,Arthur Richard,2588498
McBRINN,Sjt,Francis Alphonsus,2339050
McGAHAN,Cpl,James,2340848
McKENNA,Sgmn,John Eaton,2583567
McKEWAN,Sgmn,Arthur William,2365661
McLACHLAN,Sgmn,James,2574141
McLEOD,L/Cpl,John Stewart,2325601
McMANUS,Sgmn,James,2326759
McMINN,Sgmn,George Franklin,2334724
McNAMARA,L/Cpl,John,2335562
MEADOWS,Sgmn,Samuel,2367989
MEEK,2/lt,Robert David Gemmell,151448
MEEK,Dvr,Thomas James,2356818
METCALFE,L/Cpl,Albert Alexander Carpenter,2361034
MILES,Sgmn,William,2349074
MILES,Sgmn,Ronald,7889508
MILLAR,Sgmn,Richard David,2324118
MILLS,Sgmn,William Albert,2347175
MILROSE,Sgmn,James,2350958
MOFFAT,Sgmn,William George,2358728
MOLD,Sgmn,Jack,5886739
MOLE,Capt,Kenneth,145785
MONCUR,Sgmn,William,2350227
MONGER,Dvr,Alan,2346245
MOORE,L/Cpl,Dennis Joseph,2348734
MOREY,Sgmn,John Leslie Hayward,45262
MORGAN,Sgmn,Samuel,2331659
MORGAN,Sgmn,Parry Glyn,2334207
MORRIS,L/Cpl,George Arthur,14376959
MORRIS,Sgmn,Stanley,2368164
MORRIS,Sgmn,William Albert,2366556
MORTLOCK,Sgmn,Maurice John,2336921
MORTON,Cpl,William Wedgewood,2352248
MOULT,Sgmn,Leonard Stanley,2350031
MURRAY,Sgmn,George Archibald Brown,2335293
NAIRN,Sgmn,Henry,2326168
NASH,Cpl,George Edward,2361328
NATBORNY,Sgmn,Hyman,2333178
NEALE,Sgmn,Arthur Stanley,2354988
NELSON,L/Cpl,R,14924601
NEW,Sgmn,Charles Arthur,2360325
NEWBOLD,Sgmn,William James,2324193
NEWBURY,Cpl,Albert Edward,2585281
NEWTON,L/Cpl,Henry Owen,2369069
NIBLOW,Sgmn,Reginald William,2334301
NIGHTINGALE,L/Cpl,Wilfred,2320904
NIXON,Sgmn,William John,2590000
NOBLE,L/Cpl,Charles Thomas,2347423
NORMAN,Cpl,John Thomas William,2594712
NORTHEY,Sgmn,Ronald Eric,2337638
NORWOOD,Sgmn,James Kerr,2369002
NUGENT,Sgmn,Thomas,2583978
NUTT,Dvr,George Albert,2350506
O'BRIEN,Sgmn,Lawrence Vincent,2341082
O'KEEFE,Sgmn,Douglas Charles,2345273
O'SHEA,Sgmn,Daniel Michael Patrick,2371592
OCKELFORD,Dvr,Frederick Jacques,2342179
OLDFIELD,Dvr,Horace,2354843
PAGDIN,Sgmn,Colin,2364828
PALMER,Sgmn,John Arthur,2327689
PALMER,Sgmn,William Evans,2336911
PANNIERS,Sjt,Harold John,2580288
PAPWORTH,Sgmn,Frederick Owen,2336793
PARFITT,Dvr,Walter Fredrick,2365685
PARKER,Sgmn,Philip George,2574415

PARKIN,Dvr,George,2343548
PARKIN,Sgmn,Ernest,2590963
PARKINSON,Sgmn,George,2364830
PATMORE,Dvr,Douglas Archibald,2330232
PATON,Sjt,Frederick Robert,2322402
PATRICK,Smgn,Cyril,2353465
PAUL,Dvr,Thomas,2357536
PAYNE,Cpl,Albert Thaorns,2365688
PEARSON,Sgmn,William,14226401
PEARSON,Sgmn,Nevill Corrie,2327369
PEARSON,Sgmn,John Cumings,2593185
PEEL,Maj,Robert,79754
PEERS,Lt,Neville Squire,200032
PEGG,Sgmn,Alfred Philip,2345841
PENNEY,Sgmn,Leslie John,2590828
PENTREATH,Sgmn,George Henry,2346251
PERCIVAL,Sgmn,Donald Oldham,2595377
PERKINS,Sgmn,Arthur Frederick,2357060
PERRY,Sgmn,Aymond Clifford,2338385
PETERS,Sgmn,Stanley,2325166
PETRIE,Sgmn,Harry Wilkinson,2346516
PETTS,Sgmn,Jack,2355692
PHILPOTTS,Sgmn,Patrick Gervase,2582706
PICKSLEY,Sgmn,William Webster,14838056
PICKTHALL,L/Cpl,Harold Byers,2352211
PINNIUCK,Sgmn,Walter James,2366146
PLEAVIN,Cpl,Robert Arthur,801557
PONSFORD,Dvr,Ernest William,2366567
PORTEOUS,Sgmn,Thomas William Shiels,2349354
POTTON,Sgmn,James William,2325135
POTTS,Dvr,Gordon Charles,2330720
POWELL,Sgmn,Sidney George Thomas,2320640
POWELL,Sgmn,John,2351257
POWLING,L/Cpl,Gordon Reginald,14593066
POWRIE,Dvr,David,2349791
PREECE,Sgmn,Bernard Victor,2324242
PRIESTLEY,Sgmn,Stanley,2329806
PRINCE,Sgmn,Hubert,2340664
PRODGER,Dvr,Albert Victor,2346257
PURCELL,Sgmn,John William,2589375
QUEEN,Sgmn,Thomas,809485
RADFORD,Sjt,Horatio George,2321301
RAMSDEN,L/Cpl,Arthur James,2335378
RANSFORD,Sgmn,Charles,2353860
RAPER,L/Cpl,Edward Simeon Walter,2359942
RASHBROOK,L/Sjt,Gordon William Edward,2579594
RATCLIFFE,Sgmn,Frank Percy,834913
RAY,Sgmn,Arthur John,2335944
RAYMISH,Sgmn,Douglas,2333286
REDFEARN,L/Cpl,Samuel,2355694
REDMAN,Sgmn,Jack Major,3059145
REES,Cpl,William Alfred,2359360
REYNOLDS,Sgmn,Hubert Morris,2366447
RIBBONS,Sgmn,Leonard Norman,2361578
RIDLEY,Sgmn,Thomas Edward,2368207
RITCHIE,Sgmn,Robert,2026157
ROBB,L/Cpl,Gordon Kenneth,2325080
ROBERTS,Sjt,Robert John,2317202
ROBERTS,Sjt,Cecil Gordon,754344
ROBERTS,Sgmn,Edward,2321727
ROBERTSON,Sgmn,John Wilson,2359697
ROBERTSON,Sgmn,Alexander Lindsey,3193921
ROBINSON,Dvr,Harry Edward Archibald,2349493
ROBINSON,Sgmn,Frederick Donald Hughes,2591866
ROBINSON,L/Cpl,George Bertrand,2343066
ROBINSON,Sgmn,Harold Sargant,2342981
RODEN,Sgmn,Thomas,2347904
RODERICK,L/Cpl,C.W.,2392211
RODLEY,Dvr,Harry,2368568
ROGERS,Sgmn,Robert,2365451

ROGERS,Sgmn,Robert Kipping,2341573
ROOTHAM,Sgmn,Laurie James,2591156
ROSENBERG,Col,Richard Louis Mortimer,13450
ROSS,Sgmn,Sidney,2579374
ROY,Sgmn,Robert,2596603
ROY,Sgmn,Leslie Frederick Noel,2345285
RUSSELL,Sgmn,Geoffrey Edward,2353471
SADLER,Dvr,Philip Ravenscroft,2588082
SADLER,Sgmn,Frederick Elliston,2358051
SAID,Sgmn,Alfred,2329580
SALTER,/Sjt,Herbert Brown,2317472
SANDERSON,Sgmn,Edward,7342840
SANDERSON,Dvr,Alexander,2349360
SAUNDERS,Sgmn,Ronald Rodney,2331959
SAUNDERS,Dvr,Clifford Trevor,2347144
SCOTT,Sgmn,Samuel Paley,2350462
SCOTT,Cpl,Frank Stanley,2601264
SCOTT,Sgmn,Jack,2368374
SEWELL,Dvr,Arthur John,2366584
SHAPIRO,Sgmn,Israel,2332221
SHARPE,Sgmn,Jimmy Ivor Griffen,2579558
SHAW,Cpl,Alfred,3759604
SHEEDY,Lt,John Robert,200663
SHEEHAN,L/Cpl,James Christopher,2346530
SHEILS,Sgmn,John,3777049
SHUFFLE,Sgmn,Alfred James,2590807
SIDWELL,Sgmn,Ronald,2320659
SIMPSON,Sgmn,Frank,2336801
SINGER,Dvr,Lewis,2359837
SKIDMORE,Sgmn,Joseph,7906875
SMART,Dvr,Thomas Henry,2336550
SMEED,Sgmn,Joseph Robert Cecil,2358660
SMITH,Sgmn,George Alfred Bence,2336115
SMITH,Sgmn,William Thomas,2325771
SMITH,L/Cpl,John Walter,2321083
SMITH,Gnr,George Ernest,2361068
SMITH,Dvr,Philip George,2361184
SMITH,Cpl,John Douglas,2363213
SMITH,Sgmn,Adam Sturdees,2368614
SMITH,Sgmn,Robert Armour,1365456
SMITH,Sgmn,Dennis Arthur,2337308
SMITH,Sgmn,Alexander Clinton,2335564
SMITHIES,Sgmn,Sidney William,2325774
SMOOTHY,Sgmn,Joseph,2352527
SNELLING,Sgmn,Thomas George,2359315
SOLK,Dvr,Benjamin Elijah,3969647
SOPPET,Cpl,Edward Benedict,2321592
SORRELL,Dvr,Henry,2351380
SOWLTER,Sgmn,Edward,2590469
SPALDING,L/Cpl,Laurence William,2326121
SPONG,Capt,Harry Charles Mbe,89855
SPRIGGS,Sjt,Leonard Albert,2322106
SPROUT,Sgmn,Frederick Henry,2353239
STARK,Dvr,David,2365457
STEEN,Sgmn,Arthur Donald,4543523
STEPHENSON,Lt,Thomas George,76365
STEVENS,L/Sjt,Alexandra Patrick Joseph,4907417
STEVENSON,Sjt,Andrew Baird,2562597
STEWART,Sgmn,Roy Maxwell,2523024
STEWART,Sgmn,Malcolm Alexander,2326877
STOCKS,Sgmn,Stephen,2351611
STOKES,Sjt,Arthur Robert,2323199
STRAKEY,Dvr,Frederick John,2369711
STRATTON,Sgmn,Walter Forbes,2366166
STUD,Dvr,Ronald George,2330734
SUGDEN,Sgmn,John,2349502
SUMMERFIELD,L/Cpl,Frederick Bernard,2571344
SUTCLIFFE,Sgmn,Donald,2593305
SWAAITS,Sgmn,John Alexander,14863566
SWANN,Sgmn,Ernest William Mathew,2350931

SWINNERTON,Sgmn,Leslie Marsden,2335699
TAFT,Sgmn,Frank,4608519
TALBOT,L/Cpl,William Alexander James,2564369
TAPSTER,Dvr,Frederick Albert,2361698
TAYLOR,Sgmn,Alfred Linford,2366268
TAYLOR,Csm,Thomas,2314110
TAYLOR,Sgmn,Ivan Hedley James,2588937
TEASDALE,Cpl,William James,2314668
TERRY,Dvr,James,2349506
THOMAS,Rqms,Lewis James,2316489
THOMPSON,Sgmn,John William,2356305
THOMPSON,Sgmn,Mark,2364921
THOMPSON,Sgmn,Jack,2359637
THOMPSON,Sgmn,George William,6009235
TINSON,Sgmn,Herbert Henry,2309642
TITMUSS,Sgmn,Frederick John,14368285
TOLLEY,Cpl,Francis William Robert,2335296
TOMKINSON,Sgmn,David,2346404
TONGE,Sgmn,Albert Edward,2365118
TOVEY,Sgmn,Thomas Edward,2333394
TRANT,Sgmn,Alfred Douglas,2345605
TRECHMAN,Maj,Richard Michael Cromar,201596
TRIGGS,Dvr,Frank William,2350481
TUCK,Sgmn,Arthur Reginald Nend,2333422
TUCKER,Dvr,Robert Wotton,2366410
TWIDDY,L/Cpl,Donald Frederick,2321865
UPTON,L/Cpl,Charles William,2352149
UPTON,Sgmn,Eric William,2343310
VAN-LOOY,Dvr,Joseph Charles,2335952
VICKERS,Sjt,Dennis Thomas,4131584
VITLER,Sgmn,Arthur Edward,2335377
VYNER,Sgmn,Lionel Conrad,2339704
WAGSTAFF,Sgmn,Richard Alfred,2597283
WAIDSON,L/Sjt,Fred,2351753
WAINWRIGHT,Sgmn,John James,2360221
WALDERGRAVE,Sgmn,Jack,2582739
WALKER,Sgmn,Albert Henry Percy,2326521
WALKER,Lt Col,Colin Percy,227310
WALLER,Sgmn,Walter Charles,2366412
WALLER,Sgmn,Reginald,2336489
WALLS,Sgmn,Thomas,2365466
WALSH,Dvr,William Arthur,2368964
WALSTOW,Sgmn,Albert Edward,2593293
WARD,Dvr,Albert,2350821
WARE,Dvr,Richard Clements,235492
WARING,L/Cpl,Ewart Gladstone,2352277
WARING,Sgmn,Austin,2359037
WARNER,Sgmn,Phillip Richard William,2354778
WARRENER,Sgmn,George,2368965
WASHINGTON,Sgmn,Horace,2329836
WATERMAN,L/Cpl,Harry Jeremy,2336103
WATERS,Dvr,Frederick Norman,2338534
WATERS,Dvr,Herbert,4914621
WATERS,Sjt,William George,2315747
WATSON,Sgmn,James,86133
WATSON,Sgmn,Herbert,2337787
WATSON,Dvr,James,2353360
WATT,Sgmn,James Templeton,2333800
WATTS,Cpl,Joseph Henry,
WEATHERLY,Sgmn,Alfred Richard,2333417
WEBBER,Dvr,William Richard,2369227
WEBSTER,Dvr,Frederick Wilmot,2343591
WELLER,Sgmn,Arthur,2371542
WELLOCK,Csm,Horace Conrad,2316473
WEMYSS,Sgmn,Charles,2328520
WESTWOOD,Sgmn,Samuel,2333360
WHALEN,Sgmn,Joseph,2326752
WHARF,Cpl,Thomas Albert,2335364
WHITE,Capt,Albert,113051
WHITE,Dvr,William,2357802

WHITTLE,Sjt,Reginald Kellaway,2317436
WHITWORTH,Sgmn,Sydney,2365173
WIGHT,Dvr,Robert,2350273
WILKIE,Sgmn,Cyril Everard,881203
WILKS,Sgmn,William Charleton,23249515
WILKS,Sgmn,Roy,2593309
WILLIAMS,L/Cpl,Ralph Bernard,2367788
WILLIAMS,Sgmn,Ralph,2351592
WILLIAMS,Sgmn,William Elsley,2334322
WILLIAMS,Dvr,Aneurin,2349517
WILLIAMS,Sgmn,Ralph,2351592
WILLS,Cpl,Gordon Owen,2386545
WILSON,Dvr,Arthur,2364930
WILSON,Sgmn,James Frederick,2345783
WILSON,Sgmn,Edwin,2592675
WILSON,Dvr,George Charles,2594741
WINSOM,Dvr,Herbert Gordon,2580462
WINSOR,L/Cpl,Ernest Herbert,2349518
WOLLAGE,Sgmn,Reginald William,
WOOD,Dvr,Thomas Alfred,2339360
WOOD,Sgmn,Donald Arthur,2366421
WOOD,Cqms,James,2322567
WOOD,Sgmn,Albert,2367028
WOODEND,Dvr,James Alfred,2351733
WORDEN,Dvr,Joseph,3781481
WRIGHT,Sgmn,Stanley Wilfred,2369767
WRIGHT,Sgmn,Alfred Walker,2333808
WRIGHT,Sgmn,Herbert Harry,2330322
WRIGHT,Sgmn,David,2358725
YARRINGTON,Sgmn,George Thomas William,2342751
YEO,Sgmn,Ronald Bernard,2342196
YEOMANSON,Cpl,Ernest Charles,2592852
YOUNG,Sgmn,Robert Charles,2360236

6 AIR SUPPLY
TURNPENNY,Sgmn,Ernest,4543311

FORTRESS
HORTON,Sgmn,Arnold,2346562
TATHAM,Sgmn,Steve,739959
TAYLOR,Sgmn,Harwood Alfred,2319490
WOOD,Sgmn,Robert Harry,2590434

27 LINE
HUNT,Sjt,Gordon Leonard,2579982
SMITH,Sgmn,Kenneth Sidney,2337950
WAKELING,Sgmn,Claude Edward,2329379

ROYAL EAST KENT
FARRIER,Pte,Walter John,14761741
PAYNE,Pte,J.S.,14854362
PAINE,Capt Qm,Jesse,278009
THORNTON,Pte,D.E.,14781114

ROYAL ELECTRICAL & MECHANICAL ENGINEERS
ADEY, L/Cpl, Dennis, 4916693
ALEXANDER, Cftn, Claude Nelson, 1572465
ALLISON, Cftmn, George Edward Hall, 4269767
ASHWORTH, Lt, Bernard, 154168
BADMAN, Cftmn, Peter Thomas, 7616267
BALSON, Cftnmn, Frank Steven Herbert, 5495030
BARKER, Sjt, John James, 1572589
BARNETT, Cftmn, Ernest Alfred, 7603419
BEAL, Cftsn, Wilfred, 7642968
BEAN, Cftn, Denis Fawcett, 7362934
BENDALL, Sjt, Bernard Owen, 759'556
BINNELL, Crftn, Samuel, 5118986
BLAXLEY, Cftmn, Maurice, 5886640
BURDEN, Cpl, Thomas William James, 7654858
BURGESS, Cftmn, Alfred John, 7636885

CHARLESWORTH, Crfmn, John William, 77144
CLAPHAM, Crfmn, Harold, 7615993
CLARE, Cfmn, 5e., 14683627
CLARKE, Arm S/m, Leonard Arthur, 7585750
CLEGG, Cftmn, Alfred Wilson, 7622633
COLLINS, L/Cpl, George Millward, 7611737
COPLEY, Cftmn, Arthur, 7651327
CRABTREE, Cftmn, Ernest Alfred, 10534675
CUBBERLEY, L/Cpl, Cecil James, 10530207
DAVIES, Cfmn, Brinley, 7643871
DAVIES, Cfmn, Evan Leonard, 7643873
DENNIS, Cftmn, William John, 7620535
DOBSON, Cftmn, Edgar Allan, 1682887
DORAN, L/Cpl, Vincent Reginald, 7596175
DOWNER, Sjt, Harold, 7624931
DRAKE, Cfmn, Thomas Charles, 10532901
DUNBAR, Capt, Harold Egan, 289016
EASTMAN, Pte, Ernest John, S/244515
EDWARDS, S/Sjt, Jack, 7592247
EDWRADS, Cftmn, Leslie George Jarvis, 7653967
EMM, S/Sjt, Arthur Richard, 874338
FAWCETT, Cpl, John, 761271O
FAWCETT, Brig, Walter Lindley (MC), 298/1A
FENTON, Cftmn, Peter, 7636649
FERGUSON, L/pl, William Richardson, 7636651
FORSEY, Cftmn, George John, 7612601
FORSTER, L/Cpl, Arthur Frederick, 7593994
FROST, Cftmn, Douglas Clarence, 7619117
FULLAGAR, Cftmn, Terence John, 7654008
GLASS, Sjt, Robert Rutherford, 7585322
GODSELL, Cftmn, Eric Victor, 7598335
GOLDING, Fmn, John, 7618331
GORE, Cftmn, James, 7651411
GRAY, Crmn, Leonard Arthur, 1572489
GREEN, Cftmn, Benjamin James, 7370771
GREENHALGH, Sjt, William Proctor, 14510796
GRIFFITHS, Crfmn, John Leonard, 10562434
HAIGH, Cfmn, Ralph, 7615782
HALL, S/Sjt, Thomas Freeman, 7625227
HARRISON, Cftmn, Walter Cryer, 1572569
HAY, Crft/n, Edwin Alexander Marmaduke, 4447244
HIGHAM, Cftmn, James, 5124411
HOLLAND, Cftmn, Jack, 7638617
HONEYFORD, S/jt, George Lee, 2041561
HUGHES, Cftmn, Douglas James, 7625164
INGLIS, Cfmn, Alex, 7639833
JENKINS, Sjt, Francis David, 7596419
JOHNSON, Crftn, George, 4277283
JONES, Crftn, Robert William, 7646913
JONES, Cftsn, David Ivor, 4201665
KERR, Maj, Harold, 300944
KING, Cftmn, Reginald John, 7651498
LEE, Sjt, Samuel, 7607621
LIVESEY, Crsm, Frank, 7623504
LONGWORTH, Sjt, Robert, 7638179
MAXWELL, Cmnft, Horace Edgar, 7639667
McCABE, Sjt, John, 7642604
McCANN, Cfmn, John Hogan, 14694260
MEARS, Arm Sjt, James Alfred, 7627531
MELLOR, Cftmn, Fred, 4693465
MELVILLE, L/Cpl, George Kinnell, 7624965
MILES, Cftmn, Charles Fletcher, 10530484
MORGAN, Cftn, James, 7626515
MORRALL, Crftmn, George Victor, 7641282
MOSS, Crftn, Charles Gordon, 7615445
MUNRO, Cfmn, George, 3323554
MYERSCOUGH, Crftn, Samuel, 7623503
NICHOLLS, Sjt, William Edward, 7627535
NICHOLSON, Sjt, Joseph, 7639395
OGDEN ARM, Sjt, James Clifford, 7608831

PEARCE, Cftmn, Cyril Alfred, 7598842
PEARCE, Cftn, Oliver Graham, 10539175
PEARMAN, Cftn, Thomas William, 7635257
PENNINGTON,Cftn,Kenneth Augustus,7654332
PEPPER, L/Cpl, George, 934466
PHILLIPS, Cftmn, Rowland John, 6016330
PORTER, Cftmn, William Hugh, 3305396
PRICE, L/Cpl, Dennis Rowley, 7638255
READ, Wo1, Arthur Alan, 7585756
RENNIE, Cftmn, Charles Hnery, 6598459
RICHARDS, Cfmn, Kenneth, 7614558
RICHES, Cfmn, Jesse Raymond, 817311
ROBSON, Crftn, Geoffrey Stein, 7638684
ROEBUCK, Lt, Edward, 181444
ROSS, Cfn, James Mcleod, 91897
SALT, Cftn, John Thomas, 7643849
SANDERS, Sjt, Eric George, 7621843
SAVILLE, Sjt, Harold, 7596752
SCOTT, Cftn, Leonard, 5121868
SHAZELL, S/Sjt, Bernard Harry Edgecombe, 7873955
SHORT, Cfmn, Stanley George Joseph, 7629938
SMART, Cftmn, Joseph, 7603547
SMITH,Crfn,Benjamin Arthur,7638954
SMITH,Cftn,Frederick Charles,7616168
SOULBY, Sjt, John Edward, 3599887
SPARE, Cftmn, Reginald Newton, 7592305
STARLING, Sjt, Frank Miles, 168004
STEEL, Sjt, Douglas, 7619144
STOGDEN, Sjt, Harry, 7589720
STREET, Cftmn, Percival, 10559757
STRINGER, Cfmn, Francis Thomas, 10540867
SUTHERLAND, Cftmn, Alexander, 7655049
SYLVESTER, Sjt, Frederick Frank, 7585959
TANNER, Cftmn, William George, 990674
TAPLIN, L/Cpl, Gordon Edward, 1873809
THOMPSON, Cftn, James, 14327657
THOMSON, Cftmn, John Speirs, 7623665
THOROGOOD, Cfmn, Ernest Frederick George, 7644947
TRIGGS, Sjt, Frank, 7607944
USHER, L/Cpl, Edwin Hobday, 14638729
WALKER, Cftmn, William, 2751061
WALKER, Cfmn, Fred, 7609977
WARD, Cfmn, George Robert, 4859953
WARN, Cftmn, John Kenneth, 5121871
WARRALLO, Cfmn, Frederick, 7619083
WATERS, Cftmn, Thomas Albert, 1572585
WESTON, Cftn, Robert, 3532798
WHITE, Cftmn, John Henry William, 10533545
WILTSHIRE, Sjt, Arthur Radclyffe, 1060030
WOOD, Sjt, Montague Frederick, 165949
YOUENS, Cfmn, Frederick William, 10559768
YUILL, Sjt, John Bexfield, 7608035

ROYAL LEICESTERSHIRE REGIMENT
ABBEY, Pte, Ronald, 823918
ALLEN, Pte, Charles, 4858537
ANNIS, Sjt, Bernard, 4857568
ARNETT, Pte, William Arthur, 4857920
ASHMORE, Pte, Thomas, 4857398
ASHMORE, Pte, Cyril, 4858959
ASKEW, Pte, Frederick, 4859989
ATKINSON, Pte, Leslie, 4857919
BAILEY, Pte, Albert, 4860101
BALL, Pte, George, 4857835
BALL, L/Cpl, Charles, 4859816
BANCROFT, Pte, George, 4858531
BARKBY, Sjt, George, 4857211
BARNACLE, L/Cpl, Walter Ronald, 4860497
BARNES, Pte, Frederick Barwise, 4865630
BARNES, Pte, Cyril Arthur, 4859824

BARNETT, Pte, Harry Thomas, 4865719
BARNETT, Pte, Thomas William, 4857581
BELL, Pte, Alfred James, 4858830
BELL, Pte, Arthur Hubert, 4862811
BENNETT, Pte, John Edward, 4857468
BENTLEY, Pte, Arnold, 4865693
BEVINS, Pte, Solomon Joseph, 4864811
BILLINGS, Pte, Isaac Martin, 4857545
BILLINGS, Pte, Alfred Mons, 4856230
BIRCH, Pte, Joseph William, 4858895
BIRD, Pte, Joseph, 4859823
BLACKHAM, L/Cpl, Thomas, 4858218
BLANCHARD, Pte, William, 4865814
BLOWER, L/pl, Dennis Jarvis, 4860175
BOCKROSS, L/Cpl, Sande, 4857720
BRAMLEY, L/Cpl, Frank Cyril, 4857501
BROOKES, Pte, Harry, 4972463
BUCKET, L/Cpl, Ernest Gordon, 4857293
BULLIMORE, Pte, George Ernest, 4857335
BURDER, Capt, Patrick Gifford, 58264
CADDICK, L/Cpl, John, 4859846
CARLING, Sjt, William, 4857758
CARRIER, Pte, Charles Herbert, 4860417
CHALLONER, Pte, Thomas, 4859980
CHAMBERLAIN, Pte, James, 4856868
CHESSMAN, L/Cpl, William, 4859689
CHESSON, Pte, Thomas Walter, 4860346
CHISWELL, Pte, Albert, 4859840
CLARKE, Pte, Frank, 4858057
CLARRICOATES, Lt, Tom Wiiliam, 159370
CLAYTON, Pte, George William, 5048096
CLOSE, L/Cpl, George, 4857232
COLEY, L/Cpl, William, 4858180
COLEY, L/Cpl, Ambrose Pepper, 4857026
COLLIER, Capt, William Thomas, 159369
COLLINS, Pte, James Wilfred, 4858478
COMINS, Pte, Harry, 4798634
COOPER, Pte, George, 4855317
COPE, Pte, Albert, 5048377
CORDELL, L/Cpl, Frank, 4857541
CORK, Pte, Edward Charles, 5494646
CORRIGAN, Pte, Michael Francis, 4121166
CORTON, L/Cpl, Leonard, 4863288
COUPLAND, Pte, Frank, 4860146
COX, Pte, Walter Lionel, 4859836
CRAIG, Pte, George Sharpe, 4857751
CRAIG, Pte, George, 4867039
CROMEYN, L/Cpl, Simon, 3382675
CROSTHWAITE, 2/lt, Patrick Guy, 1539082
CUNNINGTON, Pte, Cyril Frederick William, 4859833
CUTHBERTSON, Cpl, Reginald William, 4857845
CUTTS, Cpl, Reginald Thomas, 4857376
DAGG, Lt, William Joseph George, 222050
DALBY, Pte, George Albert, 4801886
DANIELS, Pte, Alfred Daniel, 4858200
DARBY, Pte, Cyril, 4858778
DAVIES, Pte, Frank, 4862501
DAVIS, Pte, William Henry, 4857138
DEAKES, Drmr, Hector Ronald, 4857801
DENTON, L/Cpl, John Edward, 4859850
DIGBY, L/Cpl, Frederick, 4863298
DRAYCOTT, Pte, Arthur, 4959852
EAGLES, Pte, William Arthur (served As Hill), 4858431
ECCLESTONE, Pte, Herbert Henry, 3767756
EDMANDS, Pte, Frederick Richard, 4867050
EDRIDGE, Pte, Sydney Raymond, 4857745
ELEMENT, Pte, Francis George, 4857789
ELKINGTON, L/Cpl, Frederick, 4857340
ELLIS, Pte, Arthur, 4858387
ENSOR, Pte, Robert Wiliam, 4864911

FARRANDS, Sjt, Richard, 4857841
FAULCONBRIDGE, Pte, Eric, 4859863
FAULDER, Pte, George William, 4863016
FAULKS, Pte, Henry, 2046811
FERN, Pte, Percy, 4862066
FINNEY, Pte, Robert, 4857916
FIRTH, Pte, Ronald, 4859856
FISHER, Pte, John Thomas, 4857344
FLEWITT, Cpl, Walter Douglas Haig, 4859861
FORD, Pte, Alfred, 4850064
FOSTER, Pte, Reginald, 4864606
FOX, Cpl, Thomas Francis, 4860042
FRANCIS, L/Cpl, George William, 4859148
FREER, Pte, Samuel, 4859853
FRENCH, Cpl, James Robert, 4857488
FRIEL, L/Cpl, William Michael, 4858940
GARDNER, Pte, Edwin Maurice, 4857817
GARNER, Pte, Maurice Arthur, 4860094
GARRETT, L/Cpl, Enoch Henry, 4860410
GEARY, Pte, William Stanley, 4857650
GIBBINS, Pte, Stanley, 4862860
GIBBONS, Pte, Cyril, 4858738
GIBBS, Drmr, Gwilym Thomas, 4857818
GOOCH, Pte, Ronald William, 5826715
GOODHAND, Cpl, John Henry, 4856792
GREEN, Pte, Ronald Leonard, 4864409
GREEN, L/Cpl, Herbert, 4858630
GREEN, Pte, Thomas Henry, 4856848
GRUNDY, Pte, George, 4973849
GUILFORD, Pte, Arthur Samuel, 4857526
HAINES, Pte, John Thomas, 4860385
HALL, Pte, Frederick, 4857312
HALL, Pte, Alfred Justine, 4865703
HANDLEY, Pte, Hariold, 4865733
HARRIS, Pte, Ivor Linsey George, 485976
HATHAWAY, Pte, John, 4858299 ·
HEATHCOTE, Bdsmn, John David, 4855768
HEGGS, Pte, Colin Charles Philip, 4859721
HILSDON, Cpl, Leonard Raymond, 4860087
HIND, Pte, Walter, 4860135
HINTON, Cpl, Thomas H., 4858205
HITCHCOCK, Pte, John Maurice, 4860518
HODGES, Pte, Albert George, 4862886
HOLLIS, Cpl, Leslie, 4972963
HOPKINS, Pte, William Henry, 4859798
HOPKINS, Pte, Thomas, 2694121
HORTON, L/Cpl, Alfred, 4857629
HUBBARD, Pte, Ronald George Richardson, 4858502
HUCKERBY, Pte, Ernest, 4857499
HUCKNALL, Pte, Horatio, 4860137
HULL, Pte, Frederick, 4858748
INGLESANT, Pte, John Henry, 4860462
JACKSON, Pte, Peter, 4858718
JACKSON, Pte, Ivor Maxwell, 4858333
JAKEMAN, Pte, Arthur Vincent George, 4858170
JAMES, Pte, Ronald, 4857793
JEFFERY, Pte, Benjamin Jack, 4862548
JEFFS, Pte, Richard G., 4859932
JENSON, Pte, Leonard, 4858172
JESSON, Pte, Walter, 4857399
JONES, Sjt, Robert Richard, 4858031
KINDON, L/Cpl, Ronald, 4857696
LAMBERT, Pte, John Henry, 4859891
LAMEY, Pte, George, 4858819
LANE, Pte, Eric, 4857260
LAWRENCE, Pte, Samuel, 4858085
LAYTE, Cpl, John Charles, 4858122
LEE, Pte, George Henry, 4862908
LETTS, L/Cpl, Harold, 4863375
LEWIS, Pte, Percy Valentine, 4858285

LORD, Drmr, Albert William, 4857623
LUCK, Pte, Charles William, 4856214
MADDAMS, Pte, James Kitchener, 4867110
MADDOCKS, Cpl, Walter, 4856430
MAISEY, Pte, Frederick Lewis, 4863524
MALLENDER, Pte, Willim Edward, 4860238
MALLINDER, Cpl, Edgar, 4532757
MANSFIELD, Pte, Benjamin, 4860846
MARSHALL, Pte, George Edwin, 4856441
MARTIN, Pte, George James, 4863389
MATHER, Pte, Gordon Wood, 4858334
MATTLOCK, Pte, George William, 4858480
MAYNARD, Pte, Edward Patrick, 5433859
MAYNE, Pte, Reginald, 4860463
MAYNE, Pte, Edward, 2142006
MEE, Pte, William Henry, 4857839
MEENAN, Pte, Owen, 7903698
MIDDLETON, L/Cpl, Aubrey, 4863397
MIDDLETON, L/Cpl, George, 4857328
MILLS, Pte, James Henry, 4858560
MITCHELL, Capt, Ian Desmond Vance, 71121
MONTGOMERY, Pte, Maurice, 4859892
MOORE, Cpl, Arthur, 4857752
MOORE, Pte, Albert James, 4863398
MORGAN, Pte, Leonard, 4860188
MOWBRAY, Pte, Douglas Henry, 485775
MUIR, Pte, Wilfred, 4865518
MURDY, Rqms, Sidney James, 4850864
NAYLOR, Pte, Willie, 2753167
NEA, L/Cpl, Edward, 4853365
NEEDHAM, Pte, Horace, 4863404
NEWNHAM, Cpl, James Alan, 4857834
NEWTON, L/Cpl, Charles Geoffrey, 4857632
NOBES, Pte, Ronald Charles, 4858410
NORMAN, L/pl, Harry Roland, 4860348
NUNLEY, Pte, Frederick Arthur, 4858943
NUNN, Pte, Wilfred, 4857560
O'MARA, Pte, Thomas Joseph, 4865627
OLIVER, L/Cpl, George Alfred, 4856808
OLIVER, Sjt, Benjamin, 4857116
ORCHARD, Pte, William, 4863406
PAGE, Pte, Norman, 4859906
PAINE, Pte, Albert Victor, 4857971
PALMER, Pte, Albert Henry, 4867133
PARGITER, Pte, Percival William, 4860086
PARKER, Cpl, Frederick William, 4856079
PARNHAM, Pte, Albert, 4856927
PARSONS, Cpl, Edward Ernest, 4857997
PATTERSON, Pte, Richard John, 4858217
PEARCE, Pte, Thomas Edward, 4856934
PEARSON, Pte, James Orman, 4858482
PEARSON, L/Cpl, Eric, 4973967
PEGG, Pte, George Alrnold, 4857585
PETERS, Pte, Fred, 4856217
PHILLIPS, Pte, Wilfred, 4858521
PICK, Pte, George Arthur, 4862597
PICKAVER, L/Cpl, Geoffrey, 4863422
PIDCOCK, L/Sjt, Frederick Arthur, 4853057
PILKINGTON, Bdsmn, Joseph, 4857538
PLATTS, Sjt, George Arthur, 4854206
PORTER, Pte, Robert, 4857435
PRATT, Pte, Lewis Harold, 4863429
PRIESTLEY, Gnr, John Norman, 4859773
PRITCHARD, Pte, Hugh, 7880208
PRITCHARD, Cpl, John, 4856789
RADFORD, Pte, Jack, 4858660
REDDING, Pte, Arthur Charles, 4867149
REDFERN, Pte, Leonard, 4858120
RICHARDSON, L/Cpl, George, 4857772
ROBINSON, L/Cpl, James William, 4857111

RODWELL, Pte, Wilfred Roy, 4857322
ROLLETT, Pte, Herbert Aiden, 4960055
ROPER, Pte, Douglas Cambrai Butchart Bentley, 4859911
ROSE, Pte, William Clarence, 4857926
ROSS, Pte, Paul Frederick, 4857271
ROWBOTHAM, Pte, Frank, 4858817
RUSHBY, Cpl, John, 4856901
SALE, Pte, John Herbert Thomas, 4863437
SALT, Pte, Levi, 4858119
SALT, Pte, Frank Dennis, 4860382
SANDY, Pte, Eric John, 5884354
SAVAG, Cpl, Arthur, 4857657
SAVAGE, Pte, Walter, 4857016
SAXBY, Pte, C E, 4858673
SCASEBROOK, Pte, John William, 4857167
SCOTT, L/Cpl, John Walter, 4858117
SEAL, Pte, Alfred, 4859920
SGUIRES, Pte, Frank, 4857041
SHARMAN, Pte, William Frank, 4860837
SHARPE, Pte, Leonard, 4858332
SHELDON, Pte, Lewis Herbert, 4856992
SHELTON, Pte, Horace Walter, 4859752
SHENTON, Pte, Albert, 4859918
SHEPHERD, Pte, John Francis, 4863455
SHEPHERD, Pte, John, 4863444
SMALE, Pte, Lawson Frederick, 4858216
SMART, Pte, Alfred, 4859931
SMITH, Sjt, George Albert, 4856493
SMITH, Pte, William Arthur, 4864512
SMITH, Pte, Walter Samuel, 4866996
SMITH, Pte, Robert Samuel William, 4863454
SPENCER, Drmr, Thomas James, 4800404
SPENCER, Pte, Shirley, 4865752
SPRING, L/Cpl, Percy William, 4854800
SQUIRES, Pte, George Herbert, 4858509
STAFFORD, Pte, Arthur, 4860143
STAPLEFORD, Pte, Cyril Joseph, 4859927
STIER, Pte, Robert, 4865284
STORER, Pte, Cyril, 4860211
SUTTON, Pte, William, 4859604
SWINDELL, L/Cpl, Herbert Lionel, 4859929
TATE, Pte, Philip Stanley, 4863470
TAYLOR, Pte, William James, 4856883
TAYLOR, L/Sjt, Leonard, 4851486
TEW, Pte, Leonard Joseph, 4858529
THOMAS, Pte, Leonard Alfred Lewellyn, 5496933
THOMPSON, Pte, Stanley Vurden, 4857754
THOMPSON, Pte, Stanley George, 4859797
THOMPSON, Pte, Frederick Arthur, 4859935
THOMPSON, Pte, Alexander, 4858554
THORPE, L/Sjt, Frederick John, 4856667
TIDD, Pte, George Bernard, 4859933
TOON, Pte, Walter Sidney, 4863474
TRAPP, Pte, Edwin, 3769831
TRUSLOVE, L/Cpl, George Henry, 4860052
TRUSWELL, Pte, George Thomas, 4858239
TUDOR, L/Cpl, Harry, 4857807
TURNER, Dvr, Lewis Leslie, 4855612
TURNER, Pte, Albert Henry, 4858597
VANN, Pte, Horace, 4859988
VINCE, Pte, Frederick Lawrence, 4861790
VISCOUNT, Pte, William Charles, 4914941
WALKER, Pte, Harold, 4858591
WALLACE, Pte, Verdun, 4859946
WALLER, Pte, Wilfred, 4855545
WALTON, Pte, Cyril Herbert, 4859947
WARIN, Cpl, Thomas, 4857609
WARNER, Pte, Edward, 4858284
WATKINS, Sjt, Bernard Edward, 4856541
WATKINS, L/Cpl, Ralph, 4864225

WEBSTER, Pte, George Ernest, 4858474
WELCH, Pte, Kenneth Arthur, 4860024
WEST, Pte, William, 4863486
WESTON, L/Cpl, Jack, 4863487
WHARMBY, Cpl, Arthur, 4859967
WHETTON, Pte, Thomas Ernest, 4854238
WHITE, Pte, Jonas, 4857802
WHITE, Pte, Francis James, 4863488
WHITTLE, L/pl, Thomas Herbert Geoffrey, 4859944
WILKINSON, Pte, Thomas William, 4858034
WILKS, Pte, Leslie, 4863492
WINGELL, Pte, Thomas Alert, 4863495
WOOD, L/Cpl, William, 4973880
WOOD, L/pl, Avroe Jackson, 4857005
WRIGHT, Pte, Walter Herbert, 4857510
WRIGHT, Bdsmn, Percy Edward, 4857958
WRIGHT, Pte, John Joseph, 4862680

ROYAL LINCOLNSHIRE REGIMENT
BURKINSHAW, Pte, Harry, 14907671
DAWN, Cpl, J.H., 4800977

ROYAL MARINES
BROWNLIE, Mrn, Brian Patrick, CH/X111472
INGLETON, Maj, Reginald Middleton
WARR, Mrn, Bernard Herbert, P/OX118672
WILSON, Cpl, Archibald, PLY/X105879

ROYAL NORFOLK REGIMENT
4 BATTALION
ABOTT, Pte, Leslie, 5780157
ABRAHAM, L/Cpl, Kenneth Arthur, 5775372
AINGER, Pte, Percy William, 5778922
ALLARD, Pte, Ernest, 5778673
ALLAWAY, Cpl, Edward Wilson, 5778638
AMES, L/Cpl, Arthur Edward, 5774679
AMYS, Pte, William John, 5774188
ANDREWS, Pte, William Ernest, 5573345
ANKER, Pte, John William, 5777074
ASHWORTH, Pte, Ernest Arthur, 5778642
AYERS, Pte, John William, 5774704
BALDWIN, Pte, George, 5768227
BANBROOK, Cpl, Leslie, 5573360
BARBER, Pte, Harold Edwin, 5779998
BARNES, Pte, Ernest Harold, 5778627
BARNES, Pte, Bertie Benjamin, 5774673
BATES, Pte, Harold Harry, 5776633
BEARD, Pte, Patrick Joseph, 5780110
BENDALL, Pte, Harry Henry, 5775527
BENNETT, Pte, Henry William Frederick, 5573550
BERRY, Pte, Edward Albert, 5772876
BETTS, Cpl, Robert Cope, 5774321
BIDMEAD, Pte, Arthur Henry, 5573318
BLAKE, Pte, Robert Thomas, 5573532
BLAND, Pte, Kenneth David, 5775040
BOBBINS, Pte, Bertram Ronald, 6144823
BOCKING, Pte, Hubert Arthur, 5771337
BOND, Pte, Edward, 5573398
BOOTHBY, Pte, Raymond Wilfred, 5778653
BOWELL, Pte, Ralph Ellis, 5774995
BREAM, Pte, Bertie George, 5774048
BRIDGES, Pte, George Victor, 5775317
BRIEGEL, Lt, David Roy Lindsey, 129434
BRIGHTON, Pte, James Albert, 5776159
BRITTIN, Pte, Albert Edward, 5778692
BROOKS, Pte, John Ernest Samuel, 5777686
BROWN, W/o, 1 John, 7876499
BROWN, Pte, Henry Frank, 5779129
BRYAN, Pte, Clarence, 5776619
BRYANT, Pte, Alfred Douglas, 5573364

BUCKENHAM, Pte, Robert John, 5776829
BUCKENHAM, Pte, William George, 5778685
BUCKLE, Pte, Ernest Robert, 5771861
BULLEN, Pte, Frank Horace, 5778683
BURNELL, Pte, Stanley William, 5780638
BURROWS, Pte, George Gilbert, 5773754
BURTON, Pte, Richard Walter, 5774451
BUTLER, Pte, Arthur William Thomas, 5573380
CARSON, 2/lt, Oliver Mayhew, 164470
CARTER, Pte, George Richard, 5573512
CARTER, Pte, Benjamin Albert, 5774189
CARTER, Pte, Robert Frederick, 5771376
CATCHPOLE, Pte, Alfred John, 5778695
CATCHPOLE, Pte, Bert Albert, 5824120
CHAMBERLAIN, Csm, Charles Henry, 5767244
CHAPLIN, Pte, Albert, 5772592
CHAPLIN, Pte, Ronald Leslie, 5774850
CHIVERS, Pte, Michael Ernest, 5573315
CLARK, Pte, Vivian Walter, 5573516
CLARK, Pte, Lionel Milne, 5776312
CLARKE, Pl, Edward Neslin, 5774691
CLARKE, Pte, Charles William, 2031783
CLAXTON, Pte, Frederick Richard, 5775118
CLEMENTS, Pte, George Alfred, 5774949
COK, Pte, Derek, 5772784
COLCHESTER, Pte, Claud Henry, 5774199
COLE, Pte, Albert Frank, 5573381
COLE, Pte, George Joseph, 5573531
COLE, L/Sjt, Arthur Henry, 5772385
COLE, L/Cpl, Ernest George, 5775765
COLES, Pte, James Alfred, 5573497
COLLINS, Pte, Norman Alexander, 5770060
COOKE, Pte, Charles Thomas, 5772674
COPE, Pte, Ernest, 5777013
COPPING, Pte, Eric Edward, 5781894
COSEY, Sjt, Percy William Stanley, 5771364
COZENS, Pte, David Daniel, 5779424
CRACK, L/Cpl, Donald Charles Arthur, 5773363
DANIELS, Pte, Basil Frederick, 5774514
DAVIDSON, Pte, Raymond Leslie, 5572083
DILWORTH, Pte, Walter Ernest, 5573510
DOUGLAS, Pte, Alexander Henry Beaney, 5780527
DOWNING, L/Cpl, Richard Vaynor, 5573330
DRAKE, Pte, Frederick Charles, 5772289
DRANE, Capt, James Marner, 69569
DUFFIELD, Pte, Frederick John, 5769955
DUGGAN, Pte, Albert Henry, 5573511
DURRANT, Pte, Ronald Leslie, 5775646
EADE, L/Cpl, William Patrick, 5778751
ECCLESTON, Pte, William John, 5772968
EDGINGTON, Pte, Albert Radge, 5112688
ELVIN, Pte, Frederick James George, 5775120
ELWIN, Cpl, Frank Robert, 5775630
EMERY, Pte, Bert, 5112890
ETTHERIDGE, Pte, Robert Percy, 5774515
EVERETT, Pte, Wilfred Calude, 5774513
EVERSON, Pte, Ronald William, 5774011
FARMER, L/Cpl, Ernest James, 5573424
FAWKE, L/Sjt, Evan Warwick, 5769913
FINCHAM, Pte, George Horace, 5773866
FIRMAGE, Pte, Stanley Cecil, 5773880
FORD, Pte, Jack William, 5767564
FOSTER, Pte, Newton, 5573581
FROST, Cpl, Bertie Robert, 5775121
FROST, Sjt, Stanley Allen, 5776716
FULLER, L/Cpl, Herbert Robert James, 5774687
GARNER, Pte, James Norman, 5775198
GAWTHROPE, Pte, Frederick Arthur, 5780452
GAYMER, Capt, Maurice Parke, 87892
GEORGE, Pte, Thomas, 5781802

GIBBONS, Pte, Sidney Jack, 5573433
GIDNEY, Pte, George Mack, 5782327
GILES, Pte, Stanley Frederick, 5774000
GLISTER, Pte, Herbert Kitchener, 5774364
GOLDER, Pte, Basil Albert, 5775595
GOLEBY, Pte, Clarence Victor, 5780231
GOOLD, Cpl, Percy Edgar, 5573387
GOTHARD, Sjt, Ernest H., 5774155
GOWING, Capt, Michael, 69480
GRAVELLS, Pte, Jack, 5778798
GREEN, Pte, James Charles Hobart, 5774684
GRIMES, Pte, Bertie Edward, 5773900
GRIPPER, Capt, Edward Siddans, 66512
GROM, Pte, Cyril William, 5780852
HALL, Pte, Charles Ernest, 5770294
HALL, Pte, Francis, 5775537
HANTON, Pte, William, 5774350
HANTON, Pte, Ernest Gilbert, 5774256
HANTON, Pte, Percy Arthur Noel, 5772862
HARRIS, Pte, Timothy Christopher, 3959376
HARRIS, Pte, Edward Edmund, 5773950
HARVEY, Pte, Raymond Alfred, 5771231
HEATON, Pte, George, 2571649
HENSLEY, Sjt, Gordon James, 5770098
HERWIN, Pte, Thomas William, 5774223
HITCHAM, Pte, Reginald Herbert, 5778833
HOAR, Pte, Robert James, 5573515
HOCKLEY, Lt, Hubert George, 124133
HOL, L/Cpl, Raymond, 5773941
HOLEHOUSE, Pte, Louis Raymond, 5776694
HOLKER, Cpl, Volney, 5774296
HOLLOWAY, Pte, John William, 5776614
HOLMES, Pte, William Ernest, 5774338
HOLMES, L/Cpl, Thomas Edward, 5776737
HOWELL, Pte, Berie Arthur, 5772533
HOWLETT, Pte, Oliver Verdon, 5773875
HUCKSTEP, Pte, Richard, 5773272
HUMM, Pte, Wiliam Charles, 5775479
HUNT, Pte, Harold, 5782259
HUNT, Pte, Ernest Raymond, 5774065
HUNTON, Pte, Walter James, 5780559
IMPEY, Pte, Donald James, 5779007
JACOBS, Pte, Wilfred Stanley George, 5775251
JAMES, Pte, William Arthur, 5774164
JARMEY, Pte, Robert Thomas, 5770036
JEFFS, 2/lt, Kenneth Frank, 184460
JOHNSON, Pte, Frederick William Samuel, 5779013
JORDON, Pte, Charles, 5779598
KEDGE, Pte, Clifford Arthur, 5776378
KEMP, Cpl, Frederick Ernest, 5573439
KERRISON, Capt, Roger Greville Justine, 91010
KERRISON, Cpl, Robert Herbert, 5774258
KNOTT, Pte, Edward William, 5774195
LAKE, Pte, Fred, 5770421
LARTER, L/Cpl, Harold David, 5774930
LAWRENCE, Sjt, Herbert Edward, 5768448
LEAMON, L/Cpl, Jack Raymond, 5774337
LEEDER, Pte, Henry George, 5774108
LEVERETT, Pte, George Henry, 5774845
LEWIS, Pte, Leonard James Arthur, 5573339
LOCKE, Cpl, Ernest Benjamin, 5775596
LONG, Pte, George E, 5775210
LONGSHAW, Pte, Ernest William, 5775787
LUNN, Rsm, Arthur John, 5766945
MALE, Pte, William Charles, 5774301
MANN, L/Cpl, Horace Frederick, 5769383
MARSHALL, Pte, Stanley, 5776728
MARSTON, Sjt, Frederick Thomas, 5775125
MASCALL, Pte, Graham Ernest, 5775207
MATHEWS, Pte, Walter John Keith, 5573421

McMASTER, Pte, Arthur Stanley, 5773573
MERRIX, Cpl, Denis Frederick, 6826910
MIDDLETON, Pte, Leslie Ronald, 5774033
MILLER, Pte, Douglas Carl, 5775584
MILLIGAN, Pte, William Alexander, 5573413
MILLS, Pte, George William, 5782157
MOORE, Pte, Russell Thomas, 5779030
MUSK, Pte, George Hebert, 5772199
MUSKETT, Pte, Cyril, 5773996
MYHILL, Pte, Frederick Arthur George, 5774880
NATHAN, Pte, John Charles, 5775342
NEAL, Pte, Reginald Charles Henry, 5777821
NEAL, Pte, Arthur Samuel, 5774023
NEALE, Pte, Ormonde Stewart, 5777820
NEWMAN, Pte, Joseph, 5573348
NOBBS, Pte, Ernest Reginald, 5775266
NORMAN, L/Cpl, Bernard Burnham, 5773920
OSBORNE, Cpl, Willam George, 5769804
OSBORNE, Pte, Wilfred, 7906801
OSWICK, Pte, Dennis Aubrey, 5782334
OUZMAN, Gnr, Donald Herbert, 5782334
OVERY, Pte, Cecil Norman, 5779625
PAGE, Pte, Bertie Clarence, 5776755
PAGE, Csm, Wilfred Robert, 6391589
PAGE, Pte, Roy Terence, 5774852
PARKER, Pte, Arthur Sidney, 5573503
PARSONS, Pte, Frederick, 5770889
PARSONS, Pte, Victor, 5773279
PEARCEY, Pte, Frederick William, 5573542
PEARSON, Pte, Percy Clifford, 5779364
PERCIVAL, Pte, Leonard Charles, 5774334
PERFITT, Pte, Albert, 5771196
PHILLIPS, Pte, Harry George, 5772729
PIERCE, Pte, Philip Arthur, 5773420
PLANE, Pte, William Robert, 5774239
POINTER, Pte, Harry Arthur, 5772865
POPPLE, Pte, Herbert William, 5779637
PROSPER, Pte, Walter Raymond, 5573501
PYE, Pte, William Ernest, 5777843
RICE, Pte, Leslie Leonard, 5573528
RICE, Pte, Stanley Robert, 6203037
ROBERTS, Pte, Albert Victor, 5778459
ROBINS, Pte, Frank Reginald, 5774983
ROBINSON, Pte, Frank George, 5777850
ROBINSON, Pte, James Henry, 5773208
ROSE, Pte, Charles William, 5777852
RUSSELL, Pte, Lionel Horace, 5773358
SAUNDERS, L/Cpl, William Cornelius, 5772129
SAUNDERS, L/Cpl, Louis, 5573577
SEAMONS, Pte, Harry Algernon, 5775605
SENTANCE, L/Cpl, Alfred, 5775174
SHALES, Pte, John, 5572887
SHOOBRIDGE, Pte, Frederick, 5779498
SKUSE, L/Cpl, James Douglas, 5573554
SMITH, Pte, Reginald, 5781864
SMITH, Pte, Percy Harold, 5772465
SMITH, L/Cpl, Leonard, 5777042
SMITH, Sjt, Arthur George, 6003564
SMITH, Pte, Albert Edward, 5781631
SMITH, Pte, Harry James, 5775648
SMITH, Pte, Edwin Joseph, 5773486
SNELLING, Cpl, Frank James, 5774851
SNELLING, Pte, Frederick John, 5771468
SOFTLEY, Pte, Cyril George, 5776797
SOUTHGATE, Pte, John Richard, 5779081
SOWELS, Cpl, William Francis, 5773039
SPRIGENS, Pte, Alfred, 5775528
STARMAN, Pte, Albert Edward, 5773302
STEAD, L/Cpl, John Walton, 5782343
STONE, Pte, Leslie, 5774136

STURLEY, Pte, Henry George, 5779083
STURMAN, L/Cpl, Alan Jack, 5775704
SUSSAMES, Pte, Albert Clifford, 5772593
TENANT, Pte, Leslie Eric, 5774193
TENNANT, Pte, George Albert, 5774089
THURSTON, Pte, Cyril Kenneth Sidney, 5775232
TIDSWELL, Pte, George, 577023
TOMKINS, T, John Richard Moore, 148870
TOMLINS, Pte, Arthur Edward, 5774360
TOVEY, Pte, Ronald Michael Henry, 5773276
TURNER, Pte, Frederick Joseph, 5773209
UNDERWOOD, Pte, William George, 5776816
UPTON, 2/lt, Sidney Arthur, 186044
WATSON, Pte, Desmond Howard, 5774214
WATSON, Pte, Thomas Henry, 5775441
WATSON, Pte, Bernard Cecil, 5774015
WEBB, Pte, Arthur James, 5775351
WEST, Pte, Reginald Harold, 5779733
WHALL, Pte, Albert Arthur, 5779092
WHITTAKER, Pte, Alfred, 5780678
WILLBURN, Pte, Frederick Vincent, 5774132
WILSON, Pte, Ernest Arthur, 5774378
WISKEN, Cpl, Walter, 5771946
WITHERICK, 2/lt, Brian Oliver, 164830
WOODS, Pte, Frederick John, 5773919
WRIGHT, Lt, John Hilary Carter, 138789
YOUNG, Pte, James Edward, 5573441

ROYAL NORFOLK REGIMENT
5 BATTALION
ABELL, Pte, Walter Edward, 5773570
ABRAHAMS, Pte, Victor James Donald, 5775331
ABREY, Pte, Cecil James, 579160
ALDERTON, L/Cpl, Raymond, 5777151
ALDRED, Pte, Charles Noel George, 5771491
ANDREWS, Pte, John, 5777312
ARMIGER, Pte, William Charles, 5775370
ASKER, Pte, Stanley Clifford, 5774826
ATKINS, Pte, Ernest Richard, 5777180
BAILEY, Pte, Henry Arthur, 5779996
BAKER, Pte, Albert George, 5774286
BALDWIN, Pte, Walter Valson, 5112756
BALDWIN, Pte, Frederick Henry, 5779520
BALES, L/Cpl, Idney Dennis, 5772902
BARKER, L/Cpl, William George, 5772631
BARKER, Pte, Arthur Edward, 5774808
BARKS, Pte, James William, 5888045
BARNARD, Cpl, Edward Sam, 5772941
BARNES, Pte, Arthur Reginald, 5779999
BARRETT, Pte, John Joseph, 5779524
BATTERBY, Pte, Frederick George, 5775169
BAXTER, Pte, Percy James, 5772619
BAXTER, Pte, James, 5776923
BEALES, Sjt, Isaac John, 5772249
BESSEY, Cpl, Kenneth Edward, 5776981
BETTS, Pte, Russell Walter, 5781665
BEVERLEY, Pte, Stanley George, 5774870
BLUNDEN, Pte, Lloyd George Joseph Charles, 5779120
BLUNT, Cpl, Harry Sutton, 5774829
BLUNT, Cpl, Ernest James, 5773904
BLYTH, Pte, Eddie Hall, 5775516
BOARDMAN, Capt, Stuart Cozens Hardy, 32936
BRACE, Pte, William, 5777108
BRADY, Pte, James Arthur, 5776681
BRERETON, Capt, Cloudsley Shovell Malcolm, 87629
BROWN, Pte, Frederick Charles, 5779538
BROWN, Cpl, Reginald Cyril, 5775109
BROWN, Pte, Leonard James, 5775800
BUCK, Pte, Edward Ernest, 6204756
BUCKNELL, Pte, Ernest Stanley, 5777217

BULL, Pte, James Arthur, 5777218
BULLIMORE, Pte, Theophilus William, 5774970
BUROWS, Pte, Thomas Lawrence Leonard, 5777219
BURRAGE, Pte, Sidney George, 5774718
BUTLER, Cpl, Arthur Harold, 5777077
CALEY, Pte, George James, 5776900
CAMERON, Pte, James Wiliam, 5774496
CARMEN, Pte, Arthur Ernest, 5777220
CARTER, Pte, Edward Robert, 5777158
CHAPLIN, Pte, William, 5777600
CHAPMAN, Pte, Charles William, 5775310
CLARKE, Pte, Edward Arthur, 5781783
COEN, Pte, Leslie Ernest, 5777160
COLBERT, Pte, Walter Richard, 5777225
COLE, Pte, Arthur James, 5774060
COLE, Pte, Jack Harry Barton, 5776987
COLLEN, Pte, Jim, 5774979
COLLINS, Pte, Frederick Frank, 5776664
COOKE, Pte, Thomas Harold Steward, 5777161
COOPER, Pte, Thomas Arthur, 5776704
COOPER, Pte, Ernest Charles, 5774868
COPELAND, Pte, William Charles, 5828884
COPEMAN, Pte, Walter Reginald, 5773928
CORK, Pte, Stanley Cecil, 5778728
CORSTON, Cpl, Sidney Harold, 5775318
CRACK, Pte, Frederick, 5779808
CREASEY, Pte, Dennis Albert, 5773609
CROWN, Pte, Sidney Reginald, 5777183
DACK, Pte, Bertie Reginald, 5770353
DACK, L/Cpl, Edward, 5775502
DAVIS, Pte, Alfred Oliver, 5777228
DEXTER, Cpl, James Verdun, 5776991
DICKINSON, Pte, Cyril Frank, 5773840
DIGBY, L/Cpl, Frank William, 5774906
DIPPLE, Pte, Ernest John, 5777407
DITCHAM, Pte, Raymond George Charles, 5776992
DIXON, Pte, Victor Arthur, 5777083
DUBLACK, Pte, Frederick James, 5777163
DUNTHORNE, Pte, George Arthur, 5775131
DURRANT, L/Cpl, Arthur John, 5773614
DYBALL, Pte, Robert Stanley, 5773616
EARLEY, Pte, Charles, 5779823
EBBS, Cpl, Horace Verdun, 5774273
EDWARDS, Pte, Godfrey, 5775560
EDWARDS, Pte, Cedric Graham, 5775359
EGGLETON, Pte, Kenneth, 5777085
EKE, L/Cpl, Harold Edward, 5775828
EMERSON, L/Cpl, William, 5772441
ETHERIDGE, Pte, John William, 5777050
ETHERIDGE, Pte, Ernest Alfred, 5772859
EVERITT, Pte, Robert Richardson, 5773839
FAIRHEAD, Pte, Sidney Dennis, 5777184
FARROW, Pte, Leonard Wilson, 5774643
FENTON, Pte, Richard Stanley, 5775395
FIDDY, Pte, George Edward, 5777167
FIELD, Pte, Douglas Frederick, 5776702
FIELDING, Pte, Herbert Ransom, 5777420
FISHER, Pte, Frederick, 5777185
FITT, Pte, James, 5774915
FITT, Pte, Frederick Arthur, 5776909
FITXATRICK, Pte, Dennis, 5775396
FLATMAN, Pte, Bertie James, 5777423
FLAXMAN, Pte, Frederick Arthur, 5774971
FLETCHER, Pte, Sidney Aubrey, 5773911
FORDHAM, Pte, Sidney George, 5777087
FRAMINGHAM, Pte, Peter William, 5772845
FRANCIS, Pte, Charles Frederick, 5775697
FRANKLIN, Pte, Alfred, 5779184
FREEMAN, Pte, Frederick Thomas, 5778134
FROST, Pte, Percy S Thomas, 5773090

FROST, Pte, Percy James, 5775107
FUTTER, Pte, Frederick Walter George, 5777052
GARROD, Pte, Philip, 5778136
GEE, Pte, George, 5774843
GILLOCH, Pte, Bernard George, 5775399
GINNS, Pte, George Joseph William, 5777236
GIRLING, Cpl, Frederick Stephen, 5774056
GOOCH, Pte, Reginald Charles, 5779579
GOODSON, Pte, Benjamin Henry, 5779580
GOODYEAR, L/Cpl, Harold Augustus, 5775951
GOREHAM, Pte, Harry Percy, 5778791
GOTTS, Pte, Stanley, 5775032
GRANGE, Pte, Basil William, 5779839
GREEN, Pte, Eric Wilfred, 5775033
GREENACRE, Pte, Alan George, 5775177
GRIFFIN, L/Sjt, Oswald James, 5770986
GRIMES, Pte, Frederick William, 5775179
GROOM, Pte, Arthur, 5776917
GUYMER, Pte, Christopher George, 5775221
HAL, L/Cpl, Edward Lewis, 5772889
HALL, Pte, Douglas Charles, 5774004
HALL, Pte, George Thomas, 5779582
HALL, Pte, Alfred John, 5775352
HALL, Pte, Cecil Frank, 5774113
HALL, Pte, Arthur, 5777091
HAMMOND, Pte, Ronald Herbert, 5774975
HARDIMENT, Csm, Henry Walter George, 5767940
HARROD, Pte, Theodore Ypres, 5777455
HARVEY, Pte, David Thomas, 5771657
HARVEY, Pte, James George Mckean, 5773059
HARVEY, Pte, Frank, 5775337
HAWKINS, L/Cpl, William George, 5776669
HAYES, Pte, Dennis Peter Francis, 5775518
HAYHOW, Cpl, Albert William, 5775407
HAYLETT, Cpl, William John Patrick, 5775353
HAYLOR, Pte, Leonard, 6394643
HAZELWOOD, Pte, John, 5774566
HEDGE, Pte, Kenneth George, 5777094
HENDEN, Sjt, William John, 5774610
HEWITT, Pte, Arthur James, 5773641
HIGGINS, Pte, Edgar Francis, 5777771
HIGH, Pte, Ernest Henry, 5776365
HIL, L/Cpl, John Frederick, 5772348
HILL, Pte, Charles Benjamin, 5777114
HIPKIN, Pte, Cecil Jack, 577095
HOGG, Pte, Arthur, 5776723
HORNE, Pte, Robert Thomas, 579850
HORNE, Pte, Jack Ernest, 5775875
HORNE, Pte, Robert Thomas, 579850
HORNIGOLD, Cpl, Clarence Vernon, 5775554
HORNSBY, Pte, Edward Samuel, 5773481
HOWARD, Pte, Leonard George, 5769861
HOWARD, Pte, John, 5775501
HUGHES, Pte, Joseph, 5777465
IRONS, Pte, Ernest Sidney, 5778601
JACOBS, Sjt, Frederick Alfred, 6002805
JARRED, Pte, John Edward, 5774658
JARVIS, Pte, Mark James, 5775220
JARVIS, Cpl, Jack William, 5775848
JARVIS, Pte, Arthur Leonard, 5775411
JARVIS, Pte, Harry Hansley, 5782043
JARVIS, Pte, Bertie Frederick, 5773967
JECKELLS, Pte, Henry Robert, 5777055
JENKINS, Pte, William, 5777117
JOHNS, Pte, Robert Charles, 5779228
JOHNSON, Pte, Arthur Richard, 5776677
JOLLEY, Pte, John William Stratton, 5782152
JONES, Pte, Eric David, 5773971
JONES, Pte, Ralph, 5772530
KETTRINGHAM, Pte, George, 5777176

KIRBY, Pte, William, 5774896
KNIGHT, Pte, Donald Keith, 873026
KNIGHTLEY, Pte, Dennis William, 5110633
LAND, Pte, Herbert John, 5777484
LANE, Pte, Frederick John, 5775157
LAWRENCE, Pte, Douglas Norman, 5777098
LECKIE, L/Cpl, Thomas William, 5779241
LEEDER, Cpl, Olaf William, 5774599
LEETE, Pte, Frederick Arthur, 5772973
LEIGH, Pte, Henry Harry, 5775414
LIGHTWING, Pte, Walter John, 5774604
LINCOLN, Pte, Edward George, 5777306
LOOME, Pte, James Robert, 5774840
LUMBERS, Cpl, John William, 5777122
MACKENDER, Pte, Stanley Charles William, 5778219
MANNING, Pte, Harry, 5773508
MARGETSON, Cpl, Elijah Reginald, 577209
MARSHALL, Pte, Ronald Edward, 5773346
MARSHALL, Pte, Leonard Jack, 5777101
MARTIN, Pte, Frank William, 5772985
MARTIN, Pte, Alfred William, 5775418
MARTIN, Pte, Harry James, 5775362
MASON, Cpl, Lawrence Arthur, 5774864
MASSINGHAM, Pte, James Ernest, 5777197
MAYES, Pte, Gerald Victor, 5777123
MAYHEW, Pte, Percy, 5774895
McCARTER, Pte, David Samuel, 5774115
McNEIL, Pte, Thomas Ernest, 5781118
MEARS, Pte, Albert George, 5774051
MEDLOCK, Pte, Ernest Theodore, 5775564
MEESON, Pte, George Walter, 5774579
MILLER, L/Cpl, Bernard Robert William, 5773970
MITCHELL, Pte, Reginald, 5779614
MITCHELL, Pte, Walter J, 5775079
MITSON, Sjt, Harold Douglas, 5775165
MOULTON, Pte, Leonard Maxwell, 5775558
MOWER, Pte, Russell Charles, 5773981
MOYSE, L/Cpl, Stanley, 5777243
NASH, Sjt, George Walter, 5770951
NEAL, Pte, Ernest John, 5774502
NEVILLE, Pte, Leonard Mathew, 5775035
NEWMAN, Pte, Alfred George, 5773664
NICHOLS, Pte, Miles Kitchener, 5778407
NORMAN, L/Cpl, Gordon Leonard, 5773668
NOVICK, L/Cpl, Harris David, 5775468
NUDDS, Pte, Edward Thomas, 5776960
OLDFIELD, Cpl, Frank Newland, 5774853
OSBORN, Pte, Stephen Alfred, 5774572
OVERLAND, Pte, Edward James, 5776671
OXBURY, Pte, Charles Albert, 57779724
PAINE, Pte, Francis Arthur, 5782161
PALLIOSTER, Lt, Guy Humphrey Roscamp, 138779
PALMER, Pte, Victor James, 5779273
PALMER, Pte, George Frederick, 5779628
PALMER, Pte, Robert John, 5775429
PALMER, Pte, William Percival, 5777831
PALMER, Pte, Kenneth George, 5779627
PATTERSON, Pte, Ronald William, 5774924
PATTERSON, Pte, Jack, 577503
PEARCE, Cpl, John Robert, 5776673
PECK, Pte, Herbert William, 5772900
PECKOVER, Cpl, Percy Albert, 5772761
PELLS, Pte, Herbert George, 5779956
PENTELOW, Pte, Jonas Harry, 5775562
PERRY, L/Cpl, Charles William, 5776964
PIGGIN, Pte, William Thomas, 5778436
PITT, Pte, Victor George, 5773897
PLAICE, Pte, Percy, 5772659
PLANE, Pte, Arthur Edward, 5775313
POWELL, Sjt, Percival Donald, 5772287

PUGH, Pte, Cuthbert Martin Parkhurst, 5779641
RAMM, Lt, Peter Jervis, 160928
RANDALL, Pte, Stanley Charles, 5779644
RASBERY, L/Cpl, Edward Arthur, 5775556
RATCLIFF, Pte, Frank Townsend, 7902934
READ, L/Cpl, Kenneth William, 5777248
READ, L/Cpl, George Charles, 5777205
REEVE, L/Cpl, Fredrick Allen, 5773080
REEVE, Pte, Walter Horace Jack, 5777207
REYNOLDS, Pte, Frederick Henry, 5778454
RICHARDSON, Pte, William George, 5774810
RIX, Pte, Ernest George Frederick, 5779295
ROBINSON, Cpl, Noel Frederick, 2577365
ROBINSON, Pte, Kenneth, 5776729
RODWELL, Pte, John Charles, 5775334
ROLLINGS, Pte, Leslie Charles, 5775348
ROUSE, Pte, Charles William, 5776966
RUDD, Pte, Robert, 5775097
RUDDOCK, Pte, George Edward, 5779466
RUMP, Pte, Ernest Jack, 5772563
SAUNDERS, L/Cpl, John, 5771063
SCHOLES, Pte, Robert, 5767024
SCOTT, Spr, John, 2116919
SEAGO, Pte, Cecil Edward, 5772956
SECKER, Pte, Bertie, 5777066
SEWTER, Pte, Frederick Edward, 5777209
SHARMAN, Pte, Albert George, 5776968
SHIPMAN, L/Cpl, Kenneth Hardy, 5776689
SHIPP, Sjt, Robert Arthur Jellicoe, 5772030
SHIPPEY, Pte, Frederick Stanley, 5775464
SKOULDING, Pte, Reginald George, 5782311
SLAUGHTER, L/Cpl, Herbert Orford, 5769634
SMITH, Pte, Thomas William, 5779315
SMITH, Pte, Bertram John, 5772778
SMITH, Pte, Robert, 5776970
SMITH, Pte, Frederick William, 5775432
SMITH, Pte, Cecil Jack, 5778490
SMITH, Pte, Eric Arthur, 5774962
SNELL, L/Cpl, Cyril Thomas, 5775083
SNELLING, Pte, Charles Robert, 5775899
SNELLING, Pte, Charles Albert, 5772490
SOUTHGATE, Pte, Johnnie, 5775508
SPARKES, Pte, Cyril Arthur, 5778296
SPENCER, Pte, Stanley Frederick, 5775473
STEBBINGS, Pte, Reginald Bert Sidney, 5770379
STEVENSON, Pte, Norman, 5777275
STEWARD, Pte, Norman James, 5774913
STEWARD, Pte, Charles Edward, 5779671
STOCKS, Pte, Georeg Frederick, 5775436
STONE, L/Cpl, Harry Samuel, 5777262
SYMONDS, Pte, William Edward John, 5779673
TABERHAM, Pte, Cyril James, 5779859
TAYLOR, Pte, Allured John, 5772349
TAYLOR, Pte, George Frederick, 5776756
THEOBALD, Sjt, Edward James, 5769733
THIRST, Pte, John Ernest, 5774175
TINKER, Pte, Walter Graham, 5781030
TOOLEY, Pte, Jack William, 5774900
TOVELL, Pte, Albert, 5781032
TUCK, Pte, David Lloyd George, 5769866
TURNER, Pte, Reginald Clement, 5776975
TUTTLE, Pte, Ronald Bert, 5779087
URRY, Pte, Claude Edward, 5779341
VALENTINE, Pte, George Frederick, 5774138
VINCENT, Pte, Thomas Albert, 5774926
VINCENT, Cpl, Thomas Albert, 5774926
WAGG, Sjt, Frederick Charles, 5775545
WALDEN, L/Cpl, Herbert John William, 5774873
WALKER, Pte, William Wallace, 5779866
WARD, Cpl, Victor Norman, 5771270

WARD, Pte, Russell Wilfred, 5778543
WATKER, Pte, William Charles, 5778549
WATSON, Pte, Percy, 5778551
WEBB, Pte, George Thomas, 5778554
WEBSDALE, Pte, Peter Henry, 5776861
WHILEY, Pte, Reginald Arthur, 5777267
WHITEHEAD, Pte, William Arthur, 5828325
WILKIN, Pte, Richard James, 5775663
WILSON, Pte, Harold Frank, 5777286
WOODS, Pte, Robert Stanley, 5775160
YARHAM, Sjt, Frederick, 5875650
YARROW, Pte, Gus, 5773300

ROYAL NORFOLK REGIMENT
6 BATTALION
ABEL, Pl, Ronald John, 5775608
ADCOCK, Pte, Dennis Frank, 5778168
AGGAS, Pte, James William, 5778171
ALDERTON, L/Cpl, Godfrey G, 5780714
ALDIS, Pte, Harry Peter, 5775713
ANDREWS, Pte, William James, 5780722
ARBON, Pte, Ronald Henry, 5775763
ARDLEY, Pte, John Charles, 5775381
ARMSTRONG, Gnr, George Ronald, 5774245
ARTIS, Pte, William George, 5775682
ATKINS, Pte, Thomas Harry, 5769639
ATTEWELL, Pte, Herbert Thomas, 5775750
BALAAM, L/Cpl, Herbert William, 5776142
BARFIELD, L/Cpl, Herbert Leslie, 5775767
BARKER, Pte, John Henry, 5780734
BARNARD, Pte, Frederick Benjamin, 5773580
BARNETT, Pte, Douglas, 5776143
BARNETT, Pte, Alfred, 5777026
BARON, Pte, William, 5777036
BARTON, L/Cpl, Alexander Walter, 7668354
BASS, Pte, John Edward, 5888048
BATCHELOR, Pte, Leslie Stuart, 6020806
BAXTER, Pte, George Harry William, 5780167
BEAMENT, Pte, Jesse, 5777670
BECK, Pte, Walter George, 5773747
BELL, Pte, Bernard William, 5776408
BELLCHAMBER, Cpl, Ivor, 5775012
BENISON, L/Sjt, Gordon Robert, 5774943
BENNETT, Pte, Sidney Daniel, 5775764
BETTINSON, Pte, William Arthur, 5888052
BIRD, Pte, John, 5778196
BLAKE, Pte, John Francis, 5773448
BLAND, L/Cpl, Robert Thomas, 5769517
BLOOM, Pte, Walter George, 5772273
BLOSS, Pte, Arthur James, 5778139
BLUNT, Pte, Jack, 5776606
BOUTON, Pte, Cecil Claude, 5775242
BREACH, Pte, Richard Joseph, 5776156
BROWN, Pte, Arthur Ernest, 5778150
BROWN, Pte, Bertram, 5888058
BROWNE, Pte, Eric Frank, 5778152
BRUNTON, Pte, Reginald Theodore, 5778153
BUCKLE, Pte, Geoffrey Charles, 5888127
BUMFREY, Pte, Stanley James, 5778154
BUNTING, Pte, James Robert, 5779539
BURTINSHAW, Cpl, John, 5773755
BURTON, Pte, Harry, 5774447
BURTON, Pte, Geoffrey Sidney, 5775576
CAMPBELL-ORDE, Capt, Peter Stewart, 90864
CANNELL, Pte, Ecil George, 5775579
CARLTON, Pte, Charles Henry, 5775725
CARMAN, Pte, Harold George, 5781639
CARR, Pte, Richard Henry, 5781777
CARTER, Pte, Gerald Vernon Herbert, 5776583
CARTER, Pte, Ernest, 5774615

CATCHPOLE, L/Cpl, Frederick William, 5774720
CAWLEY, Pte, Leonard, 5778163
CHAMBERS, Pte, Leonard Verdun, 5778165
CHAPLIN, L/Cpl, Denis Edward, 5775770
CHARITY, Pte, John Edward, 5888072
CHILVERS, Pte, Reginald, 5776357
CHITTOCK, Pte, Harold, 5778955
CHURCHARD, L/Cpl, Ernest William, 5774834
CLARKE, Pte, John Arthur, 5772303
CLARKE, Pte, George William Ernest, 5773311
CLARKE, Pte, John Spurling, 5775667
CLIFTON, Pte, Adam Ronald, 5888078
CODLING, Pte, Kenneth, 5776167
COE, Pte, John Franklin, 5774989
COLE, Pte, Ronald, 5773759
CONNELL, Pte, Christopher Joseph, 5779763
CONNELLY, Pte, Terence, 1430503
COOK, Pte, Walter Leslie, 5775778
COOKE, Pte, Bert Frank, 5776642
CORLETT, Pte, Frederick Joseph, 5776949
CORY, L/Sjt, Frederick, 5779554
COX, Lt, Alfred Edwin, 197120
CRASKE, C/sgt, George Thomas, 5773762
CROOKS, Cpl, William, 5769169
CROSS, Pte, John, 5776171
CROTCH, Cpl, Reginald George, 5771547
CRUMP, Pte, Frederick Charles, 796308
CULWICK, L/Cpl, John Edward, 5776645
CUNNINGHAM, Pte, Arthur John, 5773566
DARLEY, Pte, Henry William, 5770804
DEATH, Cpl, Francis Arthur, 5776177
DICKERSON, Pte, Maurice Golden, 5775783
DIGBY, Pte, Leslie Lancelot William, 5771680
DIGGINS, Pte, Douglas Haig, 5775390
DOUGHTY, L/Cpl, Leslie Norman, 5888097
DOVE, Cpl, Alec George William, 5773768
DOVEY, Sjt, Peter Alan, 5781616
DOWNES, Pte, Basil Ivory, 5776179
DUNCAN, Sjt, Donald Herbert, 5770650
DURHAM, Pte, Henry Robert, 5775642
DURRANT, Pte, Bertie Stanley, 5778119
EASTWOOD, Pte, Herbert, 5773898
EDWARDS, Sjt, Herbert Reginald, 5774723
ELLIS, Pte, Douglas Owen, 5888105
EVANS, Capt, Richard Rowland, 138780
EWELLS, Pte, Harry James, 5780823
FERROW, Pte, James, 5775344
FISKE, Pte, Sidney Harold, 5775590
FITCH, Pte, Leslkie Reginald, 5888113
FLATT, Pte, Frederick George, 5779827
FLOWERS, Pte, David Henry, 5773422
FOSTER, Cpl, John Collin, 5775631
FOX, Pte, Harry Edward, 5346040
FREEMAN, Pte, Arthur Ernest, 5774531
FRENCH, Cpl, Edward Richard, 5775677
FRYER, Pte, Jonathan, 5774027
FYFE, Sjt, John Douglas, 5888117
GARDINER, Pte, Benjamin, 5774736
GARRETT, Lt, Donald Robert Wilfred, 113761
GIBBONS, L/Cpl, Donald, 6895955
GIBBS, Cpl, Leslie John, 5888121
GODFREY, Pte, Cyril, 5780286
GOLDSMITH, Pte, William Arthur, 5780650
GOOCH, Pte, Frederick Robert, 5781804
GOOCH, Pte, Thomas Henry, 5776190
GRAY, Pte, Leonard, 5774421
GRAY, Cpl, Cyril Edward, 5773567
GRAYSON, Pte, Albert, 5888125
GREEN, Pte, John Arthur, 5771367
GREEN, Pte, John Allan Douglas, 5775728

GREN, Cpl, Sidney, 5776654
GRIFFITHS, Pte, Percy William, 5778089
GUEST, Pte, Douglas George, 5771548
GUEST, Pte, Donald, 5776198
GUYMER, Pte, Henry Thomas, 5780263
HAGUE, Pte, Samuel Arthur, 5776954
HAGUE, Pte, Douglas Henry, 5776199
HALL, Pte, Arthur Alfred William, 5778091
HALLAM, Pte, William Robert, 5888133
HAMMOND, Pte, George Charles, 5772052
HAMPSON, Cpl, Thomas, 6020894
HANNANT, Pte, Edward Herbert, 5780856
HANTON, L/pl, Mathew Hovells, 5775264
HARDWICK, Csm, Stanley William, 1669037
HARRISON, Pte, George Joseph, 5887829
HARVEY, Pte, Reginald Richard, 5780553
HAYLETT, Pte, Maurice Henry, 5775735
HAYLETT, Pte, Robert Herbert, 5779586
HENRY, Pte, William Alfred, 5774425
HERRING, Pte, Percival John, 7349408
HILDITCH, Pte, William Alexander, 6150215
HILTON, Pte, Stanley Herbert, 5780868
HINKINS, Pte, Henry William Charles, 5771037
HOLDEN, Pte, Reginald Thomas, 5776204
HOLDOM, Pte, Leonard Debonaire, 5778101
HOOK, Pte, Arthur Charles, 5772039
HOOPER, Sjt, Frederick Thomas, 5774413
HOWARD, Pte, Herbert John, 5778105
HOWARD, Pte, Henry Albert, 5772540
HOWE, Pte, George, 5778106
HOWELL, L/Cpl, Stephen Eric, 5773180
HOWES, Pte, Walter Ernest Alexander, 5775741
HOWES, Pte, Frederick, 5778197
HOWLING, Pte, Jeffrey Bernard, 5773909
HOYES, Pte, Horace, 588145
HUBBARD, Sjt, Reginald John, 5771766
HUGHSON, Pte, Herbert Harold, 5772521
HUME, Pte, Harold, 5778201
HUNT, Pte, Victor Reginald Nigel, 5776947
HURST, Pte, Geoffrey Snowden, 5774712
HUTSON, Pte, Frederick Charles, 5770623
IVINS, Sjt, Peter Dunbar, 5774395
JARVIS, L/Cpl, Alert Charles, 5778204
JEFFREYS, Pte, John Robert, 5782657
JENNINGS, Pte, Alfred Thomas, 5773035
JOHNSON, Pte, Alex Walter Rex, 5775186
JONES, Pte, Peter Charles, 5778206
KETT, Pte, Leonard Sidney Haig, 5775747
KING, 2/lt, Ronald Oliver Clayton, 145088
KNIGHT, Pte, Albert Harold, 5775730
LARTER, Pte, David John Wighton, 5776214
LIVINGSTON, Cpl, George Turner, 5779739
LOAKE, Pte, Horace George, 5776596
LUFF, Pte, Arthur Norman, 5773432
LYWOOD, Lt Col, Ian Conway Gifford, 12303
MADGETT, Pte, Raymond Ernest, 5778878
MAHONY, Pte, John William, 5778221
MARLER, Pte, Roland Leslie, 5775903
MARRISON, Sjt, Walter, 5774938
MASON, Sjt, James Edwin, 5774241
MAYES, Pte, Herbert Gordon, 5778227
McNEILL, Pte, William, 5773860
MEEK, Pte, Jack James, 5778230
MELLOR, Pte, Edwin, 5773516
MERRY, Pte, Geoffrey, 5776598
MIDDLETON, Pte, John William Barton, 5776083
MIDDLETON, Pte, Gordon William, 5773660
MILLS, Pte, Robert William, 5773988
MILLS, Pte, Sidney, 6020956
MILLS, Pte, Albert William, 5775731

MIMISTER, L/Cpl, Herbert Cyril, 5777502
MITCHELL, Lt, Michael Charles, 138784
MOBBS, Pte, Cyril, 5770928
MORETON, Pte, Herbert Alven, 5773525
MORTON, Pte, Reginald, 5778235
MOULTON, Pte, Harry Albert, 5776227
MYHILL, Pte, William, 5773993
NEAL, Pte, Richard Robert, 5780582
NELSON, Pte, Jack Leach, 5780298
NEWBY, Pte, Frederick John, 5774213
NEWSTEAD, Pte, Herbert, 5775738
NICHOLS, Pte, William David, 5776230
NIXON, Pte, Robert Stanley, 5887919
NOBES, Pte, George Samuel, 5778241
NUTT, 2/lt, Richard Harwood, 200755
OSBORNE, Pte, Edward Arthur, 5772650
OVERY, Pte, Peter Samuel, 5778246
PAGE, Pte, Donald, 5780304
PALMER, Pte, Leslie Malta, 5778249
PARKER, 2/lt, Norman Ernest, 197118
PARKER, L/Cpl, Bernard Edward, 5886855
PARKIN, L/Cpl, Albert, 5887925
PARTRIDGE, Pte, Frederick James, 5778253
PEARCE, Pte, Roy Leonard Nelson, 5778430
PEARCE, Pte, Harry William Robert, 5780587
PECK, Pte, Edward John, 5778254
PEEL, Pte, Harry George, 5775733
PEPPER, Pte, Frank Robert, 5775771
PICTON, Cpl, Eric Frank, 5773052
PIGGIN, Pte, Bert, 5774403
PINNER, Pte, Eric James, 5776240
PLACHECKI, Pte, Henry John, 5772623
PORTER, L/Cpl, Charles William, 5778261
PRENDERGAST, Pte, Thomas Joseph, 5782362
PRENTICE, Pte, Ernest William, 5776772
PRETTY, Pte, William John, 5773681
PYMAN, Cpl, Thomas Albert, 5770640
QUARTERMAN, Pte, Sidney Thomas, 5777021
RAVEN, L/Cpl, Eric, 5776775
READ, Cpl, Edward John, 5776777
READ, Pte, Percy Sidney, 5773836
READ, Pte, Frank, 5775268
REEDER, Pte, John Bertlot, 5780969
REEVE, L/Cpl, Richard Grocutt, 5887942
REEVE, C/Sjt, Cecil John, 5774459
RICHARDS, Pte, Stanley, 5777848
RICHARDSON, Pte, James, 5771733
RINGWOOD, Pte, Sandall, 5776779
RISEBROW, Pte, Henry Robert, 5774648
RIX, Pte, Arthur William, 5775589
ROBERTS, Pte, James William, 1455883
ROLFE, Pte, John Amos, 5773812
SABBERTON, Pte, Edwin Alfred, 5778470
SADD, L/Cpl, Ronald Arthur Brett, 5775650
SADLER, Pte, William Fitt, 5778278
SALKIND, Pte, Arthur, 3776850
SALTER, Pte, Joseph William, 5776707
SALTER, 2/lt, James Alexander, 176832
SAMS, Pte, George, 5779464
SANDERS, Pte, Reginald, 5780985
SANDS, Pte, Harold Walter, 5778281
SAUNDERS, Pte, Robert Stanley, 5776252
SAUNDERS, Pte, Alert Ernest, 5779655
SAUNDERS, L/Cpl, Sidney Victor, 5773693
SCATTERGOOD, Pte, Eric, 5776609
SCOTT, Pte, Arthur Richard, 5345897
SEMMENCE, Pte, Victor Ellis, 5775708
SHALES, Pte, Harold Henry, 5778289
SHARMAN, Pte, Russell Joseph Frank, 5775321
SHARPE, Pte, George, 5776595

SHELDRAKE, Pte, Maurice Robert, 5778076
SHIPLEY, Pte, Donald Stanley, 5778290
SHORTING, Pte, Frederick Raymond, 5773097
SHUTER, L/Cpl, James, 5776603
SILLETT, Pte, Sidney Keith, 5773698
SIMPSON SMITH, Pte, George Edward, 5776254
SMITH, Pte, William Neville, 5773275
SMITH, L/Cpl, Ralph, 5775718
SMITH, Sjt, Donald Jack, 5773947
SMITH, Cpl, Leslie Charles Percy, 5772995
SMITH, Pte, Willam Alan, 5776582
SMITH, Pte, Claude Donald, 5776274
SNOWLING, Pte, Raymond Verdun, 5777260
SNOWLING, Pte, William Edward, 5779666
SOANES, Pte, Harold Ernest, 5776258
SOLOMON, Pte, Harold Oliver, 5776798
SOLOMON, Pte, Amos George John, 5773706
SOUTHGATE, S L/Cpl, Bernard Gilbert, 5779667
SPELMAN, Pte, Albert Frederick, 5772916
SPINKS, L/Cpl, Robert George, 5775602
STIMPSON, Pte, Alfred Henry, 6021031
STONE, Pte, Herbert, 5779326
STONE, Pte, Edward Arthur, 5778300
STOTT, Pte, Peter Peterson, 5769728
STRATFORD, Capt, John Clifton, 90917
TAYLOR, Pte, Sidney Donald, 5775676
TIMBERS, L/Cpl, Arthur James, 5774019
TOYE, Pte, Richard Alfred, 5345899
TRETT, Pte, Stanley Charles, 5776811
TUTTLE, Pte, George Arthur, 5768628
TYRRELL, Pte, Bertie James, 5773247
UNWIN, Pte, Rupert Harding, 5772847
UTTING, L/Cpl, George Deluge, 5770357
WALLER, Pte, George Thomas, 6021056
WARD, Pte, Reginald Ernest, 5780616
WARD, Pte, Percy Kenneth, 5780351
WARD, Sjt, Bernard Harry, 5776821
WARDLEY, Pte, Charles Edward, 5777284
WARNES, Pte, William John Robert, 5772589
WARREN, Pte, Cyril Oswald, 5778314
WATSON, Pte, Reginald, 5776860
WATSON, Pte, Arthur, 5774162
WATTS, Pte, Charles Wilfred Thomas, 5776265
WESTGATE, Capt, Peter Maxwell, 67803
WEYMONT, Lt, Eric Lawrence, 184700
WHITEAR, L/Sjt, Jack Frederick, 5775720
WHITEHEAD, Cpl, George, 5776750
WHITTINGHAM, L/Cpl, Joseph Alfred, 5346147
WILKINS, L/Cpl, William Herbert, 57747411
WILLOX, Cpl, Alexander John Thomas, 6021070
WILSON, Pte, William Thomas, 5770571
WILSON, Pte, Claude Vivian, 5781878
WILSON, Pte, Arthur William, 5774306
WILSON, Sjt, Arthur, 5770728
WILSON, L/Cpl, Arthur Henry, 5777451
WINTER, Pte, James Percy, 5772687
WRIGHT, Pte, Albert Thomas, 5778571
YALLOP, L/Cpl, Ralph Edward, 5776273
YOUNG, Cqms, Frederick Richard, 759356
YOUNG, Cpl, David Daniel, 6021079

ROYAL NORTHUMBERLAND FUSILIERS
ALCUS,Fus,Joseph Alfred,2818461
ALDERMAN,Capt,Richard Harold Robert (MC),
ALEXANDER, Fus, Leslie, 4274062
BELL,Fus,George Robert Headley,4274122
BELL,Capt,William,3524382
BELL, Fus, Norman, 4276625
BENSLEY, Fus, William Henry, 4127854
BESLEY, Maj, Charles Robert Ingram (MBE MC), 37810

BISHOP, L/Cpl, Thomas Henry, 4127756
BLACK, Fus, David, 4267620
BOND, C/Sjt, Edward, 4265849
BROOKS,Csm,Albert,4270112
BROWN, L/Cpl, Frank, 4274207
BROWNBRIDGE, Fus, Harry George, 4278538
BUIE, L/Cpl, James Wishart Bainbridge, 7662455
BURNETT,Fus,Alan,4274209
CAISLEY, Fus, Charles Smailes, 4273542
CALVERT, Fus, Alexander John, 4275793
CARSLEY, Fus, George, 4127738
CASTLE, Fus, Joseph, 4275798
CHARLESON, Fus, Oliver, 4275800
CHARLTON, Fus, Thomas, 4278380
CHILMAN,2/lt,Alfred Thomas,EC/2744
CHISHOLM, Fus, Thomas William, 4273974
CLARK, Fus, Thomas, 4276638
CLARK, Fus, James William, 4273813
CLARKE, Fus, James, 4275626
COLLIER, Fus, James Howard, 4274935
COOK, Fus, John Richard, 4273814
COWAN, Fus, William Henry, 4270931
COWAN, Fus, John Richle, 4276641
CRAMPTON, Fus, Kenneth George, 4276776
CRAVEN, Fus, Charles, 4276403
CRITCHLEY, Fus, Edward, 4278386
CROWTHER, Fus, Thomas, 4276896
CUMMINGS, Fus, John George, 4276642
DEES, Fus, James Bracken, 4274961
DIROM, Fus, Gavin, 4271470
DIXON, Fus, Robert Patrick, 4278978
DOWIE, Fus, Albert, 4271693
DUNBAR,Fus,Alan,4273273
DUNLOP, Fus, John, 4274124
EAGLETON, L/Cpl, Gerard, 4127820
EDGELL, Fus, Thomas, 4278397
ELLIOT, Us, Percival, 4273336
ELLIOT, Fus, Richard Douglas, 4273911
EMERSON, Fus, James Arthur, 4274806
ERRINGTON, Fus, George, 4375254
EYTON, L/Cpl, Cecil, 4275669
FARRINGTON, Fus, Christopher, 4126733
FOREMAN, L/Cpl, George Anthony, 4271537
FORSTER, Cpl, John Alexander, 4273913
FROMSON, Fus, Thomas Milburn, 4274908
GARDNER, Fus, John, 4277417
GARSIDE, Fus, Harry, 4275066
GRAHAM, Fus, George, 4263171
GREGSON, Fus, Henry, 6210596
GRUNDY, Fus, Harry, 4127724
HALL, Fus, John Henry, 4277071
HALL, Fus, John, 4279329
HANLON, Fus, Denis, 4126886
HINE, Fus, Gordon, 4275565
HOGG, Fus, James, 4268899
HOLLYWELL, Fus, James, 4273556
HUMPISH, Cpl, John, 4264905
HUNTER, Fus, Herbert, 4273651
IONS, Fus, Harold, 4449243
IONS, Fus, Harold, 4449243
JARRETT, Fus, Geoffrey Alwyn, 5949191
JOHNSON, Fus, Lewis, 4278447
JOHNSTON, Fus, Thomas Purves, 427419
KENNEALLY, Fus, Timothy, 4271150
KNIGHT, Fus, William Douglas, 4273514
LAIDLER, Fus, Robert, 4273835
LEIGHTON,Fus,George
LONG,Fus,John Robert,4275862
LUNDY, Fus, Frederick, 4263283
MASON, Fus, Norman, 4274515

MASON, L/Cpl, Frederick, 4275559
McCABE, Fus, Henry, 6210710
McGREGOR,Fus,Walter George,4274018
McMANUS,Fus,Myles,2980548
MIDGLEY, Fus, Leslie, 4275182
MILBURN, Fus, William, 4278465
MOGIE, Sjt, Hugh Gordon, 4269643
MOLE, Fus, Joseph, 4273561
MORRIS, L/Cpl, Harold, 4277397
MULIGAN, Fus, John Edward, 4272857
MURRAY, Sjt, William, 4273884
NEWTON, Fus, Sidney, 6210474
NOCKELS, Fus, Douglas, 4274854
NUTMAN, Fus, John William, 4263937
O'HARE, L/Cpl, John Robert, 427353
OLIVER, Fus, George William Clunie, 4273940
ORMSTON, C/Sjt, James, 4273564
PALMER, Fus, Peter, 4278783
PARK, Fus, Thomas Henry, 4275510
PARKER, Fus, John George, 4275585
PARKINSON, Fus, Norman, 4276484
PEARSON, L/Cpl, Joseph, 4273941
POLL, Fus, James Elliott, 4275293
RAIPUTANA RIFLES
REAY, Sjt, Edward, 4269426
REED, Fus, Joseph, 4276545
REILLY, Fus, James, 4274136
RICE, Fus, Richard, 4274031
RICHARDSON, Fus, Alexander, 4272293
ROBERTSON, Fus, Robert, 4274099
ROBSON, L/Cpl, Luke, 4275762
ROBSON, L/Cpl, Albert Roy Russell, 4276224
ROUNDING, Fus, Thomas Lee, 4276225
ROUTLEDGE, Fus, Ronald, 4272832
RYAN, Fus, John Hnery, 4274096
SCOTT, Cpl, James Laidler, 4273855
SCOTT, Fus, Mathew, 4278276
SCOTT, Fus, John Alexander, 4273951
SCOTT, Fus, Charles, 4277329
SHEILS, Sjt, Patrick John, 7011208
SMEATON, Cpl, John, 4275766
SMITH, Fus, George, 4277334
SMITH, Fus, James Phorsen, 4270864
STANBURY, Fus, Frederick, 4275759
STAYMAN, Fus, William Foreman, 4278815
STEPHENSON, Fus, Thomas, 4449673
STEWART, Fus, John, 4275572
STONE, Fus, Noah, 4273854
SUGGETT, Fus, Harold, 4276736
SWEETING, Fus, Charles Stewart Wilcox, 4279387
TAIT, Fus, John, 4271077
TAYLOR, Fus, Norman, 4275924
THOMPSON, Fus, Arthur William, 4278291
TONKINSON, Fus, Sidney, 4278917
TOWNSLEY, Sjt, Ambrose, 4265967
WAIT, Fus, William, 4273893
WAIT, Fus, Thomas, 4273895
WANTY, Fus, Leonard William, 4272350
WARD, Lt, Mark, 121523
WARD, Cpl, John, 4278303
WATSON, Capt, Robert, 56898
WEATHERBURN, Cpl, John, 4273894
WHITE, Fus, James Joseph, 555590
WHITE, Fus, William, 4278508
WILLCOX, Fus, Henry, 4264668
WILLIAMON, Fus, Albert Bell, 4273961
WILLIS, 2/lt, George Basil, 180536
YOUNG, Fus, William Henry, 4273863

ROYAL REGIMENT OF ARTILLERY

GENERAL
ACKLAND, S/Sjt, George John, 806843
ATCHELER, Gnr, William Victor, 1799306
AVINGTON,Gnr,Henry,873706
AXTELL,Gnr,Charles Nathaniel,14727971
BADDELEY, Maj, Arthur Frederick, 70719
BARRETT, Gnr, Joseph, 1801244
BEERE, Gnr, Stanley Harold, 963577
BELL,Gnr,John Ebury,812070
BICKNELL,Gnr,Reginald Thomas,1744104
BLACKWELL, Gnr, Edward Roy, 1805017
BLAKE, Gnr, Reginald John, 1561258
BLONDEL, L/Sjt, Thomas Vernon, 863936
BOLTER, Gnr, Max, 13528
BOWMAN,Gnr,Arthur Ernest,1080695
BRACKENRIDGE,Gnr,Leslie Stuart,1879021
BROWN, Gnr, Edmund Richard William, 1806352
BROWN, Gnr, Alexander William, 1572560
BULLEN, L/bdr, Alfred R, 14994330
BURDELL, Sjt, Stanley, 854118
BUTTER,Gnr,Frederick,1787202
CARTWRIGHT, L/Sjt, Ronald Sydney, 847177
CHANDLER, L/bdr, James Harvey, 1780255
CHISHOLM, Bdr, Douglas Haigh, 1470484
CLARK,Gnr,William,800238
COCKWILL, Gnr, Percival Charles, 1786945
COLTON,Gnr,Joseph,863190
COOMBS, Sjt, Leonard Cyril, 1057059
CRISP,Gnr,Stanley C.,11054101
CUTTS,Sub Cmdr,George Thomas,838026
DAVIS, Gnr, Frederick William, 1055905
DEVENISH, Lt, Kenneth Godfrey, 143163
DREW, Gnr, Gordon Henry, 853021
EDENEDEN, Gnr, William Stewart, 1580035
ELLWOOD, Sjt, William Jenkinson, 831692
FIXTER,Gnr,Francis Jack,922763
FLORY, Gnr, Basil, 325278
FOX, Gnr, Neville Alfred, 863880
FRANKS,L/bdr,Dudley Graham,1595465
FULTON, Pte, Thomas Thompson, 1725318
GIBSON,Gnr,Thomas William,914882
GIBSON, L/bdr, Joseph, 62284
GRIMSEY,Gnr,Charles Nathan,165375148
GROVE, W//o 1, Wiliam Arthur, 1071453
HALL, L/bdr, William George, 1796106
HATCLIFF,Gnr,Frederick John,1697914
HICKMAN, Sjt, James Louis, 1523235
HILLEN, Gnr, James, 1427283
HOOPER, Sjt, George Henry, 808543
HOOPER, Gnr, George Edward, 1438729
HORTIN, Gnr, William Robert Richard, 1769787
HUNT,Bqms,Sydney Edgar Clement,1419620
IVES, Gbdr, John Anthony Gerard, 130963
JEARY, Gnr, Herbert W, 14940029
JENNINGS, L/bdr, Chares Francis, 12751
KNOX, Gnr, Maxwell, 3128906
LODGE,Gnr,Robert,1805102
LOW,Maj,Anthony Frederick Leetham,67002
LOWRY,Gnr,Henry John,1786952
MANSI,Gnr,Bonaventuro,1092749
MATHER, Sjt, Kenneth, 851729
MAXWELL, Gnr, Robert William, 1427146
MILLER, Gnr, Dennis Neilson, 880746
MORAN, Gnr, John, 1786748
MORGAN, Gnr, Bertie Thomas, 863020
NELSON, Gnr, James Ndrew, 1787312
NEWMAN,Gnr,Thomas Frederick,1438736
NORTH, Gnr, Willie, 860668

NORTON, Lt Col, Daniel Alfred Mbe Mc, 145801
O'BRIEN, Rsm, James, 1412689
OWEN, Gnr, William, 11001428
PALFREY, Gnr, Vernon David, 1779115
PALMER, L/bdr, George Mark, 1754082
PARKER, L/bdr, George Victor, 865560
PATRICK, Gnr, Arnold James, 1787267
PERRY, Cpat, Robert Michael, 64528
PHILLIPS, L/Sjt, Frank Edward Victor, 5822693
PHILLIPS, Lt, Eric Gladstone, 146774
PIPER, Gnr, Francis Edward, 1787268
PITT, Gnr, Harold Ernest, 822766
POTHAN, Gnr, Robert Frederick, 943675
POTTS, Lt, George Mathwin, 179326
PRATLEY, Gnr, Hubert, 11000579
READING, Bdr, William Hnery, 845839
RICHARDS, Gnr, Reginald Charles, 1763486
ROACH, 2/lt, Richard Langford, 166218
ROBERTS, Gnr, William Alfred, 830603
ROBERTS, Gnr, John Radcliffe, 11054811
ROBERTS, Gnr, Ernest George, 860913
ROBINSON, Gnr, Ernest Walter, 1786708
ROSE, Gnr, Alexander, 2615501
RUSSELL, Rqms, Edward Charles, 5491957
RUSSELL, Gnr, Edwin, 1574940
RYAN, Wo/1, Samuel Walter George, 791782
RYTON, Sjt, Kenneth Newton, 847458
SARGEANT, Bsm, Arthur Leonard, 1952800
SAWYER, Lt, Eric Alan, 197421
SCOTT, Gnr, Donald Allan, 11054856
SHARP, Gnr, William, 2816123
SHAW, Gnr, Jack, 1780971
SHORT, Gnr, Ernest, 1426698
SLADE, Lt, Arthur, 225154
SMITH, Wo/1, Frank Ernest, 1422087
SPENCER, Bdr, Frederick George, 4855807
SPILLER, Gnr, Frederick John, 855016
STAFFORD, L/bdr, Arthur John, 853211
STEELE, Maj, Alistair Patrick, 40639
STEVENS, Sjt, Kenneth Whigham, 876797
STURT, Lt, John Edward, 156870
TABOR, Gnr, Harry Robert, 1641568
THOMAS, Gnr, Norman Wilfred, 11001019
TRANMAR, Lt, George Edgar, 156995
TUGWELL, Gnr, Arthur John, 11001231
WALKDEN, Lt, Alan Frank, 221894
WALKER, Gnr, Edmund John, 923277
WALTER, Lt, Barrie Bleasdale, 201702
WARD, Sjt, Cyril Vivian, 860279
WARNER, Sjt, Arthur Charles, 793125
WATERS, Gnr, Richard Albun, 1777633
WATT, Gnr, Robert, 11001608
WEBSTER, Maj, C.H., 279661
WEEDEN, L/Cpl, Jack, 846901
WHELDON, Lt, Duncan Moigh, 186366
WILLIAMS, Capt, Leonard Walter Thomas, 113041
WILLIAMSON, Gnr, Albert, 11001581
WILLIS, Gnr, Edward Morris, 1712330
WILLMOT, Bdr, John Hedley,
WILSON, Sjt, John Bertram Manfield, 809818
WOOD, Gnr, James Henry, 851954
WOODFORD, Gnr, Laurence Emile, 1470573

13 ANTI-TANK REGIMENT
GEDHILL, Gnr, Ernest Cameron, 1465168
IRVINE, Gnr, Hugh, 1524547

50 ANTI-TANK REGIMENT
PARRY, Sjt, Samuel Alfred, 1073734

68 ANTI-TANK REGIMENT
WALKER, 2/lt, Rupert Reginald Mcmaster, 193553

80 ANTI-TANK REGIMENT
ALLAN, Gnr, John Harry, 854867
ARTHURS, Gnr, Ernest John, 1104500
BARLOW, L/Sjt, Fred, 851185
BARNES, Gnr, Thomas, 5495507
BARTHOLOMEW, Gnr, Albert Edward, 791382
BASS, Bdr, Harold Edward, 1511259
BATES, Gnr, Thomas Arthur, 786443
BAXTER, /bdr, George Fraser, 1450502
BAXTER, Gnr, Bartholomew, 1545381
BILES, Gnr, William Henry, 1086959
BINKS, Sjt, James Rowland, 884708
BLOOMFIELD, Gnr, Jack, 1463184
BOYNS, Gnr, Arthur, 1461069
BRADLEY, Gnr, Cyril, 1107151
BRANIGHAN, Gnr, William George Frederick, 790758
BRETTE, Gnr, Charles Edward, 1515047
BUCKLAND, Gnr, Frederick Herbert Frank, 5495384
BUCKLEY, Gnr, Clement, 821133
BUCKLEY, Gnr, Arthur James, 1094625
BULLAMORE, Gnr, John George, 8348437
BUTTERWORTH, Sjt, John, 4609605
CAMPBEL, L/bdr, Harold Andrew, 790883
CAMPBELL, Gnr, John, 866722
CAMPBELL, Gnr, Robert, 1545454
CAMPBELL, L/bdr, Donald, 1545298
CANNON, Gnr, Henry, 1510934
CAREY, Gnr, Eric Roy, 5341989
CARVELL, Gnr, Frederick Henry, 1107705
CHAMPELOVIER, Gnr, Joseph, 1107707
CLEGG, 2/lt, Peter, 166079
COCKER, Gnr, James, 1526686
CONLAN, Sjt, Charles Hendry, 3310147
CONROY, Gnr, James, 1545455
COOK, L/bdr, Albert Ernest, 880840
COOPER, Gnr, Angus Andrew, 1510879
DARBY, Gnr, Henry Wiliam, 1558155
DEAN, Gnr, Robert Allan, 1463230
DEVENNY, Gnr, Patrick Joseph, 1545205
DYSON, Bdr, Kenneth Walter, 882513
ELOY, Gnr, Henry Albert, 1107736
EVANS, Gnr, Hugh, 1545297
FLOWERS, Gnr, Robert, 1107737
FORBES, Bdr, John Donald, 1450672
FORBES, Bdr, David M;kay, 1448928
FOSBERY, 2/lt, Francis Henry Close, 190699
FRASER, L/bdr, William Pratt, 882708
GIBBS, Gnr, Charles, 1524625
GOURLAY, Gnr, David, 1727657
HALES, Gnr, George Douglas, 1524981
HANCOCK, Gnr, George Herbert, 1606738
HARE, Lt, John Edward (MC), 98854
HAWTHORN, L/bdr, John Clelland, 1545408
HIDDLESTON, Gnr, Robert Stanley, 886378
HIGHLEY, Bdr, Fred, 4614142
HOWARD, Lt, Eric Bertram, 160119
HOYLE, Capt, Peter James Denton, 92705
HUTT, Gnr, Leslie Cyril, 886379
JAMIESON, Sjt, John Thurston, 837114
JOHNSON, /bdr, John Joseph, 1515077
KELLY, Bdr, David Gray, 934906
LAWSON, Capt, Robert Mckenzie, 91861
LEARY, Gnr, William Arthur, 1524949
MALEY, Gnr, Edward, 748096
MANN, Gnr, Raymond William, 114535
MANSELL, Gnr, Reginald Harry, 1114536
MARTIN, L/bdr, James, 1460981

MEEHAN, Bdr, Thomas, 768142
MELTON, Gnr, Eric George, 1466153
MERCER, Gnr, Clifford G W, 1094948
MORRIS, Gnr, Harry, 1493884
MUDGE, Bdr, William, 1425263
MUNDAY, Gnr, George, 1078164
NELSON, 2/lt, Ronald, 172963
ORANGE, Gnr, John, 1439486
OSBORNE, Bsm, Philip Henry, 6004343
PALMER, Gnr, William James, 1525570
PARKER, Gnr, Alfred George, 1557912
PARVIN, Sjt, Herbert Frank, 5485774
PEARCE, Gnr, Leslie, 1462822
POWER, Gnr, Leonard, 996086
PROCTOR, Gnr, David, 1545368
RENDLE, Gnr, Harold Gorden, 999417
RENNIE, Gnr, Joseph, 3314048
RICHARDSON, Gnr, John Charles Frank, 1094961
ROBINS, Gnr, Benjamin, 1544173
ROBINSON, L/bdr, Edward Lewis, 1516907
RODGERS, Bqms, Robert Brown, 3309071
ROSE, L/bdr, George Frederick, 1558392
ROWE, Bdr, Henry Charles, 1558239
RUSSELL, Gnr, John Kenneth Patrick, 1516734
RYDER, Gnr, Arthur, 1104533
SCARBOROUGH, L/Sjt, Eric, 1515007
SCOTT, Bdr, Walter, 1463240
SEABY, L/bdr, Albert Victor, 1524648
SMITH, Gnr, William Urquhart, 919621
SMITH, Gnr, John Wilfred, 1465157
SMITH, Gnr, Albert William, 1469972
SQUIB, L/Sjt, Cecil Douglas, 1452559
STEWART, Gnr, Donald, 886227
STILLWELL, Gnr, Herbert George, 5496661
SUTCLIFFE, Gnr, Harry, 62014
TAYLOR, Gnr, James, 1517142
TAYLOR, Gnr, John Charles, 1107814
THOMPSON, Gnr, Angus, 1545417
TRIM, Gnr, Douglas Roland Howard, 1524652
TRITTON, L/bdr, Victor James, 1563215
TUCK, L/Sjt, Cyril, 808685
TURNEY, Gnr, Walter Thomas, 1570989
WALL, Gnr, William John, 1510846
WALSH, Gnr, John, 1469962
WARNER, Gnr, Ronald Arthur, 1516918
WATERWORTH, Gnr, George, 1087577
WHEELHOUSE, Gnr, Ernest, 1094985
WHITEHALL, Gnr, William Henderson, 1545388
WIGHT, Lt, John Robert, 359907
WOOD, Gnr, Rupert Gabriel, 5498675
WRIGHT, Gnr, Phillip Gordon, 5499976
WRIGHT, Gnr, George, 1527621
YALLOP, Gnr, Fredrick Ernest, 1515922
WHITE, Sjt, Robert Edward, 2202362

85 ANTI-TANK REGIMENT
ADAMS, Gnr, William Edward, 1455220
ARMSTRONG, Gnr, Leslie, 1107362
AUSTIN, Gnr, Fredick Henry, 1107140
BARRY, Gnr, Alwyn, 1456091
BELL, Gnr, Charles Edward, 1493626
BENNETT, Gnr, Walter Harry, 1117680
BETTISON, Gnr, William Andrew, 870128
BIRD, Gnr, Robert, 1114619
BLACK, L/bdr, William Edward, 1107554
BLACKBURN, Bdr, Leonard Cuthbert, 788661
BLYTH, Gnr, Thomas Ernest, 1103197
BOWEN, Gnr, James, 1533170
BRADLEY, L/bdr, Bernard, 4746298
BRADLEY, Gnr, Thomas Albert, 505394

BRADY, L/bdr, Harry, 1117313
BRIGGS, Gnr, Roy, 1464388
BROWN, Gnr, George William Thomas, 1493650
BROWN, Gnr, Harold Percy, 1442231
BRUMBER, Gnr, Arthur Sidney, 1099014
BUCKLE, Sjt, Cyril, 857804
BUSBY, Gnr, Ronald Lewis, 885440
CALDWELL, Gnr, Donald Henry, 1471471
CARLING, Gnr, Arthur, 1463198
CHALLIS, Gnr, Bernard Lionel, 1086528
CHAPMAN, Gnr, Cyril, 1493671
CHATTAWAY, L/bdr, Daniel, 821450
CHRISTIE, Gnr, Francis, 1076093
CLARKE, Gnr, Reginald, 1103146
CLAYDON, Sjt, Ernest John, 5379766
COLBORN, Gnr, Percy William G, 1511144
COLES, Sjt, Jack Mcpherson, 1455787
COONEY, Gnr, Stephen, 810377
COOTE, Gnr, William Henry, 1107172
CRABTREE, Gnr, John Herbert, 4612098
CROSS, Sjt, George, 1449545
CULLENDER, Gnr, William George, 1493649
DEAN, Gnr, Thomas, 1457646
ECUYER, Gnr, Alfred John, 955331
EDWARDS, Gnr, Brian Alexander, 1447734
ELLIOT, Gnr, Wilfred Arthur, 1094814
EVANS, Gnr, William John, 1457931
EVANS, Gnr, Harry Leslie, 1468434
FAGG, L/bdr, Ronald Birks, 1439335
FAULKNER, Gnr, William Garton, 1033539
FLANNER, Gnr, William Norman, 5569720
FREEMAN, Bdr, Bernard Austin, 1475880
FYFE, Gnr, George, 1076038
GARSIDE, L/bdr, Eric, 1463229
GEE, Bdr, James, 1056219
GILHAM, Bdr, Lewis John, 1439350
GORDON, Gnr, Eric, 1606733
GOULD, Gnr, Patrick Clarence, 1558331
GRAHAM, Gnr, Thomas Ronald, 1511264
GREEN, Bqms, Victor Lewis, 817818
GREENHOUGH, Gnr, Herbert, 1493762
GREVILLE, Capt, Donald Cecil Brooke, 87643
HALL, Gnr, James William, 1493771
HARDEY, Gnr, Thomas Alfred, 800496
HARVELL, Gnr, Alfred Martin, 1094796
HARVEY, Sjt, John Thomas, 1454126
HATCHETT, 2/lt, John James, 193533
HAWES, Sjt, James, 1062394
HEARD, Gnr, Harry James, 1525020
HENDY, L/bdr, Rupert Arthur Septon, 1057131
HODGSON, Gnr, Ernest, 1491384
HODGSON, Gnr, James, 1491399
HOSTY, Gnr, William, 1465143
HOUSLEY, Gnr, Charles, 1103751
HUGHES, L/bdr, Thomas, 1460840
HUGHES, L/bdr, Henry Lloyd, 4193233
INGHAM, Bdr, Jack, 1463205
INNES, Gnr, George, 884876
JAMES, Gnr, Edwin, 1117574
JEFFRIES, Gnr, George William V, 1114456
KEARLEY, Gnr, Sidney, 1094798
LAW, Gnr, John, 1465183
LAWRENCE, Bdr, Charles Francis, 6913968
LLOYD, Gnr, Robert Owen, 1082571
LORD, Gnr, Jack, 1464255
MALONEY, Sjt, Joseph, 830440
MANN, Sjt, Donald Hubert, 1457210
MARSHALL, Gnr, Ernest, 1463133
MASON, Gnr, John Thomas, 1087830
MAY, Lt, Harold Thomas Jones, 198128

McGREVY, Bdr, Lawrence, 1087828
McMILLEN, L/bdr, Mathew, 812770
METCALF, Gnr, Norman, 886109
MINETT, Gnr, Henry Edmund, 955970
MISKELLLY, Gnr, Robert, 843143
NOLAN, Sjt, John, 4191376
NORTH, Gnr, Sorin Swift, 1062341
OSBOURNE, Gnr, Ernest, 1117942
PARKER, Sjt, Richard James, 6140352
PARKER, Bdr, Richard, 1493893
PARKER, Gnr, Kenneth, 798573
PITCHES, Gnr, Walter James, 1558378
PLAMER, Gnr, Ernest Arthur, 1094824
PLATT, L/Sjt, John, 1075286
PRICE, Sjt, David Richard, 4190083
PRIOR, Gnr, Albert Reginald, 1120840
QUIGLEY, L/bdr, George, 1607389
RATLEY, Bdr, Charles Maurice, 1075134
RICHARDS, Gnr, Cyril, 1075138
RICHARDSON, L/Sjt, John Thomas, 3598110
RICHARDSON, Gnr, Frank, 1606975
RILEY, Gnr, George Archibald, 1100411
RING, Gnr, Robert Charles, 1107663
ROBERTS, Bdr, Dwin John George, 5721788
ROBERTS, Bdr, Moses, 4188311
ROBERTS, Sjt, Edward, 1460836
ROBERTS, Gnr, Caradoc, 1459408
ROSENBERG, Gnr, Joseph, 1075156
ROUTLEDGE, Gnr, John, 11515005
RYMILL, Gnr, John William, 1458177
SANSBURY, Gnr, William Lional Howard, 1457227
SAYE, Gnr, Herbert Edward, 1117349
SCATES, Gnr, Frederick Reginald, 1514687
SHANNON, Gnr, George, 1120105
SHELLARD, Gnr, Horace Peter, 1107350
SHORT, Gnr, Edward John, 1094832
SINGLETON, Sjt, John James, 4190043
SMITH, Gnr, Thomas Arthur, 3439210
SMITH, Gnr, Joseph, 1491483
SMITH, Gnr, Harold Charles, 1107800
SOMERVILLE, Bdr, Arthur Clarence, 1075194
SPENCER, Gnr, Harry, 1117238
STANEY, L/Sjt, George Haynes, 1075198
STANLEY, Gnr, Thomas James, 1454747
STEADMAN, Gnr, Frank, 1514854
STOKES, Gnr, Arthur George, 1074580
SULLIVAN, Gnr, Gerald, 1697302
SUTER, Gnr, Edwin Charles, 1515106
TAYLOR, Gnr, Sidney William, 1607366
TAYLOR, Gnr, Ronald, 4614662
TAYLOR, L/Sjt, Joseph Edgar, 857809
THOMPSON, Bdr, Frank, 1465160
THOMPSON, Gnr, William George, 1075220
TITMUS, Gnr, George William, 1074449
TRACE, Sjt, Raymond Richard, 768374
TREGARTHEN, Gnr, Henry James, 1074590
TYLER, Gnr, Samuel Arthur James, 1086708
UPTON, Gnr, Philip George, 1458646
VALANTINE, Gnr, Vincent Joseph, 1516803
WADE, Gnr, William Henry, 1455513
WAKEMAN, Gnr, Richard Henry, 851252
WALDRON, Gnr, Henry William, 1075235
WALLIS, Gnr, Archibald John, 985928
WARD, Gnr, Eric, 1509789
WEAVER, Gnt, Thomas, 777331
WEBBER, L/bdr, Charles Edward, 1094807
WEBBER, Gnr, Arthur Ernest, 5679437
WENZEL, Gnr, Stanley Adolph, 1075251
WESTWOOD, Gnr, Frederick, 1110620
WHITE, Gnr, Walter, 1094986

WHITE, Gnr, Ernest George, 1074612
WHYTE, Gnr, William Craig, 1105509
WIGNALL, Gnr, Albert Edward, 1516921
WILLIAMS, Gnr, Harold, 1558464
WILLIAMS, Bdr, Richard Alfred, 4910842
WILLIAMS, Sjt, William Arthur, 4191708
WILSON, Gnr, Alfred Edwin, 1110080
WILTON, Sjt, Lexander, 1094119
WISE, Gnr, Arthur Frederick, 1558467
WORTON, Gnr, George Arthur, 1115356
WRIGHT, Gnr, James Ebenezer Robert, 1075362
YOUNG, Gnr, John William, 1120373

88 ANTI-TANK REGIMENT
BREWSTER, Gnr, Conway Ronald, 884243

105 ANTI-TANK REGIMENT
MACKINTOSH, Lt, James Mackintsh, 100372

125 ANTI-TANK REGIMENT
AIRD, Gnr, Arthur, 913431
ALDERTON, Gnr, Edwin Arthur, 1094125
ALLAN, Gnr, Frank, 901935
ALLEN, Gnr, George, 913661
ALLMAN, Gnr, Wilfred John, 1572544
ANNIS, Gnr, George Osborne, 1104610
ARNOLD, Gnr, William, 902424
BAILEY, Gnr, Frank, 1094132
BANNIER, Gnr, Stanley Ernest, 1094134
BARKER, Gnr, Leslie, 922198
BARKER, Gnr, Charles Frederick, 1573943
BASCO, Gnr, Lionel, 1558132
BEDDOWARTH, Gnr, Arthur Richard, 1558134
BEDFORD, Bdr, Arthur, 947637
BELL, Gnr, Thomas Alfred, 947517
BLAKEMAN, Gnr, Leslie, 911876
BOWDEN, L/bdr, Samuel, 920785
BROOK, Gnr, Charles William, 911862
BROWELL, L/bdr, Ernest Douglas, 923112
BROWN, Gnr, Thomas James, 923016
BULL, Gnr, Lloyd, 1493653
BURNUKELL, Sjt, Norman, 917077
CAMERON, Bdr, John Appleton, 902443
CARNEY, L/bdr, George, 913857
CHAMBERS, Gnr, Ronald, 917864
CHANDLER, Gnr, Joseph Henry, 1107565
CHAPMAN, Gnr, Edward Paul, 923048
CLAMP, Gnr, Leslie, 944383
COATES, Gnr, Robert William, 913434
CONLON, Gnr, William Wilfred, 923046
CONSTANTINE, L/bdr, Eric Clifford, 918145
COOK, Gnr, Robert William, 917074
COWELL, Gnr, George Henry, 1114303
CRABB, Gnr, Reginald John, 1094180
CRANMER, Gnr, Charles William, 918464
CRANMER, Gnr, Frederick, 925953
CRAWFORD, Sjt, Edward William, 915168
CRAWRFORD, Gnr, John James, 907138
CROSBY, Gnr, Stanley, 919799
CROSSLEY, Gnr, Alexander, 919808
CUTTER, Gnr, Anthony, 925608
DENBY, Gnr, Alfred, 1107917
DONKIN, Gnr, Frederick, 925899
EDWARDS, Gnr, Harold, 1114392
FARRAR, Gnr, Thomas Walker, 918752
FINCH, Sjt, Albert, 779171
FULLER, Gnr, Ernest, 1094631
GALE, Gnr, Frederick George, 1544718
GAZELEY, Gnr, Allan Roy, 1525247
GLASBY, Gnr, William Edward, 946543

GOODERICK, Gnr, Benjamin Hutcheon, 910844
GOULD, Bdr, Jack, 887872
GRAY, Bdr, John George William, 1558186
GREAVES, Gnr, Alfred, 884809
GREGORY, Gnr, David William, 1107593
GUY, Sjt, George, 828963
HANDLEY, Gnr, Frederick Edward, 1558015
HANNON, Gnr, Norman, 918768
HARVEY, Gnr, Alfred Black, 923085
HENDERSON, Gnr, Norman, 958070
HERBERT, Bdr, Douglas Barker, 911891
HEWISH, Gnr, Edmund Gordon, 1557731
HOGG, Gnr, Leonard, 1107325
HOLDFORD, Gnr, Robert Joseph, 1558199
HOPE, L/bdr, Thomas William, 800703
HUDSON, Sjt, Frank William, 824015
HUTCHINS, Gnr, Arthur John, 1094228
IRONS, Gnr, George, 1107329
JAMESON, Gnr, Alan, 919791
JANE, Gnr, Charles, 958073
JOHNSON, Gnr, Arthur Wiliam, 1104098
KELLY, Gnr, Patrick Joseph, 1094273
KENNEDY, Gnr, Idney Alexander, 1078149
KERSHAW, Bdr, John, 944340
LAMBERT, Gnr, Albert, 944386
LAST, Bdr, Eric George, 836271
LAWSON, Gnr, Eric Russell, 948579
MADDY, Gnr, Edward John, 1092615
MADGWICK, Bdr, John, 917055
MALE, Gnr, Charles Frederick, 1557941
MANNING, Gnr, Herbert William Phillips, 901972
MARSH, Bsm, Herbert Cyril, 1058543
MARTIN, L/bdr, James, 4915116
MASON, Gnr, James Patrick, 1078160
MASON, Bdr, Ernest, 923096
MATON, Sgt, William Joseph, 786200
McDOUGAL, Gnr, Ernest, 946588
MEALHAM, Gnr, Arthur William, 1104629
MILBURN, L/bdr, Raymond Baket, 922342
MITCHELL, Gnr, Arthur James, 946590
MONAGHAN, Gnr, Francis Barras, 958076
MORGAN, L/bdr, William Lewis, 923106
MORRIS, Gnr, Wilfred John, 884860
MOSS, Bdr, Kenneth Fitzroy, 1557897
MURGATROYD, Gnr, Thomas, 947526
MURRELL, Gnr, Percy, 1114019
NEVIL, L/bdr, Robert Alfred, 915138
NEWTON, Gnr, Robert Lazenby, 946592
PANNIFER, Gnr, Walter Charles, 1104634
PEMBERTON, L/bdr, Joseph Francis, 812150
PERRIN, Gnr, William, 809876
PHILLIPS, Gnr, Thomas, 1557762
PHILLIPS, Gnr, H., 901972
PLUMMER, Bdr, Leslie, 923017
POTTS, Gnr, Henry John Thomas, 798627
RAINE, Gnr, Gordon, 923031
RAINE, L/sgt, William Thompson, 917058
RAY, Gnr, Frederick Edward, 1094294
REEVES, Gnr, George, 900720
RICH, Lt, Ernest Hammill, 89451
RIDDELL, Gnr, George William, 900672
RITCHIE, Gnr, John, 958075
ROBLOU, Gnr, Frank, 1107647
ROBSON, Gnr, John Richardson, 923084
ROBSON, Gnr, William Brown, 910836
ROCHESTER, Gnr, James Lambert, 918741
ROWE, Gnr, Frederick William, 1557969
SANDHAM, Gnr, Robert, 936580
SHARPLES, Gnr, Samuel Hartley, 3659941
SLEE, Gnr, Henry Douglas, 1517083

SMITH, Gnr, Stanley Gordon, 925146
SPURGEON, Gnr, Philip Sidney, 1104644
STEPHENSON, Gnr, Robert, 922344
STOREY, Gnr, John Edward, 919807
STOTT, Gnr, Ernest, 1094333
STUART, Gnr, John, 922339
SULLIVAN, Gnr, Joseph, 909469
SUTCLIFFE, Gnr, Terence, 1114376
SYMONDS, Gnr, Frederick, 1107392
TATE, Gnr, Arthur, 923042
TAYLOR, Sjt, Norman, DIX909466
TEASDALE, Gnr, William, 1527235
TERRY, Gnr, Frank, 1078206
THOMAS, L/bdr, Thomas Robert, 1558264
THOMPSON, Gnr, Walter, 1525944
TINGLE, Gnr, Frank, 1087360
TOWELL, Sjt, Cyril, 917871
TROTTER, Gnr, George Nicholas, 910839
TUBBY, Gnr, Kenneth Walter, 1104647
TUDDENHAM, Gnr, William Thomas, 919806
TURNER, Gnr, Allan Edwin, 902401
UNDERWOOD, Gnr, Alfred Robert Kitchener, 1558270
WALKER, Gnr, Frank Robert, 1558271
WARD, Gnr, Richard, 919795
WARD, Gnr, George, 919575
WATSON, Gnr, Alan Kirtley, 915159
WATTS, Capt, John Reginald, 126009
WAUD, Gnr, Derek, 919574
WELCH, Gnr, Ronald, 925786
WHITE, Gnr, Wilfred Sinclair, 913438
WILDE, Gnr, Joseph, 1114269
WILLIAMS, Gnr, Edward, 910837
WILLIAMS, Gnr, Reginald Arthur, 1557798
WILLIAMSON, Gnr, Arthur, 1078388
WILSON, Lt, Robert Barker, 92765
WYLDE, Bsm, Richard Edward, 917882
YOUNG, L/bdr, Wiliam, 923105
YOUNG, Gnr, Archibald, 946518
ZIMMER, Gnr, Morris, 1558472

7 COAST
ARMITAGE, Lt, Stanley Rhodes, 157713
ARTHUR, Bdr, Walter Edward, 1422411
BARKER, Gnr, Douglas, 1466975
BARR, Gnr, Samuel, 7009882
BARRETT, Gnr, Albert Charles, 1739282
BARRON, L/bdr, John James, 853790
BEDDARD, Gnr, John, 1426639
BELTON, Gnr, Henry Walter Frederick, 853315
BENNETT, Bdr, William John, 872634
BERGIN, Gnr, Jermiah, 1786922
BLAYCOCK, Gnr, William Edward, 3597219
BLOYCE, BSM, Herbert Charles, 1414456
BONTOFT, Gnr, Jesse Rowland, 842714
BOON, BSM, William Arthur, 842243
BOWLER, Sjt, Frank, 2206313
BROWN, Gnr, Ronald Claude Kitchener, 834975
BROWN, Gnr, Bob, 851976
BROWN, Gnr, Alan James, 825673
BROWN, Sjt, William Henry, 819811
BROWN, BSM, John Edward, 1425636
BROWNHOOD, Gnr, Alex, 1787125
BRUSH, Sjt, Harry, 853798
BUDD, Gnr, Herbert Alexander, 853712
BURGE, L/Bdr, Victor, 851834
BURKE, Gnr, James, 1426650
BUTTERWORTH, Gnr, Kenneth, 1786841
CAMERON, Gnr, John Phillip Brickwood, 1743991
CARTER, Bdr, Leslie, 1492708

CARTER, Gnr, Edmund, 853466
CATHCART, Gnr, James, 1772784
CHAMBERS, Bdr, George Alexander, 835246
CHAMBERS, Gnr, Francis Alexander, 11003964
CHAPMAN, Bqms, Ernest, 1069163
CHAPMAN, Gnr, John, 10241869
CHEWINS, Bdr, Brian Hardwicke, 872107
CLARKE, Gnr, Leonard, 1772567
COGGINGS, Gnr, Clifford, 973236
COLLINS, BSM, Herbert Stanley, 1030737
CONGDON, Bqms, William Henry, 1412007
COOK, Bqms, Samuel, 4912761
COOK, Gnr, Robert William James, 1710662
COOMBER, Gnr, Albert James, 1061053
COOPER, Bdr, Charles Sidney, 850272
CRICK, Gnr, Philip, 1786772
CULLEN, Gnr, Arnold George, 863742
CURRIE, Bqms, Joseph Hamilton, 1049546
DAVIES, Gnr, Dewi Gyndwr, 3961338
DAY, Gnr, Albert James Ross, 1470483
DIX, Gnr, George Henry, 835377
DONOVAN, Gnr, Lawrence, 1493217
DRURY, Gnr, James Leonard, 1710669
DYE, Gnr, Ralph Joffre, 850331
DYSON, L/Bdr, Alfred, 845425
EAST, BSM, Harold Henry, 847403
EDEMA, Gnr, Gordon Patrick, 1470491
ELLIOT, Lt, Orlando Grahame, 69278
FIDLER, Gnr, Thomas, 1031920
FLYNN, Gnr, Thomas, 856932
FOGG, L/Bdr, Leonard, 850829
FORDER, Gnr, Victor Stephen, 6395526
FOWLES, Gnr, Albert Thomas, 1786896
FRENCH, Gnr, Kenneth, 4977454
GALBRAITH, Gnr, William John, 853539
GALE, Gnr, Frederick Thomas, 1061618
GALLOWAY, Gnr, Arthur Wellesley, 3186775
GARDENER, L/Sjt, Stanley William, 781481
GARVEY, Gnr, James, 1426653
GEISS, Gnr, Joseph George, 1577720
GEORGE, Sjt, Thomas Henry, 802702
GEORGE, Pte, Alfred Stephen, 1808566
GERMANEY, Gnr, Alexander, 1759245
GILL, Gnr, James Francis, 1787233
GOBLE, Gnr, Thomas Henry James, 6138142
GOUGE, Gnr, Joseph William George, 973684
GRAFTON, L/Bdr, James Alfred, 1492760
GREEN, Gnr, Leonard Leslie, 1821040
GREEN, Gnr, Joseph, 851939
GREENHAM, Bdr, Alexander Victor, 1062043
GUTHRIE, Gnr, Jacob Boag, 1574540
HALSTEAD, Capt, Henry Norman Peter Robert, 113037
HAMMOND, Gnr, Harry Bernard, 1786729
HANDLEY, Gnr, Joseph Kenneth, 908760
HARDING, Bdr, Kenneth, 850830
HARPER, Gnr, Herbert Robert, 975795
HARRIS, BSM, Frank William Harries, 800304
HARTLEY, Gnr, James, 3385878
HAWKEN, Gnr, Clifford Dingley, 11005534
HESKETH, Gnr, John Jellicoe, 847957
HIL, L/Bdr, George Valentine, 835266
HILL, Gnr, Stephen, 1426921
HILL, Gnr, Raymond, 872024
HIRST, Gnr, George William, 868388
HOBBS, Gnr, Frank, 1744043
HOLLAND, Gnr, Harry, 1787102
HOLLAND, Gnr, John Lional, 1470489
HOLMES, Gnr, Alfred, 1765150
HOOPER, Gnr, Reginald, 845900
HOWARD, Bdr, Thomas Reginald, 850288

HUMPAGE, Gnr, George, 850322
HUNT, Gnr, George Graham, 845394
HUNTER, Bdr, Thomas Tory Anderson, 799437
HYDE, L/bdr, Walter, 884804
JAMES, Gnr, George Henry, 1724622
JAMES, L/bdr, Douglas Frederick, 1493032
JOSEPH, Gnr, Gomer, 1438760
KILPATRICK, Gnr, Thomas, 7009812
KIMBER, Gnr, William John, 1058737
KIRK, Gnr, Albert Victor, 2614260
KNIGHT, Gnr, Thomas George Porrote, 856988
LANGFORD, Gnr, Reginald F, 3855958
LEWIS, Gnr, Sidney Frederick, 1786134
LOW, Gnr, Robert, 2878917
MAHONY, Gnr, James, 863511
MANGAN, Gnr, Thomas, 835510
MARTIN, Gnr, Alan, 11054574
MATTHEWS, Gnr, Walter Thomas, 845309
MAXWELL, Gnr, Reginald, 835003
MAYO, BSM, Walter, 802731
McCONNELL, Gnr, Thomas, 6977741
McLEAN, Gnr, James, 872445
McMORROW, Gnr, Patrick, 1697952
MENMUIR, L/Bdr, Frederick James, 879989
MORRIS, Gnr, Albert John, 6401465
MULLEN, Gnr, Edward, 1077103
NEARY, Gnr, Ronald Raymond, 1493082
NEVILLE, Sjt, John Edward, 1065669
NOLAN, Gnr, Christopher Patrick, 850096
NOLAN, Gnr, Denis, 1568324
O'SHEA, Gnr, Michael, 850606
OSBORN, Gnr, Sidney Ernest, 11054672
OXFORD, Gnr, Samuel Lewis, 1058962
PAGE, Gnr, John Horton, 1787195
PALIN, Gnr, Albert, 840177
PATERSON, Gnr, William, 890905
PATIN, Gnr, Leon George Harry, 11000463
PATMORE, BSM, Percy Maurice, 1055483
PAYNE, Gnr, Albert William, 851467
PEARCE, Gnr, Charles William, 1431029
PEARCE, L/Sjt, George Alfred, 1018561
PEGLER, Lt, Gerald Francis Jack,
PETERSON, Gnr, Charles Graham, 11001586
PHILP, Sjt, Harold Cecil, 845907
PLUMSTEAD, Gnr, Joseph Robert Louis, 862963
POLLARD, Gnr, George, 1808438
PRIDHAM, WO/1, Arthur, 1414868
PRINGLE, L/Sjt, Douglas, 851043
PRITCHARD, Sjt, George Edward, 842181
PRITCHARD, Gnr, Jack, 824396
REYNOLDS, Gnr, Joseph, 1426910
RICHARDS, L/Bdr, Harold Joseph, 1438739
RICHARDSON, Sjt, Ernest, 845247
ROBERTS, Gnr, Herbert, 1492522
ROBERTS, Gnr, Horace, 1711736
ROBINSON, Gnr, Harry, 835652
ROBINSON, Bdr, Ernest, 842342
ROSEVEARE, L/Bdr, Ernest Victor, 5616746
ROWBOTTOM, Gnr, Harry, 1787272
ROWLAND, Bdr, Albert Tewis, 845890
RUSHBY, L/Bdr, Leslie Charles, 1492884
SCHOFIELD, Gnr, Wilfred, 1787075
SHAW, Gnr, William, 1787152
SHUTER, Gnr, James, 863518
SIBBALD, Gnr, Alexander, 1787322
SIMPSON, Bdr, Herbert, 872625
SIXSMITH, Gnr, James, 1825137
SMITH, Gnr, William A, 1431390
SMITH, Gnr, Sydney Lawrence, 1739275
SMITH, L/Bdr, Albert Joseph, 2048662

SMYTH, Gnr, John Reginald Walter, 872147
SOLLARS, Gnr, Joe Thomas, 1786966
STAFFORD, Gnr, Thomas, 1786909
STEER, L/Bdr, Frank Thomas, 836130
STEVENS, Bdr, Albert, 1438750
STOKES, Bqms, John, 1415430
STUBBERFIELD, Gnr, James Ernest John, 1697985
STUBBS, L/Bdr, Bernard Joseph, 1426651
SULLIVAN, BSM, Ernest Walter Edward, 1419760
SWIFT, Gnr, Harry Edward, 1752605
TATE, Gnr, John, 819649
THORNHILL, Gnr, Ralph, 1787079
THORNTON, Gnr, Nathaniel, 1771067
THURGOOD, Gnr, Graham Sidney, 872344
TIBBLE, Gnr, Thomas Charles, 1756354
TOMLIN, Gnr, George James, 727930
TOWERS, Gnr, Brenard, 1492559
TUMULTY, Bdr, Clarence Edward, 6200068
TYLER, Gnr, Stanley Frederick, 845275
VENEABLES, L/Bdr, Ronald Stuart, 871455
WARD, Gnr, Leslie Arthur, 1807799
WATTS, Gnr, Roger Haddock, 11001579
WELSH, Gnr, Alexander Peter, 850955
WHITE, Lt, Alexanda Augustus, 186367
WHITESIDE, Gnr, Carrol Eugene, 1770691
WILKS, L/Bdr, Harry, 818699
WILLIAMS, QMS, Leonard Frank, 1412202
WILLIAMS, Gnr, Wiliam Henry, 2567664
WILLIAMS, Sjt, Richard Lewis, 2957770
WIMPENNY, Gnr, James Percy, 1775460
WINSHIP, Gnr, Charles, 830321
WOOD, Gnr, Harry Leonard, 4000412
WORSDELL, Gnr, Ernest Eric, 856180
WRAY, Bdr, Robert Morrison, 853309
YARROW, Gnr, Bernard Cecil, 1787274

8 COAST

BROWN, S/Sjt, Samuel, 822236
DENNETT, Bqms, Francis Leslie, 847065
DENNISON, L/Sjt, Norman, 833887
HART, Gnr, William Henry Edward, 6202039
HILTON, Capt, Frank William, 71817
HOLE, Gnr, William Lenard, 856082
MATHEWS, Lt, Vivian Ratcliffe, 146689
MAYNARD, L/Bdr, John Vernon, 872299
McEWAN, Gnr, Henry, 845360
McMENAMIN, Gnr, Patrick Gerard, 1725327
MILLS, RSM, James, 1062585
THOMPSON, BSM, Robert Stephen, 1068858
THORPE, Gnr, Horace William, 5879560

9 COAST

ABBOTT, Gnr, Ernest Webster, 2037137
ABRAMS, Capt, Thomas Edwin, 164292
ACTON, Bdr, James Benjamin, 843833
ADAIR, Gnr, Mathew, 1427087
ALDRIDGE, Gnr, John Cook, 1786916
ALLEN, Gnr, Henry Chapman, 1426843
ANDERSON, Gnr, Sidney, 1426791
ASTLEY, Gnr, William Edward, 1492596
BADMINTON, Gnr, Sidney William, 833630
BAIRD, Gnr, David Ritchie, 984137
BALL, Gnr, James William, 868473
BANKS, Gnr, George Edmund, 853226
BARBER, Gnr, Harry, 850708
BARR, Gnr, Stanley Herbert, 11055871
BARRETT, L/bdr, Joseph, 850961
BARTLEY, Gnr, Maurice Seymour Thomas, 11053926
BATEMAN, 2/Lt, Arnold Charles, 153556
BEECH, Gnr, Harold, 1426797

BEEDIE, Sjt, James, 707104
BELFORD, L/Sjt, James Patrick, 826450
BENNETT, Gnr, William, 872364
BENTLEY, L/Bdr, Alfred, 863016
BENTON, Gnr, William Thomas, 1427282
BEVAN, Bdr, Willam Robert, 860801
BICKERON, Gnr, Robert, 843557
BIRCH, Gnr, Edwin, 1426708
BLACKSTOCK, Bdr, Edward Kenneth, 83858
BLAKE, Gnr, Francis Henry, 1818199
BOOTHBY, Gnr, Harry, 860998
BOWTELL, L/Bdr, George William, 5884236
BROWN, Gnr, Thomas James, 872327
BROWN, L/Bdr, George William, 2610433
BROWN, BSM, Alfred Edward, 781840
BROWN, Gnr, Austin, 1743843
BROWN, Gnr, Charles Henry, 1808641
BRUMPTON, Sjt, John William, 840334
BRYANT, Bdr, John Charles Frederick, 828276
BUCKLEY, Gnr, Thomas, 1065462
BURNELL, Gnr, Harry, 1427590
BURTON, Gnr, Arthur Sidney, 872423
BUSFIELD, Gnr, Ralph, 1784214
CADDICK, Gnr, Raymond, 863877
CAIRNS, Gnr, George, 1066629
CANELLE, Gnr, Cecil Albert Edward, 851151
CARLISLE, Gnr, George Frederick, 1063785
CARTER, Gnr, William, 1818271
CARTWRIGHT, Gnr, Sidney Arthur, 1786768
CATCHPOLE, Gnr, John Siddall, 851408
CEREXHE, Bdr, Maurice Arthur W Rockford, 842938
CHADWICK, Gnr, John James, 876942
CHAMP, L/Bdr, James, 1057009
CHEESEMAN, L/Bdr, Harold Anthony, 872087
CHIVERS, Gnr, Ernest, 847651
CLARGO, Gnr, Ernest Thomas Edwin, 11055178
CLARK, Gnr, Harold Robert, 1427549
CLARKSON, Sjt, Cedric, 793769
COCKBURN, Gnr, Malcolm, 979500
COLE, Gnr, Wilfred, 1066495
COLEMAN, Lt, Robin Benjamin Bunch, 87490
COLIN, Gnr, Reginald, 1786770
CONNORS, Gnr, Francis, 853116
COOK, Gnr, Cecil, 860633
COOKE, Gnr, Ernest Arthur, 1470588
CORAM, Gnr, Edward Charles, 1058054
COUSENS, Gnr, Walter Charles, 851813
COVE, Gnr, Ernest John, 872613
COX, Sjt, Cyril Reginald, 1068160
COXON, Gnr, James Henry, 835824
CRABTREE, Gnr, John, 863401
CROOKS, Gnr, Arthur, 7446797
CROSS, L/Sjt, Gilbert Henry, 1061873
CULLY, Gnr, Thomas Henry, 850145
DAISLEY, Gnr, Herbert, 11055388
DARGIE, Gnr, John, 1787344
DAVEY, L/Bdr, Reginald James, 1063419
DAVIES, Gnr, Charles Royston, 837579
DAVIES, Gnr, Joseph James, 1492341
DAVIES, Gnr, Lewis, 1492724
DAVISON, BSM, Thomas Bruce, 798990
DAVISON, Gnr, John Edward, 863923
DAY, L/Bdr, George Reginald, 754558
DEWHIRST, Gnr, Frank, 876550
DODSON, L/Sjt, Thomas Sefton, 1425311
DOWNING, Gnr, Edgar William, 1803929
DRUMMY, Gnr, Stanley John, 851842
DUCKWORTH, Gnr, Albert, 1469836
DULLEY, Bdr, David Charles, 863389
EPPS, Bdr, Sidney Jesse, 1417270

FAWCETT, Gnr, Herbert Terence, 759085
FERGUSON, Gnr, Francis, 3307692
FINCH, Gnr, Alfred Henry, 1426864
FLETCHER, Gnr, Stephen, 3307674
FLINDERS, Gnr, Thomas, 853304
FLORENTINE, Gnr, Joseph Sidney, 4452338
FURLONG, Gnr, Robert, 1493232
GARNE, Lt, Denis Arthur, 109362
GEARING, Bdr, Charles Thomas, 1426687
GEARY, Gnr, David James, 860820
GEE, L/Bdr, Percy Leonard,1426858
GIBBS, Gnr, Ronald Charles, 1427565
GIBSON, Gnr, Peter, 800411
GILDON, Gnr, Arthur Lawrence, 838738
GILES, Sjt, Walter, 847959
GOLDSMITH, Gnr, Frederick Albert, 880575
GOODMAN, Gnr, John Claydon, 880328
GORMAN, Gnr, Michael George, 3763444
GRANT, Gnr, George Arthur, 872407
GRAY, Gnr, Ernest Edward, 1438605
GREEN, Gnr, George, 5106169
GREEN, Gnr, Arthur, 850067
GRIFFITHS, Gnr, James Denis, 853198
GRIFFITHS, Gnr, Hugh, 4195658
GROOMBRIDGE, Bqms, Alfred Frank, 1047098
GUTCHER, Gnr, T.T., 860601
HAIG, Gnr, Thomas Douglas, 845454
HALEY, Bdr, Ernest Claude, 791731
HALL, Sjt, Ralph, 1062169
HALL, Gnr, George, 840283
HALLAS, Gnr, Albert Edward, 851582
HAMER, Bdr, George, 845098
HAMERTON, Gnr, Robert Sanley, 1493006
HAMILTON, Bqms, Robert William, 1416695
HAMPTON, Gnr, Charles, 1786730
HARDIE, Gnr, William Ronald, 1822094
HARRIS, Gnr, Joshua Theodore, 880580
HARVEY, Sjt, Frederick, 808865
HATELEY, Gnr, Cyril, 1054995
HAWKINS, Gnr, Norman Harold, 1427350
HAYNES, Gnr, Peter, 872413
HAYWARD,Gnr,Eric Claude,1426682
HEATON, Bdr, Leonard, 876464
HELLEN, Gnr, Alfred Henry, 11034357
HICK, S/Sjt, Charles William, 1413555
HICKFORD, Gnr, George, 853418
HIGGINBOTTOM, Bdr, Walter Augustine, 1018043
HILL,L/Bdr, Harold, 840112
HILL, Gnr, Thomas, 1426716
HILLIER, Gnr, Edward Frederick, 5332816
HILLMAN, L/Bdr, Wyndham John, 872405
HINDMARSH, Gnr, James, 975802
HINLEY, Gnr, Francis Alfred, 843617
HIPKISS, Gnr, William, 1427571
HOGAN, Gnr, Charles, 1427552
HOLMES, Gnr, Fred, 1426893
HOMAN, Gnr, Joseph Leonard, 1427505
HOOD, Gnr, Charles William, 844593
HORN, Gnr, Leslie, 157104
HOWELL, Gnr, Sidney George, 1438636
HOWELL, Gnr, Harold William, 845221
HUDSON, Sjt, Ralph Herbert, 812399
HUGHES, Gnr, Joseph Frederick, 1426750
HUGHES, Gnr, Hugh John, 868326
HUITSON, Gnr, Norman, 1426855
HULL, Gnr, John Frederick, 1765100
HUME, Gnr, Colin, 850970
HUNTER, Gnr, Donald, 1427206
INGARFIELD, Gnr, Harry, 1426678
INGLEY, Gnr, Richard, 1427575

JARRET, Gnr, Harry, 2755409
JARVIS, Gnr, Joseph, 1426891
JEFFRIES, Gnr, Graham John, 1427395
JESSOP, Gnr, James Thomas, 851141
JOHNSON, L/Bdr, Anthony, 863857
JOHNSTON, Gnr, Lancelot Storey, 1744073
JOHNSTON, Gnr, William, 1668539
JOWETT, Gnr, Charles Edward, 797564
KENDALL, Gnr, Joseph, 1818292
KENNY, Gnr, James Danial, 863089
KING, Gnr, Frederick, 3764339
KNOTO, Bdr, Joseph Young, 838764
LEAR, Gnr, Ronald, 3959479
LEAVER, Gnr, David George Houlford, 853514
LEWIS, BSM, Lionel Vivian, 1412438
LINDLEY, Gnr, Henry, 1822078
LUNNON, Gnr, Victor Claydon Home, 1427550
MACWILLIAM, Gnr, Charles Alexander, 1547052
MANN, Gnr, Henry George, 1427482
MANNING, Gnr, Eric Albert, 5182509
MASKELL, Gnr, Henry Albert, 886405
MASON, Gnr, James Henry, 851512
MASON, Sjt, Herbert, 824231
MAYLIN, Gnr, Gordon Angus, 1438702
McCANN, Gnr, John, 872575
McMULLEN, Gnr, Samuel, 1821120
MEAKIN, Gnr, Albert Edward, 1786867
MELLOR, Gnr, Wilfred, 3521558
MENZIES, Gnr, Stewart, 860616
MILLARD, L/Bdr, Henry Ernest, 845411
MILLERGILL, Gnr, William Newbery, 4856197
MINSHULL, Gnr, John William, 1786689
MOORHEAD, Bdr, Joseph, 839963
MORBEY, Gnr, Edward, 987354
MORTON, Gnr, George, 1787071
MUIR, Gnr, Alexander Munro, 1470084
MURFIN, L/Bdr, Ronald, 40824
MURPHY, Gnr, John Patrick, 1427603
NEEDHAM, Bdr, Dennis, 860401
NELSON, Gnr, Frank, 868021
NICHOLLS, Gnr, Albert William, 843732
NICHOLS, Gnr, Ronald, 1427589
NICHOLS, Gnr, William, 1786056
NORTH, Gnr, Ernest, 835481
NUGENT, Gnr, Patrick, 833408
O'HARE, Gnr, John, 1427449
OATES, Gnr, Edwin Armitage, 1075780
OGILVIE, Gnr, Alexander, 1820004
OSBORNE, Gnr, Alec, 5109374
OXLEY, Gnr, Thomas, 2569652
PAGE, Bdr, Bert Cecil Walter, 842858
PARKER, Bdr, William Edward, 843546
PAYNE, Gnr, Edward Fredeick, 1427597
PEARSON, Gnr, Alan, 860561'
PETRNOSTER, Gnr, Herbert, 868970
PHILLPOT, Gnr, Arthur John, 1427312
PHIMISTER, L/Bdr, George Gordon, 788596
PINK, Gnr, Ernest William, 863163
POUNDER, Gnr, Joseph Alfred, 850323
POWERS, L/Bdr, Alfred, 847522
PRENDERGAST, Gnr, John, 3597380
PRICE, Gnr, James Henry, 863176
PRITCHARD, Gnr, George William, 843640
PURVES, Gnr, John Sinclair, 916118
RADCLIFFE, Sjt, Robert Edmund, 1069714
RAE, L/Bdr, Colin, 1426958
RAFFERTY, Gnr, George, 845829
RALPHS, Gnr, Reginald, 851142
REDFERN, Gnr, Frederick Arthur, 4859359
REDGERS, Gnr, Thomas Henry, 844932

REDPATH, Gnr, John Robert, 872393
REES, Gnr, Clifford William, 4859575
REVILLE, Gnr, Anthony, 43399575
RICHARDSON, Gnr, Harry, 2042186
ROBERTSON, Gnr, Henry, 1820024
ROBINSON, Gnr, Joseph, 828431
ROBINSON, Gnr, Charles Geoffrey, 1427123
ROUND, Gnr, Raymond, 1427546
ROWELL, Gnr, John, 800880
ROWLANDS, Gnr, Edward, 1786980
ROWLANDS, Sjt, Walter John, 815186
RYAN, Gnr, John Joseph, 863298
RYAN, Gnr, John, 863328
SAUCIER, Gnr, Kenneth Robert Joseph, 1427569
SAUNDERS, Gnr, Richard Charles John, 1776800
SAUNDERS, Bqms, Cyril, 4380965
SCOTT, Gnr, Edward, 1427168
SEAL, Gnr, George Edwin, 1781858
SHARP, Gnr, Cyril James, 863096
SHAW, Gnr, Thomas, 1426846
SHAW, Gnr, James William, 853213
SHAW, Gnr, Arthur, 1787150
SHIPSEY, Gnr, Frederick George Gordon, 860942
SILVESTER, S/Sjt, Albert, 856063
SIMPSON, Gnr, James William, 4912284
SLADE, Gnr, Frederick, 797779
SLATER, Gnr, Samuel, 1427241
SMITH, Gnr, William, 850342
SMITH, Gnr, Thomas, 833834
SMITH, Gnr, George William, 2821116
SMITH, Gnr, Percy Benjamin, 1424140
SNELL, Gnr, Cyril, 863090
SODEN, Gnr, Eric Scott, 832161
SOUTHGATE, Gnr, Eric Cecil Ferneaux, 6895611
SOUTHWORTH, Gnr, James, 3712059
SPENCER, Gnr, Freeman, 863855
SPILSBURY, Gnr, Alfred, 552423
SPINKS, L/Sjt, Henry Tenant, 851606
SPRATT, Gnr, Trevor William, 1818135
SPROUTING, Gnr, Albert William, 5670320
STAINTON, Gnr, William, 1811768
STATE, Gnr, Ivor William, 1427191
STEVENS, Gnr, Alfred Henry, 1712301
STEWART, Gnr, James, 842018
STILLWELL, Gnr, Peace, 872342
STOKES, Gnr, Albert Norman, 1525070
STRACEY, Gnr, George Henry, 5109334
STYCH, Gnr, Samuel John, 856041
SUNSHINE, Gnr, Edward, 1426946
SWINBURN, Gnr, Leslie, 842437
THEWSEY, Sjt, Henry, 809461
THOMAS, Sjt, William Griffiths, 808007
THOMAS, Gnr, Royston, 3962045
THOMPSON, Gnr, George, 5771941
THOMSON, Gnr, James, 1433290
THORNTON, Gnr, Thomas Allan, 868143
THORPE, Gnr, Walter, 3711630
TODD, Gnr, Francis Fox, 1469876
TODD, Gnr, Edwin Douglas, 846687
TRAFFORD, Gnr, George William, 845925
TROTH, Gnr, Frederick, 1438640
TUNE, Gnr, William James, 853238
TURELL, Gnr, Robert Sydney, 8600068
TURNER, Gnr, Ephraim Ivor, 4076834
VIGGERS, Gnr, Thomas John, 831491
WADE, Gnr, Ernest, 5570275
WAINWRIGHT, L/Bdr, Joseph William, 850890
WALKER, Gnr, Arthur Nicholas, 845146
WALKER, Gnr, William, 1426849
WALSH, Gnr, Michael, 1769585

WATSON, Gnr, Robert, 1070222
WATSON, Gnr, Ernest, 812680
WATTS, Gnr, William James, 850487
WEBBER, Gnr, Peter Ambrose, 871205
WEST, Gnr, John James Bailey, 1061068
WESTGATE, L/Sjt, Wilfred Owen, 1426240
WHEELER, L/Bdr, Peter David, 850918
WHITMORE, Gnr, George Tuskall, 1470600
WILKES, Gnr, George Douglas, 838126
WILKINS, Gnr, George Thomas, 1060726
WILKINSON, Gnr, William, 797442
WILLIAMS, Gnr, Stanley, 1492929
WILLIAMS, Gnr, Francis Horation, 827841
WILLS, Gnr, Harold James, 847572
WILSON, L/Sjt, Ernest Hart, 798117
WILSON, Gnr, Charles Gordon, 1438673
WILSON, Gnr, Joseph, 843423
WILTSHIRE, Gnr, Gordon Victor, 838027
WOOD, Gnr, Henry William, 851187
WRIGHT, L/Bdr, Enoch Charles, 840436
WRIGHT, Bsm, Harry Wesley, 1047573
WRIGHT, Sjt, George Derek, 853209
YATES, Gnr, William Chambers, 1470589

11 COAST

ASHER, Capt, John Reid, 132019
CARTER, Lt, Herbert Henry, 159085
CURTIS, Gnr, Henry, 1577652
DEACON, Gnr, Henry John, 1786948
DENT, L/Bdr, Desmond Alfred, 853538
DRY, Gnr, Alfred George, 1577712
FIEDHOUSE, Gnr, Leslie, 1787083
HALLETT, L/Sjt, William Waller, 845849
HASTINGS, Gnr, Walter William, 1577729
HAYWARD, Gnr, Richard George, 1577731
HUGGETT, Gnr, Bernard Owen Edward, 1577732
ISTED, Gnr, George Thomas, 1427562
JAMES, L/Sjt, Robert Henry, 856663
JOHNSON, BSM, William Smethurst, 800585
JOHNSON, Gnr, Albert, 1787105
KENNA, L/Bdr, John, 869390
McGORAN, Gnr, John, 1577866
MOULE, Gnr, Frederick John, 1541719
O'BRIEN, Gnr, Frederick William, 860089
PEARS, Gnr, John Pinder, 1452361
PICKERING, Gnr, Charles John, 1577757
PLACE, Gnr, Charles Stephen, 1577759
PURDEY, Gnr, Thomas Henry, 1577762
RAMSDEN, Gnr, Arthur, 177775
RUDKIN, Gnr, Wilfred, 1770686
SINNOTT, Gnr, William, 1769647
SMITH, Gnr, William Henry, 1578021
SPOKES, Bdr, Frank Edward, 842057
STEWART, Gnr, Alexandrer Brooks, 1577767
STONE, Gnr, Albert George, 1577788
WELLS, Gnr, Frederick James, 1577805
WILKINSON, Gnr, Frederick Albert, 1577812
WILTON, Capt, Arthur Cyril, 164300

12 COAST

ATKINS, L/Bdr, Arthur, 860937
BANHAM, BSM, Thomas William George, 545435
BIRKINSHAW, L/Bdr, Albert Edward, 840346
BUCKLEY, Gnr, Leslie, 5498761
COCKLEY, Gnr, Alfred Arthur, 1712337
FOSTER, Gnr, John Arthur, 872412
LUCKETT, L/Bdr, William George, 828266
MARTIN, Gnr, Douglas Herbert, 6012515
MASON, Gnr, James William, 1715095
McCONNELL, Lt, Thomas James Courtney, 221172

ROWLEY, Gnr, William Thomas, 1521732
RUNYARD, RSM, George, 1414046
TAVENDALE, Sjt, Ian Ross, 833477
TUBB, Gnr, Cecil, 6394452

16 COAST
GREENSTEIN, Gnr, Harry, 1787350

31 COAST
WEST, Gnr, Clifford, 1772940

37 COAST
DELLA CASSA, Gnr, Achilles, 1764738
JAMES, Gnr, Arthur, 1537703

47 COAST
PATON, L/Bdr, Hugh Mair, 1750907

48 COAST
NOWELL, Gnr, Frank Herbert, 1805362

49 COAST
CLARK, L/Bdr, Frederick Charles, 1754481

50 COAST
CURNOCK, Gnr, James William, 1789599
SMITH, Gnr, Eric Arthur, 1805404
SMITH, Gnr, Robert, 1808778

51 COAST
SANDERS, Gnr, George, 11001989

52 COAST
RUSSELL, Gnr, Robert Charles John Sidney, 1805151

16 DEF
BACKHOUSE, Bsm, Roger Alexander, 1052316
FOLAN, Gnr, Joseph Martin, 863058
HASLETT, Gnr, Howard Wynne, 863654
HENDERSON, Bdr, Siddle Dixon, 838221
IVES, Gnr, Charles Thomas, 838570
ROCHE, Gnr, Thomas Joseph, 856951
SMITH, Gnr, Ernest William, 11001566
STOAKLEY, Gnr, Ralph Oliver, 1787252
THOMPSON, Gnr, John Clark, 2818204

FR
CARTER, Gnr, John Thomas, 86706988
CAWTHORNE, L/bdr, Walter, 814460137
FARMER, L/bdr, John Charles, 950052155
SEED, L/Sjt, Henry Norman, 85739288

4 FR
PREST, Maj, John Sabine Stanley, 63506

5 FR
ADAMS, Gnr, John Stanley, 863961
ANDREWS, Gnr, Stanley Edward Thomas, 815281
ARCHER, RQMS Wilfred, 843448
ASHWORTH, Gnr, John Henry, 856767
AYSCOUGH, Gnr, William Edward, 4613972
BAKER, Gnr, Edward Percy Nelson, 985523
BELTON, Gnr, Charles Frederick, 1083824
BEMBRIDGE, Bdr, Rufus William, 847616
BISHOP, Gnr, Herbert John, 860035
BLAND, Maj, William Fraser, 45047
BONNER, Gnr, James Hercules, 840483
BRADLEY, L/Sjt, Albert Oliver, 840882
CLARE, L/Bdr, Gregory, 857794

CLARK, L/Bdr, Bernard, 923899
CLARKE, Gnr, Colin Arthur, 985724
CORNICK, Gnr, John Bence, 831300
DANCER, Gnr, Reginald Keith, 942662
DARE, Gnr, Ivan Benji, 1092722
DAVIES, 2/Lt, Henry Peris, 164971
DEAKIN, L/Bdr, Harold Victor, 856774
DRING, Gnr, Trevor Aubrey, 889944
ELLIS, L/Bdr, George Kenneth, 988020
FARMER, L/Bdr, John Charles, 95005215
FLACK, Gnr, Albert, 1086305
FORSTER, Gnr, James, 843119
FOX, Gnr, John Joseph, 893905
FOXCROFT, Gnr, Cecil Donald, 893596
GREEN, Gnr, Ronald William Frank, 1077370
HADLOW, Gnr, George Henry, 1110134
HALLIWELL, Gnr, James, 1082736
HARRISSON, L/Sjt, Edward Richard Charles, 838852
HILL, Gnr, Frank, 872929
HOBSON, Gnr, Fred, 995429
HOLBURN, Gnr, John Allen Kingsley, 853993
HOWARD, Gnr, James Henry, 4612810
HUNT, Capt, Robert William, 69467
JARVIS, Bdr, Frederick R, 6397906
JONES, Capt, Derlin Brynford, 166234
LENTON, L/Bdr, George, 863208
LOGAN, L/Sjt, Simon, 842391
LOVEDAY, Gnr, Stanley Richard, 867052
LOWDON, Gnr, Frederick, 802561
LYON, Gnr, Raymomd, 899190
MALES, Gnr, John Philip, 957820
MARGETSON, Gnr, Charles, 1077622
MATHEWS, Bdr, Richard, 843409
McNULTY, Gnr, Wilfred, 845426
MIDDLETON, Gnr, William Harold, 987653
MILLAR, Gnr, John, 991669
MITCHELL, L/Bdr, Maurice William, 5618380
MOORE, Gnr, Reginald Alfred, 993642
MOORE, Gnr, Patrick Plunkett, 876536
MORAN, L/Bdr, Frank, 836561
MORGAN, Gnr, Sidney Lawrence, 1110793
NEIL, Sjt, Bertram William, 810947
NELSON, Gnr, Kenneth, 968761
NICE, Gnr, Oscar Claude, 1088015
ORMROD, L/Bdr, Thomas, 860656
OWEN, Gnr, Frank, 847410
PARKER, Gnr, Allan, 893601
PARMINTER, Gnr, John Moore, 1461834
PAYNE, Gnr, Edward Alexander, 1110047
PEACH, Gnr, John Wesley, 847000
PRICE, Gnr, Ceroig Rhys, 941711
QUENNELL, Gnr, George Ralph, 3778350
RICHARDSN, BSM, John Charles, 812370
ROBERTS, Gnr, John Henry, 860458
ROBINSON, Gnr, James Sidney, 932372
ROSS, Gnr, William Henry, 5664660
ROYAL, Gnr, Albert George, 998761
RYDER, Sjt, John Henry, 805417
SHEPHERD, Gnr, Fred, 975699
SHEWING, Gnr, Edward John, 863302
SIMPSON, Gnr, Norman, 1068438
SMITH, Gnr, Douglas, 1525417
STEVENS, Gnr, John Arthur George, 993778
STEVENS, Gnr, Robert, 869478
TATE, Gnr, Fred, 1425329
TODD, Gnr, Harry, 1470082
TOOKE, Sjt, Percy, 851433
TREW, Bdr, Reginald John, 758266
TUNE, Gnr, Ronald, 942942
WALSH, Gnr, Patrick John, 1514758

WARNOCK, Gnr, John Sergeant, 993781
WHTEHEAD, Gnr, Ernest William, 880104
WILLIAMS, L/Bdr, Trevor, 850658

8 FR
READ,Gnr,Ernest,1118303
WOODS,Capt,William Thomas,78898

11 FR
ROSE,Gnr,Lionel John,14351545
SHARP,Sjt,Lan Edward,8997739

12 FR
CROSS,Gnr,Kenneth,912679

55 FR
FARMER,L/Bdr,John Charles,9500521
68 FR
WILSON,Gnr,Henry,905586
85 FR
ORD,Gnr,William Clement Stewart,898795

88 FR
ARCHIBALD, Gnr, Andrew, 1109050
ARMSTRONG, Gnr, Henry Bolton, 1082000
ARTHUR, L/Sjt, Ernest Albert, 788861
ATHERTON, L/Bdr, Harry, 890965
ATKINS, Gnr, Norman, 1123200
ATKINSON, Sjt, Albert Victor, 1415917
BAKER, Bdr, Michael Joseph, 820222
BARLEY, Gnr, William Edward, 1119927
BARTLE, L/Bdr, Dennis Ernest Court, 980377
BARTLETT, Gnr, Ronald William Ernest, 974427
BATE, Gnr, George Hennry, 1089095
BEAL, Gnr, Eric, 890968
BENNETT, Gnr, James, 1458187
BENNETT, Gnr, George, 861804
BERGIN, Gnr, Norman, 1119452
BERRY, Capt, James Thomas, 75000
BILLS, Gnr, Wiliam, 1092339
BURGIN, L/Bdr, Albert George, 955218
BUSBY, RSM, Eric James, 6607404
BUSBY, L/Sgt, Albert, 841602
CABLE, Gnr, Edgar William, 959203
CADMAN, Gnr, Gerald, 1085742
CARLISLE, Sjt, Stanley, 768941
CATES, L/Bdr, Alfred, 1044488
CLARK, Gnr, Archibald, 1041730
CLAYTON, Gnr, Walter, 891813
CLAYTON, Gnr, Harry Noel, 1119437
COLE, Gnr, Charles Tidal, 1092360
COLLIER, Gnr, Frank, 902157
COLLINS, Gnr, Walter, 828382
CONNOR, Gnr, Daniel, 1077702
COOPER, Bdr, Frank Coltman, 835223
CORLESS, Gnr, Francis James, 801494
CORNAL, L/Bdr, Charles Vivian, 903421
DACRE, L/Sjt, William, 3592842
DAWES, Gnr, Francis, 862151
DICKSON, Capt, Anthony Chambre, 70153
DRAKE, Gnr, Douglas, 984350
ECCLESTON, Sjt, James, 801303
EDWARDS, Gnr, Philip George, 1089614
ELEY, Gnr, John Frederick, 923904
ELLIS, Gnr, John Albert, 1085761
FARNSWORTH, Gnr, James Edward, 903403
FIELDS, Gnr, Herbert, 1017912
FLETCHER, Gnr, William, 891732
FOX, L/Bdr, Cyril, 902169
FOX, Gnr, Frank, 894779

GALE, L/Sjt, Arthur Maurice, 830400
GARDNER, Gnr, Harry, 855810
GARDNER, Sjt, Leslie Sands, 818591
GOADBY, Gnr, Fdward, 1085566
GRAVES, Gnr, Harry James, 805068
GREEN, Gnr, William John, 1058664
GREGSON, Gnr, John Elston, 892643
GRICE, Gnr, Cyril, 1115636
GRIFFITHS, Gnr, Alfred George, 821960
GROVER, Gnr, John Henry, 987481
GROVES, Gnr, Harry Asquith, 1504966
GUMSLEY, Gnr, William Stanley, 1085567
HALLWORTH, Gnr, Frank, 1119444
HALSTON, Gnr, Sam, 1115275
HANLON, Gnr, William, 968413
HARE, L/Bdr, Henry Thomas, 800790
HARPER, Gnr, George Henry, 1092437
HARRISON, Gnr, James Norman, 871220
HARVEY, Gnr, Leslie William, 974417
HARWOOD, Gnr, Leonard Charles, 984112
HASLAM, L/Bdr, William, 910192.
HEAP, Gnr, Ernest James William, 34106
HEARMAN, Gnr, Eric Bertram, 876354
HEAVER, Gnr, Arthur Edward, 956624
HENDEN, Gnr, Albert William, 980350
HEWITT, Gnr, Charles William, 904257
HILL, Pte, George Sleightholme, 1072232
HINDLEY, Gnr, Herbert, 1119414
HIRST, Bdr, Leonard, 861253
HITCHING, Gnr, John Edward, 1108929
HODKINSON, Gnr, John Bernard, 871410
HODSON, Gnr, Frederick, 858164
HUCKLE, Gnr, Frank, 1085702
HUDSON, Gnr, Arthur, 946428
HUXTABLE, Lt, Adrian Anthony, 182100
INGHAM, Gnr, Kenneth, 1115070
INGRAM, Gnr, William, 901484
INGRAM, Gnr, John, 855368
JACKSON, Gnr, Leonard, 1115069
JACKSON, Gnr, John, 905032
JAY, Gnr, Joseph Frederick, 990199
JENKINS, Gnr, Charles Frank,11050431
JENKINSON, Gnr, George Maxwell, 897895
JOHNSTON, Gnr, James Ian, 845275
JOHNSTONE, Gnr, William, 967512
KEEGAN, Bdr, Francis John, 955192
KEOGH, Gnr, Thomas, 1118178
LAMBERT, Gnr, David, 954236
LAMPLUGH, Gnr, John Stanley, 941331
LAWTON, Gnr, Kenneth Willam, 1113481
LEA, Gnr, Ronald Percy, 1115278
LLOYD, Gnr, George William Revenhill, 1094249
LOCKYER, Sjt, John Henry, 1072570
MACKELLAR, Gnr, James, 1112544
MALAM, Gnr, Norman, 1115661
MARSH, L/Sjt, John Albert, 2730252
MARSHALL, Gnr, Clarence George, 1085605
MARTIN, Gnr, Michael Gerard, 1119447
MASON, Gnr, George David, 1417074
MAWSON, Gnr, Arnold, 895411
MAXWELL, L/Sjt, Arthur Vincent, 915429
MAYNARD, Gnr, Claude, 1108826
McGILLICUDDY, Gnr, Peter Thomas, 982814
MIDDLETON, S/Sjt, David, 810148
MILLER, Gnr, Edward, 1119448
MILLS, Gnr, Ronald Mirven, 843734
MITCHELL, L/Sjt, William, 902158
MITCHELL, Gnr, Lewis, 895985
MOORE, Gnr, Albert Victor, 958330
MORRIS, Gnr, Gordon Eric, 930734

MOSS, Gnr, John Roger Stuart, 891727
MOULE, Gnr, Stanley Harold, 1118278
MOUNT, Gnr, Robert, 870971
MULRENAN, Gnr, Michael Terence, 955631
MUNRO, Gnr, Randolph Anderson, 1105842
MUNSON, L/Bdr, William Edward, 980356
MURRAY, Gnr, James, 858916
NASH, Gnr, Arthur Samuel, 964198
NELSON, L/Bdr, Thomas, 861704
NEWMAN, Gnr, Frederick William, 6405401
NEWMAN, Gnr, Raymond Arthur, 941946
NEWTON, Bdr, Douglas, 900352
NICKSON, Gnr, Frederick, 903463
NOBLETT, Gnr, Walter, 898749
NOYCE, Gnr, Geoffrey, 963068
O'CONNELL, Gnr, John Gordon, 1087680
O'CONNOR, Gnr, Denzil Raymund, 1087681
O'DOWD, Gnr, Colin, 1090819
ORMEROD, Gnr, Richard, 834824
OVERTON, Gnr, Albert Edward, 1094275
PALMER, Gnr, John, 990055
PARKINSON, Gnr, George Rutherford, 905582
PARRY, Bdr, George William, 1068791
POOLE, L/Bdr, Harry, 891094
REEVES, Gnr, Walter Edmund, 947563
RIGGAL, L/Bdr, Eric, 950030
ROBERTS, Gnr, Charles Henry, 145938
ROBINS, Gnr, William Frederick, 1098348
ROBINSON, L/Bdr, Walter Stanley, 956653
ROBINSON, Gnr, John, 779733
ROSCOE, Gnr, Joseph Anthony, 878898
ROURKE, Gnr, Burnett Thomas Ramsay, 1421440
RUDD, L/Sjt, John James, 812509
RUDD, Gnr, Jacob, 966543
RUFFELL, Gnr, Ronald Richard, 959667
SHAW, Bqms, Alfred, 1021736
SHIELD, Lt, George Edward, 129207
SIBILIA, Gnr, Aldo, 1119424
SIMPSON, Bdr, Sidney George, 930712
SIMPSON, Bdr, Edward, 923114
SINGLETON, Sjt, James, 885723
SMITH, Gnr, John Albert, 1119228
SMITH, Gnr, Henry, 982262
STEPHENS, Sjt, George Francis, 882179
STEVENSON, L/Bdr, George Telford, 910785
STONES, Gnr, George Sydney, 1120606
STOREY, Gnr, Sydney George, 1113108
SUMMERSGILL, L/Sjt, Thomas Robert, 895372
SUMNER, Gnr, Anthony Myers, 887115
SWINHOE, Sjt, George, 1071583
THOMAS, Gnr, George, 869998
THORNE, Gnr, Albert, 908392
TITCHENER, Gnr, John Jack, 948399
TOLLEY, Gnr, Frederick Charles, 899388
TONKS, Gnr, Jack, 1092571
TRETHEWY, 2/Lt, Ronald George, 174696
VAUGHAN, Gnr, Harold, 891729
WADE, Gnr, Charles Edward, 1108596
WALKER, Gnr, Thomas Wilson, 855388
WALLIS, Bdr, Leo, 895038
WALLIS, Gnr, George William, 1092600
WALSH, Gnr, James, 1113242
WALSH, Gnr, John, 896408
WATERHOUSE, Gnr, Arthur, 1119454
WATSON, Gnr, John Leonard, 908197
WATTS, BSM, John F E, 1055189
WHATLING, Sjt, Edgar, 816592
WHITELY, Gnr, John Harold, 896409
WHITTLE, Gnr, Edward, 879115
WILKINSON, Bdr, John Nelson, 870012

WILKINSON, Gnr, Cyril, 1119426
WILLMOTT, Sjt, Joseph Wiliam, 1073133
WILSON, Gnr, Richard Frederick, 941676
WINDER, L/Bdr, Harold, 912216
WINTERSGILL, Gnr, Edward Walter, 953953
WOLFE, Gnr, Henry Edwin, 899258
WOODWARD, L/Bdr, Peter Norman, 953824
WORDEN, L/Bdr, Richard, 857723

96 FR
CLAXTON, Gnr, James, 14793612
EGAN, Gnr, George Alfred Leonard, 860047
EVANS, Gnr, Rhys Henry, 1141841
HARDY, Bdr, Leslie, 14273913
McDONALD, Gnr, William M, 14575193
SHARPE, Gnr, Hubert Leslie, 14566710
WAY, Gnr, John Frederick, 1150738

114 FR
BETHUNE TAYLOR,Maj,Derek Beresford (MC),121686
HARKELL,Gnr,Geoffrey,14668060

118 FR
ALLSOPP, Gnr, William Henry, 1108691
AMER, L/Bdr, Robert William, 901373
ANSELL, L/Bdr, Clifford Peter Heasman, 908540
ASHFORD, Gnr, Charles James, 1112973
AYRES, Gnr, George Edward, 1089342
BADWELL, Gnr, Bertram George, 910575
BAKER, Sjt, Charles Erbert, 902323
BALDOCK, Gnr, Victor Alfred, 1074819
BALL, Sjt, James William, 946124
BALL, Gnr, W.F., 6205587
BAMPTON, Gnr, Ernest John, 964371
BARNES, Gnr, Alfred Edward, 1112245
BASTON, L/Bdr, Donald George, 943422
BAYLIS, Gnr, Edward, 1112247
BENDON, Gnr, Elias, 1101504
BONE, Gnr, Albert Raiseberry, 901348
BOODLE, Gnr, Thomas, 1078817
BOWN, Gnr, George Charles Atton, 944677
BRADLEY, Gnr, Frederick, 908509
BRETT, L/Bdr, Edgar, 954491
BRIERS, Sjt, George William, 818455
BROOME, Gnr, Ronald Peter, 1085908
BROWN, Gnr, Jack, 964476
BROWN, Gnr, Ernest William, 1112256
BROWN, Gnr, Arthur Thomas William, 1112255
BUBB, Gnr, Leonard, 1106199
BUCK, L/Bdr, Maurice William John, 901390
BURCHELL, Gnr, Arthur Edward Gerald, 1112260
BURROWS, Gnr, Thomas, 1119516
BUSBY, Gnr, Robert George, 1106333
BUTLER, L/Bdr, Bernard Frank, 915391
CAMPBELL, Gnr, James Tom, 984867
CARTWRIGHT, Gnr, Roland Albert, 910108
CHALK, Gnr, Henry Humull, 964383
CHALMERS, Gnr, Joseph Allen, 1087624
CLELLAND, Gnr, John, 1076097
CODDRINGTON, Gnr, George Albert, 1103289
COLEMAN, Gnr, Frank, 909984
COLLIER, Gnr, Henry Victor, 1084191
COLLINSON, Gnr, Cyril, 1123239
COLLISCHON, Gnr, Kenneth Charles G, 1089179
CONSTABLE, Bdr, Robert William George, 900318
COOPER, Gnr, Alfred John Charles, 911261
CREES, Bdr, Benjamin James, 901307
CREW, L/Sjt, William Charles, 910692
CREWE, Gnr, George Haydn, 3960229
CROCKER, Gnr, Henry,1087631

CROFTS, Capt, Peter Henry Francis, 92517
CROXFORD, Gnr, John Dennis, 950247
CULPIN, Gnr, William, 1098140
CURRIE, Sjt, Harry, 816987
DADD, Gnr, George Henry, 1106350
DAVEY, Gnr, Fredcrick William, 908523
DICKINS, Bdr, Peter Hambleton, 915378
DILLEY, Gnr, Harry Elliss, 964193
DOBIE, L/Bdr, Ernest, 901321
DONNELLY, Gnr, James, 1108626
DREWRY, Gnr, Charles Stewart, 1119521
DRU, Bdr, Graham Ernest, 905171
DUDLEY, Bdr, George Thomas Harry, 904518
EATON, Gnr, Eric Lawrence, 964168
EREIRA, Gnr, George Walter, 1101512
EVANS, Gnr, Arthur John, 969166
EVANS, Gnr, Henry John, 904537
EWIN, Gnr, John Arthur, 900327
FERGUSON, Gnr, Malcolm James, 906771
FOLEY, Gnr, William Henry, 1116228
FORSYTH, Gnr, Sidney, 1310075
FOSKETT, Gnr, Alfred Wilson, 902313
FOSTER, Gnr, Daniel Edmund, 990319
FRANCIS, Bdr, Ernest Thomas, 915013
FREEMAN, L/Bdr, Arthur George, 910577
GARDNER, Gnr, John William, 11230113
GARDNER, Gnr, Trevor Thomas, 1089352
GARDNER, Bdr, Gerald Charles, 900325
GARTON, Gnr, Charles Maurice, 908484
GAUNT, Gnr, Albert Charles, 1119411
GILBEY, Sjt, Bernard Victor, 837699
GOSLING, Gnr, Norman Arthur, 908742
GOSLING, Gnr, Ernest Sidney, 909327
GRAHAM,Gnr,Eric Gordon Rishworth,963824
GRANGE, Gnr, William James, 910644
GRAY, Sjt, Edmund George, 914065
GRIGGS, Gnr, Albert Mons Kitchener, 1547331
GRIMLEY, Gnr, John, 1108629
HAGGAR, Bdr, Charles Roy, 941899
HAILWOOD, Gnr, John, 1123015
HALLIWELL, Gnr, Ralph, 907125
HAMLYN, Bdr, Henry Harry, 757963
HANNEY, Gnr, Henry William, 914836
HANSON, Gnr, John, 946170
HARPER, Gnr, Derick George, 911880
HARPER, Gnr, Harry William George, 909318
HARRISON, Capt, William Walter, 103603
HART, Gnr, Robert Charles, 909979
HARWOOD, Gnr, William James, 909331
HATCHER, Bdr, John Arthur, 8906035
HAWKE, Gnr, Edward Rawlings, 1112384
HAYWOOD, Gnr, Charles William, 904862
HAZEL, Lt, Richard Roland William, 166631
HEAL, Gnr, Eric Frank, 909319
HEAL, Gnr, Brian, 908659
HEAL, Gnr, Eric Frank, 909319
HEATH, Gnr, Frederick Henry James, 945395
HEYWOOD, Gnr, Samuel, 1119413
HEYWOOD, Gnr, David, 1108338
HILL,L/Bdr, William Alfred, 908621
HILL, Gnr, Arthur Ernest, 1113315
HILLIARD, L/Bdr, Leonard George, 964477
HOBBIS, Gnr, Charles Victor, 947558
HOGG, Gnr, Graeme Scott, 1113467
HORLOCK, Gnr, Kenneth Audsley, 913381
HOWITT, Gnr, Wilfred, 911268
HUDSON, Gnr, Dudley Parker, 964418
HUGHES, Gnr, William Stanley, 1109185
HULL, Gnr, Jacob Elliot, 1106365
HUNWICK, Gnr, Thomas Edward, 901332

HUTTON, L/Sjt, Albert Henry, 910591
IRWIN, Gnr, Arthur Leslie, 1123139
IVISON, Bdr, William George, 904861
JAMES, Gnr, Ernest Arthur, 1558431
JASPER, Gnr, James Douglas, 909973
JEPPESEN, Gnr, John Niels Peter, 1101518
JOHN, Gnr, Thomas William Saint, 1089358
JOHNSON, Sjt, Dennis Howard, 908615
JONES, Bdr, Douglas Cartwright, 901345
JUNEMAN, Gnr, Henry James, 1101520
KEEN, Gnr, Leonard Arthur, 910109
KELF, Gnr, Thomas James, 911258
KEWELL, Gnr, Reginald, 911883
KIMBER, Gnr, George Robert, 990341
LITTLE, Gnr, James Henry, 901305
LOUGH, Gnr, Ernest William, 1089452
MANN, Gnr, William Charles, 1084839
MARTIN, Bdr, Francis Bernard, 908525
MARTIN, Maj, Arthur Denis, 50007
MARTIN, Bdr, Lester Dudley, 908744
MASON, Gnr, Arthur Rushworth, 990354
MATHEWS, Gnr, John, 1094257
McCARTHY, Gnr, Edward, 914693
MEAD, Sjt, Robert Edward, 912991
MEADOWS, Gnr, Ernest George, 910649
MEGGS, Gnr, Frank, 908634
MIDWINTER, Gnr, Harold Arthur, 915393
MILLER, Gnr, Richard, 1607268
MITCHELL, Gnr,George Henry, 1115673
MITCHELL, Gnr, Thomas James, 1101527
MORAN, Gnr, William James, 1101528
MORLEY, Gnr, Eric, 1557750
MURRELL, Sjt, Keith Edward, 907815
NASH, Gnr, William, 946088
NEILL, Gnr, Charles Henry, 1101530
NELLER, L/Bdr, Arthur Alfred, 902299
NORRIS, Gnr, James, 1084032
NUNN, Gnr, Alec, 1119532
OCKENDEN, L/Bdr, Eric William, 945400
OVENDEN, Gnr, Joseph, 902283
PARHAM, Gnr, Leslie Harold, 990363
PATERSON, Gnr, William Leonard, 1115158
PAWLEY, Gnr, Edward Wilfred, 909320
PEARCE, Gnr, Ernest George, 1101531
PETHYBRIDGE, BSM, Alan Bradshaw, 909539
PHILLIPS, Gnr, Robert John, 955386
PILBEAM, Gnr, Douglas Harry, 941890
PINCOMBE, Gnr, Thomas Charles, 990368
PLUMMER, Gnr, Ronald Patrick, 1101532
PLUMRIDGE, Gnr, Henry Charles Arthur, 964473
POOLEY, Gnr, Maurice Fred, 907161
PROCTOR, Gnr, James Robert, 1606950
PURDOM, Gnr, Richard, 1108347
RADFORD, Gnr, Edward Leslie Horace, 902281
RICHARDS, Gnr, Alfred James, 1103375
RICHARDSON, Gnr, Henry Charles, 11054802
RIST, L/Bdr, Edward Arthur, 910646
RIXSON, Sjt, Ronald Alfred, 909989
ROBERTS, Gnr, Arthur Charles, 945396
ROBINS, L/Bdr, Sidney Francis, 914205
ROWLES, L/Sjt, Maurice Cameron, 946047
RUTHERFORD, Gnr, Henry, 1108644
RYAN, Gnr, John William, 968931
RYDER, Gnr, Victor Charles, 1074550
SABOURIN, Gnr, Leonard Charles, 901311
SADLER, Gnr, William, 1115702
SALE, Gnr, John Trevor, 990000
SALMON, Sjt, Ronald Charlwood, 914832
SAMPSON, L/Bdr, Ernest Thomas, 964190
SEAGER, Gnr, Percy Leonard, 964449

SIGGINS, Gnr, Charles Henry, 908508
SIMPKIN, Gnr, Christopher, 1112166
SIMPSON, Gnr, James Henry, 1525859
SIMPSON, Gnr, William Harry Ernest, 946004
SMALE, Sjt, Reginald George, 944649
SMITH, Bdr, Harry, 964467
SMITH, Gnr, Ronald Arthur, 913315
SMITH, Gnr, Leslie Thomas, 909342
SMITH, Gnr, Frank, 1115891
SOWERY, Gnr, John James, 964401
SPOONER, Gnr, Charles Henry, 990286
SPURLING, Gnr, Robert Willam Edward, 915620
STANDBRIDGE, BSM, Leonard Arthur, 915807
STRAND, Gnr, Thomas William, 602269
SUMPTER, Gnr, Albert Edward, 1106390
SWIFT, L/Bdr, Ralph George, 913380
TAGGART, Gnr, Mathew, 1123025
TAYLOR, Gnr, James Patrick, 1606954
TEDDER, Gnr, Frederick Walter Francis, 1112123
TERRY, L/Sjt, Albert William, 910640
THOMPSON, Sjt, Victor John, 909987
TICKEL, L/bdr, Richard Henry, 904538
TRENELL, Gnr, Stanley, 893690
UNDERWOOD, Gnr, Henry Leonard, 1101539
VERNON, L/Sjt, Henry William, 946029
VOAK, Gnr, Frederick James, 901325
WADE, Gnr, Norman Harold Alan, 836497
WALKER, Gnr, William Roland, 945531
WALL, Sjt, Robert Charles Croft, 901347
WALTER, Gnr, Cyril Bertie Alfred, 944950
WATTS, Gnr, James, 1087515
WEBB, Bdr, Stanley Richard, 901796
WEBB, Sjt, Charles George, 907833
WEIR, Gnr, Thomas Joseph, 1123155
WELLS, Gnr, Roy Albert, 945539
WENNELL, Gnr, Walter Stanley, 908737
WEST, Bdr, James Frederick William, 909982
WHARTON, Gnr, Arthur, 1119537
WHITING, L/Bdr, Leslie, 907860
WILKINS, Bdr, Ronald Gordon, 945393
WILKINS, Gnr, Christopher Arthur, 901386
WILLIAMS, Gnr, Frederick, 945529
WILLSHIRE, BSM, John Ralph, 758495
WILSON, Gnr, Jack Ewson, 912993
WINTER, Bdr, Charles Abrassia, 5826675
WORTH, Bdr, Ronald Willitt, 908514
WRIGHT, Gnr, Douglas Allen, 964196
YOUNG, Gnr, William George, 902248
YOUNG, Gnr, Stanley, 891190
YULE, Gnr, Sidney Richard, 907811

122 FR
ADRISON, Gnr, Edwin Robert, 963757
ALLAN, Lt, George Albert Thomas Boris, 359855
AMBLER, L/Bdr, Frederick, 963760
BARR, Gnr, George, 981652
BEASTY, Gnr, John Thomas, 963771
BOND, Gnr, Sidney, 986367
BOWES, Gnr, Clifford, 963776
BRANTON, Gnr, Roy, 1504850
BRUNT, Bdr, William Harold, 843013
BURGESS, Gnr, Urban Charles, 975346
CHARLESWORTH, Gnr, Frank, 940648
CHRISTOPHER, Bdr, Joseph, 963728
COLBROOK, Gnr, Jack, 926788
COMINS, Cap M, Colin Frederick Innes, 29939
CORE, Bdr, Gilbert Allenby, 908709
COX, Gnr, Lewis, 907891
CROWTHER, Gnr, Herbert, 907865
DAVIES, Gnr, Thomas Allan Cecil, 925992

DYSON, Lt Col, George St John Armitage (MC), 8409
ELLIS, Gnr, Arthur Ronald, 926789
EVANS, Gnr, Ernest, 963810
FARRAND, Gnr, Walter Edward, 963813
FOLLON, Gnr, Martin, 963818
FOSSEY, L/Sjt, Stanley, 912686
FRANKLIN, Gnr, Percy, 940714
GARRET, Gnr, Albert Edward, 986435
GILES, Gnr, Gordon William, 984196
GREEN, Gnr, Frank Wiliam, 940707
HALL, Gnr, Frank, 918687
HANSON, Gnr, Eric, 919259
HARNESS, Gnr, Jack, 845755
HEPTINSTALL, Gnr, Harold, 918446
HIDE, Gnr, George Edward, 963836
HINDLEY, L/Bdr, Henry, 908688
HITT, Gnr, Arthur, 940685
HODGSON, Gnr, Arthur Carrigan, 963839
HOLT, Gnr, Stanley, 984200
HOWARTH, Gnr, Harry Haslam, 921588
HUMPHREYS, L/Bdr, Daniel Gwynolwyn, 1072152
ILLINGWORTH, Gnr, Jack Bradley, 963845
INNES, Bdr, Harry, 1066996
KEIGHLEY, Gnr, William Arthur, 892991
KERR, Lt, Graham Callow, 92937
KINSLEY, Gnr, Arthur, 914466
KNOTT, Bdr, Frank, 918472
LAWRENSON, Gnr, Edward, 984204
LOUTH, Gnr, Leslie Thomas, 940705
MARKIN, Gnr, Sydney Osborne, 952299
MARTIN, Sjt, Henry James, 1050718
MASON, Gnr, Albert Thomas, 940737
MASON, Gnr, James Edward, 963864
MILLEN, Gnr, William Arthur, 969995
MILNE, Gnr, Harry Russell, 987055
MOORE, Lt, John Lawson, 113173
MORAN, Gnr, Edward Albert, 888451
MORTON, Gnr, Horace, 919783
MOWAT, Gnr, David Reid, 987067
MURTOUGH, Gnr, James, 963742
NEWTON, Gnr, Ernest, 921613
NUTTALL, Gnr, John Albert, 934958
OLDFIELD, Gnr, George, 896127
PAGE, L/Bdr, Ernest George, 958051
PARKER, Gnr, Hugh, 940727
PEACOCK, Gnr, Percy Donald, 975292
PICKLES, Bdr, Gordon, 915538
POLL, Gnr, George Albert, 975295
PRING, L/Bdr, Ronald George, 940738
PROCTOR, Gnr, George, 984235
QUEST, Gnr, Walter J., 969830
RAYNE, Gnr, Arthur Helliwell, 922316
RHODES, Lt, Robert Lionel Mitchell, 92941
RIDER, Gnr, Herbert, 908694
ROWLES, Sjt, Sidney, 914469
RUSHWORTH, Gnr, Frank, 963898
RUSTON, Gnr, George William, 963899
SAGAR, Lt, Anthony Durban Gordon, 92942
SELLERS, Gnr, Frank, 963983
SMITH, Gnr, Donald, 919771
STEAD, Gnr, Harry Foster, 926790
STEED, Gnr, John Robert, 969965
SUMMERSGILL, L/Bdr, Arthur Whitaker, 918631
TAPPENDEN, Gnr, Henry, 973496
THORNLEY, L/Bdr, Arthur Edward, 925624
TOWNSEND, Gnr, Thomas Daniel, 1074588
TRIGG, Gnr, Jack, 901368
TUCK, Gnr, James William, 1074346
VALENTINE, L/Bdr, Walter Reuben, 940690
WADE, Gnr, Richard Woodcock, 963126

WALKER, Sjt, William, 913174
WALSH, Gnr, George Joseph, 926005
WARNER, Gnr, Frederck Graham, 981023
WATKISS, Gnr, Geoffrey Mansbridge, 963947
WATSON, RQMS, Alfred, 1421557
WEBB, Gnr, Leonard James, 935601
WELSH, Gnr, Alexander, 901385
WEST, Gnr, Cyril, 940712
WHITEHEAD, Gnr, Harry Douglas, 975232
WHITWORTH, Sjt, James, 825666
WILLIAMS, Ronald George, 831976
WILLIAMS, Gnr, Job, 955796
WILSON, L/Bdr, Raymond, 963965
WOOD, Gnr, Frank, 963955
WOOD, Gnr, Edward, 963754
WOOD, Gnr, Norman, 921134
125 FR
WILLIS, Gnr, Cyril Edward, 1557855
MAGRILL, L/Sjt, Jack Harold, 902520

135 FR
AKASS, Gnr, George Seppings, 1122083
ALDIS, Gnr, Charles Burton, 1098357
ALLEN, Bdr, Jack Stanley, 948874
ANDERSON, L/Sjt, Dennis Patrick, 962475
ANDERSON, Gnr, George, 994855
ATKINSON, Sjt, Herbert George, 837045
ATTRILL, Gnr, John Thomas Henry, 1092982
BAKEWELL, Gnr, Vernon Joseph, 943484
BARKER, Gnr, Parram Edwin Augustus Walter, 1115106
BARRETT, Gnr, Benjamin Thomas, 1094136
BARTON, Gnr, Thomas, 1111233
BEAVIS, Gnr, John, 1092907
BEL, L/bdr, Kenneth, 920935
BELCHER, Gnr, Sidney Ernest, 996192
BELLIS, Gnr, Vyrnwy Allison, 1076445
BELSHAM, Gnr, Stanley George, 1104081
BELT, Sjt, Harry, 848960
BINES, Sjt, George William, 852698
BOLTON, Bdr, Victor Peace, 940897
BRANNAN, Gnr, Patrick, 996199
BRANT, L/bdr, Reginald Hary, 943493
BRIGHTWELL, Gnr, Thomas William, 1092995
BROWN, Gnr, Leslie Albert, 1104083
BROWN, Gnr, Harry, 923527
BROWN, Gnr, Wallace, 893872
BROWNE, L/bdr, John, 1113486
BRYANT, Sjt, William Charles, 890210
BRYCE, Gnr, James Bellingal, 1092983
BULLARD, Gnr, Reginald, 897394
BURGESS, Gnr, Ronald Lelsie, 7663115
CANNON, Bsm, Roye Frank, 855012
CARR, Gnr, Mathew Stafford, 1092863
CASBON, Gnr, Walter John Harry, 940900
CASWELL, Sjt, Richard William, 914347
CATHIE, Gnr, Chrighton Arthur, 903279
CHAMBERLAIN, Gnr, George Charles, 943471
CHAMBERLAIN, Gnr, Roland, 896161
CHAPMAN, Gnr, Walter Harry, 922770
CHAPMAN, Gnr, Arthur, 1098213
CHAPMAN, Gnr, Victor Roy, 923479
CHAPMAN, Gnr, George William, 996201
CHARNLEY, Gnr, Roy Edward, 921154
CLARKE, L/bdr, Kenneth Frederick, 969859
CLASPER, Gnr, Frederick, 1085031
CLEGG, Gnr, Frank Bewley, 1098214
CLEMENTS, Gnr, Leonard Charles Aubrey, 923478
COCKROFT, L/bdr, Thomas Geoffrey, 996337
COKE, Sjt, Robert, 839740
COLES, Rsm, George D, 733511

COOLING, Sjt, Raymond, 921421
COOPER, Gnr, Major, 996206
COOPER, Gnr, Jack, 1104085
COWLING, Gnr, Frederick.W, 1102539
COX, Gnr, Norman Douglas, 919933
CRADDOCK, Gnr, George William, 1104086
CROMBLEHOLME, Gnr, Francis William, 894851
CUNNINGHAM, Gnr, John Goring, 1085203
DRING, Bdr, Thomas Eric, 915797
ECCLES, Gnr, Harold, 1098217
ELLIOTT, Gnr, Frederick Thomas, 922904
EMBLOW, Gnr, Edward Sydney, 905119
EVANS, Gnr, Thomas Henry, 1111238
FARR, Gnr, Arthur Edward, 996210
FEARNETT, Bdr, Alfred Cecil, 1077007
FENN, L/Sjt, George Wiliam Frederick Henry, 924090
FISHER, Gnr, Reginald Leslie Dudley Stewart, 1094198
FOLK, Gnr, Cecil Henry, 1092860
FROST, Gnr, William Ivor James, 1721559
FROST, Gnr, William John Percy, 1094200
GABRIELSON, L/bdr, George, 1072304
GAILLARD, Bdr, Robert Philip, 954943
GALE, Sjt, John Wilfred Christopher, 916878
GAMBLIN, Gnr, John, 948882
GARDINER, Gnr, Daniel Stephen, 1094202
GEORGE, Gnr, Ernest John Lewis, 950501
GIBSON, Gnr, John, 993687
GILBERT, Gnr, Christopher Leslie, 1094204
GILBY, Gnr, William Clarence, 920975
GILHAM, Gnr, Alfred David, 896763
GOODLAND, Gnr, Ernest, 1085384
GOTLIEB, Gnr, Gerald, 962481
GRAHAM, L/bdr, John, 977350
GRAY, Gnr, Frederick James, 913649
GREENWOOD, Gnr, George, 981933
GROMBAKH, Gnr, Boris, 1098335
GROVES, Gnr, Albert, 1111239
HAILEY, L/bdr, Claude, 878022
HAMPSHIRE, Gnr, Frank, 1092975
HARDING, Gnr, Henry Wyatt, 1123097
HART, L/bdr, Marshall Raban, 892172
HAWKING, W/o 119, Henry Halton, 914339
HAYWARD, Gnr, Jethro Hadney, 920936
HILL, Gnr, Ernest Georgc Edward, 922775
HOCKEY, Gnr, Edward Walter, 9214127
HOUGHTON, Gnr, Percy, 881826
HUMBLE, Gnr, John Jnes, 979782
HUMFRYES, Gnr, Henry, 1087663
HUNT, Gnr, Frederick William, 1104097
IVINS, Bdr, Charlie, 905481
JOHNSON, Bsm, Arthur, 785471
KEEBLE, Gnr, Stanley Charles, 962429
KEMP, Gnr, Cecil Vincent, 7662763
KING, Gnr, Arthur Eric, 948896
KIRK, Gnr, Alan Godfrey, 1123162
KNIGHTON, Gnr, George Henry, 834360
LEWIS, Bdr, Ivor Wells, 808595
LEWIS, Bdr, Albert Stanley, 940892
LIVINGSTONE, Gnr, Andrew, 994869
MAILE, Gnr, Roy Hugh Wiltshire, 927947
MARSHALL, Gnr, Hary Lester, 1094255
MARSHALL, Gnr, Edward, 1082447
MEARS, Bdr, Walter, 914345
MERRITT, Gnr, Albert Walter, 1056218
MILNE, Gnr, James, 994871
MONK, Gnr, Edwin James, 1104105
NEVILLE, Gnr, William, 915812
NEWLAND, Gnr, Jack, 924091
NICHOLLS, Pte, Bernard, 5933898
NICHOLS, L/bdr, William Thomas, 1104108

NICHOLS, Bsm, Frederick Walter,
NORFIELD, Gnr, Oliver George, 1104633
NORRIS, Sjt, John Cyril, 896155
O'CONNOR, Gnr, John Raphael, 1087682
PARKER, Gnr, Henry, 1092872
PARKES, Bdr, Arthur, 1056248
PATERSON, Gnr, Robert, 994874
PATMORE, Gnr, George Henry, 878024
PEACHEY, Bdr, Frank, 962425
PERCY, Bdr, Wiliam Henry, 897393
PETTENGELL, Sjt, William James, 923508
PHILLIPS, Gnr, Edward John, 1085302
PICKING, Gnr, Stanley H, 1104637
PILLATT, Gnr, Frank Bertram, 1123260
POPELEY, Gnr, Alfred Edward, 5932363
PROBERT, Gnr, Thomas William George, 1092510
PRYKE, Gnr, Lawrence, 885407
RAYNOR, Lt, Rowland, 161784
REEVE, Gnr, John William, 1085278
REMON, Gnr, Victor Edward, 962444
RICE, Gnr, Percival, 1094297
RICHARDS, Gnr, Cecil Charles, 949699
ROBERTS, Gnr, Ernest William, 1103755
ROBERTSON, Gnr, James Richard, 994875
ROBINSON, Gnr, Wiliam Thomas, 953014
RUSSELL, Gnr, Harold Thomas, 922761
SANDERS, Gnr, Stanley Ivor, 1098848
SAYWOOD, Bdr, Douglas Thornton, 922748
SEAMANS, L/bdr, Herbert George, 962432
SHARP, Gnr, Wilfred Amos, 890847
SHERWOODS, Wi Gnr, Arthur Richard, 962476
SMITH, Gnr, Raymond, 1085191
SMITH, Bdr, Walter Bernard, 5828175
SMITH, L/bdr, John Richard, 856318
SMITH, Gnr, Philip Henry, 810116
SMITH, Gnr, Gerald Dean, 922755
SMITH, Gnr, Bert Leslie, 920931
SPINK, Gnr, Albert Edward, 962426
STACEY, Gnr, Frederick, 5720898
STARNES, Gnr, Walter George, 1076731
STEBBING, Lt, Ralph Edward Arthur, 92991
STEED, Gnr, Henry Charles, 1076733
STEELS, Gnr, Arthur Edward, 885649
STEGEMAN, Gnr, Edward, 954718
STONE, Gnr, Frederick Harold, 1094331
TAGG, Gnr, Donald Walter, 6094981
TAYLOR, Gnr, Robert, 903288
THOMPSON, Gnr, James, 1779956
THOMPSON, Gnr, Ernest, 1517299
THOMPSON, Gnr, Harry George, 943428
TOKENS, Gnr, Albert Edward, 895162
TROTMAN, Gnr, Thomas Douglas, 1083132
TUCKER, Gnr, Charles, 1104116
TUNNICLIFFE, Bdr, Albert Cyril, 943462
TURNER, Gnr, Alfred Charles, 923500
VANN, Gnr, John Henry, 943466
WADDINGTON, Gnr, Dennis, 1121282
WALKER, Gnr, Percy, 946421
WARBURTON, Gnr, Geoffrey, 957288
WATSON, Gnr, Frederick George, 913640
WESTWOOD, Gnr, Douglas, 948324
WHICKER, Gnr, Alfred Walter, 1119590
WHINCUP, L/Sjt, Bernard Eric, 915817
WHITE, Gnr, Bertie, 1076786
WHITEHEAD, Sjt, Edwin, 920681
WHITTEN, Gnr, Frank Charles, 1087725
WILIAMS, Sjt, Arthur Henry, 405866
WILLIAMS, Gnr, Henry Lloyd, 1088050
WITHERS, Gnr, Arthur Richard, 962476
WOOD, Gnr, Stanley, 883858

WOOD, Gnr, Philip Clifford, 1094364
WOODS, Gnr, Charles Leonard, 1094365
WRIGHT, Gnr, Frederick Charles, 905440

137 FR
ALFF, Gnr, William, 1099744
ANSTICE, L/Bdr, Kenneth Humphrey, 1097412
ASHWORTH, Sjt, Eric, 944855
ASKEW, Gnr, Richard, 932046
BAKER, Gnr, John Henry, 1099745
BAKER, Gnr, Stanley, 948893
BAKER, Gnr, John, 948039
BAKER, Sjt, Charles Henry, 1038788
BANKS, Gnr, William, 944556
BARKER, Gnr, William John, 1080671
BARRITT, Gnr, Frank, 948118
BARTON, Gnr, Alexander Frederick, 1080674
BAUM, Gnr, Henry, 1080677
BAYLISS, Gnr, Albert William, 1115196
BONNEY, Gnr, Walter, 933105
BOWKER, L/Sgt, William Hubert, 882432
BOWLES, Bdr, George John, 1034027
BROUGHTON, L/Bdr, Raymond, 905035
BULLOCK, Gnr, Ernest, 850871
BURNS, Gnr, Thomas, 902561
BURNS, Gnr, Edward Arthur, 1080711
BUTLER, Gnr, Mathew John, 906315
BUTON, Gnr, Harry, 944576
CANNELL, Gnr, Charles Henry, 950893
CAPP, Gnr, Oliver Norman, 980542
CARNE, Gnr, Alfred, 1099753
CARTER, Gnr, Cyril, 930785
CHADWICK, Gnr, William Henry, 950947
CHALLONER, Gnr, Dennis, 903546
CHAMBERS, Gnr, Edgar Arthur, 833078
CLARK, Gnr, Roland Walter, 952496
COHEN, Gnr, Harry, 1099755
COOKSON, Gnr, Frederick, 900410
COOPER, Gnr, George, 930822
COOPER, Gnr, Kenneth Finlay, 908416
CREWE, L/Bdr, Arnold, 905040
CROOK, Gnr, George, 948091
CROSSLEY, Gnr, John Ralph, 896321
CUERDEN, Gnr, James, 890564
CULPIN, Gnr, Francis William, 1099759
CUMBERBATCH, L/Bdr, Richard Elkin, 931467
DAMON, Gnr, Alfred George, 1097360
DAVIES, Gnr, Sidney Clifford, 1116470
DEATH, Bdr, Walter Herbert, 906307
DIXON, Gnr, James, 948033
DONELLY, Gnr, Thomas, 1119461
DONNELLY, Gnr, Terence Patrick, 948053
DOSWELL, Gnr, Edward Albert, 1099762
DULSON, Gnr, Harold Ernest, 950863
EATON, Gnr, Cyril Albert, 1119323
EDGE, Gnr, Harry, 905608
ESDELL, Gnr, Robert James, 1099764
ETTRIDGE, Gnr, George Arthur Thomas, 1099765
FOLEY, Bdr, Arthur Edward, 897910
FORSYTH, Gnr, James Plenderleith, 1787349
FREAK, Gnr, George Henry, 845147
FROST, L/Bdr, Walter, 879032
GARNER, Gnr, Arthur, 950943
GLYNN, Gnr, Harry, 903448
GOSSAGE, Gnr, Frederick William, 1099770
GRAY, Gnr, Joseph, 908397
GRAYSON, Gnr, Kenneth, 948071
GREGORY, L/bdr, Kenneth, 908441
GREGSON, Sjt, John, 904258
GROSSET, Gnr, John Arthur, 1093545

HALL, Gnr, Herbert, 964784
HALL, Gnr, William Charles, 1099773
HALLWORTH, Bdr, Leslie, 903543
HAMER, Gnr, Charles Frederick, 905089
HAMPSON, Bdr, George Talbot, 944557
HANCOCK, Gnr, Frederick George, 964719
HARMER, L/Bdr, Reginald Claude, 1080823
HARTLEY, 2/Lt, Robert, 153633
HAYTON, Gnr, Ronald, 930727
HEARNSHAW, Gnr, Albert, 964234
HIRST, Gnr, Frank, 896002
HITCHEN, Gnr, Thomas, 93435
HOLDEN, Bdr, Norman, 902525
HOLME, Lt Col, George Dodgson, 37672
HOPKINSON, Gnr, Ernest, 964790
HORSMAN, Bdr, Peter, 896402
HOWARTH, BSM, Eric, 787517
HOYE, Gnr, George, 1096974
HUGHES, Gnr, Lionel Henry, 1099779
HULME, Gnr, Thomas, 950937
HURSTFIELD, L/Sjt, Leslie Arthur, 916530
JACKSON, Gnr, Henry Carlisle, 1099781
JACKSON, Bdr, James Walter, 905587
JAQUES, Gnr, George William, 1099782
JOHNSON, Gnr, Joseph, 898809
JONES, Sjt, George, 5104932
JONES, Gnr, Thomas Frederick, 950889
JONES, Bdr, Edward Victor, 948123
JONES, Gnr, Thomas Frederick, 950889
KELLET, Gnr, Andrew, 950917
KING, Gnr, Eric, 950903
KIRBY, L/Bdr, Stanley, 921396
LAHEY, Gnr, John, 899370
LEE, Gnr, Fred, 944575
LINGARD, Bdr, Sidney James, 950951
LISTON, Capt, John Frederick Gordon, 71020
LITTLE, Sjt, Edward, 904404
MACHIN, Gnr, Walter Ernest, 943887
MARSHALL, Sjt, Leonard Norman, 908189
MARTIN, Gnr, Peter Laing, 1093566
MAY, Gnr, Ernest Richard, 1116243
McKEOWEN, Sjt, Henry, 897908
MICHELL, L/Bdr, Ian James, 905754
MILLER, Bdr, George Gordon, 908442
MILLER, Gnr, Albert, 950866
MOORE, Gnr, George, 951185
MORETON, Gnr, Raham Ernest Henry, 998062
MORGAN, Gnr, Harold Wilfred, 948037
MORGAN, Gnr, Jack, 964716
MORRISON, Sjt, George Dunhill, 895355
MOSS, Lt, Halliwell Sutcliffe, 90351
MUFFETT, Gnr, Wiliam Henry, 1119218
MURPHY, Gnr, Patrick Thomas, 823214
NEWBY, Gnr, Leslie, 960813
NICHOLAS, Sjt, Peter, 908238
OAKES, Gnr, William Frederick, 949459
OSMON, Gnr, Richard Frederick, 1119585
OXLEY, Gnr, Walter Edgar, 953986
OXLEY, Gnr, Ronald, 964743
PALTRIDGE, Gnr, William John, 909615
PARKER, Bdr, Roy, 908200
PARKINSON, Bdr, Norman, 948048
PARKINSON, Gnr, Verden, 948058
PEARSON, Gnr, Cuthbert, 961291
PEARSON, Bdr, Roy, 908195
PENDLETON, L/Bdr, William, 950940
PITT, Gnr, Ronald Henry, 800084
PRESTON, Gnr, William Kenneth, 950933
PRICE, Gnr, Leslie David, 1119330
PULLEN, Gnr, Reginald George Henry, 1099794

RADLEY, Gnr, Frederick Charles William, 1099795
REYNARD, Gnr, Henry Edwin, 1080975
REYNOLDS, Bdr, Lionel Selby, 899328
ROBBINS, Gnr, Thomas Henry, 1080979
ROBINSON, Gnr, William, 781905
ROSCOW, Gnr, Alan, 908233
ROWSE, Gnr, Harry Arthur, 1119588
RUSSELL, Gnr, Alfred, 1097287
SALKELD, L/Bdr, William Edward, 953987
SANDERS, Gnr, Gilbert Arthur, 908435
SAUNDERS, Gnr, John Ernest, 1099797
SEABRIDGE, Gnr, Jack, 848138
SEDGWICK, Gnr, Leonard, 940935
SEWARD, Gnr, Charles William, 1080994
SHENTON, Gnr, Albert, 892714
SHORE, Capt, John Hamilton, 85529
SLENEY, Gnr, Eric Leslie, 963913
SMITH, L/Bdr, James, 950883
SMITH, Gnr, Christopher Brummell, 11131598
SOUTHWORTH, Gnr, Joseph Aloysius, 905531
SPENCE, Pte, Derrick Alexander, 906298
SPENCER, L/Sjt, Joseph Butterworth, 908194
STEELE, Gnr, Leslie, 964703
STONE, Gnr, Louis, 1093613
STRINGFELLOW, Gnr, Albert, 948051
STUBBS, Gnr, Arthur, 903393
TAFT, Gnr, George Edwin, 1081752
TAYLOR, Gnr, Robert, 895377
TAYLOR, Gnr, Ernest, 961459
THOMAS, Gnr, Wilson David, 1119334
THOMPSON, Gnr, Gerard, 948099
TOMMANY, Gnr, James, 849754
TURNBULL, Gnr, James Terence, 906312
WAITE, L/Sjt, Edgar Noel, 902513
WATERMAN, Gnr, David, 1099803
WEBSTER, Gnr, William Henry, 1099804
WEST, Gnr, Frank, 98124
WHITE, Gnr, William Walter, 1081788
WHITTLE, Gnr, Stephen, 109805
WHITWORTH, Bdr, Allan, 906308
WILSON, Gnr, George, 924270
WOOD, Gnr, John, 950874
WOODWARD, L/Bdr, Edward Henry Walter, 1081807
WRIGHT, Gnr, Herbert, 907044
WRIGHT, Gnr, Samuel, 1081814
WRIGHT, Gnr, Ernest Edward, 1099807

145 FR
HARRIES, Gnr, William Hubert, 14206517

148 FR
ADAMS, Gnr, Gordon Arthur Richard, 1110371
ADAMS, Gnr, Neville, 915467
ALLEN, Bdr, Jonathan William, 854440
ALLEN, Gnr, John Herbert William, 898752
ASKEW, Gnr, James Arthur, 891310
BAILEY, Gnr, Kenneth, 918241
BAKER, Gnr, George, 1024042
BALL, Gnr, Arthur, 941919
BARR, Gnr, John, 1084097
BARTLETT, Bqms, Leslie Robin, 865764
BAVISTER, Gnr, Joseph, 916646
BELL, Lt, David Dunwoody, 140727
BINGHAM, Gnr, Arthur, 941923
BIRD, Gnr, Edward Frank, 921530
BISHOP, Gnr, Robert Victor, 943508
BLAIR, Gnr, John, 1096599
BLOUNT, Gnr, Charles Eric, 1104265
BOYD, Gnr, George Edwin, 1087616
BRACEWELL, Gnr, Ezra, 874900

BRAWN, Gnr, Eric Jack, 945029
BROWN, Gnr, Ernest, 921534
BURD, L/Bdr, Harold Leonard, 900698
BURKE, Gnr, John, 1099289
BUTLER, Gnr, Harold, 1103030
BUTTEN, Gnr, Henry, 1104267
CAFFELL, L/Bdr, Gordon Walter Joseph, 924778
CAGGAN, Gnr, Leon, 998880
CANE, Gnr, Frank Charles, 993909
CARTER, Gnr, George Henry, 948846
CARTER, BSM, John James, 1059473
CASSWELL, Gnr, Howard John, 1119460
CHALKLEY, Sjt, Horace Frederick, 921540
CHAMBERS, Gnr, John Lytton, 1104268
CLARK, Gnr, Frank, 962447
COLLETT, Gnr, Arthur Henry, 1094173
COLLINS, Gnr, Thomas, 1096657
COOPER, Gnr, Leslie, 867238
CRAWLEY, Gnr, Allan, 917297
CROOK, Gnr, William Daniel, 899822
CRUMP, Gnr, Basil William, 967213
CURTIS, Gnr, Albert Edward, 5947145
DALTON, Gnr, Joseph Jasper, 1087633
DANIELS, L/Bdr, Lawrence Rufus, 948856
DAVIES, Lt, Philip Austen, 121697
DAVIS, BSM, Kenneth Isaac, 1064841
DENNISON, L/Sjt, Ronald Henry, 871353
DICKIN, Gnr, Albert, 1098216
DRAPER, Gnr, Richard James, 948866
EGGINTON, Gnr, Howard, 943507
EVANS, Gnr, Clifford Stephen William, 1116344
EVANS, Gnr, Ronald Charles, 1088797
FARRINGTON, Gnr, Percy William, 9662506
FIELDEN, L/Bdr, Thomas Herbert, 1098218
FINN, Gnr, Edward, 1092728
FLINT, Gnr, Walter, 1113953
FOSSEY, L/Sjt, Henry Thomas, 5946042
FOWLER, Sjt, Frederick Norman, 887505
FRENCH, Sjt, Thomas John, 809817
FROST, Gnr, Leslie Harold, 927335
GAULTON, Gnr, Percy Frederick, 1094203
GAUNTLETT, Gnr, Glyndwr, 904426
GILBERT, Bdr, Harold Kenneth, 900696
GORDON, Gnr, Lional David, 998222
GRIGG, Bdr, George Stanley, 916771
GROOM, L/Bdr, Stanley, 918237
HAMER, L/bdr, Norman, 1098220
HARRISON, Gnr, Ronald Charles Frederick, 996218
HART, Bdr, Stanley Frederick, 925369
HART, Bdr, James William, 962453
HART, Gnr, Leslie John, 996276
HARVEY, Sjt, George Arthur, 1425795
HEDGES, Gnr, Bernard Frederick Russell, 917289
HEPPENSTALL, Gnr, Harold, 941935
HEWARD, Gnr, Harry, 996278
HICKMAN, Gnr, Ernest, 941936
HILLMAN, Gnr, William Major, 892417
HOLT, Gnr, John William Ambrose, 1104277
HORN, Gnr, John Arthur, 918247
HORNE, L/Sjt, Donald Edwin, 873278
HORNE, L/Sjt, Dennis Alfred, 917317
HUCKLEBRIDGE, L/Sjt, Frank Haworth, 858909
HUGHES, Gnr, Hugh Frederick, 1123342
HUGHES, Gnr, Robert William John, 1104278
HUMFREY, Gnr, Robert Alfred, 917355
HUMPHRYS, Gnr, Stanley, 996282
HUNT, Gnr, John Gordon, 1108425
HUNT, Bqms, Arthur George, 924158
HYDE, Bdr, Roland Charles, 862144
ISAACS, Gnr, William Henry, 864027

JOHNSON, Gnr, George Sidney, 1094232
KEARNEY, Gnr, Edward, 915521
KEEBLE, Gnr, Harold Ivan, 1088802
LAMB, Gnr, Cyril Edward, 855583
LOFT, Sjt, Albert Arthur, 917291
MACLURE, Gnr, George Richard, 911711
MAJOR, Gnr, George James, 955904
MARTIN, Gnr, Pat William, 1119581
MASON, Gnr, Ronald, 943509
McALLISTER, Gnr, James, 3185975
McCANN, Bdr, James John, 1054050
McCLEARY, Gnr, Albert, 996224
McCRACKEN, L/Bdr, James, 900897
MERRY, Maj, William Haslam, 35984
METCALF, Gnr, Robert, 1110423
MILES, Bdr, Arthur George, 1032404
MILLER, Gnr, Ian Campbell, 1096709
MILLWARD, Gnr, Francis Edward, 1123164
MISSENDEN, Gnr, Norman Mayo, 923006
MOORE, Gnr, Alfred Kenneth Sedgwick, 996327
MOORE, Gnr, Daykin, 996226
MORRIS, Gnr, John Saph, 1103604
MOULD, Gnr, John Thomas, 904034
MULLETT, L/Bdr, Sidney David, 941945
MUSGROVE, Gnr, Joseph, 923004
MUSK, Gnr, George Arthur William, 996229
NEVILLE, Sjt, Philip Alfred, 916735
NEWSTEAD, Gnr, John Kenneth, 996230
NORMAN, Gnr, William Ford, 956440
NORMAN, Gnr, Norman Royston, 985402
NORTON, Gnr, Joseph Michael, 996231
O'ROURKE, Sjt, Herbert, 864809
OWEN, Gnr, Brinley, 925383
PAGE, Gnr, Sidney Lewis, 869451
PAGET, L/Bdr, Thomas Leslie, 948857
PALMER, L/Sjt, Leslie Herbert Joseph, 1065467
PAYNE, Bdr, Irving William, 900898
PEARSON, Gnr, Walter Leonard, 913799
PENRICE, Gnr, George, 1115990
PETTY, Gnr, Harry, 1090817
PHILLIPS, Gnr, Bernard Power, 1087687
POLLARD, Gnr, Lewlie Arthur, 927417
PRICE, Capt, Henry Antony, 99375
PROCTOR, Gnr, James Arthur Edwin, 918243
PURCELL, Gnr, Percy Chandos, 1088810
QUINCE, Gnr, Edward William, 916679
RANDALL, Gnr, Edward George, 1088446
RAYNER, L/Bdr, Eric George, 941951
READ, Gnr, Frederick George, 900693
REDFERN, Gnr, Eric, 1113706
RICK, L/Sjt, Pery Edward, 962455
ROBINSON, Gnr, Herbert Alfred, 962441
ROCK, Gnr, Dennis Graham, 1116363
ROGGERS, Gnr, Gilbert, 922105
ROSS, Gnr, William Edward, 1096549
ROUY, Gnr, Felix Patrick, 1119587
SAVILLE, Gnr, Ernest, 913740
SCALES, Gnr, Henry Percy, 924167
SHAW, Bdr, Frederick John, 941954
SHEWARD, Gnr, Henry, 1104295
SIMMONDS, Bdr, Willis, 921527
SIMPSON, Bdr, Samuel William, 1425561
SLATER, L/Sjt, Raymond Gordon, 903891
SLIMMON, Gnr, David Locherbie, 991759
SMART, Gnr, Walter, 1083922
SMART, Bdr, Harold Alfred Stephen, 894928
SMITH, Gnr, David Paul, 925387
SMITH, Sjt, Patrick Clare, 1056061
SMITH, Bdr, John Thomas, 1055553
SOUTHGATE, Gnr, Bernard Philip, 1088456

SPARY, Gnr, Albert Arthur Mons, 2031600
STEVENSON, Sjt, Kenneth Edmund, 877697
STOTEN, Gnr, Desmond Arthur Henry, 925386
STUART, Gnr, Cecil Herbert, 948867
TARRY, Gnr, Reginald, 921531
TENNANT, Gnr, Andrew, 991620
THOMPSON, Gnr, John, 890929
TITE, Gnr, Jeffery, 956443
TOYER, Gnr, George Frederick, 924354
TOYER, L/Bdr, Ronald, 903805
TURNER, Sjt, Harry Boyd, 948851
TURVEY, Gnr, Frederick George, 885194
WALKER, Gnr, George, 1103049
WALTON, L/Bdr, Norton, 943448
WEBB, Gnr, Rhys, 1123354
WEBBER, Bdr, John Henry, 1087721
WELHAM, L/Bdr, Robert William Charles, 923013
WELLS, L/Bdr, William Henry, 873318
WENZERUL, Gnr, Edward, 962443
WHEATLEY, L/Bdr, Richard James Henry, 917851
WHITE, Bdr, Frederick Charles, 873280
WHITE, Bsm, Francis John, 1669584
WHITE, Gnr, Eric Charles, 917852
WHITEHEAD, Gnr, Roy, 4983015
WHYTE, Gnr, Thomas Anderson, 991819
WILDMAN, Sjt, Wilfred, 825927
WILLIAMS, Gnr, Harry, 962468
WILLIAMS, L/Bdr, Harold Trevor, 923011
WILLIAMS, Gnr, Arthur, 1094359
WILSON, Gnr, Arthur George, 948850
WOOD, Gnr, Kenneth Albert William, 901388
WOOD, Gnr, James, 935940
WORMALD, Gnr, Walter, 1090016
WRAY, Gnr, Edward, 923008

149 FR
JACKSON,Gnr,James Woodruff,993691

155 FR
ANDERSON, Capt, Michale Lewin, 129328
ANNISS, Bdr, Fredeick Arthur, 942866
ASKEW, L/bdr, Harold, 974739
BAILEY, Gnr, Henry Alfred, 919354
BARNES, Gnr, Ernest, 942756
BARNES, L/Sjt, Edward Frederick, 954912
BARTLETT, Bqms, Alfred Charles, 740690
BENNETT, Bdr, George John Edward, 929697
BILLINGS, Bsm, Francis John, 1423985
BYERS, Gnr, William James Johnstone, 325657
CADDELL, Gnr, David, 977280
CALLAN, Gnr, Ronald, 977218
CARROLL, Gnr, John Joseph, 318003
CAVERS, Bdr, Alexander Sutherland Lawson, 326263
CHRISTIE, Gnr, Alexander Hunter, 325669
COLES, Capt, Guy Roger, 146967
CRAWFORD, Gnr, Thomas, 1105160
CUNNINGHAM, Gnr, William, 977313
CUTHBERTSON, L/bdr, Samuel, 309572
DONNELLY, Gnr, Thomas Francis, 317907
EDEL, L/bdr, Bernard, 934634
EDGAR, Gnr, Thomas, 1075337
EMERY, Gnr, Thomas Alfred, 854813
EUSTACE, Capt, Maurice James Reginald, 118417
EVANS, Bdr, John Henry, 915076
FLINT, Bdr, George Victor, 950227
FORSTER, Cpt, Alfred Donald, 91544
GRAHAM, Gnr, George Mcintosh, 977348
GREIG, Gnr, John, 977355
GRIERSON, Gnr, William John, 322020
HAL, L/bdr, Maurice Waldon, 936272

HALIFAX, Sjt, John, 318264
HENDRY, Gnr, John, 977232
HOSKINS, Gnr, Fred, 950242
JAMES, Gnr, John Wilfred, 963195
JOHNSON, Gnr, Edward, 961098
LOGAN, Gnr, Robert, 977233
MURDOCH, Lt Col, Alan Td, 25586
PARKER, S/Sjt, John James, 1069558
PATERSON, Gnr, John Mcelroy, 1105136
PENNINGTON, Bdr, Robert Cyril, 802800
QUERTIER, Gnr, Albert George, 930602
SCOTT, Gnr, Ian, 326279
SHUN, Gnr, Charles William Alfred, 963487
SINCLAIR, Bdr, Thomas Andrews Stewart, 977210
STEWARD, Gnr, Ernest, 953819
STREET, Gnr, Alfred Charles, 880103
TADMAN, L/bdr, Thomas William, 963490
TAYLOR, Gnr, George, 942188
VANSTONE, Gnr, Richard Henry, 996455
WAIN, Gnr, Frederick, 953823
WEBSTER, Gnr, Edgar, 4687344
WILSON, Maj, John, 42299
WINSLOW, L/bdr, Walter, 960021
WYNNE, Lt, Jack Garstang, 164312

178 FR
COMBER,Gnr,Dennis Charles,14710014
DANCE,Gnr,Eric Lawrence,1134123

1 H AA
ALDRIDGE, L/Bdr, Bertram Charles Frederick, 988440
ARMITAGE, Gnr, William Samuel, 984218
ASTLEY, Gnr, Sidney, 1732865
BAILEY, Capt, Charles Henry, 75673
BOTTLE, Bqms, Arthur George Victor, 1007380
BROTTEN, Gnr, John George, 1781666
BROWN, Sjt, John Frederick, 833673
BSTIN, Gnr, Donald Frederick, 1784395
BURROWS, Bqms, Earnest John, 840419
CHELLINGSWORTH, Sjt, James Kenneth, 1437803
CHEYNE, Bdr, George, 825715
CLOSE, Lt, John Christopher (MC), 74503
COLLINGS, Bdr, Cecil, 1493197
COLQUHOUN,Bqms,Thomas,1017570
CONROY, Gnr, Charles, 1781633
COXALL, L/Bdr, Cyril Frank, 1784139
CREGEEN, Bdr, Winston, 1474744
CROLL, L/Sjt, James Cargill, 1063870
CROOK, Gnr, Jack, 993287
DARLEY, Gnr, Frank, 1781644
DAVIDSON, Lt, John Duncan, 76552
DAVIES, Gnr, Sylvester, 1778094
DAVIES, L/Bdr, David Durand, 1530007
DAWSON, Gnr, Charles James, 1590367
DEWSNAP, Gnr, Sidney Wardle, 1780200
DIXON, Lt, John Neville, 145938
ENGLAND, Bdr, Jack, 812557
EVANS, Lt, Rupert Edgar, 102875
FERGUSON, Gnr, James, 1542871
FINCH, Lt, Peter Terence Trimmer, 76355
FOSTER, Gnr, Harry, 1778624
GARDNER, Gnr, Albert Edward John, 1470503
GEMMELL, Lt, Richard Francis, 109917
GRIBBLE, Lt, Herbert William, 180950
GRIFFITH, Lt, Hugh Stanley Lemon, 165304
HAWKS, Maj, George Ronald Langford (MC), 34454
HEWITT, Lt, David Edward, 186652
HINTON, Bdr, Donald, 1440018
HORNE, Bdr, John Patrick, 4199389
HOULTON, Lt, John Charles Freeman, 194457

HOY, Gnr, Harold Stanley, 978260
HUGHES, Gnr, Thomas James, 851158
HUNTER, Maj, Charles Reginald George Whish, 53256
HUTCHINSON, Bdr, William, 872644
JENKINS, Lt, Samuel Morley, 155418
JERMYN, Lt, Peter, 73050
JOHNSON, Lt, Guy Herbert, 172664
JOHNSON, Bdr, Charles George, 866439
LANSLEY, L/Sjt, Philip Edwin, 1071766
MARTIN, Lt QM, Oriel Alfred Augustus, 157127
MASLEN, Lt, John Nicholas Eaden, 138385
MATHESON, Gnr, Kenneth, 1750774
McNAB, Gnr, Joseph, 1474227
MEAD, Bdr, Andrew, 793857
MILLER, Bdr, Donald Frank, 1460158
MOON, Gnr, Valentine Henry, 1756775
NEILL, Lt, Eric, 201704
NOON, Lt, John, 86082
NORRIS, Lt, Benjamin Robert Herbert, 89591
NURSE, Gnr, Thomas William, 1573184
PRETLOVE, Bqms, Thomas James, 794455
REAH, Bdr, Thomas Albert, 869131
REYNOLDS, Sjt, Herbert, 1546558
RICHARDS, Lt, Cyril Corbett, 169546
ROBERTS, Bdr, Harry, 850953
RUSHMER, Sjt, George, 776315
RUTHERFORD, Bqms, Alfred William, 1487732
SALMON, Lt, Peter John, 214688
SAMPSON, Gnr, John Alfred, 934927
SANDIFORD, Bdr, Joseph, 3446184
SCULLY, Gnr, Norbert Hugh, 1470559
SIMPSON, Gnr, W., 878848
SKELDON, Gnr, Harry Edwin, 1779839
SMART, Gnr, Roy Hugh, 1602965
STEPHENSON, Gnr, William George, 1783344
SWINGLER, Gnr, John Edward, 1089482
TAYLOR, Gnr, Harry James, 1707573
TILLMAN, Bdr, William, 1478100
TOTHAM, Sjt, Bernard Arthur, 1476644
TOWNSEND, BSM, William Charles, 1475655
TUCK, Sjt, John Friend, 811470
WALTER, Lt, Barrie Bleasdale, 201702
WELBOURN, L/Bdr, James Henry, 1427117
WELLER, Gnr, Edward, 1780636
WILBY, Gnr, Leonard William, 981003
WILCOCKSON, Gnr, Leslie Herbert, 1771041
WILSON, Gnr, William Rowe, 1721238
WIMPENNY, Gnr, Vivian Harold, 4394979
YOUNG, 2/Lt, John Denis, 190136

2 H AA
BEDFORD, Lt, James Wilson, 148084
BENN, L/Bdr, Stephen Thomas, 1727393
BENNETT, Lt, William Frank, 194408
BENNETT, Sjt, Robert Henry, 6895053
CAPPER, Gnr, Harry, 1779885
COLEBY, Lt QM, Albert Edward, 191983
COX, Gnr, Richard Charles, 1603286
FRAGLE, Gnr, Ather, 5038611
GIBSON, Lt, Michael Charles, 186637
GLASBY, Sjt, Fred William, 819287
GOLD, Bdr, Charles Holt, 1467981
GREENWOOD, Maj, Frank, 63693
HILL, Lt, Brian O'neill, 172635
MARTIN, Gnr, Walter, 6975341
OSCROFT, Sjt, Ronald, 1427074
PALK, T, Patrick Brian Ussher, 194502
PHILLIPS, Gnr, Cyril Graham, 318355
PICKFORD, Capt, Joseph, 78282
PORTEUS, Gnr, Wilfred George, 4684717

REES, Bdr, John Haydn, 1485821
REES, Gnr, Benjamin Davies, 1605252
RIGBY, Bqms, Arthur Thomas, 1424286
ROERTSON, Lt, David Ronald, 158708
ROWLANDS, Gnr, Albert Owen, 3716111
SMITH, Sjt, James Crickton, 845159
SMITH, Lt, Geoffrey Ernest Marcel, 158730
THOMAS, Gnr, David, 1703236
WIEBKIN, Lt, Peter Murrey John, 190126
WOODHEAD, Lt, Robert George, 186368

3 H AA
ABBOTT, L/Bdr, John Thomas, 872656
ANDREW, Lt, Lionel Derek Mc, 151926
ARNOLD, Gnr, Owen Orlando, 1427477
ATKINSON, Gnr, Thomas, 1603414
ATKINSON, Gnr, Fred, 1603413
BAGGETT, RSM, Isaac Thomas, 1421287
BAIGENT, L/Bdr, Michael George Wiliam, 1445376
BAILEY, Maj, John Evans, 47825
BAKER, L/Bdr, William George Albert, 821899
BALL, Gnr, George Lloyd, 1427147
BANNISTER, Gnr, Howard, 1815388
BARNES, Gnr, Frederick, 872686
BARNEY, 2/Lt, Frank Douglas, 165296
BARNWELL, Gnr, Charles Haynes, 1810440
BAXTER, Bdr, Harold, 846287
BAXTER, Bdr, George Charles, 856628
BEDWORTH, L/Bdr, George, 3187909
BEEDIE, Gnr, David, 872710
BELT, Sjt, Robert William, 840011
BENEY, Gnr, Ronald John, 1605137
BENFORD, Capt, M Edward Charles Frederick, 113940
BENSON, Gnr, John Robert, 4388135
BENSON, Gnr, William John, 860364
BISHOP, Gnr, Stanley Wilfred, 1427573
BLAKE, Gnr, Frederick, 1605319
BLOOR, Gnr, Wilfred Alwyn, 818124
BLYTHE, Gnr, Eric, 1499959
BOULDING, Bdr, Geoffrey Castledene, 1550481
BOWERING, Gnr, Alfred John, 1547967
BOYES, Gnr, Wilfred Hadyn, 903147
BRIDGES, Sjt, Alfred Edward, 4385140
BROWN, Gnr, William John, 1605228
BROWN, Gnr, Walter Henry, 1603130
BURGE, Bdr, Sydney Frederick, 1543915
BURKE, Sjt, Richard, 872441
CASSIDY, Gnr, Benjamin, 1427376
CHAPMAN, L/Bdr, George, 4746643
CLARK, Bdr, Arthur James, 841371
CLEMENTS, Gnr, Thomas Herbert, 1811400
COBB, Gnr, William, 1811401
COMBER, Gnr, Ronald Arthur, 1603284
COOK, Gnr, Lister, 1603234
COOK, L/Sjt, John, 2925623
COOKE, Gnr, Arthur Lennard, 868600
COTTRELL, Gnr, Walter Edward Guy, 872109
COUSINS, Gnr, John, 872033
CREEDON, Gnr, Dennis Kitchener, 1603346
CROSSE, Gnr, John, 872149
CROWDER, Bdr, William Edwin, 851135
CROWHURST, Gnr, Henry William, 4029649
CURTIS, Lt, Ronald Henry, 19059
AVIES, Gnr, Simon, 1605287 DAVIES,
Sjt, Frank William, 842915
DAY, Gnr, Walter, 850190
DEAN, Gnr, Ronald Leslie, 872464
DENNIS, Gnr, Henry, 1729073
DONACHIE, Gnr, Eric Crawford, 854663
DOYLE, Gnr, Patrick, 1438699

DRAPER, Gnr, Walter, 1603241
DUNBAR, Bdr, Harold, 1426798
EVANS, Bdr, Edward Hugh, 1489085
FLANDERS, Gnr, John, 1427402
FORD, Gnr, Tom, 1604942
FOWLER, Sjt, John Bain Mckay, 850544
FRANCIS, Gnr, Ronald Lewis, 1605293
FRY, Gnr, Alfred Thomas, 872036
GALISTAN, Gnr, Edgar, 1470518
GARDNER, Gnr, Ralph Deane, 812832
GASPER, Gnr, George Edgar, 1460543
GEORGE, Sjt, Arthur Harrington, 812331
GIBBONS, Gnr, Thomas, 872326
GILL, Gnr, James Stewart, 1603431
GIRLING, Gnr, Harry Edwin, 483899
GLEASON, Gnr, George Henry, 872440
GOODBURN, L/Bdr, George, 1603033
GOODE, Gnr, Edward Walter, 1811439
GOODWIN, Bdr, Arthur Ridley, 850249
GRANGE, Gnr, Alfred Henry, 847799
GRAY, Gnr, John William, 1470548
GRAY, Gnr, Alexander Mclachlan, 847366
GRAYSON, Gnr, Kenneth, 856742
GREEN, Gnr, Walter, 1805863
GREGORY, Bdr, Frederick William, 827092
GRIFFITHS, Gnr, John Charles, 1605295
HADDEN, Gnr, Norman, 1470595
HAMMOND, Gnr, James Percival, 1780531
HAMP, Capt, Patrick Thomas (MC), 73783
HAMPTON, Bdr, James Walter George, 1603304
HARGREAVES, Maj, Frank, 51851
HARRIS, Gnr, Thomas Henry, 1603436
HARTAS, L/Bdr, Harry, 816546
HASLAM, Gnr, Charles, 842151
HAWTHORN, Sjt, Robert Henry, 6911263
HAYES, Gnr, John Francis, 939216
HENSHAW, Gnr, Roland, 1426827
HILL, Gnr, Leanord Cooper, 1811457
HOBLEY, Gnr, Arthur Goodwin, 1427028
HOLLAWAY, Gnr, Ernest H, 1810535
HOOLEY, Gnr, Wilfred Stanley, 1811460
HORLOCK, Gnr, Walter John, 845191
HOWELL, Gnr, George Harry, 1427716
HUGHES, Gnr, Harold Henry, 1810546
HUMPHREYS, Gnr, Peter, 1426945
HUNTINGTON, Lt, Nigel John Saranoke, 180966
HURST, L/Bdr, Ernest, 1603445
HUTCHINS, Lt, Donald Jack, 179236
IRVING, Bdr, James Blackie, 856745
IRWIN, Gnr, Johnston, 7009917
JACKMAN, Gnr, George Patrick, 1603147
JENKINS, Bdr, Isaac John, 1605211
JERVIS, Gnr, Leonard Vincent, 1603260
JOHNSON, Gnr, Ernest, 1427736
JONES, Gnr, Ernest, 1488641
JONES, L/Bdr, Richard Treharne, 1605217
KILNER, Gnr, Frederick, 1811096
KING, 2/Lt, Leslie John, 158644
LAW, L/Bdr, Joseph, 1427225
LEWIN, Gnr, Charles Leonard Needham, 1630925
LILLEY, Bdr, John Gilbert, 1603339
LOCKE, Gnr, Samuel, 850367
MAGEEAN, Gnr, Patrick, 872609
MALPASS, Gnr, Ernest, 1781178
MARRS, Bdr, Joseph, 851195
MARSH, Gnr, Robert, 814089
MASON, Gnr, James, 872568
MATTHIEW, Gnr, Kenneth Leicester, 1470521
McCORMICK, L/Sjt, Robert Thompson, 850373
McKEE, Gnr, Ralph Albert, 5497805

MEREDITH, Gnr, Emrys George, 1605170
MICKLETHWAIT, Gnr, William Reginald, 973860
MILLINGTON, Gnr, William, 1470513
MILNE, Gnr, George Sutherland, 1603098
MILSOM, Gnr, Stanley Thomas, 845947
MOLES, Gnr, Arthur Leonard, 1810608
MONAGHAN, Gnr, Joseph, 1810617
MONK, Gnr, Frederick James, 845475
MOORE, Gnr, Harry, 872705
MOORE, Gnr, Arthur, 1811487
MORGAN, Gnr, Edward Lewis, 1605307
MORRIS, Gnr, Ernest John, 1427316
MORRISON, Bdr, William, 1427308
MORTIMER, Gnr, Harry, 1427059
MOUNT, Gnr, John Thomas, 872697
MOXON, Gnr, Harry Raymond, 869224
MRRRIMAN, Gnr, Francis, 872010
MUSSON, Gnr, Rowland, 1693272
NEWMAN, Gnr, George Henry, 1427091
NIXON, L/Bdr, William Robson, 872557
NOBLE, Gnr, John Robert, 868014
O'CALLAGHAN, Bdr, Peter Eric, 860066
OLIVEIRO, Gnr, Raymond Godfrey, 1470526
PADDISON, Bdr, Alfred, 851012
PAGE, Gnr, Samuel Bernard, 1605033
PAGET, Gnr, Harold John, 1810657
PARRY, Gnr, Victor Charles, 1605180
PHILLIPS, Gnr, Frank, 1470529
PHILLIPS, L/Bdr, Reginald, 872063
PINDER, Gnr, Robert Vincent, 1602854
POTTER, Gnr, Ernest Henry, 845249
POWELL, Gnr, Ivor Thomas, 1605186
POWER, Gnr, John, 3660113
PRATT, Gnr, John, 1603102
RAMPTON, Sjt, Wilfred Charles MM, 835643
RAMSEY, Bdr, Thomas, 850364
RATCLIFFE, Gnr, James, 1810665
RAY, Gnr, William George David, 872288
REARDON, Gnr, Timothy, 1605304
REAY, Gnr, Edward, 1810672
RIBBENS, Gnr, Arthur, 1426697
RICHARDS, Gnr, Ivor, 838130
ROBERTS, Sjt, Wilfred John Henry, 820369
ROBINSON, Sjt, John Kenneth, 791870
ROBINSON, Gnr, William Lelsie, 1427118
ROBINSON, Gnr, James, 872689
ROCKLIFFE, Gnr, Charles Beresford, 3385671
ROGERS, Gnr, Dennis Stanley Freeman, 1779033
ROLLINGS, Gnr, Albert Ernest, 850113
ROSS, Gnr, Arthur Leonard, 872662
RUNNALS, Gnr, Reginald John, 1810661
SAYE, Gnr, Charles Leonard, 853146
SAYERS, Gnr, Roland William, 1603469
SCALES, Gnr, Harry, 1605357
SCARTH, Gnr, John, 1810694
SCOVELL, Gnr, Benjamin George, 1810687
SELLARS, Gnr, Robert, 1601873
SHACKLETON, Bdr, Arthur, 1427449
SHANKLIN, Gnr, Henry, 1427444
SHELTON, Gnr, Gerald Owen, 1811531
SHORT, Gnr, Alan Richard, 1602962
SIMPSON, L/Bdr, Robert Strachen, 834752
SIMPSON, Sjt, Joseph, 872524
SINEY, Gnr, Alfred Thomas, 1508000
SMITH, Gnr, George Abner, 809555
SMITH, Bdr, Frederick Stanley, 856749
SMITH, Gnr, Donald Richard, 1603305
SMITH, Gnr, John Edward, 1605066
SMITH, Gnr, Herbert, 872683
SOAR, Lt, William Godfrey, 148038

SOUTH, Bdr, Arthur Alexander, 1737511
SPENCE, L/Bdr, Henry Richard, 1426744
SPRASON, Gnr, Leslie Clarence, 1605374
STEEL, Gnr, Arthur, 872598
STEPHENS, Gnr, Howard, 872458
STRICKLAND, Gnr, Terence George, 1470558
SUTTON, Gnr, William H, 5378004
TAYLOR, Gnr, Raymond, 843092
TAYLOR, Bdr, Albert, 872517
TAYLOR KANE, Gnr, Frank, 2050213
THOMAS, Sjt, Vernon, 845049
THOMSON, Gnr, James, 1427362
THORPE, Gnr, Ronald, 1603322
THURLING, Gnr, Ronald Arthur, 911598
THURSTON, Gnr, Charles Joseph, 1067343
TUNNICLIFF, Gnr, Cyril Randolph, 1806028
VALENTINE, Gnr, Christopher, 842629
VANDERBECK, Gnr, Maurice William, 1470553
WADSLEY, Gnr, William, 1603326
WALKER, L/Bdr, Henry Watson, 3050675
WALLACE, Gnr, John Norrie, 1427447
WALLEY, Gnr, Ernest Leonard, 1470568
WARD, Gnr, George, 853631
WARD, L/Bdr, John, 1427381
WARD, Gnr, Frank, 2055505
WATSON, Bqms, William Edward, 1068850
WATT, Bdr, William, 845380
WEAVER, Gnr, Raymond Charles, 5108253
WEAVERS, L/Bdr, Jack Veri, 872632
WEINMAN, L/Bdr, Wiliam, 872349
WETHERILT, Gnr, Frederick Louis, 1603211
WILKINSON, Gnr, Robbie, 4534555
WILLIAMS, Gnr, Walter, 1426894
WILLIAMS, Gnr, A J, 147545
WILLIAMS, Gnr, Griffith, 1603382
WILSON, Gnr, Ronald George, 1427428
WILSON, Bdr, George, 850149
WINTER, Sjt, Eric, 1441494
WITHYCOMBE, Gnr, Basil Frederick, 851705
YORK, L/Bdr, Herbert Arthur, 859180

5 H AA
BALL, Gnr, Leonard Walton, 1490617
BANKS, L/Sjt, William, 779082
BARRACLOUGH, Bdr, Leslie Charles, 825468
BENTLEY, Sjt, Sydney Maurice, 2039618
CAMPBELL, Gnr, Thomas Reynolds, 872768
CLARKE, Bdr, Stanley Reginald, 838446
DAVIES, Bdr, Eli Robert, 842976
EVANS, L/Bdr, David Daniel, 918830
FRANKLIN, L/Sjt, John Henry, 863711
GRIEVE, L/Bdr, John, 1708010
GRINT, Gnr, William Henry, 4532721
HARNESS, Gnr, Thomas Edward, 838377
HARRINGTON, Gnr, Robert, 1426857
KILGORE, Gnr, John, 872531
KING, Gnr, Frank Gordon, 842287
KYLE, Gnr, Hubert, 833155
LAVIS, L/Sjt, Arthur George, 1422526
LING, Gnr, Kenneth Robert, 1426671
MORGAN, Sjt, Wilfred, 1049726
OWENS, L/Bdr, Ernest A Maldwyn, 840444
PHILLIPS, Gnr, John, 1414646
REID, Gnr, Mark Thomas Anderson, 1502328
SARGENT, Sjt, William Horace George, 824892
STARCK, Gnr, Charles Roy, 840312
THOMPSON, Gnr, Charles, 1438819
WHEELER, L/Bdr, Harry, 5569552
WOOD, L/Sjt, Frank, 845902

6 H AA
ADAMS, Gnr, George, 815241
ALLISON, Gnr, John, 1460879
AMES, Gnr, Harry, 865453
AMIES, L/Bdr, Sidney George, 1063331
ANSTEE, Gnr, William Edward, 820116
ARMISTEAD, Gnr, Alex Martin, 1073966
ASHTON, Gnr, Frederick John, 777423
AYRES, Gnr, Leonard, 1726195
BACKWAY, Gnr, Percy William, 1426424
BAKER, L/Sjt, William, 812965
BALL, Gnr, Kenneth Stanley, 1817008
BANKS, Gnr, Walter, 1427472
BARBER, Gnr, John Henry, 55914
BAREHAM, Gnr, Harry Walter, 1764021
BARKER, Gnr, George Frederick, 1817009
BARLOW, Gnr, Henry, 3857636
BARMBY, Gnr, Wilfred, 842520
BARNARD, L/Sjt, Harry Reginald, 819377
BARNBROOK, Gnr, Albert Reginald, 230114
BARTON, Gnr, Francis, 1695561
BARTON, Gnr, George Frederick Thomas, 1748708
BAXTER, Bdr, Hugh, 786193
BEARD, Gnr, James William, 1793880
BELSHAW, Gnr, John Reginald, 1568459
BENNETT, Gnr, John, 809160
BERRY, Gnr, Dare, 1580612
BESSANT, Gnr, Thomas Edmund, 781554
BILBIE, Gnr, Samuel, 1808154
BISHOP, L/Sjt, William Arthur, 845539
BLAKEY, Gnr, Frederick William Thomas, 2049365
BOYLE, Gnr, Thomas, 790912
BRANDON, Gnr, Sidney Charles, 1426949
BRAY, Bqms, Arthur John, 790513
BRIDGES, Gnr, Walter Henry, 822282
BROGDEN, Bdr, William, 1073124
BUCK, Gnr, Benjamin Robert, 1427327
BURDETT, Gnr, Harry, 1502840
BURNS, Gnr, Walter Robert, 791869
BUROWS, Gnr, Percy Wilfred, 4968035
BURTON, Gnr, Ernest, 1805836
CARD, Gnr, William Frederick, 1646045
CARR, Gnr, Frank, 1676375
CARTER, Gnr, Frank Ernest, 1696381
CASEY, Gnr, James, 1569577
CHARLES, Gnr, John, 1472376
CHORLEY, Gnr, Wilfred, 1569040
CLARKE, Gnr, Alfred, 1818221
CLARKE, Gnr, William, 402224
COLEMAN, Gnr, John Joseph, 847816
COLHOUN, Gnr, Richard Campbell, 819047
COLLINS, Gnr, Albert James, 1747978
CONQUEST, Gnr, Bertram Edward, 1502871
COOK, Gnr, Thomas Joseph, 1600635
COOLEY, Gnr, Frank, 847924
COPELAND, Gnr, Herbert Lawrence, 1760369
CORLETT, Gnr, Percy, 1524187
COTTERILL, Bqms, Harry, 1018483
CRUTCHLOW, Gnr, Noah, 1502883
CUNNINGHAM, Gnr, Kenneth Gordon, 822663
DAVIES, Gnr, Charles Albert Calvert, 1618576
DAVIS, S/Sjt, John Westacott, 1467515
DEACON, Gnr, George Arthur, 1426634
DEEPROSE, Gnr, Reginald Alfred, 1797526
DEW, Gnr, John Walter, 1789479
DIXON, L/Bdr, William George, 1425594
DOBBINS, Gnr, Alfred Edward, 1817065
DORRICOTT, Gnr, Jonathan, 1811148
DOUGHERTY, Sjt, Jeffrey, 779231
DOWNEND, Gnr, Frank, 1427173

DWYNE, Gnr, Eric, 1725591
EDWARDS, Gnr, Harry Dudley, 797196
ELLIS, Gnr, George, 1063502
ELLIS, Gnr, James, 1818009
EVANS, Gnr, William Ernest, 1719549
EVANS, Gnr, William John, 1817086
EVANS, Gnr, Evan Gwyn, 1818014
FAIRFAX, Bdr, William, 545131
FEATHERSTONE, Gnr, Albert Edward, 824772
FENNEY, Gnr, George Nicholas, 4387270
FIELD, Gnr, Frank Eric, 824967
FISHER, Gnr, Frank, 3529020
FORD, Gnr, Joseph, 1065862
FORREST, Gnr, Arthur Stanley, 1738779
FORSTER, Gnr, Richard Ernest Albert, 918100
FOSTER, L/Bdr, Oscar, 797474
FOULKES, Sjt, Kenneth, 828643
FOULKES, Gnr, George Valentine, 816887
FRANCIS, Gnr, George, 1580883
FROSTICK, L/Bdr, Ernest, 1525610
FROWEN, Gnr, William George, 1818240
FRY, Gnr, William Henry, 1811648
FRYER, Gnr, Harry, 822003
GALLOWAY, Maj, James Buchanan, 64137
GARDNER, Gnr, Thomas, 4447406
ARDNER, Gnr, Leonard Victor, 6345522
GILBY, Lt, Edwin (MC), 105870
GILLINGHAM, Gnr, Allan George, 1757759
GINGELL, Gnr, Christopher Sydney, 1714916
GINN, Gnr, Henry Robert, 1414579
GLEED, Gnr, Raymond Oswald Edwin, 1746900
GORE, Gnr, Albert Edward, 1817395
GRAYSTONE, Sjt, Thomas James, 1426503
GRIFFITHS, Gnr, Farnham, 1817097
GRIFFITHS, Gnr, William Samuel, 1817099
GUDGE, Gnr, Richard Alfred, 1427473
HALL, Gnr, Arthur William, 1725610
HALLIDAY, Gnr, Harold Mcdonald, 4190999
HAND, Gnr, George, 863337
HANRAHAN, Gnr, James, 847469
HANSON, L/Bdr, John MM, 847784
HARRIS, Gnr, Walter Thomas Ralph, 5722449
HARRIS, Gnr, Raymond John, 1811608
HARRIS, Gnr, Henry John, 1697911
HARRISON, L/Bdr, Sydney Samuel, 1793693
HATTER, Sjt, Walter Allwood, 781576
HAWTIN, Gnr, George, 822186
HEANAN, Gnr, John, 1609683
HERD, Sjt, William John, 1073490
HERLEY, Gnr, James Michael, 1746331
HERRING, Gnr, Horace John, 822309
HIBBERT, Bdr, Wiliam, 8162149
HIGGINSON, Gnr, Thomas Henry, 860867
HILES, Gnr, William Richard, 1717110
HILL, Gnr, Sidney George, 1643289
HILL, Arm Sjt, Harry, 7629627
HINSLEA, Bdr, Frederick Richard, 1467422
HOLLINGWORTH, Gnr, David Arthur, 1428422
HOLMES, Gnr, Charles Thomas, 1720230
HOOPER, Gnr, Eric, 2051781
HORN, Gnr, Jack, 1569303
HORNE, Gnr, Alfred Bishop, 895020
HOWARD, Gnr, William, 872438
HUGHES, Gnr, Ernest, 1817114
HUNTER, Gnr, John Edward, 1426245
HUNTER, Sjt, James, 835260
HUNTER, Gnr, William, 1427112
HURIDGE, Gnr, Harry, 1427260
IRVING, Gn, Robert, 868788
JACOBS, Gnr, Thomas Henry, 1580786

JAMES, Gnr, Glyn, 1817116
JAMES, Gnr, Samuel Edward, 1065758
JENKINSON, Bdr, Thomas, 1073904
JOHNSON, Bdr, Frederick, 5044523
JOHNSON, Gnr, Albert, 3855392
JONES, Gnr, Norman, 1427229
JONES, Gnr, William John, 1817140
JORDON, Bdr, George Jordon, 1426161
KENT, Sjt, George Harry, 1066216
LEDGER, Gnr, Charles, 4120319
LETCH, Gnr, Alfred Edwin, 2208787
LEWINGTON, Gnr, Arthur Frederick John, 5490611
LEWIS, Gnr, William Thomas, 1817274
LLOYD, Gnr, Charles Roger, 1817153
LOMAS, Gnr, Walter, 4527180
MACDONALD, Bdr, James Alfred William, 982792
MATTHEWS, Gnr, John James, 1528640
McCALLUM, Lt, Malcolm, 156926
McCLUSKY, Gnr, John, 797650
McDONALD, Gnr, Thomas, 1738087
McDONALD, Sjt, Duncan, 835854
McLATCHIE, Gnr, Hugh Boyd, 1774707
McLELLAN, Gnr, William Charles, 1779537
McVEY, Gnr, William John, 1713742
MEADOWS, Gnr, James, 3856946
MELLOR, Gnr, Harold, 1072709
MERCR, Gnr, Frederick William, 1696515
MICHELL, Gnr, Arthur Albert, 1643445
MINTON, Gnr, Robert, 1530175
MONTEITH, Sjt, Hugh, 7642594
MOODY, Gnr, Thomas Walter, 794542
MORGAN, Bdr, William Cecil, 809651
MORTON, Gnr, Robert, 1073072
MOSS, Gnr, Ronald Arthur, 1766373
MURPHY, Gnr, James Edward, 1537327
MURPHY, Gnr, James, 826416
NAUGHTON, Gnr, Henry, 868364
NEVILL, Gnr, John Louis, 1475012
NICHOLLS, Gnr, Thomas William, 1580671
NICKOLAY, Gnr, George Arthur William, 1817324
NUTTY, Gnr, Edward, 11053546
O'SHAUGHNESSY, Gnr, Francis, 1643466
OAKLEY, L/Bdr, Robert Henry, 1063227
OSBORNE, Gnr, Frederick Charles, 3194681
OXBY, Gnr, Owen Reginald, 323095
PADFIELD, Gnr, Roderick Frank, 1726135
PALMER, Gnr, Albert Frederick, 1643469
PARSONS, Gnr, Frederick George, 1643474
PEARSON, Gnr, Harold, 877738
PHILLIPS, Gnr, George Sidney, 1817188
PIGOTT, Gnr, Cyril, 1748911
PITMAN, Gnr, Sidney Oliver, 882486
POWELL, Gnr, Albert, 864377
PRIE, Gnr, Jeffreys, 839426
PULLIN, L/Bdr, Henry John, 1073830
READ, Gnr, John, 1749526
READ, Gnr, George Thomas, 872454
REID, Gnr, William, 2872020
RENNARDSON, L/Bdr, Arthur William, 1749003
RENNIE, Gnr, John, 826603
REYNOLDS, Gnr, Leslie Charles, 1514294
RHODES, Gnr, Eric Peter Geoffrey, 1427109
RICKETS, Gnr, Charles, 777867
ROBERTS, Gnr, John Henry, 1817208
ROBERTS, Sjt, Edward Arthur, 545610
ROBINSON, Gnr, Edwin Thomas, 826502
ROOKER, Sjt, Joseph Harold, 818029
RUDDICK, Gnr, George Edward, 788969
RUSHTON, Gnr, Albert, 781602
SALTER, Bqms, Allan Henry, 874036

SANDS, Gnr, Richard, 1748640
SAVAGE, Gnr, Robert, 1746426
SCOTT, Gnr, James Henderson, 1489680
SEABROOK, L/Bdr, Frederick, 1072029
SEDDON, Gnr, William, 1733567
SEVIOUR, Gnr, Hubert Charles, 777106
SHATWELL, Gnr, James, 818750
SIMMONDS, Gr, Frederick, 774380
SIPPINGS, Gnr, William Martin, 1524972
SKELTON, Gnr, Harry, 1643341
SMITH, Sjt, David James, 791150
SOUTTER, L/bdr, William Albert, 836697
STADDEN, Gnr, William, 1716837
STANLEY, Gnr, Sampson Edwin, 1770727
STANLEY, Gnr, Charles, 1068356
STANTON, Gnr, Alfred Arthur, 1745269
STAPLES, Gnr, Albert Edward, 1643356
STEED, Gnr, William, 1502670
STEEDMAN, Gnr, E, 1439392
STEVENS, Gnr, Thomas Percy, 1726146
STEWART, Gnr, Christopher, 1738111
STORR, Gnr, Henry George, 815954
STUART, Gnr, David Arthur, 1800894
STUTCHFIELD, L/Bdr, Challis Crescens Charles, 4529905
TART, Gnr, Joshua, 822311
TAYLOR, Gnr, George Horace, 966663
THOMAS, Gnr, Tom, 1580723
THORNETT, Gnr, Archibald William James, 1065901
TINGLEY, Gnr, Frank, 1726151
TOOLE, Sjt, George Michael, 1427519
TOWILLS, Dvr, Herbert, 2065053
TRICE, L/Sjt, Edward Charles, 772441
TRICKETT, Gnr, Jack, 1580909
UNDERHILL, Gnr, George Henry, 782342
UNTERMAN, Gnr, Francis Rene, 1427564
VARNEY, Gnr, Thomas Edward, 1502708
VAUGHAN, Gnr, David, 790353
WALSH, Gnr, Patrick, 3382944
WARD, Sjt, Charles William, 1061364
WATERS, Gnr, William John, 1643490
WAYMAN, Gnr, Christopher Thomas, 1065009
WEAVER, Bdr, Frederick, 7877791
WEAVER, Gnr, Ronald, 1749569
WESTON, Gnr, Stanley, 797493
WHEBLE, Gnr, Jack, 1643497
WHEELER, Gnr, George Henry, 790021
WHITE, Gnr, Tom, 818020
WHITEHOUSE, Gnr, Frederick John, 790388
WHITTAKER, Gnr, David Beavis, 1687164
WHYATT, L/Bdr, Christopher Charles, 1793534
WILKINSON, Lt, Dennis Wilfred, 85514
WILL, Gnr, Arthur, 866894
WILLIAMSON, Gnr, John Herbert, 847891
WILLSON, Gnr, William John, 1561724
WILSON, L/Sjt, Thomas Henry, 842112
WILSON, Gnr, James Stanley, 1738265
WILSON, Gnr, William James, 2646346
WINDOWS, Lt, Harry Bernard, 172845
WINKWORTH, Gnr, Charles Alfred, 6087473
WOOLF, Gnr, William Henry, 808768
WYKES, Bdr, Raymond Walter, 1437267
YOUNG, Lt, Philip Henry, 109991

9 H AA
HAYKIN, Bdr, Norman, 788076
PARSONS, Sjt, Joseph, 822144

12 H AA
COULSON, Maj, Nevil, 67887

16 H AA
EVANS, Gnr, Frederick George, 6009485
METCALFE, Gnr, Thomas, 1073948
SIBLEY, Gnr, Walter Albert, 805245
WOODS, L/Bdr, Alec Alfred, 1793202

29 H AA
WILSON, Lt, Norman, 86912

54 H AA
NAIRN, Capt, Peter Thompson, 73398

55 H AA
EDDLESTON, Gnr, William Henry, 1492736

77 H AA
AGAR, Gnr, John Robert, 975543
ARGUST, L/Sjt, Thomas John, 858461
ASHPOOL, Gnr, Harold Leslie, 1529320
ASHTON, Gnr, Thomas Charles, 1582248
ASKEW, Gnr, Thomas Andrew, 1738167
AVRIALL, Gnr, Reginald A.C., 6205376
AYRES, Gnr, Frederick George, 1645939
BAKER, Gnr, Thomas Charles, 1729649
BALLANS, Gnr, Edward, 1791061
BANTON, Gnr, Hector, 1807462
BARNES, L/Bdr, Ivor Glyndwr, 870186
BARRETT, Gnr, Reginald Walker, 1646062
BARTLETT, Gnr, Thomas Henry, 867420
BATES, Gnr, Arthur, 1770770
BAXTER, Gnr, Nelson Frederick Robert John, 1646452
BAYLIS, Gnr, Peter Henry, 1646453
BEARD, Bdr, Kenneth, 883260
BECKETT, Gnr, Leslie Kitchener, 975566
BELLANGFORD, Gnr, Walter Brinley Bell, 869856
BENTLEY, Gnr, William, 1623453
BEVAN, Bdr, Idris, 855542
BIRCH, Gnr, George, 771108
BLACK, Gnr, Frederick, 1794655
BLAKE, Bdr, Horace George, 1771730
BLANCHARD, Gnr, Idris George, 1764658
BORRILL, Gnr, Percy Atherton, 1636562
BOWSKILL, Gnr, Frank, 1794659
BRADSHAW, Gnr, Ronald Henry, 1807493
BRICKNELL, Gnr, Leslie William Court, 1646025
BROOKER, Gnr, Charles Frederick William, 2064749
BROWN, Gnr, Percy Charles, 1582263
BULLETT, Gnr, Ivor, 1717146
BURGEON, Gnr, Edward, 1794666
BURGESS, Gnr, Edward George, 1777621
BURROWS, Gnr, William Leonard, 1721779
BUTCHER, Gnr, Albert John, 1792475
BUTLER, L/Bdr, William Henry, 1706299
BUZZACOTT, Gnr, Sydney John, 1491669
CAMPBELL, Gnr, James, 918574
CARRIGAN, Gnr, William Henry, 1638486
CARTER, Gnr, William John, 1771692
CHANDLER, Gnr, Herston George William, 1627503
CHAPMAN, Gnr, Stanley Edward, 1633482
CHAPMAN, Gnr, Ernest Herbert Charles, 1737584
CHATWIN, Gnr, William Charles, 1706364
CLARKE, Gnr, Albert Stafford, 839063
CLAYTON, Gnr, Herbert Thomas, 1633497
CLEMENTS, Gnr, Lionel Arthur, 857501
CLIFTON, RSM, Charles Thomas, 1061621
COLEMAN, Gnr, George John, 1491692
COLEMAN, L/Bdr, David Clifford, 1444944
COLEY, Gnr, Charles William, 1646085
COLLINS, Gnr, Albert William, 1706351
CONNELLAN, Bdr, Trevor Frederick, 887501

COOK, Gnr, Charles Henry, 1777579
COOPER, Gnr, George, 1609557
COUGHLIN, L/Bdr, Michael, 857848
COULEY, Gnr, Thomas, 1706343
COWELL, Gnr, Raymond William Frederick, 1444948
COX, 2/Lt, Donald Patrick, 214249
COX, Gnr, Charles Ronald, 1807520
CRABBE, Bdr, Bertie, 869552
CRABTREE, Gnr, Leonard, 1794620
DAVIES, Gnr, William Lwyn, 1779354
DAVIES, Bdr, John Samuel, 1474423
DAVIS, Gnr, Frederick George William, 1635984
DAVISON, Gnr, Kenneth, 1807526
DAWSON, Gnr, George, 1794662
DUTTON, Gnr, Charles, 1472571
EDWARDS, Sjt, Glyndwr, 810955
EDWARDS, Gnr, George Henry, 1447283
ELLIOT, Gnr, Stephen, 1796392
ELLIS, Gnr, Albert Edward, 1794627
ELLWOOD, L/Bdr, Bernard, 1743083
ELMES, Bdr, William Frederick Horace, 1491758
EVANS, Gnr, Frank, 1636545
EVANS, Gnr, Daniel John, 1835138
EVANS, L/Bdr, Albert George, 1582306
EV0ANS, Sjt, Albert Edward, 765982
EWINGS, Sjt, John, 1455594
EYNON, Gnr, Dorrien, 883314
FARRANT, L/Bdr, Ernest Frank, 1491772
FAWCETT, Gnr, John, 1434031
FENN, Gnr, Robert George, 1808726
FERGUSON, Gnr, Robert Alfred, 1623465
FIELDING, Gnr, Walter, 1566359
FIRTH, Gnr, Eric Haig, 1794630
FITZGERALD, Bdr, Thomas Christopher, 1449127
FLANAGAN, Gnr, William, 1730089
FOWLE, Gnr, Norman Percy, 1808730
FRANKS, L/Sjt, Jack Anthony, 1535408
FREEMAN, Gnr, Wilfred Stanley, 1807547
FRITH, Gnr, Jack, 1794521
FRY, Gnr, Percy Cyril, 1587611
GARNER, Gnr, Walter, 1609535
GAY, Gnr, William Alexander, 1587840
GEE, Capt, Reginald Lawrence, 113035
GELL, Gnr, William Percy, 1807736
GIDMAN, Gnr, Robert, 1636508
GLOVER, Sjt, John James, 920191
GOODIER, Gnr, Clifford, 1733525
GOSLING, Gnr, William Ernest, 1646355
GRADY, L/Sjt, Maurice Eugene, 1491824
GREAVES, L/Bdr, Joseph Thomas, 1491825
GRIFFITHS, Bdr, David Morris, 1449675
GUEST, L/Bdr, Harold, 1591190
GUILAR, Pte, Peter, 918269
GULLEY, L/Sjt, Thomas Edwin, 1449679
HADLEY, Gnr, Arthur, 1706476
HALL, L/Bdr, Jack Percy, 4189392
HALL, Gnr, Frederick Noel, 1807561
HARDING, Gnr, Cecil Hemslie, 2063179
HARPER, Gnr, Sidney, 1636470
HAYES, Gnr, Leslie James, 1587853
HAYWOOD, Gnr, Cecil Thomas, 1807575
HEALEY, Gnr, Stanley Ernest, 1604973
HERBERT, Sjt, Clifford, 1438436
HEYHOE, Gnr, Walter, 1794648
HIDES, Gnr, Ronald, 1794590
HILLIER, Bdr, Herbert George, 1646112
HILLS, Sjt, Leslie Patrick, 1457986
HISCOCK, Gnr, John, 1595042
HOARE, Gnr, Donald, 1645985
HOLLIS, Gnr, Henry George, 1808748

HOLMES, Gnr, John Henry, 1807585
HOWELL, L/Sjt, John Jeffrey, 887590
HUMPHREY, Gnr, Harold Arthur, 1808664
HURREL, L/Bdr, Leonard, 1517804
ILES, Gnr, Richard John, 749649
IRVINE, Gnr, William, 900568
JAMES, Bdr, Roy William, 1587861
JAMES, Sjt, Gwyn Towyn, 1452857
JARRETT, Gnr, Wilfred, 1780803
JENKINS, Bdr, Haydn, 1452858
JENKS, Gnr, Alfred Smith, 1794599
JOHN, Gnr, Leonard Westley, 1443870
JOHNSON, Gnr, Donald, 324835
JOHNSON, Sjt, Reginald, 1458464
JONES, Gnr, Alfred Thomas, 1433302
JONES, Gnr, William John, 858192
KIDD, Bdr, Charles Frederick, 1491895
LANCASHIRE, Gnr, Bernard, 1807744
LANGLEY, Gnr, James Leonard, 1808675
LESTER, Bdr, Frederick William, 1491906
LEWIS, S/Sjt, John, 795614
MACKENZIE, Gnr, Donald Maclean, 1727624
MANSFIELD, Gnr, Cornelius, 3914100
MARSH, Gnr, James Henry, 1591196
MARSHALL, Gnr, Arthur William, 3914436
MASKILL, Gnr, Raymond, 1794617
MASTERS, Gnr, Edward, 1807619
McDADE, Gnr, Andrew, 916391
McLEAN, Gnr, Robert Thomas, 1632312
MEDWAY, Gnr, Reginald Percy, 1645950
MEE, Gnr, James, 1807626
MEGINS, Gnr, David Thomas, 1835097
MILLER, Gnr, Arthur, 1609570
MILLER, Gnr, Henry Allen, 1602488
MILLS, Capt, James Francis Dawson, 73787
MILLS, Gnr, Lorraine George, 1582396
MILLS, Gnr, George Victor, 1491948
MILNER, Gnr, Henry, 1807628
MITCHELL, Sjt, Henry William, 1794561
MITCHELL, Gnr, Frank, 1794561
MORGAN, S/Sjt, Vivian, 1460050
MORGAN, Bdr, Daniel Haydon Lewis, 1455531
MORRIS, Gnr, Frank Victor, 1706524
MORRISON, Gnr, Charles Watson, 753072
MORROW, Gnr, Alex, 1657365
MOSES, Gnr, Leslie Vincent,
MOULTON, L/Bdr, Ernest, 1587875
MURRAY, Gnr, James, 1793083
NAYLOR, Gnr, Cooper, 1636090
NEWLOVE, Gnr, William James Yorke, 1793084
NOAKES, Gnr, John Percival, 5337489
NORRIS, Gnr, George, 1591198
O'MAHONY, Gnr, Lawrence Richard, 885710
OSBORN, Gnr, Reginald Victor, 1646529
OWEN, Gnr, Arthur, 1706561
OWENS, Gnr, Edward, 1627446
OXLEY, Capt, Melvill Hayes, 2049
PALMER, L/Sjt, Henry John, 1434295
PALMER, Gnr, Cyril, 1789498
PARKER, Gnr, Gerald, 2100929
PARSONS, Gnr, Frederick James Henry, 1458305
PEARCE, Gnr, David George, 1459957
PERRY, Gnr, Harry, 1710479
PLANT, Gnr, Sidney, 1627584
POLLARD, Gnr, James Davidson, 835504
POPE, Gnr, Ivor Aleck, 1627486
POVEY, Gnr, Edward Albert, 1587785
PRICE, Gnr, Henry, 1627583
PRIOR, Gnr, Victor Gordon, 6897326
PRITCHARD, Gnr, Frederick John, 1732105

PRITCHARD, L/Sjt, William John, 1447887
PUGH, L/Sjt, Lewis, 830773
PUGH, Gnr, John, 858970
PYKE, Gnr, John Augustus, 1645953
RANSOME, Gnr, James Arthur, 1808708
RAW, Gnr, Edward Harper, 1635360
REEVES, Gnr, Bert Ephraim, 1706596
ROBERTS, L/Sjt, William Grenville, 1458772
ROBERTS, Gnr, Thomas Glyn, 1717208
ROBERTSON, Gnr, Robert Charles, 1582438
ROBINSON, Gnr, Thomas, 1605469
ROBINSON, Gnr, Francis William, 1587767
RONALDS, Gnr, William David John, 885247
ROWE, Bqms, Reginald Herbert, 748122
ROWLEY, Gnr, Robert, 1627511
ROWLEY, Gnr, John James, 1627447
RUSSELL, Gnr, William John, 1433529
RUSSELL, Gnr, Frank, 1442940
SAGE, L/Bdr, Norman, 1626641
SAUNDERS, Bdr, Norman Eric, 1751252
SCARBOROUGH, L/Bdr, Henry Thomas, 1064369
SCHOLES, Gnr, James, 1784071
SCOURFIELD, Gnr, Sidney Benjamin, 1710050
SHANKS, Gnr, John, 1640874
SHEPPARD, Gnr, Ronald, 1645959
SIMMILL, Gnr, Herbert, 1706613
SMALLMAN, L/Bdr, Norman Edward, 866186
SMEDLEY, Gnr, Joseph Edwin Ernest, 1807689
SMITH, Gnr, Walter, 1794584
SPRAGUE, Gnr, Alan John, 1645956
STANTON, Gnr, John, 1721631
STONE, Gnr, Ernest John, 1646008
STUBBS, Gnr, John, 1591205
STYLES, Gnr, George Jesse, 1529504
SULLIVAN, L/Bdr, Daniel, 1449695
SUMMERS, Gnr, Charles, 1807695
SUMPTION, BSM, Edward, 747928
SUTTON, Gnr, Eric John, 1706628
SWAIN, Gnr, Stanley Charles, 1807696
TARRANT, Gnr, Douglas John, 1627200
TAYLOR, Lt, Kenneth Landale, 148107
THOMAS, Gnr, William Charles, 1447543
THOMAS, Sjt, Hayden James, 871106
THOMAS, Gnr, Evan Lloyd, 964697
THORPE, Gnr, Frank, 1807699
TIMLIN, Gnr, Lawrence, 1794543
TINSLEY, L/Bdr, Charles Willie, 81855
TOON, Gnr, Alfred Ambrose, 1807700
TOWERS, Gnr, George, 1794544
TOWNSEND, Gnr, Sidney James, 1646102
TUCKER, Gnr, Harold, 1646054
TURNBULL, Gnr, Robert, 919468
WALKER, Bdr, Jack, 984512
WALTERS, L/Bdr, Thomas Samuel, 1453838
WARDELL, Gnr, Mark William, 1706719
WATKINS, Gnr, David John, 870994
WATKINS, Gnr, Clifford, 1635347
WATTS, L/Bdr, Francis Joseph, 1458782
WEBB, Sjt, Charles Oliver, 833203
WEBB, Gnr, Allenby Foch, 1507596
WEIR, Gnr, Walter, 1730348
WHITEFIELD, Gnr, Frederick Francis, 1807712
WHITMAN, L/Bdr, William John, 1808716
WHITTET, Gnr, John Wilmer, 1808717
WILLIAMS, Gnr, Emrys, 1706703
WILLIAMS, Gnr, William, 1783349
WILSON, Gnr, Frank, 1794556
WOOD, Gnr, Francis Henry, 1636241
WOOD, Gnr, Harry, 1706684
WOODWARD, Bdr, Richard, 1706699

79 H AA
BAILEY, Gnr, Leonard John Edward, 1491630

85 H AA
EAVES, Gnr, George, 1120813
HOWORTH, Gnr, Wilfred, 1465180

HONG KONG & SHANGHAI
IEVERS, Maj, Frederick Robert, 44913

3 LT AA
BEAUMONT, L/Sjt, William Arthur, 1072241
BIRCH, Gnr, Clifford, 607192
CORNWELL, Gnr, John Laindon Jackson, 986085
COUZENS, Sjt, John Philip, 90419
DAWSON, Gnr, Leslie Weston, 922255
GUTTERIDGE, Bqms, William James, 812061
HASLAM, Capt, Harry Jack, 91743
HYNE, Gnr, Claude George, 5615198
JENNINGS, Gnr, Harry, 1543986
KITCHEN, Gnr, Maurice, 1569966
MOORE, L/Sjt, Robert William, 1642614
NEWINGTON, Capt, Claude Desmond, 63528
O'CONNOR, L/Sjt, Alexander Dallas, 845989
ODHAMS, Gnr, Michael Anthony, 1470142
PERLS, Lt, Ormond Israel Rodney, 197700
POWER, Lt, Patrick Michael, 149892
RACKHAM, Lt, Arthur Wray, 151237
RAWSON, Gnr, John Leslie, 1542741
SAMPSON, 2/lt, William Anthony Pennycuik, 145341
SANDERS, Lt, Hugh Allen, 158715
SHEAFF, Sjt, William George, 1020192
SPRANKLEN, Sjt, Sidney Richard, 1415761
THORNE, Bdr, Lionel, 1482104
TRUMAN, Lt, Richard Henry Francis, 148410
WARD, Gnr, Leslie Harold, 1484136
WARD, Gnr, George Henry, 59606

5 LT A A
ALDRED, Gnr, Harry, 6129453
EATON, Gnr, Leslie Thomas, 1709743
HARRIS, Gnr, Fred, 1629583
SIVYER, Gnr, Robert Sidney, 771868

21 LT AA
ADAMS, Gnr, David Francis, 1614691
ADRIAN, Gnr, William, 1753250
ANDREWS, Gnr, Harold, 1821279
ANGEL, L/Bdr, John Lindsey, 1552212
ARCHIBALD, Gnr, Thomas Miller, 1826533
ASHMORE, Gnr, Harold, 1818392
AVENELL, Gnr, Robert Berry, 1768731
BAKER, Gnr, Reginald, 1734152
BARNES, Gnr, Frederick William, 1624395
BARNETT, Gnr, John William, 5103648
BARTLETT, Gnr, Arthur Edwin, 1563244
BAULCOMBE, Gnr, Henry John, 1753256
BENN, Gnr, Edward Thomas, 1549477
BENNELL, Gnr, William John, 1555676
BENNETT, Gnr, Albert Sidney George, 1653987
BLACK, Gnr, Leslie Wylie, 1826537
BODEN, Bdr, John, 1622419
BRABBIN, Gnr, Stanley, 1824274
BUCHAN, Gnr, John Ford, 1653996
BUDD, Gnr, Thomas Arthur, 1485971
BULL, Gnr, Stanley George, 1737444
BURDEN, Gnr, John James, 1487049
BURDETT, Gnr, Noel, 1523544

BURNNETT, Gnr, Reginald John, 1548346
BUTT, Gnr, Arthur Ashley, 1736369
BUTTERWORTH, Gnr, James Robert, 2821102
CANHAM, Gnr, Rex, 1802595
CANN, L/Cpl, Walter George, 45230
CARVER, Gnr, Percy, 1760033
CASEY, Gnr, Albert Edward, 1654002
CAST, Gnr, Francis John, 1821338
CHANDLER, Gnr, Frederick Winslow, 1811325
CHANDLER, Gnr, Harold, 1735808
CHARLESWORTH, Gnr, Robert Spink, 1722457
CHARMAN, Bdr, Wilford Harry, 1616543
CLACK, Gnr, Arthur George Berkley, 1532604
CLARK, Gnr, William Samuel, 1655712
CLARKE, Bdr, Cecil Budd, 1485577
COCKADAY, Gnr, William Bob, 1735528
COE, Gnr, Albert James, 1654010
COLLINS, Gnr, Enoch, 1823289
COMPTON, Bdr, Arthur Frank, 1552186
COOK, Gnr, John Harold, 1654011
COX, Gnr, James William, 1833690
CROFT, Gnr, Ernest William George, 1624414
CROFT, Gnr, Samuel, 1622420
CROWDELL, Gnr, Oliver, 1511317
CROZIER, Bdr, John Emanuel, 1527498
CRYER, Gnr, Ernest, 1724978
CUNLIFFE, Gnr, Calvert, 1809144
CUNNINGHAM, Gnr, Walter Frederick, 1826556
DAVENPORT, Gnr, Richard James, 1719728
DAVIS, Gnr, Alfred John, 1764042
DOYLE, Gnr, James, 1543186
DRAKEFORD, Gnr, Arthur Francis, 1769005
DRING, Gnr, Edwin, 1654019
EADEN, Sjt, Ronald Stuart, 1484235
ELLIS, Gnr, Norman, 1678970
EMMS, Bdr, Douglas Charles, 1614637
EVANS, Gnr, Thomas Festubert, 1827284
EVERETT, Gnr, Harry, 1624364
FEAST, Gnr, Alfred Harold, 1624366
FENNER, Bdr, Raymond Arthur, 1481404
FIELDING, Gnr, Thomas Owen, 1736236
FILBEY, Gnr, Charles Herbert, 1827434
FITCH, Gnr, Leslie Ernest, 18807016
FOSTER, Gnr, Charles Herbert, 1614639
FOSTER, Gnr, John, 1826509
FRATER, Gnr, Arnnold, 3448705
FROST, Gnr, Norman, 1482073
FROST, L/bdr, Dennis Anthony, 1779965
GANE, Bdr, John, 1478319
GARRETT, Gnr, George Terence, 1807025
GILLIGAN, Gnr, John, 11263042
GLUE, Gnr, John William, 1833216
GOLDFINCH, Gnr, John Thomas, 1736187
GOODALL, Gnr, Edward, 1822322
GOODWORTH, Gnr, Harold, 1781571
GRANT, Gnr, Gerald Lockhart, 1822265
GRAY, Gnr, Robert, 1812952
GRIFFIN, Gnr, James Ypres, 2042674
HARRIS, Gnr, Wilfred John, 1833348
HASLAM, Gnr, Frank Evan, 1824485
HAYWARD, Bdr, Stanley Alfred, 1478315
HAZZARD, Gnr, Ernest John, 1817400
HEAD, Gnr, John Edward, 1807157
HENSHALL, S/Sjt, Norman Henry, 7630609
HEWITT, Gnr, Hubert William, 1490211
HIGGINS, L/Bdr, Jeffrey Herbert, 1735213
HILLS, Gnr, Nelson John, 1653876
HINDE, Sjt, John, 1694160
HOCKING, Gnr, Joseph, 1548784
HOLDER, Gnr, Charles James, 1817403

HOLLAND, Gnr, George Frederick, 1737682
HORN, Gnr, Edgar, 1812964
HOULDSWORTH, L/bdr, Robert, 1694191
HUDSON, Gnr, Thomas Henry, 1809178
HUGHES, Gnr, Joseph John, 15413180
HUNTER, S/Sjt, Ronald Thomas, 1483127
JACKSON, Gnr, James, 1771843
JAMES, Gnr, Brinley, 1818777
JUDD, Gnr, William Charles, 1817265
KILLICK, L/Bdr, Albert George, 6401331
KING, Sjt, George Herbert, 1453589
LANGTON, Gnr, James Willis, 1779960
LOBB, Gnr, Walter Edward, 891879
LOCK, Gnr, Charles William, 2051230
MACKIE, Gnr, Andrew, 1774706
MADELEY, Gnr, John William, 1826599
MAGUIRE, Gnr, Joseph, 1543128
MANSELL, Gnr, Ppercy Stuart John, 1548785
MANSI, Gnr, Lawrence Leonard, 1563176
MARSHALL, Gnr, Gavin, 1826695
MARSLIN, Gnr, William, 1591841
MARTIN, Gnr, John Russell, 1482079
MARTIN, Gnr, Harold Laurence John, 6401712
MASON, Cftmn, Edward James, 7621809
McCRORY, Gnr, James, 1822703
McKENNA, Gnr, John, 1826684
McLEOD, Gnr, Thomas J, 1822769
McMAHON, Gnr, Henry, 1478716
McMENEMY, L/Bdr, Daniel, 1828416
McNAB, Gnr, Cyril Peter, 1771927
MEDLAR, Gnr, Sidney Ernest, 1735606
MITCHELL, Gnr, Robert, 1826700
MIZEN, Sjt, Alexander, 1542969
MOORE, Gnr, Alfred John William, 1556169
MORTON, Gnr, Hugh Richmond, 1826701
MOTH, BSM, John Bevington, 1456257
NAYLOR, Gnr, Leonard, 1807274
NEWALL, Gnr, John Eric, 1733113
NORTON, Gnr, Bernard, 1791497
OAKHAM, Gnr, George Joseph, 1599632
ORR, Gnr, James, 1568330
PADBURY, Gnr, Charles Frederick, 1807286
PARKER, Gnr, Leslie Norman John, 1548600
PARKER, Gnr, Fredrick William, 4797820
PARKS, Gnr, Kenneth, 1455182
PASCOE, L/Bdr, Michael Bennett, 1555980
PAYNE, Gnr, Benjamin, 1550073
PEARSON, Gnr, Albert Reginald, 1590224
PENN, Gnr, Edward William, 1681252
PERRY, Bdr, Gordon Hardy, 1485584
PICKLES, Gnr, Harry, 1774576
POLLOCXK, Gnr, Thomas Maitland, 11253460
POOLE, Gnr, Jack, 1556108
POPE, L/Bdr, Charles Edwin, 1563098
PRENTICE, L/Bdr, Dennis Eric, 1481396
PRETLOVE, Gnr, John, 1549478
PRIOR, Gnr, Frank Desmond, 1807309
RABINOVITCH, Gnr, Simon, 1592417
RAMSBOTTOM, Gnr, Percy Randolph, 1826635
RAYNER, Gnr, Joseph Charles, 1592418
RIGBY, Gnr, Peter, 1826603
RILEY, L/Bdr, John Lawrence, 1779878
ROBERT, L/Bdr, William Lloyd, 923333
ROBINSON, L/Bdr, Arthur Watson, 1826671
ROCKER, Gnr, Sidney Stanley, 1771878
RODDEN, Gnr, Michael Joseph, 1828420
ROGERS, L/Bdr, Eric Ralph, 1772638
ROLFE, Lt, Ian David, 359128
ROOKWOOD, Bdr, Leslie John, 1481395
RUSHTON, Gnr, William, 11060960

RUSSELL, Gnr, Hereward Gilbert, 1592423
SABAN, Gnr, Cyril Victor, 1807346
SCRIVENER, Gnr, George, 1824295
SEABORNE, Gnr, Alfred, 1563158
SEAMARKS, Gnr, William H, 1828366
SHARP, Sjt, Harry, 1498952
SHIMMIN, Gnr, John Joseph, 1534698
SHIPLEY, Sjt, George, 1483130
SHRUBSHALL, Gnr, William Frank, 1465066
SIME, Bdr, John Rodger, 1592521
SIMMONDS, Pte, Thomas Jesse Noel, 1574392
SIMPSON, Gnr, Benjamin, 1592522
SKILBECK, Gnr, Ernest, 1490053
SKINNER, Gnr, John Robert Alexander, 1483416
SMITH, Gnr, Kenneth, 1826738
SMITH, Gnr, Edward Charles, 1563818
SMITH, Gnr, Albert Edward Walter, 1548866
SNAPE, Gnr, William, 1826607
SPARKE, Gnr, John James, 1817355
SPENCE, Sjt, Leslie Frederick, 1482054
STEARN, Gnr, Sidney, 1736274
STEPHENSON, Gnr, Allen, 1826610
STEVENTON, Gnr, George Victor Henry, 1549377
STOCKWELL, Gnr, William John, 1592526
STONEHAM, Gnr, Stanley William, 1807387
SUNLEY, Gnr, Lawrence Henry, 822321
TANT, Gnr, Frederick Charles, 1549050
TASKER, Bdr, Ernest Leslie, 1478296
THOMPSON, Gnr, James, 1779956
THOROUGHGOOD, Sjt, Charles Richard, 910445
TOMINAY, Gnr, Thomas, 1820579
TREVORROW, Gnr, Henry David, 6199585
TROKE, Gnr, Hubert, 1828699
TUNKLE, Gnr, Benjamin, 1552262
TWOMAY, Gnr, James Dennis, 1735260
WALKER, Sjt, Norman George, 1595423
WARWICK, L/bdr, Albert William, 1549851
WATKINS, Gnr, Frederick James, 1818926
WEBB, Gnr, John, 1527314
WEBB, Gnr, Edwin George, 1833305
WEBSTER, Gnr, Archibald Bernard, 1817377
WEBSTER, Gnr, William Henry, 1828489
WELLS, Gnr, Gordon James, 1556203
WELSFORD, L/Bdr, Norman Outram, 1482082
WESTON, Sjt, Ronald James, 1452499
WHIOTESIDE, Sjt, George William, 1674928
WHITTLE, Gnr, Thomas Charles Hope, 1826645
WILKINSON, Gnr, George Frank St George, 1545761
WILKINSON, Gnr, James Leonard, 1807869
WILLCOX, Gnr, Henry, 1827132
WILLIAMS, Gnr, Trevor Conway, 1818943
WILLIS, Qms, Frederick Alfred John, 744583
WILSON, Gnr, William, 1602019
WILSON, Sjt, George Edward, 1490050
WIX, L/Bdr, Donald James, 1549189
WOODMAN, L/Bdr, Leslie Harold, 1555770
WOODS, Bdr, Edward Arthur, 1478001
WOOLBAR, Bdr, Richard Charles, 1478303
WORTHINGTON, Gnr, Thomas Elvyn, 1818946
WRIGHT, Gnr, James, 1735786
WRIGHT, Gnr, George, 1811565
WRIGHT, Gnr, Albert Edward, 1592537
WRIGHT, Gnr, Alfred Randolph, 1781386
YORK, Gnr, William Richard John, 1592538
YOUNG, Gnr, William, 1592540
YUDKIN, Gnr, Abraham, 1819219

33 LT AA
FRY, Sjt, George John, 1483232

34 LT AA
BOULTON, L/Bdr, Ezra, 797441

35 LT AA
ABBOTT, Gnr, Albert Frank, 1543347
AKERS, Sjt, Frank, 529309
ALLSOPP, Gnr, William Henry, 1700401
ANSELL, L/Bdr, Horace William Haywood, 1700403
ARDY, Gnr, William Albert, 1773841
ARMSTRONG, Gnr, Percy, 1831416
ASHTON, Gnr, Ernest, 1793059
ATTEWELL, Gnr, Arthur, 1700399
ATTWELL, L/Sjt, Arthur Frederick, 2620137
AYRE, Gnr, Albert, 1700407
BACON, Gnr, Dennis Walter, 2044898
BAKER, Gnr, William Reginald, 1799969
BAKER, Gnr, Reginald Stanley, 1439411
BAKER, Gnr, Henry George, 1801737
BALCH, Gnr, Paul Farmer, 1799970
BARTLETT, Gnr, Bert, 1573055
BASS, Lt, Eric Walter, 166810
BASSETT, Lt Col, John, 15258
BAXTER, L/Bdr, Joseph Henry, 1539977
BILLINGHAM, Gnr, Stanley Clifford, 877075
BILLS, Gnr, Raymond Thomas, 1777963
BLINKO, Sjt, Alec Mark, 542937
BOSTOCK, Gnr, Cyril, 1700373
BOULDING, Gnr, Walter Frederick, 1801754
BROWN, Gnr, Alec James, 1777966
BROWN, Gnr, Charles Freddy, 1563417
BROWN, L/Bdr, William Ptere, 1760081
BULLOCK, Maj, Edward, 97594
BURGESS, Gnr, Alfred William, 1831431
BURTON, Gnr, William George, 1549685
BUTLER, Gnr, William, 1794159
CALLAGHAN, Gnr, William, 1773966
CANE, Gnr, Frederick Ernest, 1831260
CANNON, L/Bdr, Ronald Frank, 1524347
CARR, Gnr, James Weatherall, 1827295
CARRIS, Gnr, Laurence, 1782171
CHAMBERS, Gnr, Edward Maddock, 1700348
CHANCE, Gnr, Philip James Jethro, 1831435
CLARK, Sjt, William Arthur, 1550115
CLARKE, L/Bdr, Arthur Edmund, 1700354
CLARKE, Gnr, Victor Alfred, 1546330
CLARKE, Gnr, Frederick William, 1757632
CLAYTON, Gnr, Eric, 1831473
CLOGG, Gnr, John Henry, 1799360
COLLINS, Gnr, Harry Kitchener, 1556046
COOPER, Gnr, Thomas James, 1760042
COOPER, Gnr, John Henry, 1777876
CORBETT, Gnr, William, 1760044
CRAIG, Gnr, James, 1790089
CRAWFORD, Gnr, John Wood, 1700311
CRICKET, Dvr, George Frederick, T/91632
CROSS, L/Bdr, Oswin Leslie, 1572754
CUTBUSH, Maj, Harold William, 44989
DANCE, Capt, Eric George, 106005
DAVIES, Bqms, John Robeerts, 1481592
DAVIES, Gnr, Henry George, 1831442
DAWSON, Gnr, Clement Wallace, 1800374
DENTON, Gnr, Reginald, 1831488
DICKENS, L/Bdr, Henry, 1700322
DOWLING, Sjt, George Thomas, 1714852
DREW, Gnr, Alert Stephen, 1573056
DRIVER, Gnr, Ernest Arthur, 1777887
DUNN, Gnr, John Raymod, 1572920
DUNN, L/Bdr, Arthur Edmund, 1481590
DUPLOCK, Gnr, James Alfred, 1770390
DUTTON, Gnr, Alfred Edward, 1773983

EASTGATE, L/Bdr, Arthur Leonard, 1700329
EDMONDS, Gnr, Albert Henry, 1772595
EDWARDS, Gnr, Ernest Harry, 1831491
EPTON, Gnr, John William Herbert, 1481589
EVANS, Gnr, William Benjamin, 1807010
FALCONER, Gnr, Herbert King, 1074199
FAWDEN, Gr, Herbert, 1782191
FENSOME, Gnr, Harold Victor James, 1831493
FINCH, Gnr, Ernest, 1486474
FKETCHER, Gnr, Harold, 1700281
FORD, Gnr, Samuel, 1789900
FRANCIS, L/Sjt, Frank, 1700287
FRANCIS, Gnr, Frank, 1831497
FRANKTON, L/Bdr, Thomas George, 1700288
FRIDD, Gnr, Thomas W, 1788821
GALLAGHER, Gnr, James, 1644035
GAMON, Gnr, Edward William, 1785885
GILES, Gnr, Frederick Charles, 1555804
GINMAN, Gnr, Harry Thomas, 1788829
GOLDING, Gnr, Cyril Ernest, 1543345
GRAY, Gnr, Victor, 1806163
GRAY, Bdr, Edward Gordon, 1552488
GRAY, 2/Lt, Stanley Arthur Gordon, 207162
GREENFIELD, Gnr, David Harry, 1478927
GREENHILL, Gnr, Joseph James, 1788867
GREENWOOD, Gnr, William H, 1788838
GRIEVES, Gnr, John, 1792687
GRILLS, L/Bdr, George, 1547696
GUNN, Gnr, George, 1790104
HABBERLEY, Gnr, Henry Thomas, 1797160
HABGOOD, Bdr, Leslie James, 1549568
HALE, Gnr, George Thomas, 1834088
HALL, Gnr, Frank, 1544538
HAMMOND, Gnr, Frederick Spencer, 1831445
HANSEN, Sjt, John, 1547025
HARDING, Gnr, Harry Victor, 1545940
HARDY, L/Bdr, John William, 1700259
HAROLD, Gnr, Edgar, 1443424
HARRISON, Gnr, Leslie James, 1700266
HATTON, Gnr, Montague Francis, 6630613
HAVERCROFT, Gnr, Wilfred, 1782214
HAWKINS, Sjt, Joseph James, 1552184
HAYERS, Gnr, George William, 1562901
HAYWARD, Grn, Willie Daniel, 1808516
HERBERTS, Bdr, Harold, 1700214
HIGGS, Bdr, Edward John, 1483243
HILL, Sjt, Frederick, 1483245
HILTON, Gnr, Edward Alfred, 13021277
HINTON, Sjt, Stanley Charles, 1488339
HODDINOTT, S/Sjt, Henry Francis, 1483246
HOLLIMOULD, Gnr, Leslie, 1700222
HOLMES, Gnr, Cyril, 1732009
HOPKINS, Bdr, Alfred Henry, 1549831
HUGGINS, L/Bdr, Frank Ernest, 1700228
HUGHES, L/Bdr, Elwyn Llewellyn, 1714859
HUNTER, Gnr, Alexander, 1738981
HURRICKS, Gnr, Reginald Charles, 1799493
HUTCHINSON, Gnr, Harold W, 1700230
IBBOTSON, Gnr, Sidney, 1550113
JACKSON, Lt, Frederick William, 180967
JAMES, Bdr, Leslie, 1556296
JENKINS, Gnr, Evan John, 1808538
JENKINS, Gnr, Frank Edward, 17155450
JEPSON, L/Bdr, Frederick, 1700233
JERVIS, Gnr, Harry, 1737869
JOHN, Bdr, William Albert Johnnie, 1540118
JOHNSON, Gnr, Bert Richard, 1540119
JONES, BSM, Bernard Noel, 1479513
KNOWLES, Gnr, John, 1826673
LAKIN, Gnr, Eric Wilson, 1700186

LAMBERT, L/Sjt, Frederick George, 1483258
LAMBOURNE, Gnr, William Ernest, 1519899
LEACH, L/bdr, Herbert George, 1563010
LEE, Gnr, Charles William, 1834050
LEE, Gnr, John William, 1782233
LILLEY, Gnr, William Eric, 1700196
LONGHURST, Gnr, Edward, 1573264
LOWE, Gnr, Ernest Wilfred, 1777858
MACRAE, Gnr, Alexander, 1766458
McHUGH, Gnr, Thomas, 1782238
McINTYRE, Gnr, Hugh Douglas, 1750843
McMANUS, Gnr, Stephen, 179858
MEAKIN, Gnr, William, 1700161
MEIKLE, Gnr, William, 1750777
MELLOR, Gnr, Sidney, 11263050
MELLOR, Gnr, Stanley, 1700162
MERRIMAN, Gnr, George Reid Michael, 1552493
MILLARD, Bdr, Roland, 813507
MITCHELL, Gnr, Roy Warnerford, 1550516
MOSS, Gnr, Alfred Aaron, 1753154
MOTH, L/Bdr, Horace, 6083529
MUNDY, Gnr, George Shaylor, 1456810
MUNTON, Gnr, Harry, 1735867
MUSSON, Gnr, John Wilfred, 1777870
NAPTHINE, Sjt, Eric Sidney, 1520482
ORRAH, Gnr, Francis William, 1643087
OWENS, Gnr, Henry, 1700123
OXLADE, Bdr, Douglas Allan, 1572935
PARKER, Bdr, Henry, 1700127
PASSENGER, Gnr, Robert Arthur Charles, 1523717
PAYNE, Gnr, John David, 1759952
PAYNE, Gnr, Frank William, 929806
PENMAN, Gnr, John, 1540188
PERRY, Gnr, Wiliam H, 1688866
PIGG, L/Bdr, John Thomas, 973843
PIKE, Gnr, Edgar Reginald, 1486661
PINKNEY, Gnr, Thomas George, 1642431
POWELL, Gnr, Henry Charles, 1734094
PROUTTEN, Sjt, George, 7586000
QUINNEY, Gnr, John Owen, 1700142
RAHNSFORD, Gnr, Anthony John, 1779217
RAINEY, Sjt, Ernest William, 1522719
RANSCOMBE, Gnr, Arthur Francis William, 1549644
RASITRICK, Gnr, Oliver, 1781189
RAWLES, Gnr, Leonard Albert, 1540199
REDGRAVE, Gnr, Harry Leslie, 1545919
RICHARDS, L/Bdr, Bernard Alfred, 1489517
RICHENS, Sjt, Frederick Robert, 1483286
ROBINS, Gnr, Edward Frank, 1601713
ROBINSON, Gnr, George, 1700097
ROBINSON, L/Bdr, Ernest, 1562822
ROWLAND, Gnr, James Walter, 1573039
ROWLAND, Gnr, Jack, 1782368
RUTTER, L/Bdr, John Henry, 1543466
RYAN, Bdr, Rudolph Michael Oasen, 1549403
SADLER, Gnr, Edwin, 1700103
SAUNDERS, Gnr, Charles James Hudson, 1785940
SCOTT, Sjt, Arthur Douglas Claude, 1456147
SHARP, Gnr, James, 1700110
SHAYLER, Gnr, Frank, 1483275
SHELDON, Gnr, John Edward, 1782243
SHELDON, Gnr, Arthur, 1700115
SHEPHERD, Gnr, Eric Blake, 1807358
SHORT, Gnr, Ernest Edward, 1801865
SILVER, Gnr, Samuel, 1801866
SIMES, Gnr, Rgeinald, 1757520
SIMMONDS, Gnr, Percy Albert, 1790071
SINFIELD, Gnr, Reginald Sidney, 1548813
SLACK, Gnr, John Byron, 1700062
SMALL, L/Bdr, Charles Thomas, 1700064

SMELT, Gnr, James, 1700066
SMITH, WO/1, Wilfred, 2041648
SMITH, Gnr, Arthur George Peter, 1799435
SMITH, Gnr, Ronald William, 1799437
SOUTHGATE, Gnr, George, 1635313
SPENCER, L/Bdr, Ralph, 1700078
STACY, Gnr, Henry, 1828138
STAGG, L/Bdr, Albert Frederick, 1573220
STANLEY, Gnr, Arthur Ernest Jesse, 1700080
STRANGE, Gnr, Robert Ernest, 1550525
STREET, Gnr, Thomas Stanley, 1760086
STURGESS, Gnr, Stanley, 1782251
SULLY, Gnr, Benjamin Charles, 1753086
SUSSEX, Gnr, Basil Jack, 1714878
SWAIN, Gnr, Albert Edwin, 1700088
TAYLOR, Gnr, John, 1700090
TAYLOR, Gnr, Eric George, 1700031
TAYLOR, Bdr, Edwin James, 1700032
TAYLOR, Gnr, Robert, 1788711
THEAKER, Gnr, Thomas George, 1700036
THOMPSON, Gnr, James Edward, 1549714
THOMPSON, Gnr, William, 1735996
TILLING, L/Bdr, Thomas Harry, 1547026
TIZZARD, Gnr, Stanley, 1700038
TROTH, Gnr, Arthur, 1777947
TURNER, Gnr, Alfred James, 775353
VANSTONE, Gnr, Joseph Ernest, 1776966
VAREY, Gnr, David, 1824328
WAGHORN, Gnr, Charles Edward, 1759185
WALDER, Bdr, Frank, 1627816
WALKER, Gnr, John, 1824268
WALKER, Sjt, Eric Bertie, 1479525
WALSH, Gnr, Stanley, 843076
WARD, Gnr, Samuel, 1569907
WARD, Gnr, Richard, 1821028
WARD, Gnr, George, 1547780
WARD, Gnr, Francis, 1782263
WARREN, L/Bdr, Albert, 1554024
WATKINS, Gnr, Edgar Bruce, 1550416
WATSON, Gnr, Robert Leslie, 786171
WEBB, Gnr, John Henry, 1700002
WEIR, Bdr, James, 1798902
WELFORD, Lt QM, Kenneth William Dampier, 150046
WEST, Bdr, Eric Douglas, 1524210
WHEELER, Bdr, Joseph, 1483295
WHITEHEAD, Gnr, John Bernard, 17729978
WHITFIELD, Gnr, Joseph, 15726113
WHITING, Gnr, Christopher, 1552303
WHITLOCK, Gnr, Leslie Ethelbert, 1489035
WICKSON, Gnr, Frank, 1483298
WILKINS, Gnr, Robert Edward, 1633945
WILLIAMS, Sjt, William James Christopher, 1546111
WILSON, Gnr, James Wilfred, 1777919
WINSTON, Gnr, Lionel James, 1573301
WITTS, Gnr, Samuel, 1700019
WOOTTON, Gnr, Lewis Charles, 1700023
WRIGHT, Gnr, Albert Charles, 1715475
WRIGHT, Gnr, Peter Clarence, 1563480
WRIGHT, Gnr, Frank Hugh, 1827135
YATES, Gnr, Fred, 1700029
YOUNG, L/Sjt, Walter Ernest, 1483240

44 LT AA
DAVIS, Gnr, Jack, 1762524

48 LT AA
ADAMS, Gnr, Percy Albert, 1736093
ALLEN, Gnr, John, 11052160
ALLEN, Gnr, Gordon Robert, 1796021
ANDERSON, Gnr, Jack, 1792823

ANDERTON, Gnr, William Cyril, 1808928
APLIN, Gnr, Clifford Ernest, 1734002
BAGWELL, Gnr, Arthur Alfred Charles, 1758991
BALDWIN, Gnr, Horace Charles, 1696922
BALL, Gnr, Ernest Walter, 5875932
BANNER, Lt, Melville Stewart, 119605
BARDEN, Gnr, Alfred Ernest, 1549483
BAREHAM, Gnr, William James, 1548153
BARKER, Gnr, Maurice Edward, 1639343
BARNES, Gnr, Eric Reginald David, 1614349
BAXTER, Gnr, Alexander Orr, 1696930
BEARDWOOD, Sjt, Edward, 3856955
BEECH, Gnr, Reginald Edwin, 1649483
BIGGS, Gnr, Victor Maurice, 2651476
BIRD, Gnr, Frank Leonard, 1549846
BIRD, Gnr, James Patrick, 1736103
BISS, Gnr, Ernest, 1734164
BLADON, Gnr, Frederick Charles, 5989180
BRESNEHAN, Sjt, John William, 1681733
BROWN, Bdr, Robert Herbert, 11052208
BUCKINGHAM, Gnr, Henry Frederick, 1679320
BURGESS, Gnr, Richard, 11052489
BURKE, Bdr, George, 6550836
BUTT, Sjt, Herbert Jack, 1522707
BUTTERWORTH, Gnr, James, 11052252
CAMP, Gnr, Robert James, 1681747
CAMPBELL, Gnr, Thomas Mcgowan, 11052492
CANE, Bdr, Richard Oliver, 1479799
CARRUTHERS, Gnr, William, 1697486
CARSON, L/Bdr, Charles, 1543769
CLARKE, Gnr, Arthur G, 1802638
CLARKE, Gnr, Edwin, 1783208
COLLIER, Gnr, Ernest Henry, 1717712
COOK, Sjt, Percy Victor, 1465809
COOK, Sjt, Sidney William, 1477453
COPPIN, Gnr, Ernest John, 1481518
COSTELLO, Gnr, Michael, 1609558
COX, Gnr, Arthur James, 1799368
CRETTEN, L/bdr, William Richard, 1735774
CROMBIE, Gnr, Robert, 11052500
DAVIS, Gnr, Edward, 1687169
DAVIS, Gnr, Laurence Arthur, 1833259
DAY, Gnr, Frank Arthur, 1547776
DEE, Bdr, Harry, 1523299
DERBYSHIRE, Gnr, John Robert, 11052164
DERRY, L/Bdr, Sydney Horace, 1735554
DIXON, L/Bdr, Richard Frederick, 1478346
DODD, Gnr, Alfred Henry George, 5780129
DONNELLY, Gnr, John George, 1792659
DOUGLAS, Gnr, Gilbert Georgeson, 1822310
DUFFIELD, Gnr, Gerard, 1623463
DUNNINGTON, Gnr, William C.H., 1800378
EAST, Gnr, Edgar James, 1718393
EAST, Sjt, William Godwin, 1479642
ELLIOT, Gnr, Thomas William, 1821316
ENGSTROM, Bdr, Robert Catchside Barnes, 11052571
EPSTINE, Gnr, Adrian, 11052572
FAIRBAIRN, Gnr, Frederick, 1687181
FARRANT, Gnr, Leonard Henry, 1549844
FAULKS, Gnr, Chares Henry, 1801594
FILLINGHAM, Gnr, lwilliam, 1824279
FINLEY, Gnr, Thomas, 1439163
FINNIGAN, Gnr, William, 11052575
FOLKES, BSM, Robert, 1545764
FORSTER, L/Bdr, John Walton, 11052577
FORSTER, Sjt, John Joseph, 1653727
FOSTER, Gnr, Eonard, 11051978
FOWLER, Bdr, George Frederick, 1653730
FRIEND, Gnr, George James Robert, 1653739
FROST, Gnr, William George, 1653743

FROST, Gnr, William John, 1549689
FULLER, L/Bdr, Frederick James, 1653632
GANMSBY, Gnr, John William, 1649397
GARDNER, L/Bdr, George, 1602188
GIGG, Gnr, John Henry, 1801598
GOODRUM, Gnr, Horace Ambrose, 1653719
GREEN, Gnr, Horace William, 1653681
GREGSON, Gnr, Alfred, 1105288
GREWCOCK, Bdr, Lawrence Henry, 1560157
GRIMSEY, Gnr, Charles Nathan, 1653751
GROVES, Gnr, Frederick, 1550169
HAGGER, Gnr, Jocelyn Alfred James, 1653756
HALL, Pte, John Edward W, 4436237
HALLSEY, Gnr, George Thomas, 1550136
HAMILTON, Gnr, John James, 1490118
HARDACRE, Gnr, George, 1808998
HARDING, Sjt, Alexander Sidney, 1653772
HARLAND, Gnr, William Taylor, 1487212
HARRISON, Gnr, Leslie, 11051992
HARVEY, Gnr, Thomas Henry, 1785740
HARVEY, Gnr, Leslie Ronald, 1687338
HASTIE, Gnr, John, 788277
HAYLETT, Gnr, George Sydney, 162653
HAZELTINE, Gnr, John, 1793073
HAZELTON, Bdr, George Ernest, 1486768
HEATHCOTE, Gnr, Cecil Arthur Clarence, 6214563
HESSEY, Gnr, Samuel, 11052510
HEYWOOD, Gnr, Clifford Joseph, 1738670
HILL, Gnr, William Roland, 1793075
HIRSTLE, Gnr, Lewis, 2085011
HODGKINSON, Gnr, Derek, 11052273
HOLDEN, Gnr, James, 1807912
HOLDER, L/Sjt, Hersey Jack, 1614385
HOOD, Gnr, Arthur, 11051943
HOPKINSON, Gnr, Henry, 11052169
HOTSTON, Gnr, Frederick, 1775968
HOWARTH, Gnr, William, 3313041
HOWETT, Gnr, James Alfred, 1687291
HUMPHREY, Gnr, Percy, 1696705
HUSBAND, Gnr, William Seymour, 1792616
IRON, Bdr, Edward James, 1678796
JAMES, Gnr, Stanley Edward, 1801620
JARDINE, Gnr, Albert, 11051585
JENMKINS, Gne, Albert William Edward, 1801622
JONES, Gnr, Brynley James, 1714865
KEENAN, Gnr, James Henry, 4454767
KING, Gnr, William George, 849796
KING, Gnr, Leslie Ernest, 1801627
LIPMAN, Gnr, Nathan, 1757667
LUCKETT, Gnr, Reginald Walter Frank, 1787429
MANNIX, Gnr, James, 11052533
MARSDEN, Gnr, James, 11052209
MASON, Gnr, William, 1809130
MAY, Gnr, Frank, 1782357
MAYHEW, L/Bdr, Herbert John, 1771509
McDONNELL, Gnr, William, 11051588
McKENNALL, Gnr, Edward, 1796166
McMEECHAN, Gnr, Charles, 1481925
MELLOR, Gnr, Edward, 11052238
MILES, Gnr, George Arthur, 1801526
MILLER, Sjt, Harry Lewis, 1482805
MILLS, Gnr, William James, 1490291
MOORE, Sjt, John Edward, 1560196
MORRIS, Bdr, Ronald, 11052176
MORRIS, Gnr, Reginald Sydney, 1801645
MOUG, Gnr, Stanley Snith, 1784627
MYERS, Gnr, Steve, 1801649
NORTHFIELD, Gnr, Alan, 11051912
O'HARA, Grn, George, 1809186
O'HARA, Gnr, Michael, 1605907

OLIVER, Gnr, Harry Samuel, 1801656
OWEN, Gnr, Leonard William Austen, 1520178
PAGE, Gnr, William Frederick, 1801660
PARSONS, Gnr, Ernest Frederick George, 1736040
PATRICK, Gnr, Frederick William, 11052549
PATTERSON, Gnr, Thomas, 1808947
PEEL, Gnr, Joseph, 1794569
PENROSE, Bdr, Samuel Herbert, 1611674
PHELAN, Gnr, Peter, 1801665
PICOT, Gnr, Edward John, 1684046
PLATT, L/Bdr, James Samuel, 11052180
POOLEY, Gnr, George, 1735753
PORTSMOUTH, Gnr, Ronald Arthur, 1801666
POTTER, Gnr, Ernest Rodhouse, 1801667
POWER, Gr, William, 1594951
PREW, L/Bdr, John, 1801670
PYLE, Gnr, Leslie Frederick Walter, 1556021
RAFFERTY, Gnr, James, 11053325
RAWLINGS, Gnr, Daniel, 1801690
READ, Gnr, James, 1809011
REDHED, Gnr, John Edward, 1801692
REID, Gnr, Kenneth William, 11051564
RELF, Gnr, Alexander Theodore Royston, 1550563
RICHARDS, Sjt, Thomas Herbert Ivan, 1717708
RICHARDS, Gnr, Darando, 1771494
RICHARDSON, Gnr, William Harold, 1801695
ROGERS, Gnr, Josiah, 1796224
ROGERS, Sjt, James William, 851182
ROSS, Gnr, James Godfrey, 1621236
ROUND, Gnr, Horace, 1495484
RUDLING, Gnr, John William Parker, 1488316
RUTHERFORD, Gnr, Ian Francis Hamilton, 1621240
SALTER, Gnr, James Henry, 5622407
SAUNDERS, Bdr, Ernest Frederick, 1544358
SAVILLE, Gnr, Walter, 11051931
SCOWEN, Sjt, Alfred William, 1486763
SHEALS, Gnr, Peter, 1784606
SHEARSMITH, L/Bdr, Douglas, 11051876
SHIPPEN, Gnr, John William, 1632166
SHORE, Gnr, Solomon, 1563035
SHUFFLETON, Gnr, James Albert, 11051567
SIMS, Gnr, William Arthur, 1827635
SKELT, Gnr, Robert Edward William, 1523356
SLADE, Gnr, Arthur Edgar, 1684076
SLEE, Gnr, John Robert, 1720477
SMITH, Gnr, Frank, 1761146
SMITH, Gnr, James, 1769308
SNEDDON, Gnr, Thomas, 1687386
SOMMERVILLE, Gnr, John Weir, 1828427
SPERRING, Sjt, Arthur John, 1736581
SWEENEY, Gnr, Michael, 1687396
TABBERER, Bdr, John Henry, 1569412
TAYLOR, Gnr, Cyril, 1554935
TAYLOR, Gnr, Albert Lenhurst, 1801686
TAYLOR, Bdr, Ralph Ambrose, 1482800
TERRY, Bdr, Leonard Lawrence, 1490292
TESTER, Gnr, Eric John Richard, 1563443
THOMAS, Gnr, Tudor Samuel, 1796246
THOMPSON, L/Bdr, Arthur, 11052607
THORPE, Gnr, Arthur George, 1547322
THURSTON, Gnr, Robert George, 1801699
TONKIN, Gnr, Jack, 11052188
TONKINSON, Gnr, John Steven, 1710408
TURNER, Gnr, John, 1807899
TUTTY, L/Bdr, James Gerald, 11052203
WARD, Gnr, Robert, 1784372
WASHINGTON, Gnr, Jim, 1753219
WATSON, Gnr, Peter, 1826753
WATTS, Gnr, Rupert Algernon, 1522895
WELLER, Gnr, Ernest Hamilton, 1801707

WESSENDORFF, Gnr, Jame Gordon, 1795289
WHITTLE, Gnr, William, 546730
WILLIAMS, Gnr, Arthur Owen, 1548161
WILLIAMSON, Gnr, John, 1827755
WILSON, Bdr, John, 1765808
WILSON, Gnr, Charles John, 1801710
WRIGHT, Gnr, William Robert, 1760227
YATES, Gnr, Albert Henry, 1717722
YATES, Gnr, Reginald Claud, 1801714

SEARCH LIGHT
DONKIN,Gnr,Richard Whitfield,16414105
SALTER,Sjt,Frederick Hobbs,8609715

5 SEARCH LIGHT
ADOLPH, L/bdr, Edward Joseph, 2089412
ARNALL, Gnr, Charles Oslwald, 1592818
ATKINSON, Bdr, Thomas, 856893
AYLWIN, Bdr, George Alfred Morrice, 2044384
BACK, Gnr, Willliam Frank, 2024954
BAINES, Gnr, Richard Charles, 2059076
BANKS, Gnr, Thomas, 1629455
BANNERMAN, Gnr, George Crombie, 1078333
BARBER, Gnr, William Leonard, 1686336
BARKER, L/Sjt, James, 872336
BAXTER, Gnr, William Edwin, 1696931
BEARD, Gnr, Cyril, 1629512
BELL, Gnr, Thomas, 5728123
BENNETT, Gnr, Dennis, 6967898
BERESFORD, Gnr, George, 1709676
BERRY, Gnr, Edward, 1629484
BISHOP, Bdr, Frederick Charles, 838292
BLACKLOCK, Gnr, Donald, 1629545
BOOTHBY, Gnr, Harold, 1709738
BRADLEY, Gnr, John, 1644058
BROPHY, Gnr, George, 1607461
BROUGHTON, Gnr, Rayomnd Thomas, 1717361
BRYAN, Bdr, Joseph, 827834
BURGE, Gnr, Leslie J, 1541589
BUTCHER, Gnr, Frank, 2061975
CADDY, Gnr, John Albert, 1709706
CAMMACK, Gnr, Charles, 1686046
CAPERS, L/bdr, Victor Frederick, 872279
CARROLL, L/bdr, William James, 1629485
CARTER, Gnr, Frank, 1644089
CARTER, Gnr, John Vernon, 2056840
CARTIN, Gnr, James, 1629486
CHEESEMAN,Bdr,Eric Victor,6286906
CLAGUE, Gnr, James, 1709586
CLOWES, Gnr, Alexander, 1709707
COLEMAN, Gnr, Harry Frederick Joseph, 2056078
COLES, Gnr, Ernest Martin, 2025946
COLGAN, Gnr, James, 1613510
COLLEY, Gnr, Sidney, 1629011
CONWAY, Gnr, William Thomas, 1629575
COOK, Gnr, Clement, 1709678
COOKSON, Gnr, Wilfred, 1709708
COOPER, Gnr, George, 1709679
COPER, Gnr, Frederick Joseph, 1592793
COURAGE, Gnr, Charslay John, 5726602
COX, Gnr, Francis Ralph, 1686349
DAVIE, Lt, Peter Hamlyn Wilson, 170158
DAWES, Bdr, Fred, 2045478
DOBSON, Gnr, George Mortimer, 1429464
DOYLE, Gnr, George Frederick, 1629465
DUNKLAY, Gnr, Alfred, 2048135
ELLERSHAW, L/bdr, Thomas Sedgwick, 1613548
FAIRBROTHER, Gnr, George, 1629579
FARLEY, Gnr, Douglas, 1613526
FIGG, Gnr, Albert, 3649636

FORD, Gnr, Michael Thomas, 1607466
FORD, Gnr, Albert, 1709686
FOX, Sjt, Edward James, 799349
FREELAND, Gnr, Samuel, 847375
FULLEN, Gnr, Edward Bernard, 1709712
GLYNN, Gnr, Alfred, 1644060
GODDARD, Bqms, William George, 1424537
GREENLAND, Gnr, Frank Thomas, 2050994
GRIFFITHS, Gnr, George, 1709714
GRIFFITHS, Gnr, Harold, 1709533
HAL, L/bdr, William Frederick, 2038814
HALL, S/Sjt, Robert, 863998
HALSALL, Gnr, William, 1629467
HARE, Gnr, Thomas William, 1607469
HARMAN, Gnr, Peter John, 6287515
HARRIS, Gnr, George Robert, 1686286
HARTLEY, Gnr, Arthur Martin, 1629523
HEAD, Sjt, Frederick Maurice, 2035224
HEDGER, L/bdr, Douglas Alfred, 2054916
HENDY, Gnr, Norman Frank, 6287215
HERMITAGE,Gnr,Jack Frederick,1788158
HERSON, Gnr, Myer, 1709715
HEWITT, Gnr, Thomas, 1644063
HEYS, Gnr, Tom, 1514199
HIL, L/bdr, William Henry, 872717
HILLIER, Bdr, Charles Albert Frederick, 2049436
HINCHCLIFFE, Gnr, George, 1709596
HOBBS,Gnr,Alfred James,2038324
HOOPER, Gnr, George Henry, 1629582
HORLEY, L/bdr, Henry James Frederick, 2050524
HORTON, Gnr, Arthur, 1709689
HUBBARD, Bdr, Charles, 872387
HUCHINSON, Gnr, Leslie, 1709690
HUGHES, Gnr, George, 1644095
HUNT, L/jt, Eric Thomas, 5109079
HUTTON-TAYLOR, L/bdr, Eric Sydney, 2085023
HUXLEY, Gnr, Edward, 1629553
IRISH, Gnr, Thomas Henry, 2047759
JACKSON, Gnr, Arthur, 1709753
JAMIESON, Gnr, Richard, 1709572
JAQUES, Gnr, William, 154368
JARDINE, L/bdr, Sanley, 1629554
JARVIS, Gnr, James, 2081724
JOHNSON, Gnr, Frederick, 1573751
JOHNSON, Gnr, Charles Thomas, 1629470
JOHNSON, Gnr, Patrick, 1709718
JOHNSON, Gnr, Frank, 1629586
JONES, Gnr, Arnold, 1629471
JONES, Gnr, James Bower, 1709751
KEETON, Gnr, Valentine, 1686112
KENT, Gnr, Sydney Harold, 1696567
LATIMER, Gnr, John Thomas, 1641466
LEGG, Bdr, Cyril Albert, 2054196
LILLEY, Gnr, Arthur Leonard, 837440
LINDSEY, Gnr, Leonard, 1613546
LLOYD,Gnr,James Patrick,1709600
LOADER, Gnr, Harold Thomas, 5726185
LOVE, Gnr, Stanley, 1585451
MARKEY, Gnr, John Reginald, 1709664
MARKLAND, Gnr, Frank, 4181571
MARSDEN, Gnr, James, 1644148
MARSHALL, Gnr, Mathew Speed, 2057105
MATTERFACE, Gnr, Ernest William, 5726895
MEADE, Gnr, Francis Penrose, 1629496
MILLAR, Gnr, William Stanley, 1709755
MILLER, Gnr, James William Fergie, 1641427
MOORE, Bdr, Ronald, 842575
MORTON, Gnr, Allan James, 1649516
MULKERN, L/Sjt, Hubert Cowell, 2082504
MURRAY, Gnr, Vincent, 2087427

NAPPIN, Gnr, Frederick Charles, 6203841
NEKREWES, Gnr, Ronald Thomas Service, 1628962
NEWLAND, Sjt, Edward Thomas, 826388
NORRIS, Gnr, Stanley Jack, 1627882
NORRIS, Gnr, Henry Arthur, 1507247
NOWELL, Gnr, Leslie, 1676833
OLDHAM, Gnr, Louis Vincent, 1629498
OLLIVANT, Gnr, Walter, 1788884
OLROG, L/Sjt, William John Christian, 6140098
ORMESHER, Gnr, Robert Edward, 1607481
PALMER, Sjt, Thomas, 819027
PARKIN, Bdr, Edward, 865676
PARROCK, Gnr, John Henry, 1709697
PARROTT, Gnr, Frank, 1709545
PEDDLE, Gnr, Maurice George Charles, 1497988
PERROTT, Bdr, William George Lecky, 835997
PETTIT, Gnr, Arthur Alexander, 1592836
PHILLIPS, L/bdr, William Albert, 1629590
POTTER, Sjt, Frederick James, 825915
RADFORD, Bdr, Harold, 872579
REHM, Gnr, Dennis Patrick, 1713949
RIMMER, Gnr, William Joseph, 1726364
ROBERTS, Gnr, Harold, 1709607
ROGERS, Gnr, John Elsley, 1592839
ROWLINSON, L/bdr, Richard, 1057548
RUSH, Gnr, John, 1629593
RYCROFT, Bdr, Arthur Martyn, 845251
SAMBRIDGE, L/bdr, Alfred James, 1592812
SENIOR, Gnr, John Thomas, 1629503
SHAW, Gnr, James, 1629597
SHAW, Gnr, Arthur, 1676908
SILLS, Gnr, Herbert, 1709730
SIMS, Gnr, William George, 2051712
SIZER, Gnr, Arthur, 1686223
SMART, Gnr, Wiliam, 1629535
SMITH, Gnr, Harold, 1686312
SMITH, Gnr, Walter, 1709549
SMYTH, L/bdr, William James, 1719305
SNOOKS, Gnr, Samuel, 1807370
STACE, L/Sjt, Philip Henry, 859370
STANTON, Gnr, William, 1709671
STOCKER, L/bdr, Howard Walter, 2088540
STUBBS, Bdr, Robert, 2034318
SWALLOW, L/Sjt, William George Rufus, 2035324
TEMPEST, Gnr, John William, 1644155
THOMAS, L/Sjt, George Ronald, 850807
THOMAS, Gnr, Albert Henry, 1709702
THOMPSON, Gnr, George Arthur, 1709731
THRELFALL, L/Sjt, John Edgar, 845330
TIDD, Bdr, William, 2042771
TOLOND, Gnr, Frederick, 1625937
TURNER, Gnr, Ben Alfred, 1709732
VICKERS, Gnr, William Hugh, 1709704
WAGHORN, Gnr, Thomas, 1709734
WALSH, Gnr, William Henry, 1629568
WARDLE, Gnr, Ernest, 1709551
WARMAN, L/Sjt, William, 802087
WELBELOVE, Sjt, Sidney, 1073551
WEST, Gnr, Ewart Edward Ralph, 1613525
WHEELER, Gnr, Leonard Victor, 2041713
WHITAKER, Gnr, Donald Marsland, 1538599
WHITE, Gnr, Philip Horace, 2039520
WINSTANLEY, Gnr, George, 1709553
WITHERSTONE, Gnr, Edwin, 1709552
WOOD, Gnr, Thomas William, 1709554
WOODHEAD, Gnr, Frederick, 1676933

30 SEARCH LIGHT
TEASDALE, Gnr, Eric, 2061680

ROYAL SCOTS
ANDERSON, Pte, Colin Kindness, 3053544
BELL, Pte, Thomas Baxter, 3054412
BLACKIE, Cpl, Arthur Henry, 3054165
BOOTH, Sjt, James Dunbar, 2874392
BOWES, Lt, George William, 205366
BUTTERFIELD, Pte, Edward, 3055692
CHALMERS, Cpl, Andrew, 3054504
COYLE, Pte, Hugh, 3055188
CRICHTON, Cpl, Thomas Easton, 3050013
CUTHBERTSON, Capt, Norman Henderson, 74594
DUFF, Pte, Joseph Parkerson, 3054089
DUNNELL, Pte, Kenneth Stanley, 3053771
EDGAR, Pte, Robert, 3054528
FARMER, Pte, George, 3059158
FERGUS, Sjt, John, 3052141
FRASER, Sjt, William Noble, 3049325
GOODFELLOW, Esm, Isaac, 3050915
GOUGH, Drmr, Albert Stanley Howard, 3053530
GRAY, Pte, Ian, 3055728
GREIG, Pte, Joseph, 3055733
HALL, Pte, Ralph, 3054843
HARLOW, L/Cpl, Harry, 3059154
HART, Lt, Colin James, 177486
JAMES, Pte, William Anderson, 3054486
LAWSON, Pte, Alexander Brown, 3053784
LEEN, Pte, Edward, 7047747
McLARNEY, L/Cpl, Joseph, 354207
MERCHANT, Pte, David Johnson, 3053641
MILLER, Pte, Alan, 3059109
MORROW, L/Cpl, John Alexander Wilson, 3059290
MOYES, Bndsn, Henry, 3054403
MYLES, Pte, James, 3055407
PARK, Cpl, E Hamilton White, 3053694
PATTULLO, Pte, David, 3053616
PHILLIPS, L/Cpl, Joseph, 3054068
RAE, Pte, Thomas, 3054394
ROUGH, Pte, Harry Robson, 3055925
SCOTT, Pte, William, 3053613
SINCLAIR, Pte, Alexander George, 3063759
STANNARD, Pte, William Witherden, 3063763
TAYLOR, C/Sjt, Alexander, 3051885
TOOTHILL, Pte, Robert Ernest, 3059144

ROYAL SUSSEX REGIMENT
HARLEY, Pte, Eric, 14842337
HISCOCKS, Pl, Thomas John Richard, 5576992

ROYAL WELCH FUSILIERS
BLAKE, Sjt, Albert Eadon, 6456400
CHEERS, L/Sjt, Frederick Merlyn, 14867436
COLLINS, W/o 1, Walter, 6003140
PRICE, Fus, R.S., 14996277
ROBERTS, Fus, Harold, 19001817
SIMS, Fus, Arthur, 1438615

SEAFORTH HIGHLANDERS
DAVIE, Lt, Ronald James, 362889
DAVIES, L/Cpl, James, 3447680
KIRKWOOD, Pte, John Knox, 14833957
LEE, Maj, S.J.S. (MC), 112874
OWENS, Pte, M E, 14467270
ROWEL, L/Cpl, John Gordon, 2978983
ROY, Pte, David, 2818472

SHERWOOD FORESTERS
ATKIN, Pte, Harold, 4972390
BANNISTER, Cpl, Sidney, 4974065
BARBER, Pte, Reginald Stanley, 4978013
BARKER, Pte, William, 4975655

BARROWCLIFFE, Pte, Albert, 4978033
BATEMAN, L/Cpl, James Walter, 4656029
BAYLEY, Pte, Albert Elfred, 4756030
BEARD, Pte, Richard John, 4756031
BECK, Pte, John Frederick, 4979567
BEDDOES, Pte, James, 7903779
BELL, Pte, James Wiliam, 2573995
BENNETT, Pte, Frederick William, 4756033
BERESFORD, Sjt, William Henry, 4966491
BETHEL, Capt, Charles, 93927
BETTS, Pte, Charles William, 4976711
BIGLEY, Sjt, John Henry, 4968257
BLOWERS-WRIGHT, Pte, Derrick, 4619384
BONSER, L/Cpl, Frank, 1078817
BRADY, Pte, Percy John Alford, 4620516
BRANDON, Pte, John William, 4756039
BRANSTONE, Pte, Robert Stephen, 4620517
BRIERS, Pte, George Frederick, 4974716
BROO, Pte, John, 4979459
BROOKS, Pte, John William Jobson, 4975578
BROWN, Pte, Reginald Norman, 4984518
BROWNRIGG, Lt, John Forrester, 71179
BRYANT, Pte, Frederick Thomas William, 4750596
BULLING, Pte, Joseph, 4619378
BUNYAN, Pte, Donald Hankins, 4981054
BURCH, Pte, Cyril, 4978113
BURKE, Pte, Herbert, 4978121
BURROWS, Pte, Charles George, 4981840
BYRNE, L/Cpl, Frederick Charles, 4750555
BYRON, Pte, Peter, 4984584
CARDIGAN, Pte, Eugene, 7932670
CARR, Pte, William Walter, 4977565
CARRINGTON, Sjt, Jack, 4970089
CARTER, Pte, Robert Victor, 4619737
CARTER, Pte, Thomas Claude, 4750034
CARTWRIGHT, 2/lt, John Robert, 165817
CASTALLETTE, Pte, Arthur Harold, 4978366
CLARE, Pte, Arthur, 4981402
CLIBBENS, Pte, Walter Robert, 4656057
CLIFFORD, Cpl, Francis, 5045141
CLIFTON, Pte, Thomas, 4978782
COLE, Pte, Charles Frederick, 4756058
COLE-BOWERS, Pte, Sidney, 4976071
COX, Pte, William John, 4985363
COX, L/Cpl, James Edward, 4756062
CRACKLES, Pte, Cecil Walter, 4756063
CRIPPS, Pte, Walter Winston, 4976588
CRISPIN, Pte, Thomas William, 4756064
CRONIN, Pte, Frederick, 4982764
CURR, Pte, Stanley Jack, 4756068
CUTBILL, Pte, John Thomas (MM), 4756069
DALE, Pte, John, 4975652
DANSKIN, Pte, Alfred Scott, 4620556
DAVIES, Pte, George Ronald, 4976592
DAVIS, Pte, Sidney, 4978085
DAVIS, Pte, Lawrence, 4975962
DENMAN, Pte, Ronald, 4979890
DENMAN, L/Cpl, Wilfred, 4976593
DICKENS, Pte, Arthur Newell, 4756075
DODGE,Pte,Stanley Cyril,4975813
DRAPER, Pte, Reginald, 4978046
DUFFIELD, Pte, John, 4756078
DUNNE, Pte, Victor, 5112680
DUROSE, Pte, Ernest Edward, 4977301
EAST, Pte, Harold, 4620568
ECCLES, Pte, Joseph, 4981376
ECCLESTON, Pte, Thomas, 4079476
ELLIOT, Pte, Henry Arthur, 4753916
FAIRBROTHER, Pte, Leonard, 4971523
FARMER, Pte, John Charles Sydney, 4620573

FELTON, Pte, George William, 4756084
FISHER, Pte, Jack, 4978067
FITCHETT, Pte, Edwin, 4979486
FLETCHER, Pte, Seth James, 4976527
FORD, Pte, Walter Douglas, 4978082
FOSTER, Pte, Bertie Walter, 4756085
FOULK, Pte, Ranall, 4976650
FREEMAN, Pte, Reginald James, 4756088
FRESHWATER, Pte, Arthur David, 4750560
GADSBY, Pte, Arthur Gordon, 4978066
GARNHAM, Csm, Horace Herbert Williams, 4971163
GEE, Pte, William, 4747976
GIBBS, Pte, Reginald Walter, 4619786
GILBERT, Pte, Leonard Charles, 4756091
GIRDLESTONE, Cpl, Horace, 4978130
GOLDING, Pte, Reginald Spear, 4756093
GOODALL, Pte, Henry, 4978131
GREASLEY,Pte,Frank Frecknall,4978104
GREEN, Pte, Gerald Frank, 4756098
GRICE, Pte, Ivan Verdun, 4978112
GROVES, Sjt, Robert William Melville, (K/N)
HALFORD, Pte, John Hartshorn, 839801
HALL, Pte, Leslie, 4983583
HALL, Pte, Granville, 4977671
HALL, Pte, Walter Leonard, 4619445
HARDWICK, Pte, George Alfred, 4977090
HARDWICK, Pte, Reginald, 4978047
HARDY, Pte, John, 4978070
HARE,L/Cpl,Henry Charles,4619448
HARGREAVES, Pte, James, 4977944
HARPER, L/Cpl, Enneth Leslie, 4750691
HARRISON, Pte, Jack Verdun, 4857664
HARVEY, Pte, Harold Ernest, 4978058
HAWLEY,L/Cpl,Leslie Wiliam, 4977593
HAYES, Cpl, Herbert, 4978200
HAYWOOD,Pte,James Frederick,4078012
HENSON, Pte, George, 4983292
HEPHER, L/sjt, Albert Arthur, 4756112
HILL, Sjt, Harry, 47742247
HILL, Sjt, Edgar, 4978148
HILTON, Pte, Eric Bertrand, 4982391
HINCHCLIFFE, Sjt, Charles Robert, 4972075
HINES, Pte, John Clements, 5773126
HINKS, Sjt, Alfred Ernest, 4977499
HOLDEN, Capt, Peter Vivien Shuttleworth, 52663
HOLMES, Pte, William Keith, 4978021
HOLYOAK, Pte, Ernest George, 4976836
HORNE, L/Cpl, Albert, 4966425
HOROBIN, Pte, William, 4972315
HOUGHTON, Te, Frederick Victor, 4756117
HOWELL, Sjt, Frederick, 4976627
HUBBARD, Pte, Dennis Gordon, 4974854
HYMAN, Pte, Maurice, 4756120
JEBSON, Pte, Ernest Edward, 4977650
JEFFS, Pte, Henry James, 4620617
JEPHCOTE, Pte, John William, 4976299
JEPHCOTE, Sjt, Stanley Thomas, 4967329
JOHNSON, Pte, William Manifold, 4977486
JONES, Pte, Leonard, 4983622
KEIR, Pte, George Thomas, 4755998
KIDGER-PRESTON, Pte, Dennis, (K/N)
KISS, Pte, Charles Edwin, 4618499
KRIEGER, Pte, Alfred, 4750648
LAYTON, L/Cpl, John, 4978521
LOWE, L/Cpl, George Wilfred, 4976056
LUDLAM, Pte, Frederick William Harrison, 4976302
LYONS,Pte,Alfred George,4756128
MADIN, Pte, Thomas, 4977672
MALAN, Pte, Henry, 4982422
MARKEY, Pte, Fred Charles, 4619678

MARRIOTT, Pte, Bertie, 4967751
MARSDEN, Pte, William Edward, 4978050
MEAKIN, Te, Herbert, 4983655
MEE, Pte, Lewis Claude, 4982837
MEE-BISHOP, Pte, Thomas, 4970700
MELBOURNE, Pte, Walter, 4976073
MILLER, Pte, George D, 4750574
MILWARD, Pte, Thomas Henry, (K/N)
MOSLEY, Pte, Thomas Henry, 4973001
MOXHAM, Pte, Frank William, 4756140
MULROY, Lt, Terence Patrick, 203861
NADIN, Pte, Sidney, 4978024
NASH, Cpl, Roy Kelvin, 4620660
NEAL, Csm, George Ernest, 4967912
NEARY, Pte, Frank, 4981461
NEILL, Pte, Henry Francis, 4984560
NETTLETON, Pte, Horace Wilkins, 4620662
NEWBOLD, Cpl, Clifford Arthur, 4978105
NORRIS, Pte, George Albert, 4620666
OLDERSHAW, Cpl, Robert Arthur, 4978351
PALMER, L/Cpl, William Edwin, 4750578
PALMER, Pte, Charles Henry, 4976937
PARKER, Pte, William Stanley, 4750554
PARKER, Pte, Samuel Charles, 4978702
PARKIN, Pte, John Albert Maurice, 4754097
PARKINSON, Pte, Herbert, 4976363
PEARCE, Pte, Edward, 4976104
PHILLIPS, Cpl, William Benjamin, 4976091
PILKINGTON, Pte, George William, 4620678
PLUMMER, Pte, George Henry, 4978603
POLLINGTON, Pte, Frederick Claude, 4981264
PORTER, Cpl, Frank Dennis, 4977491
PURLAND, Pte, Arthur, 4756163
RAYNOR, Pte, Gordon, 4978113
REED, Pte, Albert Ernest, 4756168
ROBERTS, Pte, Fred, 4976427
ROBINSON, Pte, John Edward, 4620691
RODEN, Pte, Robert, 4914222
RODWELL, Pte, Arthur Charles Stab, 4750570
ROOK, Capt, Peter, 67912
ROTHWEL, Pte, Albert, 4981465
SADLER, Pte, Arthur George, 4978373
SAMUELS, Pte, Kenneth Douglas, 4983723
SANDERSON, Pte, James Edward, 4975770
SCUDDER, Pte, Leonard, 4983730
SELBY, Pte, Arthur, 4982867
SELLORS, Pte, Frederick Allan, 4983157
SEVERN, Pte, Walter, 4981755
SHAW, Cpl, Horace, 4978064
SHEPHERD, Pte, Frederick, 5112673
SIMMONDS, Pte, Harry, 4756182
SIMMS, Pte, Eric, 4975884
SIMPKIN, Pte, Lewis, 4974936
SKEEN, Pte, Harold, 4981363
SLEVIN, L/Cpl, Nicholas, 4977549
SMALLWOOD, Pte, Herbert Kenneth, 4858990
SMITH, Pte, Ambrose, 4975643
SMITH, Pte, Herbert, 4971975
SPALLACY, Pte, Robert, 4984600
SPAUL, Pte, Alfred, 4756190
STANLEY, Cpl, Leslie Robert, 4978258
STANLEY, Pte, Joseph, 4974933
STENTON, Pte, Charles Reggie, 4978022
STEVENSON, L/Cpl, John, 4978385
STILES, L/Cpl, John Thomas, 4756192
STIRK, Pte, Kenneth Harry, 4976401
STORER, Pte, George Edward, 4756194
STUART, Pte, Walter, 4756198
SUMMERS, Pte, John Henry, 4756199
SWIFT, Pte, Francis Ernest, 4978623

TAFT, Pte, Albert James, 4981776
TAYLOR, Pte, James, 483166
TAYLOR, Pte, Cyril John Arthur, 4978065
TAYLOR, Pte, James, 4983167
TAYLOR, Pte, Herbert Charles, 4756204
THOMPSON, Pte, Percy, 4978135
THORLEY, Sjt, Frederick, 4974041
THORNTON, Capt, Lionel Cuthbert, 51476
THORP, Pte, Harry Osborne, 4756209
THORPE, Pte, Roland, 4978132
TOMLIN, Pte, Robert, 4972330
TRUMAN, Pte, Percy Edward, 5981786
TRUMAN, Pte, Douglas, 4978719
TURTON, Pte, George, 4978885
TYLER, Pte, Frank Edwin, 4977439
VINER, L/Cpl, Edward Thomas, 4749872
VINTEN, Pte, Walter Stanley, 4756221
WAKEFIELD, Pte, Charles Frederick, 4756224
WALKER, Pte, Leslie, 4976303
WALKER, Pte, Henry Joseph, 4756225
WALKER, Pte, George, 4981792
WALKER, Pte, Andrew Leslie, 4981298
WARD, Pte, Joseph Richard Bell, 4974987
WARD, Pte, Harry, 4979360
WARFIELD, Pte, Frank Ronald, 4956232
WARNER, L/Cpl, Charles Arthur, 4978074
WATSON, Cpl, Ernest, 4756238
WEATHERBURN, L/Cpl, Thomas Leslie, 4756241
WEAVER, Pte, George William, 4981452
WEBB, Pte, Frederick Oliver, 4756243
WHITBREAD, Pte, William Henry, 4978001
WHITBREAD, Cpl, Arthur, 4982907
WHITE, L/Cpl, Reginald Victor, 4756253
WHITE, Lt, Francis John, 165816
WHITEHEAD, Pte, Arthur William, 4978035
WHITTAKER, Pte, Cyril Douglas, 4978143
WHITTINGHAM, Sjt, Arthur Wilfred, 4976028
WHYATT, L/Cpl, Arthur, 4976013
WHYMAN, Pte, Douglas Lawson, 4975166
WILES, Cpl, George, 4743294
WILES, Cpl, George, 4743294
WILKINS, Cpl, Leonard John, 4919598
WINDLE, Pte, Harry, 4978280
WISE, Pte, Edward Walter, 4756263
WITCHLOW, Pte, Arthur John Charles, 4756264
WOODCOCK, L/Cpl, William, 4978334
WOODGATE, Pte, Eric Arthur John, 4756267
WOODWARD, L/Cpl, Harry Charles, 4971782
WOOLLEY, Pte, Daniel Wilson, 4978658
WOOTTON, Pte, Sydney Lawrence, 4981528
WORTHINGTON, Pte, Stanley Thomas, 4980072
WOTHERSPOON, Pte, Hugh Strickland, 4978015
WRIGHT, Pte, William Ernest, 4620750
WRIGHT, Pte, George William, 4756271
WRIGHT, Pte, Arthur Cyril, 4973316
WRIGHT, Pte, Joseph William, 4981813
WYATT, Pte, Albert Ernest, 4756273
YEATMAN, Pte, Edward Arthur, 4981787
YEOWELL, Pte, Bernard, 4756274

SOMERSET LIGHT INFANTRY
FRANCIS, Cpl, Frederick George, 5673095
VILE, Sjt, Frederick Daniel, 5667460

SOUTH LANCASHIRE
HAINWORTH, Wo/1, Harold Burt, 3657419

SOUTH WALES BORDERERS
EVANS, Pte, Thomas, 4074883
FLYNN, Pte, James, 2718011

HAWKINS,Pte,William Walter,5577505

SUFFOLK REGIMENT
4 BATTALION
ABBOTT, Pte, Charles Ernest William, 5833165
ADCOCK, Cpl, Davis Angus, 6018959
ALDRIDGE, Pte, Reginald, 6028662
ALLISTON, Pte, Jack Ernest, 6020671
ANDREASON, Pte, Eric Julins, 5828161
ANDREWS, Cpl, Ernest Albert George, 5830635
ARBON, Pte, Sidney James, 5829871
ARCHER, Lt, Humphrey Frewen, 117644
ARCHER, L/Sjt, William John, 6918934
ARNOLD, Pte, Donald Smith, 5831135
ARNOLD, Pte, Sidney Allan, 5833755
ASHWORTH, Pte, Thomas, 5827895
AUSTIN, Pte, Frank, 5829846
BABBAS, Pte, Alfred George Ellis, 6020675
BAILEY, Sjt, Percy Leonard, 5825358
BAINBOROUGH, Pte, George, 5829634
BAKER, Pte, Fredderick Lawrence, 6019167
BALDRY, L/Cpl, George Herbert, 5828245
BALDRY, Pte, Gordon George, 5827415
BALDRY, Pte, Cyril Ronald, 5827169
BALES, Pte, Arthur William, 5827078
BALL, Pte, Robert Henry, 5828999
BALLS, Pte, David William, 5834324
BALSTER, Cpl, Douglas Percy, 5830293
BANKS, Pte, Richard, 6028544
BARNSLEY, 2/lt, Francis Albert, 184112
BARRETT, Pte, Ernest John, 5827897
BEAN, Pte, Roy Francis, 5833205
BEARMAN, Pte, Frederick John, 6020083
BEECROFT, L/pl, Bernard Victor, 5830621
BERRY, Pte, Granville Arthur, 5828253
BIRD, Pte, Ronald Elija, 6019053
BIXBY, Pte, Cyril, 6020612
BLAKE, Pte, Alfred Douglas, 5828241
BLAKE, Pte, William George, 5828252
BLOWERS, Pte, Stanley Frederick, 7370732
BRAYSHER, Pte, Roland Norris, 5933280
BROWN, Capt, Noel Anderson, 68093
BROWN, Maj, John Anderson, 47940
BROWN, Pte, Cyril George, 5832937
BUCK, Cpl, Cyril, 5827907
BUCKLE, Pte, Leslie Wiliam, 5827079
BUTLER, Pte, Thomas, 6020763
CAHILL, Pte, Alec, 5829614
CALVER, Pte, George Dennis, 5828218
CARABAJAL, Pte, Edgar Ammaldo, 5835243
CARNE, Pte, Thomas Charles, 5832943
CARRIER, Pte, Percy Frederick, 5832945
CARTER, Pte, Frank Henry, 5827475
CATCHPOLE, Pte, Gordon Ernest, 5828086
CATTERMOLE, Pte, Harry Thomas, 5829784
CHAPMAN, Pte, Cyril, 6020689
CHAPPIN, Pte, Dennis Alfred, 5830327
CHENERY, Pte, Cecil John, 5828072
CHERRY, Pte, Arthur Eric, 5828993
CHITTOCK, Pte, Bert, 5827502
CLACK, Pte, Ronald Ward, 5830665
CLAPTON, Sgmn, Eric Frank, 2359413
CLARIDGE, Pte, Cyril Charles, 5829885
CLARKE, Pte, John Alfred, 5832953
CLAYTON, Pte, David, 5829611
CLEMENTS, Pte, Allan Louis, 5828007
COATES, Pte, Charles Edward, 5828150
COLBRON, Sjt, John Rice, 5825375
COLE, Pte, Russell Bernard, 5827258
COLE, L/Cpl, William George, 5826828

COLLETT, Pte, Francis Robert Charles, 5826640
COLLINS, Pte, George Edward, 5825484
CONNOLLY, Pte, Richard James, 5829625
CONSTANCE, Pte, Frederick Leonard, 5828149
COOPER, Pte, Albert Rahere, 5829621
COOPER, Pte, Fred Charles, 5828206
COOPER, Pte, Charles Alfred, 6013469
CRANE, Pte, Eric Edward, 5835478
CRITTEN, Pte, John Henry, 5829639
CROSS, L/Cpl, James Charles, 5828198
CROSS, Pte, James, 6020764
CUTHBERT, Pte, William John, 6013915
DAUNTER, Pte, Leonard, 6028695
DAVIES, Pte, Stanley William Edward, 6028580
DAY, L/Cpl, Stanley John, 6020742
DAY, Pte, William George, 5828231
DAY, Pte, Peter Eric, 5828096
DEVONSHIRE, Pte, Victor James, 5829642
DICKERSON, Pte, Arthur Ronald, 5828008
DILLOW, Pte, William Thomas, 5827802
DOCKERILL, Pte, Harry Charles, 5830189
DOE, Pte, Stanley Alfred, 5829612
DOLBY, Pte, George Leslie, 5832971
DOUBLE, Pte, Frederick Charles, 6019071
DOW, Pte, Arthur, 6028813
DURN, Pte, Stanley Edward, 5834079
DYAS, Pte, Ernest John, 6024306
EAGLE, Pte, Charles William Henry, 5827075
ENGLISH, Pte, Neville Percy, 5832979
EVANS, Pte, Robert Thomas, 5828214
EVERETT, Pte, Bertram Joseph, 5834362
FAIRHEAD, Sjt, Alfred William, 5826435
FAITH, Pte, Alfred Charles, 5833436
FARRINGTON, Pte, Sidney, 5828074
FAYERS, Pte, Albert Edward, 5834612
FEAKINS, Pte, John Percy, 6020606
FELLGETT, Pte, George Leslie Mons, 5828190
FISHER, Pte, William, 5828272
FLATT, Cpl, Victor Albert, 5825877
FLEET, Pte, Frederick Archie, 5831092
FLEMMING, Pte, Reginald James, 5826829
FLEMMING, Pte, Reginald James, 5826829
FOLKARD, Pte, Ivan Sranley, 5828226
FORD, Pte, Eric Peter, 5828236
FORD, Pte, Ernest Henry, 5831281
FORTUNE, Pte, Reginald Percy, 5832989
FOULGER, Pte, Robert, 5827512
FOX, Pte, Horace Raymond, 5827792
FRANCIS, Pte, Alfred James William, 5827514
FRANCIS, Pte, Reginald George, 5827359
FREWEN, Pte, James William, 5836310
FROST, L/Cpl, George Albert Mills, 5830369
FULLER, Pte, George, 5834371
FYSON, Pte, Ernest, 5833178
GAME, Pte, George Thomas Cecil, 6021106
GARDNER, Pte, Robert Allan George, 5827115
GARRETT, Cpl, Nelson Robert, 5827164
GARROD, Cpl, Ronald Frank, 5825934
GILES, Pte, John William, 6018982
GIRLING, Pte, Reginald Stanley, 5827144
GLANFIELD, L/Cpl, Charles Herbert, 5825955
GOODAY, Pte, Norman George, 6019078
GOODCHILD, Pte, Kenneth Charles, 5830606
GOODING, Pte, Ronald Francis, 5827631
GOODING, Pte, George William, 5828133
GOODWIN, Pte, Joseph Charles, 5829865
GORDON, Pte, Peter Connal, 6020032
GRANT, Pte, Albert Frederick, 6018985
GRAY, Pte, Reginald Henry, 6021115
GREEN, L/Cpl, Jack, 5826143

GURNER, Pte, Leonard George, 5832627
GUYVER, Pte, James, 6121117
HALES, Pte, Bertie, 6021171
HAMPTON, Cpl, Walter C, 5827264
HARKNESS, Pte, William, 6020617
HAYES, Pte, Patrick, 6020064
HAYES, Pte, George Arthur, 5832641
HAYWOOD, Cpl, Frederick Harry, 5830650
HEATH, Pte, Arthur Herbert, 6020099
HEATHER, Pte, Frederick James, 5828977
HENDRY, Pte, William Henry, 6018200
HENNIGAN, Pte, David, 5836230
HENRY, Pte, Stanley Maurice, 6019219
HERITAGE, L/Cpl, Ronald Frederick, 6020062
HERRON, Pte, Arthur, 5830637
HEWETT, L/Cpl, Victor Arthur, 5830653
HOLLOWELL, Maj, Walter James, 41824
HOLMES, 2/lt, Rex Alec, 180099
HOPKINS, Pte, Thomas James, 5774190
HOWARD, Pte, Frank, 5826780
HOWARD, Cpl, Charles Albert, 5826704
HOWARD, Pte, John Thomas Alfred, 5830955
HOWLETT, Pte, Reginald Charles, 5827161
HOY, Pte, Edward, 6020488
HUGHES, Pte, Thomas Alfred, 6018988
HUGMAN, Pte, George, 5826497
HUMPHREY, Lt, Lionel Dudley, 138473
JAMIESON, Pte, Walter Edward, 6021140
JARVIS, Pte, Sydney John, 6020618
JAY, Pte, John Charles, 5826896
JEFFRIES, Gnr, Philip Henry John, 6020649
JONES, Pte, William Francis, 5833183
JONES, Pte, Thomas Patrick, 5830784
KENNETT, Lt, John Nevil Pollard, 130024
KETTLE, Pte, George William, 5835513
KNIGHT, L/pl, Hubert William, 5828183
LAMBERT, Pte, William John, 3827165
LEE, Pte, James, 5827546
LEECH, L/Sjt, William James, 5825646
LEEK, Csm, Frederick George Henry, 5823687
LINDER, Pte, Horace William, 5826462
LLOYD, Pte, Albert Cecil, 5830612
LOCK, 2/lt, Norman Ingram, 193369
LORD, Pte, Reginald Arthur, 5828194
LUCAS, Pte, William Arthur, 5825378
LUCAS, Pte, Norman, 5829608
MACE, Pte, George William, 5826232
MANSFIELD, Pte, Wilfred David, 5827424
MARLER, C/Sjt, George, 7814212
MARSH, Pte, Tom Charles, 5830573
MARTIN, Pte, Robert, 752546
MARTIN, Pte, William Charles, 5823924
MAYHEW, Pte, Harry, 5827038
McDONALD, Cpl, Richmond Morrison, 5833044
MEADOWS, L/Cpl, Cecil George, 5828249
MEADOWS, Pte, Harold Jack, 6023193
MILLER, Pte, Thomas, 4270818
MINTER, Cpl, Stanley Ernest George, 5824986
MITCHELL, Capt, Albert Edward, 88976
MOORE, L/Cpl, Robert James, 6020492
MOORE, Pte, Leonard Eugene, 5827273
MORRIS, Pte, George Douglas, 6020659
MOSS, Pte, Olaf Ambrose, 5828095
MOSS, Pte, Harry Alan, 6010474
MUNNINGS, Pte, Leonard William, 5833064
MURRAY, Pte, Harold Joseph, 5826901
MYNOTT, Pte, Henry, 5834724
NEEDHAM, Pte, Herbert John, 6018995
NEWELL, L/Cpl, Leonard, 6019248
NORTON, Pte, John, 5836084

O'BRIEN, Cpl, Stephen, 58293215
OLIVER, Pte, Sidney Robert, 5830600
OWEN, Pte, William Ernest, 6020667
OWEN, Sjt, Arthur Lewis, 5828066
PARKER, Pte, Victor George Albert, 5830651
PARKER, Pte, Gordon Ernest, 5825423
PARR, Pte, Reginald John, 6018335
PAWSEY, L/Cpl, Joseph Richard, 5828747
PECK, L/Cpl, Wesley Ernest George, 5827739
PERKINS, Lt, Michael Bernard, 140667
PINNEY, Pte, George Robert, 5833718
POPE, Pte, James Henry, 5833628
POWELL, Pte, Charles, 5833094
PRATT, Pte, Dick, 5833095
PRICE, L/Cpl, Arthur, 5828984
PROBIN, Pte, Alexander Henry, 5829650
PRYKE, Pte, Amos Arthur Thomas, 833955
PUNT, L/Cpl, Sidney Edward William, 6020628
PYKE, Pte, Robert James, 5837068
RACE, L/Cpl, Kenneth Clifton Emerson, 5830642
RAMSEY, Pte, Basil Morris Alfred, 5828189
RANSOME, Pte, Charles, 5833862
RAPSON, Pte, Frederick Edwin Joseph, 6028709
RAWE, Pte, Henry F., 6020183
REEDER, Pte, Leonard Harry, 5828147
REYNOLDS, L/Cpl, Herbert, 5830824
RICHARDSON, Sjt, Frederick David, 5825059
RICHARDSON, Sjt, William Sidney Francis, 5824068
RIDGE, Pte, Harold James, 5830825
ROPER, Pte, Reginald Henry, 6018381
ROPER, Pte, Leonard Percy, 6029000
ROSE, Pte, Dennis Arthur Robinson, 5828228
ROUND, Pte, Joseph, 5830680
ROWE, L/Cpl, Frank, 5830829
ROWE, Cpl, Cecil Charles, 5826012
ROYCE, Pte, Ernest Edward, 6019260
RUSH, Pte, Albert Henry, 5827449
RUSS, Pte, Edward Harry, 6029056
RYLAND, Pte, Cecil, 6028743
SADLER, Pte, Bertie Wiliam, 5835294
SANDERS, L/Sjt, George Douglas, 5829632
SANDERSON, Pte, Stephen Jacob, 5835570
SAVAGE, Pte, John Joseph, 6028625
SAVAGE, Pte, Reginald George, 5830601
SAVIN, Pte, Kenneth, 5830831
SAYER, Pte, Percival Walter, 5826960
SCOTT, Lt, Sidney Etherington, 148881
SCURRELL, Pte, Charles Sidney, 5826214
SHEMMING, Pte, Herbert William, 5823115
SHIED, Pte, Joesph Albany, 5830833
SHILLING, Pte, William, 5833647
SINKINS, Pte, Frank, 6019816
SKEELS, Pte, Edward John, 5826769
SMITH, Pte, William George, 6019042
SMITH, Cpl, Arthur William, 5828234
SMITH, Pte, Ralph, 5826465
SMITH, Pte, Joseph Horace, 5830836
SMITH, Cpl, Harold James, 5828223
SMITH, Csm, Leonard Clarence, 5824922
SOUTHGATE, L/Cpl, Walter Charles, 5825872
SPOONER, Pte, Philip Edward, 5828076
SPRULES, Pte, Frederick, 5833465
SQUIRES, L/Sjt, Francis John, 5828128
STONE, Pte, Henry John, 6020714
STOW, Pte, Albert James, 6020715
STRAWSON, Sjt, Gordon Edgar, 5933857
SUTTLE, Pte, Raymondcharles William, 2616096
SUTTON, Pte, Ronald Leonard, 5826778
TATTMAN, L/Cpl, William Charles, 5833658
TAYLOR, L/Cpl, Richard Victor, 5833188

TEMPLEY, Pte, Ernest Charles, 5830604
THEOBALD, Cpl, Frank William Isaac, 5826775
THIRKETTLE, L/Sjt, Charles Ernest, 5829803
THOMAS, Pte, Roland Frederick George, 888052
THOMPSON, Pte, Peter Richard, 5834818
THOMPSON, Pte, Charles Frederick, 6019046
THOMPSON, Pte, Sidney Edward, 59835315
THORPE, Pte, Walter John, 5933142
TINK, Pte, Arthur James, 5829618
TRACE, Pte, Ronald John, 5829607
TRASK, L/Cpl, George Reginald, 6020717
TUFFIN, Pte, Leonard Ralph, 6028793
TUNMORE, Sjt, William Edward, 5823510
TURNER, Cpl, Edmund John, 5828345
TUTTLE, Pte, Donald Edward, 5827326
TYLER, Pte, William Alfred, 5833147
TYLER, Cpl, George, 5825881
UNCLE, Pte, Albert William, 6024480
UPSHALL, Pte, Fred, 5827044
WALKER, Pte, Andrew, 6021181
WALLIS, Pte, Cyril William, 6019286
WARNE, Pte, Edward James, 5827027
WATERS, Pte, Joffre Douglas, 5826847
WATSON, 2/lt, Walter, 153886
WATTS, Pte, Edward Harry, 6020721
WAY, Pte, Donald, 6028631
WEAVING, Pte, John, 6028568
WELHAM, Pte, Frederick Archie, 5828113
WELLS, Pte, Clement George, 5828229
WESLEY, Pte, John Edward Creek, 5830912
WESTWOOD, Pte, Bernard, 5835556
WILKINS, Pte, Thomas Edward, 6013909
WILSON, Lt, John Edmund, 165646
WINTER, L/Cpl, Albert, 5951860
WOOL, L/Cpl, Cyril Walter, 5825494
WRIGHT, Pte, Arthur, 5833474
WRIGHT, Pte, Albert George, 5825510
WYTHE, Pte, Robert James, 5830591

5 BATTALION
ADDISON, Cpl, Frederick George, 3828683
ALDERMAN, Pte, Henry, 4805278
ALLEN, L/Cpl, Garnet Alfred, 5827018
ANDREWS, Pte, George, 5834455
APPLEBY, Pte, Herbert Alfred, 5828158
ASHDOWN, Pte, Cecil Joseph, 5832442
ATKIN, Pte, Charles William Leslie, 5833502
AVIS, Pte, Alfred William, 6020166
BARKS, Pte, Thomas William, 4805286
BARNES, Pte, John, 5834524
BARNES, Cpl, Maurice William, 5952171
BARTLETT, Pte, Eric, 5950454
BAYFIELD, 2/lt, Alan David, 193368
BBEAR, L/Cpl, Albert Charles, 5828492
BEDWORTH, Pte, Edward Albert, 5832466
BERRY, Pte, Frank, 6020003
BIRD, Pte, Wilfred Reginald, 4805284
BLACKBURN, Pte, Albert, 5835260
BLANCHARD, Pte, John William Arnold, 4805236
BLEW, Pte, Albert Victor, 5832480
BLUMSON, Pte, James William, 5832927
BOLTON, Pte, Howard Gerald, 6020683
BRADBURY, Pte, Percy, 5833402
BRADFORD, Pte, Edward Charles, 583451
BRANCH, Pte, Harold Stephen, 5826653
BRETHERICK, Pte, William John, 5828577
BREWIN, Pte, Robert, 4805308
BRIGGS, Pte, Stanley, 4805303
BROWN, Pte, Wilfred Henry, 5824691
BROWN, Pte, Kenneth, 4805311

BRUCE, L/Cpl, Edward James, 5828442
BUCKLES, Pte, Leslie Raymond Henry, 5835461
BUCKLES, Pte, Frederick William, 5828153
BULLEN, Pte, William Randle, 5835462
BUNGAY, Pte, Ronald Percy, 5828649
BURCH, L/Cpl, John Henry, 5832499
BURGESS, Pte, Kenneth, 5933926
BURNS, Cpl, Victor, 5831409
BURTON, Pte, Arthur C., 5827910
BUSBY, Pte, Edward Alfred, 6020737
BUTCHER, Pte, Percy Levi, 5828702
CAHILL, Pte, Philip Ronald, 5828494
CANDLER, Sjt, Richard Victor, 5828292
CANDLER, Pte, Cecil William, 5834564
CANSDALE, Pte, Reginald George, 5627402
CAPPS, Pte, Maurice Pierson, 5838674
CARRIAGE, Pte, Reginald Arthur, 6020080
CARROLL, Pte, John Joseph, 5950370
CATT, Pte, Nigel John, 5828470
CECIL, Pte, George Harry, 5828305
CHAMBERS, Cpl, Arthur Edward, 5825876
CHATFIELD, Pte, William Henry, 5824759
CHESMAN, Pte, Alfred, 4805319
CHISNELL, Pte, Frederick, 5828663
CLARK, Pte, Joseph Francis, 5828929
CLARKE, L/Cpl, George Alfred, 5825172
CLARKE, Pte, Albert Victor, 5832954
CLEGG, Cpl, Richard, 5827916
CLEMENTS, Pte, Arthur Edward, 5828340
COLLETT, Pte, Alfred Edwin, 4805315
CONNOR, Pte, Cyril Frank, 5832538
COOK, Pte, James Frederick, 5832441
COOK, Pte, Frank Sidney Walter, 5828408
CORBETT, Pte, Harry, 5834061
COUSINS, Pte, Maurice James, 5828529
COX, Pte, Leonard, 6020697
COX, Pte, Harold Percival Graham, 5828974
COX, Pte, Bernard, 5950374
COX, Pte, Frederick William Isaac, 5833741
CRACKNELL, Pte, Albert Edward, 5832097
CRANE, Pte, Vincent William, 5933693
CREASEY, Pte, Richard, 5829670
CREEK, Pte, Harold Edwin, 5828927
CROXON, Pte, George Eric Bray, 5827605
DALE, Pte, Harold James, 5825965
DEARLOVE, Pte, Herbert Allenby, 4805333
DENCH, Pte, Dennis Edward, 5828780
DENNIS, Pte, Albert, 13021224
DENNY, Pte, Stanley Charles, 5832557
DEWAR, Pte, Peter Hamilton, 5834073
DODDINGSON, Pte, William George, 2608993
DRIVER, Pte, Jack, 5834600
DUPUIS, Sjt, Frederick, 5824844
DURANT, Pte, William Stephen, 4805326
DURRANT, Pte, Spencer Kitchener, 5832566
EADY, Pte, Bertie, 5828610
EASTAFF, Pte, Frederick, 5832569
EBDEN, L/Cpl, David Henry, 5832570
EDGELEY, Pte, Harry John, 5834603
ELLIS, Pte, Frederick Charles Henry, 6021100
EMMINGTON, Pte, James William, 5830913
EVANS, Sjt, Charles Headford, 5828484
EVERETT, Pte, Stanley Albert, 5834609
EYRE, Pte, James, 4805334
FELLGET, Pte, Stanley Fred, 5832983
FISH, Pte, Norman Douglas, 5828937
FLETCHER, Pte, Charles William, 4805339
FOLKARD, Pte, Alfred Charles, 5828188
FREEMAN, Pte, John William, 5832596
FRENCH, Pte, John Ernest, 5827948

FRENCH, Pte, Leonard Albert, 5834625
FROST, Pte, Frederick Arthur, 5828611
GARNER, Pte, Ronald, 4805241
GATHERCOLE, Pte, Jack, 5828644
GILBEY, Pte, George, 6021111
GIRDLESTONE, Pte, James Willioam, 5768161
GOODCHILD, Pte, John Mowbray, 5832376
GOULD, Pte, James Felix, 5827207
GREEN, Pte, Alan Hewitt, 5950522
GREEN, Pte, Arthur Jack, 5832622
GROOM, Pte, George William, 5830607
GUSTARD, Pte, Mathew, 5834644
GYNGELL, Pte, Lawrie Francis, 5836074
HALES, Pte, Francis Henry, 4805369
HALL, Pte, William George Villiers, 6023684
HAMBLING, Pte, Alfred Edward, 5826572
HAMMOND, Pte, Francis Edward, 5828688
HART, Cpl, Ernest Herbert, 5950620
HAWKINS, Sjt, Edward, 5826751
HAWKINS, Pte, Alfred, 5952336
HAYDEN, Pte, Leonard George, 5830919
HEARN, L/Sjt, Geoffrey Charles, 5828465
HIGHTON, Pte, Hubert Thomas, 4805364
HILL, Pte, Ivor Robert, 6023696
HILLS, Pte, Douglas William, 5830952
HOGGINS, Pte, Isaac, 4805358
HOLMES, Pte, Sydney Charles, 5832394
HONEYBALL, Pte, Thomas William, 551029
HOUSEGO, Pte, Charles, 5826753
HUNT, Pte, Albert, 4805368
HUNT, Pte, Eric John, 5828540
JARMAN, Pte, William Reginald, 5830959
JARMAN, Pte, John, 5834118
JARVIS, Pte, Frederick Russell, 5830194
JEFFERY, L/Cpl, Arthur William, 5821941
JOHNSON, Pte, George Edward, 5825248
JORDON, Pte, Patrick Joseph, 5834470
KEMP, Pte, Charles, 5827432
KING, Pte, Howard Walter, 5835514
KING, Pte, Raymond Theophilus, 5828796
LANGTON, Pte, Raymond Percy, 4805391
LING, L/Sjt, Leslie Warner, 5828526
MALTBY, Csm, George William, 5821945
MAPLESTONE, L/Cpl, Frederick William, 3836533
MASKELL, Pte, George Edward, 5827301
MAYES, Pte, Thomas, 5828520
McINTYRE, Cqms, Robert Mcansland, 5828303
MILES, Pte, Ernest Arthur, 5952526
MILLER, Pte, William, 5830438
MULLEY, Pte, Ephraim Sidney, 5826758
NIGHTINGALE, Pte, George Herbert, 5830908
NORWOOD, Pte, Frederick William, 5832427
NUNN, Pte, Albert Edward, 5828689
OWEN, Pte, John Reuben, 5830924
OXFORD, Pte, William Harry, 5826906
OXFORD, Pte, Frederick Charles, 5828422
PAGE, Pte, Francis Leonard, 5950493
PAGET, Sjt, Gerald Danial, 5826760
PARKER, Pte, Charles Dennis, 5884541
PARSONS, Pte, Donald, 5834747
PARTRIDGE, Pte, Leslie Thomas, 5830889
PAYNE, L/Cpl, Frederick George, 5950478
PAYNE, Cpl, Arthur William, 5825138
PEACOCK, Pte, Frederick Oswald, 5832412
PEACOCK, Pte, Percy Harold, 5828681
PEARCE, Pte, Ernest William, 782371
PEARS, Pte, Anthony, 6021146
PECK, Pte, Jack Samuels, 5827463
PEER, L/Cpl, Percy Henry Alexander, 5830662
PEET, Pte, Harold, 5950583

PHILLIPS, Pte, Walter Sidney, 5828808
PICKARD, Pte, Horace Arthur, 5830934
PLUMB, Pte, Arthur William, 5833089
POMROY, Pte, Rufus Claude, 6021174
PORTER, L/Cpl, Arthur George, 5950456
POWELL, Pte, Leslie John, 6028561
PRYKE, L/Cpl, Sidney, 5828499
RAVEN, Pte, Geoffrey Lional, 5835344
READ, Cpl, Douglas Herbert, 5828444
REED, Pte, William, 5834414
REGAN, Pte, Morris Joseph, 5834765
RIDGEON, Pte, Walter John, 5828316
ROGERS, Pte, Francis Eeward, 5950504
ROPER, Pte, Gordon Arthur, 5828438
ROSE, Pte, William Edward, 5834772
ROSE, Pte, Geoffrey Edward, 5833105
ROWE, Pte, Donovan Gordon, 5828956
RUTTERFORD, Pte, Cyril Wilfred, 5933587
SAUNDERS, Pte, Charles Albert, 5950429
SAYER, Cqms, Donald William Ormrod, 2030349
SCARFF, Pte, Ray William, 5828793
SCRIVENER, Pte, Walter Ernest, 6344548
SENTON, Pte, Ira Sinclair, 5827274
SHIRLEY, Pte, Charles Richard Jenkin, 5951294
SIMPSON, Pte, William, 5950749
SIMS, Pte, Joshua John, 5950634
SMITH, Cpl, Frank Ernest, 5828557
SMITH, Sjt, Douglas Herbert, 5830916
SMITH, L/Cpl, Eric Francis, 6020758
SMITH, Pte, Aubrey John, 5834196
SMITH, Pte, Edward George, 6021175
SNEESBY, Pte, Sidney, 5830929
SNEESBY, Pte, Henry James, 6020712
SNEYD, Pte, Albert William, 5830693
SPARKS, Pte, Roy Eric, 5827299
SPRAGUE, Pte, Ronald Francis, 6020767
STANNARD, L/Cpl, John Robert, 5828460
STEBBEDS, Pte, Reginald Arthur, 5828585
STEELE, Pte, Geoffrey James, 5829655
STEPHENSON, Pte, John William, 5828583
STEVENS, Pte, George William, 5834203
STEVENS, Pte, William Henry, 5827431
SWAN, L/Cpl, Ronald Charles, 5950586
SWANNELL, L/Cpl, William Arthur, 5950399
TARLING, Pte, Leslie James, 5828512
TAYLOR, Pte, Ronald, 5828403
TAYLOR, Pte, George, 5834501
TAYLOR, Pte, Edward Augustus, 5828486
TAYLOR, Pte, Bernard Edward, 5833138
THORNTON, Pte, Frederick, 5951185
THORPE, Pte, Leslie William, 5830926
TOOKE, Pte, Eric Walter, 5832830
TRICKER, Pte, Vernon Edward, 5828581
TUCK, Pte, Arthur Reginald, 5828653
TURNER, Pte, Peter Walter, 5828399
UPSON, Pte, Leonard George, 5828459
WADE, Pte, William Charles, 5833148
WALES, Pte, Frederick Charles, 5828299
WALKER, Pte, Arthur James, 6021182
WALLACE, Pte, George, 5830698
WALTERS, Pte, Frederick John, 6028749
WALTERS, L/Cpl, Cyril Harry, 888701
WALTON, Pte, Norman, 5833476
WALTON, Pte, Frederick Herbert, 5828734
WARD, Cpl, John, 6142462
WARD, Pte, Alexander, 5949912
WATTS, Pte, Fred Thomas, 6020722
WEBB, L/Cpl, Leonard George, 6021154
WENT, Pte, Horace Edwin, 5950457
WESLEY, Pte, Reginald Charles, 5828518

WEST, Pte, Stanley Arthur, 5834832
WHAYMAN, Csm, George Cecil Henry, 5821066
WINFIELD, L/Cpl, Frederick George, 5950622
WOODLEY, L/Cpl, Frederick Albert, 5828805
WOODS, Pte, Charles Donald, 5828383
WOOLLEY, Pte, Sidney John, 5828369
YARROW, Pte, Arthur Wilfred, 5834849
YARROW, Pte, Alfred, 5835326
YOUNG, Pte, Leonard James, 5836272

SUSSEX
GRAY,Pte,Douglas Ronald,6411881
LAKER,Pte,Peter John,14266811

TERRITORIAL ARMY NURSING SERVICE
ANDERSON,Sister,L.H.M.V.,N/1075
ELSMORE,W/o 2,Winifred Ethel,W/297044
GALE,Sister,Margory Eveline,213310
INGHAM,Sister,Alice Ann,213559
STRACHAN,Sister,Elizabeth,215508
WILSON,Sister,Edith Mary,215779

VOLUNTARY AID DETACHMENT
BRITISH RED CROSS
BRADFORD,Cad Ens,Chaslyn Mary,19772
BROOKS,Nurse,Ruby Margaret,W/513046
COOPER,Nurse,Diana Mary,W/552169
SUGDEN,Nurse,Dorothy.M.M,

WEST YORKSHIRE REGIMENT
BROWN,Pte,Norman Gattis,14808627
CALLAGHAN,Pte,P,14580476
CHILVERS, Pte, Charles, 14641095
EVE,Capt,Donald William John,331690
EXTON, Pte, Reginald, 6985651
GILL, Pte, Robert John, 4456164
HORNE, Cpl, Ernest, 1785943
MARSHALL,Pte,H.,14167500
NICHOLSON,Pte,P.J.,19676082
SCHOLLIC, Pte, T W, 14778017
SWALLOW, Pte, Harry, 14701365
TOOTHILL, Pte, C., 19093314
WRIGHT,Sjt,Kenneth,4535177

WELCH REG
BARNES,Sjt,Maurice Reginald,5569347
CHASE-WIGGINS,Sjt,Richard,5576714
SMITH,Sjt,Alexander John,3975862

WORCESTERSHIRE REGIMENT
KENDRICK,Pte,J,14172304
TYRWHITT,Capt,Cuthbert,50924

YORK & LANCASTER REGIMENT
MEGSON,Sjt,Leslie,4744928

YORKSHIRE LIGHT INFANTRY
MAYOH,Pte,D,19038765
MORTON,Pte,James Sydney,19033400

Royal Air Force

GENERAL
ABBOTTS,Lac,George,1159570
ABEL,Ac1,Cyril,1675425
ABLETT,Ac1,Cyril,1381697
ADAM,Ac1,William,1136597
ADAMS,Cpl,Laurence Carey,571321
ADAMS,W/o,Alexander,1186109
ADLEY,Ac1,Ronald Charles,633816
AGER,Lac,Arthur Samuel,926709
AISTON,Fl/off,Frederick,129439
AITKIN, Ac1, James Smith Robertson, 1021595
ALCOCK,Ac2,Alfred Huddlestone,1117235
ALLAN,Cpl,Samuel,521623
ALLAN,Cpl,John Ferguson,591275
ALLAN,Cpl,John,519628
ALLEN,Cpl,Alfred,326343
ALLISON,Sjt,John William,2222658
ALLISON,Fl/off,Fred Illingworth, 129052
ALLITT,Fl/lt,Robert Edward (DFC),40594
ALLSOP,W/o,Kenneth Henry,751161
ANDERSON, Fl Off, Stanley Walter, 45211
ANDERSON,Sjt,William,509519
ANDERSON,Ac1,Thomas Henry,1354271
ANDREWS,Lac,Eric William,918239
ANSELL,Ac1,Alfred Leslie,1330456
ARDERN,Cpl,Alfred,985471
ARNOLD,Cpl,Cecil William,516938
ARNOTT,Fl/off,David Blair,116974
ARTIS,W/o,Harry Albert,343043
ASHLEY COOPER,Fl/off,Thomas George Duncan,116290
ASHURST,Ac1,Jack Hall,1082219
ASHWORTH,Pl,Stanley Glendon,935929
ASTLEY,Sgt,Richard David,530447
ATKINSON,Ac1,Harold,990223
ATKINSON,Ac2,Arthur Frederick,1335806
AUSTEN,Lac,Geoffrey Frank,539289
AUSTIN,Ac2,Jack,1400348
AVERILL,Sjt,Edward Marwood,536124
AVIS,Ac1,Frank,1074066
AYNSLEY,Lac,Ronald Peter,1308244
BAGULEY,Ac1,Leonard,1121082
BAILEY,Ac1,Walter,1229788
BAILEY,Cpl,Ronald Arthur,537579
BAKER,Lac,Norman Frederick,11063133
BAKER,Lac,Eric William,954762
BAL,L/Cpl,Arthur James,537877
BAL,L/Cpl,Frank James,6327908
BALDWIN,Cpl,Herbert Leslie,591238
BALLARD,F/Sjt,Albert William Henry,366033
BARBER,Lac,George John William,1132321
BARCLAY,Cpl,George,996234
BARKER,Cpl,Eric Ernest,646513
BARLOW,Ac1,Eric Joseph Nutley Leighton,547349
BARNES,Ac1,Leslie Stuart,1251664
BARNETT,Ac1,Kenneth Lewis,548705
BARRACLOUGH,Ac2,Leonard,1104245
BARRAH, Ac2, Thomas John, 927801
BARRINGTON,Cpl,Henry Herbert,3962924
BARTON,Lac,Walter Frederick,1064901
BARWISE,Sjt,William,1685683
BASSNETT,Sjt,Herbert,530959
BAYLEY,Ac1,Samuel John,2275970
BEALES,Lac,Robert Henry,924269
BEAN,Lac,Arthur Kennedy,539447
BEARDSLEY,Ac1,John,1530389
BEATEY,W/o,Thomas Atkinson,1104751

BEAVIS,Cpl,Victor Frederick,640149
BECKETT,Lac,Kenneth Douglas,647524
BELL,Ac2,William,1040478
BELL,Ac2,George Alexander,1371918
BELL,Ac1,Edward Burrow,1354076
BELL,Ac2,Clephan William Hamilton,931888
BELL,Lac,Albert,644334
BELL,Ac2,Francis Wilfred,107371
BENNETT,Lac,Leslie Gordon,1282242
BENNETT,Ac1,Alfred,956244
BENNETT,Lac,Alec Henry,847141
BENNETT,Flt Sjt,Charles Whitfield,638469
BENNIE,Lac,William Pretsell,530232
BENNIER,Lac,Frank Harold,1052169
BENSLEY,Lac,Charles Brightmore,1160850
BENT,Fl/lt,Arthur Le Baldwin,118154
BINDING,Ac2,Donald James,906685
BINGHAM,Lac,William Alfred,956494
BIRCH,Lac,Windham Thomas,592687
BIRCH,Ac1,Edward,1087236
BIRKETT,Cpl,Joseph,533921
BIRTWHISTLE,Fl/Sjt,Herbert Joseph,569393
BISS,Lac,Cyril William Alfred,1833639
BISSETT,Ac1,Robert,1019329
BLACK,Lac,Robert,991147
BLACKWOOD,Ac2,David,1023130
BLAIR,W/o,Robert,1365950
BLAIR,Lac,Charles,1002683
BLAKELEY,Lac,Alfred George,634798
BLANCHARD,Lac,Ramon Keith,952856
BLANCHARD,Lac,Eric William,933812
BLANCHARD,Cpl,Arthur Charles,962616
BLOW,Ac1,Donald Edwin,1259149
BLOWERS,Sjt,Bernard Paul,526774
BLUCK,Lac,Harry George,1201580
BOAGS,Lac,George,1557346
BODEMEIDE-BURBAGE,Ac1,George Albert,1030835
BONNER,Lac,Ivanhoe Frederick,654650
BOOTH,Ac1,Frank,1069332
BOTTING,Ac1,Arthur Francis,1304692
BOUCKLEY,Ac1,Harold John,959911
BOUGHTON,Ac1,George William,1082133
BOULTON,Cpl,Bcn,1152607
BOWEN,Ac1,Thomas Brendon,1255228
BOYD,Sjt,Trevor Barkley,1145139
BRACEGIRDLE,Ac1,Phil,1265463
BRACKENBURY,Lac,Kenneth Stephen,912488
BRACKENBURY,Ac1,Norman James,622722
BRADLEY,Cpl,Peter William,1874335
BRADSHAW,Ac2,James Samuel,1142354
BRAIN,Lac,Albert Leslie,637253
BRANT,Ac1,Joseph Eric,1156249
BRASS,Sjt,George Wilson,567436
BRAY,Lac,Leslie,946522
BREMNER,Cpl,Ian,636346
BRENCHLEY,Sjt,Harold Bryan Spencer,524960
BRETT,Lac,Stanley Herbert,1169298
BRIGHT,Sjt,Roland Bernard,2222977
BRIGHTWELL,Fl Off,Frederick Charles,108934
BRIMLEY,Ac1,Charles John,1620132
BRINSDON,Cpl,Bernard,1057153
BRINTON,W/o,Leslie Ronald,517611
BROADHURST,Sjt,James,522691
BROCKMAN,Ac2,George Reginald Henry,14440802
BROMLEY,Ac1,Thomas,1368857
BROOKER,Ac1,Donald Archie,1231177
BROUGHTON,Ac1,Derrick Graham,959088
BROWN, Sjt, Cyril John Ambrose, 366040
BROWN,Ac2,William Edgar,1073368
BROWN,Ac1,Robert Aitken,950438

BROWN,Cpl,Leslie,524715
BROWN,Ac2,Joseph,3209015
BROWN,Ac1,Harry Charles,1155365
BROWN,Lac,Arthyr Edward,1207379
BROWN,Ac1,Albert Edward,702279
BROWN,Cpl,Albert,941969
BRYANT,Sjt,George Percy Firtzgerald,560529
BRYANT,Lac,Frederick John,1398164
BULLOCK,Sjt,Walter Herbert,512515
BULLOCK,Ac1,Reginald Clifford,1285897
BUNHILL,Lac,Henry Arthur,1263545
BURDIS,Sjt,William,521598
BURFOOT,Lac,Wilfred Arthur,1221119
BURGESS,Fl/off,Humphrey George,63906
BURNHAM,Lac,Walter Harvey,1527073
BURNS,Sjt,William,528321
BURNS,Lac,Robert,1006267
BURROUGHS,Cpl,John George,746177
BURT,Cpl,Walter,958014
BURTON,Sjt,Derrick Charles North,1739627
BUSHELL,Sjt,Alfred John,531231
BUXTON,Cpl,Thomas Roose,1050785
CAMERON,Ac1,John,990419
CAMPBELL,Lac,Archie,1073796
CAMPBELL,Sjt,Ernest,572371
CANDY,Lac,Richard Stafford,1390039
CARLIN,Cpl,Joseph Ernest,991671
CARSON, Ac1, Macduff Stuart, 648972
CARTWRIGHT,Sjt,Edwain,561497
CASTLE,Cpl,Sydney Harold Leonard,1162044
CATER,Ac2,John Lundy,42336
CAVE,Ac1,Edwin Colin,1287682
CAWSEY,Ac2,Arthur Rogerson,756298
CHAMBERS,Ac2,Sydney John Albert,1229958
CHAPMAN,Lac,William Laing,1059606
CHAPMAN,Sjt,Cecil,563626
CHAPPLE,Cpl,Ivor,623055
CHARLES,Lac,Haydn Melville,1409597
CHATT,Sgt,Eric,518522
CHEESEWRIGHT,Fl/off,Albert George Frederick,65030
CHESSON,Lac,Robert Frank,1280173
CHIGNELL,W/cmdr,Robert Alexander,24171
CHILDS,Fl/Sjt,Stanley Thomas,365210
CHILTON,Ac1,Eric Geoge,1170562
CHUDLEIGH,Fl Off,Sidney John,58079
CLARK,Ac1,Ronald Francis,926663
CLARK,Ac1,Raymond Donald Birt,1400968
CLARKE,Ac1,Horace Bernard,1330266
CLARKE,Fl/Sjt,Frederick George,1292597
CLARKSON,Ac1,James William,1086311
CLARKSON,Flt Sjt,Fred,590664
CLAVERY,Ac2,Robert Boyd,1478164
CLAYTON,Cpl,James,970707
CLEGG,Ac1,Harold Creighton,1011674
CLEMENTS,Fl/Sjt,Gordon Reginald Albrighton,1451837
CLEMENTS,Ac2,James Percival,1270614
CLIFF,Ac1,Donald,1113486
CLINCH,Sqdn Ldr,Denys Stanley,46369
CLOSE,Lac,George Alert,971273
COCHRANE,Sjt,Ronald,632633
COCKLIN,Ac1,Albert George,1384045
COFFEY,Ac1,Charles,11305181
COGGON,Ac1,Harold,1216180
COGHLAN,Cpl,Nicholas,536816
COKER,Lac,Arthur,1261651
COLE,Cpl,Robert Alec,651422
COLE,Lac,Bernard John,1257581
COLLIER,Lac,William Richard,646821
COLLINS,Cpl,Roger Trevithick,1015782
COLLINS,Ac1,Alfred Edward,1220595

COMELY, Flt Sgt, Anthony Hugh Basil, 576146
CONNELL,Lac,Gordon,1058242
CONNETTT,Lac,John Henry,1012371
CONNOLLY,W/o,Kiernan,621344
COOMBS,Lac,John,913650
CORK,Sjt,William Norman,2222037
COSSENS,Ac1,Robert Edward,1018560
COSSEY,Lac,Charles Edward,1184669
COVENTRY,Lac,John,951180
COWAN,Ac2,John Muir,1040671
COWEN,Cpl,Stanley,972302
COWLEY, Lac, Ronald, 651730
COWLEY,Fl/Sjt,Harold,1433242
COX,Lac,Ronald Leslie,649388
CRAIG,Ac1,Hugh,1082514
CRANFORD,Fl/off,Robert Geoffrey,103070
CRAWSHAY-FRY,Fl/off,Peter William,181944
CRESSEY,Fl/off,Stanley Webb,120083
CRICHTON,Ac1,William Gray,1103609
CRICHTON,Fl/off,Ronald Macalister,132578
CROFT,Ac1,Harold,1033198
CROOK,Sjt,Sydney,1495778
CROOK,Lac,Albert Leslie,1158503
CROSSLING,Ac1,Herbert,1262628
CROWTHER,Ac2,Crighton John,786095
CULLER,Fl/Sjt,W.F.,785112
CURRIE,Cpl,David Robson,979836
CURRIE,Ac1,David,1906077
CYPLES,Ac2,James Wilmot,1211367
DADDS,Ac2,Bernard George,1272037
DAFT,Ac2,William,1136563
DALTON,Ac1,Ernest,1549574
DALY,Lac,Michael,1056902
DANDY,Ac2,Gower,1429099
DATSON,Cpl,Eric John,569643
DAVEY,Cpl,Geoffrey,918031
DAVIDSON, Fl Off, Thomas, 181777
DAVIDSON,Fl/Sjt,David,1672590
DAVIES,Fl/Sjt,William Thomas Patrick,552842
DAVIES,Cpl,Ronald Noel,618793
DAVIES,Ac2,J.L.,1498158
DAVIES,Lac,George Glynn,625438
DAVIES,Ac1,Digby Charles,1159060
DAVIES,Lac,David George,1253128
DAVIS,Lac,Stewart James,1281220
DAVIS,Cpl,Arnold Percy,521814
DAWES,Lac,John Leonard,1621806
DAWSON,Ac2,John,1134142
DAWSON,Lac,Georeg,1009965
DAWSON,Pl,Dennis Bruce,974943
DAY,Cpl,Isaac John,157773
DAY,Jt,Desmond,529819
DAY,Cpl,Isaac John,157773
DE GARIS,Ac1,William James,1164152
DEACON,Ac1,William John,548711
DEAKIN,Ac2,Kenneth Lea,951048
DENMAN,Ac1,Robert Holder,963555
DEVERSON,Lac,Victor John,573063
DICKENSON,Cpl,Derrick Leslie,567515
DICKS,Ac1,Sydney William,1226089
DIMENT,Cpl,Ralph Francis,638113
DIMMICK,Lac,Douglas Ronald John Elton,97704
DIXON,Ac1,William,1031192
DIXON,Flt Sjt,John Walter,363913
DOBSON,Lac,Maurice,1104873
DOBSON,Ac2,James Howe,1005360
DODD,Ac1,James William,632100
DODDS,W/o,Roy Alexander,985788
DODDS,Fl/off,Richard Denis,108922
DODDS,Ac1,Richard,1096473

DODDS,Fl/Sjt,John Alfred,520562
DOLMAN,Ac1,James Heber,1177613
DONALD,Fl/off,Alexander Watt,78989
DONOGHUE,Lac,Kenneth Frederick,553176
DOUGALL,Ac1,Thomas,1101967
DOVE,Ac2,George,1016010
DOWN,Lac,Aubrey John,1084986
DOWSE,Lac,Albert James,757017
DRANSFIELD,Ac1,Kenneth Joe,553635
DREW,Ac2,Richard Ernest,1282873
DREW,Ac2,John Samuel,940560
DRON,Cpl,Charles Philip,1204528
DRYSDALE,Ac2,James Douglas,1217792
DUFF,Lac,Hector Anthony Campbell,538092
DUNCAN,Lac,James Bowman,949483
DUNLOP,Cpl,Ronald Albert,548567
DUNPHY,Ac2,Cyril Thomas,1265129
DURK,Cpl,Wilfred Brazier,805454
DURRANT,Cpl,Robert Joseph,962177
DURRANT,Lac,Robert Henry,1251220
DURRANT,Lac,Alan Bevan,1281375
DYER,Lac,William Victor,643028
DYER,Cpl,Ernest James,970189
EASTHOPE,Ac2,George,1112029
EDDEN,Lac,Stanley Victor,1208841
EDDY,Lac,Obed,977983
EDIS,Lac,Jim,903009
EDWARDS,Ac1,Leonard,1134200
EDWARDS,Ac1,Edward Arthur Sidney,1263069
EDWARDS,Fl/off,Arthur,176689
ELIAS,Ac1,Thomas Slwyn,1286282
ELLIOTT,Cpl,Douglas Croft,747446
ELLIOTT,Cpl,Donald Vernon,574596
ELLIS,Lac,Leslie,1528846
ELLISON,Fl/lt,Henry Victor,60903
ELLISON,Ac2,Edward,1484330
ELTON,Ac1,Walter John,921552
ELVY,Ac1,Stanley Alfred Gaydon,912865
ELWARD,Cpl,John Vivian,536267
EMERY,Lac,Francis Ronald,1053493
ENTWISTLE,Ac2,Stanley,1004122
ETCHELLS,Fl/Sjt,Thomas William,1432992
EVANS, Cpl, William John, 535134
EVANS,Lac,Thomas John,929550
EVANS,Lac,Thomas Daniel,1176682
EVANS,Cpl,Spencer Leigh,974895
EVANS,Lac,Richard Edward,636319
EVANS,Ac1,John Henry,913239
EVANS,Lac,John,982547
EVE,Cpl,Ashford Berridge,900839
EVERETT,Ac1,George Leonard,1286685
EYLES,Lac,William Arthur Raymond,1026512
FABB,Ac2,Leonard Norman,1209848
FAIRBRASS,Ac1,Kenneth Jonathan,1252182
FAIRHURST,Ac2,Albert,1082200
FARNELL,Lac,Arthur Sidney,1165931
FARNHILL,Wng/cmdr,Geoffrey,28039
FAWCETT,Ac1,John Vernon,987461
FAWCETT,Cpl,Henry,632931
FENN,Cpl,Norman,627990
FERRIER, Ac1, Robert Thompson, 1365248
FILMER,Ac2,Brian,1184503
FILMORE,Fl/Sjt,Frederick,359760
FINCH,Ac1,Leonard Mathew,932802
FINES,Ac2,Ronald Arthur,1052385
FINLAYSON,Ac2,William Murdoch,1341365
FINN,Ac1,Ernest John Benjamin,620115
FISHER,Ac1,William,1365456
FISHER,Cpl,Thomas William Sarginson,993389
FISHER,Cpl,Ronald Philip,1354619

FLAVELL,Ac2,John Wilfred,1090680
FLETCHER,Sjt,William Kenneth,1601738
FLETCHER,Ac2,Stanley Noel,1136363
FLETCHER,Ac1,Jack,1035626
FLYNN,Lac,Horace James,935266
FOLEY,Lac,Michael,1108527
FORD,Lac,Eric Allen,1354824
FORSHAW,Sjt,John Richard Wharton,515321
FORSTER,Ac1,Harold,1086466
FORTESCUE, Sjt, William Leonard, 563551
FOSTER,Ac1,William Alfred Randale,1157032
FOSTER,Cpl,Joseph Renton,937854
FOSTER,Lac,Edwin,991523
FRANCIS,Lac,Hrold John Money,1205964
FRANCIS,Lac,Albert William,944847
FRANKLIN,Fl/lt,Wallace Montague (DFC),115936
FRASER,Fl/lt,Francis James,66511
FREER,Lac,Stanley William,1094970
FRENCH,Cpl,Albert,1549573
FREWING,Sjt,Alec Robert,522748
FRISBIE,Fl/lt,Leslie Thomas,540234
FROST,Ac1,Leslie Alan,905642
FULTON,Cpl,Alan,1102563
GALE,Ac1,Ronald,1184094
GALE,Lac,Alan Frederick,553187
GANT, Cpl, James, 573605
GARDENER,Ac1,Henry Charles,911836
GARNER,Lac,John Harold,1157084
GARNER,Ac1,James Herman,995893
GARNETT,Cpl,John Coupland,971668
GARRAD,Lac,Eric Frederick,927421
GARRATT,Lac,Henry Charles,635417
GARSIDE,Cpl,Jack,620182
GELDER,Cpl,William,1006617
GELLING,Lac,Arthur,1141703
GEORGE,Lac,William Denis,948745
GERRARD,Pl,John Stewart,653779
GIBBS,Ac1,Yril Frank,958618
GIFFARD,Lac,Cyril,639616
GIFFEN,Ac2,William,1025146
GILDER,Lac,Arthur James,1289933
GLEESON,Cpl,Terence,546442
GLENDENNING,Fl/lt,Alexander,87519
GLOVER,Ac1,Harold Joseph,1004135
GOACHER,Ac1,Ronald,924912
GODALL,Flt Sgt,Charles Alexander,508886
GODDARD,Cpl,Leslie Malcolm Bruce,574107
GODFREE,Fl/of,John Henry Wellington,117803
GOLDBERG,Ac2,Charles,1061437
GOLDSMITH,Lac,Theodore,576580
GOODALL,Lac,Robert Arthur,963314
GOODRICH,Lac,Eustace Illingworth,1005034
GOODRUM,Ac1,Clifford William,1270486
GOODWIN,Lac,Frederick Reginald,624736
GORDON,Ac1,Victor Ernest,649850
GORDON,Fl/t,Robert,43329
GORDON,Lac,Harry Clifford,1242148
GORING, Lac, Stanley Alfred, 1881962
GRANGER,Ac1,Harold Patrick,960165
GRANT,Ac2,John,933962
GRANT,Lac,Dennis Homan,648269
GRATTAN,Flt Sjt,George Francis,521645
GRAVER,Ac2,John,1337396
GRAVES,Lac,Eric John,1621425
GRAY,Cpl,Thomas Young,535963
GRAY,Sq/ldr,Thomas Alexander,23244
GRAY,Fl/off,Anthony,198952
GREEN,Lac,Henry,1105550
GREENFIELD,Ac2,Arthur,1134110
GREENWOOD,Ac1,Harold,1021301

GREGG,Fl/off,John Francis Fitzgerald,116815
GREGORY,Ac1,Kenneth,1111647
GRENTER,Lac,Raymond John,1161972
GREY,Ac1,Fernley William,977926
GRICE,Ac2,Ronald William,994444
GRIFFIN,Lac,William,936592
GRIFFITH,Ac2,Oswald Henry,1254678
GRIFFITH,Lac,John,955915
GRIFFITHS,Lac,George William,1110896
GRIFFITHS,Lac,Ernest Stanley,937097
GROAKE,Lac,Joseph Michael,1106291
GROTRIAN,Sq Ldr,Robert Philip Brent,114591
GROUNDON,Ac1,Frederick Gordon,953230
GROVES,Fl/lt,Henry Balfour,77845
GRUNIS,Ac1,Abe,1254212
GRYNKIEWICZ,W/o,Teofil,1383357
GUEST,Sjt,Douglas Allenby,567970
GURNEY,Fl/Sjt,Cecil Charles,747910
GUY,Ac2,Graham,952345
GUYLER,Fl/lt,William David,23107
HADDOCK,Lac,Kenneth James,1067492
HALDANE,Ac1,William Hunter,621450
HALFORD,Ac1,William Bryan,1029978
HALL, Ac2, Roger Julius, 575348
HALL,Lac,Robert Joseph,648252
HALL,Lac,Leslie,1134150
HALL,Lac,Kenneth Blair,630353
HALLIDAY,Ac2,Joseph Harbottle,1480589
HAMILTON,Sjt,Robert Wishart,537357
HAMLETT,Cpl,Sidney Herbert,743333
HANCOCK,Fl/lt,Otto Lewis,60856
HANLEY,Lac,James Christopher,626473
HARCOURT,Lac,Raymond Hugh,906720
HARDING,Cpl,Frank Gerald Berrey,978788
HARDY,Lac,Robert,930495
HARDY,Ac1,Ernest,1110339
HARE,Cpl,James William,1141800
HARNDEN,Ac1,John,1210798
HARNETT,Cpl,Laurence,625750
HARRIS,Sjt,Frederick John Hugh,1322999
HARRIS,Lac,Clifford George,971093
HARRISON,Cpl,Herbert,616344
HARRISON,Sjt,Francis John,523676
HARRISON,Lac,Aubrey William,534929
HARTLEY,Ac2,Ronald,1090776
HASLAM,Cpl,Stephen John,975322
HAWKESWOOD, Cpl, Horace, 633998
HAWKINS,Lac,Clifford,1212107
HAWTHORNE,Cpl,John Mills,1104550
HAYES,Ac1,William John,1235829
HAYLEY,Ac2,Douglas Andrew Ross,1380998
HAYLOCK, Lac, Clifford Richard, 1431164
HAYWARD,Ac2,Phillip George,1166634
HAYWARD,Lac,George Leslie,624395
HAZELHURST,Lac,Gerald Thomas Edwin,98264
HEAD,Lac,Ernest John,913473
HEAP,Cpl,Michael George,523496
HEATH,Ac2,Reginald Arthur,1205956
HEDEGCOX,Lac,William,156510
HEGGIE,Fl/off,Leslie,204187
HENDERSON,Lac,Gordon,1117657
HERON,Ac1,Joseph,1141212
HESTER,Lac,William Victor,1189230
HETHERINGTON, Cpl, John Gofton, 544592
HEWITT,Fl/Sjt,William Walter,1601266
HEYES,Lac,Leslie,2209780
HICKEY,Lac,William,1797597
HICKEY,Ac1,Bernard,1112895
HICKS,Lac,Walter,1304949
HIGGIBS,Ac1,William Henry,1274270

HILL, Lac, Joseph Hubert, 960724
HILL,Ac1,Ronald Edward,3023015
HILL,Ac1,Leslie Walter,1151463
HILL,Lac,Leslie Kenneth,1380430
HILLAM,Ac1,Joseph Robson Lumsden,1020682
HILTON,Ac1,John,577354
HOBBS,Cpl,Frederick William,1180962
HODDELL,Lac,Roy Cope,553030
HODGE,Lac,William,1665618
HODKINSON,Ac1,John Eric,1104224
HOLDER, Ac2, James Henry, 2234245
HOLLAND,Fl/off,Thomas Reginald,124320
HOLLAND,Ac1,John,1273718
HOOD,Ac2,Jmes William,1077,182
HOPE,Lac,John Forster,991646
HOPKINS,Sq Ldr,Desmond Albert Morgan,41122
HORN,Fl/off,Robert Henry Wright,122732
HORNE,Ac1,Sidney Baskerville,1000041
HORNSBY,Lac,Albert Edward,1009942
HOROBIN,Ac2,William Henry,1109882
HORTON,Cpl,Albert William,956147
HOUGHTON,Fl/t,Raymod Douglas,109364
HOUSE,Cpl,John Rydon,573298
HOWARD,Ac1,Frank Ernest,1293790
HUDGELL,Lac,Harry Ernest,1185599
HUGHES,Lac,William Albert,1185203
HUGHES,Lac,Ronald William,972395
HUGHES,Lac,George John,952153
HUGHES,Cpl,Fred,620709
HUGHES,Ac1,Benjanmin Francis,1260445
HULLEY,Ac1,Patrick O'dwyer,1280482
HULTQUIST,Ac1,Ernest Theodore,1075828
HUMPHRIES,Cpl,Berkley,702115
HUNT,Ac1,Jonathan Henry,1173380
HUNTER,Lac,George Hilton,1006283
HUTCHINSON,Lac,Roy Smeaton,903136
INGHAM,Cpl,Horace,946072
INGHAM,Lac,Harry,1004986
INGLIS,Lac,Robert James,636210
JACKSON,Ac1,Philip Jefferson,990132
JAGGARD,Lac,Arthur John,929588
JAKES,Cpl,John Arthur,915334
JAMIESON,Lac,John,1349505
JARDINE,Lac,John George,628473
JAZEWKIS,Ac1,Wincas,1367070
JEFFERIES,Lac,Harry,957082
JEFFERY,Ac2,Herbert Albert,1537862
JOBSON,Fl/Sjt,James,1567017
JOHNS, Lac, Norman Edmund, 578482
JOHNSON,Ac2,William George,1120543
JOHNSON,Lac,Robert Walter,1280302
JOHNSON,Ac1,Ernest,1273387
JONES,Ac1,William Frederick,750336
JONES,Cpl,Wilfred,974068
JONES,Ac1,Tivy,1123171
JONES,Ac1,Thomas,970172
JONES,Lac,Oliver Henry,961740
JONES,Lac,Medoc Pritchard,1010911
JONES,Ac2,Leslie Douglas,909930
JONES,Ac2,Leonard William,128258
JONES,Ac1,John Edric,1022472
JONES,W/o,John Clifford,746833
JONES,Sjt,Howell Gwyn,532173
JONES,Ac1,Gordon Leslie Mccloughlin,575062
JONES,Cpl,Edgar Amphion,532739
JONES,Ac2,Andrew Gerard,1027910
JOSHUA,Ac2,Joshua Moses,785110
JOY,Cpl,Ronald Lamond Thompson,538301
JUBY,W/o,Dennis Albert,115201
KAINES,Ac1,Alfed Leonard,1214661

KANE,Ac2,James,967134
KEARNEY,Lac,Frederick William,1195700
KELLET,Lac,Stanley,1122625
KELSEY,Lac,Robert Ronald,1069636
KEMBER,Cpl,Alfred,157925
KEMMLER,Cpl,John Mortimer,574679
KENT,Lac,George Herbert,1104252
KENWRIGHT,Lac,James,856715
KEY,Cpl,Stanley,534165
KIDD,Ac1,John Thomas,1387333
KIMPTON,Lac,Richard Charles,702130
KING,Ac1,Maurice George,1309078
KING,Ac1,John Thomas,1430241
KING,Lac,Arthur Albert William,1182928
KIRTLEY, Lac, George Davidson, 581186
KITCHINGHAM,Cpl,Tom,642298
KLEISER,Cpl,Edgar Louis,911965
KNAPPER,Ac1,George William,1072004
KNIGHT,Ac1,Harold Edgar,1179850
KNIGHTLY,Cpl,George Bertram,950227
KNOCK,Ac1,William Frederick,1134274
KNOGHT,Ac2,Henry George Thomas,1194884
KNOTT,Lac,Dennis George Frederick,926359
LACEY,Ac2,John Michael,1055493
LAING,Ac1,Sidney,1072473
LAMBERT,Sjt,Alfred Charles Noel,560306
LAMONT,Lac,Daniel,632213
LARMAN,Sq Ldr,Francis,75484
LARTER,Ac1,George Robert,1129837
LARWOOD,Fl/Sjt,Reginald John Louis,621042
LAWE,Lac,Norman Edward,762154
LAWES,Lac,Neville James Alfred,1250653
LAWFORD,Lac,Alfred James,958676
LAWLEY,Sjt,Patrick Loftus Hunter,569123
LAWRENCE,Lac,Eric John,919524
LAWSON,Cpl,Harold,614399
LE-GASSICK,Lac,Francis Albert,910221
LEACH,Ac1,Ronald Chares,979864
LEEPER,Ac1,Daniel John,1286884
LEES,Ac2,John,1075362
LEES,Cpl,Francis Norman,570612
LEEVES,Lac,William,1164591
LEGG,Ac1,John Frederick,1314337
LEGG,Ac2,Henry James,1286505
LENNON,Lac,Patrick,638384
LENTON,Ac1,Fred,988052
LEVENSTON,Cpl,Louis Solomon,1905285
LEWINGTON,Fl/Sjt,Alfred Montague,1338859
LEWIS,Sjt,Marcel William,514834
LEWIS,Lac,Eric,613639
LEWIS,Lac,Alfred,1106956
LEWIS,Cpl,Basil Frank,621301
LEWIS,Ac1,Albert,1007659
LIGHTOWLER,Lac,Gerard,976566
LILLEY,Fl/lt,Edward Wilson,49567
LINCOLN,Ac1,Reginald Ernest,1286535
LINDSEY,Ac2,Samuel,1022389
LING,Cpl,Arthur Ernest,1254560
LINGE,Fl/off,Alfred James,142610
LISHMUND,Ac2,Frank Napoleon,1426018
LISTER,Sjt,Jack,1480287
LITHERLAND,Ac1,John,538172
LIVETT,Ac1,Walter Cyril,1209575
LOADER,Ac1,Donald Valentine,646062
LOCK,Sjt,John Harwood,518616
LOCKWOOD,Ac2,Jack,1094228
LOMAX,Fl/off,William Arthur Barner,165682
LOOBY,Ac2,John,1256476
LOWLE,Lac,Harold Denis,1286202
LOWSON,Fl.Off,David Austin,168019

LUCAS,Ac2,James,1068474
LUCK,Fl/lt,Rolfe Cordale (DFC),112349
LUKE,Ac2,John Elliot,986429
LUMSDEN,Sq Ldr,Carlos Gerald Hugh Edward,17110
LYON,Fl/Sjt,Bruce Deans,740053
MACEFIELD,Ac2,Eghinald George,1233923
MACEY,Ac1,Harry Vaughan,634665
MACFARLANE,Ac1,Edward Thaddeus,1351850
MACKILLOP,W/o,Douglas James,1180421
MAGEE,Fl/Sjt,Patrick Joseph,523193
MAGGS,Cpl,John Reginald,907800
MAHON,Cpl,Eugene Owen,935920
MAIR,Ac2,George,1366673
MAKEPIECE,Sjt,William Ridley,1602229
MALONE,Lac,Thomas Christopher,635181
MANN,Fl/Sjt,Peter Richard,1380272
MANN,Cpl,John Wilson,1208781
MANSFIELD,Ac2,Ubert Montague,1284632
MANSON,Lac,Ronald Stark,999142
MARCH,Ac2,Alan,930128
MARKHAM,Sq Ldr,Richard Frederick Cyprian,76479
MARKS,Ac1,Robert George,978638
MARLOW,Lac,Kenneth Thomas Paul,539280
MARRIOTT,Cpl,Patrick Charles,544332
MARSHALL,Sq Ldr,Robert William Stanley,63386
MARTIN,Ac2,Raymond James,1205241
MARTIN,Ac2,John Robert,958215
MARTIN,Fl/off,Frederick Philemon,204188
MARTIN,Ac1,Albert Henry,1153062
MARTINDALE,Ac1,Thomas Arthur,856147
MARTLEW,Ac1,Leslie,642867
MARVEN,Fl Off,Sidney Charles,45853
MASON,Lac,Edwin Henry,632671
MASSIE,Ac2,Douglas,1366185
MATCALFE,Ac1,Mathew,1174773
MATCHAM,Ac1,Victor Daniel,1252640
MATHEWS,Cpl,Hubert Edward,553145
MATTHEWS,Lac,Thomas Ronald,933429
MATTHEWS,Ac1,Stanley William,924106
MATTHEWS,W/o,Harry George,362081
MAYES,Cpl,David Hugh Vass,761158
MAYHEW,Fl/lt,Stanley Douglas,63404
MAYNARD,Lac,Vivian Foyle,570306
MAYNARD,Ac1,James Ernest,1442568
McBRIDE,Sjt,John Robert,538895
McCALL,Lac,Henry Blyth,1000937
McCALLUM,Sqn Ldr,John,43335
McCANDLESS,Ac2,Joseph Robert,539798
McCARTHY,Ac2,Joseph Anthony,1306757
McCONNELL,Ac1,William Stewart,1107403
McCORMACK,Fl/Sjt,John William,550582
McCORMICK,Cpl,William George,542444
McCRINDLE,Lac,John,702539
McDERMOTT,Sjt,Thomas Harold,358213
McDOWELL,Lac,Adam Rutherglen,1052659
McENTYRE,Ac1,John Alan,1063346
McGLADDERY,Ac1,Norman,1109886
McGUINESS,Ac1,Robert,978073
McINTYRE,Lac,Robert Anderson Shields,1056500
McKEON,Cpl,Leonard,646134
McKIE,Cpl,James,564998
McKIE,Ac1,Archibald,1162692
McLELLAN,Ac2,Robert Crosbie,1367192
McLENNAN,Ac2,Duncan Douglas,1365889
McMILLEN,W/o,Gerard Francis,1371004
McPHILLIPS,Ac1,Thomas,621000
MEADOWS,Cpl,Percy Henry,1725834
MEATHRELL,Fl/off,Douglas Campbell,142650
MEDHURST,Ac2,Henry George,1263910
MEEHAN,Ac1,Anthony,1029262

MEEK,Lac,Geoffrey Colin Wilfred,1387693
MERCER,Ac1,Shirley,633677
MERCHANT,W/o,Arthur Hedley,505712
MERRIMAN,Lac,Ronald,1014312
MESSER,Lac,Henry Charles,648503
MIDDLETON,Fl/off,Norman Edward,189433
MIDDLETON,Ac1,Charles,618585
MIELE,Ac1,George Philip,624260
MILLARD,Ac2,William Edward,1475234
MILLER,Ac2,Norman Clive,1174886
MILLER,Lac,Dennis Charles,637570
MILLIS,W/o,Ernest Thomas,513683
MILNE,Lac,John,1016606
MITCHEL,L/Cpl,Claude Edward,1166165
MITCHEL,L/Cpl,Alexander William,937975
MITCHELL,Lac,Charles Denholm,623149
MOORE,Lac,William,630847
MOORE,Lac,Sydney,624046
MOORE,Cpl,Frederick William Arthur,749641
MOORE,Ac2,Frank Arthur,925396
MOORE,Ac1,Douglas,645710
MORE,Grp Capt,James Winter Carmichael (OBE DFC),26161
MORGAN,Ac2,Gwynfor,1409877
MORGAN,Lac,Francis Albert John,980427
MORGAN,Cpl,Dennis Edwards,2216911
MORRILL,Ac1,Walter Ernest,941184
MORRIS,Cpl,Rowland Vernun,527412
MORRIS,Ac1,Leonard,1028262
MORRIS,Fl/lt,Kenneth Albert William,118470
MORRIS,Lac,John,1351858
MORRISON,Cpl,Hugh,532230
MORRISON,Lac,Samuel,1231102
MORRISON,Ac1,Dunan Baxter,1118583
MORTON,Ac1,George Samuel,1286629
MOUNSEY,W/o,Alexander,901189
MUNDIN,Ac2,Harry Kenneth,1190136
MUNDY,Cpl,Godfrey Elton,1258104
MYERS,Plt Off,Harold,58781
NAPIER,Fl/Sjt,Robert,1054912
NASH,Lac,Thomas Arthur,701757
NATHAN,Ac1,Gerald Maurice,940019
NEAL,Ac1,George,922771
NEALE,Ac1,Thomas,1141811
NEEDHAM,Cpl,Arthur,1540712
NELSON,Ac2,George Frederick,1036427
NELSON,Fl/Sjt,David,533351
NEWMAN,Ac1,Francis Ray,1376881
NICHOLSON,Lac,Robert William,1000551
NICHOLSON,Ac2,Ernest Gordon,1498296
NICOL,Ac2,Alexander,1076705
NIEHORSTER,Ac2,Geoffrey Ernest,1234542
NISBET,Ac1,Walter,1021793
NOB;E,Ac1,James Robert,616255
NOBLE,Fl/Sjt,John Stephen,1551862
NOBLE,Lac,Austin Black,573704
NORRIS,Sjt,Mathew George,574771
NORTH,Cpl,Donald Edward,615574
NOTT,Ac2,Hubert William,1375971
NUNN,Lac,Derrick Edward,1260470
OLDROYD,Lac,Henry Gordon,956432
ORANGE,Ac1,Thomas,622104
ORCHARD,Sjt,Sidney Albert,517248
OSBORNE,Lac,William,1134290
OSMENT,Lac,John Thomas,1250418
OWEN,Fl/Sjt,Albert,577571
OWEN,Ac2,William Emlyn,1441079
OWEN,Ac1,Leslie William,1054275
PAGE,Cpl,Ronald Herbert,1198247
PAGE,Ac2,Benjamin William,634559
PALMER,Ac1,Eric Archibald,1390430

PARFITT,Lac,Alfred William Charles,651872
PARKER,Cpl,Frederick Partington,523222
PARKER,Sjt,Harold Theophilis,647970
PARKES,Lac,William Arthur,11718236
PARSONS,Ac1,William George,1447475
PARSONS,Lac,Frederick William,648522
PASK,Ac1,Jack Kenneth,575669
PASSEY,Lac,Francis Maurice,942946
PATERSON,Ac1,Robert Rusell,1368486
PATERSON,Ac1,Leslie,1253054
PAUL,Fl/off,Noel Francis William,203466
PAYNE,Lac,William Ernest,995058
PEARCE,Ac2,Charles,149800
PEARSON,Cpl,James Jonas,1247670
PEARSON,Cpl,Cyril Bowes,971437
PEET,Cpl,Stanley Ernest,918527
PELAN,Cpl,Henry Girvan,648059
PELL,Ac1,Ronald Clement,1183415
PENFOLD,Ac1,Harry Thomas,753282
PENNY, Cpl, Robert Evan, 1686666
PEPPER,Ac2,William James,1496245
PEPPER,Lac,Frederick,1050190
PEPPER,Cpl,Douglas Hadrian,634946
PERIERA,Ac2,Malcolm,785917
PERIERA,Ac2,Harry.L.,785912
PERMAIN,Cpl,James,701363
PERREAU,Ac1,Vincent Ralph,785783
PERREAU,Ac2,Harold Vincent,785655
PERRY,Fl/Sjt,Victor Dennis,1575597
PERRY,Lac,Michael Christie,1263736
PERRY,Cpl,Harold Shillito,509897
PETHERAM,Lac,Kenneth Desmond George,971938
PETTITT,Sjt,Clifford John,1397619
PHELPS,Cpl,Hubert Ernest,1189278
PHILIPS,Lac,Herbert John,1376191
PHILLIPS, Lac, Ronald Durston, 3006131
PHILLIPS,Ac1,Ronald,552759
PHILLIPS,Ac1,David Glyn,1255877
PHILPOTT,Lac,Sidney,929224
PICKLES,Ac1,James,1029474
PIGOTT,Lac,Arnold Edward,642849
PIMBLETT,Cpl,Eric,572595
PITMAN,W/o,Walter Charles,363232
PITTENDRIGH,Lac,William,536640
PITTS,Cpl,Victor Charles,749903
POLAND,Sjt,Dennis Albert,1116610
POLDEN,Ac1,Leslie Walter,934876
POLEYKETT,Ac1,Albert Francis,643840
POLLOCK,Ac1,William Edward,613630
PORTSMOUTH,Sjt,Alexander,517705
POTTER,Fl/jt,Bernard Henry,1582117
POTTER,Ac2,Basil Roy,1290449
POTTER,Fl/Sjt,Arthur Alex,533811
POTTS,Ac2,Leslie George,1441975
POULSON,Sjt,Wiliam Thomas,805342
POWELL,Ac1,Edward John,1284061
POWNALL,Ac2,John Stanley,1017978
PREECE,Cpl,Sidney Charles,637297
PRESTON,Ac1,Jack,925636
PRESTON,Lac,Alfred Albert,964703
PRICE,Ac1,Dilwyn Joe,1274285
PRICE,Lac,John Tweeddale,650982
PRIDDLE,Lac,Gilbert Frank,998580
PRIESTLEY,Ac1,Dennis,1032538
PRIME,Ac1,Charles Henry,1309574
PRIME,Lac,Albert James,1158337
PRITCHARD,Fl Off,Thomas James,44422
PROCTOR,Fl/off,Edward,67126
PRYOR,Lac,Vernon,622099
PULFORD,Air Vice Marsh. (CB OBE AFC),Conway Walter Heath,

PULLEYN, F/o, Rupert Julian, 181508
PUSEY,Lac,Joseph Walter,640281
PYKE,Cpl,Stewart,550881
QUY,Ac1,Edward Charles,1250381
RACE,Cpl,William,531262
RADFORD,Ac2,Norman,1177682
RAMSAY,Ac1,Harold John,1269858
RAMSDEN,Ac1,Arthur,1309876
RANSOME,Sjt,Harry,623622
RATCLIFFE,Fl/Sjt,John Squire,1894746
RAWLINSON,Lac,Maurice Howard,622294
REAY,Lac,Reginald Frederick George,649039
REDMAN,Fl/lt,John,41952
REEVES,Ac1,George Frederick,1177473
REID,Ac2,Richard,1027881
REID,Fl/off,James Brodie,193131
REID,Lac,Ernest Montieth,1063513
REILLY,W/o,James Joseph,907049
RENDEL,L/Cpl,Arthur Francis,646127
RENNIE,Ac1,Georeg,993394
RENSHAW,Ac2,William,1108806
REYNOLDS,Ac2,William Arthur,1234773
REYNOLDS,Lac,Leonard Robert,1045886
REYNOLDS,Ac1,Herbert,1169152
REYNOLDS,A1,Arthur,1124266
RHODES,Fl/Sjt,Sidney,564006
RHODES,L/off,Arthur,170239
RICHARDS,Ac2,William,1205627
RICHARDS,Ac1,Reginald Gordon,635445
RICHARDSON,Lac,William Hailes,1043272
RICHARDSON,Fl/Sjt,Herbert Arthur,517958
RICKARD,Ac1,Thomas,1271734
RIDDLE,Ac1,Gordon Henry,1176206
RIES,Plt Off,William Edward,109327
RIGBY,Ac1,William,991984
RILEY,Ac2,Philip John,1020235
RINGROW,Lac,Frederick Charles,925034
ROACH,Sjt,Frederick,534737
ROBB,Ac1,Hector Stewart,1158722
ROBERTS,Cpl,Isaac,532208
ROBERTS,Ac1,Emlyn,1161102
ROBERTS,Ac2,Cecil Frederick,1219037
ROBERTSON,Sjt,Alexander Paterson,515540
ROBINSON,Ac1,Arthur Thomas Meanwell,1167696
ROCHE,W/o,Gerald,535178
ROGAN,Ac2,Francis Patrick Joseph,627409
ROGERS,Ac1,John,1134107
ROGERS,Lac,Gordon Frank,615228
ROGERS,Cpl,Frank,1228529
ROMAIN,Lac,Louis,1256012
ROOT,Lac,Jack Eric,939135
ROSE,Ac1,Arthur Bernard,1178453
ROSINE,Ac1,James Noel,552768
ROSS,Ac1,David P,1305204
ROSSITER,Ac2,Walter,576400
ROUCHY,Ac2,John Frederick,1231820
ROUND,Ac1,Olaf Alfred,1359997
ROUTLEY,Cpl,Leonard George,551190
ROWARTH,Ac1,John George,1326197
ROWLAND,Sq Ldr,Ian Terence Byathan,33284
ROWLAND,Ac1,Frank Wallace,1161258
ROWLEY,Ac1,Albert,1164836
RUSSELL,Ac1,Samuel Kane,1357602
RUSSELL,Sq Ldr,Asil Henry Sackville,77419
RUTHERFORD,Fl/off,Gordon,45252
RYAN, Cpl, John Joseph, 2224190
RYAN,W/o,Cecil Denis,354239
SANDFORD,Ac2,Frederick George,1291870
SANT,Cpl,Reginald Thomas,654537
SARGINSON,Lac,Joseph Edwin,543013

SCHOFIELD,Cpl,Harry,615243
SCOTCHER,Ac2,Frank Robert,1270226
SCOTT,Ac1,George,1107245
SCOTT,Cpl,Edward,568889
SCOTT, Ac2, Thomas Liddle, 1023057
SCUDDER,Ac1,George Henry,933690
SCULLION,W/o,William,511304
SECKINGTON,Cpl,Eric,642378
SEMMENS,Lac,Leonard,1818153
SEMPLE,Cpl,Tommy,549415
SEYMOUR,Cpl,Noel Arthur,552186
SHACKLETON,Ac2,Norman,938152
SHARP,Ac2,Albert,654246
SHAW,Lac,Reginald,1030209
SHEALS,Fl/off,Hubert Stanley,61116
SHEARER,Ac2,George,1126378
SHEARS,Sjt,Philip Gordon,956073
SHEERIN,Lac,Leslie,973394
SHELTON,Ac2,Clarence Douglas,1442606
SHERWOOD,Ac1,Ernest Robert,916303
SHIMMELS,Fl/Sjt,Leonard,518753
SHINE,Ac1,James Alfred Thomas,1069371
SHIRLEY,Sjt,Wilfred,523502
SHIRLEY,Fl/Sjt,George Ernest,523280
SHORES,Sjt,George Cyril,530989
SHOULER,Ac1,Derek William,906113
SHUBROOK,Ac1,Leonard,644613
SHUTTLEWORTH,Ac2,Donald Anthony,1074216
SIM,Cpl,John Hart,803509
SIMPSON,Fl/Sjt,James Alexander,946014
SIMPSON,Ac1,George William,1232047
SIMPSON,Ac1,George Arthur,944334
SIMPSON,Lac,Cyril,1166618
SKEA,Lac,Robert Allan,89166
SKELTON,Cpl,George Robert,636765
SLATER,Ac1,John Ephraim,1269900
SLAUGHTER,Cpl,Frederick Keith,628781
SMART,Lac,Jack,956483
SMART,Cpl,Owen Frank,534719
SMERDON,Fl/off,Rolf,140803
SMITH,Ac1,Samuel James,1025329
SMITH,Lac,Joseph Henry,1030298
SMITH,Lac,John Thomas,956498
SMITH,Fl/tjt,James,560485
SMITH,Lac,Herbert John,1377011
SMITH,Lac,Henry Llewellyn,1103013
SMITH,Ac1,George Bernard,1069715
SMITH,Lac,Frederick Dickens John,610526
SMITH,Cpl,Frank,1002643
SMITH,Ac2,Edward Mert,975668
SMITH,Lac,Arthur Hudson,1055923
SMITH,Sjt,Archibald,548541
SMITH,Ac1,John Charles,577173
SMITH,Flt Sjt,Henry,622986
SNOWDEN,Lac,Frank,1457872
SNOXELL,Ac1,Charles Henry,1219969
SOLLY,Cpl,Frederick Thomas,1351524
SOUTAR,Ac2,Eric Alexander,1060263
SOUTAR,Cpl,David Crabb,525345
SOUTHWELL,Ac1,John Richard,1292960
SPENCE,Cpl,Maurice,1003785
SPENCE,Lac,James,653027
SPRAKE,Ac2,Robert John Leslie,1319147
SPRIGGS,Ac2,Samuel Cecil,1376263
SPRINGALL,Lac,Victor Stephen,907918
SPUFFARED,Lac,Eric Norman,634384
STACEY,Fl/off,Bernard Frederick,101225
STANDEM,Lac,Geoffrey,921798
STANDLEY,Cpl,Peter John,573094
STANILAND,Lac,Eric John,925188

STANLEY,Lac,Clare,1102699
STANNER,Ac1,Sidney,1273418
STAPELEY,Ac1,Owen William,1387375
STAPLETON,Lac,Arthur Thomas,953390
STAPLEY,Lac,Percy Charles,1182144
STARKIE,Lac,William James,1004596
STEDMAN,Cpl,John Walter,625564
STENHOFF,Cpl,John Frederick,632575
STENTON,Fl/lt,John,47513
STEPHEN,Fl/off,Paul Steward,46557
STEPHEN,Fl/lt,James Bryden,148814
STEPHENS,Fl/jt,Ronald William,1322459
STEPHENS,Fl/Sjt,James,1294418
STEVENS,W/o,Peter Thomas Maurice,570644
STEWART,Ac2,John Stark,989432
STOCK,Lac,Arthur,1100024
STONE,W/o,Herbert Frederick John,508820
STOOKES,Cpl,Donald,641840
STRANGE,Lac,Christopher Arthur,1667867
STREATER,Ac1,Victor Sydney,1378172
STREET,Cpl,Alec,972854
STRICKLAND,Ac1,Walter Claude,1254032
STRONACH,Cpl,William,1495445
STRUDWICK,Ac2,David George,1030512
STUART,Lac,Benjamin Walter John,427036
SUGDEN,Lac,Horace Alfred,920849
SULLIVAN,Ac2,Charles John,1293472
SUMMERFIELD,Cpl,Victor,644381
SUMNER,Ac1,Edward,1128974
SUTCLIFFE,Cpl,Ellis,641082
SUTTON,Cpl,William Robert,2269585
SWAFFIELD,Sjt,Noel George,6190989
SWAN,Lac,Benjamin Gordon,559205
SWIFT,Lac,Sydney Tolson,638121
SWINDELL,Lac,George,1103688
SYMONDS,Ac1,Albert George,1017354
TADGELL,Sjt,William George,785108
TALBOT,Ac2,Stephen John,576850
TALBOT,Lac,Alan Ronald,1545529
TANGUY,Ac1,Raymond Louis,1167039
TASKER,Sjt,Charles Neville,1432828
TATE,Ac1,George Manners,1000442
TAYLOR,Cpl,William Cummings,1076948
TAYLOR,Ac1,Sidney Ivor,1014128
TAYLOR,Lac,Ronald James,986376
TAYLOR,Cpl,Owen,540659
TAYLOR,Ac1,Loftus George,1259891
TAYLOR,W/o,George Derek (DFM),1050838
TAYLOR,Ac1,Freddie,957318
TAYLOR,Lac,Frank Richard,976583
TAYLOR,Ac1,Frank,577270
TAYLOR,Ac1,Ernest William,1206929
TAYLOR,Cpl,Edward,627490
TAYLOR,Lac,Alfred,643307
TAYLOR,Sjt,William George,528043
TEASDALE,Lac,George Norman,941699
TEED,Cpl,Denis Theodore,536231
TELFER,Cpl,William Ritchie,974502
TENNENT,Sjt,Basil Gerald Roland,508150
TEPPETT,Ac2,Roy Leslie,1189937
TERRY,Cpl,Walter Patrick,617737
THATCHER,Lac,Douglas Edward Allan,3008235
THOMAS,Ac1,Ronald John,931800
THOMAS,Ac1,Ricghard Mansel,1262124
THOMAS,Fl/Sjt,Gordon David,1607426
THOMPSON,Fl/Sjt,Thomas William,1145121
THOMPSON,Lac,Stephen Thomas,816056
THOMPSON,Lac,Robert,969695
THOMPSON,Ac1,Reginald,926847
THOMPSON,Cpl,Edward Henry,1050417

THOMSON,Lac,Peter,972442
THOMSON,Lac,John,982191
THOMSON,Fl/Sjt,Robert,350627
THORNTON,Ac1,Robert William,1486926
THORPE,Cpl,James William,539848
THRIPP,Sq Ldr,Cyril,21096
TILL,Fl/off,Edward Stracey,60942
TILLEY,Cpl,Romald Kenneth,575335
TITLEY,Ac1,Arthur,1177615
TOE,Lac,Ernest George,40613
TOMKINSON,Ac2,Fred,1013110
TONGUE,Fl/off,Edwin (MM),116822
TOOVEY,Ac1,Eric Charles,1727030
TRICKETT,Ac1,Ernest Stanley,1055582
TRIGG,Fl/lt,Norman Charles,143031
TRISTRAM,Ac2,Thomas Herbert,1382165
TROUT,Ac1,Albert William Donald,1176664
TUGWELL,W/o,William Percival,621324
TURNER,F/o,Vincent,181801
TURNER,Lac,Ronald James,1352164
TURNER,Lac,Anthony William,1280138
TURTON,Sq Ldr,Jack,124816
TUTHILL,Ac1,David Henry Clarence,1242343
TYLER,W/o,Frederick,505594
TYRRELL,Lac,Mervyn Guy,1186330
TYRRELL,Ac1,Claude David,1206675
UMPLEBY,Lac,Edgar,646177
UNDERWOOD,Ac1,Alfred,1009648
UNSWORTH,Fl/lt,Laurence,150089
URRY,Lac,Fred,942171
VARLEY,Ac1,Jack Kenneth,1216911
VASEY,Lac,Frank,938572
VASS,Lac,William Kenneth,1307084
VENN,Lac,Verdun Dennis,903626
VICKERMAN,Sjt,Herbert,516884
VILLARS,Sjt,Ernest Joseph James,538950
WAGSTAFF,Lac,Walter,1055467
WALKER,Ac2,William Charles,1401823
WALKER,Lac,James Scott,937399
WALKER,Ac1,James Roland,1116173
WALKER,Ac1,Arthur Cecil Caesar,1190515
WALLACE,Cpl,Richard Anthony,1352874
WALLER,Cpl,Jonathan Walter,332584
WALMSLEY,Cpl,Mathew Whyte,304115
WALTON,Cpl,Raymond,541041
WARD,Cpl,John Edward,702288
WARD,Sjt,Charles Frederick,569300
WARD,Ac2,Charles,1569747
WARD,Lac,Arnold,652616
WARDALE,Ac1,Arthur,1379138
WARREN,Ac1,Leslie Rupert,1253510
WARWICK,Cpl,Jack,972357
WATERS,Fl/lt,Arthur Edgar,169147
WATKINS,Ac1,Kenneth Oswald,951267
WATKINSON,Lac,Reginald,1009915
WATSON,Ac2,Walter Thomas Tony,1450291
WATSON,Ac2,Roland Arthur,1358305
WATSON,Fl/lt,Edward James,81374
WATSON,Lac,Charles Percy,1287882
WATSON,Cpl,Albert John,625094
WATTS,Ac1,William Alfred Charles,1206646
WATTS,Lac,Ronald,1251128
WATTS,Grp Capt,Frank Eric,05099
WATTS,Lac,Eustace Henry,953636
WAUD,Cpl,Kenneth James,950703
WAUGH,Cpl,Stanley Jameson,548471
WEARE,Ac1,Alan Joseph,1034469
WEAVER,Ac2,Frederick Henry,1407331
WEBB,Lac,James Edward,1289591
WEBB,Lac,Hector John,611113

WEBBER,Flt Sjt,George Richard,364372
WEBSTER,Lac,Reginald,1306588
WEBSTER,Ac1,Hedley William Benjamin,1191273
WEDGE,Lac,Ernest Charles,701328
WEIR,Lac,Valentine Edward Douglas,1436429
WELCH,Ac1,Charles Arthur,1185253
WELLER,Ac2,Ronald Frederick Cyril,1391725
WELLS,Ac1,Frederick George,1292985
WHALLEY,Lac,Ronald,975753
WHALLEY,Sjt,Geoffrey Alan,2202704
WHISTLER,Grp Capt,Harold Alfred (DSO DFC),03100
WHISTON,Cpl,Percy,941158
WHISTONDALE,Grp Capt,George Frederick,16259
WHITE, Lac, James Armitage, 1561913
WHITE,Fl/lt,Thomas Roden,77510
WHITEHEAD,Ac1,Robin Mervyn,1354117
WHITESIDE,W/o,Robert Macdonald,516891
WHITFORD,Ac1,Albert,943495
WICKS,Cpl,Charles Joseph,1294824
WIDDICOMBE,Ac1,Frederick Charles,1172943
WIGGIN,Fl/Sjt,William Arthur,364753
WILCOCK,Lac,Harry Rourke,1010120
WILD,Sjt,Donald Cuthbert,1036348
WILDMAN,Cpl,Cyril,545204
WILIAMS,Ac2,Gordon Thomas Garfield,932450
WILKES,Ac1,George William Arthur,976355
WILKIE,Ac1,John Mcewan,1341518
WILKINS,Sjt,Reginald Sidney,644371
WILLIAMS,Ac1,Thomas Henry,1128182
WILLIAMS,Lac,Stanley,613679
WILLIAMS,Ac1,Ronald Harry,1089246
WILLIAMS,Sjt,Joseph Charles,615449
WILLIAMS,Ac1,Joseph,1086473
WILLIAMS,Ac2,John Lynn,1077842
WILLIAMS,Ac1,John Dewi,626147
WILLIAMS,Lac,Harold Eric John,629130
WILLIAMS,Lac,Edward Stanley,1121640
WILLIAMS,Sjt,Rene,570511
WILLIAMSON,Ac1,John,1117357
WILLIAMSON,Fl/Sjt,Claude Marriott,566818
WILLIS,Ac1,Vincent,1078896
WILLIS,Fl/Sjt,Louis Ernest,1339781
WILLIS,Lac,Charles,643501
WILLMOTH,Lac,Alfred William,957899
WILSON, Lac, William Meiklem, 1055469
WILSON,Lac,William Leonard,928855
WILSON,Ac2,Leslie,1076488
WILSON,Lac,John Lionel,1003098
WILSON,Cpl,George,567026
WILSON,Ac1,Francis,1026539
WILSON,Ac1,Benjamin,954701
WOLFE,W/o,David Augusta,341934
WOOD,Lac,Robert,612683
WOOD,Ac1,Raymond,542931
WOOD,Ac2,Percival Henry,1401948
WOOD,Ac1,James,1106457
WOOD,Fl/lt,Hugh John,152282
WOOD,Lac,Charles Harold,653402
WOOD,Wt Off,Percy Charles,358570
WOODMANSEY,Fl/off,Frank,134368
WORTH,W/o,Walter John,335324
WORTHINGTON,Lac,Robert Sherwin,965157
WORTHINGTON,Cpl,Fred Stephenson,1022139
WRAGG,Ac1,Ernest,1499501
WRIGHT,Cpl,Lawrence Stratton,2269623
WRIGHT,Sjt,Edward Cecil,534127
WRIGHT,Lac,Arthur,1112202
WRIGHT,Cpl,Oswald Allen,611696
WYATT,Lac,Arthur Reginald,1157986
YALLOP,Lac,Wilfred Edward Frank,1259752

YATEMAN,Lac,John Frederick Owen,1256684
YATES,Lac,Kenneth,633084
YEAMAN,Sjt,Robert William Cowan,1095641
YOUNG,Sjt,Leslie George,1443453
YOUNG,Fl/lt,Earl William,39593

GENERAL (VR)
ACLAND,Flt/lt,Simon John Dyke (DSC),T78340
ALLCORN,Ac1,Sidney Francis,1440792
ALLEN,Flt Lt,John Anthony,76473
ALLFREY,Ac1,E J,1294301
ASKER,Lac,Peter George,1725431
BAILEY,Ac2,Thomas,1498590
BAILEY,Cpl,Ronald Hayden,761217
BAMFORD,Lac,George,938538
BANKS,Ac2,James Hector,1127141
BEAUMONT,Ac1,George William,1141866
BECKETT,Ac1,Albert John,1055052
BESSANT,Ac1,Leslie George,1312440
BISHOP,Lac,Harold William,1183752
BISHOP,Lac,Harry Willis,1281170
BOARDMAN,Lac,Clifford,980284
BOOTH,F/lt,Philip George Nathan,80605
BRADLEY,Ac1,Charles,650917
BRAIN,Ac1,Frank Maxwell,1233279
BREACH,Ac1,Cyril Wallace Frederick,1325569
BROOKER,Lac,Edward George,910432
BURNS,2,Eric,952815
BUSSEY,Ac1,Reginald Thomas,934864
BYERLEY,Lac,Alfred Wallace John,907350
CAPON,Ac1,Walter Stanley,1256149
CARPENTER,Ac2,Gordon John,1295462
CARTER,Ac2,Reginald Jack,1028192
CHADBOND,Ac1,Austin,3039702
CHAMBERS,Ac1,George Henry,1059768
CHISHOLM,Ac2,David Galt,1340678
CHURCH,Lac,Patrick Clisby,1030299
CLARKE,Ac2,Douglas Gordon,1286242
CLAYDON,Fl/off,Francis Joseph Staff,61120
CLAYTON,Lac,Leslie Arthur,1100939
CLEMENTS,Ac2,Sidney Herbert,1236042
CLULEE,Fl Off,Leigh Walter Denis,63882
COTTON,Cpl,Roy Douglas,3077422
CURNOW,Ac2,Cecil,1246719
CUTHBERTSON,Ac1,Denis Melville,1106471
DANIELS,Ac1,Edward,1177894
DAVIES,Ac1,William Raymond,1137140
DAVIES,Ac1,Arthur Reginald,1074495
DAVISON,Ac1,Frederick Terence,1085842
DUFF,Cpl,Danial James Stewart,941229
ELIOTT,Ac2,Henry,1137138
ELWIS,Cpl,James Ronald,987209
EMERY,Lac,Wilfred,1661571
EMSLIE,Lac,Arthur Mcleod,987796
FOOT,Lac,Wilfred William John,1290409
FOX,Wt/ Off,John James,956809
FRANKLIN,Cpl,Charles Arthur,744426
FROST,Ac2,Kenneth Ernest,1239880
GANNON,Ac1,John Daniel Bert,4002920
GERRISH,Cpl,Kenneth,1313236
GESS,Ac1,George Gilbert,1176093
GIBBONS,Ac2,Cyril George,1400709
GIBBS,Ac1,Ronald Joseph,1228666
GIBSON,Ac1,William,995749
GILBURT,Sjt,Sanley Victor,1883201
GOODINGS,Fl Off,Norman Geoffrey,195875
GOSLING,Ac1,Geoffrey Lional Henry,1290040
GRAY,Ac1,William,1365956
GREAVES,Ac2,Wilfred,1067845
GREEN,Sjt,Ernest,2223070

HAIGH,Ac1,Dennis,1079816
HAIRE,Lac,Robert Henry,1002842
HALEY,Ac1,Harold Edward,1156347
HAYES,L A C,Herbert,981225
HAYLOCK,Lac,William John,1215414
HEPPERSTALL,Ac2,William,1142478
HETHERINGTON,Ac1,William Murphy,1266649
HEWITT,Lac,Samuel Stephen,1637004
HIGGINBOTHAM,Ac2,James Edward,1218592
HILLS,Ac1,Denis Harold,1446359
HODGKIMSON,Cpl,Donald Christie,992162
HOLLANDS,Ac2,Sydney Frank,1283706
HOLMES,Cpl,Charles George,923937
HOPWOOD,W/o,Lewis,1125666
HUBBARD,Ac,Edward Ernest,922659
HUTCHINSON,Ac1,Herbert William,1350885
INGRAM,Cpl,Frank,540918
JACKSON,Fl Off,Raymon Bensley,116817
JACKSON,Lac,Harry,957898
JACKSON,Flt Sjt,Philip Paul,1899244
JOHNSTON,Ac1,William Goodwin,1176696
JONES,Lac,William Charles,1074824
JONES,Ac1,Albert Derrick,1021708
JONES,Cpl,James Henry,1226173
KEELEY,Flt Sjt,Percy Norman,785003
KIRKLAND,Lac,Andrew,1303238
KNIGHT,Ac2,Robert Michael,1294829
LANCASTER,Ac2,George,1141295
LANSDELL,Ac1,Martin Gordon,1211773
LARKMAN,Lac,Sidney,964890
LAUNDER,Ac2,Charles Henry,1425224
LEETCH,Ac1,Bertram Percival,748811
LEVINSON,Ac1,Sydney Henry,1262684
LEVY,Ac1,Alfred,942855
LEWIS,Ac1,Gwyn,1401156
LEWIS,Cpl,Reginald William Roper,1035295
LEWITT,Ac2,Arthur Alfred,1075677
LINDLEY,Ac2,Harry,1053805
LLOYD,Crl,Frederick Desmond,905706
LOGAN,Ac1,John William,1015956
LONGBOTTOM,Lac,Jack,1103624
LYLE,Lac,Horace John,1205847
MAJOR,Cpl,Robert Abraham,1053692
MALKIN,Lac,Reginald Alexander,949570
MANSFIELD,Ac1,Henry Frederick,3009085
MARTIN,Flt Lt,Guy Joseph Marie (DFC),161289
MASSEY,Fl Ff,Joseph (DFM),185868
MAY,Ac1,Arthur Charles,925981
MAY,Ac1,Arthur Charles,925981
McCORMACK,Ac1,John,1529456
McEWAN,Ac2,Ronald Alexander,1054041
McLACHLAN,Lac,Ronald Graham,3024743
McMILLEN,Ac1,William Henry,701454
MEREDITH,Ac1,Francis,972615
MOORE,Ac1,Stanley John,2274559
MORT,Lac,William,1112822
MORTON,Lac,John Russell,1366825
MOSES,Ac1,Robert,1033850
MUDGE,Lac,Henry James,926507
NELSON,Ac1,Ernest William,914057
NORTH,Cpl,John Hurst,1645022
ODDY,Lac,Charles William,982151
OSBORNE,Ac1,Clifford,1049754
PATCHETT,Ac1,Albert,1080636
PHILLIPS,Lac,Edgar Herbert Harrison,1061702
PLEAVIN,Cpl,Basil,968522
POCKLINGTON,Lac,Stanley,1007940
PORTER,Ac2,William Joseph,1126454
POUNDER,Lac,Winston,984840
POWELL,Lac,William Charles,1357971

PRATT,Lac,William,1113446
PRICE,Lac,Eric Cyril,965151
PRINCE,Ac2,William John,1047125
PRIOR,Lac,Gilbert Ronald George,1307269
REAKES,Lac,Thomas Bloomfield,1410910
REES,Ac1,Thomas Howard,1297832
REGAN,Ac2,Charles,1079339
RENNIE,Lac,William Taylor Coghill,988181
RENNISON,Ac1,George,2269982
REYNOLDS,Lac,Henry James,805425
ROBB,Ac1,James Emslie,992367
ROBINSON,Ac1,Arthur David,1046886
ROSSER,Ac1,Leighton Howell,1255740
ROWAN,Ac1,William Erwin,993604
RUSSELL,Lac,Charles Bruce,932333
RYDER,Lac,William,1010437
SALTER,Ac1,Wiliam,1305421
SCOURFIELD-EVANS,Fl Off,Richard,87789
SEE,Ac1,Jim,964496
SERVICE,Ac2,Archibald Stevenson,1054724
SHARROCK,Ac2,Harry,1064357
SHOEMAKE,Lac,Charles,1250108
SIMPSON,Ac1,Robert Arthur,1204023
SMITH,Ac1,Thomas Duke Gibson,922106
SMITH,Ac1,Francis John,1261534
SMITH,Ac2,Gerald,1071456
SMITH,Flt Lt,Harry,164703
SMITH,Ac2,Gerald,1071456
STANFORD,Sjt,John,1607530
STENT,Ac1,Donald William,916710
STEVENS,Lac,William Henry,1069427
STIFF,Ac1,George Edward,927911
STRATFORD,Ac1,Albert Charles,1193840
TAYLOR,Ac1,Stanley Arthur,1032221
TAYLOR,Lac,George Alfred,1031456
THOMAS,Ac2,Hilton Lloyd,910377
THOMPSON,Ac1,Thomas Percy,1176692
THOROWGOOD,Lac,Leslie Victor,1325225
TURNER,Ac1,Thomas Douglas,755212
TURNER,Lac,Edward Thomas,1107916
URIE,Ac1,John Mcleod,1024473
VENN,Lac,Francis Albert,1665081
WAINES,Lac,Francis Herbert,991345
WARNE,Ac1,Henry Ernest,907872
WATKINS,Wng Comm,Trevor James Legrew,76472
WEBB,Ac1,Vincent Bertram,1275416
WEIR,Cpl,Frederick Edward,1303050
WELCH,Ac2,Reginald William,3202033
WEST,Ac1,James Charles,1085840
WHITE,Lac,George,931735
WHITE,Ac2,Edward Charles,4004763
WILES,Lac,George Andrew,976969
WILLIAMS,Lac,Gordon Alfred,1281525
WILLIAMS,Lac,Albert Graham,1705343
WILLIAMSON,Cpl,Arthur,967008
WINDMILL,Ac1,Colin Victor,938547
WIRE,Lac,Benjamin Lloyd,931153

2 SQUADRON
ATKINS,Ac2,Stanley Harold,1270724
BULL,Fl/lt,Sir Stephen John,87153

5 SQUADRON
CAMERON,Fl/Sjt,Robert Dyce,776154
CAMPBELL,Fl/Sjt,Christopher Gordon,1001176
LEE,Fl/t,William John Newton,112434,DFC
THOMAS,Fl/Sjt,William Geoffrey,655563
WILSON,Fl/off,John Ernest,1246410
WOOD,Sjt,Alan Tyson,785063

10 SQUADRON
BEER, Fl/off, Henry Albert, 197600
COOPER, Fl/off, William Kenneth, 180306
GORLEY, Fl/lt, William (DFC), 169474
HUMES, Fl/off, George Fewster, 167174
MAIN, W/o, David, 1568281
REDFERN, W/o, Denis Clifford, 1578892
RHODES, Fl/Sjt, John Edward Laurence, 1894239
ROBINSON, W/o, Frank Barrow, 1697566
ROBINSON, W/o, Frank, 2207214
SHAW, Fl/lt, Frederick Brian, 170625
STEDMAN, Fl/off, Berkley George, 56186
WELCH, W/o, Leslie Ernest, 1606977

11 SQUADRON
AULT, Sqn Ld, Kenneth, 33214
BELL, Sjt, James Charles Alfred, 970852
BIGGS, Sjt, Sidney Charles, 1164957
COLMORE, Fl/lt, David Martin, 107982
FOREMAN, Cpl, Leonard Wiliam, 575828
HUTTON, Sjt, Charles Peter, 573547
KITE, Pilot, Edward John, 568320
MACKAY, Sjt, John Macleod, 1564693
PARKINSON, Sjt, Kenneth Reginald, 1800761
PENNINGTON-LEGH, Wg Cmdr, Alan William, 37687
RICHARDSON, Sjt, Eric, 1684515
ROWAN, Sjt, Gordon, 1069929
SMITH, Sjt, Merville Keith, 97479
VEITCH, Fl/off, Peter Michael Craven, 145073
WHILES, Fl/Sjt, Stanley Dennis, 776023

11 SQUADRON (VR)
HARDS,Ac2,Peter,1890274
QUICK,Flt Lt,Desmond O'conner,160257
THOMPSON,Flt Sjt,Robert Sydney,2200083

13 SQUADRON
HANSON,Fl Off,Jeffrey Graydon,55136
MACKENZIE,W/o,Roy,1393402
O'NIELL,W/o,John Gerald,1439445

17 SQUADRON
ALEXANDER, Fl Off, David Hugh, 57718
BROOKS, Fl/Sjt, Donald Charles, 655341
COOPER, Sjt, Arthur Walvin, 1819819
CRAVEN, Fl/Sjt, George Philip, 1685324
CRAWFORD, Sjt, Derrick, 1522990
HOLT, Fl/off, Ronald Thomas William, 165389
IRVINE, Fl/off, Frederick David, 178975
PEPPER, L/off, Frederick Foyle, 149512
STEVENS,Fl/Sjt,William George,1852685

17 SQUADRON (VR)
COOKE, W/o, William Markland, 1476452
GRAY, W/o, Anthony James, 1567857

20 SQUADRON
ALDERSON, Lac, Joseph Batty, 539725
BAILEY, Fl/off, Keith Vincent, 170403
BURKILL, Fl/Sjt, Ronald Frederick, 1530598
HOLMAN, W/o, Reginald James, 1387923
STILLING, Wng Cmdr, Stanley Gordon (DFC), 39579
WHITEHALL, Sjt, William Henry, 1434984
WILKINSON, Fl/Sjt, Francis Bernard, 1576373
WILLIAMS, Lac, Raymond James, 953620

21 SQUADRON
CARROLL,Ac2,Robert,1098479
McKENZIE,Fl/off,David,134713
MUCKLE,Cpl,Thomas Paterson,633896

22 SQUADRON
BAILEY, Fl/Sjt, William Archie, 1600853
CLIFFORD, Fl/Sjt, Ronald Geoffrey, 1621165
GRIFFITH, W/o, Colin Henry, 1579261
HEDDERLEY, Fl/Sjt, William Arthur, 1604155
IRELAND, Fl/Sjt, Francis John Madden, 541264
MACKAY, Fl Sjt, John Mair, 1569418
MAGUIRE, W/o, Leonard, 1452576
MARTIN, Fl/off, Horace, 152449
MORTON, Fl/off, Norman Storrs, 151472
NICHOL, Fl/jt, Charles Frederick, 553344
SAVORY, Fl/off, Robert Glyndwr, 152676
STUART, Fl/Sjt, Norman Harold Wallace, 1578805
TAYLOR, L/Sjt, Alexander Fraser Watson, 1552276
YOUNG, Fl/Sjt, Gordon, 1512073

23 SQUADRON
MACKENZIE,Fl/Sjt,Norman William Munro,1672269
MINTON,Lac,Frederick Albert,1112966

27 SQUADRON
ARNOLD, Lac, Edmund Thomas, 571572
BARNES, Fl/Sjt, William Stanley, 1684976
BEAMAN, Sjt, Denis, 542557
BRITTER, Fl/Sjt, John Stapleton, 1314401
BUCHANAN,W/o,Stanley,1553519
CHIPPENDALE, Fl/off, Malcolm George Rea, 174371
COLLINGWOOD, Sjt, William, 1379130
COOPER, Sjt, Stanley James, 956082
CROSS, Fl/lt, Eric Samuel Collins, 129365
CULLEY, Fl/Sjt, Leonard Pinfold, 1802431
DODD, Sjt, Reginald Henry Noel, 1426811
FAIRCLOUGH, W/o, Paul John, 1379077
FINCH, W/o, Norman Francis, 1801643
FINN, Lac, Hugh, 974733
HACKETT, Sq Ldr, Charles Desmond, 33165
HASSELL, L/off, John Desmond, 119742
HERBERT, Fl/off, Kenneth Esward, 121565
ILLINGWORTH, Sq Ldr, Kenneth (DFC), 41708
LUFF, Fl/off, William Charles, 157193
MANSEL-LEWIS, Fl Off, John, 42248
MATHEWSON, Fl/Sjt, James, 970362
McDOWALL, Fl Sjt, Ian Alexander, 1556367
MERRETT, Fl/Sjt, Robert Joseph, 1421404
OSGUTHORPE, Sjt, Albert Edward, 1239576
PAINE, Fl/Sjt, Kenneth Frank, 1388175
PEARCE, Cpl, Ronald Arthur, 1263422
PLUMMER, Fl/Sjt, William Clive, 1091873
RHODES, Sjt, Ronald Mckenzie, 639637
RONUIRES, Ac2, William, 1350516
SANDS, Ac2, Arthur Mcgeoch, 1374118
SHAW, Sjt, Alick, 1620574
SILK,Dvr,Arthur Albert,2345194
SOKELL, Fl/Sjt, Frederick Ronald, 132014
STEPHENS, Ac2, William Kenneth, 102395
THOMAS, Sjt, Robert Mark, 1435315
THOMAS, W/o, Marcel Cabot, 1309736
VINCENT, Fl/off, Ronald Stuart, 169090
WHITE, Fl/lt, Frank Furley, 124831
WIGGLESWORTH, Ac1, Leslie Harry, 1005976
WILLOWS, Sjt, Michael Ransford, 771742
WOOD, Ac1, Joseph Milton, 996864

28 SQUADRON
CADE,Fl/Sjt,Edwin George,1337730
DRAYCOTT, Fl/Sjt, Kenneth Alfred Alfred Edward, 1385688
FARQUHARSON, Fl/off, Robin Lachlan Shand, 162238
FOSTER, Fl/off, Stuart Wykes, 128627
HOBART, Fl/off, Bernard, 171213
INGRAM, Lac, Rodney Lever, 1862099

PANNELL, Sq Ldr, Edward Geoffrey, 86680
PERRY, Fl/lt, Frederick James, 119140
PHILLIPS, W/o, Robert Christopher, 1336497
RED, Fl/off, Jack Miller, 48911
RHIND, Sq Ldr, John, 41954
SINCLAIR-HULL, Fl/off, Nigel, 185146
THOMSON, Fl/lt, Douglas Stuart, 47298
TITMAN, Lac, Leonard, 1872912
WILD, Fl/Sjt, Donald Hugh, 1583540

30 SQUADRON
GEFFENE, Fl/off, Donald, 64861
KEMBER, Sjt, Peter Brian, 1314908
LAWRENCE, Fl/Sjt, George Edward, 1251047

31 SQUADRON
AUBREY, W/o, Alfred William Henry, 1178104
BATTEN, Fl/off, Herbert James, 165194
BELL, Fl/Sjt, David Frank Boyce, 779857
BENNETT, L/Sjt, Ronald Sidney, 1607104
BOUGH, Fl/lt, Norman Lee (MC), 43524
CARDEN, Sjt, Thomas Herbert Boothman, 1321750
CAREW-GIBBS, Fl/Sjt, Alan Michael, 1383610
CUMING, Fl/Sjt, Richard William, 1339994
DIGHT, Fl/off, Raymond George, 164945
FORSTER, Sjt, Humphrey Rex, 1261889
HENRY, Sjt, John, 1119246
HINTON, Sjt, Raymond George, 1256736
HOWE, Fl/off, Alexander Munro, 199514
JOHN, Sjt, Edwin Maurice, 16562847
JOHN, Lac, Albert George, 576350
LAMOND, Sjt, Kenneth Edward, 771983
MILNER, W/o, John Austin, 1389666
MOORE, Fl/Sjt, Robert, 1586681
NICHOLS, Fl/Sjt, John Orson, 1377419
O'CONNOR, Sjt, Gerrard Patrick, 1614509
SCOTT, Sjt, David Horne, 1066843
SINGLETON, Lac, Leonard Herbert, 1206949
SMETHURST, Fl/Sjt, Neville Walker, 1066794
SMITH, Fl/off, Thomas Keith Burgoyne, 181712
STORRIE, Fl/Sjt, Eric Forrester, 1560944
WAGLAND, Cpl, Percival Thomas, 1179345
WALENN, Fl/Sjt, James Bernard, 778727
WALKER, Fl/lt, James Arthur (DFC), 40768
WILLIAMSON, Ac1, Thomas Gladstone, 1082946

34 SQUADRON
BISHOP, Cpl, Peter Conway, 568798
BUTLER, Fl/Sjt, Douglas Edward, 1615752
CARR, Fl/Sjt, John, 580507
CLEMENTS, Fl/Sjt, John Frederick, 577401
COX, Cpl, Albert, 567358
ELLIOT, Sjt, Alfred Gordon, 1056224
ELLIS, Lac, James William, 642037
FORD, Flt Sjt, Thomas, 619749
FOSTER, Ac1, Douglas Moore, 619906
GOMM, Ac1, John Henry, 573384
GOODWIN, Ac1, Samuel Busby, 61824
GREAVES, Sjt, Francis Murray, 1259996
HAYLOCK, Lt Lt, Basil Geoffrey, 39664
HILL, Fl/t, Ronald Edwin, 40705
HILLEBRAND, /o, Petrus Helgard, 580565
HYLAND, Fl/Sjt, Edward, 966813
JAMES, Flt Sjt, Roy Frank Richard, 564864
JULIAN, Fl/Sjt, John Phillip Reginald, 1018129
KING, Fl/Sjt, Kenneth Michael Omar, 1232306
KITCHING, Ac1, Tom Appleton, 546577
LERIGO, Ac1, Alfred Charles, 614754
LISHMAN, Fl/off, Thomas Geoffrey, 50512
MATTHEWS, Sjt, Robert Henry Pardoe, 1259647

MOORE, W/o, Charles Henry, 612425
MOORE, Ly Off, Dennis Clive, 45212
MORGAN, Ac2, Ronald George, 912211
MULLER, W/o, Jack Roland, 1386950
O'DRISCOLL, Sq Ldr, Finan, 39109
OLSON, Flt Sjt, Harold Bryan, 551372
RAYNER, Fl/Sjt, Robert John, 580380
SIMM, W/o, Jack Lawrenson, 563690
THWAITS, L/off, John Henry, 80219
WINDDRUM, Lac, James Kenneth Mark, 619843

34 SQUADRON (VR)
CHANEY, W/o, Pilot George Edwin, 1318357
CONDLIFFE, Ac1, Arthur, 1104226

35 SQUADRON (VR)
AISBITT, Sjt, Thomas, 3040082

36 SQUADRON
BARRON, Sjt, Samuel Edward, 809003
CALLICK, Fl/lt, Basil Bernard, 44977
CHATFIELD, W/o, Charlie William Noel, 335809
EINARSON, Sjt, Ivan Paul, R/65764
GOLDSWORTHY, Ac1, Leonard, 912826
GRIMES, Lac, Eric Harvey William, 619292
HADRILL, Ac1, John Pinnell, 1360698
HAGGAN, Fl/Sjt, Owen, 612057
HARRIS, Fl/Sjt, Bernard Vernon, 755290
HESLOP, Cpl, Francis Quinlan, 526856
HICKS, Fl/Sjt, Humphrey Frank, 755320
HOLMAN, Lac, Archibald Leslie, 1157359
LANGLEY, Fl Off, Kenneth Ernest, 44969
LAPISH, Sjt, Joseph, 548892
LYALL, Fl/Sjt, Ernest, 580214
MACDONALD, Jt, Angus, 566979
MAXWELL, Lac, David, 979553
MILLARD, Cpl, George Samuel, 639229
MITCHEL, L/Cpl, Albert Edward, 573922
MITCHELL, W/o, Reginald Lionel William, 590489
MITCHELL, Sjt, Kenneth Thomas William, 570372
MORGAN, Ac1, Hayes William, 1360504
MORRIS, Flt Sjt, Sidney Waler, 551556
PECK, W/o, George Bryan William, 564350
POWELL, Lac, William Albert James, 524069
RICHARDSON, Fl/lt, George Sidney, 40017
ROWELL, Sjt, William, 619635
SEATON, Fl/Sjt, John Binning, 535269
SHARPNELL-SMITH, Flt Lt, Thomas Edward, 37562
SHAW, Fl/off, William, 40571
SHAW, Lac, Ernest, 619485
SHORT, Cpl, Victor George, 566093
WITNEY, Sqn Ldr, Graham Felix, 39251

36 SQUADRON (VR)
DUFFY, Lac, John Francis, 1103600
HARRIS, Flt Sjt, Bernard Vernon, 755290
HATHERALL, Lac, Arthur Mathias, 91186
MILLER, Flt Sjt, John Christie, 563466
RICHARDSON, Flt Lt, George Sydney, 40017

42 SQUADRON
SHIELDS, Fl/lt, Lwyne Robert Peirce, 124416

42 SQUADRON (VR)
NEWHOUSE, Cpl, James, 9685232

45 SQUADRON
ASHWORTH, Sjt, Gordon Herbert, 1622404
BARGH, Fl/jt, George William, 1582355
COOK, Fl/Sjt, Geoffrey, 1569006

GOODWIN, Fl/lt, Charles Ronald, 123113
PINKERTON, W/o, Robert Leonard Cecil Conrie, 1342807
POTTS, Fl/off, Samuel, 136488
PROCTOR, Fl/lt, Gordon Hayter, 60769
PROCTOR, Fl/lt, Arthur Vincent, 150674
SIDDLE, Fl/Sjt, Sidney, 996543
TONKS, Fl/lt, Geoffrey John, 1151120

47 SQUADRON
DADEN, W/o, Edward Albert, 1335460
FILSON-YOUNG, Wg/cmdr, William David Loraine (DFC), 39725
ILLINGWORTH, W/o, Kenneth, 1434004
LAING, Fl/off, Orace Francis, 200528
LORAINS, W/o, William, 1451677
TUCK, Fl/Sjt, George Edward, 1607464
WATERS, Fl/lt, Roger Claude Vaughan, 142344

48 SQUADRON
ANDERSON, Cpl, Martin Morrison, 545634
BANKS, Cpl, Norman George Wedd, 920154
BELL, W/o, James Dfm, 1511709
BROWNING, Fl/off, Cyril Reginald Arthur, 165962
CROSS, Sjt, Ivor John May, 1609666
HANNINGTON, W/o, Phillip James Emmanuel, 1459471
HARRISON, Fl/Sjt, Reginald Sydney, 1815501
JACKSON, Lac, William Edward, 1595841
MARTIN, Sjt, Stanley Wilfred, 1239540
MULLUCKS, Fl/Sjt, Victor William, 1894841
SMITH, Fl/off, Edward Albert, 179337
SPENCER, Fl/off, James Rightson, 58390
THOMAS, W/o, Leonard, 1892300
THURSFIELD, Fl/Sjt, Joseph, 1071768
TILBURY, W/o, Donald George, 1802461
WATSON, Fl/lt, Henry De Landre, 148537
WROE, Fl/lt, Herbert, 119828

52 SQUADRON
CALLANDER,Ac1,James Cowan,1343103
CLAYDON,Fl/Sjt,Maurice Leonard,1390884
COLLARD,W/o,Edward Douglas Haig,1270759
OLIVER,Fl/Sjt,Henry Alan,551534
SMELT,Fl/Sjt,Alfred William,1216530

52 SQUADRON (VR)
WESTON,Ac2,Arthur,2279038

53 SQUADRON (VR)
JONES,Sjt,Ernest Francis,1053798

56 SQUADRON
WATTS,Fl/lt,John Selwyn,1580173

57 SQUADRON
SKINNER,Sq Ldr,Leslie Harold,85652

59 SQUADRON
GARRARD,Sq/ldr,Paul (DFC),44191
RICHARDS,Fl/off,Robert,89301

60 SQUADRON
AYRES, Sjt, William Arthur, 610542
BATES, Sjt, Ernest, 1059831
BIGMORE, Plt Off, Thomas Herbert, 48085
BROWN, Sjt, Donald Horace, 745217
BROWN, Sjt, Cyril, 1183446
CLARKE, Fl/Sjt, Thomas Lewis, 544010
COLEMAN, Fl/Sjt, Andrew John, 576820
COLLETT, Sjt, Alexander Albert, 138398
CONNELL, Sjt, Kenneth, 610272
COX, Fl/off, Herbert Lionel, 48058

DOBSON, Fl/lt, Joseph Adlington Ballantyne, 39597
DREW, Sjt, John Francis, 1259412
DUNCAN, Fl/off, Michael, 102140
EDWARDS, Fl/off, Leslie Cosmo (DFM), 45719
ELIAS, Fl/off, David Charles Martin, 181246
FOWLER, Sjt, Ernest Frederick William, 537770
GILL, W/o, Charles Sydney, 566013
GRIFFITS, Fl/Sjt, Patrick Gordon, 1385052
HESELTINE, Sjt, Richard, 563144
MOCKRIDGE, Fl/off, George Albert, 45431
MONIN, Lac, Douglas Constantine, 977222
PYLE, Fl/Sjt, Robert Joseph Henry, 580701
RYSDALE, Sjt, Geoffrey, 1058516
SMITH, Fl/Sjt, George Robert, 562896
TOMPKINS, Ljt, Reginald John, 565827
WEBB, Sjt, Ronald Arthúr, 639130
WEST, W/, Ralph Percival, 580705
WESTROPP-BENNETT, Sq Ldr, George Patrick, 37950

61 SQUADRON
GRENIER,Sjt,Guy Bertram Christopher,771978

62 SQUADRON
ADSHEAD, Fl/Sjt, Percy James, 1152717
BARKER, Fl/sgt, Ronald Frederick, 759017
BERE, W/o, Claude Henry, 515790
BOWIE, Fl/Sjt, John Walter Coutts, 56106
BROWN, Sjt, William Edward Harold Leslie, 755140
BURBIDGE, Fl/Sjt, Ronald Vincent, 562968
COATES, Fl/off, Raymond Aubrey, 60805
COMPTON, Flt Lt, John, 70136
COUZENS, Sjt, Garnett, 546805
DAWSON, Fl//Sjt, George Harold Desmond, 580258
DODDS, Fl/Sjt, James Angus, 966370
DURRANT, W/o, Robert Harold, 1437395
EDWARDS, Fl/off, Ian Albert, 179194
ELIAS, Fl/off, Sidney John, 201252
FIFOOT, Fl/off, Reginald, 172714
FIRTH, Fl/jt, John Grenville, 1475139
FRYER, Ac2, Dennis Harry, 961691
GRAHAM, Sjt, Ernest, 1356099
GRAVESON, Lac, James, 611159
GUTERSOHN, Fl/Sjt, Gordon Charles Wager, 968251
HAIGH, Fl/off, Geoffrey William, 81335
HALE, Ac1, Cecil Bertram, 905828
HALLIWELL, Flt Lt, Robert Frederick, 33341
HARVEY, Fl/off, Kenneth Foreman, 106581
HARVEY, Sjt, Colin William, 966005
HASWELL, Ac1, Kenneth Eugene, 1172752
HEADLAND, Lac, Alfred John, 935113
HEALEY, Fl/jt, Edward Anthony James, 754053
HERBERT, Fl/off, Dennis Jack (AFC), 162946
HIGGINS, Fl/Sjt, William Howard, 1293715
HILLS, Lac, Eric George, 624212
HOROBIN, Fl/Sjt, George Henry, 939826
HOUSTON, Fl/Sjt, William Frederick, 637005
HUNTER, Fl/Sjt, John Charles Herbert Layle, 1310870
JOHNSON, Fl/off, Richard Arthur Chaffen, 100543
LANCASTER, Fl/lt, Norman Douglas, 40397
LLOYD, W/o, George Henry, 1234511
MARTIN, Fl/jt, William Watson, 536352
MARTIN, Fl/off, Frank, 80560
MASLEN, Sjt, Arthur Leonard, 918580
MATSON, Fl/off, Francis Cedric Richmond, 116990
MAUGHAN, Fl/off, George Oliver (DSO), 50662
McNEIL, Sjt, Neil, 110880
MERCER, Sjt, Joseph, 987916
POOLE, Fl/Sjt, Geoffrey, 955799
RAMAGE, Fl/Sjt, Tom, 1113612
RAVEN, Ac2, Ernest Frank, 963940

RIDING, Sjt, Stanley John, 1654300
ROBERTSON, Fl/Sjt, James, 751555
ROBERTSON, Fl/Sjt, Alexander, 1567164
ROBINSON, Fl/off, John Stewart, 89331
ROGERS, Cpl, Jack, 567816
ROWE, Sjt, Norman Francis, 566992
SALTER, Ac1, Richard Frank, 1155359
SAUNDERS, Sjt, Derek Vaughan, 914592
SCARFE, Sq Ldr, Arthur Stewart King (VC), 37693
SCULLY, Sgt, Gordon, 1456856
SEWELL, Fl/Sjt, Christopher Gordon, 956121
SHANNON, Lac, Patrtick Gilbert, 618333
SHAW, Ac2, Vincent Thomas, 1019586
SMITH, Lac, Donald, 972275
SMITH, Fl/Sjt, Colin Graham, 1322739
SMITH, Cpl, George, 575109
SPRINGMAN, Fl/off, Paul Eyre, 61227
TEARNAN, Sjt, Allan Arthur, 996312
TEMPLETON, Fl/Sjt, William, 745908
UTTING, Ac2, Harold, 1208373
WALKER, Sjt, Percy Yeomans, 561258
WALTON, Ac2, Allan Noel Cliffe, 1023094
WATERS, Fl/off, William Thomas De Rouffignac C, 62342
WATSON, Ac1, Wilfred Albert, 1010759
WILCOCK, Fl/off, Charles, 46167
WILLIAMSON, Fl/Sjt, John Charles Wilson, 1566290
WILLIS, Fl/Sjt, John Lewis Francis, 527205
WINTERS, Fl/Sjt, Ernest Joseph, 658330
YARR, Sjt, Terence John, 925204

62 SQUADRON (VR)
CASEY, Sjt, Hubert William, 751915
EDWARDS, Ac2, Ronald, 1023159

63 SQUADRON
MORRIS, Ac1, Harry, 625407

64 SQUADRON (VR)
FORRESTER, Ac2, Alxander, 1064304

67 SQUADRON
BLIGHT, Fl/t, Peter Harden Goyen, 101036
CARROLL, Lac, George Henry, 614093
HARRIS, Fl/Sjt, John Hugh Raymond, 1314260
MUGGLETON, Fl/jt, Reginald Gordon, 1258443
PINCKNEY, Fl/lt, David John Colin (DFC), 52520

73 SQUADRON
CROSS, Cpl, Edward, 538515

79 SQUADRON
BARTON, Sjt, Charles Henry, 1111461
DELEMERE, Sjt, Fred Herbert, 1330961

79 SQUADRON (VR)
OUTEN, Ac1, Wiliam Thomas, 926814

81 SQUADRON
CAMPBELL, Fl/Sjt, Alexander Vernon, 1386500
WHITTAMORE, Sq Ldr, William Michael (DFC), 102107

82 SQUADRON
BECKENSALL, Fl/off, William, 145516
BLACK, Sjt, Ronald Erskine, 1588358
CARTER, Fl/lt, Edward Albert, 104344
HAYES, Fl/off, Gwilym Griffiths, 173232
PARKES, W/o, Enos George, 751760
TATCHELL, W/o, Harry, 957040

84 SQUADRON

ALLEN, Lac, William Thomas, 956303
AUSTIN, Ac2, Thomas Hollister, 1278350
BEATTY, Cpl, Maurice Alfred Albert, 626496
BELL, Sjt, Geoffrey George, 915140
BOTT, Fl/off, James Edwin Warwick, 84718
BOVINGDON, Lac, Frederick Henry, 638428
BRENTNALL, Fl/off, Alfred Sidney, 47467
BUDD, W/o, Herbert George, 1316397
BURRLUCK, Sjt, Alfred Owen, 511787
BYNG, Lac, Geoffrey Meallin, 574149
CARY, Cpl, Norris Robert, 968737
CHANDLER, Pl, Henry George Ernest, 645028
COATES, Ac1, Bernard, 1016297
COLLINGWOOD, Cpl, Richard Anthony, 537707
COLLINGWOOD, Sjt, Albert Edward, 1816943
COLVIN, Fl/off, Walter, 194362
DANIELS, Lac, George James, 638546
DARWEN, Sgt, Geoffrey George, 539874
DAVIDSON, Lac, Robert, 1001982
EDWARDS, Lac, John, 652344
EDWARDS, Ac1, Gwynfryn, 1018697
ELLIS, Fl/off, John Frederick, 136727
EVANS, Lac, Idris Morton, 637368
FAIRGRAY, Cpl, Nelson, 633556
FRETWELL, Lac, Albert, 746615
GORRINGE, Lac, Thomas E, 650570
GORST, Ac2, Fred, 1056822
HAMBRIDGE, Lac, Alan Richard Victor, 901652
HARDING, Lac, Alan Vernon, 1530954
HARRIS, Lac, Bertie, 972747
HARRIS, Wo/1, Norman, 1579508
HAYES, Cpl, Harry, 966176
HERBERT, Lac, John Ernest, 1350924
HEWITT, Cpl, Arthur Gilbert, 633090
HOLDSWORTH, Cpl, John Vernon, 636112
HOLMES, Sjt, Keith Wheatcroft, 551029
HOUGH, W/o, Howard Henry, 1252122
HOWARTH, Sjt, George Lloyd, 542946
HOYLES, Ac1, Frank, 991586
JACKSON, Ac1, James, 1088016
JOHNSON, Cpl, John, 1063849
JONES, Ac2, Harry, 1042255
JONES, Ac1, Cuthbert Edward William, 978595
KENNY, Lac, Thomas Stanley Philip, 1281600
KING, Ac1, William, 1109052
LUCK, Pl, Henry William, 520586
MAKIN, Pilot 11, David, 576921
MARTIN, Sjt, Norman, 568268
MATTHEWS, Cpl, George William, 736632
McBRIDE, Sjt, Alfred Henry, 358842
McLEAN, Cpl, Angus, 1062210
MERRICK, Lac, Edward Charles, 1164294
NIX, Ac1, Harold James, 1309569
NORTHWOOD, Lac, William Samuel, 948273
OGBURN, Lac, William Henry, 920019
OLDCORN, Ac1, Leslie, 1535364
PHILLIPS, Ac2, Albert Victor, 1151993
POPE, Ac1, Philip Frederick, 631904
PORTER, Cpl, John, 546847
PRATT, Sjt, Stanley Horace, 551169
RATCLIFFE, Ac1, Leonard, 1006943
RICHARDSON, Ac1, Alfred, 1137513
ROBERTS, Cpl, William Frederick, 636552
ROBERTSON, Ac1, Albert, 1340008
ROBSON, Ac1, John Edward, 1019835
ROSS, Sjt, Andrew, 565384
RUSSELL, Lac, Dvid Geddes, 1007171
SALMON, Lac, Edward, 1309871
SCRUBY, Ac1, Lawrence Frederick, 964338
SHAW, Ac1, Denis Joseph, 925195

SHAW, Cpl, Ronald Francis, 650188
SLEE, Fl/Sjt, William, 560903
SMALL, Lac, Stanley Richard, 1156987
SMALL, Fl/Sjt, Leonard Edward, 581356
SMITH, Cpl, Arthur Bertram John, 1261758
SMITH, Ac1, Albert Edward, 1284538
SMITH, Sjt, Andrew Wood, 537660
STREET, Cpl, William Charles Knapp, 622091
SUMNER, Cpl, David Henry, 528883
TULLY, Sjt, William Edwin, 550100
TWEEDIE, Lac, George, 995075
VINCENT, Ac1, Donald Raymond, 944211
WARNER, Ac1, Charles William, 1245672
WARWICK, Lac, Donald William, 1309880
WESTFIELD, Lac, Charles Henry, 626939
WRIGHT, Lac, Kenneth, 624725
WRIGHT, W/o, George Cranston, 511113

84 SQUADRONDN (VR)
ARDEN, Ac2, George Thomas, 1116623
BAUGH, Ac1, Henry William, 912991
DUFFIELD, Lac, Royden William, 1173695
HADRICK, Lac, Fred, 1004389
MALTESE, Fl Off, Francis Reginald Anthony, 202942
MARLAND, Lac, Frank Joseph, 1017170
MELLOR, Cpl, Donald, 1817941
MERRALLS, Cpl, Leslie, 1162106
PALMER, Wo, Geoffrey Clifford, 958283
REGAN, Ac1, John Bailey, 1058387
RICHARDSON, Lac, Lawrence William, 959271
WRIGHT, Cpl, Wiliam Leslie, 991919

89 SQUADRON
CLAPHAM, W/o, Allan Charles, 1330225
OTTER, Fl/t, Robert Colin Michael, 144337
OWEN, Fl/pff, Ernest Trevor, 195198

89 SQUADRON (VR)
KNAPP, Lt Lt, George, 150298
STEVENS, Lt Lt, Jack Trevor (DFC), 151116

96 SQUADRON
WHITE, Lac, Peter Eric Godlongton, 701305

99 SQUADRON
ADAIR, Fl/off, John Thomas (DFC), 187101
BEBE, Sjt, Robert Charles, 2211019
BOOTH, Fl/off, Stephen Dion, 160692
BRANFELD, Fl/Sjt, Arthur Herbert, 1643005
BURNS, Fl/off, James Conway (DFC), 190022
CHANDLER, Sjt, Leslie Victor, 1415783
CLEMENT, Fl/Sjt, George Wiliam, 1335299
CRAGG, Sjt, Frank Raymond, 1038422
CUFF, Fl/off, Philip John, 113934
CULBERT, Fl/off, Bernard Douglas, 159393
DACEY, Sjt, Alan, 1319215
DREW, Fl/off, Leslie Samuel (DFC), 182355
DUCKLES, Sjt, Stanley, 1594025
DUNN, Fl/Sjt, Richard John, 1323985
EGLEN, W/o, Raymond, 1594256
FARROW, Fl/Sjt, James Edward Joseph, 1387116
GRIMSHAW, Fl/Sjt, John Francis, 1590681
HAMPSHIRE, Fl/Sjt, Arnold, 1045238
HAWKINS, Fl/Sjt, Kenneth, 1529018
HIGGINS, Fl/Sjt, Kenneth, 1083308
HUGHES, Fl/Sjt, William Peter, 1593469
JOHNSON, Fl/Sjt, John, 1675263
JOYNSON, Sjt, Albert Louis, 1379347
MANN, Sjt, William Mill, 1595543
McCOLLEY, Sjt, John Edward, 1335703

McINTOSH, Fl/Sjt, Angus, 1783260
McNERNEY, Sjt, Patrick, 1798175
MOSS-VERNON, Jt, David Keith, 1670858
NASH, Fl/Sjt, Reginald Charles, 1204043
PICKUP, Fl/Sjt, Harry, 1591976
PUGH, Sjt, William James David, 1398672
RADMORE, Sjt, John Leonard, 1600558
RICHARDS, Sjt, Gordon William, 576072
ROBERTSON, Sjt, Robert, 1825400
SANGER, Fl/Sjt, Reginald Ernest Shackleton, 1601861
SCHONBERG, L Sjt, Michael, 1564344
SMITH, Fl/Sjt, Sydney Richard, 1397725
STEELE, Sjt, John, 1825981
TOPPLE, W/o, John Edward, 1874884
TUDOR, Fl/Sjt, Gerald Ernest, 1414899
WARD, W/o, William Henry Carlisle, 2205873
WEBB, Fl/off, Peter Walton, 50919
WEBB, W/o, Peter, 1523895
WHITE, Fl/lt, Hugh Cecil Lovat, 49590
WORTHINGTON, W/o, Arthur Tattersall, 1600279
WRIGHT, Fl/Sjt, George Donaldson, 1569523

99 SQUADRON (VR)
SIMMONS, Sjt, Frederick Victor, 974060

100 SQUADRON
BENNETT, Flt Sjt, George, 245454
BIRDSALL, W/o, Stephen Dale, 551090
BORRAS, W/o, Cyril John Samuel, 561982
BURRY, Flt Sjt, Frederick Charles, 362810
CHARLESWORTH, Fl/Sjt, Jack, 519352
COOK, W/o, Edward Cecil, 1600777
DAVIES, Sgt, Walter, 541173
DUNN, Flt Lt, James Henderson Whitefield, 39970
FAWCETT, Cpl, Albert, 618589
FILES, Ac1, Frank, 1360261
FORBES, Fl/off, Gilbert Strachan, 44049
GIBSON, Sjt, John Forster, 759001
GRANT, Sjt, John, 744970
GURNEY, Ac1, Selwyn George, 978686
LAMB, Fl/off, Reginald Robert, 44974
LAWLEY, Sjt, Henry Thomas Herbert, 813086
MORGAN, W/o, David Landeg, 530137
MORRISON, Fl/off, John Edwin, 45944
PETTS, Lac, Ritson Finlay, 524461
PICKLES, Lac, Stanley, 542200
RYDER, Fl/off, Dennis Eric, 40023
SINGLETON, Cpl, Eric Norman, 571871
SLADDEN, Ac1, William, 1256699
SONE, Lac, William, 612169
TILLOTT, Sq Ldr, John Dorrell, 39400
TOZER, Lac, Leslie Raymond, 591817
WAKE, Cpl, Sidney Charles, 572130
WIGGLESWORTH, Sjt, Leslie John, 437848
WILTHEW, Lac, John, 1054364

100 SQUADRON (VR)
ALMEROTH, Ac1, Albert Arthur Sturry, 917329
COPE, Ac1, Kenneth Frank, 1264600
CROMPTON, Ac2, Samuel, 1064265
FRYER, Ac1, Leonard Edward, 1204573
MILLS LT, Sjt, Henry Arthur Herbert, 755295
POWELL, Sjt, Robert, 755314
SMEATON, Ac1, George, 1020752
WHELPTON, Flt Sjt, Clifford James, 759310
WOODWORTH, Sjt, Desmond Henry, 741304

110 SQUADRON
ALLEN, Fl/Sjt, Wilfred Louis, 1397716
BLOWER, Fl/ff, Stephen Hugh, 197845

BULLMAN, L/Sjt, John Edward, 553594
CHARMAN, Sjt, Peter James, 1381658
DARLOW, Fl/t, Arthur Eric, 174017
FINLEY, Fl/lt, Patrick Bernard, 121286
HAWKINS, Fl/lt, St John, 143892
HEMINGWAY, Fl/Sjt, Anthony Sidney, 771997
HURST, Fl/off, Lawrence Goddard, 148030
LAWTON, Sjt, Thomas Hume, 1305442
McMASTER, Sjt, Walter, 304970
SAUNDERS, Wng Cmdr, Arthur Ernest (OBE), 37052
TAYLOR, Fl/lt, Thomas Leonard, 159577
TURNER, W/o, Philip Edward, 1483339

113 SQUADRON
AITKEN, W/o, John Seaton, 580933
ANDERSON, Sjt, George Edmund, 624878
BALL, W/o, Henry John, 1382843
BANKS, Fl/Sjt, Frederick Cecil, 1286602
DENNETT, Fl/Sjt, David Greig, 1048316
DENT, Ac2, Laurence, 1134235
DRAKE, Sjt, William, 946468
HARPER, Sq Ldr, Clifton Watt (DFC), 42221
HERBERT, Fl/off, Aubrey Lloyd, 149096
HINDS, W/o, William Victor, 745452
LANCASTER, L/Sjt, Alan Norman, 1147535
LOWCOCK, Fl/Sjt, David Dean, 920706
WOOD, Cpl, Wilfred Owen, 549948

113 SQUADRON (VR)
BRIGGS,Sgt W/o,Douglas Eric,759056

117 SQUADRON
BALL, Fl/Sjt, Richard Beart, 1320457
BATCHELOR, Fl/off, Dennis D'arcy, 148538
BATEMAN, Fl/Sjt, Derek, 1439024
BLIGHT, Fl/jt, Frederick Richard, 1586711
BRIDGE, Fl/lt, Bernard, 133818
BUCKMAN, Fl/Sjt, Derek William Ellerton, 1803124
BYRNE, Floff, John Clifford, 137167
CLARK, Sjt, Albert, 1021191
CUTHBERT, Fl/lt, James Forbes (DFC), 120967
DAVIES, Sjt, Alec Youlton, 1268125
EASON, W/o, Granville Mundon, 798713
ELLIS, Fl/jt, Bruce, 567365
GOAD, Fl/Sjt, Kenneth Harold, 1802394
HUMPHREYS, Fl/off, Thomas Watkin (DFC), 171357
HUYGENS, Fl/off, Stanley Ernest, 171358
KENT, Fl/off, Anthony Charles, 179998
LORIMER, Fl/off, John Dundee, 176873
LUSTED, Fl/off, Albert Jack, 17130
McIVOR, W/o, Harry, 967573
McLOUGHLIN, Fl/Sjt, Eric, 1080599
O'RIELLY, Fl/t, Brian Gerrard Levins (DFC), 47367
PARKER, W/o, Edward James, 1165708
ROSS, Fl/off, John Mcpherson, 164723
ROWSON, Sq Ldr, Richard Neville, 79145
SAMSON, Wng Cmdr, Arthur James (DFC), 78850
SELLEY, Sgr, Edward Charles Mitchell, 1607826
SHALLOW, Fl/Sjt, Augustus Arthur, 798798
SHARLEY, Sjt, Cyril George, 1167816
SISSONS, Fl/off, Edwin Maurice, 179971
SQUADRONUIRES, Fl/off, Roland Henry Traviss, 163768
STANSFIELD, L/off, Bernard Barker, 178369
TRAIL, Fl/jt, Eric William, 1566944
WARRINGTON, Fl/off, Edward Gordon, 183794
YOUNG, Fl/off, Hugh Crawford, 186542

123 SQUADRON
DAVIES,Fl/lt,Arthur William Bowen,80289
STEWART,Fl/off,Andrew,130642

135 SQUADRON
BALDWIN, Cpl, Peter Charles, 574459
EDGE, Sjt, Roy William, 1312872
GIDDINGS, Sq/ldr, Herbert Selwyn, 37283
GOLDNEY, Fl/Sjt, John, 567030
MARRACK, Fl/lt, Richard Fitzgerald, 139943
PRINCE, Fl/off, Raymond Aubrey, 69478
ROBERTSON, Fl/Sjt, Donald Peter, 1262780
WHISKIN, W/o, Dennis Richard, 1314711

136 SQUADRON
BROWN, Fl/lt, Eric (DFC), 102143
DODDS, Fl/Sjt, John Bonnell, 1432353
GILLIES, Fl/lt, James (DFC DFM), 47317
HACKFORTH, Fl/off, Samuel Nicholas, 119105
HENDERSON, Sjt, Ronald Balfour, 1346430
HIGGINS, Fl/Sjt, William, 1183689
KEARON, Fl/off, Arthur Brodie, 54854
PICKARD, Fl/off, Frederick John, 130323

139 SQUADRON
FREHNER,Sjt,John Robert,1261851

144 SQUADRON
MUMBY,Fl/lt,Thomas Leonard (DFM) ,49752,

146 SQUADRON
HIGDON,Sjt,Peter William,1605075
ORTON,Fl/Sjt,Kenneth Thomas,1322067
VERITY,Sjt,Frank Clive,957723

152 SQUADRON
BERRY, Fl/Sjt, Richard Charles James, 1390084
BURNETT, Sjt, Cecil Royston Forster, 626748
COLE, Fl/Sjt, Charles Thomas, 1316347
FOSTER, L/Sjt, William Patrick, 907568
SHORT, Lc, Kenneth George, 1168328
WILLIAMS, Lac, Laude Reginald, 910168

155 SQUADRON
ALLEN, Fl/off, Derek Arthur, 114662
BUGGE, Fl/Sjt, Ronald, 1294983
CALLICOTT, W/o, Kenneth Stanley, 1315731
GENTRY, W/o, Charles Walter, 1386480
HEELEY, W/o, Peter Joseph, 1239294
McCLUMPHA, Fl/off, Roy Colvin James, 109781
RATHIE, Fl/lt, Peter (DFC), 88467

159 SQUADRON
ADAMS, Fl/Sjt, James, 1403958
ALEXANDER, Sjt, Stanley, 1895231
AMBLER, Fl/Sjt, Eric Edwin, 1058886
AYRES, Sjt, Arthur Cecil, 1398784
BAILEY, Fl/Sjt, Dennis Harold, 1394253
BEACH, Fl/Sjt, John Albert, 926857
BROCKMAN, Sjt, Percy John Friend, 1397213
BURGESS, Sjt, Desmond Riversdale Anthony, 1659085
BURN, Fl/Sjt, Arthur Robert, 1319428
CHALCT, Jt, Stanley William, 1807507
CHRISTMAS, Sjt, Frederick Merville, 1164379
CLIFTON, Floff, Bernard (DFM), 50589
COLES, Fl/Sjt, Leslie James, 1493989
DENNERLY, Fl/Sjt, Norman, 1623291
DOAK, Fl/Sjt, David Phillip, 947752
EVANS, Sjt, Arthur Vincent, 1389705
FLETCHER, Sjt, John Mcgibbon, 1306199
GARDEN, Fl/off, Quentin, 88614
GURR, Fl/jt, Douglas Charles, 1393437
GWYNN, Fl/Sjt, Thomas James, 1281616
HALL, Sjt, Leonard, 1532286

HALL, Sjt, John, 1493867
HETHERINGTON, Fl/Sjt, James Carruthers, 2210508
HILTON, Fl/jt, Donald Denis, 1233506
HOGAN, Sjt, Patrick, 1522977
HOLFORD, W/o, Charles John, 1268205
HOLT, Fl/Sjt, John Horace, 1171383
HUGHES, Fl/jt, Edward Francis, 2210463
HUMPHRIES, Fl/lt, Geoffrey Robert, 82962
JONES, Sjt, Thomas John, 1581255
KELLY, Fl/Sjt, Donald Anthony, 3030010
KENWRICK-COX, Fl/off, Charles Desmond, 102113
KERNOHAN, Sjt, George, 1796515
KING, Sjt, John, 1804662
LEAK, Sjt, John Henry Starmer, 1682798
LEWIS, L/Sjt, Ronald John, 1582372
LOCKWOOD, Fl/off, Clifford Ernest, 184464
LOWERY, Fl/off, Williamn James John, 157576
MAUDE, Fl/Sjt, Allan Haigh, 1590962
McCREERY, Fl/Sjt, Hubert Brindle, 551364
McKINNON, W/o, John, 1550526
PANNELL, L/Sjt, Stephen Frederick, 627985
PATERSON, Fl/jt, William Noble, 1345502
PLANK, Sjt, George Alfred Charles, 1435434
PRICE, Fl/Sjt, Arthur Ronald, 564169
PRITCHARD, Sjt, Kenneth Gordon, 1424322
RAINE, Flsj, Thomas Vernon, 1000570
RICH, Fl/Sjt, Cyril Guy, 935019
ROBINSON, Fl/off, Clifford, 151549
SKINNER, Wng Cmdr, Clifford George, 29148
STANLEY, Fl/lt, Edward James Douglas, 114064
STEVENSON, Fl/off, James Crighton Dfc, 64282
STEWART, W/o, Arthur James Lander, 1394873
STOUT, Sjt, Ansel Ernest Bklackburn, 771563
TASSELL, Fl/Sjt, William Charles, 1378543
TAYLOR, Fl/Sjt, Victor Gordon, 1684358
THOPSON, Fl/lt, George Norman, 109491
TOWERS, Sjt, Kenneth, 1494991
UNDERHILL, Fl/off, John William, 153104
WARDHILL, Fl/Sjt, Leslie Ernest, 1305419
WATSON, Fl/jt, Ronald, 1210078
WHITEHALL, W/o, Victor Ernest, 1262742
WHITELEY, Fl/jt , Michael John, 1803437

160 SQUADRON
BALL, Sjt, Leslie, 1262451
BLOSS, Sjt, Fred, 1016941
CALDER, Fl/off, Walter Allen, 120600
CAMERON, Sjt, Andrew, 1566579
CAMPBELL, Fl/off, John Waran, 120498
CRUST, Sjt, Hillyar Raymond, 1253122
DEENY, Fl/Sjt, Henry, 1066646
DUNKLEY, Sjt, Jack, 1580251
HARRISON, Sjt, Ronald William, 943631
HAYNES, Lac, Tom, 1750158
LECKEY, Fl/Sjt, Thomas, 1023458
MACDONALD, L/off, Duncan Farquhar, 134739
MACGREGOR, Sjt, Cyril Raymond, 1271486
McDONALD, Sjt, George, 798529
MORGAN, Sjt, Roland, 1187248
NAYLOR, Sjt, Francis Edwin, 572011
OWEN, Sjt, Arthur James Newnham, 1377681
PALLET, Fl/off, Taverner Richard, 120793
SOMERVILLE, Fl/Sjt, Frank, 1381952
WILLCOCK, Fl/Sjt, Harold Ivan, 1255724
WILLSON, Fl/off, Harry Patrick, 120801
WISEMAN, Fl/Sjt, William Robert, 1432804

173 SQUADRON
HARPER,Lac,William Joseph,535820

176 SQUADRON
HALBEARD, Fl/lt, Geoffrey Reeve, 102540
HUGHES, Fl/Sjt, Charles Ronald, 1029801
LAWRIE, Fl/Sjt, James Morrison, 1550898
TAYLOR, Fl/Sjt, Harold Stanley, 658245

177 SQUADRON
BLOOM, Fl/Sjt, Francis Gerald Durrant, 1333762
BUCKLEY, Fl/off, George Herbert Eversley, 130837
CALLINGHAM-WOODS, Fl/Sjt, Philip, 1096861
CLOUGH, Sjt, John Arnold, 1239662
DINHAM, Fl/Sjt, Gerald Albert, 1337887
EDE, Fl/off, Alexander James, 152523
FORBES, W/o, John Cuthbert, 1383979
HALL, Sjt, Thomas Albert, 1575982
HART, W/o, Henry William Gwyn, 1319247
HAWKINS, W/o, Ronald Arthur, 1333580
HIGHFIELD, Fl/Sjt, Hawtrey Ian Geoffrey, 1379685
HOLLAY, W/o, Dennis Arthur Stephen, 1320620
HOUSTON, Fl/off, Donald James, 129366
HUDSON, W/o, Walter Jack, 1388715
HUMPHREYS, Fl/Sjt, William Unitt, 1208786
JACKSON, Fl/off, William Thomas, 154544
JAMES, Fl/off, Ronald Gwyn, 191284
LINDSELL, Fl/off, Edward Stratton, 129342
McKAY, Fl/off, John Angus, 151282
MILLIS, Fl/off, John Edward, 53252
MORGAN, Fl/Sjt, Cyril Stanley, 1210551
PLATT, Fl/off, Arthur Joshua, 137629
REYNOLDS, W/o, Leslie Frederick, 1388270
SEARY, Fl/off, Lelsie Arthur, 127461
SMITH, Fl/Sjt, Joseph Kenneth, 1578244
STUART-COX, Fl/off, Alfred Edward, 182116
WELSH, Fl/Sjt, Robert Henry, 1548731

194 SQUADRON
CROSS, W/o, Ernest, 1040039
GREENWAY, Fl/off, Ernest John, 201468
INGLES, Fl/lt, William Frederick, 102968
KEMP, Sjt, Royden Maxwell, 3033533
MANTLE, Fl/jt, John Haydn, 1254045
PILE, W/o, Ronald George, 926789
ROBERTS, Sjt, Robert, 1684904
SCOTT, Fl/lt, James Ronald, 124545
SHEPHERD, W/o, Stephen James, 1166190
WOOD, Fl/lt, Peter William Henry Frederick, 121419
WRIGHT, Fl/Sjt, Edwin William, 1602119

203 SQUADRON
BALL, Fl/off, Edmund Russell, 164683
BERNARD, Fl/Sjt, William, 1825309
CHURCHILL, Sjt, John Frank Dawes, 1867412
COLLINS, Sjt, Wilfred Arthur, 1312970
GRAINER, Sjt, Raymond Knight, 1250280
GRANT, Fl/off, Louis Mary Joseph, 153776
HERD, Sjt, Angus Forrest, 1829311
LANG, Sjt, Alexander Murdoch, 404759
LAW, F/off, John Alexander (DFC), 185341
LEFTWITCH, L/Sjt, Ernest Edward, 1337779
LENNOX, Fl/gr, Gordon Leonard, 1801628
OAKDEN, Sjt, Dennis Clifford, 1895383
OLDEN, Fl/Sjt, Dudley Ernest, 1585962
PETERS, Fl/Sjt, Eric, 1894482
PICKERING, W/o, Kenneth Charles, 1265423
PROSSER, Fl/off, John Vernon, 164532
SILKSTONE, Fl/Sjt, John Douglas, 1318346
STEWART, Fl/Sjt, Wilfred, 168513
STEWART, Fl/off, Gordon Alfred, 184025
TAYLOR, Lac, William Rdevers, 1507318
WATKINS, W/o, Griffith Trevor, 1316918

WENNING, Fl/off, George Anthony, 150857
WEST, Sjt, Paul, 1104572
WILLIS, W/o, John Victor, 1231312

205 SQUADRON
ABRAM, Sjt, Stanley, 909403
ALLEN, Fl/Sjt, Ernest Arthur, 751374
ALTHAM, W/o, Edwin John Thurston, 508800
ARCH, Sjt, Joseph Henry, 751857
ATTWOOD, Ac1, Alfred Charles, 977888
BAILEY, Sjt, Edward Alexander, 567431
BEDELL, Fl/off, Patrick Edwin, 81334
BEEDLES, Sjt, John Edward, 578145
BISHOP, Fl/Sjt, Gifford John, 566869
BOAM, Sjt, Albert Montague, 1355813
BOWDEN, Fl/Sjt, John Alonzo, 362816
BRETT, Sjt, Philip James, 565691
BURNETT, Ac1, William Thomas David, 1004210
BYE, Sjt, Henry John, 958431
CANNON, Sjt, William, 1017511
CHAPMAN, Lac, Arthur Henry, 967971
CLAYTON, Sjt, Neil Douglas, 755558
COKER, Sjt, Ernest Edward, 1390840
CURTIS, Fl/off, Maurice George, 126701
DANIELLS, Sjt, Lexander Thomas Edward, 566129
DAVIES, Fl/Sjt, Charles, 1081692
DODD, Sjt, William Cecil Friscourt, 525263
DOYLE, Fl/Sjt, Peter Francis, 1497150
DRAPER, Sjt, Roger Maxwell Temple, 621213
DUNN, Sjt, William, 1370893
EATON, Sjt, Peter, 755182
ECKETT, L/Sjt, Thomas William, 1895942
ELLERBY, Fl/Sjt, Henry, 541218
FAIRHURT, Fl/Sjt, Fred, 972020
FARRAR, Sg/ldr, Maxwell Francis Campbell (DFC), 37498
FURNESS, Fl/Sjt, Thomas Raymond, 1066742
GARNELL, Fl/lt, Hugh, 70897
GOGGIN, Sjt, Terence John, 911581
GRAHAM, Fl/lt, James Ramsay, 44127
GRANT, Fl/Sjt, Percy Allen Eric, 1313736
GRIER, W/o, William, 976155
GRIEVE, Fl/off, Andrew Terras, 76483
GRIFFIN, Sjt, Frederick, 529437
HALL, Fl/Sjt, Cedric Herbert, 902161
HOGG, Fl/Sjt, Derrick Norman, 1600551
JACOBS, L/Sjt, Albert Sydney, 1383819
JEFFERIES, Fl/Sjt, Alec Samuel, 1384658
JEFFRIES, Fl/off, Harold Alfred Stephen, 138912
JOHNSON, Sjt, Reginald Lakin, 1084403
LAMBERT, Sjt, William Duncan, 544437
LEACH, Fl/lt, Harold David Tamsett, 40926
LEAK, Fl/Sjt, William, 532008
LEWIS, Lac, Idris, 616394
LEWIS, Sjt, Harold Victor, 406146
LINN, Fl/Sjt, Sydney Charles, 1483304
LITTLEWOOD, W/o, Edwin Leslie, 935211
LOWE, Fl/lt, John Conyers, 33498
MADDOCK, Sjt, Keneth Alfred, 1076647
MARKLAND, Sjt, William Gibbons, 1055984
McKIERNAN, Sjt, Christopher, 965540
NEWHAM, L/Sjt, Eric George, 755444
O'KEEFE, Lac, Arthur James Henry, 913831
REGAN, Fl/Sjt, Frank Richard, 812251
RUST, Fl/off, Richard, 131115
SHAW, Fl/off, Douglas, 44050
SHERRIFF, Lac, Frederick Charles, 752181
SKINNER, Ac2, James Alfred, 913878
STAMMERS, Fl/Sjt, Arthur George, 529174
STANTON, Sjt, Arthur Frederick Raymond, 1150670
STEPHENS, Cpl, John Clifford, 569396

STEWART, Fl/Sjt, Francis William, 1551684
TEASDALE, Lac, Frederick, 619844
TODD, Sjt, Sidney William, 568813
WALKER, Sjt, Robert Douglas, 568505
WALKER, Fl/lt, Donald Ernest, 60574
WALMSLEY, Fl/off, Herbert Lofthouse, 139492
WEBB, W/o, William Edward, 590711
WESTBY, W/o, William Henry (DFM), 524787
WHEELER, Sjt, Leslie Cornelius, 921515
WHITEHOUSE, D Sjt, Raymond William, 1153661
WHITTICASE, Sjt, John Leonard, 937670
WIDOWSON, Lac, Geoffrey Allan, 991319

206 SQUADRON
LAWLESS,W/o,Cormac,535548

209 SQUADRON
TINKLER,Flt Lt,John Walter,47318
WHEELER,Cpl,Edward John William,647430

209 SQUADRON (VR)
EVANS, Fl Off, David John, 181341
HATTON, W/o, Albert Donald,
LA NAUZE, Flt Sjt, Peter Claude, 1891328
McKAIG, Flt Sjt, Robert Alexander, 1568821
PEACOCK, Lt Sjt, Wilfred, 1033463

211 SQUADRON
ANDERTON, Ac1, William Bramwell, 1120401
ANDERTON, Ac2, James, 1085594
BAKER, Ac2, Stanley James, 927430
BARBER, Cpl, Dennis William, 946718
BEVERIDGE, Ac2, James, 1361272
BEWSHER, Fl/Sjt, Robert, 1042107
BICKLEY, Ac1, Geoffrey Arthur, 1003848
BLAXALL, W/o, Albert Walter, 1318859
BLAZLEY, Ac1, Thomas William, 1330503
BLYTH, Ac1, Johnstone William, 1366139
BOON, W/o, Ernest Moreton, 1233069
BOULTON, Cpl, Fred, 632480
BOUTCHER, Sjt, Donald Gerald, 565512
BURTON, Ac2, George Harold, 814176
CARTER, Ac2, Evan William, 1315262
CHAMBERS, Sjt, Roy Arthur, 1463571
CLARK, Cpl, Alfred Charles, 923452
CLUTTERBUCK, Fl/lt, Julian Dennes William Hugh, 42300
COLE, Lac, Percy William, 940191
COLES, Fl/lt, Rodney Maxwell, 41553
COOK, Fl/Sjt, Stanley Charles, 1396062
COSHAM, Ac2, Kenneth Frank, 1293357
CROSTON, Lac, Thomas, 530013
DALBY, Ac1, James Edward, 917767
DAVEY, Ac1, Raymond Thomas, 920886
DAVIES, Ac2, Thomas Benjamin, 1232082
DAVIES, Fl/Sjt, Geoffrey Preston, 1213620
DAVIS, Ac1, Christpoher, 1317077
DAWSON, Fl/lt, Donald James, 88828
DONALDSON, Fl/Sjt, William John, 778767
DONALDSON, Lac, John, 954800
DUNNETT, Fl Off, Stephen Falconer, 179774
ENGLAND, W/o, Arthur Eric, 1270380
FAIRLESS, Lac, Thomas, 1236651
FELTHAM, Ac1, Montague Roy, 1211363
GATES, Ac1, Alfred Izzard, 1099099
GIBBONS, Cpl, Derek Arthur Laslie, 624374
GIBSON, Cpl, Walter, 552272
GIBSON, Cpl, Walter, 552272,
GILMORE, Fl/Sjt, Ivan Alexander William, 1072498
GOLLOP, Ac1, Walter David, 1317118
GORE, Fl/Sjt, James Arthur, 563780

GROOMBRIDGE, Lac, James Gilbert, 913137
HAMBLIN, Lac, Reginald Charles, 1170132
HAWKINS, Ac1, William Reginald, 1211134
HAYES, Ac1, Patrick Henry, 1336730
HOLLERAN, Lac, John, 946913
HOLMAN, Lac, Robert Fenton, 908080
HOWCROFT, Sjt, Fred Batty, 549616
HUMPHRIES, Ac1, William George, 1059747
JACOBS, Ac2, Alec, 1237236
JEFFERIES, Ac2, John Paul, 1055869
JONES, Ac1, Oswald, 1019069
KAY, Ac1, Raymond, 1073264
LEA, Ac2, Henry Rickerdy, 113641
LEE, Ac1, William Alexander, 622386
LINTON, Fl/lt, Kenneth, 41037
LOCK, Fl/Sjt, Silas, 1548317
LOVELL, Fl/Sjt, Cyril Walter, 1580895
MARSH, Cpl, Ernest Aubrey, 641845
MASON, Ac1, George, 645752
MAWDSLEY, Cpl, Joseph Anderson, 633465
MAYLAM, Ac1, Harry Edward, 1257180
MILLAR, Lac, Peter Richard, 539095
MINISHUL, L/Cpl, Alan, 621508
MORLEY, Ac2, Allan Ivan, 1202564
MORRIS, Ac1, Leslie Herbert, 1152386
MORRIS, Ac1, John Aloysius, 977552
MOSS, Fl/Sjt, Claude John, 1288253
MULLANEY, Lac, James, 1105761
NEWMAN, Ac1, Francis Kenneth, 1294019
NEWMAN, Fl/lt, Eric Walter, 128462
NEWSTEAD, Fl/Sjt, Herbert Grant, 747854
PAINTER, Fl/off, Raymond Sydney, 152568
PARKER, Ac2, Roger Conway, 1198371
PULLEY, Lac, Henry Jack, 621841
QUAINTANCE, Fl/Sjt, Daniel Roy, 1418377
RATCLIFFE, Ac2, William Walmsley, 1058262
READ, Ac1, Leslie Walter, 1296836
ROBERTS, Cpl, Arthur, 968386
ROBSON, Ac1, James Boland, 1106425
SAWARD, Lac, James Edwards, 1185335
SEAL, Ac1, Cyril Arthur, 1120396
SHELDON-BISHOP, Fl/off, Gabriel, 112244
SIMS, Ac2, Eric, 1195232
SINCLAIR, Ac1, Robert, 1171745
SKEDGE, Ac2, Maurice Henry, 931023
SMITH, Ac1, Douglas Leonard, 1152228
SOUTHALL, Ac1, Henry Charles, 1169108
STEVENS, Ac2, Ronald Victor John, 1336749
TAYLOR, Lac, Arnold Lindsey, 940964
TOUT, Lac, Robert Ernest George, 647676
WELLER, Lac, Arthur Leonard, 940195
WHITE, Ac1, Thomas Dillon, 1287897
WHITTAKER, Cpl, Robert Arthur, 626386
WOODALL, Fl/off, Jack, 136062
WOOLLEY, Fl/Sjt, Philip Noel, 1198789

211 SQUADRON (VR)
CONWAY, Lac, Patrick Richard Barrington, 1282160

215 SQUADRON
ADAMS, Sjt, William David, 3050579
BADKIN, Fl/Sjt, Thomas Henry, 1285033
BAILEY, Fl/off, William James, 127788
BEAR, Fl/lt, Lawrence Howe, 116409
BROWN, Fl/sgt, Robert Wishart, 1345713
CLEGG, Sjt, Ronald Frank, 926648
CONVENTON, Fl/off, Alan Walter, 200774
CROSS, Fl/Sjt, Robert, 1153491
DAWSON, Fl/Sjt, Harry, 1541705
EDWARDS, W/o, John Arthur, 1387114

FULLER, Sjt, Bert Lawrence George, 1377586
HILL, Sjt, George, 946109
HINGOTT, Sjt, Donald Francis, 1203701
HOLMES, Fl/off, Arthur, 174367
JONES, Fl/Sjt, Dennis Robert, 1801507
KERRY, Sjt, Ronald Vivian, 927-53
MULLIGAN, Sjt, Kevin Barry, 1574487
NESBITT, Fl/off, James Hepworth, 164352
NEWTON, Fl/Sjt, John Henry, 1384199
NICE, Fl/Sjt, Harold Raymond, 939368
PARRIS, Sjt, Redvers Cyril Malcolm, 912784
PITCHERS, Fl/off, David Alexander, 123453
READ, W/o, Alfred Thomas, 1333702
RIDDLE, Fl/Sjt, Denys Walter, 1382695
ROBSON, Sjt, Thomas, 946307
RONUIRE, Fl/Sjt, Ernest, 1316095
SMITHSON, Sjt, Harold Thomas, 1050942
SYKES, Fl/off, Peter Roy Crompton, 130128
WATLING, Sjt, Norman Claude, 953426
WELCH, Sjt, Arthur Norman, 1873607
WILMOR, Fl/Sjt, James Watson, 1071529
YARNELL, Fl/off, Stanley Gordon James, 109034

216 SQUADRON
JONES, W/o, Arthur, 1025984
MITCHELL, Fl/Sjt, William Frank, 657900
ROBINSON, W/o, Kenneth Edwin, 1260270

217 SQUADRON
LUND, Fl/off, Richard, 125152
PLOWS, Sjt, Frank, 1307375
WALLIS, Fl/off, Stanley George, 120342
WALMSLEY, Sjt, Philip, 1188194

224 SQUADRON
DOUGLAS, Ac, Wilfred Stanislaus, 1325396

230 SQUADRON
BENNETT, Fl/lt, John Wallace, 127271
BONNER, Fl/Sjt, Alfred James, 1312925
COX, W/o, Thomas George Henry, 1385145
CRAWFORD, W/o, David Nicholson, 1553185
DAVIES, W/o, David Maxwell, 1578994
GILBERT, Fl/lt, Alfred Basil, 120787
GREEN, Fl/Sjt, Charles Alfred, 1804043
HAWTHORNE, Fl/Sjt, Francis, 1767656
JUFFS, W/o, Reginald Frederick, 1431231
LEVY-HAARSCHER, Fl/lt, Richard Simon, 127181
UNDERWOOD, Sjt, Dennis Walter, 1691951
WALLIKER, Fl/off, Reginald Frederick, 56210
WILLIAMS, Fl/Sjt, Dgar Reginald John, 1312874

232 SQUADRON
BLACKLEDGE, Fl/lt, Raymond George, 84844
BROOKES, Lac, Alec, 634480
CHRISTIANSON, Fl/Sjt, Charles David Gordon, 970186
DANIEL, Fl/off, Rian Philip, 102144
DAY, Ac2, Wilfred Arthur, 1114611
DEARLOVE, Fl/off, Walter Albert John, 195889
DEERY, Fl/Sjt, Robert James, 1522872
DUFF, Ac2, Joseph, 1366743
EMMERSON, Fl/off, Leslie Archibald, 102077
FARTHING, Fl/lt, Hugh Arthur, 40900
GILROY, Ac2, William, 1005787
GOLDSWORTHY, Fl/lt, Stuart Edward, 151101
HILDER, W/o, Leonard William Edward, 1270683
JARVIS, Fl/Sjt, Dennis Jack, 915910
KILPATRICK, Ac1, Hugh, 1113156
LANDELS, Sq Ldr, Leslie Inian, 84695
LLEWELLIN, Sq Ldr, Arthur John Alexander, 39998

LOWE, Sjt, Peter Dania, 1107461
MARCHANT, Sjt, Frederick Henry Harold, 1320334
MARCHBANKS, Fl/off, Alphonso Calvin, 100523
RATCLIFFE, Sjt, Leslie, 564972
SWEETMAN, Fl/off, Ronald George, 187483

233 SQUADRON
MOULDER,Fl/lt,Jack George,119807
SACH,Fl/off,Cyril James,165390

234 SQUADRON
BALDWIN,Sjt,Mervyn John Fitzhardinge,771896

240 SQUADRON
BENN, Flt Sjt, Edward, 1080445
CHAMBERLAIN, Fl/Sjt, Jack, 904415
DENMARK, Fl/Sjt, Edward William George, 1294159
FREEMAN, W/o, Eric John, 1320699
HAWORTH, Cpl, Fred, 1199771
JAMIE, W/o, Arthur, 1555612
McAREE, Fl/Sjt, John Desmond, 1344910
MOORE, Fl/off, Douglas Cowan, 141350
MOXHAM, Sjt, John Denzil Marcus, 938960
PARAMORE, Fl/Sjt, David James John, 1581676
SIMS, Flt Sjt, Geoffrey, 982448
SPEARING, Fl/Sjt, Eric George, 1585079
UNDERWOOD, Lac, Ernest Robson, 1379081

242 SQUADRON
ABBOTT, Cpl, Walter James, 1308868
AINDOW, Cpl, Gilbert Henry, 631215
BADCOCK, Lac, Ingerson Keith Fey, 926840
COUSINS, Ac2, Arthur William Charles, 1531976
DOE, Ac2, James Henry, 1296952
FALCOLNER, Ac1, Leslie Charles Gilling, 1002213
GILES, Ac2, William Henry, 1085148
GUY, Ac1, Clifford William, 1165265
HARRIS, Ac1, Leonard Stanley, 1289843
HATTON, Lac., James, 855017
HEWITT, Ac1, James William, 633562
HIGGINS, Ac1, Thomas Henry, 1279933
HIGHTON, Ac1, James, 1111403
HUGHES, Ac2, Alec John, 1218482
HYNES, W/o, Cyril Austin, 563799
INESON, Ac2, Edward Cyril, 1141305
ISDALE, Sgt (pilot), Donald John Blake, 1375259
JAMES, Ac2, Roland William, 1012167
LANCHBURY, Jt, Graham Douglas, 551039
MASON, Lac, William Dennis, 1234797
MORRIS, Ac1, Ernest William, 1292710
PERRY, Lac, Charles Frederick, 620015
REID, Lac, Leo David Roy, 925905
RILEY, Ac1, Alec, 1129434
SAUNDERS, Lac, Alan Alfred, 926131
SHICKLE, Ac1, Alfred William, 1124579
SLATER, Ac1, George Henry Reid, 1282087
STANNARD, Sjt, Robert Patrick, 522249
THWAITES, Ac2, John Edgar Edward, 1239436
TUCKER, Cpl, Arthur Leonard Frederick Samuel, 619807
WALSHMAN, Sjt, James Ernest, 552008
WEBSTER, Cpl, William, 358244
WIGLEY, Ac2, George Virgo, 1235505
WIGLEY, Lac, Charles Arthur Henry, 1173220
WING, Ac2, Francis Jesse, 1316108

242 SQUADRON (VR)
BRANDON, Lac, Charles James, 936802
EVANS, Ac1, John Cecil, 1139486
FAULKNER, Ac1, Francis Robert, 1408176
FRY, Lac, Charles Ernest, 1008584

HOARE,L A C,Cyril,1202993
KINSEY, Lac, Thomas Bowen, 1012164
LE FEVRE, Lac, Wilfred, 964949
SLATER, Cpl, John Francis, 936838
STEELE, Lac, Eric Alfred, 747931
SYRETT, Ac1, Victor Edward, 1288621
TAYLOR, Ac2, Frederick Edmund, 1213253
TENNANT, Ac2, William Murrey, 1551641
WILLIAMS, Ac1, Edward, 1195042

243 SQUADRON
CHALMERS, Cpl, William, 537913
CHAMPIN, Ac2, Spencer Charles, 1284112
CHECKETTS, Lac, Cecil Walter, 952844
DAVIS, Ac2, Thomas Edward, 1375889
DIMON, Ac1, Donald William, 1285998
DUNCAN, Ac1, Keith Presgrave, 927951
EVANS, Ac1, James Stanley, 1262829
GREIG, Lac, William Mcqueen, 947547
KINNAIR, Ac1, John, 998121
LUCAS, Ac2, Victor William, 1128260
SAUNDERS, Cpl, Charlie, 980128
SPARKES, Cpl, Athur Henry Francis, 957096
STEPHENS, Ac1, Reginald Gwynne, 1067937
VAUX, Lac, Robert Norman, 970332
WILLS, Lac, Frank Denzil, 915548
YARDLEY, Lac, Herbert Lawrence, 1180663

243 SQUADRON (VR)
BAILEY,Ac1,Frederick Douglas,1168446
WILLS,Flt Lt,Alec Percy Stanley,32134

246 SQUADRON
TUCKER,Lac,Walter Frank Frederick,1151261

249 SQUADRON
BOTTING,Cpl,John James Arthur,930078

250 SQUADRON
SADLER,Ac2,Joseph,1226745

251 SQUADRON
BRASH,Fl/Sjt,William Hendry Stewart,1123529

258 SQUADRON
ADAMS, Ac1, James, 1066083
ADAMSON, Fl/Sjt, Philip John, 1334388
BRIGHT, Ac1, Willam John, 1379575
BROWN, Lac, Lawrence, 981315
BROWN, Fl/lt, Arthur, 102062
CAMPLING, Lac, Frederick Stratford, 927033
DAWSON-SCOTT, Fl/off, Keith Desmond, 102149
EAMES, W/o, Noel Charles, 1385263
GLYNN, Sjt, Kenneth Arthur, 1174909
HARVEY, Cpl, Leonard John, 1356673
LANSDOWN, Fl/off, Desmond William Burt, 184368
McFADDEN, L/lt, Aubrey, 42510
MOORE, Sjt, Frank William, 1699152
PERRY, Fl/Sjt, John Richard, 1626796
ROBERTS, Sjt, William George, 656237
SLATER, Lac, Kenneth Blundell, 1110976
THOMAS, Lac, Robert, 1103502
TIDDY, Fl/off, Alastair James, 145680

258 SQUADRONN (VR)
WILSON, Fl Off, James Edward Malcolm, 159979

261 SQUADRON
BOWIE, Fl/off, David Price, 137299
COOPER, Gnr, Richard Denis, 14930065

GEE, W/o, Alen Denis David, 1283017
HANKINS, Fl/Sjt, Lyn, 1577648
PHILLIPS, Fl/Sjt, Dennis Robert, 1317412
STRICKLAND, Fl/off, John, 125585

267 SQUADRON
BRIGGS, Fl/Sjt, Jack, 1622995
BRODIE, Ac2, William Forbes Petrie, 1622995
CURSONS, W/o, Graham Walter, 1603390
DONALDSON, W/o, William Henry, 1568647
GREENSLADE, Fl/off, Clifford, 199508
HOGG, Fl/off, Capel Wilson, 167138
NEWSOME, W/o, Ronald, 1081851
SCOTT, Fl/Sjt, Walter Alan Thomas, 1651236
TREACY, Fl/Sjt, Robert Francis, 1796178
WALTON, W/o, William Henry, 1443476

273 SQUADRON
BISHOP, Ac2, Verdun, 530720
CROW, Fl/off, Stanley Gerald, 157063
WILLIAMS, Fl/off, John Denys, 40583

282 SQUADRON
TAYLOR, Fl/lt, Edwin Murrey, 85259, (DFC)

292 SQUADRON
RUDDOCK, Fl/Sjt, Lawrence Lloyd, 1335353
SILVER, Sjt, Raymond George, 1896848

352 SQUADRON
TAYLOR, Fl/off, Norman Charles, 112758

353 SQUADRON
ALLARD, Fl/off, William Stanley, 1864359
CLOVER, Sjt, Arthur, 1058469
CROSY, Gr Apt, Leonard John, 29064
ENSOR, Sjt, Norman David, 1166158
FOOT, Fl/off, William Easton, 131123
RABY, Fl/off, Jack, 203533
SHOVLIN, Fl/off, William, 101589
SMALL, Sq Ldr, David Lawrence, 79143
STURT, Fl/off, Donald Ian Paul, 201103
WHEELER, Sjt, Robert Gerald, 1034197
WILSON, Sjt, Ronald, 1050944

354 SQUADRON
AGNEW, Jt, David Lawrence, 1339644
BAKER, Fl/Sjt, William Albert, 1334782
CHESTER, Sjt, Richard Howard, 1451246
DAY, Fl/Sjt, George Herbert, 1496430
LANNANE, Sjt, James, 1863110
LEESE, Fl/off, Charles Edwin, 163697
MAXTED, Sjt, Frank, 2221326
McCREESH, Fl/off, Donald George, 176957
MOULD, Jt, Dennis Leonard, 1819680
PARKER, Sjt, Gordon, 1685728
SLATER, Fl/lt, Cyril John, 156021
SMAIL, Fl/Sjt, William Derek, 578230
STRINGFIELD, Sjt, Norman John, 1021370
SUTCLIFFE, Sjt, John, 980740

355 SQUADRON
AUSTIN, Sjt, Eric Wiliam, 1577655
BELL, Sjt, Robert Taylor, 1826150
BENFELL, Sjt, Leslie, 1557907
BREACHMORE, Fl/Sjt, Graham Bevis, 1530515
CALLAND, Fl/off, John, 101427
CAMERON, Fl/jt, Donald Urquhart, 1823810
CAMPBELL, W/o, Hugh, 977546
CHOAK, Sjt, Kenneth Henry, 1585634

DUCKWORTH, Fl/off, Robert James, 197862
DUNN, W/o, Malcolm James, 908867
EMERSON, Fl/jt, Harold Walter, 1804316
FLOYD, Sjt, Anthony Henry Edward, 576113
GREETHAM, Fl/Sjt, Robert Frederick, 939059
GRIFFITHS, W/o, William, 657359
GROUCOTT, Fl/Sjt, Eric Richard, 1416098
HELSBY, Sjt, Laurence, 1755315
HIGGINBOTHAM, Fl/Sjt, Thomas, 1030948
HILL, Fl/off, Brian, 163701
HOLLAND, Fl/Sjt, Sidney James, 1851590
JOHNSON, W/o, Harry, 655366
McALHONE, Sjt, Denis, 652432
McDOWELL, Fl/Sjt, John Herbert, 1522985
McPHERSON, Fl/Sjt, Robert Murdock Bannerman, 1380358
MORGAN, Fl/off, Ieuan Anthony, 187828
MORRISON, Fl/off, Mathew, 164290
NICOLSON, Wng Cmdr, James Brindley (VC DFC), 39329
RICHARDSON, Fl/Sjt, James Leslie, 992879
RUMSEY-WILLIAMS, Fl/off, Frederick Edward (DFC), 179043
SPILLARD, Fl/off, Jack, 195438
TOTHAN, Fl/off, Rowland (DFC), 177155

355 SQUADRONN (VR)
LAW, Sjt, (bomber) Harry, 1579345
NUNN, Flt Sjt, Charles, 1320361
HARRISON, Fl/Sjt, Harold Norman, 1575095
MARTIN, Sjt (Air Gunner), Hugh Cecil, 1796212
PAGE, Flt Sjt, Roy, 996520,

356 SQUADRON
AARONS, Fl/Sjt, Sidney Solomon, 2200115
BLAKEY, Fl/Sjt, Jack, 1582692
BROMFIELD, Fl/off, John Trevor, 166369
DOVEY, Fl/off, William Kenneth, 166352
GOODACRE, Fl/off, Frank Winston, 605687
MASON, Fl/off, Edward Donald, 166082
PENFOLD, Fl/off, Ernest Albert, 164096
RAYBOULD, Sjt, Jack Joseph Richard, 1583053
ROSS, Fl Sjt, William, 2213814
ROSS, Fl/off, Thomas Douglas Munro, 165752
SKIPWORTH, Fl/off, Walter Frederick Mons, 195479
SNEWING, Fl/Sjt, George James Harry, 1641867
STEWART, Fl/Sjt, John, 1802355
TOWELL, Fl/Sjt, Raymond Arthur, 1624252

356 SQUADRONN (VR)
CLARKE, Sjt W/o, Leonard George, 1601980
HARRISON, Fl Off (navy), Robert Francs, 165719
NEALE, Sjt, Philip Anthony, 1583422
PASSEY, F/officer, Norman Edgar, 165782
TAYLOR-WALKER, Sjt, Ian, 2218721
WINCHESTER, Flt Sjt, Reginald Charles,

357 SQUADRON
BINNS, Fl/Sjt, Alfred, 1598599
BOLINGBROKE, Wo/1, Ernest Joseph Leonard,
CALDER, Fl/Sjt, Alexander Fraser, 1894540
CLARK, Sjt, E M, 1318743
FRANCIS, Sjt, Charles Raymond, 1321173
HARTLEY, W/o, Jack, 1534015
HERDMAN, Fl/jt, Roy Metcalfe, 1473480
LONGHURST, Fl/Sjt, James Leslie, 1395543
McLEMAN, Fl Sjt, Daniel, 1565046
MILNE, W/o, Joseph Reid, 658498
MOUAT, Sjt, Duncan, 1597461
NATHANIEL, Fl/Sjt, Thomas Porteus, 2209199
PONSFORD, Fl/lt, James Cecil Spencer, 80801

WILKINSON, Fl/Sjt, Joseph, 537086

357 SQUADRON (VR)
FRANCIS,Plt Off,Dennis Leslie,189477
MASTERS,Flt Sjt,Peter George,1850121

358 SQUADRON
ADAMS, Sjt, William Thomas, 1294384
ALDRIDGE, Sjt, Ivor Keith, 1626326
BARKER, Fl/Sjt, Eric Wilfred, 1586121
BULL, Fl/off, Walter Henry, 165575
BUTT, Fl/Sjt, Victor Arthur Frederick, 1800854
CLARKE, Fl/Sjt, Thomas Frederick Courtney, 636459
DAVIDSON, Sjt, Robert Hay, 1013215
DUFF, Fl/off, Arthur Herbert, 182369
GITTINS, Sjt, George, 1458467
GRIFFITHS, Fl/off, Barry John Carrington, 167414
HOLT, Fl/Sjt, John Hewitt, 1522039
HUGHES, Fl/off, John, 164129
MERRIMAN, Fl/off, James Ashley, 167426
ROBERTSON, Sjt, Albert William, 1800541
ROBINSON, Fl/lt, Richard William, 51159
ROBINSON, Sjt, James Alfred, 976434
SIMON, Fl/off, Joseph Walter Burrows, 166544
STORRAR, W/o, Kenneth John, 1459361
TUFFNELL, Fl/Sjt, Derek, 1674764

358 SQUADRON (VR)
BROWN, Flt Lt, Thomas Andrew, 135527
HAZELWOOD, Sjt, Leonard William, 1584988
JOHNSON, Fl Off(nav), Herbert John Alec, 165517
PARKER, Fl Off, Philip Percy, 165276
PINCKNEY, Sjt, William John, 1805139
POOL, Flt Sjt, Brian Richard, 1434100
PUMPHREY, Sjt, Gerald Mathew, 798789
SMART, Fl Off, John Brown, 171567
SMITH, Sjt, William Watts, 1479656
WISE, Sjt, Joseph Ronald, 1587400

413 SQUADRON
HENZELL,Sjt,John,641447
HOUSLEY,Sjt,Derek Laxton,915310

505 SQUADRON
BLAKE,Fl/Sjt,Errol Walter Joseph,785051

514 SQUADRON
CHILDS,Sjt,Victor George,1890418

548 SQUADRON
CANNON,Fl/off,Roy Albert Arthur,142064
CLINTON,Fl/off,Basil,198796
COOK,Fl/lt,Thomas John Donald,124854
FOX,Fl/off,Peter,188187
WELBURN,Sjt,James Kenneth,5785703

605 SQUADRON
BELFIELD,Lac,Eric, 576986
BERESFORD, Ac1, Arthur Henry, 1046884
BROADMORE, Lac, Jack Alfred, 805521
BROWN, Ac2, Victor Lewis Clarke, 1407313
BURGE, Lac, Stanley Percy, 1352074
CARMICHAEL, Lac, Ian Ross, 1220075
CHECKETTS, Ac1, Ernest Edward, 1211362
EARL, Ac1, Colin Stuart, 1143310
EVANS, Lac, Wilfred Campbell Lloyd, 1031309
FOAN, Ac2, Maxwell, 1276504
HALL, Ac1, Frank Herbert, 1311294
HARRIS, Lac, John, 955111
HARRIS, Ac1, Alfred Frank, 1213243

JAMES, Cpl, Harold Vincent, 54822
KEMP, Fl/Sjt, Stanley, 531925
McLAUGHLIN, Lac, John, 996085
PALMER, Cpl, John Eden, 903290
PARRY, Sjt, Ivor Glynn, 341249
PERKS, Lac, Alfred Arthur, 805493
PONT, Lac, Alfred Leslie Frank, 1012421
PUGH, Ac1, Charles Gilbert, 1046887
RUSSON, Lac, Arthur Frederick, 805512
STEVENS, Cpl, Joseph, 622575
TASKER, Lac, John Norman, 805411
TOOTH, Lac, Yril Geoffrey, 805530
WARD, Cpl, Alfred William, 1168448
WHITEFIELD, Lac, William Harry Herbert, 641669
WOOLDRIDGE, Fl/Sjt, William George, 560735
WRIGHT, Fl/off, Harold Lewis, 80597

605 SQUADRONN (VR)
DOWDING,Lac,Fred Charles,1255254
GREENWOOD,Ac1,Ronald,1504765
NEI,L/Cpl,Donald Carden,1352105

607 SQUADRON
ANDREW,Fl/off,James Richard,172188,DFM
GOODWIN,Fl/Sjt,William Geoffrey,853856
NEWSAM,W/o,Raymond,1452618
SHAW,Fl/off,Johnston Roger Watterson,1616640

615 SQUADRON
HYDE,Fl/off,Arthur Reginald,169440
KOSTROMIN,Sjt,Edgar Charles,528577
MADDOCKS,Sjt,Raymond,1081228
McKAY,Fl/Sjt,James Bordro,1387314

628 SQUADRON
GARCIA,Fl/sgt,Abraham,1320156
HOLLAND,Sjt,James William,1196990
OWEN,Sjt,Robert Higginson,1571602,
WHITBY,Sjt,Henry,1119325

650 SQUADRON
DOUGLAS,Ac1,Colin Frederick,1294625
LOVE,Ac1,Cecil Frank,1046901,

681 SQUADRON
BARNETT, Fl/off, Redmond Lewis, 111237
BRINDLE, W/o, Henry Alec, 580360
DAVIES, Fl/lt, Cecil Brian Powell, 111244
GORDON-WHITE, Fl/off, Lynden Kingsley, 128566
HARRIS, W/o, Mervyn Harold, 656354
HORSEY, Fl/off, Michael John, 61497
HYNDS, Fl/off, William John, 161672
WALTERS, W/o, Lawrence, 1316296
WEIGHILL, Lac, Benjamin, 1253670
WOODHOUSE, Fl/lt, Thomas, 55003

681 SQUADRONN (VR)
CHAPMAN,Lac,Tudor,1652113

684 SQUADRON
BURY, Lac, Ronald Stancliffe, 1522216
BUTLER, Lac, Eric Henry John, 1866566
COTTON, Fl/off, Eugene, 115187
EARL, Fl/off, William Mclure, 198134
FAWKNER, W/o, James Alfred Harry, 1382899
JONES, Fl/lt, George Hayward (DFC), 152650
LOWRY, Wng Cmdr, William Michael (DFC), 33193
MUNDAY, Fl/off, Jacob Indian, 202399
NEWMAN, Fl/lt, Kenneth John, 125705
PRESTON, W/o, John William, 1579759

REDFERN, Fl/off, Benjamin, 141847
ROBISON, Fl/lt, Neil, 109915
SUTCLIFFE, Fl/lt, Esmond James, 123501
WHITEHOUSE, Lac, John Leslie, 1498188
WOODS, Fl/Sjt, Raymond Ewart, 1288560
WORKMAN, Fl/lt, Michael Charleton, 129389

689 SQUADRON
PLATER,W/o,Sidney Jack,1386875

721 SQUADRON
RITH,Fl/Sjt,Clifford James,560600

805 SQUADRON
GOODACRE,Fl/off,George William,179053
LEWIS,W/o,Colin Graham,1411410
WATLER,Fl/Sjt,Chrisopher Stanley Horace,1613408
WHITE,Sjt,Robert Edward,2202362

2896 REG (VR)
McCONNELL,Lac,James,1552044

5005 AIR CON SQUADRON (VR)
FARREN,Lac,James Patrick,1903877

5012 AIR CON SQUADRON
BOOTH,Ac1,Arthur.J.,1433067

Hong Kong Forces

HONG KONG DEFENCE
ANGUS, Pte, George Ian
ASHTON-HILL, L/Cpl, Robert
BEARMAN, Pte, George Henry
BLAIR, Sjt, Younger Ralph
BLAKE, Pte, David Samuel
BREWIN, Pte, Alan
BUTCHER, W/o, Eric Robert
CLAYTON, Pte, Bernard
CRABBE, W/o, William Gordon
CURD, Sjt, W J J
DEACON, Sjt, George William
FLEMING, Pte, William
FOREMAN, Pte, Herbert George
GOW, Sjt, David
GRANT, Pte, Kenneth
HOOD, Cpl, John Mair
HORSWELL, Maj, Sydney James
JACK, Rsm, James Ackenzie
JUPP, Wt Off, John Edmund
KNIGHT, Sjt, W.C.
LEE, L/Cpl John Stirling
MACKINNON, L/Cpl, John Mcdougal
MANN, Pte, Alexandr Leonard
MAY, Pte, Francis Cecil
MILL, Sjt, William Frederick
MULLETT, Wo, L A
OGLE, Pte, George Henry
ORGAN, Pte, William Henry
SHAW, Sjt, Willis
SHUSTER, Cpl, Edward
SMITH, Sjt, Harrry
STONEHAM, Pte, William Thomas
THELIN, Pte, Henry Antonia
TYNEMOUTH, Sjt, Robert
TYRER, Pte, Robert Frederick
WALKER, Bsm, William Laird
WISE, Pte, Reginald John Joseph Samuel
WORRALL, W/o, Geoffrey Clare

Indian Forces

ADAMS, Lt Col, David Abro, 139
BELL, Lt, Alan Cowburn Lascelles, 225577
BROWN, 2/lt, Leslie Muir, 225869
COTTE, Maj, Jean, 03378
CRAWFORD, 2/lt, Donald Torrance Paterson, 221751
DARBY, 2/lt, Oliver, 225879
DAVEY, Capt, Harold George Aldridge, 223662
EDWARDS, 2/lt, Allen Edgar Alexander, 363894
GRAHAM, Lt, Ronald, 225884
HARDING, Lt, Frederick John Atkin, EC/8868
HARVEY, Lt, William Percy, 68285
HUTN, Lt, Leslie George Richard, 223262
PINHEY, 2/lt, Robert Douglas,
PRIOR, Lt, T.G., 350699
RAND, 2/lt, Guy Widdrington, 225862
REID, Lt, John, 225863
RIGBY, Capt, James, 343921
RIX, 2/lt, Henry Rodnay, 205480
ROACH, Lt, H S L, 270634
ROBINSON, Lt, William Stanley, 225864
ROSS, Lt, Harold Robert, 325365
SCOTT-SKOVSO, Lt, Algot Erling, 225851
SMYLLIE, Lt, Thomas Marshall, 225852

STEPHEN, Lt, Geoffrey Francis Dixon, 202209
STEWART, 2/lt, Duncan Blair, 363893
STUBINGTON, 2/lt, William Henry, 225853
TAYLOR, 2/lt, Lslie Henry William, 225847
THOMAS, 2/lt, Albert William Jesse, 366188
TREMLETT, Lt Col, Frederick Innes, 52505
TYSON, Capt, Bryan Frank, 371943
VANRENEN, Lt, Frank Campbell, 28000
WHYTE, Cpat, Donald, 350861
WRIGHT, 2/lt, Francis Henry, 363895

BALUCH REGIMENT
COOMBE, Capt, George Allen, A1/818
HARVEY-KELLY, Capt, Hume Dairmid, EC/276
HILDER, 2/lt, Gerald Hall, EC/1346

DOGRA REGIMENT
CELLARS, 2/lt, Andrew Geddes, EC/18710
FRAZER, 2/lt, Patrick Desmond George, EC/3763
FRANK, Capt, Geofrey Neal, IEC/11511
HAYNE, Capt, Desmond Peter Thomas Patrick, EC/2841
HENDRICK, Lt Col, Charles Albert, A1/809
MEIKLE, Lt, John L, EC/16317
RICHARDSON, Capt, Bernard Ian, EC/712
THORPE, 2/lt, Owne Edwin, IEC/182

FRONTIER FORCE RIFLES
ACWORTH, Lt Col, John Pelham, A1/387
DENT, Maj, Richard Clinton Wilkinson, A1/353
GAUVAIN, Maj, Rowland De Putron, A1/500
GELL, Capt, Paul Brian, 1A/1260
GORDON, Lt, Arthur Hamilton, EC/1360
HARVEY, Capt, Bernard Wilfred, EC/128
HODSON, Capt, Michael Harry, A1/889
PATON, Capt, John Ramsay, 1A/1054
PHILLIPS, Lt, Herbert Baker, EC/840
POMEROY, Capt, Ugene Cowles, EC/15868
WILLIAMSON, Lt, Norval John, EC/5441

GURKHA RIFLES
BUCKNALL, Capt, Richmond Drummond Hay, 1A/1342
DEACON, Gnr, Richard Thomas, 71444756
FULTON, Lt Col, John Oswald, 37/1A
GATES, Lt, Digby, EC/16341
HANCOCK, Capt, Bernard Cunningham, EC/1888
HODGETT, Capt, David Alexander Hynes, EC/477
HOGG, Capt, George Christopher Graham, 1A/914
JONES, Capt, Christopher David, EC/13434
MARTIN, 2/lt, Norman Piers, EC/2257
MODERATE, Gnr, James Rodger, 8215796
MOONEY, Capt, Thomas Arthur, EC/207
MURREY DUNCAN, Lt, Robert Eanraig, EC/15699
RIDOUT, Cpat, William Awton, IA/985
RYDER, Maj, Earnle Terrick Dudley, 55/IA
SEAWARD, Capt, William Gay, 841/A1
STREATFIELD, Lt, James Champion, 2955
TAYLOR, Capt, William Norman,
WILLIAMS, 2/lt, Arthur, EC/2852
WOOLCOMBE, Lt Col, Geoffrey Harley Douglas, 75/IA
YATES, 2/lt, Kenneth Robert, EC/16324

HYDERABADS
DARLING, Lt, Austin Eaton, EC/871
DAVIDSON-BROWN, Maj, Alan A.1., 937
HARRIS, Capt, Vere Walace, A1/913

INDIAN ARMOURED CORPS 100 LT TANK
ALFORD, Maj, Jack, 1/220

INDIAN ARMY
EDNIE,Sub Cmdr,James,

INDIAN ARMY CAVALRY
HENEKER,Capt,Patrick Allason Holden,1A/54

INDIAN ARMY ORDNANCE CORPS
ANSELL, Capt, Charles Arthur, EC/1112
ATKINSON, Capt, John Surtess, A1/788
BARSTOW, Maj General, Arthur Edward (CIE MC COM)
CARPENTER, Maj, Elgious Victor (MBE),
DOUGLAS, Lt Col, William Abbot Gale, 818/1A
EDWARDS, Lt, Cecil Menzies, OS/275
ELLIS, Capt, Francis Robert Bloye, E/C19
GILL, Lt, James Frederick Horace,
HILL, Maj, Henry John Carwardine, IA/11700
HORSFIELD, Capt, Stanley Rostron, EC/12839
LETTS, Condr, Frederick William,
LYONS, Maj, Patrick Owen,
ROSS, Ass Sur, Leonard Douglas,
STAMP,Maj,Robert Verdun,EC/23
WALKER, Capt, John Tait,
WEBB, Capt, Alfred Horace Benjamin, OW/135

12 INDIAN INFANTRY BRIGADE
PARIS,Brig Comander,Archibald Charles Melvill (MC) ,6515

45 INDIAN INFANTRY BRIGADE
DUNCAN,Brig,Herbert Cecil,

INDIAN MEDICAL SERVICE
BAMFORD, Maj, Percy Vivian, EC/481
EASTWOOD, Sister, E, Z/19590
FROST,Lt Col,Robert Lewis,MZ/8226
RETZ, Capt, Gilbert Charles,
SMITH, Condr, Robert Henry, 22419
TAPSALL,Capt,Godwin Lionel Robbins,
WHITE,Maj,John,MZ/1278

INDIAN MOUNTAIN ROYAL ARTILLERY
STRONG,Capt,Cecil Warwick,EC/2739
HORDER,Lt,Laurence,EC/12156
HART,Maj,John Goodwin Lancelot (DSO),EC/3403

INDIAN ROYAL ARTILLERY
KING,Gnr,Douglas,924589
SMITH,Gnr,Raymond Bruce,1116026
SWINGLER,Gnr,John Edward,1089482

INDIAN RED CROSS
HENSMAN,Wel Off,Lalitha (MBE),35

INDIAN ROYAL ENGINEERS
HENDERSON,C S M,Stanley Charles,132428

INDIAN ROYAL SIGNALS
HARGREAVES,Capt,Allan Samuel,
SMITHIES,Sgmn,William Joseph,2335899
SNEDDON,Sgmn,James,2594997

INDIAN ROYAL SIGNALS
BILLSBOROUGH,Sgmn,V.E.,14754692
STEEL, Sgmn, Maitland, 2594893
STOKES, Dvr, Harry, 4969494
THOMPSON, Sgmn, Fred, 2347788
WHEELER, Sgmn, Gordon Frederick, 2337025
WOOD, Sgmn, William Hackney, 2363025

JAT REGIMENT
BREAKS,Maj,Kenneth Gough,463/A1

COPE,2/lt,F.B.,EC/429
DYER,Capt,Anthony Derrick,EC/1336
EVANS,Capt,David Creighton,734/A1
GRAY,Spr,John Lindsey,
HOLDEN,Capt,Cyril Beresford Vivian,1033
LEE,Capt,Brian,EC/72
PERRY,Lt,Frederick William Donald,
WHITE,Maj,Edward Purchase Hall,A1/106
WILLIAMS,Lt Col,John Whittaker,A1/117

KING GEORGE V LANCERS
FITZE,Lt,Kenneth Stewart Samuel,EC/14866

MAHRATTA
HART,Maj,John Goodwin Lancelot (DSO),EC/3403
HORDER,Lt,Laurence,EC/12156
MIDDLEMISS,Capt,Thomas Wilmot Dean,EC/6358
STRONG,Capt,Cecil Warwick,EC/2739

PUNJAB REGIMENT
ALABASTER,Capt,Christopher James Clifford,A1/811
ANDERSON,Maj,Frank Graham,A1/633
ANDERSON,Lt Col,Victor Dennistoun Winstanley,A1/531
BAPLE,2/lt,.D.R.,EC/7153
BATES,Lt Col,Ronald Charles Sidney,A1/12 CDG
BELCHEM, Capt, John, A1/440
CATT,Maj,Charles Erling Bernard,426/A1
CLIBBORN,Capt,Edward Barclay,1/895
DICKIE,2/lt,Alexander Carswell St Clare,EC/1853
DURRANT,2/lt,Christopher James,EC/1804
FINLAYSON, 2/lt, Graham Alexander, EC/16724
GETHIN,2/lt,David,EC/2758
GILES,Capt,Foster Abney,A1/529
GRAHAM,Capt,John Onslow,881/A1
HAMMOND,Capt,Deryck Charles Eckron,1A/1028
HARNACK, 2/lt, Waldo, 34498
HEENAN, Capt, Patrick Stanley Vaughan, 547/A1
HOLMAN,2/lt,George Anthony,EC/3860
JARMAN, Capt, John Dennis, 694/1A
JENNINGS,Capt,Maurice Irving,731/A1
JONES,Capt,Felix Robert Fenwick,EC/768
LARKIN, Lt Col, Henry Sloan, 922
LUCK,Capt,Henry Oswald,376/1A
MACKINTOSH, Capt, Stanley Mcleod (EC), 12389
McLENNAN, Capt, Kenneth Lesliea, 1/11666
MOORHEAD, Lt Col, Henry Dawson (DSO), A1/717
NEWMAN, 2/lt, Cyril Leonard, EC/4926
RINGER,2/lt,Vanya,EC/1858
SHARP, Capt, John Martin, A1/1147
SKYRME,2/lt,Edgar Frank,EC/3759
SLATTER,Capt,Arthur William Donald,A1/413
STAPLES,Maj,Aiden Joseph,A1/32
STOKES,Lt,Col Cyril Lovesy Lawrence,A1/600
THATCHER, Capt, John Anthony Ranulf, EC/453
TRAYNOR,Capt,Norman Egar Robert,A1/543
WAKEFIELD,Maj,George Colin,EC/162
WHITE,Lt,Frank Edward,EC/2759
WILLIAMS,Maj,Patrick Robert,418
WILSON,2/lt,C.L.M.,EC/3717

RAJPUTANA RIFLE
AIRD-SMITH,Brigdr,William,
MARTYN,Lt,Richard Valentine Cleeve,1/A1126
TRAVERS SMITH,Capt,Arthur Denis,EC/83
WARREN,2/lt,Stephen John,EC/3738

ROYAL GARHWAL RIFLES
BERRYMAN,Capt,Martin Edward Feilding,1A/1080
BINGHAM, (k/n), Pat Leonard Ranworth, A1/451
BRYHAM, 2/lt, Peter William, EC/3772

CASHMORE, 2/lt, John Westcott, EC/3774
COMBE, Lt, David Boyce, 1A/1269
CONRAN-SMITH,2/lt,Kenneth Freman,EC/2843
DALLAS SMITH, Capt, Alexander Charles M`C, 1A/1216
FOX,Maj,Edward Lionel Wakefiled (MC),A1/852
FRENCH,2/lt,Richard John,EC/3773
LANDRAY, Capt, Harry Gilbert, RO/1248
MYLES, Lt, John Stanley Noel, EC/462
NUGENT, Capt, David Richard, 1A/1081
SMITH,Lt Col,Claude Hutchinson,A/1868
SYMES,Capt,Arthur David,1A/1209
TRUSCOTT, Capt, Bevil Gilbert, 1A/1210
WARD, 2/lt, Robert Adrian Horace, EC/4822
WOOLRIDGE,Lt Col,James Hugh Capleston,A1/843

ROYAL INDIAN ARMY SERVICE CORPS
ADAMS, Lt, Alfred Cyril, ST/162
BOWKER, Lt, John Vernon, EC/2460
CLAPHAM,Sjt,Richard Brinsley,3711627
COKKE, 2/lt, H.O.P., EC/2459
COLEMAN, Lt, William Desmond, 132871
DEAN, Lt, Colin Blacklock, EC/3314
GERRARD, Lt, George Hardman, 12698
HOWELL,Capt,Frederick William Henry,ST/29
NAPIER, Capt, John Charles Francis, 3957
NEWLAND, Capt, Henry, EC/2057
SHELDON, Capt, Dennis Lawrence, EC/562
SHINER, Lt Col, Leonard, EC/15052
STEVENS, T Col, Cyril Walter, 609/1A
THOMAS, Lt, John, EC/2543
WHITTAKER, Capt, Hugh, EC/2499

Malayan Forces

FEDERATED MALAY STATES VOLUNTEER FORCE
AGNEW, Cpl, Arthur Brian
ALLAN, Cpl, George Peat, 13928
ALLEN, Pte, Walter, 13740
ANDERSON, Sjt, William, 13700
ANGUS, Cpl, F.D.
ANGUS, Pte, Roderick John
ATKINS, Lt, Alfred Percival
AVERY, Lt, James Thomas, 5958
BAKER, Pte, James Alison
BALDOCK, Pte, William Frederick
BANCROFT,Capt,Kenneth Humphrey
BARKER, Cpl, Josiah Wilson, 13916
BARNES,2/lt,Harvey Hickman,
BEARDMORE, Gnr, John Owen, 7978
BEELEY, Gnr, Fred, 6108
BELL, Pte, A.J.
BELLINGHAM-SMITH, Capt, Oliver (MID), 6878
BEST, Cpl, Leslie .H., 13232
BEST, Pte, C.C.
BILLINHURST, Pte, Charles William
BINNIE, Pte, Alexander Charles
BLAIR, Pte, Daniel Dunlop, 13014
BLAKELEY, Pte, Donald Frederick, 13336
BOND, Pte, Robert Narramore, 13504
BOYS, Pte, Richard, 13622
BROOKS, Csm, Edward Arthur John
BROWN, Sjt, R.B.
BROWN, Pte, H.S.
BROWN, Sjt, Thomas William, 13413
BRUCE,Plt/off,James Chisholm
BRYSON, 2/lt, Hugh F.
BURGESS, Lt, Cecil Henry
BURGESS, Pte, George, 6975

BYRNE, Pte, R.W.
CALLARD, Sjt, Eric Mortimer
CAMERON, Pte, Robert Hugh, 12957
CAMERON, L/Cpl, James Wallace, 6169
CAMERON, 2/lt, Maxwell Field, 13923
CAMPBELL, Gnr, Richard James Berry, 13879
CARRUTHERS, Csm, William James, 6741
CARTER,Capt,Reginald Rudolph Childers,205478
CARUTH, Cpl., R.A.Y.
CHALMERS, Sjt, Ian, 7616
CHAPMAN, Pte, Albert Stephen, 14031
CLARK,Maj,Adrian John (OBE)
CLARK, Pte, John William, 13709
CLARK, Cqms, Stanley James, 5900
COCKMAN, Maj, Herbert James (DFC EDI)
COKER,Flt Sjt,Henry John
CONAGHAN, L/Cpl, Thomas E.
COPE, Sjt, Thomas Wynn Oswald
CRAIG, Lt, Colin James George
CRAIK, Pte, Thomas Baldwin, 7929
CROFT,Capt,William Owen Glendower,EC/2973
CROSBIE HILL, Lt, Antony
CROSSE, Capt, Edward Castlemain, 152
CROWTHER SMITH, Capt, Charles Vernon
CROXFORD, Cpl, M.P.
CUNYNGHAM-BROWN, Pte, Robert Cheyne, 13513
CURRIE, Capt, Ulric Lgernon
DAKERS, Capt, Colin Hugh (MC)
DALGETTY, Cpl, Bain, 7512
DALY, Capt, Augustine Joseph (MC), 4353
DANE,Fltlt,Henry (DSO)
DAVID, Pte, William Michael, 13590
DAVIES, Maj, John Glover
DAY,Cadet,George L.
DE WITT, Pte, Ivor Henry
DEANS, Pte, Alexander Gribbon, 13244
DEIGHTON, Sjt, Lawrence Wilfred, 6558
DERBYSHIRE, Pte, William Andrew, 13895
DICKSON, Pte, W.R., 7569
DOUGHTY, Pte, Reginald Leonard Carter
EARLE, Spr, Marcus Erasmus, 1275
EDGAR, Cpl, Thomas Forsyth, 6041
EDWARDS, Sjt, Lloyd George, 6782
EGAN, Pte, J.O'dowd, 14037
EGAN, Pte, J.O'dowd, 14037
ELLABY, Spr, Edward Watts, 1277
ELLIOT, L/Cpl, Robin Aylmer, 80825
FALLOWS, Maj, Albert Edward
FERRIDAY, Sjt, Leslie Richard, 13737
FITZPATRICK, Pte, Ernest Edward
FRASER, Sjt, Eustace David William, 13009
FYFE, Pte, Norman
GILCHRIST, Pte, Wiliam
GILES, Sjt, Joseph Alfred, 80468
GILLESPIE, Pte, William, 6637
GOOCH, Sjt, John Francis
GORE,Cqms,Ross St John
GRAHAM, Pte, L Frank, 7988
GREETHAM, Lt, Albert Edward
GRUNDY, Sjt, Hugh Desmond, 13888
HADOKE, Pte, Patrick Oswald Fitzgerald, 13016
HAGGITT,2/lt,Graham D'arcy,223334
HAGGITT, Spr, Graham D'arcy
HALL, S/Sjt, Frederick Wilson, 7540
HAMILTON, S/Sjt, Andrew, 7734
HANNAY, Pte, Harry Campbell, 4783
HARRISON-JONES, 2/lt, Charles Archibald
HART-BARRY, 2/lt, Lionel Henry, 375004
HARTLEY, Pte, R.H.
HARVEY, Pte, David Warnock, 13675

HEIGH,Pte,Thomas Robert
HENVILLE, Pte, Laurence Arthur, 6860
HOGAN, Pte, L.
HOGAN, L/Cpl, Gordon Llewelen, 80431
HOGAN, Sjt, O.E., 20177
HONEY, Pte, Arhtur George, 5036
HOOPER, Cpl, Roger Alfred, 5615
HORSBURGH,Capt,John Thomson,205914
HUBBLE, Cpl, Peter Wintworth, 13007
HUMPHREYS, Gnr, Richard Clive, 7400
HUTCHINGS, Pte, Nevis Watkins, 13857
INGRAM, Gnr, Samuel Guy, 13823
JAMES, 2/lt, John Colquhoun
KNIGHT, Maj, Harry
LANSDALE-RUTHVEN, Sjt, Hugh Peter
LAWRIE, Spr, George Walker, 967
LEE,Qms,Lawrence George
LONG, Pte, Robert Ernest Gladstone, 5650
MAJOR, Gnr, James Stewart, 13536
MALET, Capt, Harry F.G.
MALINDER, L/Cpl, Leopold Robert, 13283
MANNING,L/Cpl,Keith Wilson,
MATHESON,Sup,'t David Roderick Lister
McBAIN, Cpl, George Murrey, 5598
McCRACKEN, Pte, Henry Maxwell Geddes, 13539
McCROW, Sjt, John Robertson Craig, 7837
McCUBBIN,Spr,William John,1219
McDOUGALL, Pte, Donald Campbell, 6749
McLEOD,Pte,Aden
McMICHAEL,L/Cpl,William Alexander,
McNEILL, Pte, Neil Francis, 13809
McWILIAM, Pte, George Leighton, 6172
MEIERS, Pte, John Willibald, 13660
MELROSE, Pte, John Halliday
MENARY, Pte, James Smyth, 6785
MILBOURNE, Pte, Thomas Reginald Lister, 7932
MILLER, Sjt, Edgar
MILLS, Capt, Michael Gray
MILNE, Sjt, John Norman
MISSEN, Sjt, Reginald Sidney, 13512
MITCHELL, Pte, Albert John Malcolm, 13826
MITCHELL, Pte, James Gordon
MITCHELL-INNES, Pte, Arthur Charles
MONEY-TAYLOR, Spr, John Derek, 1274
MORE, Pte, John Cecil, 6024
MORRICE, Lt Col, George Frederick, 14007
MORRISON, Cqms, Dennis Home, 7207
NEAVE,Capt,John Richard (MC)
NOBLE, Cqms, Rodeick, 13104
NONE, 2/lt, Herbert Deane
O'NEILL, Pte, F.O.C.
OGILVIE, 2/lt, Thomas Yelton
OSBORNE, Pte, William, 6025
OVERALL, Gnr, Alan, 13165
PAGE,Lt,Harold Lewis
PARSONS, Csm, Harold Arthur, C/7259
PASCOE, Cpl, Samuel Alexander
PATERSON, Sjt, William Smith, 6975
PATERSON, Sjt, William Dunbar
PATERSON, Lt Col, John Frederick, 18180
PATERSON, Sjt, James Campbell, 7921
PEALL, 2/lt, Richad Harcourt, 7564
PEARCE,Sup,T Lawrence Henry
PERRIN,2/lt,Arthur Victor
PHILLIPS, Pte, Reginald
PIRNIE, Pte, Jackson Graham, 13298
PRICE, 2/lt, Richard E, 13309
PRIGGE, Pte, Arthur Chambers, 13879
PUGH, Sjt, Edward Cecil Mills, 5374
PYKE, Cpl, Edwin Ernest, 13717

RAINNIE, Pte, Robert Albert
RAYNER, Cpl, Benjamin William
READ, Cpl, Frederick Edward, 13439
REASON, Gnr, Albion George Herbert, 7071
REEVE, Lt, Eric Wilfred
REGAN, Pte, Daniel
REILLY, Pte, F H, 13347
RICHARDS, Pte, Harold George Lorn
RICHARDS, Pte, Cuthbert Aubrey, 25289
RICHARDSON, Pte, Edward Milbourne, 13965
RIDGEWELL, Sjt, Harold James
ROBERTSON, Sjt, William Guyan
ROBERTSON, Sjt, George Campbell, 5613
ROWE, Pte, William Treza, 13679
SADLEIR, L/Cpl, Cedric William Mussett, 7863
SAMUAL, Pte, P, 13454
SANDS, Lt, Norman Herbert, 956
SAUNDERS,Sjt,Francis Wiliam
SCOTT, Pte, William James Sage, 13388
SETH, Cpl, Philip Aviet, 25215
SHELTON, 2/Lt, John Melville Scott
SHELTON PALMER, 2/lt, Patrick Arthur
SHEPTON, Sjt, Henry Mcintyre
SHORT, Pte, Charles Hatton, 13667
SHRIMPTON, Cpl, Francis, 7890
SIMPSON, Pte, Hugh
SLY, 2/lt, Laurance Pontifex
SMITH, Cpl, John Charles, 13179
SMITH, L/Cpl, Eric Thomas Rivers, 13392
SOWDEN, L/Sjt, George Charles, 13798
SPINKS, Capt, Kenneth Lewis, 13962
STEPHENS, Sjt, Michael Vivian, 7804
STEWART, Pte, James Arnold, 13648
STOKES, L/Cpl, Wilfred, 6102
STORCH, Pte, Adolph George, 13411
SULLIVAN, L/Cpl, T P, 13464
SULLIVAN, Pte, Lancelot K, 13853
TATHAM,Cpl,Terence P.H.,
TAYLOR, L/Cpl, Arthur John
TETLEY, Lt, John Lewis
THOMPSON, L/Cpl, Christopher, 13218
TYNDALE POWELL, Sjt, Reginald Oliver
VEITCH, Cpl, Robert, 7953
VIETCH, Capt, Robert, 7953
WAKEFORD, Gnr, R, 12485
WALES, Pte, Henry Price, 4810
WALLER, Pte, Keith Inet, 13658
WALTERS, Sjt, John Colville, 5395
WARD, Lt, Leonard George William, 6363
WARREN, Cpl, William Charles
WEMYSS, Pte, Alfred Home
WHITCHURCH, Sjt, Walter William, 13490
WHITE, Sjt, Thomas Leslie, 7558
WILKIE, Pte, Donald John Talbot, 13453
WILLIAMS, Capt, Frank Leslie
WILLIAMS, Pte, Clarence James, 7450
WILSON, Pte, J M B
WOOD, Cqms, Geoffrey Ashlin, 13946
WOODING, Spr, Cecil Henry
WOODROFFE, Maj, Arthur Stanley
WYLDE, Maj, John G
WYNNE,Dep Insp,S S
YOUNG, Csm, John Robert Grey (MM)

STRAIT SETTLEMENTS VOLUNTEER FORCE
ANDERSEN,Sjt,George Axel,5355
ANDERSON, Spr,Kenneth James,966
ANGUS,Pte,Hugh Shelley,25266
ARCHER,Pte,George Fletcher Beldam,13823
ATHERTON,2/lt,Brian Brenard

BAKER,Gnr,Victor Philip,13545
BAKER,L/Cpl,James Morris,12993
BANNER,Gnr,Leonard Alexander,6017
BAYLEY,L/Cpl,George,
BENNETT,Lt,Paul Johnson,
BIGELOW,Gnr,Norman Percival,5415
BIRD,Pte,Gerald L.,113
BLACK,Pte,Thomas,12087
BLACKISTON,/pl,William Alfred,80450
BLANDY,Rqms,John Marett,13804
BLEAKLEY,Capt,Robert James,
BOIZOT,Spr,George Edward,13867
BRANT,Spr,Ronald Vickers,1282
BRENT,Capt,Lional,
BROWN,Cpl,Edward Geoffrey,13276
BURSTALL,Lt,S.T.,
CAMPBELL, Pte, William,
CAMPBELL,L/Cpl,Kenneth Royston,80629
CARLOS,Cpl,E.R.,
CARSON,Pte,Brian Hardy,5369
CARVER, 2/lt, Alfred Correli,
CHAMBERS,L/bdr,William Herbert,13433
CLARK,Pte,Dennis Cecil,5467
COLATO,Pte,Silvio,
CORKHILL,Csm,W A.,10697
CRABB,Csm,Charles Henry,13092
CROMBIE,Lt,John Milward,
CROSBIE,Gnr,Martin Stewart Stanley,13840
CULLEN,Capt,A.,
DEVONSHIRE,Sup,T George Edward,
DONALDSON,Capt,William Lee,
EAST,L/dr,Frederick George,13012
ECKFORD,Sjt,Errol Frederick,5528
EDGAR,Cpl,Thomas Forsyth,6041
EDWARDS,Pre,Eric,R.13749
ELSWORTH,Sjt,Arthur,12532
EVANS,Lt,Donald Kingsford,
FABER,Pte,Homme,
FERGUSON,Cpl,William,28181
FRASER,Lt,Douglas James (MC),
GARDINER,Gnr,Gordon Hebert,13478
GILBERT,Maj,Arthur Charles,
GODBER,Pte,James Gordon,5413
GOODMAN,Rqms,Harry Evan,
GOWANS,Pte,Andrew,13512
GRAHAM,Gnr,James Edward Dundas,13810
GRAHAM,Spr,James Dempster,13319
GRANT,Pte,James Henry,5617
GRAY,L/Cpl,Douglas George,
GROSSE,Pte,J.A.,20318
GULLAND,Pte,Donald Robertson,7374
HAGGER,Inspector,Sidney Arthur,
HALLETT,Cqms,Bertram W.,
HAMILTON,Pte,John Rollo Alexander,13108
HARRISON,Pte,Patrick Howard,13132
HAY,Capt,Alistair William,
HENDERSON,L/Cpl,Jonothan,2876372
HOWARD,Pte,John,6027
HUTCHINGS,Maj,P T, SING
HUTCHINGS,Gnr,Brydon Leonard,13862
HUTCHINSON,2/lt,John Lyall,
JEPSON,Pl,Vernon B.
KENT,Spr,Robert Francis,
LAFFAN,Cqms,Thomas Gleeson,12196
LAMB,Pte,J B G,6026
LIVINGSTONE,Ass Sup,Etndnt George Logan,
LUETCHFORD,Pte,Harold Charley,
MACCALLUM,Lt,Alistair Ian,
MACLEOD,Lt,Robert,
MARTENS,Pte,Frederick Claude,

McEVETT,Pte,John Catherwood,
McINTYRE,Pte,Anthony Joseph,20324
McLEAN,Pte,Colin G,13460
MILLEN,Pte,Seymour Jay,5256
MILLER,2/lt,James Vincent,
MITCHELL,Pte,Alexander George Brian,13874
MULVEY,L/bdr,William Thomas,12931
PARR,Capt,Alfred Cecil,
PHILLIPS,Pte,Andrew Michael,
PICKARD, Pte, Robert Henry, 13436
PITT,Gnr,John Weston,5433
PLUNKETT,Lt Col,John Oliver,
PURDIE,Pte,Donald,13785
RIDLEY,Sjt,Ranulph Paul,
RITCHIE,Sjt,Geoffrey Oscar,12646
ROBERTSON,Spr,G.,983
ROCHESTER,Pte,Arthur,5389
ROWLAND,L/Cpl,Frank Edward,5520
RUSSELL,Pte,John William,12661
SHAW,Csm,Samuel,6030
SMITH,Sjt,Frederick N Joseph,12846
SMITH,Pte,Cyril,13331
SPARE,Pte,Gordon Henry,6070
STARK,Pte,Bruce Charles Kirkpatrick,5007
STAYNES, Pte, Cf.,
STIFF,Bdr,Francis George,
SWALLOW,Maj,John Francis Alan,
TAYLOR,Lt,Graham,
THESEIRA,Cpl,I.J.,20050
THOMAS,L/Cpl,Horace Samuel,80466
TREWHITT,Cqms,Robert,
TRUDGIL, L/Cpl, Ernest, 13207
TURCAN,Gnr,James Prentice,13828
USHER,Pte,Gerald John Douglas,13800
WAGSTAFF,Gnr,Alex Wheatley,12979
WALKER,2/lt,George Anthony Gilbert,
WARK,Cpl,David,5346
WATERS,Lt,David Ross,
WATSON,Cpl,Henry,13429
WATSON,Maj,G C .,
WAYMAN,Capt,Frank Sydney,
WEBSTER,Sjt,R.J.,13017
WELSH,Gnr,John,13768
WILLIAMS,Pte,Grenville George,4871
WILLOUGHBY,Pte,John Charles,13815
WINTON,Pl,Kenneth Frederick
WOODFORD,Pt,C H,
WRIGHT,Pte,Barry James,4618

Army

ARGYLL & SUTHERLAND HIGHLANDERS
BAIN, Pte, Edward James, 3322726
BALFOUR, Cpl, James, 838872
COLE, Pte, Sidney, 3321672
DICK, Pte, James, 2979938
DOANLD, Pte, George, 3324609
FOLLAN, Pte, Michael, 2975265
JACKSON, Pte, Harold, 332280
JAMES, Pte, Walter, 4622902
JOHNSTON, Pte, David Easton, 2990039
JOHNSTONE, CQMS, James Kay, 2023032
KANE, Pte, Alexander, 3312150
KENNEDY, Pte, Hector, 2979282
LANDSBOROUGH, L Cpl, Samuel Cord, 3131219
LAPSLEY, Capt, John MacDonald, 67451
LEAHY, 2/Lt, John Barham, 274700
LOWES, Pte, John, 3322835
LYON, Pte, Philip, 2989157
LYON, Pte, John, 2987551
LYONS, Bdsmn, John Dennis, 2979647
MACDONALD, Maj, Charles Angus, 56135
MACDONALD, Pte, Robert, 2978391
MACDONALD, Pte, Roderick, 297740
MacLEAN, 2/Lt, Kenneth, 193888
MACPHERSON, Pte, John, 3323251
McARTHUR, Pte, Duncan, 2974440
McCALMAN, Sjt, John, 2967356
McCOLL, Pte, Richard Dick, 1985938
MCDERMOTT, L Cpl, William, 2979298
McDONALD, Sjt, William, 2979495
McDOUGALL, Pte, Hugh, 2979872
McDOUGALL, Cpl, Thomas, 845774
McEWAN, Pte, Henry Edwardson, 2974997
McFADYEN, L Cpl, James, 2979377
McGUIRE, Pte, Joseph Myles, 3130595
McKEE, Pte, James, 2980606
McKNIGHT, Pte, William James, 2979756
McLACHLAN, Pte, Richard, 3326707
McLACHLAN, Pte, William, 2979908
McLAUGHLIN, Pte, Francis, 3326708
McMENEMY, Piper, Charles, 2979693
McNAIRNEY, Pte, Thomas, 3324741
McNEISH, Pte, Mark Doran, 3323250
McNICOL, Pte, Daniel, 2977810
McQUEEN, Pte, Robert, 2979579
REARDON, Pte, Malcolm, 3318432
STEWART, Pte, William Barclay, 2976402

BEDFORDSHIRE & HERTFORDSHIRE REGIMENT
BACON, L Cpl, Ronald Jack, 5951341
BILNER, Pte, Reginald Alec, 5955497
BONATHAN, Pte, Harold Archibald, 5953930
BONE, Pte, Frederick Albert, 5955505
CHAMBERS, Pte, Douglas George, 5953207
CLARK, Pte, Basil John, 5956248
CLARK, Pte, Stanley, 5951265
CLARKE, Pte, Charles, 5950308
CLEWS, Pte, Cyril, 5953824
COBBOLD, Pte, George Albert, 5953027
COOK, Pte, Arthur Frederick, 5950135
COWLING, Pte, Kenneth George, 5828437
COX, Pte, Charles Alfred, 5949272
DALY, Pte, Dennis, 5953036
DAVIES, Pte, Arthur, 5956265
DAWSON, Pte, Frederick Charles, 5948868
DAWSON, Pte, Stanley Albert, 5950976

DAY, Pte, William John, 5951061
DEACON, Cpl, Ralph Malcolm, 5949633
DEACON, Pte, William Henry, 5951358
DENNEY, Pte, David Beatty, 5955533
DEVONSHIRE, Pte, Charles Sidney, 5955535
DUDLEY, Pte, Francis William, 5950452
EVISON, L Cpl, Harold Thorn, 5951125
FELLOWS, Pte, Reginald Hardwick, 5952198
FORTNUM, Pte, Ralph Ernest, 5960359
GRACE, Pte, Alfred Charles Henry, 5951369
HALL, Pte, Charles John, 5956297
HALL, Pte, Sidney James, 5953065
HAMBLIN, Pte, Francis Joseph, 5950043
HARWOOD, Pte, Richard William, 5950612
HAUGHTON, Pte, Derrick Basil, 5952464
HAYDAY, L Sjt, Thomas Victor, 5951383
HIGGINS, Pte, Samuel, 5951380
HILLYARD, Pte, Stanley Walter, 5951385
HUMMERSTONE, Pte, Percy William, 5951891
IRONS, Pte, Willian Charles Alfred, 5953090
IVES, Pte, Raymond Hentry, 5955606
IZZARD, Pte, Cecil William, 5949582
JACKSON, Pte, Harry, 5953093
JACOB, L Sjt, Herbert Arthur, 5948816
JANES, Pte, Arthur William, 5955609
JOHNSON, L Sjt, Arthur Charles Frederick, 5952942
JONES, Pte, Allan, 2060055
JONES, Pte, David John, 5955612
KARMY, Cpl, John Joseph, 5950118
KIERLE, Pte, Frederick, 5953098
KIRBY, Pte, Morris, 5955624
KNIGHT, Pte, Douglas Edward, 5950166
LARMAN, L Sjt, Cyril Bonar, 5952341
LAW, Pte, John Frederick, 5952002
LAWRENCE, Pte, Ronald Charles, 5952003
LAWRENCE, Pte, Gordon, 5951726
LAY, Cpl, William James, 5952632
LEANEY, Pte, John, 5959900
LEMMON, Pte, Douglas James William, 5955634
LETT, Sjt, Albert, 2217764
MacDONALD, Pte, Alistair Charles, 5951396
McCUE, Pte, Bernard, 5951754
MEAN, Pte, Leonard John, 5955460
MERCER, Pte, Wilfred Herbert, 5950438
MIMER, Pte, Alec, 5951452
MONK, Pte, Albert Frederick, 5950941
MORRIS, Pte, Leonard Charles, 5953706
PHILIPSON, Pte, Harold, 5946267
PITTS, Pte, Ernest Lawrence, 5950394
PRIESTLEY, Pte, Henry, 5956691
PUPLETT, Pte, Robert, 5950155
ROWE, Pte, Arthur James, 5956449
SCARGILL, Pte, Leslie Alfred, 5950435
SMITH, Pte, Henry Charles, 5953159
VERNEY, Pte, William, 5959118
WHEATLEY, Pte, Walter John, 5953180
WRIGHT, Sjt, Arthur George, 5950048

1 CAMBRIDGESHIRE REGIMENT
BAINES, Pte, Kenneth Frederick, 5933426
BISHOP, Pte, Leslie Herbert, 6028545
DARE, Pte, Kenneth George, 6028549
DAVIES, Pte, William Thomas, 5827443
DAY, Pte, Charles Edward, 5835267
DEARING, Pte, Edwin William, 6020854
DORLING, Pte, Cecil Herbert, 5833804
DUHIG, Cpl, Terence, 6019344
FRANCIS, Cpl, Percy, 5932983
HILL, Pte, Ronald William, 5827377
INWARDS, Pte, Harold, 5831213

JAKES, Pte,George Walter James,5933691
JACOBS, Pte, Leslie Robert, 5933766
JORDAN, CQMS, Jack Horace, 5932428
KEMPTON, Pte, Robert Henry, 5932386
KESTER, Pte, Victor David, 5932422
KIMPTON, Pte, William, 5933224
KNIGHTLEY, Cpl, Samual Matthew, 6019119
LAMBERT, Pte, Russell Stanley, 5932624
LEUTY, Pte, Cecil Bernard, 6020942
LINFOOT, Pte, Jonathan John, 5833826
McGONAGLE, Pte, Herbert Charles, 6019124
McGRATH, Pte, Brian, 6018923
PETTIT, Sjt, Clarence Leslie, 5946673
RYAN, Pte, John Henry, 6028649
STACEY, Pte, Douglas Walter Laventie, 6028833

2 CAMBRIDGESHIRE REGIMENT
BLAND, Pte, John, 5826660
CHAPMAN, Pte, Percy Henry, 5933502
DALE, Pte, John Thomas, 5933042
DANIEL, Pte, Frank Lewis, 58238832
DAWSON, Pte, Richard Adrian, 5833426
DURRANT, Cpl, Reginald, 5825312
FOSKETT, Pte, Ernest, 5832590
JACKSON, Pte, Harry, 5835120
JEEPS, Pte, Laurence, 5933761
JEFFERSON, Pte, Archie, 5933457
KEMP, Pte, George William, 5933600
KING, Pte, Percy, 5933602
LANE, Pte, Leslie William, 5830971
LAW, Pte, John William, 5831012
LE PLA, Pte, Aubrey William, 5835518
LEACH, Pte, Jack, 6019492
LEE, Pte, George William, 5831221
LONG, Sjt, Horace William, 5933789
LORD, Cpl, William Thomas, 5830430
LOWINGS, Pte, Ronald Webster, 5933454
LUTKIN, Pte, Percy, 5933921
McFADDEN, Pte, Myles, 6026948
PEARSON, Pte, Tom, 5933719

4 CAMBRIDGESHIRE REGIMENT
LAWRENCE, Pte, Peter Daniel, 5830943
MACKENDER, Pte, Stanley, 5831523
MATTOCK, Pte, Robert George, 5830613
McFEELEY, Pte, John, 6028740
MORGAN, Pte, Gerard Austin, 5833057
MOTT, Pte, George Stanley, 5833062
MUTIMER, Pte, William Ypres, 5833065
NORTON, Pte, Sidney Walker, 5833070
PEMBERTON, LCpl, Cyril Victor, 6013919
PILBEAM, L Cpl, Reginad F, 5831363
PILGRIM, Pte, James, 6019037
PORTER, Pte, Thomas Arthur, 5830984
POTKINS, Pte, Albert Charles, 5833093
POTTER, Pte, George Edwards, 6019255
REDGEWELL, Pte, Cyril, 6020708
RUSH, Pte, Samuel, 5831230
RUSSELL, Pte, Joseph William, 6020600
RUTTERFORD, Pte, William Frank, 5833106
SWEETING, Pte, John, 6021190
TAYLOR, L Cpl, John Henry, 6021160
TIPTON, Pte, Jerry, 5830838
WEST, Pte, Basil Charles, 5834440
WHITE, Pte, William Verden, 6021186

5 CAMBRIDGESHIRE REGIMENT
LANGLEY, Pte, Horace John, 5933676
LAYFIELD, L Cpl, Norman, 5833031
MOWER, Pte, Sidney John, 5833063

NEWBOUND, Pte, Conrad William, 5832424
NORMAN, Pte, Arthur John, 5834404
REYNOLDS, Pte, Roy Lewis, 6019259
SEARLES, Pte, Leonard, 6020710
SMITH, Pte, Percy, 5833118
STEDMANS, Pte, Harry, 6028746
STEELS, Pte, Frederick Leslie, 5830917
WAKEFIELD, Pte, Albert John, 6028630
WRIGHT, Pte, John Henry, 6023842

EAST SURREY REGIMENT
DAY, Pte, Dermot Gerald, 6147743
DENNIS, Pte, Robert Plumber, 6139673
HAWKINS, Cpl, Jesse Lewis, 6284132
JEFFERY, Pte, Ronald, 6141294
JEFFRA, Pte, Arthur George, 879000
JENKINS, Pte, Donald, 6141300
JOHNSON, Pte, Eric Red Bradbury, 6141070
JOWETT, Sjt, Frederick, 315795
KEATS, Cpl, Desmond Charles, 6140967
KINGSLEY, Pte, Reginald, 6142278
LAMB, Pte, Norman, 6141885
LAWRENCE, CQMS, William John, 6455277
LEIGH, Pte, Ronald John, 6141877
LEONARD, L Cpl, Jack, 6140610
LIVERMORE, Pte, Reginald, 6147418
LORAINE, Pte, Albert, 6141887
MACE, Pte, Albert Sydney, 6147428
McAULIFFE, Pte, Edward Timothy, 6147424
McLEARY, Pte, John McDonald, 6140746
MERCER, Pte, Frederick, 4344088
NEWMAN, L Cpl, Wilfred, 6147450
REED, Pte, George, 6144893
STEPHENS, L Cpl, Alfred Ernest, 2048705
TOBIN, Pte, William James Patrick, 814253
WARMAN, Pte, Ernest, 6147523

CORP OF MILITARY POLICE
AGNEW, L Cpl, Arthur, 7689875
AYLWARD, L Cpl, James, 7688872
BENTLEY, L Cpl, Duncan, 4532583
BLOW, L Cpl, Leonard William, 6007163
BRUMHILL, L Cpl, Horace, 7690504
CANNON, L Cpl, Leonard, 5437925
CASBURN, L Cpl, Philip Montague, 7690231
COLE, Cpl, Leonard William, 7684602
COWAN, L Cpl, George, 3194338
COWAN, L Cpl, Joseph, 6920277
DAVIS, L Cpl, Cyril, 7690132
DOWNHAM, L Cpl, Edwin Price, 7687580
DUNN, Cpl, Richard, 2655020
FOSTER, L Cpl, George Alfred, 7689790
GILRUTH, L Cpl, Peter, 1026738
GOODING, L Cpl, Horace Charles, 7690373
HADLEY, L Cpl, Arthur Edward, 7690083
HAMBROOK, L Cpl, William Victor, 7689903
HILL, L Cpl, Rowland John, 1744224
HOCKEY, L Cpl, William , 7688656
HUMPHREY, L Cpl, Herbert Hardwick, 7690040
JAMES, L Cpl, Leslie, 7688717
JONES, L Cpl, Frank, 2613515
MACKENZIE, L Cpl, William Steven, 2816696
MARTIN, Cpl, Thomas, 2692623
MCQUILLEN, L Cpl, Robert Oliver, 4345336
MOLLETT, L Cpl, William Henry, 2613087
NIXON, L Cpl, Frederick Howard, 4273780
PRIOR, L Cpl, Albert Edward, 7689948
ROSE, L Cpl, Thomas Albert, 5381079
SENIOR, L Cpl, Maurice Hilton, 7688746
SHEARING, L Cpl, John Elliott, 7684606
SINCLAIR, L Cpl, James Ireland, 7689857

STONE, Cpl, George, 2656295
SWEENEY, L Cpl, James, 3311859
TAIT, Sjt, Archibald, 2695122
TARN, Cpl, Robert William, 4340904
TAYLOR, Sjt, Harry, 2613491
THOMPSON, Cpl, Samuel Edgar, 3382573
TURNER, L Cpl, Charles Frederick, 7685238
TWEEDALE, L Cpl, Duncan, 7688532
WALKER, L Cpl, Alexander, 2983277
WATTON, L Cpl, Reginald Wilfred, 7686872
WELLSTEAD, L Cpl, Arthur John, 7690147
WILLIAMS, L Cpl, David Ivor, 7683759

DEVONSHIRE REGIMENT
BALL,Capt,Richard Graham,117930
MASON,Pte,Oliver,5882672

FEDERATED MALAY STATES VOLUNTEERS
ALEXANDER, Pte, Douglas Adam, 5400
ALLEN, Pte, Charles Edward, 13358
ALLEN, Pte, Everard Reginald, 6078
ANDERSON, CQMS, Alexander Findlay, 13599
ANHOLT, Pte, Henry, 13398
AROOZOO, Pte, H M, 20280
BAILEY, Pte, Harry Lawler,
BARRIE, Pte, Allan Robertson, 13136
BENTON, Pte, Joseph, 5699
BOYD, Cpl, Andrew Conor, 13615
BROCKMAN, Cpl, A G, 5635
BROWN, Pte, Robert, 7745
BULLOCH, WO II (CSM), John Ross, 7887
BURNS, Sjt, Alexander, 13464
CASSELS, Pte, Ronald Rene, 13623
CONNOR, Pte, George Sherwood, 13470
COOKE, Pte, Walter Hicks, 20243
CORDEIRO, Pte, LS, 20042
CRAWFORD, Pte, George Ransom, 6828
CRUMLEY, Pte, C Edward Hugh, 12758
DALTON, CQMS, James Joseph, 6887
DARBY, Gnr, Richard, 7927
DAVID, L Cpl, , 13825
DAVIS, Cpl, William Edward, 80475
DAY, Pte, George Moreton,
DENNIS, Pte, J P, NX
DICKENSON,Lt,Peter
DINGLE, Cpl, Walter Hugh, 50528
DUKE, Lt, Richard Barry,
DUKE, L Cpl, Basil Barry, 19
DUNCAN, Capt, Harry Stuart,
DURANT, Cpl, Charles Cecil Lord,
EDMISTON, BQMS, Alec Ingram, 13428
GREBBY, Sjt, Leslie Norman, 12799
HAMLYN, Cpl, Treleon Courtenay, 12513
HARVEY, Pte, William Martyn, 6645
HUTCHINSON, Sjt, Alfred Johnstone, 80037
INGLIS, Cpl, J G, 7666
INGRAM, Spr, John, 7584
JAMES, Lt-Col, Harold Morton MC and Bar,
JAMES, 2/Lt, John Colquhoun,
JOHNSTON, Pte, William Lawrie, 13046
JONES, Lt, Thomas Patrick Desmond, 204896
JONKLAAS, L Cpl, St John Bevan,
KEIGHTLEY SMITH, Cpl, Arthur,
KENNEDY, Cpl, Albert Roy,
KNIGHT, Pte, Stanley, 13498
LAIDLAW, L Cpl, James Armstrong, 12954
LAUB, Capt, George,
LAURIE, Pte, William Irving, 13790
LEBERT, Pte, William Henri, LEE, Pte, David LA, 687
LEE, Pte, HS, 684

LEECHENG KUAN, Pte, ,
LEIJSSIUS, L Cpl, Irving, 13329
LENNANE, Cpl, Wyndham Quin, 12927
LEON, Pte, Raphael Patrick, 611
LITTLE, 2/Lt, Ronald B,
LOCKE, Pte, Alfred Charles Spencer, 13474
LONGLAND, 2/Lt, Harold Albert,
LORD, Sjt, Allan Owen, 12886
LOVEDAY, Pte, Joyce Alistair, 13889
LOVEWELL, CSM, Francis Douglas, 6805
LOW, Pte, Anthony, 35073
LOWE, 2/Lt, George Gerald,
LYE, Pte, Douglas, 30203
LYNCH, Pte, Michael Breen,
MACDONALD, Capt, Giffard Douglas,
MACKAY, Lt, Thomas Dodd, 257472
MACKENZIE, Pte, Ian Macdonald, 13506
MCARTHUR, L Cpl, Ian, 938
McCONIGLEY, Pte, John, 13471
MCCREA, Pte, Arthur George, 3059
MCCREADIE, L Cpl, G W, 12691
McCUTCHEON,Cpl,A Q,13404
McDOUGALL, Pte, George Hamilton, 6031
MCGUFFOG, CQMS, Robert Nicholas,
McGUGAN, Pte, Frederick James, 13515
McGWIRE, Lt, Brian Walter,
MCINTOSH, Pte, Douglas, 5144
McLEAN, Pte, Colin G, 13460
McLENNAN, Capt, Kenneth Leslie, A.I./1168
McNEILL, Pte, Neil Francis L, 13809
MITCHELL, Sjt, Lewis Mackay,
MOORE, Pte, Arthur, 13726
MOORE, Pte, Olaf Ernest Fine, 7441
MOULDING, Lt, Harry Graham,
MURRAY, Pte, Allistair Hamilton,
NAUN, Sjt, John Charles, 5387
NISBET,Sjt,William,
NONIS, Cpl, JL, 20109
NORGATE, Sjt, Robert Le Grys, 80490
OGDEN, Pte, Fred, 7670
PARR, Pte, FA, 20073
PEEL, Cpl, Charles Edward, 13812
PESTANA, Pte, AC, 20254
PHILIP, Sjt, Charles Alexander, 7702
PHILLIPS, Pte, Martin Baxter, 13132
PIRRIE, Pte, Alan Ball,
QUARTLEY, Pte, Henry Douglas, 7813
RAMSAY, Pte, Sydney, 13659
REDFEARN, Pte, George James,
REDMAN, Pte, Robert Carne, 13172
RUSSELL, Pte, Leslie, 13653
SCOTT, L Cpl, Dennis Lindsay Walters, 13158
STEVENS, CQMS, Kenneth B Havelock,
STONE, Bdr, Peter Duncan, 7777
TEMPLER, Spr, George Devereaux, 920
THESEIRA, Pte, John E I, 20159
WALKER, Pte, James Cadenhead, 5474
WATT, Spr, Leslie Ian, 13866
YOUD, WO II (CSM), Clifford Maurice, 12722

GORDON HIGHLANDERS
ANDERSON, L Cpl, Frederick, 2879163
BOURNE, Pte, Henry Joseph, 3321650
BRIERS, Pte, Frederick John, 3321837
CALDER, CQMS, William Alexander, 2872624
CARR, Pte, William, 830999
CHALMERS, Cpl, James, 2877937
DAY, Pte, Edward, 2889847
DEPO, Pte, David, 836369

DICKSON, Pte, Thomas, 2885780
DICKSON, Pte, Frederick, 857642
DUFFY, Pte, John, 2879008
DUNCAN, Pte, John, 841047
DUNCAN, Pte, James, 2876736
DURWARD, Pte, William, 2876339
DUTHIE, jt, Robert Easton, 2876457
GERRARD, Pte, William, 2876650
GOODLAD, Pte, William, 2876581
HALL, Pte, Robert Arthur, 2876304
INGRAM, Pte, James Barclay, 2876257
INNES, Pte, Alexander, 2986059
INNES, Pte, James, 2876415
JAFFREY, Pte, Robert Ingram, 2876509
JAMIESON, Pte, Andrew John, 2876448
JARDINE, Pte, Michael, 2974394
JOHNSON, Sjt, Donald Vivian, 2975608
JOHNSON, Pte, Victor, 859165
JOSS, Pte, Gordon, 2876262
KEITH, Pte, George, 2875889
KEMP, Pte, George, 2874064
KEMP, L Cpl, William, 2876320
KINGHORN, Pte, William Craven, 2979968
LAING, Pte, Douglas, 2885228
LAIRD, Pte, William, 2876398
LINDSAY, Pte, James Robb, 2885144
LOVIE, Pte, Hector, 2876624
MACAFFERTY, Pte, James, 2824558
MACDONALD, Pte, Donald, 407734
MACKIE, Pte, Edward, 2876852
MACKINNON, Sjt, Donald, 2978471
MACLEOD, Pte, Alexander, 2982101
MACNEIL, Pte, Richard Peacock, 2982002
MATTHEW, Pte, Albert, 2876839
McALLISTER, Pte, James, 2876734
McCAFFERTY, Pte, Philip, 2984610
MCDONALD, Pte, John Rogers, 2880690
McDONALD, Pte, Dvid Ritchie, 2879285
McDOUGALL, Pte, James, 2980727
MCGREGOR, Pte, Scott, 2876365
McGREGOR, Pte, Alexander Milton, 2879072
McGREGOR, Sjt, Ronald, 2875459
McHARDY, Pte, Charles Stewart, 2876254
MCINNES, Cpl, Roderick, 2876187
McKNIGHT, Pte, James Hughes, 2986112
McLARDIE, L Cpl, Robert, 2981666
McLEAN, Pte, John, 2985962
McLEAN, Pte, John Currie, 2982022
McLEISH, Pte, Frank Watson, 2879002
McLEOD, Cpl, Alexander SB, 1661787
McLEOD, Drummer, Edward, 2982017
McLEOD, Pte, Harry, 2875021
McLEOD, Pte, Hector, 2876758
McNALLY, Pte, John, 7681724
McNIVEN, L Cpl, John Alexander, 2982058
MCQUEEN, Pte, John, 2989540
MCROBBIE, Cpl, George, 2875976
McVEY, Pte, William, 2987350
MYERS, Pte, James, 2989074
PIRIE, Pte, William, 2876251
ROBERTSON, L Cpl, Alexander, 2875838
SCORGIE, Pte, John Alexander, 2888446
SCOTT, WOII (CSM), Randall, 2868908
SHERWOOD, Pte, Ian Thelwell, 2890066
SIMMONS, Pte, Anthony John, 2889827
SMITH, Pte, Alistair, 2876724
STRUTHERS, Pte, John G C, 2885710
TAYLOR, Pte, James, 2883818
TOUGH, Pte, Ernest, 2885244
WOOD, Pte, Thomas, 3322264

YOUNG, Pte, Alexander, 2874092

INTELLIGENCE CORPS
JAMIESON, Pte, John, 2871098
LESLIE, Sjt, James, 2876246
LIVESLEY, Cpl, Charles Stewart, 10350188
O'NEIL, L/Cpl, Henry, 3526874

LEICESTERSHIRE REGIMENT
ASTILL, Pte, Francis Arthur, 4860331
DAWES, Cpl, Harold, 4857329
HOLLINGSWORTH, Pte, John William, 4800333
INGLESANT, Pte, John Henry, 4860462
JEFFERY, Pte, Benjamin Jack, 4862548
JENSON, Pte, Leonard, 4858172
JESSON, Pte, Walter, 4857399
JOHNSON, Sjt, Harold Ernest, 4857601
JONES, Pte, Frederick William, 4973591
KING, Pte, John Eric, 4859889
KING, Pte, Ronald Stephen, 4863370
LAMBERT, Pte, Horace Cecil, 4857127
LEWIS, Pte, Albert William, 3383149
LEWIS, Pte, Jack, 4858495
LISSENBURGH, Pte, Charles Forrest Seymour, 4857281
LOCKTON, Pte, William Frederick, 4863380
MOORE, Pte, George, 4863400
PAGE, Pte, George, 4864646
RUDIN, Pte, Charles Thomas, 4863434
WHITEHOUSE, Sjt, Thomas, 4856881

LOYAL REGIMENT
AINSWORTH, Tpr, Henry, 3859188
ALEXANDER, Tpr, Albert, 3857282
CAMERON, Pte, James, 3854701
CHAPMAN, Pte, Harold, 3856180
CHARNLEY, Pte, John, 3857666
CHRISTIAN, Pte, Eric Edward, 3391041
DAWES, L Sjt, Harry, 3855546
DICKSON, Pte, James, 3855679
DILLON, Pte, Joseph, 3860634
DOOTSON, Sjt, John, 3857390
EDWARDS, Pte, Eli, 3858515
FOWLES, Pte, Stanley, 3859510
GRAY, Cpl, Cecil, 3856815
GREEN, Tpr, James Richard, 3858364
GREENHALGH, Pte, Frederick George, 3860361
HALSTEAD, Pte, William, 3854794
HARGREAVES, Tpr, Joseph Winston, 3858385
HARWOOD, Sjt, Albert Roylance, 3858036
HASLAM, Pte, Leslie Ronald, 3855778
HEWITT, Tpr, Samuel, 3534995
HINKS, Tpr, Joseph, 385256
HINKS, Pte, Joseph Samuel, 1733854
HOLCROFT, Tpr, John, 3850655
HOLLAND, Tpr, Ernest Johnson, 3864844
HORRABIN, Tpr, John, 3856744
HORROCKS, Tpr, James William, 3858369
HOWARD, Cpl, George Henry, 848025
HOWARD, Sjt, William James, 3857309
HUNT, Tpr, Walter Alfred, 6916720
JACKSON, Pte, James, 3848668
JACKSON, Drummer, John, 3852226
JACKSON, Pte, John, 3855979
JACKSON, Cpl, Eric, 3856391
JAMES, Pte, Jonathan William, 3851046
JONES, Pte, Horace Paspuill, 3854868
JONES, Pte, John Robert, 3854972
JONES, Pte, William, 3855383
JONES, Tpr, James, 3859262
JONES, Cpl, John Edward, 3857370

JONES, Pte, Alfred, 3856215
KEITCH, Tpr, Rodney Stuart Dacre, 4133401
KELLY, Pte, Thomas, 3856905
KELLY, Tpr, Thomas Anthony, 3856392
KENNEDY, Pte, Martin, 3860671
KENYON, Sjt, Henry, 3855089
KERSHAW, Tpr, James Howarth, 3858399
KIRBY, Pte, William Patrick, 3863869
KNIGHT, Tpr, Albert Edward, 6915339
KNOCKTON, Pte, Dennis, 3855908
LATCHFORD, Pte, James Morris, 3858427
LAWSON, Capt, Arthur Hamilton, 75799
LAWTON, Tpr, Richard, 6915238
LEACH, Pte, Francis, 3856389
LEE, Cpl, Albert, 3854674
LEE, Cpl, Cyril Charles, 3858418
LEIGH, C Sjt, Thomas, 3854810
LINNEY, L Cpl, Thomas, 3856420
LITTLE, Sjt, Stanley Wells, 3855148
LITTLEFAIR, Pte, Arthur, 3856520
LOCKE, Pte, Henry, 3852192
LONGDEN, Tpr, William, 3857122
LOWRY, Pte, Frederick, 3856440
LUCAS, Tpr, Lawrence, 3859111
LYTHGOE, Tpr, Peter, 3856528
MARSDEN, Pte, John, 3858572
MARSDEN, Pte, Joseph, 3854119
MARSON, Tpr, Arthur Ernest, 6969216
MASSEY, Tpr, Sidney, 4133296
MCARDLE, Tpr, Albert, 3859279
MCCARTHY, Pte, William, 3954300
McDUFF, Sjt, George, 3855399
McFADDEN, WOII (CSM), Hugh, 3851920
MCFARLAND, WO II (SSM), Douglas George, 3858373
MCFARLANE, Pte, David, 3855690
McGRATH, Tpr, Patrick Edward, 3857095
McGRORY, Cpl, John, 3315841
MCGUIRE, Cpl, John Munro, 3311890
McGUIRE, Sjt, James, 3855762
McGUIRE, Tpr, Thomas, 3310949
MCIVER, Pte, George, 3857701
MCKEON, Sjt, Thomas Peter, 3855325
MORRIS, Tpr, Walker Charles Thomas, 3859110
MULLEN, Tpr, Joseph, 3857387
NOWLAND, Pte, James Joseph, 3851970
O'CONNELL, Bdsmn, Michael, 3855030
PALMER, Pte, William, 3856193
PAXTON, LCpl, James, 3859191
PHILLIPS, Tpr, James, 4133269
PRIESTLEY, Pte, John, 3319117
PRIOR, Sjt, Thomas, 3854144
PYE, Pte, William, 3856416
RICHARDS, Tpr, Thomas Couch, 4132824
RICHARDS, Tpr, William Cyril, 4133377
ROE, Tpr, William Nicholas, 4133219
ROPER, Tpr, Harold, 3859202
ROSTRON, Tpr, Henry, 3855868
SANDERSON, Pte, Alfred, 3854638
SHAW, Pte, John, 3858915
SHAW, Pte, Thomas, 3859550
SHIPP, L Sjt, Ken William, 3854676
SHORE, Tpr, Robert Taylor, 4131663
SKERRETT, Tpr, Joseph, 3859311
SMALL, Tpr, Jack, 3855291
SMEDLEY, Tpr, William, 3857366
SMETHURST, Tpr, James, 3857243
SMITH, Pte, Arthur, 3851623
SMITH, Tpr, Henry, 3865430
SMITH, Pte, Robert Henry, 3856196
SNELL, Pte, Vincent Roy, 3855026

SOUTHWARD, Pte, Jack, 3858618
TAYLOR, Tpr, Henry, 4133274
TAYLOR, Tpr, Jonathan, 3865206
TERRY, Cpl, John, 3855492
THORPE, Tpr, Joseph, 3854145
TURNER, Tpr, Alfred, 3858396
WADESON, Tpr, Albert, 3522224
WALKER, Tpr, Peter, 3856809
WALLACE, Tpr, Alec Henry, 3857375
WEBSTER, Tpr, John, 3859335
WEEDS, Pte, Charles, 3855050
WEST, Tpr, Frederick, 3855885
WHITE, Pte, Cecil James, 3855774
WHITE, Tpr, Arthur Alfred, 3533216
WHITTLE, L Sjt, Frank, 3857142
WILSON, Pte, Ronald, 803722
WOOD, Tpr, John William, 3859333
WOODHOUSE, Pte, John Henry, 3854350
WOODS, Sjt, Albert, 3855327
WORDEN, Tpr, Richard, 3856874
WRIGHT, Pte, Thomas Arthur Leslie, 3769524

MANCHESTER REGIMENT
ALLISON, Pte, Geoffrey Amos, 3530481
ARCHDALE, Pte, James, 3535904
AXON, L Sjt, John, 3525605
BARBER, Drmr, Arthur, 3523637
BARCROFT, Pte, Arthur Weaver, 3526628
BARLOW, Pte, Ernest, 3533995
BARNES, L Cpl, John Stephen, 3534705
BARTLEY, L Pte, Maurice, 3528421
BAXTER, Pte, Arnold, 3533260
BAYBUTT, Pte, Ernest, 3529192
BEAVAN, Pte, Dennis, 3529493
BEECH, L Cpl, Howard, 3533994
BENNETT, Pte, Arthur, 4124925
BENNETT, Pte, Thomas Frederick, 3529281
BENZ, Pte, William, 3536013
BERESFORD, Pte, Albert, 3531139
BERRY, Pte, William Ernest, 3528955
BETHELL, L Sjt, Stanley, 3523132
BIRCH, Pte, William, 3528790
BIRKIN, Pte, Arthur, 3527903
BLOUNT, Sjt, Percy, 3526477
BOARDMAN, Pte, Frank, 782196
BOSTOCK, Cpl, Harry, 3529632
BRANT, Pte, Harold Edwin, 3526576
BROAD, Pte, William, 3530014
BROWN, Pte, Arthur, 3532988
BROWN, L Cpl, Jack, 3533726
BULLARD, Pte, Jack, 3529585
BURGESS, Pte, Leo, 3531371
BURKE, Pte, William, 3528294
CAIRNS, Pte, William, 3525579
CALE, Pte, George, 3534632
CARTWRIGHT, Pte, John, 3525912
CASSIDY, Pte, James, 3526926
CHADWICK, Pte, Jack, 3528720
CHAMPION, Pte, John, 3529456
CHILTON, Pte, Thomas, 3532970
CHINN, Pte, James, 3525866
CHURCHILL, Pte, Cyril Harry, 3526840
CLAYTON, Pte, James, 3533839
CLAYTON, Bdsmn, John Joseph, 3527995
CLEMMET, L Cpl, George, 3532956
CONNOR, Pte, Edward, 3529305
COONEY, Pte, Stephen, 3526890
COPE, Cpl, Arthur, 3526875
CORNWELL, L Cpl, Leslie Corless, 3534668
COX, Pte, Stanley, 3525934

CRIMES, Pte, Thomas William, 3534021
CROMPTON, Pte, Joseph Henry, 3533019
DALTON, Pte, Ernest, 3531435
DANDO, Pte, Ernest, 3525720
DARLINGTON, Pte, William, 3528089
DAVENPORT, Pte, Thomas, 4125064
DAVIES,L/Sjt,John,3527196
DAVIS, Pte, Edward R, 3535922
DENTON, Pte, Richard, 3521848
DICKENS, Pte, Thomas, 3534672
DIFFIN, Cpl, David, 3527018
DIMELOR, Sjt, Arthur, 3528206
DOUGHTON, Pte, Lewis Arnold, 3529676
DOWLING, Pte, Dominic, 3534008
DOWNES, Pte, Edward, 3528208
DUCKWORTH, Pte, Joseph, 3528508
DUNHAM, Pte, Willard Fred, 3534658
DURHAM, Pte, Charles, 3528348
DYSON, Pte, Fred, 3528227
EATON, Pte, Cornelius, 3530308
EDDLESTONE, Pte, Frank, 3535923
ELFORD,Pte,Herbert,3529631
EVANS, Pte, Benjamin, 3530348
EVANS, Cpl, Thomas, 3527820
FIELDEN, Pte, John, 3536024
FINNEY, Pte, John, 3534025
FISH, Pte, James Ralph, 3528937
FLANAGAN, L Cpl, Michael, 3527762
FORSTER, Pte, Norman, 3534113
FRANCIS, Pte, Ernest Robert John, 5829782
FRISBY, Pte, Leonard Ernest, 3527007
GAIDA, Pte, John Frederick, 3532879
GALLAGHER, L Sjt, Francis Angus, 3528337
GALLAGHER, Pte, Joseph, 3534116
GARNER, Pte, Harold, 3534681
GASKIN, Pte, Arthur, 3528419
GIBB, Pte, Donald, 3533938
GILBODY, L Cpl, Thomas Edward, 3533791
GILLIGHAN, Pte, John Michael, 3534722
GOLDSTONE, Pte, Bernard, 3535927
GRAHAM, Pte, Allan Beatham, 3526683
GREEN, Pte, Thomas Charles, 3528631
GREENWOOD, L Cpl, Harold, 3534729
GREENWOOD, Pte, Stanley, 3534028
GREGG, Pte, Allan, 3529075
GREGG, Pte, Frank, 3528293
GRIFFITHS, Pte, Cyril, 3528211
HALL, Pte, Clifford, 3533002
HALLOWS, L Cpl, Albert, 3523721
HALLSOR, Pte, Samuel, 3534646
HALLWORTH, Pte, Thomas, 3532993
HANLEY, Pte, Harold, 4613915
HARDY, Pte, Fred, 3528270
HARGREAVES, Pte, Harry Henry, 3529832
HARTLEY, Pte, Albert, 3534647
HASTE, Pte, John Frederick, 3534648
HEATON, L Cpl, Robert, 3533894
HESLOP, Pte, Herbert, 3526464
HIGGINS, Pte, Thomas, 3528452
HIGH, Pte, Alfred, 3534707
HILTON, Pte, Fred, 3534129
HINTON, Pte, Charles, 3530312
HOLLAND, Pte, Arthur, 4746950
HOLROYD, L Cpl, Joseph, 3526818
HOUGHTON, L Cpl, John, 3525406
HOWARTH, Pte, Herbert, 3532964
HOWARTH, Pte, John, 3529294
HULLEY, Pte, Joseph Edward, 4612581
ISHERWOOD,Lt,George Herbert,93646
JACKSON, L/Cpl, John, 3528007

JACKSON, Pte, Fred, 3534048
JACKSON, Pte, John, 3528193
JACKSON, Pte, Thomas, 3529270
JEFFERS, Pte, Matthew, 3529602
JONES, Pte, William Alfred, 3532422
KELLY, Pte, Stanley, 3527617
KILGARRIFF, Pte, Bernard, 3533874
KNIGHT, Pte, Cyril Reginald, 3529774
LANE, Pte, George, 2054067
LANE, L Cpl, Wilfred, 3523834
LANGFORD, Pte, David, 3529595
LAWTON, Pte, William, 3526159
LE PAGE, WO II (RQMS), Edward, 3514357
LEATHWAITE, Pte, Victor Oliver, 3534662
LEE, Cpl, Fred, 3526892
LEE, Pte, Thomas, 3534698
LEWIS, Pte, William, 5048412
LIGHTFOOT, Pte, Joseph, 3525868
LUCY, WO II (CSM), Joseph, 3521762
MAGUIRE, L Cpl, John, 3533055
MARKEY, Pte, Robert, 3535899
McDONALD, Pte, James Leitch Lommond, 3526896
McGLYNN, L Sjt, Martin, 3524972
MCMILLAN, Pte, George William, 3572931
MERRY, Pte, Charles Norman, 3526124
MOORES, Pte, Frank, 3527283
MOSS, L Cpl, Edward Richard, 3528347
NOLAN, Pte, Thomas, 3527187
O'GARR, Pte, Cyril Charles, 3528185
O'NEIL, LCpl, Abraham, 4613689
O'REILLY, Pte, George, 3533999
OXLEY, Pte, Charles Clifford, 3534635
PARKINSON, Pte, Edward, 3529601
PATTEN, Pte, James, 3528260
PIKE, Pte, Arthur Leslie, 3528741
PLATT, Cpl, John, 3528066
PODMORE, Pte, William Albert, 3533005
PRITCHARD, Sjt, Sidney Allen, 3526893
PRIZEMAN, Pte, Frederick James, 3526564
PRUDEN, Pte, Cecil Peter, 3530202
RAGGETT, Pte, Alfred, 3526943
REID, Pte, Charles, 3529613
REYNOLDS, Pte, Edwin, 3526769
RICHARDS, L Cpl, Austen Edward, 3533765
RILEY, Pte, Frank Hugh, 3522940
ROBINSON, Pte, Harry, 3532950
ROBINSON, Pte, William, 3527588
RODAN, Pte, William Percy, 3528718
ROGERS, Pte, Thomas William, 3530483
ROGERS, Pte, William, 3532942
ROWBOTTOM, Pte, Thomas, 3528297
ROYLE, L Cpl, James, 3533836
RUDD, Pte, Albert William, 3530394
RUDD, Pte, James, 3532965
SATERLEY, Pte, John Frederick, 3528422
SHAW, Pte, William, 3527858
SIDLOW, Pte, Frederick Arthur, 3524363
SMITH, L Cpl, Eric, 3533973
SMITH, Pte, Harold, 3532927
SMITH, Pte, James, 3535969
SMITH, Pte, James Alfred, 4125490
STANTON, Cpl, Maxwell Taylor, 3528123
SWINSCOE, Pte, George Heald Fenton, 3528186
TAYLOR, Pte, Alan George, 3526216
TAYLOR, Pte, Frank, 3526394
TAYLOR, Cpl, James, 3445333
THOMAS, Pte, Walter Leslie, 3526690
THOMAS, Pte, William, 851137
TOPPER, Pte, Albert, 3385126
TOWNLEY, Pte, Harold, 3525986

TREVOR, L Cpl, Kenneth, 3533947
VALLELY, Pte, Robert, 3526953
WALSH, Pte, David, 3530376
WALTERS, Pte, Stuart Vaughan, 3533953
WALTON, L Cpl, James, 3529752
WATSON, Pte, Thomas, 3524022
WHYATT, Pte, Joseph, 3532166
WORTHINGTON, Pte, Thomas Henry, 3522483

NORTHAMPTONSHIRE REGIMENT
MASON, Pte, Oliver, 5882672

PIONEER CORPS
JONES, Pte, Hugh, 4194743
LIPTROTT, Cpl, Sidney, 13056229

QUEEN ALEXANDERS IMPERIAL ARMY NURSING SERVICE
JONES, Principal Matron, Violet Maud Evelyn, 206238
LE BLANC SMITH, Sister Beatrice, 206286
McCLELLAND, Sister, Alice Margaret Colquhoun, 208809

RECONNAISSANCE CORPS
ASHCROFT, Tpr, Wilfred, 3858398
BAXENDALE, Tpr, Joseph Henry, 3859139
BERVOETS, Tpr, William John Baker, 4132790
BIRD, Tpr, George, 4201196
BLINKHORN, Tpr, Robert, 3865286
BROWN, Tpr, Thomas, 3846310
BURROWS, Trp, Ernest, 3857284
BURTON, Tpr, Harold, 3860418
CASWELL, Tpr, Thomas, 3865410
CHALLINOR, Tpr, Thomas Frederick, 3858014
CONNOLLY, L Cpl, Andrew, 3859220
CROMPTON, Cpl, Albert Milnes, 3859212
CULLEN, Tpr, Francis, 6918678
DEARDEN, Tpr, James, 3856664
DONOVAN, L Cpl, Thomas Henry Peter, 6915460
ECCLES, Tpr, Wilfred, 3859133
FARISH, Tpr, Joseph, 3859150
FINAN, Tpr, John, 3860915
FORSTER, Tpr, Henry Robert, 6914842
PAGE, Tpr, Alfred James, 6915007
PARKER, Tpr, Jack, 3859185

ROYAL ARMOURED CORPS
JARVIS, Cpl, Frank William, 554343
JONES, Tpr, Hamilton Harold, 5567732
KING, Tpr, Harold Percival, 7925299
MACLACHLAN, Tpr, Robert, 7899119

ROYAL ARMY ORDNANCE CORPS
ALMOND, Pte, William James, 7652059
AMBROSE, Pte, Charles Frederick, 4349770
BARRS, Cpl, Jack Alwyn, 7650949
BASS, L Cpl, Alfred, 4984791
BATES, Pte, George, 10533164
BEECH, Sjt, Jack, 7610254
BEETON, Pte, Joseph Ernest, 10535956
BENNETT, Pte, Wilfred Horace, 5441576
BOYLE, Cpl, Edward, 7632643
BRANDISH, Pte, William, 3440742
BRIDGELAND, Pte, Herbert Charles, 7604782
CAIRNS, Pte, Herbert, 10559347
CONNELL, Pte, John Edward, 6898976
COPESTAKE, S Sjt, Arthur, 4189961
DAVIES, Pte, Fred, 10532443
DAVIS, Pte, Jack Reginald, 7624424
DAY, Sjt, Leslie George, 7610726
DEARLE, Pte, Frank Henry, 2566771
DEDMAN, Pte, Edgar, 10535114

DONALDSON, Pte, George Thomas, 7626509
DOYLE, WO/1, John Henan, 5335423
DRIVER, Pte, Arthur Edward, 10535151
DURRANT, Pte, Norman Sidney, 10532202
ENTWISTLE, Pte, John James, 10553196
FRAPWELL, Sjt, Ronald Harrison, 7628250
GILES, Pte, James, 3311919
GILL, Pte, Albert Edward, 7633132
GILLETT, Pte, Arthur, 7604123
GREENACRE, L Cpl, John William, 7603777
GRIFFIN, Pte, Kenneth Compton, 10541955
HAMILTON, Cpl, James, 7609254
HARBISHER, Sjt, Gordon, 7628319
HARWOOD, Lt, George Herbert, 171616
HAYES, Sjt, Robert Cecil, 7648503
HEIRONS, Pte, William Alfred, 10561346
HINDLE, Cpl, Edward, 7610058
HOLMES, Pte, George William, 7626846
HONEYBOURNE, Pte, Alfred William Charles, 7632312
HUGGARD, Pte, Cecil Robert, 10555628
HUGO, L Sjt, James, 7587401
HYLES, Pte, Arthur Leonard, 10552280
IRVINE, Pte, John, 3045511
IVES, Lt-Col, Augustus Harry, 70684
JACK, Pte, James, 7655764
JAMES, Pte, John Frederick, 7607558
JARVIS, Cpl, Frank William, 554343
JERVIS, Pte, George, 7643273
JOHNSON, Pte, Albert Edward, 764597
JOHNSON, L Cpl, Reginald William, 7635518
JONES, Tpr, Hamilton Harold, 5567732
JONES, S Sjt, George Spencer, 7618054
JONES, Pte, John Frederick, 5243803
JONES, sjt, John Trevor, 7607620
JONES, Sjt, John William, 7607976
JONES, L Cpl, Kenneth, 7607977
JUDD, Pte, Alfred A, 1054474
KERR, Pte, John Harrison Alexander, 7613759
KETTLE, Pte, Sidney George, 7630592
KING, Tpr, Harold Percival, 7925299
KINSLEY, Pte, Cecil Gordon, 7654688
LALLY, Pte, William, 3864847
LAMBERT, WO II (SQMS), Howard Reginald, 7592627
LAWRENCE, Pte, Peter, 7607779
LLOYD, Pte, Robert Charles, 7628676
LOUDON, L Cpl, Eric Douglas, 7604859
LOWN, Pte, Sidney Herbert, 7635424
LUCAS, Pte, Francis Godfrey, 7592071
LUMBER, Pte, William George, 5730112
MACKIE, Sjt, Alfred, 7642587
MACLACHLAN, Tpr, Robert, 7899119
MAUND, Pte, Royston, 10556875
McCOLM, Sjt, Arthur John, 7588959
McIVOR, Cpl, William John, 2877464
McKERCHER, WO II, Ewen Kennedy, 7591412
McMEEKIN, Pte, William Gamble, 241080
McSWAN, Pte, Donald, 10548548
NAPIER, Pte, Archiblad, 6469650
NICHOLLS, Cpl, Reginald Albert, 7664816
OSBORNE, Pte, Albert Arthur, 7648058
PEACE, Cpl, Clarence Alban, 7622365
POLLARD, S Sjt, Cyril Jack, 7585470
PRESTNEY, Pte, Jack Ernest, 7649980
PYLE, Pte, Albert William, 7607961
RALPH, Pte, Leonard Ernest, 7647408
RAVEN, WO I (Sub Condr), Ronald Eric, 7609654
RENFREW, Sjt, Arthur, 7662261
RICHARDSON, Pte, Frederick Thomas, 7654958
RITSON, Pte, George, 13068313
ROBERTS, Pte, Harry, 3137014

ROBINSON, Pte, Eustace Henry, 10550009
ROGERS, Pte, Ernest Jack, 10533358
SHIMMIN, Pte, John, 3781486 SIMPSON, Pte, Richard, 7632947
SMITH, L Cpl, Donald George Armstrong, 7648438
SMITH, Sjt, William James, 5763672
SPENCER, Pte, Arthur William, 7651695
STEPHEN, Pte, Allan Garth, 7649054
SYMINGTON, Cpl, John Patrick, 7609461
TEGG, Pte, Fredrick George, 11057220
THOMAS, L Cpl, Francis, 2929076
WHITE, WO I (Condr), William, 759613
WHITTON, Cpl, Jack Herbert, 7618441
WHYTE, Pte, Robert Clark, 7622611
WILLIAMS, Pte, Harry Idris, 7618622
WILSON, L Sjt, Arthur Robert John, 7639921
WILSON, Pte, Philip, 1579641
WINBORN, Pte, Adrian Herbert Dudley, 7636119
WOODHALL, Pte, Kenneth, 10558863

ROYAL ARMY MEDICAL CORPS
ADAMS, Pte, Roger, 7394281
ALEXANDER, Dvr, David George, T/81208
ASHWORTH, Pte, Charles, 7394190
BELTON, Pte, Arthur Reginald, 7374104
BIGNELL, Pte, Arthur Edward Victor, 7347978
CAMPBELL, Pte, Francis Patrick, 7346496
CAUSEBROOK, L Cpl, Francis Charles, 7520270
CLARK, Pte, Reginald Arthur, 7368806
DEAN, Cpl, Reginald Albert, 7344310
DEVERELL, Capt, Henry Alexander, 122725
DOVE, Pte, Leonard Maple, 7391385
DUTTON, Pte, James Henry, 7394225
EVANS, S Sjt, William Prys, 7518179
FITZPARTICK, Pte, Patrick, 7380523
FRANCIS, Pte, Arthur Walter, 5434600
GALLIARD, Pte, Ronald Arthur, 7359944
HAMILTON, Cpl, John Alexander, 7386509
HOARE, L Cpl, Reginald Slader, 7368906
INNES, Pte, J A, 7532596
IRVINE, Lt, Donald Ferguson, 223811
ISAAC, Cpl, Idris Owen, 7519883
JAQUES, Sjt, Wilfred, 4033251
JOHNSTON, Sjt, Gilbert, 7263144
JONES, Pte, John, 7357936
JONES, Pte, Robert, 7362219
JOSEPH, Pte, AW, 7524566
KENNETH, Amb Sep, , 86976
KENNEY, Pte, Kelvin, 7535040
KIM LYE SENG, Pte, , 7524511
KLYNE, Cpl, Martin Phillip, 7532504
KNOX, Sjt, Leslie, 4683662
LAYCOCK, Pte, Kenneth, 7374015
LAZAROO, Pte, L,
LEE, Pte, Eric Joseph, 7533060
LEONARD, Sjt, Bert, 7260525
LEWIS, Lt, Arthur Elroy, M/22266
LEWIS, Maj, Clifford Longden, 58964
LEWIS, Pte, Raymond, 7372833
LILLICO, Capt, James Walsh, MZ/17462
LIM, Pte, Herbert, 7524474
LOGAN, Pte, John Hunter, 2885202
LOGAN, Maj, William Robert, 223436
LOVESAY, Pte, Edward, 7266227
LOY KEK KOOK, Pte, ,
LUA PECK JIM, Pte, , 7524491
MACE, Cpl, Jack Vere, 7261427
MacKENZIE, L Cpl, Donald John, 7262383
MARTIN, Pte, William Henry, 7519520
McDOUGALL, Pte, Thomas, 7519446
McKEEGAN, Pte, Hugh, 7392185

MELLOR, Pte, George Henry Thomas, 7374095
PUDNEY, Pte, Eric Ernest, 7368826
SAGGERS, Pte, William John, 5989364
SHORT, Sjt, Jack, 7262401
STRINGER, Cpl, Douglas Neville, 7374065
UNDERHILL, Cpl, Harry, 6400858

ROYAL ARMY SERVICE CORPS
ABLE,Dvr,Frederick, T/242430
ABLEWHITE,Pte,Donald Leslie,S/6093480,
ACKLAND, WOI (MSM), Albert Thomas, T/86803
ADAM,Cpl,Henry Venters,S/2979711,
ADAMS,Lt Col,David,Abro/139,
ADAMS,Lt,Alfred Cyril,T/162,
ADAMS,Dvr,Richard Thomas,T/142645,
ALBERTS, Dvr, Alfred,T/3390643
ALDERTON,Cpl,John Leslie,S/158759,
ALEXANDER,Dvr,David George,T/81208
ALIMONDA, Pte,Lewis Augustus,S/261134
ALLAN, Dvr, William, T/97685
ALLEN, Sjt, Albert George, T/97695
ALLEN,L/Cpl,Percy Scott,T/154768,
ALLEN,Cpl,Campbell,T/100575,
ALLEN, Sjt, Albert George, T/97695
ANDERSON,Dvr,John,T/112585,
ANDERSON,Dvr,Percy,T/156324,
ANDREW,Sjt,George Simpson,S/1983921,
ANDREWS, Maj, Alfred James, 101227
ARCHER, Dvr, Philip Allen, T/141006
ARMSTRONG, Pte, Robert Joseph, T/214228
ARNOLD,Maj, John Gooday,135351,
ARNOLD,Dvr, J,T/14914742,
ARNOLD,L/Cpl, John, 276035,
ARNOTT,Cpl,Frederick John,T/7876-81,
ARNOTT,L/Cpl,T,T/14834080,
ASHBY, Sjt, George Geoffrey, S/116920
ASHLEY, Sjt, Reginald Joseph, S/862147
ASHTON, Pte, John, S/243216
ASKEW,Dvr,David Charles,T/168451,
ASPINALL,Dvr,Thomas Henry,T/199982,
ATKINSON,Cpl,Russell, A/11,
AULT,Pte,John Thomas,T/187071,
AUSTIN, Dvr, Frederick Charles, T/276415
AUSTIN,Dvr,Stanley,T/274096,
AYLETT, Pte, Cyril Henry, T/259085
BACON,L/Cpl,Albert,T/5572520,
BAILEY,Pte,William Percy Adolph,S/261135,
BAILEY,Pte,Ronald Arthur,T/206106,
BAKER, Sjt, Dennis, 10714194
BAKER, Dvr, Charles Henry James, T/219889
BALL,L/Cpl,Leslie,T/181569,
BANKS, Dvr, Victor William, T/217698
BANKS,Cpl,Michael Francis,T/3854595,
BANKS,Dvr,Cyril,T/50262,
BANKS, Dvr, Victor William, T/217698
BARDSLEY,Dvr,Herbert,T/281552,
BARKLEY, Capt, Edward Trevor Yarker, 123336
BARLOW, Dvr, Harry, T/125749
BARLOW,Cpl,Stanley,T/3529686,
BARLOW,L/Cpl,James,T/255329,
BARNES,Dvr,Reginald Albert George,T/273821,
BARNES,L/Cpl,Frederick Stephen,S/252189,
BARNETT,L/Cpl,Norman Joseph,T/177882,
BARNETT,Pte,Charles Joseph,S/143866,
BARNSLEY,Pte,Leonard,T/170440,
BARROW,Dvr,Frederick,T/58830,
BARTLE, Pte, Jack, T/229796
BARTLETT, Dvr, Leslie Maurice Frederick, T/5730153
BARTROM,Dvr,John Robert,T/231020,
BASHFORD, CQMS, Charles, T/36766

BASTON, Dvr, George William, T/194638
BATE,Dvr,Joseph,T/113659,
BATES,Dvr,Edward George,T/67550,
BEATTIE,L/Cpl,William,T/3460571,
BECK,Sjt,Graham Eugene,T/108045,
BELL, Dvr, William Sparks, T/55814
BELLRINGER, Cpl, Francis Arthur Herbert,T/118234
BENISON, Lt, Eric William Archdale,71839
BENNETT, Dvr, Leslie John, T/203516
BENNETT,Dvr,John,T/160562,
BERESFORD, L Cpl, James, T/114202
BEVAN,Sjt,Charles,T/1049795,
BIBB,Pte,Alfred George,T/261138,
BICKFORD,Dvr,William Alfred,T/864290
BIGGS, Dvr, Reginald Mortimer, T/151814
BILLINGS, Dvr, Ernest Albert, T/233016
BINSTEAD, Dvr, Joseph George, T/279754
BIRD, W/O, Frederick Arthur, S116904
BISHOP,Dvr,Joseph,T/155790,
BLAKE, Cpl, Frank Richard, S/4539112
BLANCHARD, Dvr, Sydney John, T/1022523
BLOCH, Sjt, Mark, S/3533811
BLOXHAM, Sjt, Stanley James, T/87646
BOAM, Dvr, William Austen, T/108085
BOLAM, Dvr, John William, T/58090
BOLTON, Dvr, Terence Gordon, T/75064
BOSOMWORTH, Sjt, Ernest Donald Frederick, T/108246
BOWELL, Dvr, Sidney George, T/214091
BOWEN,Pte,George Thomas,S/259088,
BOWES, Dvr, Raphael,T/7045724
BOWMAN,Dvr,Harry,T/88461
BOWTLE, Pte, Leonard George, S/130233843
BRADBURY,Dvr,George,T/182738,
BRADLEY, Dvr, Arthur, T/202191
BRADNAM,Dvr,Frederick,T/245399,
BRANWHITE, Pte, Herbert Ernest, S/257948
BRATT, Pte, Eligah, T/209509
BRATT, Dvr, John Alan, T/80748
BRATT, Pte, Eligah, T/209509
BRATT, Dvr, John Alan, T/80748
BRAY, Pte, Alan George Downer, 257457
BREAME, Pte, Sidney Jonathan, T/90280
BREW,Dvr,Leonard Charles,T/253742,
BRIANT, Dvr, Henry Frederick, T/185001,
BRIGGS,Sjt,Edward,T/56089,
BRODRICK, Dvr, Cecil Bertram, T/248149,
BROOKS, Cpl, James, S/272813
BROOM, L/Cpl, John Henry, T/163272
BROUGH,L/Cpl,Arthur,T/3662562,
BROWN,Cpl,Douglas Edward,T/112377,
BROWN,Pte,James Edman,S/6149291,
BROWN,Dvr,John,T/141788,
BROWN,Dvr,John Robert,T/168164,
BROWN,Dvr,Thomas Norman,T/217950,
BROWN,Dvr, F,T/1493597,
BROWN,Dvr,Albert Arthur,T/170512,
BROWN,Dvr,Leslie,T/267504,
BRUCE, Pte, Wallace Frederick, T/2354270
BRUNTON, Dvr, George Robson, T/138652
BRYSON, Dvr, John, T/203496
BUCKTHORPE, Dvr, Thomas, T/275307
BULLIVANT,Dvr,Henry Edwin,T/80689,
BULLOCK, Dvr, Herbert Patrick, T/221848
BULMER, Sjt, Douglas, S/54485
BURKE, WO/1, Leo Joseph, S/12666
BURNETT, Capt, Joseph Duthie, 178737
BURNETT,Pte,Thomas,S/254964,
BURNETT,L/Cpl,William,T/3044168,
BURNETT, Capt, Joseph Duthie, 178737
BURRIDGE, Dvr, Edgar Thomas, T/193795

BURT, L Sjt, Frederick Joseph, T/62810
BURTON, Dvr, Arthur Frederick, T/219913
BUSBY, Sjt, J F, T/14663151
BUSH,Dvr,Thomas Henry,T/3662393,
BUTCHER, Pte, Frederick William, S/5775474
BUTCHER, Dvr, Herbert Samuel, T/279759
BUTTERWORTH, Dvr, Harry, T/187242
BUTTERWORTH, Dvr, James, T/197776
CAMERON, Dvr, Crawford McFarlane, T/179738
CAMERON,L/Cpl,Charles Fox,T/206056,
CAMERON, Dvr, Crawford McFarlane, T/179738
CAMPBELL, Pte, Daniel, T/86350
CARNEGIE,Dvr,Alexander,T/234415,
CARSON, Sjt, John Gilbert, T/61640
CARTER, Dvr, Thomas Roland, T/234722
CASTLE, Pte, Douglas Lewis, S/254701
CHADWICK, L/Sjt, Walter, T/166252
CHANDLER, Cpl, Edward, T/169695
CHAPMAN,Dvr,Frederick William,T/231141,
CHAPMAN, Dvr, William Henry, T/37702
CHAPMAN, Dvr, C C G, T/14941623
CHARLES, Pte, Arthur Eric, S/7662255
CHARNAUD, Maj, Kenrick Archibald Worsley, 89027
CHELL, Cpl, Reginald, T/14366451
CHERRETT, Dvr Arthur Edward, T/204524
CHRISTIAN,Dvr,William Lawrence,T/3780756,
CLARK,Dvr,Walter Charles,T/275479,
CLARK, Dvr, Henry William, T/142245
CLARKE, Pte, Arthur Reginald, S/274905
CLARKE, Cpl, Reginald Horace, T/5241278
CLARKE,Sjt,Fred,T/25458,
CLARKE,Pte,Geoffrey,S/57286,
CLARKE, Pte, Arthur Reginald, S/274905
CLARKE, Cpl, Reginald Horace, T/5241278
CLDER,Dvr,Frederick,T/5339471,
CLEGG, Dvr, John Henry, T/107161
CLEWS, Pte, Bernard Henry, S/4749673
CLIST, Pte, Herbert John, T/107158
COE-WELCH,L/Cpl,Eric,T/162374,
COLE, Cpl, G F, S/14676884
COLES,Dvr,Charles Philip,T/179379,
COLLINS, Pte, Patrick Barrington, S/3863786
COLLINS, Dvr, Thomas Samuel, T/170504
COLMAN,Pte,Raymond Arthur,T/272827,
COLMER, Cpl, Thomas Lewis, T/67667
COLTMAN, Dvr, Noel Birbeck, T/185007
CONNELLY, Pte, Alfred William, S/191011
CONWAY, Dvr, Donald Somerville, T/281554
COOKE, 2/Lt, H O P, EC/2459
COOMBES, Dvr, Charles William, T/168726
COOPER, L Cpl, Herbert Henry, T/125119
CORNISH, Dvr, William Harold, T/226728
COUCHMAN, Dvr, William Thomas James, T/250228
COULTON, Dvr, George Jackson, T/3712203
COWLEY,Pte,Harold Ernest,T/208023,
COWLING, Dvr, Sidney, T/139801
COX, S Sjt, Charles Harry, S/74514
COX,Sjt,Samuel,T/65017,
COX,Maj,William Charles,216439,
CRABTREE, Dvr, John Leslie Francis, T/131221
CRICKETT, Dvr, George Frederick, T/91632
CROSSLEY,L/Cpl,Pearson,T/275802,
CROWTHER, Dvr, Allan, T/279213
CRUIKSHANK, Dvr, Joseph Brooks, T/3194308
CUBBIN, Dvr, Harry, T/272655
CULE, Pte, Raymond Thomas, S/143578
CULLEN, Dvr, Edward, T/1031954
CULLINANE, Cpl, James, T/2876333
CUNNINGHAM, Dvr, Charles, T/197207
CURSON,Dvr,H,T/1497742,

CURSON, Dvr, Benjamin George, T/266599
DAGNELL, Pte, Richard Joseph, T/244951
DALTON, Pte, Charles William, S/261144
DANGERFIELD, Sjt, John, T/49045
DANIL,Pte,J,A/428,
DARVELL, Dvr, Albert Charles, T/6723084
DAVEY, Pte, Norman Reuben James, 10631134
DAVIDSON, Pte, Alfred Francis, S/3859829
DAVIES, Pte, Albert, T/194107
DAVIES,Dvr,Reginald John Herbert,T/170158,
DAWES, Dvr, Cyril Raymond, T/164653
DAWKINS, Dvr, Thomas James, T/265198
DAWNEY, Dvr, Albert Joseph, T/254306
DAWSON, Dvr, Walter, T/236901
DAWSON, Dvr, Philip, T/14446431
DE-CRUZ, Pte, Donald, A/8679
DEADMAN, Dvr, Tom, T/273826
DEAMER, Dvr, Stanley, T/227538
DEDMAN, Dvr, Frederick Charles French, T/163297
DENGERFIELD, Pte, Walter John, S/225755
DENNIS, Pte, Alexander George, S/68648
DEVESON, Sjt, Richard George, T/6279721
DEVINE, Pte, Percy Henry, S/248270
DIBBEN, Pte, Arthur, S/6214541
DICK, Pte, Albert Francis, S/271543
DICKIE, Sjt, William, T/48772
DICKIE, Dvr, Alexander, T/168814
DICKINSON, Dvr, John Franklin, T/275324
DICKSON, S Sjt, James Johnston, T/65753
DINGLEY, Pte, Ernest Ralph, T/4922511
DIPNALL, Dvr, John Denton, T/92451
DOBBS, Dvr, William, T/163585
DOBNEY, S/Sjt, John Gordon, S/57071
DOLAN, Pte, John, T/115301
DONALD, Sjt, Frank, T/29791890
DONALDSON, Dvr, James Murrey, T/274164
DOONER, Cpl, Edward, T/7813190
DOUGLAS, Dvr, Thomas Lennie, T/83156
DOWTHWAITE, L Cpl, James Henry, T/163590
DOYLE,Cpl, Patrick Joseph Benedict, S/137947
DRUMMOND, Pte, Victor, S/7662263
DUNCAN, Dvr, James Cameron, T/246354
DURBRIDGE, Dvr, John Arthur, T/6711094
DURWARD, Dvr, Lawrence Chapman, T/185044
DYE, Pte, Walter Howe, S222902
DYKINS, Dvr, Osmond Kenneth, T/198401
EADE, Dvr, Harry Hubert, T/164709
EASTMAN, Pte, Ernest John, S/244514
EDGELL, Dvr, William Albert, T/14420957
EDGERLEY, Lt, Cecil Beresford, 227380
EDMONDSON,Dvr,Frank,T/3456500,
EDWARDS,Sjt,James Osbourne, 116917,
EDWARDS, Cpl, Robert Henry Albert, T/173820
EDWARDS, Dvr, Benjamin, T/65335
EDWARDS, Dvr, Sydney Thomas, T/217746
EDWARDS, L/Cpl, Albert, T/79105
EDWARDS, Sjt, Leslie Ernest, T/14430497
EGGINTON, Dvr, Albert Edward, T/1063892
ELLIOTT, Dvr, John Denholm, T/279103
ELLIOTT,Pte,John Charles,S/243241,
ELLIOTT, Dvr, John Denholm, T/279103
ELLIS, Dvr, David Edward, T/1064063
ELLISON,Dvr,William Henry,T/182525,
EVANS, Sjt, Robert Myrddin, T/199120
EVANS, Pte, Arthur John, T/227164
FAHY, Dvr, John Walston, T/242216
FAINT, Dvr, James William, T/205181
FAIRWEATHER,Dvr,Robert,T/254315,
FARNELL, Dvr, Robert, T/279540
FEATHER, S/Sjt, George, T/50777

FEATHERS, Capt, John Normansell, 138995
FEEHALLY, Lt/Col, John Tarrant, 40614
FELTON, Cpl, Edward Ernest, S/159113
FERGUSON, Dvr, Robert Sproat, T/110996
FERNIE, Dvr, Ernest Alexander, T/168605
FIELD, Pte, Joseph Henry, S/248984
FIELDEN, Pte, Richard John, S/5504180
FIRTH, L/Cpl, Ernest, T/75809
FITCHES, Dvr, Leonard Charles, T/226451
FITZGERALD, Dvr, Edward, T/249824
FORBES, Dvr, George, T/274168
FORSTER, L/Cpl, William Tweedy, S/806461
FOSS, Capt, C H, 320248
FOSTER,Cpl,John Robert,4033734
FOSTER, Dvr, George Monty, T/155605
FOWLER, Pte, Eric, S/259620
FREARSON, Pte, Alan Stephen, T/183685
FROST, Dvr, Frederick Douglas, T/168371
FRY, L/Cpl, James George, T/226118
FULLER, Pte, Jim, S/5957314
GALLAGHER, L/Cpl, John Martin, T/272470
GALSWORTHY, Dvr, Lewis Thomas, T/181578
GAME, Pte, James Alfred Walter Leslie, T/177910
GARBETT, Sjt, Alfred Leslie, T/142371
GAREY, Dvr, John, T/549830
GARNETT, Dvr, Edward Alfred, T/242471
GARTON, Dvr, Mervyn Frederick George, T/142236
GASS, Dvr, Reginald Albert, T/217759
GEDDES, Cpl, Ian Douglas, S/3859383
GIBBONS,SQMS,William Charles,T/116909,
GIBBS, Dvr, George Anderson, T/273930
GIBBS,Cpl,Albert George,T/181560,
GIBSON, Dvr, Andrew Stewart, T/111355
GILBERT, Pte, Douglas William, S/265415
GILL, S/Sjt, Arthur Charles, S/10670014
GILLINDERS, Cpl, Samual, T/232813
GILSON, Dvr, Leonard Samual, T/175394
GLAYZER, Lt, Edward Donald, 132811
GOLDING, Dvr, Charles Joseph, T/144048
GOLDSWORTHY, Sjt, Ernest Frederick, T/76451
GOODE, Dvr, James Alfred, T/178946
GORDON, Dvr, Reginald, T/128512
GOSS, Pte, Leslie, T/183530
GOUDIE, Dvr, Charles, T/227400
GOUGH, Cpl, John, T/66020
GOULD, Dvr, Arthur David, T/259622
GOULDER, Dvr, William, T/1037349
GOULDING, Dvr, Daniel, T/202170
GOWRIE, Dvr, Charles Millar, T/3061176
GRADY, Dvr, Thomas, T/255999
GRAHAM, Pte, Harold Gilberd, T/6350926
GRAHAM, Sjt, William Hussey, T/35480
GRAHAM,Dvr,S,T/192575,
GRANT, Cpl, James, T/2876752
GRASSING, L/Cpl, Sidney John, S/244244
GRAY, Cpl, Robert, T/2876275
GREY, Sjt, William Prior, T/74474
GRICE, Dvr, Leslie Clifford, T/168139
GRIFFIN, S Sjt, John Joseph Peter, S/753778
GRIFFITHS, Dvr, George Milton, T/221766
GRIFFITHS, Pte, Hywel, T/166237
GROUT, Dvr, Frederick William, T/274399
GUDGEON, Pte, Mathew William, T/3194395
GUNN, Pte, Charles Munro, T/260595
GUYLL, Dvr, George Cedric, T/274584
HACKETT,Cpl,Reginald Victor,T259307,
HADLEY, L/Cpl, Major, T/1063932
HAIG, Pte, John, S/282335
HALLAM, Dvr, John, T/274585
HALLAS, Pte, Percy, S/183150

HAMILTON, Pte, George Herbert Alexander, S/5345352
HAMMERSLEY, Sjt, Howard, T/39489
HAMMOND, Capt, E V, 355484
HANCOCK, Dvr, Sidney Bernard, T/1064240
HANKINSON, Pte, James, S/209707
HANSEN, Pte Laurence Frederick, S/265776
HARGREAVES,Pte,W,14160649,
HARGREAVES,Sjt,Thomas William,T/14160649,
HARRIES, Sjt, Emlyn, T/91304
HARRIS, Dvr, Norman Charles, T/223737
HASLAM, Dvr, Walter Philip, T/279926
HATCH, Pte, George, T/131040
HATCHER, L/Cpl, Robert James, T/222085
HATCLIFFE, L/Cpl, Harold, S/4348203
HAWDIN, Cpl, Harry, S/179534
HAWES, L Cpl, Thomas Andrew, S/5775629
HAWKES, Cpl, Vincent Keith, T/129732
HAWKES, Cpl, William Thomas Henry, T/160254
HAWKRIDGE, Dvr, Clifford, T/114720
HAWLEY,Lt,Jack Drew,216609,
HAY, Dvr, Alfred, T/109516
HAY, L/Cpl, William, S/3056490
HAYNEL, Sjt, Richard Vernon, T/190092
HAYNES, Pte, William, T/238038
HEALEY, Dvr, Thomas Edward, T/257879
HEATHCOTE, Capt, George Harry MBE, 154879
HEDGINGTON, Cpl, Allan Victor, S/137704
HEININK, Pte, Anthony Frank, S/3863451
HELLENS, L/Cpl, Mathew Henry, T/175819
HENDERSON, S/SM, Samuel, S7733822
HENWORTH, Sjt, James, T/142337
HERRIOTS, Dvr, Frederick George, T/175200
HESKETH, Cpl, Harry, T/192284
HEWITT, Dvr, Sidney Charles, T/170511
HEYWARD, Dvr, Ronald Sidney, T/259177
HICKLING, Dvr, Albert George, T/176435
HILL, Pte, Gordon Edward James, S/271547
HILL, Dvr, Richard, T/259434
HODGES, Pte, Cedric Harold, T/270409
HODGSON, L Cpl, William Earl, S/69665
HODGSON,Dvr,Hugh,T/240056,
HOLCROFT, Sjt, John Henry, T/121069
HOLE,Dvr,John Edward,T/131311,
HOLE,L/Cpl,William Leonard,T/4970081,
HOLFORD, Pte, Henry Arthur Victor, T/165791
HOLLAND, L/Sjt, George William, T/207845
HOME, L Cpl, James Laurence Forrest, T/198606
HONEY, Dvr, Montague Victor, T/168545
HORNE, Capt, Leslie Ernest, 160151
HOUGHTON, Dvr, Stanley Shakespear, T/162340
HOWARD, Dvr, William Sutton, T/3774381
HOWELL,Capt,Frederick William Henry,ST/29,
HOWELL, Sjt, Cyril Charles Henry, T/180791
HOWELL, L/Cpl, Charles, T/92509
HOWES, Dvr, Horace William Ernest, T/262774
HUGHES,S/Sjt,Wesley Arnold,S/5951321,
HUGHES, Dvr, Edward Hugh, T/235164
HUMBER, Cpl, Thomas Heywood, T/106795
HUMPHREY, L/Cpl, Joseph Harold, T/252644
HUNT,Dvr,Norman Arthur,T/169750,
HUNT, Cpl, Walter Henry, T/168551
HUNTER, Dvr, Bernard, T/65103
HUNTER, Dvr, Gordon Haig, T/92445
HUSTLER,Dvr, Harry,T/209299,
HUTCHINSON, Dvr, Harry, T/5946364
HUZZEY, Dvr,Newton Edmund, T/199510
HYDE, L/Cpl, Denys John, S/227622
HYSLOP, Dvr, John Davidson, T/91970
INCE, Dvr, George William, T/4041415
INMAN, Sjt, Cyril Henry, T/203191

IRESON, Dvr, Leonard Arthur, T/62811]
IRVINE, Cpl, John, T/3309922
IVES, Dvr, George, T/270164
JACKSON, Pte, Arthur, T/259537
JACKSON, Sjt, John, T/77004
JAMES, Dvr, James Sidney, T/170516
JAMES,Pte,Cyril David Rushton,S/191065,
JAMES,Dvr,Francis Parry,T/3911936,
JAMIESON, Pte, William, S/280531
JARDINE, Dvr, William Andrew Wright, T/186350
JARVIS, Pte, Frank William, S/13040750
JAYES, Dvr, George Charles, T/6099332
JEFFREY, Cpl, John, T/10699049
JENKINS, Dvr, Arthur William Sydney, T/275497
JENKINS, Dvr, Elvyn, T/225194
JESSETT, Sjt, William, T/61379
JOHNSON,Sjt,Eric Greyston,T/81442,
JOHNSON,Dvr,Thomas,T/2765655,
JOHNSTON, Sjt, Albert, T/45200
JOHNSTON, L Cpl, William Edward, T/3192815
JONES, Sjt, Albert David, T/4026676
JONES, Sjt, Basil, T/859534
JONES, S Sjt (Mech), Denis Oswald, T/44862
JONES, Gnr, Harold Thomas, T/66284
JONES, Sjt, Harvey Orlando, T/184700
JONES, Dvr, John Henry, T/3660151
JONES, Sjt, Stanley Cuthbert, T/203217
JONES,L/Cpl,Leonard,T/219374,
JONES,Dvr,Reginald,T/218004,
JONES,Dvr,Sam,T/259743,
JONES,Dvr,Thomas Eyton,T/178179,
JONES,Pte,T Stafford,S/14908676,
JONES,Dvr,William Edward,T/275988,
JONES, Sjt, Albert David, T/4026676
JONES, Sjt, Basil, T/859534
JONES, S Sjt (Mech), Denis Oswald, T/44862
JONES, Gnr, Harold Thomas, T/66284
JONES, Sjt, Harvey Orlando, T/184700
JONES, Dvr, John Henry, T/3660151
JONES, Sjt, Stanley Cuthbert, T/203217
JORDON, Capt, John William Charles, 73462
JOWETT, Pte, Jack, T/2142547
JOWITT, Dvr, Raymond Hugh, T/121530
JOYCE, L Sjt, Arthur Ernest, T/163123
JUCKLES,Dvr,Reginald,T/175389,
JUDD, Pte, A W, T/14432959
KAUFMAN,Dvr,Harry,T/217809,
KAY, Dvr, Thomas Howarth, T/182567
KAYE, Dvr, Norman, T/220072
KEARNEY, Pte, Jack Namur, S/5118891
KEEGAN, Dvr, John Robert, T/59605
KEEHGAN,Dvr,Thomas,T/2765655,
KEGGEN, Capt, Hubert Stanley, 129799
KELLEWAY, Dvr, Alfred William, T/92389
KEMP, Dvr, Prince William, T/171750
KENNAN, Maj, Lionel Williams MBE, 66657
KENNEDY, Dvr,Patrick, T/273942
KETTLE, Sjt, Stanley Rowland, S/148665
KEYS,DVR,Noel Daniel Richard,7905572
KIBBLE, Pte, Edward, S/97325
KIDD, Dvr, Leslie George, T/137954
KING,Pte,Raymond Leonard,T/191074,
KING, Cpl, Thomas James Alfred, T/214422
KING, Dvr, Sydney John, T/232702
KIRKBY, Dvr, Thomas William, T/89366
KNIGHT, WO II (SQMS), Ernest James, S/54348
LACEY, Dvr, Ronald Frederick, T/217813
LAMBERT, L Cpl, Aubrey Charles, S/227628
LAMBERT, Pte, Victor Henry, T/2322477
LANG, Dvr, Arthur, T/125975

LAPISH,Dvr,John William,T/171757,
LATER, Dvr, Thomas, T/175260
LAUNDER, L/Cpl, Ronald, T/71005
LAVERICK, Dvr, John Thompson, T/194785
LAWRENCE,Cook,J,GSF/53832
LAWSON, Dvr, Robert Oswald Lionel, T/271508
LAWSON, Dvr, Frederick, T/242430
LAY, Dvr, Robert Charles, T/244264
LAYFIELD, Dvr, Alan, T/182922
LAYTHAM, Pte, John, T/227275
LAYZELL, Pte, Sydney Charles, S/248296
LE CLERCQ, Pte, Charles Phillips, T/151639
LE MESURIER, Capt, Basil Guy, 108056
LEFEVER, Cpl, Alfred Newman, T/142677
LENNI, Pte, Charles, S/3134182
LETTS, Condr, Frederick William,
LEVITTON, L/Cpl, Henry Louis, T/245125
LEWIS, Pte, Henry John Edward, T/248492
LINDLEY, Dvr, Ralph, T/62771
LINFORD, Dvr, Roy Wilfred, T/1638315
LITTLE,Cpl,Thomas John Watson,T/3596961,
LLOYD, Sjt, Herbert, S/57235
LLOYD, Dvr, William, T/255590
LOBLEY, Dvr, William, T/275358
LOFTHOUSE, Dvr, William, T/77854
LOMAS, Dvr, George Thomas, T/3659933
LONDON, Dvr, Howard Walter, T/274821
LONGMUIR, Dvr, Arthur, T/274597
LOUGHRAN, Dvr, Leslie Allen, 216626
LYNCH, Dvr, John, T/274568
LYTTLE, Capt, Claude Edward Wilson, ST/84
MACDOUGAL, Dvr, Donald, T/264849
MACKENZIE, Pte, Robert, S/2822476
MAGUIRE, Sjt, Walter, T/3377191
MALCOLM, Cpl, Alexander, T/2753338
MALLINSON, Sjt, William John, T/45001
MANSELL, Pte, Herbert, S/123496
MANTLE, Dvr, Edward Harold, T/220677
MAPPLEBECK, Dvr, Joseph, T/66644
MARKHAM, Cpl, Alfred, T/2209730
MARKIN, Dvr, Horace John, T/177084
MARKS,Sjt,Gordon,T/122405,
MARSHALL, Cpl, Allan George, T/185611
MARTIN, Dvr, Sidney John, T/170442
MARTIN,Dvr,James Arnold,T/168572,
MARTINDALE, L Cpl, Fred, T/73020
MATHESON,Dvr,Marcus Sutherland,T/58797
MATHEWS, Dvr, George, T/156992
McCANN, Pte, George, S/99028
McCARTHY,Dvr,Michael,T/65373,
McCARTHY,Dvr,George Dennis,T/245454,
McCARTHY, Pte, Joseph Henry, T/222104
MCCRACKEN, Cpl, Clifford Richard, T/203611
McCULLOCH, Pte, Charles Henry, T/97916
McGLONE, Dvr, Thomas, T/186950
McGURK, Dvr, Brian Donald, T/7047342
MCINTOSH, Dvr, Andrew, T/279136
McKEOWN, Dvr, Brian Allan, T/66731
McLEAN, Sjt, Henry Bernard, T/215837
MCMASTER, L Cpl, Archibald, T/235397
McPHEE, Dvr, Angus, T/220810
MERCER, Dvr, John Bernadine, T/154453
MERRICKS,Dvr,Arthur William,T/202292,
MILES, Dvr, George, T/218243
MILLARD, Sjt, Ernest John, S/217176
MILLER, WOII (CSM), Robert, T/170388
MILLER,Pte,Denis James,S/14574465,
MILLINGTON, Cpl, Bertram, T/3517046
MILLS,Dvr,James,T/250967,
MILNE, Cpl, Leslie, T/2877033

MILTON, Cpl, Henry Alfred, T/ 165718
MINNS,Dvr,Stanley,T/247931,
MINTON, Dvr, John, T/209796
MITCHELL,Pte,Dennis Roy,T/203875,
MOCK,Pte,Staffard,S/7662278,
MOFFITT, Dvr, Frank Gilbert, T/92684
MONK, Pte, William Fred Charles, T/111939
MONTIETH,Pte,Edwin,T/76955,
MOONEY, Dvr, Andrew, Joseph McCormack, T/139689
MORGAN,Dvr,William Kenneth,T/142835,
MORGAN, L/Sjt, Herbert, T/45960
MORLEY, Dvr, Ronald George, T/188520
MORRIS, Dvr, John Solomon, T/120888
MORRIS, Pte, Herbert James, S/5189164
MORRIS, Cpl, Thomas, T/187738
MORRIS, Dvr, Walter, T/77123
MORRISON, Pte, James McIntosh, T/206451
MORRISON,S/Sjt,Duncan Clelland,S/57141,
MORRISON,L/Cpl,Hector Marcus Avery,T/273236,
MORRISON,Dvr,Robert,T/3064226,
MOSS, Dvr, Charles James, T/176518
MULLINGER, Pte, Frederick John, T/6281643
MUNN, Dvr, Robert White, T/3137085
MURPHY, Pte, Oswald, S/13087254
MURREY, Pte, Norman McLEOD, T/92258
NAUGHTON, Dvr, Arthur, T/3779194
NEAL, Dvr, Maurice Albert, T/274601
NEARY, Dvr, Harold Thomas Joseph, T/2633021
NELSON, Pte, Robert, S/3319606
NEYLON, Dvr, James, T/204159
NICHOLAS, Pte, John Llewallyn, S/166240
NICHOLSON, Dvr, Albert, T/218467
NICHOLSON, Dvr, Ben, T/136624
NICHOLSON, Sjt, Ronald William Charles, T/217372
NICHOLSON,Dvr,Arthur Albert,T/275123,
NIMMO, Cpl, Robert Alexander, T/116781
NORFOLK, Dvr, William, T/193233
NORMAN, Pte, Leslie, 7374029
NORRINGTON, Cpl, Thompson,Walter, T/92723
NORRIS, Dvr, Frank, T/273841
NOTSON, Capt, Ernest Henry, 107027
O'LOUGHLIN, Dvr, Arnold, T/186378
OAKLAND, Pte, Leonard, T/213631
OFFORD, Dvr, Sidney George James, T/219219
OLDS, Dvr, Robert Arthur Edward, T/247954
ORAM, Dvr, Arthur William, T/272373
OSBORNE, Dvr, John, T/155210
OTTLEY, Sjt, Reginald Charles, S/1467746
PARAMORE, Pte, Leslie, 271568
PARKER,Dvr,Arthur,T/168730,
PARKER, Dvr, Albert Edward, T/236041
PARKES, Dvr, Eric, T/120916
PARKIN,Pte,K H W,S/14960447,
PARROTT, Cpl, John William, S/170426
PARROTT, L/Cpl, Leslie James, T/168497
PEARCE, Pte, Bernard Philip, S/5259442
PEARSON, 2/Lt, Edward, 201115
PEAT, Dvr, Reginald William, T/272009
PECK, L/Cpl, C W, T/181061
PECK, L/Cpl, Leonard William, T/181061
PEGGIE, Dvr, Walter Baillie, T/171470
PENNY, Dvr, George Arthur, T/156980
PENROSE, Dvr, George, T/174906
PERRY, Dvr, William Frederick, T/139794
PHILLIPS, L Cpl, Joseph Ronald, T/185169
PHILLIPS,Dvr,David Thompson Cameron,T/139651,
PHILLIPS,Cpl,William Benjamin,T/7812765,
PHILLIPS,Sjt,F V, T/245585,
PHILLIPS,Sjt,Robert Herbert,T/215074,
PHILLIPS, L Cpl, Joseph Ronald, T/185169

PICKETT, Pte, Trevor Owen, T/135334
PILGRIM, Dvr, Gordon, T/81665
PLATT,Lt,William,168458,
POOLE, Dvr, Walter Robert Beeney, T/169794
POTTER, Pte, Ashley Arnold, S/14884751
POULTON, Pte, Bernard George, T/230430
POWELL, L/Cpl, Albert Edward, T/276804
POWEWR, Cpl, Patrick Joseph, T/3855334
PRATT, Pte, George William, T/259129
PRICE,Dvr,Marshall,T/231274,
PRICE, Sjt, Charles William, T/69948
PRICE, Dvr, James, T/252310
PRINCE,Sjt,Henry,T/95621,
PROUD,Dvr,Cyril Alexander,T/14742389,
PULLEN, L Cpl, John Frederick, T/273548
PYNCHES, WO II (CSM), Carlton Holden, T/61309
PYPER,Lt,Joseph Richard MC,225674,
QUICK, Dvr, Ivan Levi, T/262418
RAMSEY, Dvr, George Mathew Stewart, T/242498
RAWLEY, Dvr, Frederick James, T/219810
REDBOND, Pte, Ronald Luther Charles, S/151754
REDRUP, Dvr, George Thomas, T/56274
REED, Sjt, George, S/197911
REES, Dvr, Aerwyn Thomas, T/225227
REID, Cpl, Frederick William, T/7344533
RENNIE, S Sjt (Mech), William Charles, T/35230
REYNOLDS, Dvr, William Henry, T/276246
REYNOLDS, Dvr, David George, T/280960
REYNOLDS, Dvr, George James, T/279415
REYNOLDS, Dvr, Arthur, T/276131
RHEESTON, Dvr, Douglas William, T/126128
RICE, Dvr, Charles Arthur, T/276133
RICHARDS, Dvr, William Thomas, T/175734
RICHARDSON, Cpl, Douglas, T/137840
RICHARDSON, Pte, Charles Samuel, T/257497
RICHARDSON, Dvr, Alfred, T/235403
RIDDELL, Cpl, James, T/31893335
RIDGEWAY, Dvr, Thomas Edward, T/232977
RIDSDALE,L/Cpl,H C,A/7,
RILSTONE, Pte, Richard,S/5957414
RIMMER, Dvr, John, T/229939
ROACH, Dvr, Michael, T/275387
ROBERTS,L/Cpl,Edward,T/252525,
ROBERTS, Sjt, William John, T/44797
ROBERTSON, Pte, John, S/244642
ROBERTSON, L/Sjt, Cyril John, T/82111
ROBERTSON, Dvr, William Hunter, T/163150
ROBINSON,Cpl,Ernest William,T/6142619,
ROBINSON, Pte, Leslie Allen, S/238853
ROCHE,Pte,P B,19125910, *
ROSS, Dvr, Albert Donald, T/1062031
ROSS, Dvr, William, T/866808
ROUGH, Dvr, Albert, T/2765468
ROUTH, Dvr, Albert, T/64988
ROWLANDSON, Pte, Alfred John, S/212487
ROWSE, Cpl, Frederick Alan, S/5731874
RUMSEY, WOII (CSM), Gordon Reginald Jack, T/57636
RUNDLE, Pte, Leslie George, S/5681568
RUSSELL,Sjt,Francis John,T/66946,
RUSSELL, Pte, John Butler, S/7386937
RUSTON, M/SM, Norman, T/33633
RYAN,Dvr,Ronald William,T/276655,
SADLER, Dvr, William Frederick, T/254127
SAINSBURY, Cpl, Kenneth Arthur, T/128285
SAKNE, Dvr, John Theodore, T/231275
SALMONS, Pte, George, T/235215
SAMUALS, Sjt, Peter William, T/6089416
SANDS, Dvr, Robert, T/3196977
SAUNDERS, Sjt, Cecil John, T/105402
SCHOOLAR, Cpl, Aubrey, S/134378

SCOTLAND, Sjt, John Hutchinson, T/48605
SCOTT, Dvr, James, T/3050103
SCOVELL, Dvr, Kenneth Thornton, T/7685384
SEARS, Dvr, Leslie Charles, T/261093
SELF, Dvr, Ronald Edward, T/921425
SERVANT, Dvr, David, T/3196543
SEXTON, Dvr, Augustine John, T/193638
SHANNON, Dvr, James Henry, T/279463
SHEATHER, Cpl, Wilfred Ethelbert, T/104617
SHEPHERDSON, Dvr, Ronald, T/245753
SHINER, Lt Col, Leonard, EC/15052
SIDEBOTTOM, Dvr, Samuel, T/271382
SIGGINS, Dvr, Sidney Ernest, T/230445
SIGHE, L/Cpl, George, T/3662446
SILVESTER, Cpl, John Arthur, T/88398
SIMMONS,SQMS,Victor Henry,T/116911,
SIMMONS, Capt, George Raymond Baskerville, 74896
SIMON, Dvr, John Francis, T/185010
SLATER, Dvr, Bernard Charles, T/279418
SMALL,Sjt,James Norman,S/116351,
SMITH, Pte, James, T/157718
SMITH,Cpl,Charles Frederick,T/133780,
SMITH,Sjt,Donald Andrew,T/277692,
SMITH,Sjt,Douglas,4860100,
SMITH,Dvr,Ernest Samuel,T/174575,
SMITH,CQMS,Norman,T/175911,
SMITH,Pte,Andrew Phillip Wilson,S/259137,
SMITH,Dvr,Joseph Stephen,T/209840,
SMITH,Dvr,Ralph Talbot,T/180047,
SMITH,Cpl,Robert,T/179559,
SMITH,SQMS,Ronald Arthur,S/5828240,
SMITH,Dvr,Ronald David,T/275262,
SMITH,Dvr,William Oswald Impey,T/268967,
SMITH,L/Cpl,Trevor Leslie,T/165022,
SMITH,Dvr,Charles,T/2765590,
SMITH, Pte, James, T/157718
SMYTH,Capt,George Paton,71369,
SNASHALL, Dvr, Stanley Ernest, T/17-543
SNOOK, Sjt, Harold, S/5730820
SOPER, Capt, Michael Paul, 112975
SPENCER, Dvr, Harry Thomas, T/224490
SPENCER, Dvr, Sidney George, T/135884
SPILLMAN, Pte, Bert Talbot, T/246760
SPINALL, Dvr, Thomas Henry, T/199982
STEVENS, Cpl, Robert, T/6141481
STEWART, Dvr, Charles, T/275268
STEWART, Dvr, Archibald McIntyre, T/138733
STRAHAN, Dvr, Philip Keenan, T/131521
STREET, Dvr, Walter, T/275397
STUART, Dvr, Duncan, T/3196979
STUBBS, Cpl, Peter, T/1572510
STURMAN, Dvr, Cyril Edward, T/170471
SUFFOLK-ASHLEY,Sjt,Reginald Joseph,S/862147
SULLIVAN, Dvr, George William, T/279598
SWAIN, Pte, George Kenneth, T/236738
SWALWELL, Pte, Thomas, T/248952
SWANN, Pte, Jack, S/4694506
SWARBRICK, L/Cpl, A T, T/1465277
SWEENY, Sjt, Ronald Rouston, T/89779
SWINGLEHURST, Pte, John Hartley, T/213608
SYMES, Dvr, Victor John, T/281119
TALBOT, Dvr, David, T/188302
TAWTON, L/Cpl, Arthur, S/151471
TAYLOR,Cpl,Walter Edward,S/6140667,
TAYLOR,Dvr,Thomas C,T/248241,
TAYLOR,Cpl,D W,A/5MT,
TAYLOR, L/Cpl, Raymond Barton, T/10664234
TEASDALE, Pte, Frank Ellery, S/6149242
TELFORD, Dvr, James Sidney, T/63178
THIRKELL, S/Sjt, John Edward, S/426648

THOMAS, Dvr, William Emanuel, T/276518
THOMPSON, Dvr, John Frank, T/178810,
THOMPSON, M/SM, James William, T/33401
THORPE, Dvr, Albert, T/157214,
THORPE, Cpl, Jack, T/1572584,
TILLETT, Dvr, Charles Henry, T/50194,
TILT, Dvr, Joseph Lambert, T/168755
TIMBS, L/Cpl, Walter Harold, T/178366
TIMMINS, Pte, Henry Walter, T/250309
TIMPERLEY, Dvr, Arthur, T/1102835
TIPTON, Dvr, Robert, T/3656936
TITCOMBE, Cpl, Roland Eric, T/179669
TOLAN, Pte, Bernard, S/3458176
TOMLINSON, Dvr, John, T/272029
TOMPKINS, L Cpl, Raymond Buxton, T/161947
TOMPKINS, Dvr, William John, T/276030
TOMS, Dvr, P R, T/14937297
TONGE, Dvr, Arthur Walton, T/225243
TOWLER, Pte, Paul Norman, S/212492
TRANTER, Pte, Samuel, T/158089
TREGASKIS, Dvr, William Joseph, T/68799
TRIGG, Pte, Albert John, T/1060148
TRIGG, Pte, William Patrick, S/4808661
TROTT, Dvr, Albert Edward, T/275274
TRUE, Dvr, Percy Edward, T/169744
TUCKER, L/Cpl, Charles Edward, S/128240
TUNSTALL, Dvr, Leonard, T/279054
TURNER, Dvr, William Edward, T/217910
TURNER, Dvr, Willian James Stephen, T/219251
TURNER, Dvr, John Harold, T/4038049,
TURNER, Dvr, Herbert, T/283762
TURRELL, Dvr, John Henry, T/187628
UMNEY, L/Cpl, Arthur Charles, T/266498
UNWIN, Pte, W S, S/11451508
UPTON, Dvr, John Leslie, T/167933
VAIL, L/Cpl, John, T/228849
VALE, Pte, Sidney William, T/248546
VALLE, Sjt, Edward John Frederick, S/75744
VANNER, Dvr, John Edward, T/2765609
VARLEY, Dvr, Harold, T/183944
VARNEY, Dvr, Charles, T/123745
VASEY, Dvr, Douglas, T/259972
VAUGHAN, Sjt, Ernest Reginald George, S/56506
VAYRO, Dvr, Ernest, T/251199
VEREKER, Dvr, William Michael, T/225245
VERITY, Dvr, Ralph, T/272032
VINCE, Dvr, George James, T/170260
VIPOND, Dvr, Frank, T/91085
WADD, Cpl, John, T/199740
WADEY, Pte, Reginald Maurice Harold, S/265466
WAINWRIGHT, Dvr, Harry T, T/100785
WAINWRIGHT, Pte, Arthur, T/235542
WAITE, Dvr, George, T/222011
WALKER, Dvr, Joseph, T/240081
WALKER, L/Cpl, Bernard, S/7663125
WALKER, Dvr, William George, T/5576464
WALLACE, WO I (MSM), James M, T/72527
WALLIS, L Cpl, Colin, T/112856
WALLIS, Pte, George, T/196566,
WALLIS, L Cpl, Colin, T/112856
WALTON, Dvr, Frank, T/240148
WALTON, Dvr, John, T3660143,
WANN, Pte, William, T/263336
WAPLE, Dvr, Ronald Edwin, T/85374
WARD, Pte, Edward George, T/246632
WARD, Dvr, Frank, T/276005,
WARDLEWORTH, Dvr, Thomas, T/261772
WARREN, L/Cpl, Francis John, T/180115
WATKINS, Pte, George Henry, T/74642
WATLING, Dvr, George Victor, T/275410

WATSON, Pte, Thomas, S/7662002
WATSON, Dvr, Jack, T/7046761
WATSON, Dvr, Wilfred, T/272033
WATT, Dvr, George, T/178680
WATT, Pte, William Hutchison, T/263348
WATTS, Dvr, Harry Albert, T/174745
WEBB, L/Cpl, John H, T/2765485
WEBBER, Pte, Charles William, T/229640
WEBSTER, Pte, Frederick Albert, T/162468
WEEKS, Dvr, Albert Henry, T/175940
WEEKS, Cpl, Harold William, S/93247
WEIR, Dvr, Walter Edward, T/165138
WELCH, Dvr, Albert James, T/175636
WELLINGTON, L/Cpl, Albert, T/223653
WELLS, Cpl, Reginald Charles, T/4800290
WEST, Pte, John WiliamM, S/13056969
WEST, Dvr, Jack, T/206777
WESTLEY, Dvr, Charles Henry, T/159634
WESTON, Cpl, Robert Thomas, T/185934
WHATLEY, Dvr, Frederick, T/225250
WHITBY, Dvr, Wilfred Raymond, T/139438
WHITE, Pte, Kenneth Douglas, S/181715
WHITING, Pte, Henry Thurston, S/5629690
WHITTAKER, Capt, Hugh, EC/2449
WHITTAKER, Dvr, Samuel, T/281577
WHITTLE, Dvr, George Edward, T/259725
WIGGS, Pte, Arthur Leonard, S/6476131
WIGMORE, SQMS, Alan Herbert, S/54611
WILCOCK, Cpl, Fred, S/14278605
WILKINS, Dvr, Robert John, T/259217
WILKINS, Dvr, Stanley John William, T/245515
WILKINSON, Dvr, Albert, T/245918,
WILKS, Dvr, Harold Arthur, T/3197161
WILLIAMS, Cpl, Duncan Charles, T/6141316,
WILLIAMS, Dvr, John, T/273970,
WILLIAMS, L/Cpl, John Cable, T/10511212,
WILLIAMS, Dvr, Richard Percy, T/276033,
WILLIAMS, Sjt, William, T/1016931,
WILLIAMS, Pte, Edward Ronald, S/13049322,
WILLIAMS, Dvr, George Roland, T/247912,
WILLIAMS, Dvr, John Henry, T/276007,
WILSON, Dvr, John, S/139668,
WILSON, Lt, Noel Edmund Thomas, 191770,
WILSON, Dvr, Archibald, T/2752433,
WILSON, Dvr, Geoffrey, T/272037,
WINTER, Dvr, Tom, T/258393
WINTERS, Dvr, Frederick Robert, T/63874
WISDOM, Sjt, Archibald John Erward, T/50255
WITTY, Dvr, Richard, T/276404
WOOD, Dvr, Walter Thomas, T/225256,
WOOD, Dvr, Gilbert, T/168448
WOOD, Dvr, Walter, T/203821
WOODBERRY, Pte, Jack, S/5674768
WOODHEAD, Dvr, Cyril, T/135434
WOODS, L/Cpl, Richard Anthony, T/82194
WOOLNOUGH, Pte, Albert Samuel, T/109817
WORDLEY, L/Cpl, Frank H, T/175531
WORSWICK, Pte, Thomas, T/258467
WORTHINGTON, Pte, James, T/3776869
WRIGHT, Pte, Alwyn Rodney Gilbert, S/150629
WRIGHT, Dvr, William, T/276153
WRIGHT, Dvr, John, T/83896,
WRIGHT, Pte, Alwyn Rodney Gilbert, S/150629
WRIGHT, Dvr, William, T/276153
WRIGHT, Dvr, James Harold, T/259072
WRIGHT, Dvr, John, T/83896
WRIGHT, Dvr, Leslie Harold Desmond, T/139427
WRIGHT, Dvr, Joseph Dudley, T/231865
WURR, Pte, Russell Gordon, S/271577
WYMER, Dvr, Walter David, T/749942

WYMER, Dvr, Charles Clifford, T/266424
YOUNG,Cpl,Charles Anthony Christopher,S/14958472,

ROYAL ARTILLERY
ACOCK, Gnr, Alfred, 4746270
ADAMS, Gnr, Charles Thomas, 1070832
ADAMS, Gnr, Percy Murray, 922398
ALLEN, Gnr, William James, 1119433
ANDERSON, Gnr, Archibald William, 1112241
ANDERSON, Gnr, Sidney Charles, 902254
ATHERTON, Sjt, Robert William, 3449815
ATKINSON, Gnr, Norman, 1123200
BACHE, Gnr, Walter Clarke, 1810438
BANKS, Gnr, John, 3856638
BASHAM, L Bdr, Bennett Thomas, 913693
BASHAM, L Bdr, Sidney Robert, 913698
BATE, Armr S Sjt, Charles Henry, 7582935
BATTING, Gnr, Lloyd George, 818585
BAXTER, Gnr, Leslie, 1782402
BEAVEN, Lt, John Alfred Disraeli, 146148
BENNETT, Gnr, William Arthur, 3772016
BICKNELL, Gnr, Sidney, 1805249
BISHOP, Gnr, Gordon Morris, 980264
BLAKEBOROUGH L Bdr, L Bdr, George Richard, 1057341
BONE, L Bdr, Gordon Henry, 1544950
BOWLER, Gnr, Ronald, 943435
BRADLEY, Gnr, Robert William, 1064468
BRAND, Gnr, Cyril Frank, 962463
BREACKER, Sjt, Ronald Victor, 905157
BREAKSPEAR, Gnr, Albert William, 1101506
BRIGGS, Gnr, Henry Walter Jesse, 965840
BROADHURST, Gnr, William Charles, 1558475
BROOKES, Gnr, Horace Gilnow, 7174155
BROOKS, Gnr, John Henry, 2046058
BROOKS, Gnr, Wilfred, 4687248
BULL, L Bdr, Arthur James, 938509
BUNN, Bdr, Godfrey Frederick William, 2027675
BURNS, Gnr, Alan Douglas, 1108695
BURNS, Gnr, Fred, 941143
BURT, Gnr, Harry Ernest, 1084190
BUTTERS, Gnr, Frank George Arthur, 902321
CAVALIER, Sjt, Albert William, 861758
CHAMBERS, Gnr, William James, 1608910
CHRISTIAN, Bdr, George Frederick, 908678
CLARKE, Bdr, James Frederick, 845739
CLEMENTS, Bdr, William Charles, 850775
CLEWER, Sjt, William Thomas, 842161
COATES, Gnr, George William, 944338
CODD, Gnr, Derek Ernest, 980799
COLE, Gnr, John Ronald, 1108488
COLES, Bdr, Walter Ambrose, 847130
CORNS, Bdr, Frederick Ronald, 906313
CORY, Gnr, Andrew William, 946126
COX, L Sjt, Harold Stephen, 901360
CURD, Gnr, Maurice Frederick, 1558367
CURTIS, Gnr, Roderick John, 998187
D'ARCY, Gnr, Charles Frederick James, 1121226
DADD, Gnr, George Henry, 1106350
DAINES, Gnr, Charles, 1811412
DALY, Gnr, William, 1105162
DARBY, Gnr, James Harold, 941926
DARKE, Gnr, Francis Edward, 871247
DATWEN,BSM,Charles Richard,749224
DATLEN, Gnr, Victor Allan, 941186
DAVENPORT, Gnr, Alec, 950856
DAVEY, Gnr, Henry Heber Thomas, 5122402
DAVIES, Bdr, Thomas, 850915
DAVIES, Gnr, John Vincent, 1817055
DAVIES, Gnr, Trevor, 798297

DAVIES, Gnr, George, 1733546
DAVIES, Gnr, David Douglas, 1492340
DAVIES, Gnr, Thomas, 1062364
DAVIS, Gnr, John Henry, 896032
DAVIS, L/Bdr, David, 917869
DAVIS, Gnr, John Edward, 895545
DAVIS, Gnr, George, 1787207
DAY,Bdr,Rodney,803602
DE SANTI, Gnr, Leonard, 855893
De WHALLEY, Sjt, Geoffrey Richard, 896984
DEEBANK, Gnr, William Harry, 910639
DEER, Gnr, James Ernest, 1110846
DEMPSEY, Gnr, John Thomas, 947523
DENISON, Gnr, Eric, 906305
DENMEAD, Gnr, Arthur John, 1115167
DENNINGHAN, Gnr, Joseph, 840439
DENNY, Gnr, George Edmund, 964210
DENT, L/Sjt, Francis,
DENTON, Gnr, Aubrey Ronald, 921496
DENTTEN, Gnr, Arthur Ernest John, 1492352
DIBBEN, Gnr, Neville Moore, 1088910
DICKENS, Gnr, Leonard Charles, 885963
DICKSON, Bdr, Charles Alexander, 1444829
DIXON, Gnr, Norman, 851537
DIXON, Gnr, Frank, 940733
DIXON, Gnr, Joseph Francis, 1111037
DOBSON, Gnr, Harry, 956452
DOBSON, Bdr, Frederick George, 872467
DOHERTY, Sjt, James Nichol Currie, 843483
DOLAN, Gnr, James, 911927
DOLPHIN, L/Sjt, William, 851877
DOWLEN, Gnr, Francis John, 1119757
DOWNER, Gnr, Philip, 1543081
DOWNES, Gnr, William Henry, 1085753
DOWSETT, BSM, Bertram Harry, 917938
DOWTHWAITE, L/Bdr, Maurice, 1784060
DRAPER, L/Bdr, Harold, 875614
DREWRY, Gnr, ohn Allen, 1605328
DRIVER, Bdr, Leonard Cecil, 872386
DUCE, Gnr, Edward Cecil, 947829
DUDDLE, L Bdr, John, 852314
DUGGAN, Gnr, Michael esmond, 902311
DUNKERLEY, Gnr, Harold, 1651388
DUNN, Gnr, William Arthur, 856728
DUROE, L/Bdr, Charles, 940656
DYKE, Gnr, Henry George, 961313
DYNES, Gnr, George Thomas, 6285850
EDHOUSE, Gnr, Edward, 950217
FAULKNER, Bdr, Leonard Stanley, 1442304
FAWCETT, L Bdr, Frank, 924162
FISH, Bdr, Harold, 908413
FITCHES, Gnr, William, 922100
FODEN, Gnr, Robert Charles George, 1789402
FOSTER, Gnr, Robert Michael, 1427321
FOUNTAIN, Gnr, William, 877321
GARDNER, Gnr, Eric Pickering, 1463177
GILL, Gnr, Thomas Henry, 1631249
GORDON, Gnr, George, 998847
GOUGH, Gnr, Frederick Walter, 1604954
GRAHAM, Gnr, Leslie, 1426720
GRAY, Gnr, Richard Brewer, 1811442
GREENBANK, Bdr, Herbert, 849664
GUNN, Gnr, William Alfred Charles, 1112273
GUY, Gnr, Clive, 853378
HAMMERTON, Gnr, William George, 1778709
HARDING, Gnr, Alfred Edmond, 1099774
HARDY, Gnr, Thomas Frederick, 1686284
HARE, Gnr, Thomas, 860053
HARRIS, Gnr, Frank, 1603495
HATTON, Gnr, William Cornelius G, 868926

HAWKINS, Gnr, Cyril Sidney, 6405095

HEATHCOTE, Gnr, Harry, 815143

HEWARD, Gnr, Joseph Kitchener, 967440

HILL, Gnr, William Albion, 853324

HILTON, Gnr, Edgar Dickinson, 885056

HODGSON, Gnr, Ronald, 1083660

HOWELLS, Gnr, Sidney, 1438609

HUDDLESTONE, Gnr, Edward Joseph, 1119525

HUGHES, Bdr, Brian Kenneth Kiffyn, 1476245

HUMPHREY, Gnr, Herbert James, 1805346

HUTCHINSON, Gnr, Mark, 1085585

HUTCHINSON, Gnr, Norman, 863250

INGARFIELD, Gnr, Harry, 1426678

INGHAM, Bdr, Jack, 1463205

INGHAM, Gnr, Thomas, 894613

INGRAM, Gnr, John, 855368

INGRAM, Gnr, William, 901484

INNES, Gnr, Walter Robb, 1096565

IRISH, Gnr, Thomas Henry, 2047759

IRVING, Gnr, Robert, 868788

IRWIN, Gnr, Arthur Leslie, 1123139

IRWIN, Gnr, Johnston, 7009917

ISTED, Gnr, George Thomas, 1427562

IVES, Bdr, John Anthony Gerard, 130963

JACKSON, Gnr, Arthur, 1709753

JACKSON, Lt, Frederick William, 180967

JACKSON, Bdr, James Walter, 905587

JACKSON, Gnr, John, 905032

JACOBY, BSM, Harold Cecil, 1478314

JAMES, Bdr, Leslie, 1556296

JAMES, Gnr, Arthur, 1537703

JAMES, Gnr, Brinley, 1818777

JAMES, L Bdr, Douglas Frederick, 1493032

JAMES, Gnr, Edwin, 1117547

JAMES, Gnr, George Henry, 1724622

JAMES, Gnr, Glyn, 1817116

JAMES, Gnr, John Lewis, 1492795

JAMES, L Sjt, Robert Henry, 856663

JAMES, L Bdr, Roy William, 1587861

JAMES, Gnr, Stanley Edward, 1801620

JAMIESON, Sjt, John Thurston, 837114

JANES, Gnr, Ronald Edgar, 922101

JAQUES, Gnr, George William, 1099782

JARDINE, Gnr, Albert, 11051585

JARDINE, L Bdr, Stanley, 1629554

JARRET, Gnr, Harry, 2755409

JARVIS, Bdr, Frederick R, 6397906

JENKINS, Gnr, Albert William Edward, 1801622

JENKINS, Pte, Elwyn William, 7612436

JENKINS, Bdr, Haydn, 1452858

JENKINS, Lt, Samuel Morley, 155418

JENNINGS, Gnr, Harry, 1543986

JERMYN, Lt, Peter, 73050

JERVIS, Gnr, Harry, 1737869

JESSOP, Gnr, James Thomas, 851141

JOHN, Gnr, Thomas William Saint, 1089358

JOHNSON, Bdr, Charles George, 866439

JOHNSON, Gnr, Charles Thomas, 1629470

JOHNSON, Sjt, Dennis Howard, 908615

JOHNSON, Gnr, Ernest, 1427736

JOHNSON, Gnr, Frank, 950930

JOHNSON, Gnr, Frederick, 1573751

JOHNSON, L Bdr, Frederick, 5044523

JOHNSON, Lt, Guy Herbert, 172664

JOHNSON, Gnr, Harold Clifford Alwyn, 872658

JOHNSON, Bdr, Leonard Samuel, 899322

JOHNSON, Gnr, Sidney, 11053323

JOHNSON, Gnr, Thomas, 1552580

JOHNSON, Gnr, Thomas, 4130609

JOHNSON, L Bdr, Thomas Jack, 1512208

JOHNSON, Gnr, Walter William, 1805904

JOHNSTON, Gnr, Archibald McCallum, 1808054

JOHNSTON, Gnr, George, 1629587

JOHNSTON, Gnr, Joseph, 764188

JOHNSTON, Gnr, William James, 3239062

JOLLIE, L Bdr, John Wilkie, 915323

JONES, Gnr, Lewis, 1580632

JONES, Gnr, Alun Pierce, 909510

JONES, Gnr, Bernard Walter, 883016

JONES, Lt, Cecil Hugh Eversley, 86779

JONES, Gnr, Claude Albert, 1483253

JONES, Bdr, Cyril, 11052206

JONES, Gnr, David Benjamin, 1098440

JONES, Gnr, Ebenezer, 1690886

JONES, L Sjt, Edward, 868617

JONES, Gnr, Edwin Bernard, 1482052

JONES, Gnr, Frank, 1532755

JONES, Lt, James Clifford, 164302

JONES, Sjt, John, 822452

JONES, L Bdr, John Edward, 822522

JONES, Gnr, John Griffith, 1120827

JONES, Gnr, Joseph, 1457641

JONES, Gnr, Joseph, 872253

JONES, L Bdr, Joseph, 1459243

JONES, Gnr, Joseph William, 1459948

JONES, L Bdr, Thomas John, 1110548

JONES, Gnr, Thomas William, 816755

JONES, Gnr, William, 419764

JONES, Sjt, William John, 3439328

JONES, Gnr, William Joseph, 1605162

JONES, Gnr, Winser, 1442911

JOSEPH, Gnr, Joseph Harry, 1548354

JOY, L Bdr, Kenneth Charles, 1479512

JOYCE, Gnr, Allan Browning, 900180

JOYES, Gnr, Arthur Edward, 1483043

JUGGINS, Gnr, Sydney, 839317

KAEO, Gnr, Charles Raymond V, 11052172

KAY, Gnr, Ernest Albert, 6460102

KAY, Bdr, Leo, 398459

KEABLE, Gnr, Leslie Arthur, 1735580

KEAVENEY, Gnr, Patrick Edward, 11052201

KEEBLE, Gnr, Norman, 1792626

KEEN, L Sjt, Oliver James, 791190

KEEP, Gnr, Willaim Joseph, 948410

KEEVIL, Sjt, Joseph Jesse, 805169

KEIRLE, Gnr, Francis William, 1118052

KELLEY, Gnr, John Leslie, 1108450

KELLY, Gnr, Francis, 1821140

KELLY, Maj, John Ernest, 31139

KELLY, L Bdr, John Mackay, 326276

KELLY, Gnr, Michael, 3521039

KELLY, L Bdr, Robert, 1426994

KELLY, Gnr, Sylvester, 847409

KENDALL, Gnr, Archibald Bertram, 5568967

KENDALL, Gnr, Stanley Dawson, 950928

KENDREY, Gnr, Donald Walker, 903380

KENNEDY, L Sjt, David Joseph, 879001

KENNEDY, L Bdr, Leslie Howard, 13227

KENNEDY, WOII (BSM), Richard James McDonald, 1062264

KENNEDY, Gnr, Samuel, 967514

KENNETT, Gnr, Charles Marshall, 1113861

KERSLEY, Gnr, Cecil, 1084923

KEW, Sjt, Leslie, 1694225

KEWELL, Gnr, Edwin, 911887

KEY, Bdr, Frederick Leonard, 1073700

KEYES, Gnr, Peter, 1438698

KEYS, Capt, Fred, 92419

KIDBY, Sjt, Herbert G, 1486999

KILLIEN, Gnr, George Peter, 1625734

KING, Gnr, David, 4451965

KING, Gnr, John Barr, 151889
KING, L Bdr, William Frederick, 908565
KINGSHOTT, WO II (BSM), Robert William George, 840146
KINGSNORTH, L Sjt, Frank William, 1557742
KIPLING, Gnr, Harry, 7150494
KIRBY, Gnr, Mark Edward, 921606
KIRKHAM, Gnr, Robert McGovan, 1469976
KISTELL, Gnr, William Bosanko, 1591078
KITCHEN, Gnr, Eric, 1469942
KITSON, Bdr, John Richard, 856831
KNEALE, Gnr, George Edward, 903800
KNIGHT, Sjt, Alan R, 5496978
KNIGHT, Gnr, Charles Ivor John, 1467165
KNOTT, Gnr, Richard Albert John, 912994
KNOWLES, Gnr, Thomas Archibald, 752389
KNOWLES, Gnr, Walter Robert, 1808704
KREIKE, Gnr, William Henry, 1427507
LABROCK, Gnr, James, 909707
LACEY, Gnr, Robert John, 845840
LAING, WO II (BSM), Ronald, 6343400
LAIRD, L Bdr, George, 767440
LAMB, Gnr, Benjamin Thomas, 923920
LAMB, L Bdr, Donald, 815566
LAMBERT, Gnr, Harry, 2042048
LAMBERT, Gnr, John, 1764423
LAMBERT, L Bdr, Lawrence, 885349
LAMBOURNE, WO II (BSM), Thomas Edward James, 1058477
LANCE, Gnr, Eric, 1569486
LANDELLS, Gnr, William Kirby, 1639049
LANGFORD, Gnr, Arhtur Russell, 1108680
LANGLEY, Dvr, James, T/3782097
LANGSTEAD, WO II, Ian Roderick McDonald, 802350
LARBEY, Gnr, Ernest Alfred, 1112181
LARGE, Gnr, Wesley Harold, 1607059
LARNEY, Gnr, John William, 2651344
LARVIN, Gnr, George Henry, 986956
LASCELLES, Gnr, Frank, 875987
LAUNDY, Dvr, Royston, T/139971
LAVEY, Sjt, George Edward, 3384670
LAVIN, Bdr, James William, 409151
LAVRACK, Gnr, William Henry, 1091985
LAW, Bdr, Donald Robert, 6607693
LAW, L Sjt, Harold John, 913912
LAW, Gnr, Richard George, 1763388
LAWES, L Bdr, Wilfred Albert, 941009
LAWRENCE, Gnr, Dennis Raymond, 948876
LAWRENCE, Gnr, Ernest Frederick James, 2029978
LAWRENCE, L Bdr, James, 903858
LAWRENCE, Gnr, Robert Arthur, 1099785
LAWRENCE, Gnr, Stanley Walter, 1426659
LAWSON, Lt, John Lawrence, 182793
LAWSON, Gnr, Norman, 4388828
LAWTON, Gnr, Ashley Norman, 1782791
LAWTON, Gnr, William, 856617
LE-BON, Gnr, Walter, 3313361
LEA, Gnr, Albert, 863422
LEA, Gnr, John, 1115657
LEACH, Gnr, Fred, 1114311
LEACH, Bdr, George Henry, 833110
LEACK, Gnr, William, 923907
LEAKE, Gnr, Arthur, 975663
LEAMON, Gnr, Edward John, 886336
LEANEY, Sjt, William James, 1422482
LEDGARD, L Bdr, John Henry, 4534786
LEDWITH, Gnr, Thomas Christopher, 1607473
LEE, Gnr, Joseph Alfred, 5485976
LEIGHTON, Gnr, John, 1113517
LEITCH, Gnr, John, 1577853
LESLIE, Gnr, John Andrew, 1986305
LENO, Bdr, Ronald, 887488

LERWILL, Gnr, Leslie Thomas, 1613530
LETCHFORD, Gnr, Alfred John, 948897
LETHAM, Gnr, James Demptster, 1826529
LEWIS, Gnr, Harold Bowes, 849665
LEWIS, Gnr, John, 884429
LEWIS, Gnr, Oscar Thomas, 1645999
LEWIS, L Bdr, Percy, 1068953
LEWIS, Sjt, Robert, 1669410
LEWIS, Gnr, Ronald Cecil, 791037
LEWIS, Gnr, Stuart Charles, 882723
LEWIS, Gnr, Thomas Douglas, 1492458
LEWIS, Gnr, William David, 1472953
LEY, Gnr, Joseph Collin, 1709571
LIDDLE, Gnr, John George, 1108341
LILLEY, Gnr, Edward, 917068
LILLICRAP, Gnr, William Thomas John, 1448271
LILLIE, L Sjt, Roy, 812643
LILLINGTON, Gnr, Stephen William, 5726631
LINFORD, Sjt, Charles Wiliam, 819642
LINTOTT, Bdr, Sidney John, 1563570
LITSTER, Gnr, John Hill, 1101524
LITTEN, S Sjt, Albert John Edwin, 1483259
LITTEN, Gnr, Frederick John, 851681
LITTLE, Gnr, Thomas Gibson, 317888
LLOYD, Gnr, John Henry, 1582380
LOCKE, L Sjt, Charles Alfred, 1587717
LOCKE, Gnr, Mark, 863045
LOCKHART, Gnr, John, 1826674
LOCKWOOD, Gnr, William, 1700199
LOMAS, L Sjt, A, 843801
LOMAX, Gnr, Harold, 946522
LONG, Gnr, Edward Alfred, 1645948
LONG, Gnr, George, 1801632
LONG, L Bdr, Reginald Alan, 1719123
LONG, Gnr, Ronald, 948849
LONGFIELD, Bdr, Edward Telford, 881569
LONGHURST, Gnr, Lawrence Edward, 875205
LONGWORTH, Gnr, Thomas, 1591194
LORD, Gnr, Francis, 1629472
LORING, Capt, Gerald Nele, 69042
LOUGH, Gnr, Ernest William, 1089452
LOVAGE, Gnr, George, 854107
LOVELOCK, Gnr, Robert Cornwall, 1796156
LOWE, Gnr, Francis Ernest, 1810590
LOWE, L Bdr, George, 921315
LOWE, Gnr, Joseph Henry, 996222
LOWE, Gnr, Sidney, 1810596
LOWERY, Gnr, John, 872289
LOWES, Gnr, Joseph Cuthbert, 848602
LOWN, L Bdr, Clifford William, 822525
LOWNDES, Gnr, Eric, 1119397
LUCAS, Gnr, , 25486
LUCAS, Bdr, Albert Henry, 1753139
LUCAS, Lt, Henry Arthur, 98862
LUDLOW, Sjt, Robert James, 1064310
LUGG, Gnr, Richard Harry, 958992
LUSCOTT, Gnr, Thomas, 11051563
LUXFORD, Gnr, Sydney Harold, 1746273
LUXTON, WO I (RSM), Frank Herbert, 1066858
LYNESS, Gnr, William, 947515
LYON, Gnr, Joseph, 896992
MacARTHUR, Gnr, James, 1517178
MacBEAN, Lt, Alexander, 182803
MACBETH, Gnr, James Eymons, 2053379
MacDONALD, Gnr, James, 1080893
MACE, Gnr, Arthur Frederick, 1719997
MACFARLANE, Lt-Col, William Alston, 22713
MACKENZIE, Gnr, Leslie, 1709542
MACKIN, Gnr, Stephen, 1789628
MACKINTOSH, Lt, James McIntosh, 100372

MACRAE, Gnr, Alexander, 1766458
MacWILLIAM, Gnr, Charles Alexander, 1547502
MADDISON, L Bdr, Wilfred, 1603452
MAGEE, L Bdr, Eric William, 872077
MANNING, Gnr, Henry Walter, 1104284
MANSFIELD, Gnr, George James Henry, 902247
MARLAND, Gnr, Edward, 948054
MARSDEN, Gnr, Leslie, 1811477
MASON, Gnr, John George, 860511
MATTHEWS, Gnr, Edward, 906431
MAY, Gnr, John Lacey, 1098248
MAYOR, Gnr, Alfred, 855752
McAUGHTRIE, Gnr, Thomas, 838982
McAULAY, Gnr, Francis, 987082
McCALLUM, Gnr, Gilbert, 1444272
McCALLUM, Dvr, Robert, T/3064085
McCANN, Gnr, Matthew Berrill Desmond, 1801634
McCARTEN, Sjt, Daniel, 780536
McCARTHY, Gnr, Florance William, 1786904
McCORMACK, Gnr, Frnk, 4263481
McCORMICK, Gnr, Ernest William, 847280
McCOUBREY, Capt, Robert Taylor, 164294
McCRUM, L Bdr, Thomas, 782894
McCULLOCH, Gnr, Robert, 1787304
McCULLOCH, Gnr, William Henry, 1779808
McCULLY, Gnr, Stanley, 925136
McDERMOTT, Gnr, Roland Alexander, 828534
McDERMOTT, Gnr, Thomas, 1045495
McDONALD, Gnr, George Thomas Christopher, 893063
McDONALD, Gnr, James, 977235
McDONALD, Gnr, John Augustine, 1543177
McDONALD, Gnr, Michael, 1805939
McDONNELL, Gnr, James Carlisle, 7008388
McDONNELL, Gnr, Patrick, 5047056
McELVEEN, Bdr, Thomas, 835569
McEVOY, Gnr, William James, 859698
McEWEN, Lt, Edgar, 165311
McFARLANE, Gnr, David Sage, 1820793
McGARVA, WO II (BSM), Joseph Simpson, 833620
McGINLEY, Gnr, Peter Patrick, 1070727
McGLENNON, Gnr, James, 912217
McGOUGH, Gnr, James Hartley, 1610200
McGOVERN, Gnr, James, 1517252
McGROTTY, Gnr, James, 1545345
McGUINNESS, Bdr, Brian O'Rally, 1545438
McGULL, Gnr, James, 856404
MCILROY, Gnr, Jmaes Mellon, 1096582
McINNES, Gnr, Isaiah, 1545416
McINTOSH, Gnr, Frederick Charles, 996225
McINTYRE, Gnr, James, 872539
MCKAY, Gnr, Donald McIntosh, 889471
McKEVITT, Bdr, Albert, 835285
McKIE, Gnr, George Daniel, 858666
McLATCHIE, Gnr, Hugh Boyd, 1774707
McLEAN, Gnr, James, 872445
McMAHON, Gnr, Henry, 1478716
McMEECHAN, Gnr, Charles, 1481925
McMENEMY, L Bdr, Daniel, 1828416
McMILLAN, L Bdr, Matthew, 812770
McNAB, Gnr, Cyril Peter, 1771927
McNAB, Gnr, Joseph, 1474227
McVEY, Gnr, William John, 1713742
MILBURN, Gnr, William, 794874
MILLER, Gnr, Alfred Anthony Henry, 998946
MITCHELL, Gnr, Harry, 851966
MITCHELL, Gnr, John James Walker, 889861
MOIR, Gnr, Roy Lewis, 13391
MOON, Gnr, Douglas, 948056
MOORE, Gnr, George, 1094263
MUIR, Bdr, James Leslie, 894915

MURDY, Gnr, Frederick Charles, 996228
NICKSON, Sjt, Charles, 871224
O'BRIEN, BQMS, Michael, 1061150
O'CONNEL, Gnr, William Maurice, 1055683
OKEY, Gnr, Fredrick, 840010
OVERELL, Bdr, Frederick William, 849361
OWERS, Gnr, Alfred Robert, 1089363
PARKER, Gnr, Ronald, 1811494
PAYTON, Gnr, Francis, 1810642
PICKERING, Gnr, Frederick Walter, 947562
PICKFORD, Gnr, Ronald J, 5184574
PLAYFORTH, Gnr, Bernard, 900426
QUAYLE, Gnr, Frederick, 1629538
RAND, Gnr, Frank Neale, 1123224
REAST, Gnr, Reuben Edwards, 1603276
RENDELL, Gnr, George William, 1061045
RICHARDSON, Gnr, Harry John, 1475742
ROBERTS, Bdr, Frederick Charles, 1622644
ROBERTS, Gnr, Shadrach, 1092527
ROBINSON, Bdr, Robert Eric, 794036
ROBINSON, Gnr, William John, 892044
ROGERS, Gnr, Arthur, 1603055
ROGERS, Bdr, Kenneth Douglas, 950886
ROPER, Gnr, John Henry, 1101534
RUSSELL, Gnr, Frederick Henry James, 2031886
SALTER, Gnr, Henry Ernest, 904424
SAMPSON, Gnr, Dennis Grenville, 909735
SANDERSON, L Bdr, William, 895370
SAUNDERS, Gnr, William, 941916
SCOTT, Gnr, Charles Sidney, 946055
SCRIVEN, Gnr, Ivor, 1605258
SHAND, Gnr, Henry Henderson, 994876
SHAW, Gnr, James Edward, 1811518
SHELDON, Gnr, Bernard, 1786964
SIGSWORTH, Gnr, Harry Raymond, 1794766
SILLS, Gnr, Harold, 1786878
SIMMONS, Gnr, Lawrence Frederick, 964177
SINFIELD, Gnr, Ronald John, 921537
SISSONS, Gnr, George Alan, 1547265
SLATER, Gnr, Cecil Frederick, 904409
SLY, Gnr, James Charles, 1810680
SMALL, Gnr, Arthur Victor, 1467379
SMITH, Gnr, Enock Joseph, 1810689
SMITH, Gnr, Harry William, 6141214
SMITH, Gnr, Thomas Henry, 850937
SMITH, Gnr, William, 1427246
SPURRELL, Gnr, Victor Charles George, 908620
STANLEY, Bdr, Lawrence, 941956
STEVENS, Capt, Kenneth James Cloete, 102296
STEWART, L Bdr, James Pollock, 799003
STIMPSON, Gnr, Fred, 1602935
STONE, Gnr, Dennis Richard, 860027
STONLEY, Gnr, James George Phillip, 860459
STOREY, Lt, John Dennis, 90357
STOTT, Gnr, Edward Hargreaves, 938110
STOUT, Gnr, Ernest Charles, 990386
SURRIDGE, L Bdr, Paul Leslie, 1576422
THOMAS, Lt, Matthew David, 124089
THOMAS, Gnr, Thomas David, 1605265
THOMPSON, Gnr, Thomas, 1787328
TREVENA, Gnr, Arthur Herbert, 907148
TRIBE, L Sjt, Francis Charles, 1068720
TURNER, Gnr, James Walter, 6203326
WAKE, Gnr, John Arnold, 948909
WALKER, Gnr, John Arthur, 921145
WALL, Gnr, George Ernest, 968257
WALSH, Gnr, William, 1438748
WARD, L Bdr, Cyril James, 990066
WARD, Gnr, John, 906164
WARDELL, Gnr, Robert Henry, 901320

WATERS, Gnr, Arthur Leslie, 1605270
WAUGH, Gnr, Maurice Bertram Athur, 962462
WEST, Gnr, John, 1570679
WESTAWAY, Gnr, Edgar James Alfred, 1524656
WESTON, L Bdr, William Thomas, 6143215
WIBLEY, Gnr, Charles William, 895423
WICKERSON, Gnr, Sydney, 909393
WICKS, Gnr, Cyril Joseph, 964435
WICKSON, Gnr, Harry Victor, 1483299
WIGHTMAN, Gnr, Reuben, 1568620
WILLIAMS, Gnr, Denzil, 881814
WILLIAMSON, Gnr, Stephen, 945537
WILLIS, Gnr, Robert Robson, 1603487
WILSON, Gnr, Victor Charles, 904589
WINSTANLEY, Gnr, David, 860380
WINTER, Gnr, Ronald, 1088927
WOODFINE, Gnr, William, 880058
WRIGHT, Gnr, Charles, 835634
WRIGHT, Gnr, John William, 1104300
YARWOOD, Gnr, Frederick Augustus, 1805203
YOUNG, Gnr, John George, 886451

ROYAL ARMY CATERING CORPS
COOK, Pte, Joseph, 10630583
GREEN, Sjt, Ivor Charles, 1605196
REID, Pte, William, 10631515
SMITH, Pte, Norman Arthur, 5828127
WELLS, Pte, Henry Thomas, 10631054

ROYAL BERKSHIRE REGIMENT
CLUTTERBUCK,Pte,John Charles,6011792
HEMMING,Pte,Charles Donald,5334431

ROYAL CORPS OF SIGNALS
AGAN, Cpl, Urwin, 2336948
ANSELL, Sigmn, George Edward, 2589109
BAILEY, L Cpl, George, 2591332
BAILLIE, Sigmn, Jack McLoud, 2762373
BANKS, L Cpl, James, 2322283
BAYLISS, Sigmn, Charles Edwin, 2365573
BENNET, Sigmn, Duncan, 2340873
BIGGAR, Sigmn, Ernest, 2353692
BRISTOW, Sigmn, Frederick Gordon, 2337038
BUCKINGHAM, Sigmn, Herbert Edward, 6405361
CARR, Sigmn, Stephen Rennison, 2332077
CARTER, Cpl, Bernard Jack, 2350843
CHADWICK, Cpl, Harold Arthur, 2348422
CHAMBERS, Sjt, Ernest William, 2317221
CLEM, Sigmn, John Albert, 2332626
CORBETT, Lt, Dawson Gilbert, 180835
CROCKER, Sigmn, Walter Cecil, 6028953
DACKHAM, L/Cpl, Ernest Edward, 2324209
DANBY, Dvr, Owen Edwin, 2338493
DAND, Sgmn, Reginald Cecil, 597470
DARBY, Sgmn, Henry Joseph, 2588917
DAVIES, Sjt, Charles, 5495085
DAY, Cpl, Wilfred Dennis Arthur, 2336266
DEAN, Dvr, George, 2317333
DEIGHTON, Cpl, Thomas William, 2321855
DENNY, Sigmn, Frederick Arthur, 2333158
DIGHTON, L/Cpl, William Thomas, 2346965
DIXON, Sgmn, Ellis, 2333048
DOUGLAS, Sgmn, James, 2350441
DOYLE, CQMS, Edward James, 1414353
DUNCALF, Sgmn, Thomas Ashley, 2343082
FARADAY, Sigmn, Robert Edwin, 2326975
FINLAYSON, Sigmn, William Drummond, 2343365
GAFFIN, Cpl, Merton Eugene, 2341202
GALLERY, Cpl, Henry, 3519995
GARNET, Sigmn, Peter, 235682

GERRISH, Lt, Archiblad Victor, 168890
GRIFFIN, LCpl, George, 3307920
GRIFFITHS, L Cpl, Ivor James, 2353493
GWYN, Sigmn, John David, 2364853
HIKIN, Sigmn, William Clinton, 2343481
HILL, Sigmn, Peter Raymond, 2329693
HOLDSWORTH, Sigmn, Harold, 2344553
HORSBURGH, L Cpl, George Gair, 392044
HOUSE, Dvr, William George Norman, 2323135
HOWARD, Sigmn, Leslie Arthur Malcolm, 2336786
HUGHES, Sigmn, William John, 2351764
IRWIN, Sigmn, William George, 2341232
JAMES, Sigmn, Edward Robert, 2367227
JAQUET, Sigmn, Edwin Dennis, 2337270
JARRETT, Cpl, Ronald David, 2353496
JOHNSON, Cpl, Kenneth Alfred, 2359829
JOHNSON, Sigmn, Wilfred Thomas, 2348087
JONES, Sigmn, Ernest, 2367018
JONES, Sigmn, Meirion Wynn, 2333667
KANE, Sigmn, William, 2365402
KENDRICK, Cpl, Eric, 2591476
KENNEISON,Sgmn,A R, 259135
KING, L Cpl, Fred, 2350711
KIRKBRIGHT, Sigmn, Ronald William, 2353412
KIRTLEY, Sigmn, William Oswald, 2319143
KNIGHT, Dvr, Peter William, 2343500
KNIGHTS, Cpl, William Henry, 2315852
KNOWLES, Cpl, John Henry, 2596745
LAW, Sigmn, Adam Flemming, 3245395
LAWCOCK, Dvr, Colin Edwin, 153993
LAWRENCE, Cpl, George William, 2319244
LEANG, Dvr, James, 2350772
LEASON, Sigmn, James William, 2356209
LECLERCQ, Sjt, Richard Raoul, 2576710
LEDGER, L Cpl, Kenneth Leonard, 6458086
LEE, Sigmn, Arthur Fletcher, 2332281
LEE, Sigmn, Herbert John, 2349314
LESLIE, Sigmn, Raymond Eric, 2589672
LEWIS, Dvr, Val Alexis, 5336958
LINDSAY, Cpl, James, 2353302
LIPSCOMBE, Dvr, Dyson Harry Neal, 2591463
LLOYD, Sigmn, Richard, 2364798
LUND, Sigmn, Cyril, 2370030
MACDONALD, Sigmn, Thomas Andrew Walter, 2331258
MACHIN, Cpl, Harry Gordon, 2336105
MACPHERSON, Dvr, Ian, 2580832
MARLOW, Sigmn, Arthur William George, 2345596
MASTERS, Sigmn, Douglas Neville, 2336232
McAULIFFE, WO II (CSM), John, 2316938
McDONALD, L Cpl, John Vincent, 2590199
McDONALD, Sjt, Paul, 2322204
McDOUGALL, Sigmn, James, 2358089
McDOWELL, L Cpl, Edward Barr, 2359560
McHUGH, L Cpl, Patrick Joseph, 2346442
McMANUS, Sigmn, James, 2326759
MINSHULL, Sigmn, Andrew, 2586896
MONTGOMERY, Sigmn, John, 2583954
MORGAN, Sigmn, Victor, 2346336
MORLEY, Sigmn, William, 2356705
NEWTON, Sigmn, Albert Thomas, 2353676
OATES, LCpl, Norman Murgatroyd, 2347830
OLDFIELD, LCpl, Geoffrey, 2356710
PERRY, Sigmn, Gordon Eric, 2361980
PIERCE, Sigmn, John Henry, 2323342
PLATT, Sigmn, Fred, 2340800
POPE, Lt Col, Francis Thew, 11997
RAYNOR, Sigmn, William Henry, 2346192
REEVES, Sigmn, Bertie Edwin, 2364103
RENSON, Sigmn, Reginald Harry, 2595729
RIGG, Sigmn, Douglas Stuart, 2331540

ROBERTS, Sigmn, Ivor Hugh, 2590580
ROBINSON, Dvr, William, 2364649
ROBY, Signmn, Albert Thomas, 2358008
RUSSELL, Sjt, John, 2325059
SANDERSON, Cpl, Robert Henry, 2323751
SLADE, Sigmn, Albert Thomas, 2336862
SMITH, L Cpl, Albert Charles, 2318022
SUDDES, Sigmn, John Edward, 2332563
SUTTON, Sigmn, Arthur Aubrey, 2325115
SYDNEY, Capt, Ian Duncan, 153453
THOMPSON, Sigmn, Robert Douglas, 3190226
THORNE, CQMS, Norman Walter, 2361087
WEBB, Dvr, Derrick Leeson, 2571711
WILLIAMS, Sigmn, Leslie Harold, 2326016
WOOD, Dvr, Frederick Henry, 759070
WOOD, Dvr, William, 2333707

ROYAL ENGINEERS
ABBOTT, Spr, Donald Luke, 1991272
AUSTIN, Spr, John Henry, 2002291
BAIRSTO, Spr, Joseph Arthur, 2145692
BAKER, Spr, William, 1870953
BALLARD, Spr, Clifford, 3855038
BARBER, Dvr, Joseph, 1983253
BARNES, Spr, James, 1877450
BARNES, Spr, John William, 2092575
BARRETT, Cpl, Keith Cecil, 2090349
BATES, Spr, Arthur John, 1888782
BATLEY, Spr, Donald George, 2003078
BAXTER, Spr, Wallace Noel, 2120306
BEECH, Spr, Victor Wallace, 1888803
BENNETT, L Cpl, Stanley, 1871986
BROOKS, Spr, Joseph Sylvesta Richardson, 844661
BROOM, L Cpl, Herbert Edward, 5828457
BUGLER, L Cpl, William Charles, 1897661
BUTCHER, Spr, Alfred William, 2090354
BUTCHER, Dvr, Stephen Roy, 2003401
CATE, Spr, Arnold Arthur, 1873298
CATTERMOLE, Spr, Cyril William, 2069981
CHILDS, Spr, Albert Edward, 2068897
CLARK, Spr, William, 2077821
CLEAVER, Dvr, Samuel Alexander, 2090379
COLE, Dvr, John Horace, 2091173
COOPER, Dvr, Stanley, 2091259
COOPER, Spr, William Henry, 3858499
CORNWELL, Spr, Percy Denis, 2062104
DANT, Spr, William Albert, 2069998
DIX, Spr, Clifford Benjamin George, 2077957
DODD, Spr, Arthur, 1897823
DOWSETT, Spr, Dennis Cyril, 6016722
DRIVER, Cpl, Alfred, 2077087
DUCKER, Spr, Douglas Stanley, 2090489
DYSON, Spr, Harold, 3854769
ELLIOTT, WO II (ECQMS), Wilfred George, 1869132
FAWKES, Spr, Frank Sidney, 1873748
FLAHERTY, Spr, Thomas Allen, 2000515
FORD, Spr, Frederick John, 1915156
FRANKS, Spr, George William, 2091248
FRIEND, L Cpl, Sydney Neville, 2092130
GAUTREY, Spr, Neville Claude, 2073577
GRANT, Spr, Richard George, 1918810
GRAYSON, L Cpl, Noel, 1871213
HART, L Cpl, Cecil Kenneth, 2090360
HART, Spr, Joseph William Lionel Alfred, 941750
HAYLOCK, Dvr, Herbert Armistice, 2093005
HEATH, Dvr, Graham Gerald Lancelot, 2091186
HEK, Spr, Ronald Alexander, 1871122
HOLLAND, Spr, Edward Roy, 2090361
HOLMES, Sjt, John Henry, 1869672
HORNE, Spr, Joseph, 1888704

HOTSON, Dvr, Thomas Harold, 2090380
HUCKLE, Cpl, Eric Holmes, 2073568
HUMPHREYS, Spr, George Wallace, 1873827
HUNT, Spr, Harry Ronald, 2075269
IVES, Spr, Bertie John, 1892414
JARVIS, Spr, Harry, 2128766
JEFFERSON, Spr, Montie Louis, 209334
JELLINGS, L Cpl, John, 2070119
JERVIS, Spr, George Ronald, 2013581
JOHNSON, WO II (CSM), Herbert Ivo, 1867685
JOHNSON, Spr, Louis Alfred Edward, 1861650
JONES, L Cpl, Jack Joseph, 2092133
JONES, Spr, Wynn Clwyd, 4033397
JUDE, Sjt, Harold Albert, 2091253
KEENAN, Cpl, Thomas, 1872898
KEMPTON, Spr, James Alfred, 1874826
KENNARD, Spr, Frederick John, 1874769
KERBY, Spr, Gilbert John Haig, 5671161
KING, Spr, Donald Sydney, 2070126
LAND, Maj, Frank Henry, 111262
LARGE, Sjt, George Henry, 5823083
LARKING, Spr, Edgar Arthur George, 1872448
LAW, Spr, Albert Edmund, 2194205
LAW, L Cpl, John McKenzie, 1892268
LEE, Spr, Geoffrey Edward, 1922088
LEIGH, Cpl, Harry Ambrose, 1869472
LEWIS, Dvr, Ronald William Vernon, 20922134
LILLYCROP, Cpl, Reuben Edgar, 1869248
LISTER, L Cpl, Alfred Paul Sutton, 2072253
LISTER, Spr, Arthur Noel, 1873768
LOGAN, Spr, Robert Walter, 1951097
LONG, Sjt, George Frederick, 1861980
LUCAS, Spr, Alfred John, 1874263
MANUEL, Spr, Joseph Percy, 1906635
MARSH, Spr, Bertie Charles, 1903892
MATTLESS, Spr, Henry, 5933472
MAWDESLEY, Spr, George Ernest, 2013232
McCRAW, Spr, Dennis John, 2130530
MCGINLEY, Spr, Richard Taylor, 2000525
MCGREGOR, Spr, Walter, 1871697
MENTON, Spr, Stanley, 1874099
MILLER, Sjt, Frederick John, 2090365
MYERS, Dvr, John, 2003414
NICHOLLS, Dvr, Victor, 2003415
PAINTER, Dvr, Denis Edward Benjamin, 2003416
PARRIMAN, Spr, Harold Herbert, 1897800
PECKOVER, Cpl, John William, 1871858
PENTELOW, Spr, Bernard Raymond, 2090367
RANKIN, Spr, Hugh McKinnell, 1873167
REED, Spr, Fred, 1922505
RICHARDSON, GnrEric, , 888776
ROBERTS, Spr, Arthur, 2091546
ROOKE, Cpl, Frank Charles, 2069997
ROSS, Spr, George, 1907065
ROTE, Spr, George Andrew, 1906330
SALMON, Spr, Eric Arthur, 2092137
SCOTT, Spr, Frederick John, 1947425
SEALY, Sjt, George, 2204208
SIMPOLE, Spr, Jack William, 2092136
SMITH, Dvr, Ronald George, 2003424
SPIVEY, L Cpl, Albert John, 2077673
STAMMERS, Dvr, Percy Vernon, 2003425
SUNDERLAND, Spr, Hary Albert, 1873173
SWANN, Dvr, George Leonard, 2091757
THOMPSON, Spr, Walter Douglas, 1874204
TITHERIDGE, Spr, George William, 1870698
TOLLIDAY, Spr, Frederick Stanley, 2117168
TOOZER, Spr, William John, 1906385
TOPHAM, WO II (CSM), Richard Charles, 1866418
TROMANS, Spr, James Henry, 1909661

TRUMAN, Spr, William Arthur, 1922768
TRUNDLEY, Spr, Alef Alfred, 2073578
VAUGHAN, Spr, Neville Joseph, 1873636
WALLMAN, L Cpl, Ronald Thomas, 2069162
WARING, Spr, Alec Edmund, 2040755
WATTS, Spr, Fredrick Edward, 833789
WESTON, Spr, Edward Douglas, 1922615
WINDMILL, Dvr, Ronald Osborn, 2094285
WINTER, Spr, Albert Leonard, 855069

ROYAL ELECTRICAL AND MECHANICAL ENGINEERS
AITKEN, Cpl, Frederick James, 7593346
ASHBY, Crftsmn, Benjamin Silas, 7636515
BALLINGER, Crftsmn, Cedric, 1579028
BATEMAN, Crftsmn, Gerald, 7588799
BURNETT, Crftsmn, George, 7629017
BURNS, Crftsmn, Thomas, 7627243
BURROWS, Sjt, Leslie, 157536
COLLINS, Crftsmn, Basil Fred, 7617624
CONDELL, S Sjt, George, 7582953
DASHPER, Cftmn, Herbert, 7642795
DAVIES, Crftsmn, Thomas Victor, 7651798
DAVIES, S/Sjt, Sidney John, 7623092
DUNN, L/Cpl, Sidney, 86117
EDWARDS, Crftsmn, Cyril, 7599879
GATWARD, Craftsman, William George, 7637862
GILES, Craftsman, Kenneth Louis, 7641764
HELDEN, Craftsman, Denys Edgar, 5118838
HOWARTH, Craftsman, Arthur Andrew, 7637052
INGLIS, Craftsman, Alex, 7639833
JACKMAN, Sjt, Philip Henry James, 7583867
LEVEY, Craftsman, Cecil Ronald, 7614357
LODGE, Craftsman, Wilfred, 7643331
MCALEESE, Craftsman, Joseph Patrick, 7643222
MCLEAN, Craftsman, Lawrence White, 7603329
NEWELL, WOI (Armt SM), Cyril Edward, 7589927
PARRY, Craftsman, Leonard Joseph, 2045185
PARSONS, Craftsman, John Arthur, 10533288
PENDLETON, Craftsman, Stanley Collins, 7599096
PRENDERGAST, Armr Sjt, Joseph, 7612652
REX, Armt S Sjt, Edward Vernon, 2035229
ROBERTS, Craftsman, James Llewellyn, 7598873
SIMONDS, L Cpl, Frederick John, 7589168
STAINES, Sjt, Percy Ronald, 7603558
STEVENS, Cpl, Alfred Henry, 7623365
STEVENS, Sjy, Frank, 7584164
STOCKDALE, Craftsman, Alan Ernest, 326514
VEITCH, Craftsman, Henry Garnsey, 7639085

ROYAL NORFOLK REGIMENT
JOHNSTON, Pte, Kenneth Lawrence, 577
MEDLAND, Cpl, Thomas Gerald James, 5770489
NUNN, Cpl, Jack William, 5775698

2 ROYAL NORFOLK REGIMENT
HORNBY, Pte, Harry, 3858553

4 ROYAL NORFOLK REGIMENT
ARNOLD, Pte, Harry, 5774217
BARRETT, Pte, Allan Walter, 5573361
BECK, Pte, Samuel Robert, 5773746
BONNER, L Cpl, Maurice Norman, 5779370
DEEKS, Pte , Albert Frederick, 5572304
DENNIS, Pte, Noel, 5776325
DUFFY, Pte, James, 5779376
DUTTON, CQMS, Edward John Rupert, 5771746
BAILEY, Pte, Newton Charles, 5573346
ANNIS, L Cpl, William George, 5774693
CROFTS, Pte, George Albert, 1475405
HERWIN, Pte, Eric George, 5772113

BERRY, Pte, Edward George, 5771098
BROWN, Sjt, Alfred Charles, 5774340
BRYANT, Pte, Harold Roland, 5573460
CHAPMAN, Pte, James, 5573494
CROWE, Pte, George Thomas, 5778720
DAINES, Pte, Arthur Silvanus, 5781986
DAUBNEY, Pte, Frederick Reginald, 5572957
DREW, Pte, Lawrence Edward, 5774091
DURRANT, Pte, Kenneth, 5776832
DYE, Pte, Henry Robert, 5774375
EDWARDS, Pte, George, 5775482
FORD, L Sjt, Cyril Richard, 5774833
FULLER, Pte, Frederick R, 5774347
FUTTER, Pte, Clifford, 5781799
GILLINGWATER, Pte, Roy, 5775715
GOODACRE, Pte, Albert Alfred Daniel, 5775400
GOODINGS, L Cpl, Stanley J, 5778787
GRAY, Pte, Albert Edward, 5770202
GRAY, Pte, Leonard L, 5773778
HARSENT, Pte, Frederick William, 57755591
HARWOOD, Pte, George Gilbert, 5774218
HEWLETT, Pte, David Cockburn, 13031772
HOLT, Sjt, George Alfred, 576932
HOPSON, Pte, Sidney George, 5573428
HORNER, Pte, Percy James, 5778997
JACOBS, Pte, Wilfred Stanley George, 5775251
JARVIS, Pte, Cecil, 5573576
JEFFS, 2/Lt, Kenneth Frank, 184460
JOHNSON, Pte, Frederick William Samuel, 5779013
JORDAN, Pte, Alfred Albert, 5573551
KNIGHT, Pte, Harold Edward, 5780264
LARKIN, Pte, George Albert, 5781189
LAUGHLIN, Pte, Horace James, 5773951
LAWRENCE, Pte, Allen Palmer, 5772374
LINCOLN, Pte, Frederick Raymond, 5772354
LINCOLN, Pte, Percy William, 5767280
LITTLE, Pte, Frederick Thomas, 5773498
LITTLEJOHNS, Pte, Leslie Victor, 5782359
LOCK, L Cpl, Ralph Drayton, 5775614
LONG, Pte, William Richard, 5778873
MACDONALD, Lt, Alastair David, 102402
MACKLIN, Pte, Frederick George, 5573293
MINNS, Pte, Harold Arthur, 5779032
OSBORNE, Pte, Harold, 5782286
PAYNE, Pte, Norman, 5781842
PETTINGILL, Pte, Edward Thomas, 5776769
SCASE, Pte, Charles William, 5775126
SMITTEN, Pte, Harry, 5573014
SMYTH, Pte, Frank Joseph, 5573478
STURGEON, Pte, Charles William James, 5775651
TAPPIN, Pte, Alfred Jerome, 5775522
TEECE, Pte, Leonard, 5776712
VERTIGAN, Pte, William George, 5772379
WALDREN, Pte, John Elias, 5774066
WHITTALL, Pte, Edwin Oliver, 5774690
WOOTTON, L Cpl, John Reginald, 5572272
WRIGHT, Cpl, John Thomas, 5771809
YOUNGMAN, Pte, Ivan George, 5774224
KNOWLES, L Cpl, Alfred, 5772045
STONE, Pte, Edward John, 5775213
LARN, Pte, Theodore Ronald, 5778857
PRATT, Pte, George Arthur, 5774848

5 ROYAL NORFOLK REGIMENT
CHIDWICK, Pte, Sydney Alfred Noel, 5773456
DACK, L/Cpl, Edward, 5775502
DODD, Pte, Albert, 5776710
DRAKE, Pte, Reginald Victor,
DYE, L/Sjt, Colin Davey, 5770891

JENKINS, Pte, William, 5777117
JOHNSON, Pte, Arthur Richard, 5776677
JOHNSON, L Cpl, Arthur Thomas, 5773790
JONES, Sjt, Donald Alfred, 5773006
JONES, Pte, Leslie John, 5775467
KENDLE, Cpl, Cecil Robert, 5775158
LARGE, Pte, Sidney Henry, 5773905
LORRIMAN, Pte, Charles, 5773482
LOVE, Pte, Henry, 5776744
LOWTHER, L Cpl, Ernest George, 5775415
McCANN, Pte, John Edward, 5779448
McKEAN, 1/Lt, Peter Halley, 176007
NEAL, Pte, John, 5772634

6 ROYAL NORFOLK REGIMENT
BLOCKWELL, Pte, Thomas George Empire, 5778138
DEAN, Pte, John Albert, 5773849
CLARKE, L Cpl, Thomas Evans, 5776163
GRIMWOOD, Pte, Horace, 5774458
IVINS, Sjt, Peter Dunbar, 5774395
JARVIS, L Cpl, Albert Charles, 5778204
JENNINGS, Pte, Alfred Thomas, 5773035
JONES, 2/Lt, Arthur Ernest, 189213
KERRIDGE, L Cpl, Frederick Thomas, 5774406
KNIGHTS, Pte, Harry Russell, 5775777
LAMBERT, Pte, William Henry, 5778213
LANGHAM, Pte, Arthur, 5775697
LANSDALE, Pte, Ernest, 5778215
LEE, Pte, Leonard, 5773794
LEEDER, Pte, Ernest William, 5773886
LEMMON, Pte, Cyril, 5778217
MAY, Pte, James Capel, 5775187
McNEILL, Pte, William, 5773860
SMITH, L Cpl, William Archibald George, 5777563
WOODWOOD, Pte, Peter William, 5774875
HIPPERSON, Pte, Sidney James, 5774453
LORD, WO II (CSM), Cecil Victor, 5768015

ROYAL NORTHUMBERLAND FUSILIERS
ARMSTRONG, Sjt, Angus, 4273537
COUTTS, Fus, John, 4271203
CREE, Fus, Norman Alexander, 4279309
DANIELS, Fus, Robert Henry, 6210435
DODD, Fus, Joseph Thompson, 4278543
DORAN, Fus, John George, 4276646
DOUGLAS, Fus, Wilfred, 4273547
DOUTHWAITE, Fus, Lester, 4275043
HEMMINGS, Fus, Sydney, 4127779
HENDERSON, Fus, John Willis, 4274079
HUME, Fus, John, 4275592
KNOWLES, Fus, Samuel, 4278712
MILLS, Fus, Gordon Wilson, 4272872
MORTON, Fus, Ronald, 4273505
NEWTON, Fus, Mark, 4274091
NIXON, Cpl, Robert, 4273278
PATTERSON, Fus, Robert, 2982871
RILEY, Fus, Douglas Haig, 4275457
SWEENEY, Fus, Thomas, 4276942
THOMPSON, Fus, George Edward, 4271609
WHITE, Fus, George, 4273349
YATES, Pte, Frederick, 14407547

SHERWOOD FORESTERS
BANKS, Pte, Frederick Charles, 4620502
BARTLETT, L Cpl, Henry James, 4756027
BENJAMIN, Pte, Adron, 4620510
BROWN, Pte, Kenneth William, 4983484
BROWNLOW, Pte, Edward Lawrence, 4980213
CLARKE, Pte, Samuel Edward, 4975341

DEAN, Pte, George Arthur, 4976932
HARRIS, Pte, Edward, 4981659
HAYES, Pte, William George, 4756110
INGLE, Pte, George Robert, 4984654
JEBSON, Pte, Ernest Edward, 4977650
JONES, Pte, Cyril Ivor, 4756123
JONES, L Cpl, George Frederick, 4977544
KEMP, Pte, Albert Joseph, 4756125
KINDER, Pte, Harold, 4978006
KINGHT, Pte, Frederick Clifford, 4979519
KIRK, L Cpl, Joseph, 4977763
LACEY, Pte, Frederick James, 4750895
LAWTON, Pte, Edwin, 4978705
LEE, Pte, Alfred William, 4753972
LESTER, Pte, Edward, 4984590
LOCKETT, Pte, Ronald Lionel, 4750938
LOVEGROVE, L Cpl, Jack Leonard Leslie, 4859063
MACASKILL, L Sjt, Angus, 4977349
MADIN, Pte, William Arthur, 4977726
MELLOWS, Pte, Jack, 4984663
RADFORD, Pte, Lionel, 4619539
ROOME, Pte, Wilfred Harry, 4976327
SCATTERGOOD, Pte, William Henry, 4978318
SIMONDS, Pte, George Victor, 4754022
STREADER, Pte, Fredrick James, 4750775
VERRAN, Pte, John Cecil, 4756220
VICKERS, Pte, David, 4907749
WALKER, Pte, Frederick George, 4978687
WILLIAMS, Cpl, James William, 4756259
WILLIAMS, Pte, Leslie, 4978083
WILLSON, Lt, Alfred Troop, 85922
WILSON, L Cpl, Albert Harold, 4756260
WOODHEAD, Sjt, Kenneth Judson, 4977553
WRIGHT, L Cpl, Donald Arthur, 4981812
WRIGHT, Pte, George Edward, 4756272

SUFFOLK
BEAKLEY, Pte, Rowan Peter, 5933672
CRANE, Pte, Cyril, 5826179
LANCEFIELD, Pte, Charles George, 6020936

1 SUFFOLK REGIMENT
JAMES, Pte, Basil, 5830872
KEEP, L Cpl, Albert George Francis, 6020927
KERRY, Pte, Stanley Albert, 6019098
KINGWELL, L Cpl, Sydney William, 6020930

2 SUFFOLK REGIMENT
JOHNSON, Pte, William Alfred, 5932276
JONES, Cpl, Stanley Robert, 5827689
KELLETT, L Sjt, Michael John, 5825584
KING, Pte, Aubrey Frederick, 5833722
KING, Pte, Charles Russel Leonard, 5828716
KINGFISHER, Cpl, Cyril, 5824746
KITCHENER, Pte, Alec Bernard, 5833820
KNEUSS, Sjt, Paul Cecil, 5833450
KNOPP, L Cpl, John Edward, 5830418
LAING, Pte, Harold, 5831218
LAKEY, Pte, Ernest Edward, 5828945
STOPHER, Cpl, Cyril James, 5826024
WILSON, Pte, Bryan James, 5828771

4 SUFFFOLK
ADAMS, Pte, Ernest Frederick, 6019163
ANDREWS, Pte, John William Francis, 5832909
ANKER, Pte, George, 5832910
ASHBY, Pte, Charles William, 6018963
ASHDOWN, Pte, Stanley Salonika, 6020674
BACON, Pte, Leonard, 5824468
BADMAN, L Cpl, Charles Benjamin, 5827896

BAILEY, Pte, George Alfred, 5835444
BANNISTER, Pte, Arthur Horace Frederick, 6020610
BEALES, Pte, Christopher Robert, 577

4887
BEEBY, Pte, John Henry, 5835451
BENDING, Pte, George, 5827417
BERRY, Pte, Alfred Robert, 5828243
BORLEY, Pte, Reuben William Cecil, 6020734
BOWLES, Pte, Alexander Arthur, 6019179
BRANDON, Pte, Henry Percival, 6020684
BUGG, Pte, Sidney Charles, 5828171
BULLER, Pte, Henry, 5827298
BURCH, Pte, Harry Walter, 6013679
CADY, Pte, John, 5827008
CALEY, Pte, George, 5835463
CATOR, Pte, James Henry, 6018971
CHAMBERS, C Sjt, George Lorraine, 5826127
CHAPMAN, L Sjt, Edward Charles, 5826579
COOK, Pte, Cyril, 5832957
COOK, Cpl, Frank Herbert, 5826596
CORK, Lt, Timothy Everett, 164837
COTTIS, L Sjt, Percy Stanley Ernest, 6020696
CRANE, Pte, Percy George, 5827667
CRISP, WO II (CSM), Alfred Arthur George, 5822511
CRUSSELL, L Cpl, Leslie David, 6020699
DALTON, Pte, Arnold John, 874487
DAVEY, Pte, Robert Seymour, 5825975
DEACON, Pte, Charles Albert, 6013504
DEEKS, Pte, Arthur George, 6021095
DIXON, Pte, Walter Phillip Arthur, 5827933
DOOLAN, Pte, Cyril Stuart, 6019070
DRIVER, Pte, Albert, 5831194
DUNNETT, Pte, Allen, 5827167
DURRANT, Pte, James William, 5828195
ELY, Pte, F Charles, 5830616
ENGLAND, Pte, Sidney John, 6020613
FAYERS, Pte, Edward William, 6013702
FISHER, Pte, Henry Edward, 5833174
FLACK, Pte, Reginald, 5827942
FOUNTAIN, L Cpl, Jack Alexander, 5832591
FULLERTON, Cpl, Douglas Vincent, 5829591
FURZE, Pte, Gordon Phillip, 6028814
GAMMAGE, Pte, Walter, 5829598
GARNER, Pte, Olly Valentine, 5824786
GARRATT, Pte, Ronald, 5827950
GARROD, Pte, Frederick Charles, 5835273
GILLBANKS, Pte, Bernard Creamer, 6021169
GIRLING, Pte, Stephen Thomas, 5826891
GOSLING, Pte, Frederick George, 5828097
GOSTLING, L Cpl, David John, 5828782
GREATOREX, Pte, Cyril Browning, 6007831
GREEN, Pte, Wilfred Needham, 5829844
GRIMMER, Pte, Wilfred Edward, 5834987
GRIMWADE, Pte, Herbert George, 6020746
HILDER, Pte, Albert Thomas, 6013516
HODGSON, Cpl, Richard Derrick, 6013870
HORNING, Pte, Stanley James, 6020589
HUME, Pte, Walter George, 6020749
JEFFRIES, Pte, Philip Henry John, 6020649
JONES, Cpl, Henry Pryce, 5827281
KEEBLE, Sjt, Derick George, 5826483
KEEBLE, Pte, John William, 5827824
KEEBLE, Pte, Walter, 6021172
KEMP, Pte, Cyril, 6020650
KEMP, Pte, Reginald John, 5830611
KENT, Pte, Herbert Charles, 5825640
KERR, Pte, Walter Robert, 5827457
KESTER, Pte, Douglas, 5834681
KING, Pte, John William Francis, 5827721

KIRVIN, Pte, Andrew Edward, 6013650
LAW, Pte, Cecil George, 13020248
LAWRENCE, Pte, Albert, 5824200
LEECH, L Cpl, Charles, 5825374
LIFFEN, Pte, Robert Henry, 5826702
LING, Pte, Brian Samuel John, 5828197
LING, Pte, Victor George, 5830602
LLEWELLYN, Pte, Leslie George, 6020074
LOGAN, Pte, John, 5832701
MANNING, Pte, Frederick Louis, 5827815
MANNING, Pte, William Charles, 5825799
MARSH, Pte, Albert Edward, 5829619
MINTER, Pte, Arthur James, 5825712
NOYCE, Pte, George William Sydney, 5827459
PAUL, Pte, Harry Gordon, 6286716
PLUMB, Cpl, Harry, 5825180
POWRIE, Pte, John McIntosh, 5829603
REARDON, Pte, Leslie William, 5829626
RICHARDSON, Pte, Henry Arthur John, 5826837
ROGERS, Pte, John Thomas, 5829590
SCHOFIELD, Pte, William John, 5829800
SHELDRAKE, Pte, Frederick Arthur, 5828019
SKEGGS, Pte, George, 5829640
SNELLING, Pte, Alfred Ernest, 5829644
STEARNE, Pte, Roydon Samuel, 5826882
STEARNE, Pte, William Selby, 5826886
STOCKMAN, Pte, George Victor, 5829755
TRUMPETER, Pte, George Ellis, 5827067
TURNER, Pte, George, 5829975
TUTTLE, Pte, Thomas Charles, 5826634
WARNER, Pte, Geoffrey William, 58271776
WEINBLATT, Pte, Raphael Leslie, 5829641
WEST, Pte, Charles Henry, 5828978
WILDEY, Pte, Edwin James, 5828992
WYTHE, Pte, Victor Jack, 5826852

5 SUFFOLK REGIMENT
ALLEN, Pte, Frederick Jack, 5827890
BAALHAM, Pte, Frederick Charles, 5826748
BACKLER, Pte, George Wilfred, 5828404
BALAAM, Pte, Edward George, 5828591
BIDWELL, Pte, Arnold Arthur, 5933360
BLAKE, Pte, William Arthur, 5832478
BOSWORTH, Pte, Ernest Edward, 4805309
BROWN, Pte, Austin, 5830716
CHAPMAN, Cpl, Ronald Thomas, 5828635
DAVIS, Pte, Harry Douglas, 5950407
DEARSLEY, Pte, Reginald, 5827364
DEXTER, Pte, John Harry, 5835483
DOVE, Pte, Godfrey Verdan, 4805330
DULEY, Pte, Joseph William, 5835720
DURRANT, Cpl, Leslie Rushmore, 5828200
FRENCH, Pte, Peter, 5834090
FULLER, Pte, Albert Richard Lionel, 5828737
FULLER, Pte, Christopher Charles, 5828288
GLADWELL, Pte, Francis Thomas, 5828483
GREEN, Pte, Norman Henry, 5827714
HARDY, L Cpl, William, 4805372
HASLAM, Pte, Frank, 4805261
HOPKINSON, Pte, George Henry, 4805244
HOWE, Pte, Arthur William, 5828944
JAMES, Pte, Leslie Clarence, 5832667
JARVIS, Pte, Robert, 5956643
KNIGHT, Pte, Charles Frank, 5832683
KNIGHTS, Pte, Harry Thomas, 5832684
LAND, Pte, Norman, 4805393
LEE, Pte, Charles Thomas, 5949782
LEEDER, Pte, Herbert Allan, 5828391
LOCKE, Cpl, Ernest Henry, 5948738
LOCKWOOD, Cpl, Donald William, 5828711

LOCKWOOD, Pte, Frederick William, 5833041
MacGREGOR, Pte, John Alexander, 5949464
MARTIN, Pte, Reginald A, 5828947
PARTIDGE, Pte, Arthur Frederick, 5828952
PRECIOUS, Pte, Allen James, 5828955
RICH, Pte, Sidney Walter, 5828178
SARGEANT, Pte, Robert Thomas Joe, 5828659
SEAGER, Pte, Kitchener Harold, 5826529
SHARPE, Pte, Frederick Arthur, 5828152
TRAVIS, Pte, Cyril Doyle, 5179661
WARD, Pte, Edward William, 5828962
WESLEY, Pte, James Harold, 5828507
WRIGHT, Pte, Sidney Harold, 5828261
WYATT, Pte, Cyril John, 5950403
YOUNG, Pte, Robert, 6028573

TERRITORIAL ARMY NURSING SERVICE
INGHAM, Sister, Alice Ann, 213559
MacGREGOR, Sister, Annie, 213823

WEST YORKSHIRE REGIMENT
BAXTER, Sjt, Lawrence Edward, 4535425

WORCESTERSHIRE REGIMENT
LANE, C Sjt, Albert Ernest Leslie, 5249708

Royal Air Force

ABLETT, AC1, William, 1152717
ADSHEAD, W/O, Percy James, 1125707
AISBITT, Sjt, Thomas, 355 Sqn
AITKEN, W/O, John Seton, 580933
ALDERSON, LAC, Joseph Batty, 539725
ANDERTON, AC2, James, 1085594
ANDERTON, AC1, William Bramwell, 1120401
ANHOLM, LAC, Ronald, 1302851
ARMSTRONG, FL/Lt, Ronald William, 77799
ASPINALL, Cpl, Leslie Arthur, 1101999
AULT, Sq/Ldr, Kenneth, 33214
BAILEY, FL/Sjt, William Archie, 1600853
BAKER, Sjt, Dennis Harold, 1394235
BAKER, AC2, Stanley James, 927430
BALDWYN, Sjt, Mervyn John Fitzhardinge, 771896
BAMBRIDGE, Sjt, Leslie, 1262451
BANKS, FL/Sjt, Frederick Cecil, 1286602
BARBER, LAC, George John William, 1132321
BARKER, FL//Sjt, Eric Wilfred, 1586121
BARKER, FL/Sjt, Ronald Frederick, 759017
BARLOW, Flying Offr, Cyril Oscare, J/26409
BARNETT, FL/Lt, Redmond Lewis, 111237
BELL, Sjt, James Charles Alfred, 970852
BENT, FL/Lt, Arthur Lea Baldwin, 118154
BOWLES, LAC, Thomas Henry, 641958
BREWER, FL/Lt, John Edward Derrel, 113271
BRODIE, AC2, William Forbes Petrie, 993595
BROUGHTON, W/O, Rowland, 1021053
BULL, FL/Sjt, Stephen John, 87153
CARR, Sjt, Trevor, 1622921
CARROL, AC2, Robert, 1098479
CHARLOTTES, LAC, Reginald Alfred, 1204036
CHILDS, FL/Sjt, Stanley Thomas, 365210
CHIPPINDALE, Sgt, Kenneth James, 952872
CHRITIAN, FL/Sjt, Charles David, 970186
COOK, W/O, Howard Cecil, 1600777F

COOKSON, Flt Lieut (Nav), David, 50488
COOPER, Sjt, Arthur Walvin, 1819819
DAVEY, Cpl, John Edwin, 915792
DAVIES, AC2, Joyda Howell, 1409059
DAVIS, FL/Lt, Cecil Brian Powell, 111244
DAWSON-SCOTT, FL/Lt, Keith Desmond, 102149
DICKENSON, LAC, Charles, 970595
DOBSON, LAC, FH, 1169985
DRAKE, Sjt, Andrew Conway Emil, 785098
DRAPER, Fl/Sjt, John Henry, 1802379
DUNDAS, Sq/Ldr, Kenneth Crispin Vivian, DFC
DURHAM, Cpl, James Alfred, 959838
DURRANT, W/O, Robert Harold, 1437395
DYSON, LAC, James Thomas, 1002145
ELLIS, LAC, James William, 642037
EMERTON, FL/Off, Leslie Archibald, 102077
FALCONER, AC1, Leslie Charles Gilling,
FROST, AC2, Kenneth Ernest, 1239880
GARDEN, FL/Lt, Quentin, 88614
GITTINGS, Sjt, George, 1458467
GONSALVES, FL/Sjt, Frank Winston, 605687
GREETHAM, FL/Sjt, Robert Frederick, 939059
GRIFFITHS, LAC, Ernest Stanley, 937097
GRIMSHAW, FL/Sjt, John Francis, 1590681
GRYNKIEWICZ, FL/Sjt, John Francis, 1578681
HALBEARD, FL/Lt, Geoffrey Reeve, 102540
HANKINS, FL/Sjt, Glyn, 1577648
HARRIS, AC2, John, 1145369
HART, Cpl, Norman Frederick, 521107
HELSBY, Sjt, Laurence, 1755315
HELSBY, , Reeve, 102540
LOUGH, LAC, William, 1352884
O'NEIL, Flying Offr (Pilot), Hugh Leo, 53988

DENNIS, AC1, George Thomas, 1216802, (VR)
GREEN, AC1, George Cyril, 1274844, (VR)
HAYNES, LAC, E, 1134761, (VR)
HILL, Cpl, William Reid, 946736, (VR)
KELLY, AC1, Denis Matthew, 970610, (VR)
MILLER, AC1, Harold, 928490, (VR)
SCOTT, AC1, Bernard, 1061473, (VR)
SHAW, LAC, Robert Nicholas, 1273480, (VR)
SINNOTT, Cpl, Alban Edward, 1052005, (VR)
SUTTON, Flt Sgt (Pilot), Arthur Clifford, 1584180, (VR)

Royal Navy

ATHERTON, Sto, Harry, C/KX171743, HMS LANKA, RN,
ATTERSOLL, Cdr, John Walter, P/JX 251209, RN,
BALSHAW, PO, Geoffrey Arnold, D/JX135023, RN,
COPPING, Ldg Sto, Norman, P/KX 86161, RN ,
DEAN, Sub Lt, Ian Trant, HMS AMEER, RN,
DUNCAN, Mrn, S G PLY/X3717, HMS REPULSE, RN,
DUTHIE, AB, Charles John, D/JX169296, HMS SULTAN, RN,
FORSTER, AB, Stanley Arnold, D/JX 184645, RN,
HOPKINS, Sto PO, Reginald Horace, P/KK78613, RN HMS Grasshopper,
LIVERMORE, Ldg Supply Asst, Charles FB, D/MX 63672, RN HMS Sultan,
ROGERS, Ldg Sto, Frederick, P/KX87726, RN HMS Grasshopper,
SCOTT, Sto 1st Cl, Frederick Jeane, D/KX102776, RN HMS Repulse,
SIMCOCK, Cook, (S) Henry Hugh, P/MX65693, RN HMS Sultan,
WARNER, AB, William Robert, D/JX152064, RN HMS Sultan,

WEAVER,Ord Sea,Jack,P/JX 162166,RN HMS Sultan,
WIGNALL,AB,Francis,P/JX189108,RN HMS Tien Kwang,

Indian Forces

JARMAN,Capt,John Dennis
JENNINGS,Capt,Maurice Irving,731/A
JOHNSTON,2/Lt,Albert Robert,EC/2745
JOLLIFFE,2/Lt,Geroge Hilbourne,7
KERR,2/Lt,John Brumhall,EC/2030,
LAMAN,Maj,Frederick Ernest Kirkland,A./611
LARSON,Capt,Canute PhilipsEC/1831
LARTER,2/Lt,Eric Anthony Ponting,EC/374
LAW,2/Lt,Sydney James,222064
LEIGH,Lt,Herbert Egerton Miller
LESLIE, Gnr, John Andrew, 1986305
LIND,Capt,Lawrence Courtenay,AI/701
LOVETT,2/Lt,Francis Hugh,EC/2260
McGREGOR,2/Lt,Russell McDonald,EC/34

The Final Figures

Since the end of the war in the far east, many estimates and calculations have been given by historians and eager authors, concerning the number of combatants involved and the number of prisoners of war taken by the Japanese. During the research for my book "When You Go Home" I was able to interview men who served with the Japanese army and others who served with the then Siam freedom fighters and although the years between have erased some of the names from their memories, the figures I obtained have always remained very similar.

In 1991, I presented my figures to John Major in a letter in which I asked the prime minister if at this late stage the government could issue a statement confirming that Winston Churchill's figures, quoted in Parliament in February 1942, were and are a complete fabrication.

The figures quoted by Churchill at that time were that 30,000 Japanese troops had overwhelmed 120,000 British and allied soldiers and he went on to state that the men fighting in the Singapore Malaya theatre had not given their best and inferred that the defenders of Singapore were cowards. Many men have died since the war, believing in their own minds that what Churchill had said was true and no one so far has ever tried to alter history by saying that what our war leader said, was just a pack of lies issued to protect his own fragile image.

The reply to my letter from John Major implies that the reason for the deception was something to do with moral. My own feelings are that it was in order to save his neck at the expense of those of my comrades who paid the ultimate price.

On the first of December 1941, Japan had accumulated over 250,000 combatants in Indo China as guests of the French Vichy government under Petain. On the 8th December 1941, just 12,000 Japanese were transported by sea across the Gulf of Thailand for the invasion of Malaya. Between the 2nd and the 6th of December, Japanese forces with the connivance of the then Siamese government had infiltrated more than fifty thousand men across the border between Indo China and Thailand, into Malaya in the area between Kangor and the Thai border. All inhabitants living in the area where the Japanese made camp, were murdered in order to maintain secrecy.

On the 7th/8th December 1941, at the same time that the Japanese invasion force were approaching the beaches at Kota Baru and Singora on the east coats of Malaya. The Japanese launched their attack from inside Malaya against Alor Star, Jitra and Kangar.

Many historians have wondered how a Japanese landing force could secure a landing at Kota Baru and suddenly be three hundred miles away attacking the rear of the British defences at Alor Star just twelve hours later.

By the 7th December the following Japanese forces commenced their attack against the British and Allied forces in Malaya which culminated in their conquest of Singapore.

Those involved were The 15th Army commanded by General Iida covering the north of Malaya and the south of Thailand with a total of 55,000 men. The 25th Army commanded by General Yamashita and Count Terrauchi with 83,000 men which included the 18th division, the 26th infantry division commanded by Lt. General Renya Mataguchi 28,000 men. The Imperial guards division which was commanded by general Nishimura 38,000 men. Two regiments of artillery with one armoured division containing 500 tanks. 500 war planes, with 80 in reserve. 2 support carriers. ten destroyers. five submarines and other ancillary craft commanded by Admiral Ozawas, giving a grand total of 265,000 trained combat troops plus 50,000 Koreans soldiers in reserve.

During the fighting in Malaya, the Japanese lost more than 25,000 killed and wounded and on Singapore alone their losses killed was in excess of 20,000 known killed.

The allied figures on the first of December 1941 was. 19000 British personnel, 15,000 Australian, 17,000 Malay and local volunteers, plus 37,000 Indians including the 11th Indian division. During the fighting in Malaya the Allied losses were in excess of 25,000, killed, wounded, missing and deserters, which depleted the overall strength to around

65,00 between the 23rd and the 29th January 1942, the British garrison was strengthened by the arrival of the 18th division, bringing the total number of defenders on the island on the 9th February 1942 to around 68,000. Although the arrival of the 18th division increased the overall manpower, twenty percent of the number were non combatants.

After the fall of Singapore a head count revealed that on Singapore alone, the allied losses were around 7,000 killed with about 2000 missing and unaccounted for.

The Japanese casualty list showed in excess of 20,000 killed and 5,000 missing or wounded.

If as the historians have quoted many times the figures which emanated from Churchill's mouth, that 30,000

Japanese overwhelmed an Allied force of 120,000 men, why was it the Japanese casualty report stated that they had lost in excess of 25,000 men, which would indicate that the initial strength of the Japanese forces to be in excess of 170,000 men.

The figures which I have stated can be verified by the commonwealth war graves report which was issued in their registers in 1956 and also by he report of Sir Basil Liddell in his book of the second world war.

The figures given by Churchill in February 1942 were a complete fabrication, for one thing, he had no knowledge whatsoever what the strength of the Japanese forces were and it was apparent that he had no knowledge either of the Allied dispositions.

Because the figures were quoted by a respected parliamentarian the general public never doubted its authenticity.

Today however everyone knows that to be a politician, one must be able to lie convincingly and sorry to say, Churchill was a past master at it.

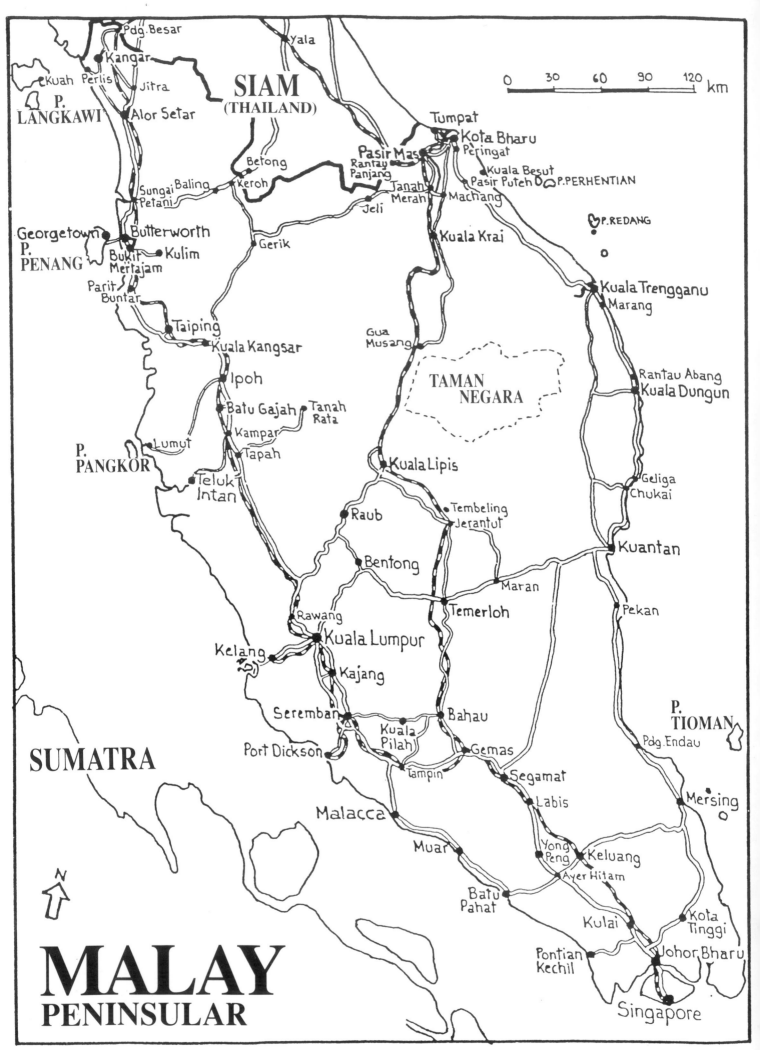

SIAM
(THAILAND)

P. LANGKAWI

P. PENANG

P. PANGKOR

SUMATRA

TAMAN
NEGARA

P. PERHENTIAN

P. REDANG

P. TIOMAN

MALAY
PENINSULAR

Note the Mass Area which was required to be defended by 82,000 Allied Forces ! !